*Routledge Revivals*

# The Russian Revolution

The revolutionary movements of 1905-1907 formed the first stage of the Russian Revolution, followed by an interval of peace and economic prosperity, but the outbreak of WWI and social unrest led to further revolutionary action in 1917 resulting in the abdication and murder of Tsar Nicholas II and the creation of the Soviet Union. Originally published in 1928, this volume traces the course and the consequences of the Revolution with Mavor emphasising the economic aspect of the Revolution as the main cause of the upheaval, considering political and military affairs in so far as their relation to the course of economic development. This title will be of interest to students of history and economics.

# The Russian Revolution

## James Mavor

First published in 1928
by George Allen & Unwin, Ltd.

This edition first published in 2016 by Routledge
2 Park Square, Milton Park, Abingdon, Oxon, OX14 4RN
and by Routledge
711 Third Avenue, New York, NY 10017

*Routledge is an imprint of the Taylor & Francis Group, an informa business*

© 1928 James Mavor

All rights reserved. No part of this book may be reprinted or reproduced or utilised in any form or by any electronic, mechanical, or other means, now known or hereafter invented, including photocopying and recording, or in any information storage or retrieval system, without permission in writing from the publishers.

**Publisher's Note**
The publisher has gone to great lengths to ensure the quality of this reprint but points out that some imperfections in the original copies may be apparent.

**Disclaimer**
The publisher has made every effort to trace copyright holders and welcomes correspondence from those they have been unable to contact.

A Library of Congress record exists under LC control number: 28026714

ISBN 13: 978-1-138-19160-0 (hbk)
ISBN 13: 978-1-315-64038-9 (ebk)
ISBN 13: 978-1-138-19161-7 (pbk)

# THE RUSSIAN REVOLUTION

BY

## JAMES MAVOR

LATE EMERITUS PROFESSOR AND SOMETIME PROFESSOR
OF POLITICAL ECONOMY IN THE
UNIVERSITY OF TORONTO

LONDON
GEORGE ALLEN & UNWIN LTD
MUSEUM STREET

*First published in 1928*
*(All rights reserved)*

*Printed in Great Britain by*
*Unwin Brothers, Ltd., Woking*

# PREFACE

THIS volume is a sequel to *An Economic History of Russia* originally published in 1914 and issued in a new and revised edition in 1925. I ventured to remark in the General Introduction of that work that " No country (besides Russia) offers the student an equal opportunity for a study of economic history. Indeed, without taking into account at least the salient features of Russian social development, general economic history cannot be written." The abrupt and fundamental social and political changes which have taken place in Russia since 1914, and the reactions to those changes throughout the world, render more than ever apparent the truth of this remark.

The second volume of the *Economic History* contains an account of the parallel growth of modern industry and revolutionary ideas. The events which form the topic of the present volume have occurred so recently that it is not easy to view them in right historical perspective. Yet an attempt has been made to look upon these events objectively and to reject systematically all statements which seemed exaggerated, whilst on the other hand giving emphasis to salient episodes.

It is not possible to separate completely economic from political history ; prominence has, however, been given to the economic legislation and administration of the Soviet Government. Though the conclusions cannot be otherwise than provisional, the book may perhaps be regarded as preparing the way for more adequate treatment, when ampler authoritative material shall be available.

What Machiavelli said of the Italians of his time is surely equally applicable to the Russians of to-day :—

" They are more enslaved than the Hebrews, more oppressed than the Persians, more scattered than the Athenians, without head, without order, beaten, despoiled, torn, overrun, having endured every kind of desolation."

I have to acknowledge gratefully the services of my old friend Professor Julius Reuter, of the university of Helsingfors, and through him the assistance of the Government of the Finnish Republic, in procuring for me valuable collections of papers of which I have made use in the following pages. I have also to thank many Russian friends for the same kind of services and for help in translation.

JAMES MAVOR.

UNIVERSITY OF TORONTO.

# CONTENTS

| | PAGE |
|---|---|
| PREFACE | 7 |
| INTRODUCTION | 21 |

# BOOK I

## THE INTERVAL OF PEACE, THE EUROPEAN WAR, AND THE COLLAPSE OF THE DYNASTY

### CHAPTER I

THE AUTOCRACY AND THE PEOPLE . . . . . . . . . . 27

Character of autocratic rule under Nicholas II—Struggle between the autocracy and the movement for constitutional government—Growth of patriotism as distinct from loyalty to the Tsar—The Dumas and their problems—The *zemstvo* movement—Union of Liberation—The peasant question—Commission on Agriculture—Fatal error of the Tsar—German propaganda.

### CHAPTER II

THE INTERVAL OF PEACE, 1907–1914 . . . . . . . . . 35

Connection between the revolutionary movements of 1905–1907 and 1917—Economic prosperity—Land legislation of Stolypin—Conflict between urban and rural interests—Conflict between peasant groups— Effects of Stolypin's legislation—Peasant ideas of property in land— Views of Peter Struvë—Unstable conditions in industry—Foreign capital in Russian industry—Vigorous enterprises—Timber—Oil— Railways—Reserves of grain—Effects of material prosperity upon peasants and artisans—Heterogeneity of Russian population—Rapidity of increase—Decline in efficiency of administration.

### CHAPTER III

THE EUROPEAN WAR AND ITS IMMEDIATE ECONOMIC EFFECTS UPON RUSSIA . 45

Declaration of war—Attitude of St. Petersburg—Lack of military and industrial preparation—Onslaughts upon East Prussia, Galicia, and Bukovina—Effect upon the campaign in the west—Retreat of the Russian armies—The people become dispirited early in the war— Re-equipment of army in spring of 1917—Discontent in the capital.

### CHAPTER IV

THE REVOLUTION OF FEBRUARY–MARCH 1917, THE FORMATION OF THE PROVISIONAL GOVERNMENT, AND THE ABDICATION OF THE TSAR . . 51

Riots in Petrograd—People call for " bread "—Revolutionists utilize the disturbances—Tsar and Government in panic—Rodzianko on the crisis—Proposed dictatorship of Grand Duke Michael—Dissolution of

# THE RUSSIAN REVOLUTION

the Duma by the Tsar—Mutinies in Petrograd—Helplessness of Government—Resignation of Cabinet—Leaders of the Duma take control and demand abdication of the Tsar—The Duma recognizes and leads the Revolution—Conflicting political aims—The abdication.

APPENDIX A . . . . . . . . . . . . . 59

Telegrams from M. V. Rodzianko to the Tsar, Nicholas II, dated March 11 and 12, 1917.

APPENDIX B . . . . . . . . . . . . . 59

Proclamation by Provisional Government, February 27, 1917 (O.S.), March 12, 1917 (N.S.).

# BOOK II

## THE DUAL AUTHORITY OF THE PROVISIONAL GOVERN- MENT AND THE PETROGRAD COUNCIL OF WORK- MEN'S AND SOLDIERS' DEPUTIES

### CHAPTER I

THE PROVISIONAL GOVERNMENT AND THE REVIVAL OF THE SOVIETS . . 63

Absence of preparation for Revolution—Petrograd Soviet—Composition of the Provisional Government—Characters of the new ministers—The Soviet system—Genesis of *Order No. 1*—Petrograd garrison and the Revolution—Character of the new army—Character of the new working men—Crumbling of the industrial system—Anarchic state of industry—Failure of the Soviets to control the working masses—Separation between ruling groups and the people—" Direct action "—Expropriation by peasants and artisans—Luga Soviet—Absence of legal local authority forces numerous functions upon the Soviet—Attitude of the peasants—Inaction of Provisional Government—Moderating influence of the Soviet over the peasants—Soviets not really representative of the population—Spontaneous growth of small local administrative bodies—Arbitrary seizures of land and timber—Destruction of manor houses—Peasant Congress at Petrograd—Central Land Commission.

### CHAPTER II

THE COALITION GOVERNMENT AND ITS STRUGGLES AGAINST " DIRECT ACTION " BY PEASANTS AND ARTISANS . . . . . . . . . 78

Arrival of Lenin, Zinoviev, and Trotsky at Petrograd—Bolshevik activities begin—Coalition Government urged by Petrograd Soviet and opposed by Trotsky—Coalition approved by Soviet—Three new socialist ministers—Peasant uprisings dismay both Government and Soviet—Government attempts to improve local administration—Grain prices fixed—Monopoly in grain established—All measures displeasing to peasantry—Government fails to secure support of mass of people—Taxation of employers—Excessive demands of workers—Difficulties of railway and other public departments—Impossibility of meeting demands—Public finances—Issue of paper currency.

# CONTENTS

## CHAPTER III

THE WORKING OF THE SOVIETS.  UNSUCCESSFUL BOLSHEVIK ATTEMPTS TO OVER-
THROW THE PROVISIONAL GOVERNMENT . . . . . . . 88

Defective tactics of Provisional Government and of the Petrograd Soviet
in relation to the Petrograd garrison—Luga Soviet—All-Russian Congress of Soviets—General approval of Provisional Government—Failure
of Lenin and Trotsky to obtain support in an attack upon it—Unsuccessful attempt to employ force—Protests from army at the front—
Bolsheviks disclaim violent intentions—Cry of " *All Power to the
Soviets* "—Disinclination of Soviets to assume the responsibility of
power—Agitation in army on calling soldiers of forty years of age for
service—Bolshevik propaganda in the army at the front—Discussion
about a Constituent Assembly—Resignation of Cadet ministers.

APPENDIX C . . . . . . . . . . . . . .

Text of *Order No. 1.*  March 1, 1917 (O.S.), March 14, 1917 (N.S.).

# BOOK III

## MILITARY, SOCIAL, AND POLITICAL DISINTEGRATION IN RUSSIA AND THE RISE OF THE BOLSHEVIKS

### CHAPTER I

DEMORALIZATION OF PEOPLE AND ARMY AND THE BEGINNING OF THE DISSO-
LUTION OF THE RUSSIAN EMPIRE . . . . . . . . 99

Epidemic of passivity and pacifism—Decline of *morale* in the army—
Propaganda by Lenin—His hypothesis of the nature and origin of the
war—Criticism of this—Kerensky's attempt to restore discipline in the
army—German attitude towards this—Disturbances in Petrograd,
July 1917—Declaration of Finnish independence—Reverses on the
Russian front—Criminal proceedings against Lenin and Zinoviev—
Kornilov's attempt to reorganize army—Revolt of the Ukraine—Capture
of Riga by the Germans—Specific causes of demoralization of army—
Specific causes of dissolution of the Russian Empire.

### CHAPTER II

THE KERENSKY–KORNILOV AFFAIR AND THE CRUMBLING OF THE FRONT . . 119

Increasing influence of Bolshevism in Petrograd Soviet—Domination
of Kronstadt by Bolsheviks—The Kerensky-Kornilov affair—Kerensky's
account—General Gourko's account—Effect of the quarrel upon subsequent events—Food riots throughout Russia in September 1917—
Bolsheviks gain a majority in Petrograd Soviet—Kamenev's Resolution
—Riots in Odessa and elsewhere—Agrarian riots—Anarchy—Wholesale
desertions—Weakness of Kerensky's administration.

### CHAPTER III

" ALL POWER TO THE SOVIETS " . . . . . . . . . . 130

Reasons for turning to the Soviet—Burtsev's warning—The Pre-
Parliament—Disturbances at Tashkent—Food riots in October 1917—

# THE RUSSIAN REVOLUTION

PAGE

Approach of German army—Nervousness of Petrograd population—Finnish Republic proclaimed—Trotsky elected president of Petrograd Soviet—Projected socialist conference at Stockholm—Dissolution of the State Duma—Bolshevization of Petrograd working men.

## CHAPTER IV

" RED OCTOBER." THE PREPARATION . . . . . . . . . 142

State of parties—Attitude of parties towards the war—Causes of political weakness of Kerensky—Reasons for the influence of the Bolsheviks—Distinction between the aims of the Bolsheviks and those of the workmen and peasants—Effects of the feebleness of Kerensky's administration—Insincerity of the propagandist cries of the Bolsheviks—Municipal elections in Moscow—Bolshevik staff organized—Importance of this staff in the promotion of the Revolution—Assembly of Soviets of the north approve of arbitrary seizures of property—Protests by Plekhanov—Protests against the conduct of the commissars sent to the army at the instance of the Petrograd Soviet—Return of Lenin to the capital—Co-operative societies opposed to anarchy—The Pre-Parliament—Cossacks of the Don hostile to the Soviet—Activities of the Bolshevik staff—Open announcement of and preparation for an uprising—Warning by Burtsev—Ecstatic oratory of Bolsheviks—Revolutionary orders by the Executive Committee of the Petrograd Soviet—Capture by the Bolsheviks of the fortress of SS. Peter and Paul " by persuasion "—Gradual winning over of army to the side of the Bolsheviks—Skilful measures taken by the Revolutionary staff—Mobilization of the Red Guard—The Smolny Institute—Scenes in it—Illusions entertained by the Kerensky Government regarding importance of the Bolsheviks—The Government fails to obtain the support of the Provisional Council of State and of the Pre-Parliament—Futile action of Kerensky—Anarchic condition of affairs.

## CHAPTER V

" RED OCTOBER." THE EXPLOSION . . . . . . . . . 155

Orders to the garrison given by the Bolshevik staff—*Aurora*, cruiser, brought up the Neva by Bolshevik crew—Investment of the Winter Palace—Railway stations, etc., occupied by Bolshevik troops—Proclamation by Bolsheviks announcing the overthrow of the Government—Sir George Buchanan's account—Flight of Kerensky—Ministers defend themselves in the Winter Palace—Siege and bombardment of the Palace—Treachery of a portion of the defending force—Fighting from room to room—Capture of ministers and of remainder of defending force—Lenin announces the new programme in the early morning of October 26th (O.S.)—Meeting of the All-Russian Congress of Soviets affirms the assumption of power by the Soviets—A Soviet Government elected—List of the new Cabinet—Alleged secret agreement between the German General Staff and Lenin, Trotsky, Raskolnikov, and Zinoviev—Von Hindenburg's reflections upon the political interference with the strategy of the Russo-German campaign—Municipal hostility to the Bolsheviks—Kerensky joins General Krassnov at Pskov—Hostilities between Cossacks and Red troops—Desertion of the Cossacks—Escape of Kerensky—Arrest of General Krassnov—Affairs in Moscow—Opposition to the Bolsheviks from the General Staff—Discordant events.

# CONTENTS

## CHAPTER VI

THE SEPARATE ARMISTICE . . . . . . . . . . . . . **170**

Efforts by Great Britain and France to keep Russia in the war—Reasons for these efforts—New Soviet Government proposes immediate armistice on all fronts—General Dukhonin being ordered to negotiate with enemy, refuses—He is dismissed and "Ensign" Krilenko appointed—Provocative order to troops—Lenin's proclamation on self-determination—Ukraine declared a Republic—Protests against a separate peace—Further disintegration of Russia—Peasants' Conference opposed to armistice —Army not yet wholly won over by the Bolsheviks—Strike of civil servants—Constitutional Democrats and ambassadors of foreign powers boycott the Bolsheviks—Numerous protests against separate peace—Sir George Buchanan advises release of Russia from her engagement to refrain from negotiating separate peace—Trotsky's *parlementaires* cross the German lines—Dissolution of Petrograd municipal council—Arrest of the mayor and some of the councillors—Hostile attitude of the H.Q.S. to the new Goverment—Revolutionary Committee formed at H.Q.—Appearance there of Krilenko followed by murder of General Dukhonin—German officers appear in Petrograd—Dismissal of Russian diplomatists—Quarrel between Soviet Russia and the Ukraine.

## CHAPTER VII

THE CONSTITUENT ASSEMBLY . . . . . . . . . . . **177**

Demands for a Constituent Assembly in 1905–1907—Decline of enthusiasm in 1917—Manner of election—Assembly favoured by the peasants—Movement among the Socialist-Revolutionaries to defend the Assembly—Indifference of the working men towards the Assembly—Passive mood in the garrison—Increase of influence of the Bolsheviks among Petrograd workers in January 1918—Parliamentarism of S.R.s and S.D.s—Projects for the Assembly—Reluctance to undertake violent opposition to the Bolsheviks—Skilful campaign of the Bolsheviks—Advantage of their position—The war committee of the S.R.s—Its plans—"The Grey Cloak" (*Sieraya Shinel*)—Illusions about the Bolsheviks and their aims—A soldiers' university—Meetings on the question of defence of the Assembly—Scene at the Semenovsky barracks—Krilenko—Opposition to armed defence of the Assembly by S.R.s—Plot to kidnap Lenin and Trotsky—Opinion of the Bolsheviks entertained by S.R.s—Attitude towards the Soviet Government of the Petrograd population—Opening of the Constituent Assembly—Scenes in the streets—Bolsheviks defeated in votes in the Assembly—Gallery packed by "invited" Bolsheviks—Closing scene—Propaganda against the Assembly—Change of attitude on the part of workers and others—Importance of the closure of the Assembly to the interests of the Bolsheviks.

## CHAPTER VIII

BREST-LITOVSK . . . . . . . . . . . . . . **202**

The negotiators—Truculent attitude of the Russian representatives—Dead-lock—Dictatorial message by Trotsky to the Allied Powers—Armistice signed—The peace negotiations—Condition of the belligerent countries—Advantage to the Central Powers of an immediate peace with Russia—Terms laid down by Russia—Ultimate design latent in these terms—Brest-Litovsk a platform for propaganda—Count Czernin at Brest-Litovsk—German proposals—Underlying meaning of these—Proposal to transfer the conference to Stockholm—Apparent object of this proposal—The Central Powers refuse to change the *locus* of the conference—Reluctance of the Bolsheviks to continue negotiations—

# THE RUSSIAN REVOLUTION

PAGE

Appearance at Brest-Litovsk of independent representatives of the Ukraine and commencement of separate negotiations with them—Trotsky arrives at Brest-Litovsk and takes charge—Speech of Trotsky—Struggle to retain control of the Baltic Provinces on the part of Trotsky—Controversy upon the employment of force by governments between General Hoffmann, representing Germany, and Trotsky—Discussion on the individuality of States—Reasons for the Russian attitude—Germany refuses to evacuate the Baltic States until after the conclusion of a general peace—Russia refuses to accept this arrangement—Breakdown of negotiations—Reasons for this—Naïve proposal by Trotsky—Refusal by Germans—Military operations resumed by Germany—Abject capitulation of Russia—Conditions of peace made more stringent by Germany—Treaties signed—Manifesto by Soviet Government denouncing the Peace.

## CHAPTER IX

THE LABOUR ARMY . . . . . . . . . . . . 217

Mistaken policy of anti-Bolshevik forces—Contrary policy of the Bolsheviks—Problem of demobilization of Red Army—Organization of four Labour Armies—Desiderata—Organization of labour for Donetz mineral region—Ineffectiveness of civil administration—Material increase of production through the Labour Army—Accompanying political and social activities—Conversion of the seventh army into a Labour Army for Petrograd district—Increase of production due to this and other measures—Dispersal of population to the villages—Diminution of the proletariat—Scarcity of labour, the Labour Armies notwithstanding—Further mobilization for labour—Withdrawal of skilled workmen from the villages—Measures for the housing of increased labour force—Services of seamstresses commandeered—Previous history of obligatory services—Sullen resistance of peasantry.

## CHAPTER X

THE RUSSIAN PEOPLE AND THE REVOLUTION . . . . . . . 223

Class organization—Inversion of social classification under Bolshevism—Return of Russian exiles from abroad—Controversies in socialist ranks—Flight of educated classes—Consequences to Russia—Character of Russian peasant—Russian and foreign opinion of the *mujik*—Peasant disturbances in 1916—Consequences of Stolypin's reforms of 1906—Difficulties of local government—Change in its character—Peasant disturbances in 1918—Incompatibility of co-operation between a communist proletarian State and a peasant State—Imitation of autocracy by the Cummunist Government—Consequences—What the peasant gained in the Revolution—Relation of the peasants to land nationalization.

# BOOK IV

## THE SOCIAL REVOLUTION AND ITS PROBLEMS

### CHAPTER I

THE CHARACTERS AND IDEOLOGY OF THE BOLSHEVIKS AND THE DEVELOPMENT OF
THEIR POLICY . . . . . . . . . . . . . 235

Intellectual inferiority of the Bolsheviks in comparison with former socialist leaders—Their attitude towards political opponents—Inertia

# CONTENTS 15

PAGE

of elements opposed to Bolshevism—Anarchic mood of workmen and peasants—Character of Lenin—Origin of the Bolshevik programme —*Osvobojdenie Truda*—G.V.Plekhanov—Movement of Blagoev—Congress at Minsk in 1898—Lenin's manifesto—Formation of Russian Social Democratic Working Men's Party—Adoption of Lenin's programme—Opposition to Lenin—Arrest of the committee of the party—Congress in London in 1903—Formation of the Bolshevist or majority faction and the Menshevist or minority faction.

APPENDIX D . . . . . . . . . . . . . . 253

Manifesto of the Russian Social Democratic Workers' Party, August 13, 1917.

## CHAPTER II

PROBLEMS OF POWER . . . . . . . . . . . 254

Lack of preparation for the task of government—Economic confusion—Illusions of the Bolsheviks—Experience of the Soviets before the October Revolution—Exaggerated importance attached to mechanical view of society—New-comers in administrative positions—Attitude of remaining *intelligentsia*—Employment of some of them in the public offices—Dialogue between two brothers—Experiences in the service of the Soviet —Social *bouleversement*—Change of opinion in the ranks of the *intelligentsia*—More departmental experiences—Working of the High Soviet of People's Economy—Incompetence of regional committees—Resolutions of the Twelfth Congress of the Russian Communist Party—*Rôle* of the party—Mercantilist views—Projected industrialization of the peasantry—Enthusiasm for great industry and for development of electrical power—Difficulties in the way—The Soviet and local government—New autonomous regions—Problems of relation between central and local authorities—The Ukraine.

APPENDIX E . . . . . . . . . . . . . . 305

Author's note with reference to hydraulic power.

## CHAPTER III

THE ADMINISTRATION OF JUSTICE UNDER THE SOVIET REPUBLICS . . . 269

Abolition of the courts of law—Judicial confusion—The revolutionary tribunals—The Soviets and the new People's Courts—The Commissariat of Justice—Organization of this body—Incompetence of the new courts —Absence of legal gradation of appeals—Example of rural justice—Incompetence of the new police—Attitude of the legal profession—Emergence of new laws without system—Lunarchasky—His views on law and on a new morality—Criticism of his views.

## CHAPTER IV

THE PRESIDIUM OF THE ALL-RUSSIAN SOVIET OF PEOPLE'S ECONOMY . . 279

The task before the Soviet—Decline in consumption of goods manufactured in Russia—Increase in number of civil servants—Stagnation of production and decay of industrial discipline—Haphazard programmes of production—Illustrative conversation in the Presidium—Corruption in industrial enterprises—Suggested explanation of grandiose schemes—Kovalevsky's views—Apparent origin of truculent communism—Superstitious reverence for "efficiency"—The membership of the Presidium in 1918 and 1919—Rykov—Oppokov—Weinberg—Karpov—Chubar—Larin—Project for the abolition of money—Difficulties in carrying this into effect—Krassin—Industrial police—Partnership of

# THE RUSSIAN REVOLUTION

PAGE

state and private enterprises—Bolshevik incompetence not a monopoly—Criticism of Soviet Government by Lenin—Multiplication of departments—Relations between Government departments—Idealization of Soviet system—Tendency towards political control and opposition to this tendency—Relation of the Soviet to the individual—Wide extension of its powers—Mingling of legislative and executive functions in the Soviet—Effect of this—Reversion to early view of the status of the sovereign—Relation of the High Soviet to local Soviets and local courts—Composition of the bureaucracy in 1918—Presence in it of counter-revolutionaries—Corruption.

## CHAPTER V

THE CONCRETE ECONOMIC PLAN OF THE BOLSHEVIKS . . . . . 296

Little progress during winter of 1917–1918—Larin's suggestions adopted—New programme recommended by him—Comments on this programme—First All-Russian Congress of the Soviets of People's Economy—Importance of this congress—Pessimistic report by Radek—Speech by Lenin—Necessity of nationalization of factories under contemporary conditions—Similar necessity of a state monopoly of foreign trade—Errors of the Bolsheviks in connection with both production and foreign trade—Grain monopoly not new nor necessarily confiscatory—Error of the Bolsheviks in connection with the grain monopoly—Attempts to force cultivation of grain—Rest-houses for working men—Collection of taxes in kind.

## CHAPTER VI

THE NATIONALIZATION OF INDUSTRY AND ITS CONSEQUENCES . . . . 306

Russia a pioneer in large-scale industry—Concentration of great industries in the northern capital—Pre-war industrial situation—Foreign investments in Russian enterprises—Effect of the October Revolution and the separate armistice—Cessation of foreign credit—Nationalization of industry economically compulsory—Intention to nationalize gradually frustrated by conditions—Haphazard nationalization—Struggle between central and local authorities—Decline of production—Alleged *sabotage* by managers of industrial enterprises—Ineffective control—Nationalization frustrated by " direct action " of workers—The High Soviet seeks to meet the crisis of under-production by universal nationalization—Difficulty of finding proper forms of action—Bolshevik opposition to revolutionary syndicalism—Scheme for associating workers' with state control—First industries to be fully nationalized—New committees appointed to carry out the scheme—Decline in the productivity of labour—Attempt to establish iron industrial discipline—Normalization of production and obligatory labour—Agrarian policy—State workng of land—Project of importing agricultural machinery—Bolshevist hopes that the *bourgeoisie*, extinguished as a class, would remain as an organizing power—Nationalization of banks and credit—State monopolies—Organization of natural exchange—Details of technique—Reasons for nationalization—Examples—" Direct action " by workers—Difficulties of gradual nationalization—Statistics of nationalization and sequestration—Nominal nationalization—Bolshevist optimism—Stages of nationalization—Nationalization of large enterprises completed in August 1918—Details of chemical industry—Decline of wages in relation to value of product—Optimist reports—Dyestuffs, fats, and matches—Policy of driving small enterprises out of business—Conversion

# CONTENTS

of munition works—Fertilizers—Relative productivity of German and Russian agricultural labour—Suggested interior loan for productive purposes—Difficulties in the way of carrying out the programme—Problems of state industrial enterprise similar to those of private enterprise—Colossal task of achieving economic equilibrium—Disappearance of the market for certain goods—Report on control of mines—Local Soviets demand organization at the centre—New mining laws—Qualifications required of mining engineers—Mining Council—Political atmosphere in industrial affairs—Friction between the local Soviets and workers in state enterprises established under the old *régime*—Multiplication of administrative organs—Hypertrophy of organization—Examples —Chronic crises—Confiscation of money and valuables—Extermination of private commerce in July 1920—Arrest of persons engaged in private commerce and condemnation to obligatory labour—Reports on the state of industry in Petrograd in 1920—Lack of raw materials—Premiums offered to peasants—Original suggestions—Communalization of dwelling-houses—Rough methods—Unlimited authority of individual members of the Communist party.

## CHAPTER VII

OBLIGATORY LABOUR, NORMALIZING PRODUCTION, AND THE SYSTEM OF RATIONING . . . . . . . . . . . . 327

Obligatory labour for non-proletarians—Method of enforcing obligatory labour—Appointment of Commission on Universal Service—System of premiums—Normalization of day's work—The Normalizing Commission—Difficulties in normalization—Optimism of official view—Scale of premiums—Wages problem still unsolved in 1923—The system of rationing—The "armoured ration"—Inadequacy of the ration—Recommendations of the Textile Workers' Union—Hostility to payment of wages in kind.

## CHAPTER VIII

THE CO-OPERATIVE MOVEMENT AND THE SOVIET REPUBLIC . . . . 335

Consumers' co-operation under the old *régime*—Widespread influence —Destruction of system by Soviet Government—This destruction a logical outcome of communism—Bolshevik definition of co-operation—Decree of April 12, 1918—Labour certificates—Cardinal necessity to Bolsheviks of controlling supply and exchange—Compulsory transformation of co-operative societies into state organizations—Resistance by the co-operators—The Moscow People's Bank—Services of the Bank to co-operation—Absorption by the Soviet State—Change of affairs on the adoption of the New Economic Policy, but rigid governmental control retained—Statistics—Proportion of exchange by means of the state co-operatives—Purpose of the policy of the Soviet Government.

## CHAPTER IX

THE CIVIL WARS, CHIEFLY IN RELATION TO THEIR ECONOMIC CONSEQUENCES 342

### (A) The South Russian Campaign.

Bolshevik manifesto directly responsible for the outbreak of the civil wars—The Volunteer Army—Four campaigns—Kornilov and Alekseiev, Denikin and Alekseiev, Denikin, and Wrangel—Political programme of Kornilov—Death of Kornilov—Denikin—Special committee—Functions of the committee—Change in programme by Denikin—Failure of Denikin and Wrangel—Reasons for failure—Reasons for

# THE RUSSIAN REVOLUTION

assistance by Great Britain and France—German officers in the Red Army—Numerous declarations of independence—Capture of Kharkov by the Bolsheviks.

### (B) The North Russian Campaign.

Situation at Archangel in the spring of 1918—"White" officers in Red Army—Landing of allied troops at Archangel—"The Provisional Government of Northern Russia"—Tchaikovsky—Flight of the Bolsheviks—Disagreeable episode—Ineptitude of the Tchaikovsky Government—The kidnapping of the Government—Reinstatement of the Government—Change of ministers—Character of the Russian troops at Archangel—School for Russian officers—General Ironside.

### (C) Siberia and the Revolution.

Movement of Potanen and others before 1865—Siberian Regional Assembly—Siberian Soviets—"Napoleon of Siberia" arrives—G. N. Potanen resigns—Derber's Government—Harbin as centre of anti-Bolshevik forces—Influence of General Khorvat, Admiral Koltchak and Captain Semenov—Mikhailov at Omsk—Czech prisoners—Causes of failure of anti-Bolsheviks—Hardships of peasants—Lenin's defence of Soviet's seizures of peasant's grain.

### CHAPTER X

THE RED TERROR . . . . . . . . . . . . . . 375

Passivity and pacifism—Assassination of the President of the *Che-Ka*—Description of the scene—The beginning of the Terror—Anarchy in Petrograd—Arrest of hostages throughout Russia—Account of the Terror by a Soviet official—Incidents of the Terror—Attitude of *intelligentsia* in Soviet service—A wise old Jew—Connection between the Terror and the old *régime*—Terror applied not merely to non-proletarian elements—Wholesale arrests—The Red Terror the result of fear.

# BOOK V

## ECONOMIC CRISIS, COLLAPSE OF COMMUNISM, AND THE NEW ECONOMIC POLICY

### CHAPTER I

THE ECONOMIC CRISIS OF THE WINTER OF 1920–1921 AND THE FAMINE OF 1921 . . . . . . . . . . . . . . . . 385

The causes of the blockade by the *Entente* Powers—Raising of the blockade—The high-water mark of nationalization in 1920—Effects of Soviet policy upon the peasantry—Increase of illegal trade—Absence of credit—The Bolshevik plan and its failure—Forcible collection of bread-stuffs—The single Direct Agricultural Tax—Resolution of the Twelfth Congress of the Communist party—Further attempts to increase production in order to relieve the situation—Dilapidation of houses in Petrograd and Moscow—The famine in rural Russia—Means taken under the old *régime* to relieve famine-stricken regions—Scarcity in 1921 even in the Black Soil region—Statistics of decline in agriculture—Measures to benefit the peasants—Epidemic of theft.

# CONTENTS

## CHAPTER II

**THE COLLAPSE OF COMMUNISM** . . . . . . . . . . 395

Decline in membership of the Communist party—The "cleaning up" of the party—Dispersal of the proletariat—Decline in production—Lenin's statement of the economical position—He blames the peasant for the failure of communism—"Bag commerce"—Lenin's threat to the peasant—Propaganda for increased production—Appeal for "work in a revolutionary manner"—Communists set an example—Indications of the collapse of communism—Reasons for the New Economic Policy.

## CHAPTER III

**THE NEW ECONOMIC POLICY** . . . . . . . . . . 403

Reasons for the adoption of the New Economic Policy (N.E.P.)—Difficulty of nationalizing small industrial enterprises—Consequent liberation of the smaller industries—Control over the larger ones maintained—Private retail trade permitted—Attempt of the Soviet Government to crush the smaller industries by developing the greater—Improved food supply resulting from N.E.P.—Partial return to a system of capitalistic enterprise—Government's efforts to stimulate agricultural "co-operation"—Partial success of those efforts—Attempt of the Government to attract foreign *concessionnaires*—Slender response to this attempt—Gradual increase of foreign trade—Agreement with Great Britain—Difficulties in the way of trade—Russo-German trade treaty—Survey of the extent and the effects of the N.E.P.

## CHAPTER IV

**SOVIET FINANCE** . . . . . . . . . . . . 412

Nationalization of banks—Purposes of institution of "natural exchange"—Differences between the Soviet budget and that of the old *régime*—Inflation of the currency—Extension of functions of the State—Consequent danger of waste—Attempt to reorganize finances—Absence of stimulus through fair and free exchange—Attempted economies in administration—First tolerable budget in 1922–1923—Large deficit—Alleged causes of the deficit—Separation of central and local government finance—Separation of budget of the Union of Soviet Socialist Republics from the budgets of the individual States—Breakdown of the system of centralization.

## CHAPTER V

**THE ECONOMIC SITUATION IN RUSSIA IN THE YEARS 1923–1925** . . . 416

Industrial conditions in 1923–1924—Comparative trade tables for those years—Russian railways—Their dislocated condition in 1920—Extraordinary Commission formed to deal with the situation—Its report and recommendations—Gradual improvement of the railway system—Improved management of national enterprises—Unemployment still serious—Education—Lowered standards in the universities—The schools—Return of officials of the old *régime*—Purchase of food-stuffs from foreign markets in 1925.

# 20 THE RUSSIAN REVOLUTION

## CHAPTER VI

THE THIRD INTERNATIONAL . . . . . . . . . . . 424

Its formation—Lenin's division of international socialists into three groups—Close relations between the Third International and the Soviet Government—Its destructive aims—Constructive aims more obscure—Not really an international movement at all.

## CHAPTER VII

CONCLUSIONS . . . . . . . . . . . . . . 428

Problem of the remoter causes of the Revolution—Tradition of a Russian message to the world—Tolstoy—Interpretation of traditional message by Struvĕ—Views and prediction of Joseph de Maistre—Absence of religious belief in Russia—Successive revolutionary movements do not suggest spiritual struggles—The literary movement of the middle of the nineteenth century—The Slavophils—Revolutionary movements in 1848 and 1870–1880—The first stage of the Russian Revolution in 1905–1906—A wave of mystical enthusiasm—Unpreparedness of the *intelligentsia* in 1917—Russian nationalism—Bolshevism the antithesis of nationalism as also of socialism—Inadequacy of an economic and political interpretation of the Revolution—Course of Revolution due to deep-seated faults in the character of the people—Has modern Russia a message for the world ?—General conclusions.

BIBLIOGRAPHY . . . . . . . . . . . . . 441

INDEX . . . . . . . . . . . . . . 447

# INTRODUCTION

THE revolutionary movements of 1905–1907 formed the first stage of the Russian Revolution, and were followed by a period of seven years of political reaction and economic prosperity, during which the prestige of the Tsar Nicholas II steadily declined. His choice of ministers became more and more open to criticism, while the extent to which he yielded to pressure from intriguing and even disreputable elements exposed him to the contempt of those who would otherwise have been staunch supporters of his throne.

The main theme of this volume is the economic aspect of the Revolution. That aspect, owing to the special character of the upheaval, is undoubtedly the most important, therefore political and military affairs can only be considered incidentally, and in so far as they are indissolubly related to the course of economic development. A full discussion of the question of the responsibility of Russia for the European War will not therefore be attempted, though the following considerations should be borne in mind.

If it be true that the German Government was bent upon war with Russia in 1914 before the military reforms upon which Russia had just entered could have their full effect, the problem of the complicity of Russia in the actual provocation of the war is reduced to one question—Did she fall willingly into a German trap or did she do her utmost to keep out of it ? Clearly the interest of Russia was to avoid a conflict with Germany at least until she could hope to wage war successfully, but did her statesmen exercise due care in making sure that she was ready for a campaign ?

Unfortunately, the Russian statesmen who were in power at that moment (June–July, 1914) were not men of first-rate ability. The President of the Council was a man of seventy-seven years, Goremikin, who had succeeded Kokovtsov in 1913. Sir George Buchanan describes him as " an amiable old gentleman with pleasant manners, of an idolent temperament, and quite past his work. He had not moved with the times, and still looked upon the Duma as an unimportant factor that could be safely ignored." (1)

The following description of Goremikin and of the moment of the ultimatum to Serbia is from a Russian hand.

" Usually at Cabinet councils, he [Goremikin] slept. In the evenings when he should have been hard at work he played *solitaire*. The most powerful minister in Russia played *solitaire* while Russia slid into the abyss !

" On one occasion, however, Goremikin showed a flash of his

# THE RUSSIAN REVOLUTION

*old self.* After Austria sent the ultimatum to Serbia and mobilized, Goremikin called a meeting of the Cabinet. He told the ministers that they must make up their minds as to the course Russia must pursue if Germany and Austria were determined on war. A hot discussion followed and Goremikin went to sleep. One minister after another spoke, and the majority were in favour of coming, if possible, to some understanding with Germany and Austria. Suddenly Goremikin opened his eyes and said : ' Well, gentlemen, I have heard all you have to say, and will tell the Emperor that you have unanimously decided that we must stand by Serbia to the end. Our honour is at stake.'

" He then went to the Emperor and suggested that everything possible should be done to preserve peace, and as a result Sazonov, the Foreign Minister, sent a circular telegram to our ambassadors in Paris, London, and Berlin, asking for . . . friendly intervention . . . between Russia and Austria. The Emperor Nicholas sent a personal telegram to the Emperor William proposing the same thing." (2)

The Government of Russia in the year of the outbreak of war was unquestionably in the hands of ministers who lacked both vigour and foresight. This circumstance was undoubtedly well known to the German Government, but if that Government counted upon Russia's refraining from war on the ground that adequate preparation for such a contingency had not been made, it failed to realize the influence of Russian fatalism. Once the Russian Government had come to the conclusion that war was inevitable, further argument was fruitless.

If, as the diplomatic papers seem to imply, Germany had for many months been resolved upon war, what was the *rationale* of such a resolution ? There appear to have been two reasons. The first was the general fear probably felt by Germany and Austria of the aggression of the Slavs and their rapidly increasing numbers.

The population of Russia has increased at a rate at least as great as that of any other country, and the increase has not been promoted by immigration, it has been wholly natural. There has, during the past fifty years, been a not inconsiderable migration from Russia. The first census of Russia was taken in 1722. At that date the population was 14,000,000 ; in 1796 it was 36,000,000 ; in 1835, 60,000,000 ; in 1859, 74,000,000 ; in 1897, 130,000,000 (3) ; and in 1914, 178,000,000. (4) Assuming that in the case of each census the same areas were included—an assumption not absolutely but approximately justified—the period of two hundred years which has elapsed since 1722 has witnessed the doubling of the Russian population during each of the earlier three fifty-year periods and the approximate doubling of it during the fourth fifty-year period. At the present time (1923) the Slavic groups comprise 45 per cent. of the total population of continental Europe. What proportion will they comprise fifty years hence ?

# INTRODUCTION

The Russian problem cannot be understood without taking into account the rapidity of the growth in numbers of the Russian people. If all Russians were peasants living upon their own farms, if there were immense reserves of land in Russia for the present and coming generations, and if the crops were annually adequate for their maintenance, interest in the numbers of Russian people . . . might for a long time be purely academic. . . . The saturation point, or the point when under the most favourable conditions the land is supporting its fullest possible quota, must one day arrive. . . . If the peasants were as proficient in agriculture as the Chinese or the Japanese, the evil day of famine might be postponed. They are not proficient, but, on the contrary, relatively unproductive. . . . This is the Russian problem, . . . which Malthus put with vivid force. Unless the hare can be put to sleep, the tortoise can never overtake it. Still less is a drowsy tortoise likely to overtake the hare.(5)

The Slavic peril in respect of the numerical growth of the Slav peoples and those whom they control may well have given cause for German alarm, because, in the event of their breaking through the western boundaries by which they are confined, Germany and Austria would be the first to suffer. Apart from the pressure of numbers, the Slavic people are normally not aggressive. They have never shone in wars of aggression ; indeed, in the last of such conflicts, the Russo-Japanese war, they were ignominiously defeated. The defences of Germany were ample to enable her to resist any attack of Russia ; but Austria was in a different position. She had within her own boundaries a large Slavic population, and had she encountered Russia alone, she would probably have been defeated by mere weight of numbers.

The second reason for dread of Russia, and for the hastening of war, was that by 1916 or 1917 the Russian army would have been greatly increased. That is true ; but the Russian army has never during the whole of its history been really well equipped, for Russian industry has never reached the point at which it could adequately equip the numbers which her vast population enabled her to put into the field. The disastrous campaign of 1915 and 1916 furnished conclusive proof of this. If, therefore, the war was due to Germany's fear of Slavic aggression, that fear was itself due to exaggeration of the real power of Russia.

So far as the people, apart from the Governments, of Central Europe are concerned, fear of a Slavic invasion was no doubt a factor to be reckoned with ; but if there was a real Slavic peril, the fatuity of German foreign policy during the past fifty years becomes apparent, for it inevitably made for the alliance between France and Russia, and that alliance, notwithstanding the collapse of Russia, involved the ruin of Germany.

The disintegration of Russia, apart from the peculiar economic system which she has adopted, produced for each of her former

## THE RUSSIAN REVOLUTION

constituent parts important economic consequences. The loss of Poland, the Baltic Provinces, and Finland deprived what was left of the former Russian Empire of the most energetic and best educated of the population, while the temporary separation of the Ukraine and Siberia cut off Central Russia from its food supply and from a large part of its fuel. Thus the civil wars which were forced on the remnant of the Russian imperial army by the policy of the Soviet Government were necessary, in order to prevent the people of Central Russia from being reduced to starvation. They could not exist without the grain and coal of the Ukraine and the products of Siberia; indeed, it was by means of these resources that the population had so greatly increased.

In the following pages an attempt is made to trace the course and the consequences of the Revolution and of the civil wars to which it gave rise.

---

### NOTES

(1) Buchanan, Sir George. *My Mission to Russia* (London, 1923), vol. i, p. 165.

(2) De Schelking, E. *The Game of Diplomacy* (London, n.d.), p 220.

(3) Brockhaus and Ephron's *Encyclopedia*, art. *Russia* (St. Petersburg, 1900).

(4) *Statesman's Year Book* (London, 1920), p. 119.

(5) Mavor, J. *My Windows on the Street of the World* (London, 1923), vol. ii. pp. 369–70.

## BOOK I

# THE INTERVAL OF PEACE, THE EUROPEAN WAR, AND THE COLLAPSE OF THE DYNASTY

# CHAPTER I

## THE AUTOCRACY AND THE PEOPLE

NICHOLAS II repeatedly announced his desire to transmit unimpaired to his successor the autocratic power inherited by himself. During his reign he made occasional concessions to demands for constitutional government, but he invariably reverted to autocratic declarations. Had his ministers been always chosen with discrimination, had they even been generally capable and honest, (1) and had the civil and military services of Russia approached the standard of these services in Central and Western Europe, the personal power of the Tsar might have survived ; but survival became impossible simply because none of these conditions existed. (2) Tsardom fell, not because the revolutionary parties were powerful, nor because despotism is an anachronism, but because the despot in question was weak, (3) and in the task of governing a hundred and eighty millions of people would not suffer himself to be guided even by such statesmanlike wisdom as Russian society afforded.

Defects in the character of the Tsar seem gradually to have become accentuated. The most serious of these were a habit of vacillation, causing him to oscillate between contradictory opinions and to agree with his ministers upon a course of action only to adopt the contrary, nervousness about encroachment upon his autocratic prerogatives, and jealousy of the influence and prestige of his ministers. This last defect caused him to consult incompetent and intriguing persons and to act behind the backs of his own self-appointed advisers. (4)

The more important forms of political struggle which were in progress immediately before the war of 1914, and which prepared the way for the fall of the dynasty, may be summarized in the following manner. (5)

### (1) THE STRUGGLE BETWEEN THE AUTOCRACY AND THE ADVOCATES OF CONSTITUTIONAL RULE.

The constitutional manifesto of October 17, 1905, drawn up by Count Witte and others, was, after much hesitation, signed by the Tsar. Witte says that he would have preferred at that moment " a military dictatorship ; but as I saw that the sovereign desired the publication of the manifesto, I insisted that my own rendering of it should be adopted if I were to be nominated Prime Minister." (6)

## THE RUSSIAN REVOLUTION

The moment of fear on the part of the Tsar which impelled him to issue the manifesto passed away. The danger of revolution seemed to have disappeared, and then came, according to Witte, " a systematic attempt on the part of the Governmental clique to annul the Act of October 17, 1905." (7) Witte resigned in the following April.

The attempt on the part of the Government to evade the performance of the promises of 1905 reinvigorated the revolutionary element, altered its character, and extended its influence. While the *intelligentsia* became more and more internationalist and antimilitarist, there grew up within the Duma among all groups a kind of patriotic fervour, (8) under the influence of which the members in general separated what they thought to be the interests of the country from the interests of autocratic government. They desired cautiously to establish progressive steps towards constitutional rule, and to do this peacefully by means of a representative system which, faulty though it was, nevertheless provided a legislative organ. (9) Since, from their point of view, change—even revolution—was inevitable, they aimed at directing that revolution into a peaceful and orderly channel in which the currents of political and social life should suffer a minimum of disturbance. The Government of the Tsar must allow itself to be interpellated and directed by the Duma and so set an example of obedience to the law. This attitude of the Duma towards the Russian political problem was the natural outcome of recent and contemporary influences and events : the defeat of Russia by Japan ; the failure of the autocracy to maintain the prestige of the country ; the irreconcilable mutual antagonisms of the socialist parties ; the threatening gestures of Germany ; and the effect upon the Russian people of liberalizing tendencies in western Europe. The Tsar apparently saw nothing in the aims of the Duma but an attempt to encroach upon his autocratic prerogative, therefore he found himself out of sympathy with the political organ which he had brought into being.

The members of the first, and to a certain extent of the second, Duma were either convinced of the need for social as well as political change, or were disturbed by the varying forms of propaganda which were being urged by the numerous socialist groups. In both Dumas the moderate parties encountered the pressure of the members of the Left, who were dissatisfied with progress by steps, as well as of those of the extreme Right, who were opposed to change of any kind. This condition gave an air of reason to the hostility of the autocracy to the first and second Dumas, and rendered criticism of the Government's action in dissolving them less effective than it might otherwise have been.

# THE AUTOCRACY AND THE PEOPLE

The first and second Dumas lasted for too short a time to leave deep traces upon legislation. The third Duma endured for the statutory period and had before it, according to M. V. Rodzianke, chiefly the problem of national defence. The defeat of Russia at the hands of Japan, a relatively small power, had been the consequence of an aggressive commercial policy in the Far East unsupported by adequate military measures. For this defeat the *entourage* of the Tsar, rather than the Tsar himself, was generally held to be responsible. It was assumed by the constitutionalists that had there been a constitutional government and a ministry responsible to the Duma and exposed to interpellation, the Japanese war would not have taken place. The issue of that war induced a feeling of " insulted patriotism," (10) and convinced almost every man in the public life of Russia, the socialist *intelligentsia* excepted, that the first task of the new legislative order must be the complete reorganization of the military system.

Thus from the commencement of its sittings the third Duma found itself confronted with the problem of national defence (11) To solve this problem it was not only necessary to increase the effectiveness of the army, but the public finances had to be put on a stable foundation and industries developed to such an extent that in an emergency they might furnish the necessary supplies for a campaign. National defence was regarded as the first necessity practically throughout the entire history of the third Duma, and as the exclusive concern of the fourth Duma during the whole course of its career until the October Revolution of 1917, hence we look in vain for any important social legislation.

The attitude of the autocracy was by no means so hostile to the third and fourth Dumas as it was to the first and second. Yet wherever a controversy arose between adherents of autocracy and those of constitutional principle and practice, the autocracy almost invariably maintained its position. In spite of attempts to interfere with the elections to the fourth Duma, the Government did not succeed in securing a majority. The alliance of the Octobrists and the Cadets, constituting the progressive *bloc*, consolidated after long discussion, furnished the Duma with a compact central party, which, in effect, controlled its deliberations and stood between the obstructive parties of the extreme Right and the equally intractable parties of the extreme Left. These latter groups occasionally voted together in opposition to the *bloc*, (12) but the progressives were able, notwithstanding, to prevent either provocative or revolutionary measures from being adopted.

## (2) The Attack by the Autocracy upon Local Self-Government.

The *zemstvo* movement, arising after the famine of 1891 and directing the activities of the *Zemstvos* towards organized local effort for the increase and continuity of production and towards unity of action among themselves, was sharply rebuked by the Tsar.(13) While Goremikin (Minister of Interior, 1895–1899) desired to recognize the work of the *Zemstvos* in certain provinces, a policy hostile to them was adopted by his successors, Sipiaghin (1899–1902) and von Plehve (1902–1904). Witte had pointed out in a memorandum, *The Autocracy and the Zemstvo*, that the growth of power must lead to local self-government and to constitutionalism, for both were adverse to autocracy. Witte stated also that the co-existence of autocracy and local self-government could not result in the education of free citizens, and would involve a struggle in which the people must be defeated because they were not educated in the methods of successfully resisting attacks upon their freedom.(14)

After the assassination of von Plehve (1904), there came the so-called " Spring " of Prince Svyatopolk-Mirsky and the petitions of the *Zemstvos* demanding the convocation of a representative assembly. This was an open declaration of the tendency of the movement. The Union of Liberation (founded January 1904) combined the *Zemstvo* or local autonomy agitation with the general demand for constitutional government. A congress was held in November 1904 at St. Petersburg, at which resolutions were passed declaring that the arbitrary conduct of the centralized bureaucracy had undermined the faith of the people in the Government, and demanding the reorganization of the *zemstvo* system upon a democratic basis, with the formation of an elected national assembly. The majority wanted a legislative chamber with full authority, but there was a minority who desired to leave the autocracy with unlimited executive and legislative powers. This congress was followed by banquets and discussions throughout Russia, but on December 27th those who took part in such demonstrations were declared to be enemies of public order, meetings were forbidden, and the *Zemstvos* were abruptly ordered to confine themselves to observance of the *zemstvo* law.

In 1902 a commission had been appointed during the ministry of Sipiaghin for the examination of the needs of agriculture. This commission was composed of Goremikin, formerly President of the Council of Ministers, Count Vorontsev-Dashkov, Viceroy of the Caucasus, Chikhachov, Gerard, afterwards Governor of Finland,

## THE AUTOCRACY AND THE PEOPLE 31

Prince Dolgorukov, and Count Sheremetev—the two last mentioned being officials of the imperial court. It lasted from January 22, 1902, till March 30, 1905, and notwithstanding its high official and bureaucratic character, it appears to have intimated clearly that in order to avoid the miseries of a revolution it was necessary to realize a certain number of liberal reforms. This commission was abruptly dissolved on March 30, 1905, as a consequence, says Witte, of the character of its projected recommendations.(15)

The attitude of the autocracy towards the *zemstvo* movement was fatal to the dynasty because the Tsar thereby deprived himself of the support of the more intelligent and public-spirited of the landowners, the main prop of his throne, and threw them into opposition, at a moment when the central authority was in a precarious position owing to revolutionary propaganda and the growing power of the urban proletariat. The net result of the unsuccessful struggle for constitutional practice, alike in respect of the State Duma as central legislative authority and of the *Zemstvo* as local administrative body, was divergence between the Government and Russian society as a whole. The Government dissociated itself from the people, and yet in governmental circles the impossibility of ruling a territory so enormous and a people racially so diverse without the aid of the educated social elements was well understood.(16) The complex of nations which constituted the Russian Empire had outgrown both the bureaucratic frame and the police *régime* by which the unity of the Empire was supported.(17) While the Government was retrograde, Russian society was forced into progress by the facts of life, and thus day by day the gulf widened between Government and people. Clearly the Government could retain its position only by destruction of the oppositional elements ; but these oppositional elements had come to comprise practically the entire Empire, and destruction of them meant destruction of the whole. The only way out of the *impasse* was the way of revolution.(18)

Revolutionary propaganda suffered a marked decline between 1907 and 1914, for the revolutionists so active in the preceding decade were dispersed in foreign countries, and propaganda in the industrial centres and villages waned, partly on account of the repressive measures of Stolypin and his successors, but chiefly because of the conflicts among the revolutionary groups themselves, with consequent discouragement and inertia. At the same time the economic prosperity of the country afforded less material for revolutionary propagandists, with the result that more moderate political and social views gained ground among all classes.

## THE RUSSIAN REVOLUTION

Demand for social development grew less, as that for political change became more insistent. The prestige of the Tsar seriously declined during the years that intervened between 1905 and 1914 ; yet whatever might be the defects of his personal character and however vacillating and inconsequent might be his policy, the unifying influence of Tsardom was still regarded by educated Russian society as necessary for the preservation of Russian national unity, and this notwithstanding the fact that at the outbreak of war in 1914 there had been in operation for some years forces which were making for the fall of the dynasty, and through its fall for the disintegration of Russia, and the more or less complete subversion of the social order.

Under these circumstances it is not surprising that an external war, especially a war of defence, appeared to some persons in governmental circles as a means of uniting the disparate elements and of securing at least the temporary support of the people. Germany and Austria together afforded the occasion for such a war. While Russian statesmen anticipated a struggle with Germany at no distant date, they had no reason to precipitate it, because, in a military sense, they were not ready, yet when the occasion arose, some of them embraced it with enthusiasm, since war appeared to be the only alternative to revolution.

German authorities do not deny that the socialist propaganda in Russia was aided and fomented by German agents during the war, but Russian authorities are inclined to the opinion that it was fostered by the Germans at a somewhat earlier period. M. V. Rodzianko, president of the fourth Duma, dates the increase of previously existing German socialist propaganda among Russian workmen from the steps taken by the Duma in February 1914 to reorganize the Russian military system.(19) It is possible, however, to exaggerate the importance of German interference in Russian affairs ; at any rate in the direct pursuit of its object, it was only moderately successful.

---

### NOTES

(1) Count Witte describes the bureaucrats and courtiers who surrounded the Tsar at the time of the Russo-Japanese war as " abject and stupid." Witte, Count. *Mémoires du Comte Witte, 1849–1915* (Paris, 1921), p. 421. Many portraits, by no means unduly harsh, are given of the *entourage* of the Tsar during the later years of his reign by Alexander Isvolsky, Minister of Foreign Affairs in the Cabinet of Stolypin. (See *The Memoirs of Alexander Isvolsky*, London, 1920.) Other memoirs confirm the general impression of the prevalence of unscrupulous personal ambition and incompetence in administration. Of Stürmer, Prime Minister and Foreign Minister in 1916, it has been said, " No principles at all,

# THE AUTOCRACY AND THE PEOPLE

and a complete nonentity." Shulgin, Basil. *The Months before the Revolution* in *The Slavonic Review* (London, 1922), vol. i, pp. 383–84.

(2) See, however, the passage from Joseph de Maistre quoted infra, p. 430.

(3) Defects disclosed themselves to observers before Nicholas II succeeded to the throne. Count Witte narrates a conversation with I. N. Durnovo, Minister of the Interior. At the time of the death of Alexander III, Durnovo inquired of Witte his opinion of their new master. Witte replied that the young Tsar was without experience, but was well brought up and intelligent ; he hoped that he would understand his business, and in that case the ship of state would voyage without danger. Durnovo replied : "I believe you deceive yourself about our young Emperor. I know better, and let me tell you his reign will bring to us much unhappiness. Note my words : Nicholas II is nothing but a new edition of Paul I." Witte, Count, op. cit., p. 158. The similarity of the characters of Paul I and Nicholas II is referred to in the anonymous article *The Tsar* in *The Quarterly Review* (London, July 1904), No. 399, p. 192. This comparison must be understood as referring to the accepted contemporary view of the character of the Emperor Paul.

(4) The character of Nicholas II is well analysed by Isvolsky, A., op. cit.

(5) The finances of Russia were afterwards reorganized by Witte ; but in 1892 the famine of 1891 had emptied the Treasury and had compelled Witte to increase the issue of paper roubles. In the adoption of this expedient, Bunge, formerly Minister of Finance, saw the beginning of the ruin of Russia. Witte, Count, op. cit., p. 40.

(6) Ibid., cf. p. 277, and cf. pp. 191–94.

(7) Ibid., p. 281.

(8) Cf. Rodzianko, M. V., *The State Duma in the February 1917 Revolution* in *Archives of the Russian Revolution* (in Russian ; Berlin, 1924), vol. vi, p. 10.

(9) Duration of successive Dumas :—

1st Duma, April 27–May 10, 1906, till July 9–22, 1906.

2nd Duma, April 20–May 3, 1907, till June 3–16, 1907.

3rd Duma, Nov. 1–14, 1907, till June 8–21, 1912.

4th Duma, Nov. 28–Dec. 11, 1912, till Feb. 26–27–11/12 March, 1917.[1]

(10) Rodzianko, M. V., op. cit., p. 10.

(11) In 1908, soon after the third Duma met, Austria annexed Bosnia and Herzegovina, and Germany assumed a truculent attitude. The military weakness of Russia at that time was universally recognized, and central European policy was shaped accordingly.

(12) Rodzianko, M. V., op. cit., p. 14.

(13) Especially in the reply (of Nicholas II in 1894) to the *zemstvo* addresses on his accession. "It has come to my knowledge that of late there have been heard the voices of people lured by senseless dreams of representatives of the *Zemstvos* sharing in the conduct of internal affairs. Let it be known to all that I, devoting all my strength to the good of my people, will maintain the principle of autocracy as firmly and steadfastly as did my late father." Quoted by Beazley, Raymond (and others). *Russia from the Varangians to the Bolsheviks* (Oxford, 1918), pp. 488–89.

(14) This reflection applies equally to the Tsarist autocracy and to the so-called "dictatorship of the proletariat." The same defects in character and training which hindered the people in overthrowing the autocracy caused them to succumb to the dictatorship.

(15) Cf. Witte, Count, op. cit., pp. 191–94.

(16) Cf. Rodzianko, M. V., op. cit., pp. 7–8.

(17) Ibid., p. 8.

---

[1] The Tsar formally prorogued the Duma in the night of February 26–27. The Duma remained sitting until it was abolished by the Bolsheviks in the October 1917 Revolution. (The dates are given according to both the Old Style and the New.)

# THE RUSSIAN REVOLUTION

(18) " Palace scandal and palace tragedy " were not wanting to complete the catalogue of occasions. When all exaggeration is removed from the accounts of the relation of Rasputin to the Imperial Court, enough remains to justify the conclusion that his influence over it was considerable and malign, and that the fact of his association with the Imperial family was regarded by wide circles of the people as discreditable. Yet the death of Rasputin did not result in appreciable change in the methods of the Court or in its relation to the people.

(19) Rodzianko, M. V., op. cit., vol. vi, pp. 15–16.

# CHAPTER II

## THE INTERVAL OF PEACE, 1907–1914

THE period from the close of the first phase of the Russian Revolution (1905–1907) to the outbreak of the European War was characterized by general economic prosperity. Various causes contributed to this state of affairs : a succession of favourable harvests, increased cultivation on great estates due largely to more frequent employment of German agronomists, (1) extension of land areas in peasant occupancy involving increase in the area of land cultivated by well-to-do peasants, transformation of the land-holding system from community-holding to peasant proprietorship, (2) abolition of the redemption payments (imposed under the Emancipation Acts), breaking up of " great households," (3) extension of credits by means of the Peasants' Bank, improved farming methods, increased production, (4) railway construction, greater export of grain inducing advance in the interior prices of agricultural produce (increased production notwithstanding), introduction of such crops as sugar-beets, new to certain regions, co-operation among peasants (stimulated by local societies of which peasants and others were members, and by *zemstvo* organization of education, and finally by advance of wages in the rural districts and industrial centres)—all these causes conduced to the economic prosperity alike of European and of Asiatic Russia.

The industrial strikes of 1905–1907, while chiefly arising from political causes, had resulted in advance of wages and amelioration of conditions of labour. The urban proletariat, through weakening of ties between village and town, had become a more compact and better organized class. Assisted by sympathetic professional men—engineers and the like—working men had acquired a certain power, and had learned that by using it they could enhance their wages and improve their position. Continuous residence in industrial towns and uninterrupted employment in the same factories, or in the same kind of factories, resulted in increased efficiency, and therefore in greater confidence and self-respect. Not yet had the urban proletariat become truculent.

While the mass of the peasantry continued to live a self-contained and frugal life, a succession of fair harvests enabled the peasants to raise their standard of comfort, and the growth of the towns and larger villages increased the volume of consumption. Thus

36 THE RUSSIAN REVOLUTION

industries found an expanding domestic market. The hostile tariff of Germany impeded exportation of Russian manufactures to that country, but contributed to the maintenance of Russian domestic prices at a relatively low level. Industry was thus expanding without the fear of over-production, although at any time an inferior harvest might diminish the power of consumption.

So far as the peasants were concerned, the land reforms of Stolypin (5) had greatly improved their general position. Those who benefited most by the change from communal to individual ownership were the peasants who had, under the previous system, been well-to-do, either because of their shrewdness and industrious habits, or because of their grasping character.(6) Though the poorer ones had not benefited proportionately, yet the peasant population as a whole had experienced a general improvement. " The purchasing power of the peasants was growing. It seemed to many of us that with one more year of such progress our country would be perfectly revived. But the political situation directed our history in another and a harder way." (7)

The political situation, however, had reactions in the economic sphere. Disturbance of traditional prices, especially those of foodstuffs, benefited the peasant, but placed the town inhabitant at a disadvantage. A conflict thus arose between urban and rural interests and became apparent in the 'nineties, when prices of foodstuffs began to rise, and it became further intensified during the pre-war period from 1907 to 1914. Although proprietors probably as a class received their rents more punctually than before, they also found that the cost of living had increased, the wages both of domestic and of field workers had advanced, and prices of everything they had to buy had risen proportionately.

Even among the peasantry conflicts of interests arose. The rich peasants were getting richer, and the poor peasants, though better off than they had been, were still poor. The latter very naturally reflected that had the system of communal redistribution of land been preserved, they might have shared more amply in the enhancement of agricultural resources.(8) They did not realize that that enhancement was due, at least partly, to the abolition of the communal system of land-holding and to the substitution of peasant proprietorship. The old system had not been communistic in the sense of division of property or income according to need ; it had been a system in which the peasant community took the place of the landowner and redistributed the land among the peasants for cultivation by them. The poorer peasant who cultivated his land without due industry or intelligence was able under this system, at least sometimes, to exchange his deteriorated land for land brought

# THE INTERVAL OF PEACE, 1907–1914

into a relatively high state of cultivation by more experienced or more industrious hands. Thus the poorer peasant was better off than he had been, until want of industry or want of skill again reduced his means of livelihood; but the skilful peasant was being deprived of the fruits of his toil upon the land for the benefit of the unskilful, and the total yield from the land was less than it might have been had he been left in undisturbed enjoyment of his improved holding. This was the *rationale* of the Stolypin reforms. Moreover, the poor and unskilful peasants were in a majority, and the reforms were by no means so obviously helpful to them as a class as they were to the well-to-do peasants—the so-called *Kulaks*. (9)

Encroachments upon the powers of the community involved in the Stolypin reforms did not merely displease the poorer peasants, but also the *intelligentsia* of Slavophil tendencies, who saw in them the destruction of the *mir* as an institution and the development of peasant life towards commercial farming of west European and American type. The reforms were also distasteful to the Social Democrats, because they offered the prospect of solving the peasant question on the basis of peasant proprietorship—a basis inconsistent with the social-democratic doctrine of landownership by the State.

The eight years which elapsed between the date of the Stolypin reforms and the outbreak of the European War afforded too short a time for the firm establishment in the minds of the Russian peasantry of a land system profoundly different from that to which they had been accustomed.

The idea of property in land was repugnant to the peasant. From his point of view even the community (local or general) must not own the land ; the utmost the community could do was to allot it for temporary use. Thus, although in 1914 quite 75 per cent. of the land was in peasant occupancy, the peasants had not yet learned to look upon their holdings as their own property, in the sense in which peasant proprietors in France and farmers in Canada and the United States regarded their respective holdings and farms. Thus peasant property in Russia, although it was established by law, " did not exist. It did not exist in this sense, that the institution of property had not made itself the habitual and firm regulating principle of the life of the masses of the people." (10)

For this reason " the institution of property was defenceless on two sides : the *intelligentsia* had intellectually renounced it, and the masses of the people had not yet arrived at it. This is the historical explanation of that lack of any conscious resistance to the Russian Revolution's attack upon property. As far as there existed elements of settled peasant property in pre-Revolution

## THE RUSSIAN REVOLUTION

Russia—to create which had been the aim of Stolypin and Krivoshein " (who continued the work of Stolypin)—" these elements were also swept away by the Revolution. The Revolution demolished equally the property of the gentry and the peasantry." (11)

Thus, while Russia at the close of the period of peace was at a very unstable stage in respect to her agrarian problems, there was just as much instability in the industrial sphere.

Iron, coal, oil, and the precious metals had been exploited by means of foreign capital, and the related industries had been managed mainly by foreigners or by Germans from the Russian Baltic Provinces. The exigencies of world-wide competition required a higher degree of efficiency than the Russian workers were accustomed to attain, and thus the administration of the larger industries appeared to them oppressive and too liable to exploitation. All kinds of socialist propaganda laid stress upon the inevitability of depression and exploitation under the capitalist system, and thus, as in the agrarian field, the *a priori* conclusions of the *intelligentsia* harmonized with the practical experience of the workers. The relatively low scale of efficiency of the Russian worker, when compared with that of the central and western European or with the American, inevitably involved a lower wage-scale, and this low scale was only rendered possible by an equally debased standard of comfort and living. Notwithstanding the inferior cost of production of certain commodities in Russia, the risks of enterprise owing to the instability of the social system were so great, especially during and after the revolutionary movements of 1905–1907, that only adventurous organizers of industry were willing to embark on Russian enterprises. Because the competition in the employment of capital was limited by the condition of social insecurity, the adventurers were in a position to make relatively large profits ; indeed, they had to make these in order to provide insurance funds against risk of total elimination of their investments by political and social revolution. Industry in Russia was thus involved in a vicious circle—inefficiency, restriction of capital investment, fear of total loss, exploitation of the individual worker, and consequent inefficiency. Had the Government been strong enough to inspire confidence either on the part of Russian capital, which was beginning to accumulate, or on the part of foreign capital, this vicious circle might have been broken, and competition of capital seeking employment in the exploitation of Russian resources might have increased the demand for labour and elevated the wages and standard of living of the labourers.

Although fear of a fresh outbreak of revolutionary activity, and doubts regarding the ability of the autocratic Government to

# THE INTERVAL OF PEACE, 1907–1914

cope with such an outbreak, hung like a dark cloud over industrial enterprises in Russia, foreign capital continued to be invested. French, Belgian, German, British, Canadian, and United States financiers and industrial concerns provided credits and organized enterprises, especially during the five years immediately preceding 1914.

At the same time, increased employment of agricultural machinery upon the large estates, erection of grain warehouses and appliances for shipping grain in large quantities at the ports of Windawa and Libau on the Baltic, and Odessa and Novorossisk on the Black Sea, together with improvements in the railway system, had increased the export trade. Siberia had developed a system of shipping cattle and dairy produce to European Russia and to the countries of eastern Europe, whilst her gold and other mines were being exploited largely by means of British capital—in short, a spirit of vigorous enterprise characterized agricultural and industrial activity in a region formerly regarded merely as a place of exile for opponents and critics of the ruling powers. Increased demand for timber made for the prosperity of Finland, and the need for coal encouraged the development of the coal-mines of south-western Poland, as well as those of the basin of the Don, whilst the oil-wells of the Baku region were vigorously exploited by foreign capital.

In European Russia the main lines of communication were improved, and in Siberia the Trans-Continental railway, formerly single, had been almost entirely converted into a double track. Railway travelling became more punctual and convenient, the Russian systems compared more favourably with others, and this improvement in communications had rendered the fear of regional famine less grave, for it was possible in lean years to send supplies of grain into many, although not yet into all, of the regions in which the harvest might be deficient. Partly due to favourable climatic conditions, there had been no such famine as that from which the region of Kazan suffered in 1899, so that for ten years before the outbreak of war in 1914 the *zemstvo* reserve stores were full of grain and every *volost* had some capital.(12) Although public expenditure, especially for military purposes, had greatly increased, the budget was balanced and the imperial finances were in a favourable position.(13)

The effect upon the *morale* of the people of the reforms in land tenure and of the social changes and economic prosperity coincident with these reforms was disturbing to the established order. As they bcame better off materially, people of all conditions, but especially the suddenly enriched peasant and artisan, lost what elements of primitive spirituality they had preserved and became

# THE RUSSIAN REVOLUTION

more and more materialistic. Formerly they had entertained a vague and sometimes poetical theory of life which satisfied them, and yet did not prevent them from acting from the most sordid motives. Even this vague theory had evaporated and, so far as one can generalize on such matters, the Russian spirit (as exemplified in the salient characteristics of the mind of the people) had degenerated into one of mere materialism. Russian society was thus in a sense prepared for the Revolution, and especially for its materialistic aspects and tendencies.

Two of the most important elements in an economic survey of Russia now remain to be considered ; these are the heterogeneous racial character and the rapidity of the increase in population.

### (1) THE HETEROGENEITY OF THE RUSSIAN POPULATION.

The complex racial composition of the population of Russia has been fully described elsewhere. (14) Probably not more than one-half of the inhabitants of the former Russian Empire were of Slavonic origin, and even in these there was much admixture of blood. The remaining half was composed of very numerous races. Alike in habits of life, in religion, in language, in the complex of elements entering into what is called " culture," these various races differed from the Slavonic peoples. The sole bond of union was the Tsardom. All of the peoples regarded the Tsar as the symbol of national unity : his personality was not a factor of moment ; what was important was his office. The racial heterogeneity of the people rendered the maintenance of the Tsardom possible, the personal deficiencies of many Tsars and Tsarinas notwithstanding ; and the same characteristic rendered extremely difficult the introduction of western European democratic and constitutional ideas. The multiplicity of languages alone made a single effective representative assembly almost impossible. When with the abdication of the Tsar and the collapse of the Tsardom the outward and visible symbol of unity disappeared, there remained no unifying influence, and the imperial system with its Tsardom of Russia, Tsardom of Poland, Grand Duchy of Finland, etc., etc., fell to pieces, and rendered inevitable the disintegration of Russia into numerous independent nationalities.

### (2) RAPIDITY OF THE INCREASE OF THE RUSSIAN POPULATION.

During the thirteen years between 1897 and 1910 the population of the Russian Empire increased by a figure almost equal to that of the population of England at the close of that period. The rate

THE INTERVAL OF PEACE, 1907–1914 41

of increase during the two hundred years which have elapsed between the death of Peter the Great and the present time exhibits a great acceleration towards the close of the epoch. (15) The mean annual increase of population between 1724 and 1897 was 6·6 per thousand, and between 1897 and 1910 it was 28·8 per thousand.

So rapid a growth of population upon a scale of such magnitude would have taxed the administrative resources of any government. The congestion in some of the regions rendered inevitable an extremely low standard of living, even when harvests were normal ; when they were deficient, there was famine and loss of life ; and even when this was not the case everywhere, the absence of effective means of communication made relief in deficient areas either difficult or impossible, for starving men could not drive starved horses to the centres of supply on the rivers or railways.

The railway system was being gradually extended and improved, while a series of favourable harvests, in spite of diminishing returns to cultivation in certain regions (17) due to the absence of fertilization, obviated the necessity for measures of relief.

Contemporaneously with improvement in the economic situation and with increase of population—largely a consequence of that progressive improvement—there was apparent a decline in efficiency of administration. This decline was due partly to the rapidity of the increase of demand for officials of competence and integrity, owing to the increase of population, and to the scarcity of the supply of such officials, and partly to the absence of elasticity in the form and practice of the Russian Government.

The frame of mind of the conscientious bureaucrat of the old *régime*, and there were many such, on the eve of the *débâcle*, is probably accurately expressed in the memoirs of C. V. Zavadsky, who was procureur of the Petrograd legal department in February 1917. He describes how, in the period immediately before the outbreak in the streets, " one could hear the noise of the solder cracking and all the governmental organization breaking. The Government had no problems of principle before it ; to go forward, it was afraid (I suppose it was too late), to go backward, it was ashamed. The only thing that was left was to do important work from day to day, like horses on a treadmill." He notices that one of the early signs of disintegration was the rapidity with which ministers were appointed and replaced—for example, four prime ministers, four ministers of the interior, and three ministers of justice held office within one year—1916. Zavadsky mentions as a significant detail that it had been customary for a man in his position to make a formal call upon a new prime minister (President of the Council) on assumption of office ; but after two changes

## THE RUSSIAN REVOLUTION

within so short a time, he ceased to observe this formality, although personally acquainted with those newly appointed. These frequent changes narrowed the already restricted circle of potential ministers. Zavadsky remarks upon the small number of men of the first rank in Russia from whom an unexceptionable choice of ministers, on the ground of integrity and ability, might be made. He does not complain of the Provisional Government appointing Kerensky as Minister of War, because similar appointments had been made under the old *régime*, as in the cases of Stürmer and Protopopov.

Instances of ignorance of usage are of minor importance compared with ignorance of matters essential to adequate performance of ministerial duties. Zavadsky narrates that Stürmer, who was at the time Minister of Foreign Affairs, did not know to what Power Salonica belonged,(17) whilst the course and consequences of the Balkan War were equally unknown to him. He also repeats the stories of Protopopov and the German fortune-teller-spy which have in other ways obtained currency.

The chief point emphasized in Zavadsky's description of the situation is the absence of support which the Government experienced. The peasants were dissatisfied, as were the workmen, the bureaucracy, the landowners, and the army. " The Government was not satisfying the front or the rear, the Left or the Right. It was not satisfying itself. . . . Power is only strong when the masses believe that it is without reproach "—or it may be added, believe in its absolutely remorseless exercise.

Zavadsky attributes the attitude of the people to the " extraordinary inertia of the Russians, who without thought preferred to be inhabitants rather than citizens, a herd rather than a society." The inertia of the people was in a sense profitable for the Government, even when it resulted in absence of education and preparation for governmental duties in educated circles, because an inert population is a conservative population, fearing change as likely to be for the worse.

During the years from 1905–1916, Zavadsky says that a distinct change was manifest. Everywhere the phrase was being used, " Things cannot be worse ! "(18) Gradually the inert mass began to move, and when it did move its very inertia prevented it from stopping.

On the eve of the war, i.e. in the early summer of 1914, the working people of St. Petersburg were full of revolutionary ideas, and these spread among other than the working groups. " Demonstrations and meetings were held, tramway cars were overturned, telephone and telegraph poles were cut down, and barricades were built."(19) This had happened in 1905–1906. " There

# THE INTERVAL OF PEACE, 1907–1914

can be no doubt," according to Rodzianko, President of the Duma, " that the excitement among the working class was the result of the activity of the German General Staff."(20) These demonstrations were going on during the visit to St. Petersburg of M. Poincaré, who was protected, while he drove about the city, by a strong military escort. (21) Rodzianko also attributes to German agency the agitation in the villages which occurred simultaneously. (22)

It is not surprising that some of the German newspapers during the months of June and July 1914 should have been drawing attention to the revolutionary movements in Russia and to the general decay of that country. (23) Yet as soon as war was declared, " there were swept aside, as if by fairy magic, all the revolutionary movements in the capital."(24)

---

### NOTES

(1) The Germans were partly from the Russian Baltic Provinces and partly from Germany. They were employed because of the scarcity of Russian agronomists and because they were able to get more work out of the peasants than could Russian overseers. The peasants disliked German foremen, but they worked hard for them out of fear.

(2) Under the law of November 9, 1906 (cf. Mavor, J., *An Economic History of Russia*, (London, 1914, revised ed. 1925) vol. i, pp. 340–57)and subsequent laws.

(3) Undivided families, several generations living under the same roof.

(4) The increased production was due to many causes ; among these must be reckoned the compulsion of higher wages and taxes.

(5) The law of November 9, 1906. Stolypin's original law was revised by the Duma, under the care especially of S. I. Shidlovsky.

(6) The poorer and " middle " peasants were in the habit of calling all peasants who were better off than themselves *Kulaks*. (Cf. Mavor, J., op. cit., vol. ii, p. 258.)

(7) Makaroff, Nicholas P., formerly Professor of Economics in the University of Moscow, *The Russian Agrarian Movement* in *World Agriculture* (Amherst, Mass., 1922), vol. ii, No. 3, p. 148.

(8) The Land Acts of Stolypin led almost immediately to anti-*zemstvo* riots which puzzled the authorities. These riots were, however, very intelligible. The Acts threw the control of local affairs into the hands of large proprietors. In the temper of the time this could not be done without risk of disorders. (Cf. Krassnov, V., *Memoirs about 1917–1920* in *Archives of the Russian Revolution*, Berlin, 1924, vol. viii, p. 110. Witte, op. cit., pp. 346–48.

(9) Witte says that his policy in regard to the land question was to establish " individual landownership and full legal rights for the peasant class. The transition from communal to individual landownership was to be gradual and free from all compulsion. Stolypin's Cabinet and the third Duma took advantage of the legislative plans which we had laid, but in doing so they distorted them to such an extent that the land reform which is now (1912) being carried out may lead to grave revolutionary complications. . . . He (Stolypin) inaugurated a policy of forcefully disrupting the time-hallowed institution of the *obshchina* (community)." Witte, Count, *Mémoires*, etc., English Translation (London, 1921), p. 388 ; French Translation, p. 348.

## 44 THE RUSSIAN REVOLUTION

(10) Struvë, Peter, *Russia* in *The Slavonic Review* (London, 1922), vol. i, No. 1, p. 33.

(11) Ibid.

(12) Rodzianko, M. V., *The State Duma in the February 1917 Revolution* in *Archives of the Russian Revolution* (Berlin, 1924), vol. vi, p. 9.

(13) " In 1914 her (Russia's) ordinary revenue, which during the preceding years had been rapidly expanding, was estimated at over £370,000,000 and the gold reserve amounted to £150,000,000." Buchanan, Sir George, *My Mission to Russia* (London, 1923), vol. i, p. 162.

(14) Cf. Mavor, J., op. cit., vol. i, pp. 573 et seq.

(15) The following table shows the growth of the population of the Russian Empire. The statistics up to 1897 include annexations by conquest or otherwise. From 1899 till 1910 there were no annexations. The figures are in millions.

| 1st Revision, | 1722 | .. | .. | .. | .. | 14 |
| 2nd ,, | 1742 | .. | .. | .. | .. | 16 |
| 3rd ,, | 1762 | .. | .. | .. | .. | 19 |
| 4th ,, | 1782 | .. | .. | .. | .. | 28 |
| 5th ,, | 1796 | .. | .. | .. | .. | 29 |
| 6th ,, | 1812 | .. | .. | .. | .. | 41 |
| 7th ,, | 1815 | .. | .. | .. | .. | 45 |
| 8th ,, | 1835 | .. | .. | .. | .. | 60 |
| 9th ,, | 1851 | .. | .. | .. | .. | 69 |
| 10th ,, | 1858 | .. | .. | .. | .. | 74 |
| 1st General Census, | 1897 | .. | .. | .. | .. | 129 |
| 2nd ,, ,, | 1909 | .. | .. | .. | .. | 160·8 |

Up to 1897, the authority is the official return as given in Brockhaus and Ephron's *Encyclopedia*, art. *Russia* (St. Petersburg, 1900), p. 75. For 1909 (January 1, 1910) the authority is the official *Recueil de données statistiques et économiques, etc.* (St. Petersburg, 1912). The movement of population since 1910 cannot be determined with confidence ; but the population of the area which comprised the Russian Empire was in 1923 about 180 millions, the population of the Federated Soviet Republics being about 132 millions.

(16) Even in the Black Soil region the yield of grain had declined owing to continuous cropping without the use of fertilizers, fallowing, or other means of permitting the regeneration of the soil.

(17) No doubt similar instances of ignorance might be found in ministers of other countries.

(18) Zavadsky, C. V., *On the Great Cleavage, The Report of a Citizen upon Life in 1916–1917* in *Archives of the Russian Revolution* (Berlin, 1923), vol. viii, pp. 5–7.

(19) Rodzianko, M. V., *The State Duma in the February 1917 Revolution* in *Archives of the Russian Revolution* (Berlin, 1924), vol. vi, pp. 15–16.

(20) Ibid., loc. cit.

(21) Ibid., loc. cit.

(22) Ibid., loc. cit.

(23) Ibid., loc. cit.

(24) Ibid., loc. cit.

# CHAPTER III

## THE EUROPEAN WAR AND ITS IMMEDIATE ECONOMIC EFFECTS UPON RUSSIA

THE last days of July and the first days of August 1914, so crowded with events in Europe, witnessed a sudden change in the temper of the Russian people, but there was no corresponding change in the government.

The declaration of war by Germany on August 1, 1914, was greeted by the articulate voices of the two capitals with as great enthusiasm as ten years earlier they had greeted the war with Japan. M. V. Rodzianko, President of the Duma, describes picturesquely the scene in the streets of St. Petersburg :—

"Who are proudly walking the streets with national flags ? Who are singing the national anthem and making patriotic demonstrations before the Serbian embassy ? I walked in the street and talked with the crowd. To my astonishment, I found that the people who were doing these things were workmen, those workmen who a few days before were tearing down the telegraph poles, overturning tramway cars, and building barricades. To my question, ' What is the cause of this change of mood ? ' I received the answer, ' Yesterday we had a mere family affair. We were demanding our rights—reforms which were planned in the legislative organizations ; these reforms were so slow in coming that we decided to have them immediately ; but now, to-day, the business has to do with all Russia. We come to the Tsar as to our flag, and we will go behind him for the sake of victory over the Germans." (1)

Suddenly Russia seemed to become " one and indivisible," party polemics and agitation were forgotten. When the Duma met on August 8, 1914, there were found to be no parties. (2) The mobilization of the army was effected without difficulty, 96 per cent. of those who were summoned responding to the call, yet in spite of enthusiasm, and of the previous economic prosperity, Russia was not prepared in any sense, political, administrative, industrial, or military, for war with a first-class power. (3)

Her unstable internal equilibrium exposed her to danger of collapse in the event of a prolonged or unsuccessful campaign. The bureaucratic administration was not conducted with adequate efficiency or integrity, (4) the industries were not sufficiently developed to provide munitions for the armies which, in respect of man power,

## THE RUSSIAN REVOLUTION

Russia was able to put into the field, the reorganization of her military system undertaken after the Japanese war required still two years to complete, (5) and the construction of strategic railways for the defence of her European frontier had not been adequately undertaken.

None of the Powers involved in the European War, not even Germany, were thoroughly prepared for five years of campaigning under the exhausting conditions of modern warfare ; but the development of industry, and the skill with which industrial plants were transformed into arsenals, provided the central and western Powers with material equipment in excess of that available for Russia, although the man power of the latter country was as great as that of Germany, Austria, and Turkey combined.

In the first onslaughts under the Grand Duke Nicholas, the Russians poured into East Prussia, Galicia, and Bukovina, driving the inhabitants before them, afterwards reaching the passes of the Carpathians and threatening the plains of Hungary. There can be no doubt that these Russian attacks, so much more energetic than either the German or the Austrian General Staffs had apparently anticipated, had an important effect upon the distribution of troops as between the western and eastern fronts and upon the strategic plans of the Germans. The Russian advance, consciously precipitate as it was, involved enormous sacrifices ; but it checked the German invasion of France by imposing upon Germany the necessity of reinforcing the defences of her eastern front. The Russians were ill-prepared to meet the additional armies now thrown into the field by Germany. (6) There were plenty of men, but the supply of munitions was deficient, and troops were sent to the front inadequately equipped, (7) with the result that they were disastrously defeated at Soldau on August 29, 1914, and had subsequently to retire from the Carpathians. (8)

Alexander Blok, the poet, regarded the year 1916 as the most critical in the disintegration of the Russian State. The symptoms of the malady were manifest in the proceedings during that year of the following personalities : the Tsar, the Tsarina, Virubova, and Rasputin. It had so deeply affected all the organs of the State that nothing might be hoped from any ordinary remedy, the only chance lay in a very complicated and dangerous operation. " No one who understood the situation," he says, " had any doubt of the necessity of the operation." The question was how it would react upon a body which was not strong enough to withstand so serious a shock.

The malady had begun before the war ; but the war greatly accelerated its progress, and in the third year (1916) the disease

# THE EUROPEAN WAR

had so shaken the governmental organism as to arrest the development of its productive forces.

" In the autumn of 1916 the Government called up the thirteenth million of peasants, ploughmen and technical workers."(9)

" During the war a stupid experiment was performed on the Russian industrial proletariat. The military specialists of the autocracy did not expect a prolonged war, (10) which would exact the use of all their technical development, a sound organization of the rear, and all the strength of those engaged. Accordingly, in the mobilization for the front, they did not spare the valuable and none too numerous skilled workers and technical industrial personnel. On the other hand, the subsequent forced growth of military industries created a new improvised working class gathered from anywhere, undisciplined, without experience, and without traditions of organized and sustained class struggles. As it became dissatisfied, this new proletariat showed itself extremely impulsive, changeable, unreliable, utterly lacking in discipline, and full of naïve faith in the 'social miracle.' Its socialism was usually of the primitive distributing and receiving variety. This section of the proletariat furnished the Bolsheviks with a great many of their fiery, but half-baked and unreliable adherents."(11)

When the huge losses incurred by the northern and southern sectors of the front became known, the enthusiasm of the people cooled, and the first signs of that depression which eventually so deeply infected them began to show itself. There was no lack of spirit in the army, but that of the people suffered a serious decline within a month after the outbreak of war, and within a fortnight after the real commencement of hostilities. The Russians can be patient in defeat, but they can at the same time be fatalistic and hopeless.(12)

The further course of the war cannot be fully described here. Our chief concern is with the effect that it had upon Russian economic life. In Russia, as in all other countries, the economic effects of the war consisted of huge losses in men through casualties and disease, increase of wages and prices, increase of paper money, increase of state debt, paralysis of industry through cessation of external demand and the drafting of workmen for the army, congestion and deterioration of the railway system by the movement of troops and munitions, the wearing-out of the rolling-stock of railways, conversion of industrial establishments into arsenals with the consequent wear and tear of machinery, scarcity of food through increased demand for army provision, diminished agricultural production, and difficulties of importation and interior transport.

# THE RUSSIAN REVOLUTION

While the peasants were feeling the actual strain of the war, the members of the Duma were criticizing the Government for the conduct of it. They were even beginning to use the ominous word " treason." On November 14, 1916, Miliukov delivered in the Duma a speech which, though forbidden by the censors to be printed, had nevertheless an enormous effect. He gave several instances of incompetent action on the part of the Government, and after each, asked the question, " Is that treason or stupidity ? " At every point his speech was applauded. Many people have thought that this was the first sign of the Revolution. Certainly the speech was courageous and probably fundamentally just. Shulgin, who was a member of the fourth Duma, remarks that Miliukov's proofs of treason " were not very convincing."(13) He admits, however, that Miliukov showed fully what an insignificant person Stürmer was, and to what extent he was surrounded by suspicious characters. That was enough ; Russia was in the throes of a great war and her affairs were in the hands of people of inferior stamp.

The assistance contributed in 1916 and 1917 by the Allies relieved the strain upon the Russian administration, and increased activity was observable in the Russian munition works. The army was equipped as never before, and early in the spring of 1917 a new spirit of confidence made its appearance among the troops. But this relief came too late ; the Russian people were defeated, and there was no support behind the army.

The blame of the defeat was inevitably attributed to the autocratic power of the Tsar, and the limitation or abolition of this power was clearly the most urgent and necessary task. Thus, in spite of the invasion of Russia by German armies, the people were not too preoccupied to turn and blame the form of government which, in their opinion, had brought about the invasion. Into a soil thus prepared by the course of events there fell, *first*, the seeds of the movement for constitutional government which for years had been conducted by the Constitutional Democrats and supported by the Octobrists, neither of these groups being anti-monarchical ; and, *secondly*, the seeds of the propaganda of the various socialist parties, whose general tendency was not merely anti-monarchical, but subversive of the existing social order.

---

### NOTES

(1) Rodzianko, M. V., op. cit., vol. vi, pp. 16–17.
(2) Ibid., loc. cit.
(3) On the part of some there were misgivings. Witte, who had disapproved of the policy that led to the Japanese war, was equally opposed to the policy

# THE EUROPEAN WAR

which permitted Russia to be drawn into the war against Germany and Austria. [See the Preface by Countess Witte to her husband's *Memoirs*, English Translation (London, 1921), p. x.] The policy of Witte as declared in his *Mémoires* (French edition, p. 375) involved the formation of a triple alliance of Russia, Germany, and France, and reduction of the land military forces of these countries with the object of creating a *puissant* naval force which would dominate the world. This was indeed a naïve project, underestimating as it did the possibilities of increase in the naval power of Great Britain and the United States, as well as the discordant ambitions of the three Powers involved in the projected alliance. Although Witte was a man of great force of character and of financial ability, his *Mémoires* reveal him as being destitute of a sense of proportion in his conception of international relations. On his view of the desirability of avoiding war with Germany see de Schelking, E., *The Game of Diplomacy* (London, n.d.), pp. 206–07.

(4) In the event of war with Germany it was inevitable that the position of Russia must be compromised by the fact that the most efficient members of the civil service (and many of the higher military functionaries) were of German extraction.

(5) This reorganization involved the reduction of the period of compulsory military service from 3½ to 2½ years, thus providing a larger number of trained troops. " In the spring session of 1914 legislation was passed in the State Duma which, implemented in two years—that is in 1917—would have made our army quantitatively, and, from the point of view of munitions, much stronger than that of Germany." Rodzianko, M. V., op. cit., p. 15.

(6) Cf. the *Memoirs* of Denikin, Gourko, etc. M. Paléologue, the French ambassador, accuses Sukhomlinov, the Minister of War, of neglect or worse in respect to the supply of munitions. (Paléologue, Maurice, *An Ambassador's Memoirs*, London, 1923, vol. i, p. 131 et seq.) So also does Rodzianko, M. V., op, cit., p. 21. But the industries of Russia were insufficiently developed and organized for the equipment of such large armies. On the efforts of the War Department, see Gourko, General Basil, *Memories and Impressions of War and Revolution* (London, 1918), pp. 100 et seq. The demands for munitions from the front were not fully met by any of the belligerent governments. Munitions in both the French and the British armies were deficient during the first year of the war.

(7) M. Paléologue relates a conversation on June 2, 1915, with a leading Russian industrial, a member of the Munitions Board :—

" The days of Tsarism are numbered. It is beyond hope. But Tsarism is the very framework of Russia and the sole bond of unity for the nation. Revolution is now inevitable, it is only waiting for a favourable opportunity. Such an opportunity will come with military defeat, a famine in the provinces, a strike in Petrograd, a riot in Moscow, some scandal or tragedy at the Palace. . . . With us (in Russia) revolution can only be destructive because the educated class is only a tiny minority, without organization, political experience or contact with the masses. To my mind that is the greatest crime of Tsarism. . . . No doubt it will be the *bourgeois*, intellectuals, ' Cadets,' who will give the signal for the Revolution, thinking they are saving Russia. But from the *bourgeois* revolution we shall at once descend to the working-class revolution, and soon after to the peasant revolution. And then will begin anarchy, interminable anarchy ! . . . We shall see the days of Pugachev again and perhaps worse ! " (Paléologue, M., op. cit., vol. i, pp. 349–50.) This prophecy is remarkable, not merely for the general accuracy of the forecast, but for the light it throws upon the fatalistic frame of mind of the educated Russian, and for the characteristic censure of the Tsardom for defects in the educated class—defects which are inherent in the Russian character and are not dependent upon any form of government. They are as apparent in the Soviet Republic as they were under the old *régime*.

(8) Yet in spite of political difficulties and intrigues in the rear, and in spite of technical difficulties and occasional instances of demoralization at the front, the Russian armies were esteemed so highly by the Germans that in January 1917,

# THE RUSSIAN REVOLUTION

near the end of the war, the German-Russian front required to oppose them 187 enemy divisions, nearly one-half of the total number of enemy forces operating on the European and Asiatic fronts. (Denikin, General A. I., *The Russian Turmoil* (New York, 1913), p. 32.)

(9) Blok, Alexander, *The Last Days of the Old Régime* in *Archives of the Russian Revolution* (Berlin, 1922), vol. iv, p. 5. Blok's work is based upon the documents and materials collected by the special committee appointed by the Provisional Government (of March 1917) for inquiry into the illegal actions of the late ministers.

(10) The military specialists of the autocracy were not alone in entertaining this view. In every belligerent country technical experts were sent into the trenches regardless of the necessity of organizing the rear.

(11) Chernov, Victor, *Disintegration of Classes in Russia* in *Foreign Affairs* (New York, 1923), vol. ii, No. 1, pp. 37–38.

(12) M. Paléologue narrates a conversation with Witte on September 10, 1914, in which Witte expressed the most gloomy views on the outcome of the war for Russia. "If we assume a complete victory for the coalition . . . it means not only the end of German domination but the proclamation of republics throughout Central Europe. That means the simultaneous end of Tsarism! I prefer to remain silent as to what we may expect on the hypothesis of our defeat." (Paléologue, M., op. cit., p. 123.)

(13) Shulgin, Basil, *The Months before the Revolution* in *The Slavonic Review* (London, 1922), vol. i, p. 387.

## CHAPTER IV

## THE REVOLUTION OF FEBRUARY–MARCH 1917, THE FORMATION OF THE PROVISIONAL GOVERNMENT, AND THE ABDICATION OF THE TSAR

THE date of the beginning of the Revolution of 1917 may be regarded as February 23rd (O.S.)–March 8th (N.S.), when riots occurred in Petrograd. These riots appear to have been spontaneous. In widely separated parts of the city crowds of people of various ranks poured into the streets, shouting " Bread ! " The scarcity and the price of bread in Petrograd were not nearly so great as they afterwards became, nor were they so serious as in the cities of some of the other belligerent countries, yet both were unusual and were ascribed by the people to the Government's continuance of the war. " Bread ! " was the dominant, if not the only, cry, and if the Government had taken prompt measures to answer it, the spontaneous street movement might have gone no farther, and cries hostile to the autocracy might not have been heard.

The revolutionary elements very naturally saw in these unorganized and spontaneous demonstrations opportunity not merely for propaganda but for direction. Red flags and revolutionary placards made their appearance. On this day (March 8th) there were strikes in over fifty establishments, involving between eighty and ninety thousand workers. Order was maintained by the police, but as a precautionary measure military forces were called up and held in readiness. (1)

Although the riots appeared as the first overt incident in the new phase assumed by the Revolution, they were not of themselves important at that moment, excepting in so far as they frightened both the Government of the Tsar (including the Tsar himself) and the leaders of the Duma. Both feared that the mob might become uncontrollable and that the spirit of disaffection might spread to the army.

The Government of the Tsar had been able to meet more than one serious crisis in which it found itself in opposition alike to the constitutionalists and the revolutionists, why was it unable to do so in February 1917 ? The answer to this question seems to lie in the attitude of the Government to the people during the three years of war. The Government was afraid to take the people into its confidence, afraid to announce the losses of the campaign,

## THE RUSSIAN REVOLUTION

and afraid to entrust the people with the organization of their forces for victory. Rodzianko says that "the readiness of the people to give all their means and all their energies for the benefit of the country was beyond necessity.(2) The Government, however, did not avail itself of the assistance of the people, though this was vital to the successful conduct of the war.

"From the beginning the Government took the wrong point of view. Instead of strengthening the monarchical prestige of the Tsardom [by trusting the people and taking advantage of their enthusiasm for service], it thought that victory would be and could be won by the Government of the Tsar alone, without immediately organizing the forces of the people and thus summoning everyone for the war. . . . Such was my opinion after conversation with persons occupying important governmental positions."(3)

The gulf between the Government and the people was too wide. The Government feared that organization of the people for victory over the enemy might prove incidentally to be organization for victory over itself, it therefore took upon its own shoulders the full responsibility for the conduct of the war. The mismanagement, especially in respect of the supply of munitions during the first two years, was fatal to its prestige. The organization of the Russian industries in the winter of 1916–1917 for the making of munitions came too late ; had it been done earlier,(4) another tale might have been told. As it was, the Government refused to be diverted from its policy of isolated action, and that policy lay at the root of the Russian military defeat and the feeble resistance of the Government to the Revolution.

On March 10, 1917, the excitement in Petrograd reached its highest point. Male and female workers in the factories on the north side of the Neva struck and marched to the centre of the city. The garrison was sufficient to deal with any violent disturbance, and there was as yet no reason to doubt the loyalty of the army, yet the crowds in the streets wore a menacing air, and it was clear that the demonstrations were primarily due to the precariousness and cost of food supplies.

Charges have been made (5) against Protopopov, Minister of the Interior, of having "provoked" the Revolution by forbidding the sale of bread in those parts of Petrograd inhabited by working people, and of preparing to shoot down the people if they made any bread demonstrations. Those who make these charges add that in the ensuing disturbances "about 5,000 people were killed."(6) Proof of these statements is wanting. Protopopov was not a competent or a popular minister. Undoubtedly he prepared, as in duty bound, to preserve order, but his failure to do so does not

## THE REVOLUTION OF FEBRUARY–MARCH 1917

prove that he wilfully intensified the bread crisis, albeit he certainly took inadequate means to meet the deficiency of food in the capital. According to Sir George Buchanan, owing to the coal shortage many factories were closed and several thousand workmen were unemployed. Many of these, after waiting in the queues at the bakers' shops, were unable to get bread ; on the evening of Thursday, March 8th, bread shops were looted, and on the following day the agitation increased. Cossacks cleared some streets, but had no collision with the crowds, for the people were not hostile to the soldiers, only to the police. On Saturday, March 10th, there were numerous strikes and the crowds were better organized than on the preceding day ; Protopopov had clothed some of the police in military uniforms and these began to shoot at the mob. On Sunday morning, March 11th, the Government gave evidence of having " determined to adopt repressive measures." General Khabalov, military governor of Petrograd, posted notices ordering the dispersal of the crowds and the return of workmen to their work. No heed was paid to these admonitions, and in the course of the day about two hundred persons were killed by the fire of the troops. In the afternoon a company of the Pavlovsk regiment mutinied, refused to fire, and had to submit to be disarmed by the Preobrashensky regiment. Sunday evening found order temporarily restored ; but discussions began in the barracks. " If the order to fire were given, were the soldiers to shoot down their own kith and kin ? " On Monday morning the Preobrashensky regiment, on being ordered to fire, shot their officers, as also did the Volhynsky regiment, till by midday 25,000 troops had mutinied. Sir George Buchanan states that according to the most reliable estimates 1,000 persons were killed. (7)

Rodzianko, as President of the Duma, convened, on March 10th, a meeting of representatives of the Government, of the *Zemstvos*, and of the municipalities. At this meeting it was agreed to entrust the immediate regulation of the food supply of Petrograd to the municipality, the representatives of the Duma guaranteeing that the necessary legislation should be passed. Rodzianko telephoned to the Grand Duke Michael Alexandrovich, who was then at Gatchina, urging him to come to Petrograd at once. He arrived on the 12th, and Rodzianko then proposed that, in the absence of the Tsar, and owing to the ineptitude of the Government in dealing with the crisis, the Grand Duke should allow himself to be declared Dictator of Petrograd, and that he should dismiss the Tsar's Ministry and announce the formation of a Cabinet, responsible, it is to be presumed, to the Duma. The Grand Duke had a conversation by telephone with the Tsar, who curtly rejected the proposal. (8)

## 54 THE RUSSIAN REVOLUTION

Rodzianko's idea seems to have been that the crux of the position lay in the attitude of the garrison. If the garrison joined the crowds in the streets the days of the Tsardom were over, but if, through the personal influence of the Grand Duke Michael, this fraternization could be prevented, the measures which had been taken immediately to relieve the food situation might avail to satisfy the people and save the situation.

In the night of March 11th–12th Rodzianko was informed by the Tsar that the Duma was dissolved. A peaceful conclusion seemed to be now no longer possible, as the only body which was, in the opinion of the people, actively discharging its functions had been dismissed.

On Monday morning, March 12th, revolts begun sporadically during the previous afternoon were continued in the Petrograd garrison. The commander of the reserve battalion of the Litovsky regiment was killed by his soldiers, and the remaining officers were arrested. They were shortly released, but the excitement had evidently spread to the garrison, and the disturbances in the streets began to assume a military complexion. During the day of March 12th the Petrograd Arsenal, the Artillery Department, and the Provincial Court House were destroyed, the Arsenal was pillaged, and guns and ammunition were taken from it and given to an extemporized battalion of what came to be known as the Red Guard. Crowds of people, armed with many kinds of weapons, filled the streets, and during the night conflicts took place between insurgents and, as yet, unaffected units of the garrison. The Government met at the Marie Palace, and there it appears to have wrung its hands helplessly. Rodzianko relates that one of the members of the Government afterwards told him that on an alarm being raised that the insurgents were marching on the Palace, lights were extinguished, and when the alarm proved false and the lights were again turned on, one of the ministers was found under the table. In the streets, during the night of March 12th, some bodies were found with their throats cut, for the Government had given way to panic, and the spirit of unrestrained violence was abroad. On the morning of the 12th, Rodzianko demanded the resignation of Prince Golitzin, President of the Council of Ministers. Golitzin refused, but during the evening of the same day he handed to Rodzianko the resignations of his colleagues and himself, and this action left the country without a government at a moment when anarchy reigned in the capital. Meanwhile the army, now well supplied with munitions, was in the trenches, and the Tsar remained silent at headquarters.

The Government of the Tsar having ceased to exist, the only

## THE REVOLUTION OF FEBRUARY–MARCH 1917 55

thing possible was for the dissolved Duma to continue without leave to exercise its functions, and to enlarge these by endeavouring to take control of the perilous situation. Then followed the demand on the part of the leaders of the Duma that the Tsar should abdicate.

By this act the Duma joined the Revolution, inchoate and confused as it was, consisting of demonstrations by women asking for bread, by soldiers complaining of their officers, by constitutionalists demanding the appointment of ministers responsible to the Duma, by workmen claiming higher wages, and peasants more land, by socialists clamouring for a state-collectivist system, by Bolsheviks demanding the dictatorship of the proletariat, by *zemstvo* representatives seeking local autonomy, and by some groups wanting more and others less centralization. To this welter of contradictory and inconsistent demonstrations and agitations there was added the danger of an epidemic of crime, for on the night of the 12th the police-stations had been attacked, those who were detained there liberated, and the buildings burned.

The Duma had no choice but to join the Revolution. Had it not done so, its members would have been killed by the soldiers in revolt, (9) and the governmental power, which fell naturally into the hands of the Duma, whose members were the representatives of the people, would have been left to be seized by any adventurous group, or even individual adventurer, who might have the skill and courage to get the ear of the mob. Such were the conditions under which the Provisional Government came into being.

Lenin's interpretation of the war and the Revolution regards the struggles of 1905–1907 as a preliminary phase and insists that without these three years of " ploughing " the second phase would not have been brought so quickly to a conclusion. During these three years " the ploughing " went " very deep " and " brought out the superstitions of centuries, woke up political life, and roused the political struggle. Millions of workers and tens of millions of peasants showed to one another, to everybody, to all classes, and to the chief parties in Russian society, their actual nature, and the actual relationship of their interests, their force, their means of action, and their future aims. The first Revolution and the Counter-Revolution which followed it showed up all the defects of the monarchy, brought it to the ' last line,' uncovered all the decay, the cynicism, and debauchery of the Tsarist gang with the miraculous Rasputin, all the rudeness, the ferocity, and brutality of the family of Romanov—those *pogromchiks* who overflowed all Russia with the blood of Jews, workmen, and revolutionaries."

## 56 THE RUSSIAN REVOLUTION

Lenin also speaks of the "landlords who were committing all sorts of brutality and crime, who were ruining and choking large numbers of citizens only to guarantee for themselves and their class the 'sacred rights of property;'" and continues: "Without the Revolution of 1905–1907, and without the Counter-Revolution of 1907–1914, it would have been quite impossible to have such self-consciousness of all classes of the Russian people . . . and to see the relationship of these classes to each other and to the Tsarist monarchy, which showed themselves in the eight days of the February–March Revolution of 1917."

After the Revolution of 1905–1907 and the Counter-Revolution of 1907–1914, some great stimulus was necessary to reawaken the revolutionary spirit. Here Lenin employs a striking and sustained metaphor. After these events, the rehearsals of the great drama, the actors knew each other, knew their *rôles*, their places on the stage, and their mode of action. But there was still necessary a strong "*régisseur*."(10) "This forcible *régisseur*, this stimulator, appeared in the form of the world imperialist war."(11)

When Lenin, with a coarseness which is characteristic of his writings, reproaches the landowners and the Romanovs with ferocity and brutality, he exposes himself to the obvious retort that these very qualities might with justice be applied to himself. But his general contention that the revolutionary movements of 1905–1907, the subsequent reaction between 1907 and 1914, and the war of 1914–1917 were indispensable preliminaries to the Revolution, cannot be gainsaid.

Lenin also says that the crisis of February–March 1917 was brought about by the defeats to which "Russia and her Allies" had been subjected, that these defeats shook the mechanism and the organization of the Government, and produced anger against the Government on the part of all classes of the population, including the army. Here also his interpretation is sound, but it is altogether otherwise when he alleges that the crisis was actually stimulated by "a union of Anglo-French financial capital and Anglo-French imperialism with the Octobrists' and Cadets' capital in Russia." He adds that "this side of the affair is very important," although "nothing is said of it in the Anglo-French press." It is on the other hand "underlined" in the German newspapers. Lenin continues: "The whole course of the February–March Revolution shows us very clearly that the English and French ambassadors with their agents and 'allies,' who were working desperately for a long time to prevent a separate treaty and a separate peace between Nicholas II . . . and William II, were working at the same time to dethrone Nicholas Romanov."(12)

## THE REVOLUTION OF FEBRUARY–MARCH 1917

No proof has yet been forthcoming, either that Nicholas II made any attempt to conclude a separate peace, or that the English or French ambassador entered into any conspiracy to dethrone him. (13) It must, however, be acknowledged that events were making for a separate peace from at least the autumn of 1916, and to these events the Tsar, had he remained in power, might have had to bend, as also the Provisional Government of Lvov and Kerensky, had it been still in authority.

The Provisional Government, according to the interpretation of Lenin, " was not an accidental meeting of persons, it really represented a new class that had attained political power in Russia, the class of capitalist landowners and *bourgeoisie* which had for a long time been ruling the country in the economic sphere." (14) It had been active in 1905–1907 and during the interval of 1907–1914, and it had been especially active in the war of 1914–1917. This class organized itself quickly for political action, took into its hands local government and education, and promoted " all sorts of congresses," controlling the Duma and organizing committees for stimulating the production of munitions.

But this Government could not give what the people wanted, viz., " peace, bread, and freedom." It could not give peace because it was " a war-government, tied hand and foot to Anglo-French imperialistic capital." Bread the Government cannot give " because it is *bourgeois*." It can only give to the people, " as in Germany generally, organized famine. . . . The people will soon know that there is bread and that it can be got ; but not otherwise than by bending before the sanctity of capital and landownership." Nor can the Government give freedom, because it is a government of landowners and capitalists who fear the people. (15)

In an article in *Pravda*, dated April 9, 1917, (16) and entitled " *Dual Government*," Lenin announced, before the fact was widely recognized, that side by side with the Provisional Government there was another. " What," he asks, " is dual government ? This, that beside the Provisional Government, the government of the *bourgeoisie*, there is another one, very weak yet, only the embryo, but in spite of all that, undoubtedly an existent and developing government, the Soviet of Workmen's and Soldiers' Deputies. What is the class character of this other government ? Proletarian and peasant, though it be dressed in soldiers' uniforms. What is the political character of this government ? That of a revolutionary dictatorship, that is to say power leading straight to revolutionary victory and to the direct help of the masses of the people from underneath, and not from the laws issued by the Central Government."

# THE RUSSIAN REVOLUTION

## NOTES

(1) Cf. Blok, Alexander, op. cit., vol. iv, p. 25.

(2) Rodzianko, M. V., op. cit., p. 17.

(3) Ibid., loc. cit.

(4) Fear of profiteering seems to account for inaction. There are other methods of dealing with profiteering than simply preventing it by allowing nothing to be done with or without profit.

(5) E.g., by E. de Schelking in *The Game of Diplomacy*, " By a European Diplomat " (London, n.d.), p. 233.

(6) Ibid.

(7) Buchanan, Sir George, op. cit., vol. ii, pp. 58–61.

(8) Rodzianko, M. V., op. cit., p. 57.

(9) Ibid., p. 59. The details of the occurrences of March 10–12, 1917, are drawn chiefly from the account given by Rodzianko, who was probably in a better position than anyone else to observe events.

(10) Lenin uses this word in the combined sense of prompter and director of the production of the drama.

(11) Lenin, N., *The First Stage of the First Revolution*, " *Letters from Far Away* " in *Pravda*, March 21–22, 1917. Reprinted in *Collected Works* (Moscow, 1923), vol. xiv, part i, pp. 5 et seq.

(12) Lenin, N., ibid., p. 8.

(13) See Sir George Buchanan's answer to rumours of this nature in *My Mission to Russia* (London, 1923), vol. ii.

(14) Lenin, N., *Collected Works* (Moscow, 1923), vol. xiv, part i, p. 9.

(15) Ibid., p. 11.

(16) Reprinted in Lenin, N., *Collected Works* (Moscow, 1923), vol. xiv, pp. 24–25.

# APPENDIX A

TELEGRAM FROM M. V. RODZIANKO, PRESIDENT OF THE STATE DUMA, TO THE TSAR NICHOLAS II, DATED PETROGRAD, MARCH 11, 1917.

"The situation is very serious. Anarchy in the capital. Government is paralysed. Transport and fuel absolutely disorganized. General dissatisfaction is growing. Riots and firing in the streets. Sections of the same regiments are firing at one another. Necessary to get someone popular in the country to form a government. Slow action useless. Praying to God that in this hour the responsibility will not fall on His Anointed."

TELEGRAM FROM THE SAME TO THE SAME, DATED PETROGRAD, MARCH 12, 1917.

"The situation is worse. Measures should be taken immediately because to-morrow will be too late. It is the last hour when the fate of the Russian dynasty is at stake."

These telegrams were duly delivered to the Tsar at his headquarters. They were not answered.

# APPENDIX B

PROCLAMATION BY THE PROVISIONAL GOVERNMENT, MARCH 12, 1917.

After the deposition (*sic*) of the Emperor Nicholas and of the rejection (*sic*) of the Grand Duke Michael, which changed absolutely the ways of ruling from which the people were suffering under the old *régime*, the Provisional Government realizes its obligations to the State. The Provisional Government takes upon its shoulders the task of implementing all the financial obligations of the State incurred by the old *régime*, such as payment of interest, payment of the state debts, obligations under treaties, payments to civil servants, pensions and all other kinds of payment due by law, or treaty, or on some lawful foundation. On the other hand, all payments which are due to the public treasury, the taxes, customs, duties, and all kinds of payments, must be paid as before into the public treasury until new laws are passed.

# 60 THE RUSSIAN REVOLUTION

The Provisional Government believes in the absolute necessity of the existing state departments being very careful in the expenditure of the money of the people. In order to emphasize this we must use the necessary measures for exercising active control. The magnitude of military expenditure at the present time, the increase of the state debt on account of the war, the increase of taxes, are all quite unavoidable. . . . .

Signed by Prince Lvov as member of the Council of Ministers.

[*Izvestia* (Helsingfors), March 14, 1917.]

*BOOK II*

# THE DUAL AUTHORITY OF THE PROVISIONAL GOVERNMENT AND THE PETROGRAD COUNCIL OF WORKMEN'S AND SOLDIERS' DEPUTIES

THE title of the Petrograd Council (Soviet) as given on pre-ceding page is the one customarily employed. The manifesto issued upon the formation of the Council on March 14, 1917, gives the title " Council of Soldiers' and Workmen's Deputies "; but the important *Order No. 1* issued on the same day gives the title as in the text. For the early history of the Council of 1905, see Mavor, J., *An Economic History of Russia* (London, 1914, 1925), vol. ii, p. 527

CHAPTER I

# THE PROVISIONAL GOVERNMENT AND THE REVIVAL OF THE SOVIETS

ALTHOUGH revival of the revolutionary spirit of 1905–1907 was anticipated by wide circles of Russian society and by many foreign observers, the actual outbreak of the Revolution of March 1917 found the Government, all the political parties (including those of revolutionary tendencies), and the population in general unprepared, the Government and the political parties in a strategic sense, and the masses of the people from the point of view of social and political development. Absence of preparation on the part of politicians was due to the fact that all of them—reactionaries, liberals, and revolutionaries—were desirous of avoiding internal struggles pending the conclusion of the war.

While propaganda had been carried on actively both in Russia and abroad,(1) there does not appear to be any evidence that the demonstrations, interpreted by Rodzianko and other leaders of the Duma as signs of revolution, were otherwise than spontaneous.

The leaders of the Duma were undoubtedly prepared for a *coup d'état* by means of which power might be transferred from a ministry responsible to the Tsar to a ministry responsible to the Duma.(2) The question of the constitutional character of the future government was reserved for decision by a Constituent Assembly soon to be convened, for the Duma had not decided to overthrow the monarchy, and the socialists had not arrived at agreement among themselves for united action. There was no one party, in the Duma or outside it, strong enough to hope for success in forming a revolutionary government. When riots occurred in the streets of Petrograd and unarmed civilian insurgents were joined by mutinous, untrained young peasant soldiers from reserve battalions(3) (which formed a large part of the garrison of the capital), the leaders of the Duma, interpreting these occurrences as the beginning of the Revolution, decided, perhaps not unwillingly, to place themselves at the head of it, and demanded the abdication of the Tsar. Some of these leaders would have been content to accept the Grand Duke Michael, brother of Nicholas II, as temporary dictator or as Tsar, but others were opposed to either of these plans, and the Grand Duke, evidently reluctant to assume a position of so great difficulty and risk, declined to accept the responsibility

## 64 THE RUSSIAN REVOLUTION

of sovereignty in any sense of the word, unless he was called to do so by a Constituent Assembly.(4)

When the Tsar abdicated(5), on March 12, 1917, a Provisional Government was formed. The members of this Government were selected by a committee of the Duma, which appears to have consulted with the Executive Committee of the newly arrived Petrograd Council (Soviet) of Workmen's and Soldiers' Deputies.(6) This body had installed itself during the early days of March in the Taurida Palace, and from that moment practically assumed the position, and discharged many of the functions of, the State Duma, which thus almost disappeared from the scene. The Provisional Government was compelled from the beginning to show deference to the Petrograd Soviet, and may be said to have owed its existence to the insurgent mob in the streets of the capital, to a few battalions in mutiny, to the State Duma, and to a hastily convened body of workmen and soldiers representing only a fraction of the population of the city. The conditions under which this Government was brought into existence rendered the speedy formation of a national policy at once imperative and impossible. It was compelled from the beginning of its career to yield to pressure from local insurgent elements without regard to the general interests of the nation, and for this reason lacked the support of the people as a whole, at the moment when the fabric of the State was shaken by the abdication of the Tsar. This Provisional Government was essentially of the middle-class ; but the Russian middle-class was not sufficiently numerous, energetic, patriotic, or experienced in political affairs to rally at once to the support of a government which had assumed the responsibility of power. Moreover, the personnel was not imposing enough to attract public confidence and enthusiasm.

It consisted of the following persons : *Prime Minister*, Prince G. E. Lvov, non-party, landowner, president of the Union of *Zemstvos* formed for war services, of unimpeachable integrity, but lacking in political sagacity ; *Finance Minister*, M. S. Tereshtchenko, non-party, Little Russian, wealthy, honest, and patriotic, but destitute of political experience and without knowledge of financial questions ; *War Minister*, A. S. Guchkov, Octobrist, energetic, honest, and capable, chairman of the military commission of the Duma, and formerly a critical opponent of Sukhomlinov while the latter was War Minister ; *State Controller*, L. Godnov, Octobrist ; *Chief Procurator of the Holy Synod*, V. N. Lvov, Octobrist (neither of the two last mentioned was a man of mark) ; *Foreign Minister*, P. N. Miliukov, Constitutional Democrat (Cadet), professor of history (for some years at Sofia in Bulgaria, during exile), a man of learning, ability, integrity, and courage, one of the leaders of

# THE PROVISIONAL GOVERNMENT

the Cadet party in the Duma, and leader of the opposition to the Government in the third and fourth Dumas, inclined to a constitutional monarchy rather than to a republic, advocate of the acquisition by Russia of Constantinople and the Dardanelles, enthusiast for the prosecution of the war in 1917, determined critic of the autocracy and of successive imperial ministers, known for his intrepid speeches in the Duma, but wanting in the political virtue of popularity among the masses, and (owing to long absence abroad) lacking direct contact with the Russian people; *Minister of Agriculture*, A. S. Shingarev, Cadet, active in the Duma, experienced politician, shrewd, sympathetic with the masses, and skilful in understanding popular currents; *Minister of Ways and Communications*, N. V. Nekrassov, Cadet, clever tactician (7); *Minister of Education*, A. A. Manuilov, Cadet, professor of political economy at Moscow, of academic temper; *Ministry of Commerce and Industry*, A. L. Konovalov, Progressivist, manufacturer, wealthy, shrewd, intelligent, and honest; lastly, as *Minister of Justice*, A. F. Kerensky, Socialist-Revolutionary, but member of the " Toil Group " in the Duma, a lawyer, eloquent, persuasive, energetic, courageous, and popular, but personally ambitious and unstable.

The Provisional Government thus consisted of 2 non-party ministers, 3 Octobrists, 4 Cadets, 1 Progressivist, and 1 Socialist-Revolutionary—11 members in all. In this small group there were two parties fluctuating in their membership. One of these parties, consisting generally of Nekrassov, Konovalov, Tereshtchenko, Godnov, and Vladimir Lvov, regarded Kerensky as their leader; and the other, consisting of Manuilov, Shingarev, and Guchkov, followed in general the leadership of Miliukov. The two leaders, Kerensky and Miliukov, one Socialist-Revolutionary and Republican, the other Constitutional-Monarchist, were personally hostile to one another. The Prime Minister, Prince G. E. Lvov, frequently threw his influence on the side of Kerensky, who thus had in the Cabinet a majority of practically seven to four.

At a moment when above all else union of forces was necessary to conduct the campaign against Germany, to avoid defeat and dismemberment of the Russian State, and to combat the elements making for internal disorder, the Cabinet was divided and contained within it the seeds of its own dissolution. The Provisional Government announced itself in a proclamation on March 12, 1917. After referring to the " deposition " of Nicholas II and to the " rejection " of the Grand Duke Michael, the proclamation went on to say that the Provisional Government had made itself heir to the old *régime*, accepting its obligations and requiring payment

## 66 THE RUSSIAN REVOLUTION

of all state taxes, etc.,(8) and would necessarily continue to employ the services of its bureaucrats.

After the revival in February 1917 of the Petrograd Council of Workmen's and Soldiers' Deputies, similar councils were formed elsewhere, and they began to exercise influence several days at least before the outbreak of the demonstrations which were interpreted as the sign of the Revolution. (9) On March 13, 1917, in the evening, a meeting was held in the salon of the State Duma at the Taurida Palace. This meeting was attended by the Executive Committee of the Council of Workmen's and Soldiers' Deputies, the Executive Committee of the officers of companies of the Petrograd garrison, delegates of officers of the garrison and of the fortress and fleet, and representatives of Republican officers. Many British, French, and Italian officers were present. Lieut.-Colonel Gusheihn, in urging the prosecution of the war, said that in order to win, it was advisable that the gap between officers and men should be closed ; he therefore moved a series of resolutions respecting the " rights " of soldiers. Official military religious service should be abolished ; every soldier should have the right to express his political, religious, social, and other views and to be a member of any party ; censorship, excepting of military correspondence, should be done away with ; forms of address by men to officers should be simplified—the expressions " sir " and the familiar " thou " should be no longer employed ; salutes should be discontinued ; services to officers should be paid for ; titles of officers (10) should be abolished ; corporal punishment should cease ; and soldiers should have the right to organize themselves. All orders contradictory to the orders consequent upon these resolutions or to the orders of the Council of Workmen's and Soldiers' Deputies were to be regarded as of no effect. (11)

These resolutions were passed. There followed as a natural consequence, on the day after this meeting, *Order No. 1* of the Petrograd Council of Workmen's and Soldiers' Deputies. (12) This order was addressed to, and was apparently exclusively intended for, the Petrograd garrison (13) ; but it was assumed in the army to be of general application. The formation of committees in the army under *Order No. 1* began immediately, and the order was recognized by the military commanders at the front and in the various garrisons. It is significant of the confusion of the time that the resolutions which led to *Order No. 1* should have been advocated and passed on the ground that the measures proposed would facilitate the winning of the war, whereas the effect of these measures was precisely the opposite. The immediate effect of *Order No. 1* upon the discipline of the army was devastating.(14) The ultimate conse-

# THE PROVISIONAL GOVERNMENT

quences were the demoralization of the army and the crumbling of the western front, the victory of the Bolsheviks over the other political parties, the Treaty of Brest-Litovsk, and the establishment of what came to be known as the Soviet Republic.

The issuing of *Order No. 1* was the first overt sign of the intention of the Petrograd Soviet to assume a dominant *rôle* in the direction of affairs. It explicitly set aside the authority of the State Duma, and infringed that of the Provisional Government.

The revolutionary press (not exclusively Bolshevik) in March 1917 discloses the state of mind of the soldiers, sailors, and workmen, rather than of the party leaders, who were at that moment merely emerging from cover in Russia, or were finding their way thither from abroad. There is observable in the revolutionary press at this time, first, a distinct demand for the stoppage of the war ; secondly, a desire for some drastic change in the character of government, with a threat of violence if the government should not be in accordance with the wishes of the army ; third, a claim for a crude communism as a means of providing food supplies.

These ideas are all expressed in the following condensed extracts :—

" The *bourgeoisie* blame us for spoiling the general unity, for setting soldiers against officers, and in so doing playing into the hands of the Germans." The *bourgeois* newspapers complain that the misfortunes of the front are due to internal lack of unity, and urge the danger to Russia of submission to Germany. " Behind these accusations there lurk two distinct aims. First : the *bourgeoisie* want to convince the soldiers that it is necessary to continue the war. Second : *bourgeois* politicians are utilizing the circumstances to sow dissensions between workmen and soldiers, to restrict the new free organization of the army, and to subordinate the army to their unlimited influence. By so doing, the *bourgeoisie* hope to achieve two results : (1) to bring the war to the end most suitable for them, and (2) to become absolute owners of the economy of the State.

" The *bourgeoisie* tell us that they are for freedom ; and that as Germany and Austria are dangerous to freedom it is necessary to continue the war to a glorious end. This is mere playing with words. These attempts of the *bourgeoisie* are not dangerous for us because, having freedom of speech and press, we shall be able to say something against them. The free army will be able to defend our freedom, but it will not shed its blood in the interest of the *bourgeoisie*. It will be very dangerous if the *bourgeoisie* separate the soldiers from the workmen. If they succeed in this, the affairs of the people will be ruined and the *bourgeoisie* will dominate the people." (15)

## 68    THE RUSSIAN REVOLUTION

At a meeting of the Soviet of Soldiers' and Labour Deputies held at the end of March 1917 a soldier deputy delivered a speech of which the following is a summary :—

" We do not want foreign land, but we will not allow ours to be taken. We will stay in the field of battle, but to stop unnecessary bloodshed we want rifles and ammunition. If factories do not have sufficient materials, let every one carry to them all the metals they possess, even door-handles. Then, if the Germans attack us, we will stop them with our breasts, and they will be broken as a crystal on a stone. Let every one write to his father and mother to carry to the factories for the good of the people and the army everything they have, so that we can continue the war. And, when we finish it, we will not put our rifles aside, but will say, ' Read us the laws you wrote for us.' And if we are not satisfied, we will change them as we like." (16)

At a meeting held on April 5, 1917, (17) and attended by soldiers and sailors, a resolution was passed in these terms :—

" We, soldiers and sailors, at a meeting of three thousand persons in the People's Hall, after discussing the question of the war, have come to these resolutions : Through the Soviet of Labourers' and Soldiers' Deputies of Petrograd we demand from the Provisional Government that they immediately declare to the fighting nations, and to all the world, that we do not want foreign land, towns, or indemnities. We demand an end of this bloody war. We protest against the cry of the *bourgeoisie*, ' War till Victory.' On the question of the land, we demand that the All-Russian Soviet of Labourers' and Soldiers' Deputies should request the Provisional Government to require that grain be immediately sown on all the land of the landowners, and on all land in possession of the churches, the monasteries, and the Government, the harvest to be divided among the population." (18)

The Revolution was not initiated by the army, but the early adhesion of large numbers of the Petrograd garrison was indispensable to its success. After the Revolution was accomplished, continued support by the army was necessary to maintain any government in power, and vigorous efforts to enlist its sympathies were made at the outset by the leaders of the Petrograd Soviet. Afterwards such efforts were relaxed ; and when attempts were made to secure the support of the army for the Provisional Government and the Constituent Assembly, these efforts were either too feeble or too late. (19)

On March 16th, four days after the formation of the Provisional Government, Kerensky addressed the Petrograd Soviet in a speech, the terms of which afford an indication of his character. " Citizens,

## THE PROVISIONAL GOVERNMENT

warriors, in the name of free Russia, in the name of the Provisional Government, I, the Minister of Justice, make you a low bow. [Furious applause.] Comrades, warriors, citizens, sailors, and officers, if you had not stood on the side of the liberated people, and if you had not helped her with your armed force, Russia would not now be a free democratic country. To all of you, honour, glory, permanent glory for all time. [Furious applause.] Comrades, I am not only a minister but I am also the Vice-President of the Soviet of Soldiers' and Workers' Deputies of Petrograd. I am an old socialist and republican. I am a member of the Socialist Revolutionary Party, and believe me that if I agreed to become a member of the Provisional Government, I am there as your representative, the representative of soldiers, workmen, peasants, republican officers, of all those who want to build up the Free Republic of Russia. [Furious applause.] Believe me and know that while I am the Minister of Justice you need not be afraid of anything ; nobody will dare to go against the new *régime* and the free people. [Furious applause.] Comrades, I am not only a minister but the Procureur-Général. All the power of punishment is in my hands, and the enemies of new Russia will not escape me. [Furious applause and shouts of ' Hurrah ! Hurrah ! '] . . . Yesterday in the Senate the Provisional Government publicly gave its oath to the people to perform its obligations, to summon the Constituent Assembly, and to transfer to it all the power which we have temporarily taken. With that power we want to do only one thing— we want to give it into the hands of the people themselves. [Furious applause.] " (20)

On March 21, 1917, in the hall of the State Duma in the Taurida Palace, a meeting was held of five hundred representatives from the troops of the Petrograd military district and the immediately contiguous areas. Resolutions were passed which placed the garrison wholly at the disposal of the Soviet of Soldiers' and Workmen's Deputies and its Executive Committee. In these resolutions no mention is made of the Provisional Government or of any authority other than the local body upon which the garrison had its representatives. (21) The troops of the capital seemed to be interested in supporting the Soviet, thus it may be presumed that they considered the Provisional Government merely subordinate and in no way hostile to the Soviet.

The war had drawn into the army the most skilful, intelligent, and best organized of the workmen in the capital and its industrial suburbs, (22) and their places had been filled by young peasants inexperienced in industrial employment. Freed from the discipline and restraint of the peasant household and village, these new groups

# THE RUSSIAN REVOLUTION

of young workmen were easily influenced by propaganda which was now open and uncensored ; indeed, they occupied a large part of their nominally working time in discussing and listening to party agitators who were eager to enlist their support.  Collectively party recruits were powerful at a moment when the social as well as the political system was in the melting-pot.  Soon the force of propaganda and the absence of governmental authority made themselves felt.  " Direct action " seemed to be the easiest and shortest path to change.  The young workmen, ignorant of the complexities of modern industry, entertained the illusion that direction, control, and industrial discipline were unnecessary, and that fair division of labour meant rotation of employment after the manner of crop rotation.  They also became obsessed with the idea that all industrial arrangements could be settled by a committee appointed by themselves, and that the less ability and learning this committee had, the less likely it was to take improper advantage of the workers. (23) With these naïve ideas in their minds, the workmen informed their employers of their intention to " take over " industrial establishments, and to employ their former employers in such a manner as the committee appointed by the workers should determine. (24)

Thus within two months of the March 1917 Revolution the industrial system of Russia had begun to crumble, not exclusively because the conditions of the war drew skilled workmen from the factories, nor because of the difficulties of import and transport and the paralysis of domestic demand (war demands having replaced normal domestic demands), and the flight of capital abroad, (25) nor again the fact that any but unskilled labour was hard to procure, but because of all these factors combined, plus the most important single cause of the disorganization of industry—" direct action " by the workers.  In seeking to save themselves from what they regarded as the oppressive exploitation of capital, they had destroyed, not merely the organization of capital and of credit, but the organization of industry, by means of which alone groups of men concentrated in towns and cities can hope to live. (26)

When the Imperial Government collapsed, the capitals and the industrial centres were left in an anarchic condition, notwithstanding the existence of the Duma and the formation of the Provisional Government.  Even the Petrograd and the other Soviets which had been formed failed to control the masses of workmen, or to direct them in the interests of the social doctrines of any of the socialist parties.  The workmen, inexperienced as they were in political action, had passed completely from under the control of those who aspired to be their leaders ; the old system of *espionage* and pervasive police management of the masses of workmen through

# THE PROVISIONAL GOVERNMENT

the trade unions was useless in the face of open revolt ; (27) and the constitutionalists, democratic republicans, and socialists of all the parties were alike too far removed from the people to understand the complex motives which were now determining their collective or spasmodic activities. (28)

The situation in the villages was not dissimilar. Violent " direct action " made its appearance in rural districts soon after the Revolution of March 1917. (29) The peasants, relieved from the restraint to which they had for centuries been subjected, resorted to the methods that they had on occasion employed in earlier periods. They simply seized the lands in their neighbourhood in the same manner as the workmen had seized the factories.

These expropriations of land by the peasants, and of factories by the workmen, were not carried out in accordance with any theories of social evolution, they were simply the outcome of reversion to primitive violence resulting from the sudden withdrawal of legal restraint. Peasants and workmen normally law-abiding, relieved from the pressure of external authority, unable to exercise self-control, and readily joined by others accustomed to lawlessness, committed acts of criminal character. The ruthlessness engendered during a long and sanguinary war was thought by some to have been responsible for these outbreaks of violence ; but it seems more likely that they were chiefly the consequence of the withdrawal of customary legal and social sanctions. In Russia, it was inevitable that a social and political Revolution involving the collapse of restraining authority should pass into this phase. (30) A well-informed and thoroughly reliable correspondent, a landowner in Tver, reports as follows :—

(1) " Excesses in the form of personal violence broke out in many places almost immediately after the March 1917 Revolution. Such instances were mostly along the war front or where there had been long-smouldering antagonism between villagers and neighbouring landowners. But these were sporadic and local, in no way an organized peasant movement."

(2) " As to land seizures and agrarian troubles, when these did occur in 1917, they began about May, generally when the ploughing season and the time for dividing the hayfields set in. All that summer the peasants around us were in a state of expectancy. The Constituent Assembly was anticipated, and in any case the peasants waited for a ' paper ' before taking active measures, and there was no seizure of the land on any large scale ; but the temper of the peasants was bad." (31)

In one case, at least, the disturbances among the peasants near the front were suppressed by troops. (32)

## THE RUSSIAN REVOLUTION

An account given by the President of the local Soviet of Luga in the Petrograd region (33) throws much light upon the actual course of events. The proceedings at Luga are not typical of Russia as a whole, because the members of the Soviet belonged to moderate rather than red groups, and because the proportion of cultivated land in peasant ownership in the neighbourhood was relatively small.

Immediately after the Revolution of March 1917 the local authorities at Luga ran away, leaving the municipality without a government. The Soviet of Soldiers' Deputies formed by the troops of the garrison of 25,000 soldiers was asked by technical workers in the factories and on the railways to allow the workers to join the Soviet, permission was given, and the Soviet became a Workmen's as well as a Soldiers' council. The union took effect in the middle of March ; three representatives of the working men, two of them being " intelligents," were elected to the executive committee, and this committee then became in effect the municipal authority pending new municipal elections. A food committee for town and garrison together was formed at once, followed by the organization of a town militia. The first experiment proved to be a failure ; it consisted in placing upon this town militia the oldest men and boys fresh from secondary schools, but these were speedily replaced by " instructors " from the garrison troops, and soon the town was as quiet as usual. The president of the Soviet acted as magistrate, and even as judge, in divorce cases and the like, and the members of the Executive Committee found themselves called upon to shoulder almost all the burdens and difficulties of the community.

When the town had been organized, the executive committee turned its attention to the villages. If in the town the people were excited and helpless when the Revolution took place and the customary authorities ceased to function, much more was this the case with the rural inhabitants. In some places mounted police controlled everything, but in others all the representatives of the former Imperial Government had fled, carrying with them public money and documents. On March 2nd peasants in the villages near the towns asked the soldiers' committee to appoint new *starschina* (reeves) and to issue new regulations. Spring was coming, bringing ploughing time, and the peasants wanted to utilize their newly acquired freedom to take the land from the landowners and to work it. In the district of Luga 70 per cent. of the land belonged to landowners, to the State, or to monasteries. Under such conditions the peasants' " need for land " was obvious, and agrarian disturbances might have been anticipated. Yet the

# THE PROVISIONAL GOVERNMENT 73

Provisional Government took no action, except to appoint district commissioners, who were required to preserve order until they received further instructions.

In the district of Luga a commissioner was appointed who had been chairman of the *Zemstvo* and was a local landowner. This man had a bad reputation among the peasants, and they refused to recognize his authority. The commissioner, fearing that he would be attacked, appealed for protection to the soldiers' Soviet. The executive committee tried to make the situation plain in Petrograd, but without success. The Provisional Government continued to draw up projects for future action; meanwhile the peasants, demanding immediate measures, became aggrieved and turned to the soldiers' Soviet as the only administrative body within reach that promised effective action. The Soviet formed a separate Village Committee, and this committee went through the villages instructing the peasants how to elect village and district committees, and for the instruction of these committees, the executive committee of the Soviet issued administrative regulations as well as some observations upon the agrarian question. These measures were the outcome of an agreement between the peasants' committees and the executive committee of the Soviet. The peasants agreed that they would not engage in arbitrary tillage of land which did not belong to them, nor would they commit violence, whilst the landowners on their part agreed to give to the peasants without payment some of the available untilled land. The authorities having charge of the treasury or State lands were more difficult to deal with, but by means of negotiation with the Ministry at Petrograd concessions to the peasants were ultimately arranged. The peasants were, however. not satisfied with the new district (34) and *volost* (35) committees, the election of which had been suggested by the executive committee of the Soviet, and decided to convene a Peasants' Congress. This Congress met, there being 102 peasant representatives present. The only subject discussed was the question of the union of peasants with soldiers and workmen in a single Soviet. After a debate, [the report (36) of which throws light upon peasant psychology and shows how slenderly prepared the peasants of the Luga region were to administer their own affairs. (37) as well as how anxious they were to have a share in administering them], the decision was reached to unite with the Soldiers' and Workmen's Soviet.

The Luga Soviet thus became the first in Russia in which " the great majority of the population was represented," (38) yet there was no representation of the landowners, the clergy or other professional classes, employers, or merchants. Like other Soviets throughout Russia, the Luga Soviet was not in any strict sense an

## 74 THE RUSSIAN REVOLUTION

assembly representing the people, but it was composed of moderate and conciliatory elements, it exhibited anxiety to aid in the effective development of new local administrative organs, and it supported the Provisional Government.

The significant point in these details is that the Imperial Government with its centralized authority having collapsed, and the local administrative machinery having ceased to function, new small administrative bodies immediately began to form themselves spontaneously in town and village, and coalescence of these small bodies took place. It is significant, also, that the peasants, finding themselves helpless, should turn to a group of soldiers merely because this group appeared to know what it was about. The executive committee of the Soldiers' Soviet at Luga, however, did not lose its head, but proceeded to organize local administration afresh and to lay the foundation of a new public order.

In many other cases, the members of the committees elected by soldiers, workmen, and peasants had not equal ability, patience, and good intentions ; and then those whom they represented were led to ruin. Yet throughout Russia, from north to south, there was manifest a spontaneous growth of new administrative organs which sprang into existence directly the former legal organs ceased to function. (39)

Arbitrary seizures of timber and land, contests between peasants over these seizures, and conflicts between villages were occurring in many different parts of Russia at least as early as May 1917, (40) that is, within two months of the March Revolution. Manor houses were burned and their contents destroyed, and as books burn slowly, the pages were torn out that they might be the more quickly consumed. The *rationale* of the destruction can readily be understood : if their nests are destroyed the rooks cannot return to them.

In May 1917 an All-Russian Congress of Peasants was held in Petrograd and a resolution was passed demanding the " transfer of all lands . . . to the people as a whole, as their patrimony, on the basis of equal possession without any payment." The resolution might mean nationalization of the land, but nationalization was precisely what the peasant did not want. Nor did he desire division on the basis of equal possession, for the town-dweller would be entitled to as much land as the peasant-householder, and to give him so much might diminish the peasant's share. To the peasant the land question was very simple. The ground he wanted was in his immediate neighbourhood, it was the gift of God to him, he had been prevented from receiving this gift by the intervention of the landowner, the landowner had been sustained in this inter-

# THE PROVISIONAL GOVERNMENT

vention by the operation of a law, this law had been passed and maintained by the government of the Tsar, that government had been abolished, therefore the law had ceased to be operative and the landlord's intervention had lost its sanction. The gift of God must now have its effect; the land must be taken; if the landlord resisted he must be driven off or killed. From the peasant's point of view, the logical process was complete and his position invulnerable.

The Provisional Government was afraid to touch the land question, so full of difficulties for any government, and therefore handed it over to the Central Land Committee, the function of which was to collect data and to draw up a scheme of land reform. Local administration meanwhile was entrusted to local land committees. (41)

---

## NOTES

(1) German propaganda was active in Russia as elsewhere, and undoubtedly it was directed towards fomenting a revolutionary state of mind. (It has been hinted that the date of the uprising was known in Berlin beforehand. (Cf. Nekludov, A., *Diplomatic Reminiscences*, London, 1920, p. 462.) The evidence is, however, not above suspicion.) Some of the revolutionists may have been in German pay, but the Germans cannot on that ground alone be held to be the originators of the Revolution of March 1917.

(2) When " representatives of the Duma and certain social circles " told General Alekseiev in January 1917 that " a revolution was brewing," it is clear that they meant that a *coup d'état* was likely to be attempted. (Cf. Denikin, General A. I., *The Russian Turmoil. Memoirs: Military, Social, and Political*, New York, 1923, p. 38.)

(3) The new reservists were well armed. Other soldiers were not so well equipped. (Cf. Voronovich, N., *Memoirs of a President of a Soviet of Soldiers' Deputies* in *Archives of the Civil War* (Berlin, 1923 ; in Russian), vol. ii, p. 30.)

(4) Had the Grand Duke accepted the throne under conditions imposed at that time by influential forces in the capital, the *coup d'état* would have been struck, and there might have been no Revolution. Kerensky, who had been taken into the group which was assuming control, opposed the offer to the Grand Duke, and not improbably convinced him of the futility of the project of continuing the monarchy at that moment. The Grand Duke Michael was murdered near the town of Perm in 1918.

(5) The Tsar seems to have made up his mind to abdicate, and even to have prepared his abdication, before the representatives of the Duma appeared to demand it. He was not, therefore, in the strict sense, deposed.

(6) Cf. Mavor, J., op. cit., vol. ii, p. 509.

(7) Nekrassov has been accused of intrigues and manœuvring between the Cadets and the socialist parties. (Cf. Tyrkova-Williams, Mrs. A., *From Liberty to Brest-Litovsk*, London, 1919, p. 31.) General Denikin describes Nekrassov as " the darkest and most fatal figure " (Denikin, General A. I., op. cit., p. 122).

(8) Quoted from a copy printed in *Izvestia* (Helsingfors), No. 4, March 12, 1917.

(9) The precise date of the revival of these bodies is difficult to determine. Reference to a council of this kind is contained in an Order of the Day issued on March 7, 1917, by Vice-Admiral Maximov, in which he appoints " a controller

# 76 THE RUSSIAN REVOLUTION

of the activities of the counter-intelligence department of the staffs of the fortress of Sveaborg (opposite Helsingfors) and of the Commander of the Fleet." This controller was Lieutenant Baravtin, who is described as the " head of the defence department of the Executive Committee of the Council (Soviet) of Deputies of the Army and the Fleet, and the workers of the fortress of Sveaborg." *Izvestia* (Helsingfors), No. 1, March 9, 1917.

(10) " Your Excellency," " Your Honour," and the like.

(11) From text in *Izvestia* (Helsingfors), March 16, 1917.

(12) For text of *Order No. 1* see Appendix, p. 94. This body will be afterwards referred to as the Petrograd Soviet ; the word " Soviet " having been adopted into the English language, although " Council " is an exact equivalent.

(13) Cf. Gourko, General Basil, *Memories and Impressions of War and Revolution* (London, 1918), p. 270.

(14) The garrison of Lutsk, however, sent deputies to Petrograd to demand that the Petrograd Soviet should not interfere with the policy of the Provisional Government, to which the army had taken the oath. (Ibid., p. 271.)

(15) *Izvestia* (Helsingfors), No. 16, March 31, 1917.

(16) Ibid., No. 17, April 1, 1917.

(17) Lenin arrived in Petrograd late that very night.

(18) *Izvestia* (Helsingfors), No. 18, April 6, 1917.

(19) An active propaganda in the army was continuously conducted by the Bolsheviks. At this time they were in a minority in the Petrograd Soviet.

(20) *Izvestia* (Helsingfors), March 21, 1917.

(21) The text of the resolutions is given in *Izvestia* (Helsingfors), No. 11, March 24, 1917.

(22) The same plan was adopted in the other belligerent countries in the first year of the war.

(23) An American employer in Petrograd informed the author that he was told by his workers that precisely this principle had determined them in electing the members of their committee. The committees were not merely shop committees : they were boards of directors as well.

(24) " Skilled engineers were obliged to spend long weeks at manual labour. In some of the Donetz mines all the office staffs, the managing director included, had to go down into the shafts and taste the joys of swinging a pick, while the miners, many of whom were quite illiterate, sat gravely in the offices. . . . When . . . they realized that technical knowledge was not altogether useless, they very soon installed the former officials in their places " (Vandervelde, Emile, *Three Aspects of the Russian Revolution*, translated by Jean E. H. Findlay (London, 1918), p. 50). In many cases the officials left and refused to return, preferring to abandon their plants rather than continue to work under impossible conditions.

(25) According to Victor Chernov : " Long before the Bolshevist Revolution, Russian capitalists manifested a growing tendency quietly to realize their capital into cash, convert it into foreign exchange, and ship it abroad " (*Disintegration of Classes in Russia* in *Foreign Affairs* (1923), vol. ii, p. 29). It is doubtful if this flight of capital from Russia could be accomplished on any important scale between March and October 1917, when there was practically no exportation from Russia. The hypothesis that the collapse of capitalism in Russia was an incident in world-wide decay of capitalism is unworthy of serious discussion.

(26) General Denikin regards the economic disorganization of Russia as having begun in the last days of the old *régime* (Denikin, General Basil, op. cit., p. 44). The Imperial Government attempted to meet the increasing charges of the Russian debt by means of government monopolies and control of industry. (Cf. Posvolsky, L., in *The Russian Review*, 1917, vol. iii, pp. 15–16.) This policy led, as it must lead everywhere, to paralysis of industrial enterprise, to diminution of the taxing power of the government, and to decline of national credit.

(27) Although probably some of the members of the *Okhrana* continued to engage in their customary activities, the Political Police was disbanded by the Provisional Government by the order of April 17, 1917.

(28) Cf. Mavor, J., op. cit., vol. ii, p. 255.

# THE PROVISIONAL GOVERNMENT

(29) Cf. Denikin, General A. I., op. cit., p. 113.

(30) Precisely similar consequences have followed the collapse of governmental restraint in China.

(31) For continuation of this report see infra, p. 228.

(32) Communicated by another correspondent.

(33) Voronovich, N., *Memoirs of a President of a Council of Soldiers' Deputies* in *Archives of the Russian Revolution* (Berlin, 1923), in Russian, vol. ii, pp. 9–102. The case of Luga is typical of a large number of Russian towns. It is taken as an example because the details available are fuller and are related with more candour than any others concerning the actual working of the Soviets.

(34) *Uezd* : a large administrative district.

(35) A *volost* is a small administrative district composed of a group of villages.

(36) Voronovich, N., op. cit., pp. 48–53.

(37) At a ballot taken at the Congress, 200 votes were recorded by 102 members ! (Cf. Voronovich, N., op. cit., p. 50.)

(38) Voronovich, N., op. cit., p. 53.

(39) For the growth of such bodies in Asiatic Russia see Price, M. Philips, *War and Revolution in Asiatic Russia* (London, 1918), p. 289.

(40) Quoted by Denikin, General A. I., op. cit., p. 112.

(41) Cf. Denikin, General A. I., op. cit., pp. 112–13. Denikin says that " the intellectuals " were, as a rule, excluded " from these local committees." When the Soviet Government came into power later, they were excluded also from the village Soviets.

## CHAPTER II

## THE COALITION GOVERNMENT AND ITS STRUGGLES AGAINST " DIRECT ACTION " BY PEASANTS AND ARTISANS

THERE appeared at Stockholm early in April 1917 a Russian *émigré* who had been living in Switzerland and who had afterwards been transported through Germany concealed from public view. On the night of April 5th he arrived at Petrograd,(1) the city which was afterwards to bear his name. This man was Vladimir Ilich Ulianov, whose party name was Nicholas Lenin.(2) With Lenin there travelled thirty-one other Russian *émigrés* who had been living in Switzerland. Among these there were nineteen Bolsheviks, six members of the Jewish *Bund*, and three representatives of the Russian newspaper *Nashé Slovo*, published in Paris. One of Lenin's Bolshevik companions was Zinoviev. In an article published in Petrograd (3) immediately before his arrival there, Lenin states that the British and French Governments refused to allow him to pass through territories controlled by the Allies. The alternative route was through Germany, and this route was arranged by the old Social Democrat, L. Martov.(4) According to Lenin, a formal agreement was drawn up between Martov and the German authorities, of which the main points were that thirty-two *émigrés* should be allowed to return to Russia whatever opinions they held on the war, that the wagon in which they were transported should be inviolable, and that those who were allowed to pass should endeavour to secure the return of an equal number of German and Austrian prisoners of war. The negotiations are said by Lenin to have been carried on by a number of international socialists, among whom he mentions Karl Liebknecht. What guarantees were exacted by the German Government are not recorded. The probability is that the Government was advised that no guarantees would be necessary.

Soon afterwards there arrived from America another *émigré*, L. D. Bronstein, whose party name was Nicholas Trotsky. (5) From the moment of the arrival of Lenin in Petrograd the Bolshevik faction of the Social Democratic party manifested increased activity. For a time Trotsky held aloof, but eventually he joined the Bolsheviks and became one of their chief speakers.

Lenin devoted himself at once to attacks on the Provisional Government. These attacks were not critical, but were merely

# THE COALITION GOVERNMENT

denunciatory. Lenin gave no consideration to the difficulties of the position of the Government, nor to the necessity, in the interests of Russia, of the united efforts of the various elements which composed Russian society and the various nations which were comprised in the Empire. Lenin attributes to " English and French imperialistic capital " the plots and intrigues by means of which the Tsar was compelled to abdicate and the Provisional Government was formed. He speaks of this Government as the simple clerks of the " milliard firm," France and England. (6)

In April 1917, about one month after the March Revolution, the members of the Soviet began to talk about a Coalition Government, that is, a government in which there should be a larger socialist representation, Kerensky being the only socialist member of the existing Cabinet. Those who opposed a coalition argued that members of the socialist parties who accepted ministerial portfolios would cease to have direct contact with the workers. The consequences would be, on the one hand, loss to the party of its most influential members, and, on the other, of direct contact of these with the masses. The party which sent its representatives to the ministry would be held responsible for the action of those representatives. Since no government of any kind could at that moment have satisfied the masses, (7) the only possible result to any government must have been loss of party as well as of personal prestige. Those who advocated a Coalition Government argued that, in a crisis, the socialists had no right to refuse to bear their part in administration; if they did refuse, the Provisional Government would fall and anarchy must ensue. The Petrograd Soviet met on May 18, 1917, to decide the question. A majority in favour of coalition was reasonably certain, since the Executive Committee had already pronounced itself in its favour. Doubt however existed because of the appearance at the meeting of Trotsky, then recently arrived from abroad. At that moment Trotsky was not a Bolshevik, he was a member of the Social-Democratic party, " standing on the extreme left flank." (8) He was known to be opposed to coalition and was thought to be likely to influence the Bolsheviks as well as those of the " March Socialists " (9) whose opinions were not yet fixed by lapse of time. The chairman of the Soviet, Chkheidze, said that he was opposed to coalition on principle, but the position was critical, and he had come to the conclusion that the Government must be strengthened by some socialist members. After Skobelov (10) had spoken to the same effect, Trotsky appeared in the tribune and received a great ovation from the Bolsheviks. He argued against coalition, made a good impression, and was applauded by all parties in the Soviet. There was no further debate, for,

## THE RUSSIAN REVOLUTION

when anyone else rose to speak, the Bolsheviks, few in number but active and noisy, contrived to make speeches inaudible. Their conduct, however, so annoyed other members of the Soviet that the vote gave a majority for coalition.

On the side of the Provisional Government there was also a movement in the same direction. Kerensky desired to strengthen his support by introducing a number of socialists, with the result that early in May 1917 a Coalition Government was formed by taking in three members representing the Petrograd Soviet, one of these members being a Menshevik, and the other two Socialist-Revolutionaries. The new members were Tseretelli, Chernov, and Skobelov. (11) The introduction of these brought the socialist representation in the Government to four, and led to the resignation of Miliukov and Guchkov, and thus practically eliminated the opposition to Kerensky. Chernov, who approved of the resolution of the Peasant Congress, was prepared to settle the land question on the basis of nationalization without waiting for submission to the Constituent Assembly. The remaining Cadet members of the Government disapproved of this plan and favoured delay.

The peasants " cared for none of these things," and thus the peasant uprisings of 1905–1907 were repeated. Just as the workmen were " in advance " of the Social-Democrats, so were the peasants " in advance " of the Socialist-Revolutionaries and Social-Democrats alike. The Provisional Government and the Soviet were dismayed, the plans of both were upset ; peasants and workmen had reverted to a primitive attitude of mind.

No doubt the Socialist Revolutionary propaganda stirred the minds of the peasants, but they paid little attention to the resolution of their Congress, although this resolution had the approval of Chernov, who was one of the Socialist-Revolutionary representatives in the Government, but Chernov's appeals to the peasants to avoid arbitrary seizures were unheeded. Tseretelli accused the local committees of organizing these proceedings. " Land is being seized and sold," he said, " agricultural labourers are forced to stop working, and landowners are faced with demands which are economically impossible. Breeding stock is being destroyed and implements plundered. Model farms are being ruined. Forests are being cut down irrespective of ownership ; timber and logs are being stolen, and their shipment prevented. No sowing is done on privately owned farms, and harvests of grain and hay are not reaped." Such conditions must " inevitably bring about endless calamities for the army and the country, and threaten the very existence of the State." (12)

# THE COALITION GOVERNMENT

The Revolution was an upheaval from beneath, and neither the Provisional Government nor the Soviets could control it. Had either attempted in the spring and summer of 1917 to resist the pressure of the workmen and the peasantry, they would certainly have been swept aside, for both were compelled to allow themselves to be carried on by the wave of Revolution, in the hope that some day they might be able to control the course of the ship of State.

Meanwhile the Provisional Government was attempting to deal with urgent administrative matters. One of the most pressing of these was the problem of local administration. Many *Zemstvos* had appealed to the Imperial Government for the rectification of their frontiers. These appeals had been neglected, and the areas of some of the administrative units had remained unaltered for two centuries. They now appealed to the Provisional Government, with the result that several new *gubernie* and forty new towns were created, and changes in the boundaries of many districts were effected. (13)

The organization of the food supply—the first issue in the demonstrations which led to the Revolution—involved fixation of prices of grain. The peasants resented this measure and resented also any interference of the Government with their arbitrary seizures. " The towns ceased to supply manufactured goods, and the villages were estranged from the towns and ceased to supply them with grain." (14)

On March 29, 1917, the Provisional Government declared that after the normal needs of the cultivator for the food of his family, for seed and fodder, had been provided for, the surplus of grain must revert to the State. Fixed prices for all food-stuffs and for commodities in common use were imposed by the Government, and the monopoly was administered by a network of food-supply bureaux, with a personnel of very varying capacity. The villages were reluctant to supply grain and to pay taxes or rents, and force had sometimes to be applied to compel them to make such payments. Undoubtedly the Provisional Government had a hard task before it when it assumed control of the administration. To save the country from calamitous defeat the armies had to be kept in the field, and required for their provision nearly one-half of the total national production. (15) In proportion as these supplies had to be increased, the total production had to be greatly enlarged. Under the conditions of industry inherited from their predecessors, (16) stimulation could not be applied by the Provisional Government without enormous difficulty. The effective measures taken by the other belligerent Governments were only possible because

## THE RUSSIAN REVOLUTION

the will of their respective peoples was behind them. This was not the case in Russia. The Government was not in reality supported by the general mass of the nation. It was a revolutionary government, with the forces remaining loyal to the previous government arrayed against it or sullenly acquiescent, with the hesitating support of forces opposed to autocracy, but unwilling, without reservation, to trust the new authority, and with open hostility of extreme parties the members of which desired to exploit the Revolution in their own interests or in the interests of their party programme.

The Provisional Government imposed war taxes upon employers, with the aim of preventing undue exploitation by them of the state of war; but through fear of the Soviets it refrained from imposing restrictions upon exploitation by workers. (17) Thus the pressure of the Soviet of Workmen's Deputies prevented the Government from uniting the forces of the nation with a view to recovering its economic position, and so serving as a means of winning the war. At the same time, the action of the Government towards employers diminished, and went far in a short time to destroy private initiative, while it led to exorbitant demands by workmen. A hostile attitude towards the Government on the part of workmen and employers alike speedily emerged. The workmen were not satisfied with the concessions, (18) but were aiming at control.

A report to the Provisional Government in May 1917 gave the following particulars : " In eighteen concerns in the Donetz basin, with a total profit of seventy-five million roubles per annum, the workmen demanded a wage increase of two hundred and forty million roubles per annum ; the total amount of increased wages in all the mining and metallurgical factories of the south was eight hundred million roubles per annum. In the Urals the total budget was two hundred million roubles, while the wages rose to three hundred million. . . . In the Putilov factory at Petrograd . . . wages rose 200 to 300 per cent. The increase in the wages of the textile workers of Moscow rose 500 per cent. as compared with 1914. The burden of these increases naturally fell on the Government, as most of the factories were engaged in executing government orders for the defence of the country." (19)

The railway administration was subjected under Nekrassov, who was for a time Minister of Railways, to " democratization." Committees were imposed upon them as upon industry in general. In his circular of May 27, 1917, Nekrassov announced : " The Ministry of Railways and its subordinate branches will work in strict accordance with the ideas and wishes of the United Railway Workers." (20) When, after four months of office, Nekrassov was

## THE COALITION GOVERNMENT

succeeded by Yurenev, the railways administration had become so demoralized that the new minister denounced as a crime against the State " the interference of private persons and organizations with the executive functions of the department." (21) At the Moscow Congress the president of the Union of Railwaymen said that " the struggle against democratic organizations was a manifestation of counter-revolution, and that the Union would use every weapon to counteract these endeavours, and would ' be strong enough to slay this counter-revolutionary hydra.' " (22) The workmen were not merely terrorizing the Government, they were terrorizing the nation.

The public finance of Russia, at the outbreak of war, was in a comparatively favourable position. The revenue was derived mainly from four sources : the profits of the spirit monopoly, which yielded about one-quarter of the revenue, customs duties, land and other direct taxes, and the revenue from the public domain and from public enterprises. The annual budget was about three and one-half milliards of roubles, the debt being about eight and one-half milliards. The abolition of the spirit monopoly and prohibition eliminated eight hundred million roubles of revenue. At the same time war expenses increased the requirements of the budget to five milliards in 1914, to twelve milliards in 1915, to eighteen milliards in 1916, and from January–July 1917 to eighteen milliards. Apart from the expenses of the war, the civil expenditure of the Provisional Government assumed enormous dimensions. The Post Office revenue, for example, was 60 million roubles, and the wages of the employees were increased by 60 millions, and afterwards an additional 105 millions were demanded. Food-supply committees expended 500 millions, land committees 140 millions, etc. The revenue suffered from a decline in the yield from taxation due to the disorganization of industry, the depletion of population in the towns because of unemployment, the absence of foreign trade, and the impossibility of collecting taxes. The Provisional Government endeavoured to meet the financial crisis by means of succession duties, taxes upon profits, income tax, etc., as well as taxes upon tea, sugar, and matches, but refused to impose a levy upon capital. Notwithstanding the fresh imposts, which, of course, did not enhance the popularity of the Government, the budget could not be balanced. For the requirements of January–July 1917, about one-half (nine and a half milliards) was obtained by internal loans ; the revenue was nearly six milliards, with a deficit of three and a half milliards.

Already before the Revolution the issue of paper currency had been increased. In the latter half of 1914, 1·4 milliards of

## 84    THE RUSSIAN REVOLUTION

roubles had been issued by the Imperial Government; in 1915, 2·6 milliards; in 1916, 3·5 milliards; and in the first half of 1917, 4 milliards. In July 1917 the total amount of paper currency in circulation was almost 14 milliards, while the gold reserve was 1·3 milliards. The amount of the gold reserve before the war was 2 milliards. (23)

---

### NOTES

(1) " Last night (April 5, 1917) at 11.30 p.m. there arrived at Petrograd N. Lenin (Ilian), the chief of the Bolsheviks, who had lived abroad since 1905." *Izvestia* (Helsingfors), No. 18, April 6, 1917.

(2) Cf. supra, vol. ii, pp. 154 on, 161, 162, and 531. Vladimir Ulianov was also known by the names " Ilich," " Ilian," " Ilin," and " Tulin." He was born on April 23, 1870, in Simbirsk, where his father was a landowner and director of elementary education. His mother had an estate in Kazan. The family consisted of three sons and two daughters. The eldest son, Alexander, while a student at the University of St. Petersburg, was accused of being a member of the *Narodnaya Volya*, and, together with the surviving remnant of the revolutionary movement of 1879, was executed on May 8, 1887. (Cf. supra, vol. ii, pp. 114–134, and Spiridovich, A. E., *History of Bolshevism in Russia* (in Russian ; Paris, 1922), p. 25.) In 1887 the father of the Ulianovs died, and Vladimir, at the age of seventeen, was sent to the University of Kazan. There he became acquainted with the doctrines of Karl Marx. In 1891 the young Vladimir entered the faculty of law at the University of St. Petersburg. When he had finished his course he became a lawyer, but he did not practise his profession. Instead, he joined the ranks of the professional revolutionists (Spiridovich, A. E., loc. cit.). While still in the university he gathered about him a group of fellow-disciples of Marx and began to form circles for socialist propaganda among the workers. Even so early as 1894, when Lenin was only twenty-four years of age, he was known by his party name, and he was engaged in a controversy with Peter Struvë. He developed his thesis in a paper read at a meeting at which Struvë was present. This paper, *The Reflection of Marxism in Bourgeois Literature*, exhibited already some Bolshevist ideas (Landau-Aldanov, M. A., *Lénine*, Paris, pp. 25–26, quoted by Spiridovich, A. E., op. cit., p. 26). Lenin insisted that in all his works Marx argued that the transition from the old to the new social order must be characterized by the sudden failure and bankruptcy of capitalism. Lenin followed Sombart in declaring that in all Marx's writings there is not a single line of ethical bearing (Landau-Aldanov, M. A., loc. cit.). In 1895 Lenin went abroad and associated himself with Plekhanov in the organization of printing and distributing social democratic literature in Russia. On his return to St. Petersburg he took part in organizing the St. Petersburg Union for Struggle for the Freedom of the Labouring Classes (cf. Mavor, J., *An Economic History of Russia*, vol. ii, pp. 158 and 161). At this time Lenin published his first propagandist brochure *Upon Punishment*. In 1895, he issued a pamphlet on *The Economical Basis of the Narodnochestvo* (cf. Mavor, J., op. cit., vol. ii, pp. 103–13). In 1896 he was arrested on the ground of his association with St. Petersburg social democrats. In January 1897 he was sent to Siberia for three years under police surveillance. He lived in Sushensky village, Yeneseisk *gub*. While Lenin was in Siberia, there was held in 1898, at Minsk in European Russia, a Marxist Congress at which the revolutionary views of Lenin were practically adopted (cf. Mavor, J., op. cit., vol. ii, pp. 161–62). In 1900 he left Siberia by permission of the Government and went abroad. He

# THE COALITION GOVERNMENT 85

became at once a member of the Central Committee of the Russian Social Democratic Labour party. His position speedily became important enough to attract once more the attention of the Political Police. On September 19, 1900, a notice was issued to officers on the frontier to arrest him if he attempted to enter Russia. The description of Lenin given in this document is as follows : " Height 5 ft. 5⅝ ins., medium build, hair on head and eyebrows slightly yellow, beard and moustache ginger (inclined to red), eyes small, head round, forehead high, nose usual, face round, features regular, mouth ordinary, chin round, ears middling." Kuprin in his *Instantaneous Photographs* (quoted by Spiridovich, A. E., op. cit., p. 26) gives the following sketch of Lenin : " Small, broad shoulders. Nothing in his bearing to attract attention ; nothing military and nothing to indicate deep thought. His forehead is large and high, but not as it appears in the photographs of him. He is absolutely bald ; but the hairs remaining in his beard remind me that in his younger days they were quite red. His hands are large and unpleasant ; but I looked at his eyes for a long time. His eyes are naturally narrow, and he has besides a habit of contracting them. This habit may be due to shortness of sight. The habit of contraction, together with sharp looks as if from the forehead, gave him a sinister and even perhaps an evil air. What struck me most was the colour of the pupils of his eyes. Last summer in the zoological gardens at Paris I saw a monkey—a lemur—the colour of whose eyes was precisely the colour of Lenin's eyes. The difference appeared only in the fact that the lemur has a large, unsteady pupil, while Lenin's are as if they were made with a fine needle, and as if they emitted a sort of blue spark " (*Obshoyé Dielo* (*La Cause Commune*), Paris, February 21, 1921). In childhood the young Vladimir is described as being " much too serious for his age, continuously at his books, friendless, and disliked by his companions." As a student, he is represented as having been " a dry, cold, calm youth," not afraid to express his opinions, and very often differing from his comrades. Lenin's later life, together with his revolutionary activities, and the consequent vicissitudes of his career, made his character very strong, hard, and heartless. The writer has been told that Lenin was subject to epileptic fits. He was a thoroughgoing Marxist. He was the most loyal, even the most fanatical, student of Marx. In putting Marx's ideas into practice, Lenin adopted the maxim that the end justifies the means, and on this ground alone defended his actions (cf. Spiridovich, A. E., op. cit., p. 17). Lenin played a part in the revolutionary uprising of 1905–1907, but he made no conspicuous appearance. He is said to have watched events from Finland. He has given an account of the events of 1905 in a volume, *The Revolutionary Year 1905, Collected Works* (Moscow, 1923), vol. vi. The rôle of Lenin in the Revolution of October–November 1917 is described in the text. He died January 22, 1924.

(3) *Pravda* (Petrograd), April 4, 1917 ; reprinted in Lenin, N., *Collected Works* (Moscow, 1923), vol. xiv, part 1, pp. 13–15.

(4) Mavor, J., *An Economic History of Russia*, vol. ii, p. 419.

(5) Leon Davidovich Bronstein, also known as " Yanovsky," " Antide Otto," " Lvov," and " Nicholas Trotsky," was born of Jewish parents in 1877 on the estate of Yanovsky, in the district of Elizavetgrad, *gub* of Kherson. His father was a wealthy landowner. (Spiridovich, A. E., op. cit., p. 28. If Spiridovich is correct, the elder Bronstein must have been a conforming or Christianized Jew, otherwise he would not have been allowed to hold land.) L. D. Bronstein was educated at the advanced technical school at Nikolaiev, and there he began his revolutionary activities. He was known among his companions as a *Narodnik* (cf. Mavor, J., *An Economic History of Russia*, vol. ii, pp. 67 and 103 ff.) for his sharp criticism of Marxism. His conspicuous characteristics while a student were honesty, energy, and self-conceit. As long as his companions were useful to him he treated them as friends ; when they ceased to be useful to him, they were discarded. He was subject to nervous attacks and occasionally to epileptic fits (Spiridovich, A. E., op. cit., p. 28). To the surprise of everyone who knew him, Bronstein became in 1897 a Marxist, and he founded the South Russian Labour Union, which began a social-democratic propaganda among the workers and

# 86 THE RUSSIAN REVOLUTION

*intelligentsia.* In this Union he met the young woman who became his wife, Aleksandra Sokolovsky. On the suggestion of Bronstein the Union obtained a multiplying apparatus and printed upon it a newspaper *Our Affair*, which Bronstein edited under the pseudonym of " Lvov." In January 1898 he was arrested, together with the members of his Union, accused of revolutionary propaganda, and sent to Siberia for four years. On the way to Siberia he married Aleksandra Sokolovsky, she being one of the party of exiles. Bronstein employed himself in writing under the name of " Otto " for *The Western Observer*, an Irkutsk newspaper. Its articles attracted the attention of the editors of *Iskra* (The Spark), of which Lenin became one of the editors in 1900. An invitation to write for this journal induced Bronstein to attempt to escape from Siberia. Leaving his wife and child, he succeeded in making his way to Europe. There he joined the Russian Social-Democratic party and began to work and write under the name of " Nicholas Trotsky." He did not at first ally himself with either of the factions into which the party came to be divided, but constituted, as has been said of him, a party by himself. He seems to have been predisposed to individual action (Spiridovich, A. E., op. cit., p. 29). His chief characteristic is said by Spiridovich, A. E. (loc. cit.), to be indifference as to the means by which his aims were attained. " In this characteristic he resembles Lenin ; in the case of Lenin it arises from mere cynicism, sometimes concealed under an appearance of idealism and party interest, whereas, in the case of Trotsky, this indifference is due to his individual egotism, and is not concerned with party, society, or government " (Spiridovich, A. E., loc. cit.). In the spring of 1917 Trotsky was in the United States. On the outbreak of the March Revolution he sailed for Russia. At Halifax, Nova Scotia, he was arrested and placed in an internment camp. On the application of Kerensky, he was liberated and permitted to go to Russia. The reason for this action was that the Provisional Government was coerced by the Petrograd Soviet to permit the repatriation of all political exiles, irrespective of party.

(6) Lenin, N., op. cit., pp. 9–10.

(7) Cf. Voronovich, N., op. cit., p. 63.

(8) Ibid., op. cit., p. 64.

(9) Those who dated their socialism from the March Revolution, 1917.

(10) Skobelov became one of the ministers.

(11) Tseretelli: Menshevik, Georgian, eloquent, little in touch with peasant life. Victor Chernov: Socialist-Revolutionary, voluminous writer, became Minister of Agriculture in succession to Shingarev. Skobelov: Socialist-Revolutionary, then Menshevik ; left Petrograd when Bolsheviks came into power, entered employment of Georgian Government at Tiflis, went on commercial missions to London and Paris, joined Bolsheviks and transacted business for them. The Soviet Government, dissatisfied with his proceedings, asked him to resign.

(12) Tseretelli, quoted by Denikin, General A. I., op. cit., p. 113.

(13) *Communist Calendar* (Moscow, 1924), p. 482.

(14) Denikin, General A. I., op. cit., p. 114.

(15) Ibid., op. cit., p. 118.

(16) Denikin blames the Imperial Government for neglecting to organize Russian industry on a " sound basis." He points out that Russian industry was too dependent upon foreign supplies of raw material, which could readily, as he thinks, have been produced within the country. " Thus, in 1912 there was a serious shortage of pig-iron, and in 1913 of fuel. From 1908 to 1913 imports of metals from abroad rose from 29 to 34 per cent. Before the war we imported 48 per cent. of cotton. We needed 2,750,000 *pudi* of wool from abroad out of a total of the 5,000,000 *pudi* used in manufacture " (Denikin, General A. I., op. cit., p. 118).

(17) The Provisional Government thus reversed the policy of the autocracy. The Imperial Government had instituted forced industrial labour without, at the same time, imposing the necessary restrictions upon industrial administration.

(18) Such concessions as, e.g., freedom of trade unions, labour exchanges, social insurance, etc., were given by means of hurried legislation.

# THE COALITION GOVERNMENT

(19) Quoted by Denikin, General A. I., op. cit., p. 119.

(20) Ibid., p. 122.

(21) Ibid., p. 123.

(22) Ibid., p. 123. This union was subsequently suppressed by the Soviet Government.

(23) These statistics are given by Denikin, General A. I., op. cit., pp. 124–26.

CHAPTER III

## THE WORKING OF THE SOVIETS. UNSUCCESSFUL BOLSHEVIK ATTEMPTS TO OVERTHROW THE PROVISIONAL GOVERNMENT

DURING April and May 1917 the influence of the Petrograd Soviet over the army began to decline. This decline appears to have been due to the gradual separation of the members of the Soviet from their constituencies. No efforts appear to have been made to inform the soldiers of what was being done by their representatives and in their name. The members of the Petrograd Executive Committee rarely went to any of the barracks, and many of them were quite strangers to the soldiers. In the early days of the Soviet, Chkheidze, Kerensky, Chernov, Tseretelli, etc., were well known and were often seen at the soldiers' meetings, but later, when the three last-mentioned became more and more occupied in their posts in the Provisional Government, they drifted away from contact with, and knowledge of, the masses, and eventually lost control of them completely. (1) The other members of the Soviet were quite unknown to the soldiers and some of them to the workmen. The resolutions of the Petrograd Soviet from May 1917 cannot therefore be said to reflect the opinions either of workmen or soldiers. (2) The contrary is said to have been the case with regard to the Luga Soviet, (3) that body priding itself upon keeping closely in touch with the electors. The majority of the members of the Luga Soviet consisted of Socialist-Revolutionaries ; the next in number were Social-Democratic Mensheviks, whilst the remaining few Bolsheviks had no influence. (4) The following significant incident took place in Luga in June 1917, according to the report of the President of the Soviet of Soldiers' Deputies at that place. (5)

Zinoviev (6) went to Luga, and proposed that the Luga Soviet should take the government into its hands. The executive committee replied that for more than three months the Soviet had been recognized by the population as the governing body. " But," said Zinoviev, " you have in Luga a government commissioner and also a commander of the garrison." " So we have," answered the soldiers, " but both were appointed by the Soviet." Zinoviev became quite angry : " Why do you not write about this in the newspapers ? " The reply was : " Because it is well known in Luga, and is nobody's business outside." (7)

# THE WORKING OF THE SOVIETS

The Luga Soviet of soldiers' deputies had four representatives in the Petrograd Soviet, and in addition two representatives in the Petrograd executive committee. (8)

While the Luga Soviet, through its representatives, who were required to report daily, had opportunity of knowing what was going on in Petrograd, the Petrograd Soviet had not the same opportunity of knowing what was going on in Luga. Moreover, the Luga Soviet was dealing with its own problems as they arose, and was only remotely concerned with the interminable and indeterminate discussions at Petrograd. The defects in the actual working of the Soviet system which the relations of those two Soviets reveal, were more clearly demonstrated in the relation between the Petrograd Soviet and Soviets in other centres. The Petrograd Soviet was indeed attempting to perform a double function for which it was not fitted, viz. that of a municipal administrative organ for Petrograd as well as an administrative organ for a vast empire.

In June 1917 the All-Russian Congress of Workmen's and Soldiers' Soviets met at Petrograd. (9) To this assembly there came from all parts of Russia representatives of workers, soldiers, and sailors, belonging to many parties. In the evenings the great corridors of the Menshikov Palace were crowded by deputies and lobbyists, and here the principal debates took place, because very few of the leaders of the various socialist parties had been elected as members of the Soviet. In the Soviet proper the tone of the speakers was generally favourable to the Provisional Government; the Bolsheviks met with " great hostility," and only Lenin and Trotsky were respectfully treated. Even they were unable on all occasions to convince their hearers. They attempted to pass a vote of " no confidence " in the Provisional Government; but, observing that the general feeling of the Soviet was opposed to them, they brought from Kronstadt a number of sailors, apparently with a view to the coercion of the assembly, but a corps of military cadets guarding the palace was enough to make them return to Kronstadt. (10) A vote of confidence in the Government was passed.

In the middle of June the Bolshevik faction determined to press their opposition to the Provisional Government and to acquire dominant influence in the Petrograd Soviet. They therefore planned an armed demonstration by the garrison for June 23, 1917. (11) On the evening of June 22nd Chkheidze denounced the scheme before the Congress. Soldiers from the front protested angrily against any attempt on the part of the Petrograd garrison to dictate to the army in the field. The Bolsheviks repudiated violent intentions, but they were not trusted by the other parties. Groups of members

## THE RUSSIAN REVOLUTION

were sent to the units of the garrison to make sure that there would be no armed demonstration. These members found that some of the units had just passed resolutions voting " all power to the Soviets," (12) which meant the deposition of the Provisional Government. The visitors realized that a serious blunder had been made by the Petrograd Soviet in not keeping in touch with the soldiers of the garrison, who had clearly fallen under Bolshevik influence, and who did not know that a majority of the members of the Petrograd and other Soviets was opposed, in the existing crisis, to the assumption of the responsibility of power.

On June 23, 1917, the day fixed for the Bolshevik demonstration, a proclamation signed by Chkheidze was issued by the Congress :—

" The Bolshevik party is calling you out on the street without the knowledge of the Workmen's and Soldiers' Deputies, without the knowledge of the All-Russian Congress, without the knowledge of the Soviet of Peasant Deputies, without the knowledge of any of the socialist parties. Comrades, in the name of millions of labourers, peasants, and soldiers in the interior and at the front, we urge you : Do not do what you are asked to do. In this dangerous moment you are called into the streets to demand the dissolution of the Provisional Government, the support of which the All-Russian Congress has recognized to be necessary, and those who are calling you to a peaceful demonstration do not realize that it may lead to bloodshed. . . . Save your forces and hold fast to revolutionary Russia." (13)

Instead of desiring to increase their responsibilities and their labours by transferring power from existing organs of government to themselves, the executive committees of the Soviets of Workmen, etc., were so overburdened with work during the summer of 1917 that some of them were even anxious " to give all the trouble of municipal government to new democratic municipal bodies." (14) The new municipal law of the Provisional Government, which included in the electoral list even the temporary members of the garrison, was approved neither by the permanent inhabitants of Luga nor by the Soviet. The soldiers were less concerned with their own aggrandizement than was the Government, and they were even desirous of insisting that the inhabitants of the town should look after their own affairs and should not trouble the Soviet about them. (15)

In the beginning of July two circumstances of importance occurred : (1) A disturbance among the soldiers of forty years of age who had been called up for service ; and (2) the resignation of the Cadet ministers. Both of these circumstances were utilized by the Bolsheviks in their continued attack upon the Provisional

# THE WORKING OF THE SOVIETS

Government. They argued with the forty-year-old reservists that if power were transferred from the Provisional Government to the Soviets, the war would be stopped at once and the soldiers would be permitted to go to their homes. The facts are that the power already lay in the hands of the Soviets in so far as these councils had exhibited any desire to exercise power, and that the Bolsheviks, being in a minority in the Soviets, had, at that time, no reason to believe that they could determine the policy of these bodies. Indeed, they had hitherto conspicuously failed to lead the Soviets, but their efforts being directed towards removing the Provisional Government, the slogan " All power to the Soviets " was as good as any other. The Bolsheviks had every reason to believe that if they were strong enough to upset the Provisional Government they would be strong enough, by means of their adherents in the army, to upset the Socialist-Revolutionaries and the Mensheviks, who together constituted their most powerful opponents in the Soviets.

The Bolshevik leaders saw clearly that they could not hope to seize power without the adherence of a large part of the army in the field. The Petrograd garrison was not enough. It was almost wholly composed of reservists who were remaining in the capital and refraining from going to the front on the plea that they had made the Revolution and must remain to prevent counter-revolution ; but this plea, in the opinion of the army in the field, did not entitle the garrison of the capital to assume the *rôle* of dictators. Therefore, although the Petrograd garrison was largely Bolshevik, it was necessary to carry on an active propaganda amongst the troops in the field in order that they might be used on the side of the Bolsheviks when the armed struggle came. Some of the more far-seeing of the opponents of Bolshevism realized what was happening ; but they were unable to offer to the soldiers the same inducements as the Bolsheviks, who were in a position to say : " We want to stop the war immediately. We want to put an end to capitalism. If we are placed in power, we shall stop the war and crush the capitalists and the landowners ; then there will be only workmen and peasants, to whom everything will belong."

Neither the executive committee of the Petrograd Soviet nor the Soviet as a whole took any notice of these efforts of the Bolsheviks. During the summer of 1917 there was much discussion in the Soviets about a Constituent Assembly (16) which was to be convened as soon as possible. The Socialist-Revolutionaries were confident that in the proposed Assembly they would have a substantial majority. The Bolsheviks on their part were equally confident. They argued that the masses of the people were war-weary, that the Bolsheviks were the only party group which proposed to put an

## 92  THE RUSSIAN REVOLUTION

immediate stop to the war, and that therefore they would be able to draw support from the war-weary of all parties.

Early on Monday, July 16, 1917, announcement was made that the four Cadet members of the Government had resigned during the night on the question of an agreement with the Ukrainian *Rada*. The Cadets objected on the ground that the settlement should be left to the Constituent Assembly, but the real reason for their resignation was probably that they found themselves always in a minority, (17) for they were adhering to constitutional forms at a moment when other parties were disregarding these. Some at least of the Cadets were men of indisputable integrity of character, and in the struggle against them there were many dark and evil forces.

Miliukov attaches blame to Albert Thomas and Arthur Henderson for their encouragement of Bolshevism. Each was sent by his Government to Petrograd in order to bring a Labour cabinet minister into relations with the Russian Revolutionary Government. Each was intended to supplant the ambassador of his country. Thomas was to replace M. Paléologue, the French ambassador, and Henderson, Sir George Buchanan, the British ambassador. Neither Thomas nor Henderson knew anything about Russia and neither of them had the least idea what importance they could safely attach either to the personalities they met or the expressions of opinion they heard. (18)

Miliukov says that two courses were open to the Provisional Government, one involving the exercise of power strong enough " to save the Revolution from its excesses," and the other involving " compromise with Zimmerwaldism," (19) which would bring about chaos, anarchy, civil war, and a separate peace. " I must state," he adds, " that the second alternative was chosen under the strong influence of M. Albert Thomas, whose authority seemed beyond dispute to our inexperienced politicians. Mr. Henderson came then to tell us that the workmen's control of factories had nothing inconvenient about it because there was already a precedent for it in the state control introduced by England during war-time." The parallel was incomplete and utterly misleading ; but here, as in the case of the Coalition Ministry and the coming offensive, these statements helped very much to push the Russian Revolution along the way which could not but prove fatal to it. (20)

---

### NOTES

(1) Voronovich, N., op. cit., p. 60.

(2) Ibid., loc. cit.

(3) For several months the Luga Soviet, representing 200,000 soldiers, workmen, and peasants, was the second in importance, Petrograd being the first (ibid., loc. cit.)

# THE WORKING OF THE SOVIETS

(4) Ibid., op. cit., p. 61.

(5) Ibid., loc. cit.

(6) See supra, p. 72 et seq.

(7) Voronovich, N., op cit., p. 62.

(8) Ibid., p. 63.

(9) The All-Russian Congress of Soviets met on Saturday, June 16, 1917. There were present 775 members. (*Izvestia*, Helsingfors, June 6–19, 1917.)

(10) Voronovich, N., op. cit., p. 67.

(11) Ibid.

(12) Ibid., pp. 68–69.

(13) Radiogram, 14 h. 40 m., June 23, 1917. From broadsheet.

(14) Voronovich, N. (op. cit., p. 70), speaking of Luga Soviet.

(15) Intimate memoirs of the attitude of other Soviets are not yet available.

(16) Cf. Mavor, J., *An Economic History of Russia* (London, 1914–1924), vol. ii, p. 185.

(17) Buchanan, Sir George, *My Mission to Russia* (London, 1923), vol. ii, p. 152.

(18) For the visit of Albert Thomas, see Paléologue, Maurice, *La Russie des Tsars pendant la grande guerre* (Paris, 1922), vol. iii, pp. 283 et seq. ; and for that of Arthur Henderson, see Buchanan, Sir George, *My Mission to Russia* (London, 1923), vol. ii, pp. 143 et seq.

(19) See p. 142.

(20) Miliukov, Paul, *Bolshevism. An International Danger. Its Doctrine and its Practice through War and Revolution* (London, 1920), p. 79.

# APPENDIX C

### TEXT OF ORDER NO. 1.

*Order No. 1.   March 1, 1917 (O.S.), March 14, 1917 (N.S.).*

To the garrison of the Petrograd district. To all the soldiers of the guard, army, artillery, and navy for immediate and absolute execution. And to the labourers of Petrograd for information.

1. In all companies, battalions, regiments, batteries, squadrons, and the different services of the military departments and in the ships of the navy, a committee must be immediately elected from the elected representatives of the low ranks of the above mentioned military departments.
2. In all the military services in which representatives to the council were not elected, one representative of each company must be elected. This representative should arrive at the building of the State Duma on March 16th at ten o'clock in the morning, with a written certificate.
3. In all matters of policy the military should submit to the Council of Workmen's and Soldiers' Deputies and to their own committees.
4. The orders of the War Commission of the State Duma should be carried out only in those cases in which they are not contradictory to the orders and decisions of the Council of Workmen's and Soldiers' Deputies.
5. All kinds of arms, such as rifles, machine guns, armoured cars, etc., should be at the disposal and under the control of regional and battalion committees, and in no case should be given to officers even on their demand.
6. In the ranks and during service soldiers should have war discipline ; but outside the service and the ranks, in their political, civil, and private life, the soldiers must not be deprived of their rights as citizens.
7. The titles of officers are abolished, e.g., Your Excellency, Your Honour, etc. For these should be substituted Mr. General, Mr. Colonel. Rudeness to soldiers of any military rank and speaking to them loftily is forbidden. Breaches of this law as well as any dispute between officers and soldiers must be brought before the company committees.

# APPENDIX C 95

This order should be read in all companies, battalions, regiments, equipages (naval units), batteries, and other commissioned and non-commissioned units.

The Petrograd Soviet of Workmen's
and Soldiers' Deputies.

(From text in *Archives of the Russian Revolution* (Berlin, 1924), vol. vi, pp. 73–74. See also *Izvestia*, Helsingfors, No. 1, March 9, 1917.) This order was confirmed by Kerensky, May 9, 1917. (Denikin, General A. I., *The Russian Turmoil. Memoirs : Military, Social, and Political*, New York, 1923, p. 174.)

## BOOK III

# MILITARY, SOCIAL, AND POLITICAL DISINTEGRATION IN RUSSIA AND THE RISE OF THE BOLSHEVIKS

# CHAPTER I

## DEMORALIZATION OF PEOPLE AND ARMY AND THE BEGINNING OF THE DISSOLUTION OF THE RUSSIAN EMPIRE

THE causes of the demoralization of the army are to be sought in the period before the Bolshevik propaganda had influenced the troops, before *Order No. 1* was issued, and before expected changes in land-ownership had begun to induce in the minds of the peasant soldiers a desire to return to their villages and share in the new distribution. Long before these incidents had any effect, demoralization had set in. (1) The chief causes appear to have been (*a*) weariness in the villages and towns arising from that exhaustion of spirit which was due to heavy loss of life (2) and to the daily spectacle of streams of wounded, (*b*) disappointment over the unexpected prolongation of the war and the apparent inability of the *Entente* Powers to cope with the military strength of Germany, (*c*) deterioration of the *morale* of the staff and officers because of the losses, and (*d*) the impossibility of a sufficiently rapid reinforcement of military units by officers as skilful and experienced as those who had fallen.

These causes combined to produce the mood of passivity and pacifism which became epidemic among the Russian people immediately after the reverses of 1915. An undercurrent of dismay and demoralization spread from the villages and towns to the front. The army offered a soil peculiarly favourable for the growth of opinions adverse to the war and to the Tsar, who was inevitably associated in the public mind with its outbreak and continuance. Regardless of the fact that the Russian people in general had acclaimed the war, both peasants and artisans blamed the Tsar for the losses entailed upon them. The newly risen middle and professional classes as well as the greater landowners felt their pride injured by military defeats ; they were not familiar with the facts relating to the theatres of war (3) other than the Russian, and they were not slow to censure the Tsar and his immediate entourage for the defeats sustained by the Russian forces.

Representatives of all classes were to be found in the army, thus it reflected the changing spirit of the whole people. The spirit of disaffection towards the Tsar and of distaste for the war spread more quickly among the troops in the field than among the people at home because of the intimacy of association. This

# THE RUSSIAN REVOLUTION

spread of disaffection induced unwillingness to submit to discipline, and, on many occasions, brought about wholesale desertion.

The Franco-Russian *Entente* had been almost exclusively an affair of " the higher spheres." Neither the peasants nor the workmen had at any time any serious interest in it. Thus when the control of the Government began to relax, and when disaffection became prevalent, the people grew suspicious of the *Entente* Powers and their policy. (4)

The spirit which characterized the Bolsheviks—aversion from authority, the breaking down of social sanctions, the relaxation of conscientiousness and of the feeling of responsibility—was to be found in the army before it had been intensified and widely disseminated by Bolshevik propaganda. This propaganda, though adapted with subtlety to particular moments and cases, derived its popularity from the fact that it expressed articulately a mood which already characterized the people. But for the Bolsheviks this mood might have been evanescent, they exploited it, and kept themselves in power by its means. The form of propaganda was derived from the speeches and writings of Lenin, who had been the recognized leader of the Bolshevist faction of the Social Democrats from the origin of that faction in the schism of 1903. It is not possible to believe that Lenin's speeches and writings could have furnished effective material for propaganda unless the course of action they urged had harmonized with the views, inarticulate as these were, which had been previously entertained by the peasants and working men who formed the rank and file of the military units. In the direct appeals to the people of Lenin and his fellow Bolsheviks, there is only the slenderest attempt at argument. They consist of continuous reiteration of phrases denouncing capitalists, especially those of Germany, England, and France, as the originators of the " imperialistic war," and demanding that all power (in Russia) be given to the soldiers' and workmen's Soviets. The promise of power was accompanied by the suggestion that it could only be realized by the destruction of the classes that hitherto had wielded it, a suggestion scarcely necessary for peasants and workmen who were already engaged in dispossessing the owners of their land and industrial plants. The following may serve as an example of Lenin's appeals. It was published in 1917, immediately after the February-March Revolution.

" It is undoubtedly an imperialistic war on both sides. Only capitalists and their ' tails '—social patriots and social *chauvinistes*— could reject or obscure this fact. The war was brought about by German, English, and French *bourgeoisie* for the purpose of destroying other countries, and in order to suffocate small nations, to obtain

## DEMORALIZATION OF PEOPLE AND ARMY 101

financial mastery of the world for division and redivision of colonies, and to consolidate the capitalist front by means of deceiving and dividing labour in all countries." (5)

A few days after the publication of the article from which the above passage is taken, and on the eve of his return to Russia, Lenin wrote urging the arming of the proletariat, the cessation of the war, and the destruction of the *bourgeoisie* as a class. He predicted that events would push the *bourgeoisie* into the proletariat. (6) For the proletariat, he contended, the war had a distinctly class character ; it was being waged between groups of capitalist countries (monarchical or republican) for the division of capitalistic booty. (7) This view of the war ignores the circumstance that Russia had any share either in the events which preceded it or in the conduct of military operations. It leaves wholly out of account the racial element in the controversy which preceded the war—the sympathy which led the Russian Government to assume the *rôle* of protector of the Balkan Slavs. It is very clear that whether justified or not in assuming this *rôle*, Russia thereby at least afforded the occasion of the war. That is a historical fact which must be appreciated in determining the origin of hostilities, and any attempt to account for the conflict by a hypothesis such as that advanced by Lenin, should connect this hypothesis in some way with the historical fact or with some other historical fact : otherwise it is surely inapplicable.

It is true that many empires engaged in the war—indeed four empires fell in it—in that sense the struggle was imperialistic. If on one side an attempt was made " to suffocate small nations "— Serbia, Belgium, Roumania, for instance—that attempt was opposed and frustrated, not at Brest-Litovsk, but in the field, by those Powers which continued to a successful issue the war against the Central Empires.

The narrative which has been given shows that imperial Russia at the beginning of the war, and at intervals later, contributed very considerably to the frustration of attempts " to suffocate small nations." (8) In so far as Lenin had any influence in the matter, he exerted it in favour of this " suffocation." Indeed, the " suffocation " of Russia by the Central Empires might have followed had the Allies not been able to secure the annulment of the treaty of Brest-Litovsk, which was the work of Lenin and his ministers.

In none of his writings or speeches did Lenin adduce any evidence to prove his thesis that the war was brought about by " the German, English, and French *bourgeoisie* to destroy other countries . . . and to obtain financial mastery of the world."

The available evidence points rather to the contrary. In Germany, Great Britain, and France, the attitude of the financial

## THE RUSSIAN REVOLUTION

and commercial world in the summer of 1914 was not favourable to war. The leading business men in Germany gave only reluctant acquiescence to a war policy under the influence of the optimism of the military authorities, who promised them a short conflict followed by greatly expanded opportunities for trade. They certainly did not promote the war, indeed many of the German men of business had from the beginning slender confidence in the judgment of the military groups. (9) In France and Great Britain, the leaders of the financial and commercial world in the beginning of August 1914 looked upon the war as a grave and terrible necessity, and no vestige of proof that they conspired to bring it about has yet been produced. On the contrary, the financial and commercial world of every country, including Germany, was completely taken by surprise and was wholly unprepared for a great war. In Germany, for example, the mercantile interests had, years before 1914, urged upon the military authorities, and upon the Government, the danger of pursuing a policy which might conceivably lead to hostilities, without accumulating supplies of food and raw material, and without making definite arrangements for these supplies to come from or through neutral countries. Practically no attention was paid to these warnings, and the consequences, from the second year of the war onwards, were most disastrous. If the mercantile interests had succeeded, either through governmental action or otherwise, in making such arrangements as would have protected the German people against famine and against the capitulation which must in the long run be the consequence of famine, and if they had then urged the German Government to declare war, there would have been validity in Lenin's hypothesis. Assuming that the financial and commercial community in Germany was apprised by the German Government, even at an earlier date than the middle of June 1914, of the likelihood of war, the notice occasioned none the less a general surprise. To provision Germany for a long campaign under conditions of partial or complete blockade was obviously impossible. Steps were taken to obtain supplies, but these steps took time, and the course of events showed that they were seriously insufficient. (10)

In countries other than Germany, the realization that war was inevitable probably came later. When it did come, towards the end of July 1914, the normal course of international trade was violently disturbed, credit was contracted, and stocks fell sharply in the markets of London, Paris, Berlin, and New York. So intense was the panic that the stock exchanges were closed everywhere. In the markets for commodities prices fell, no one wanted to buy, everyone wanted to sell. Even commodities like copper, for

## DEMORALIZATION OF PEOPLE AND ARMY 103

instance, which came to be urgently required during the coming struggle, were unsaleable on the outbreak of war. Immense sums were lost by people who were not speculating but merely pursuing a conservative course in the ordinary way of business. Speculators in general lost heavily. Capital everywhere received a shock from which it did not appreciably recover for several years.

There may have been some foolish capitalists who " brought on the war," but if such had been discovered in the early days of August 1914, they could scarcely have escaped lynching, not by Bolsheviks, but by their fellow-capitalists whom they had involved in their own ruin.

A short war might conceivably benefit financially some groups of capitalists, and so also might one of long duration. It is conceivable that under certain indispensable conditions, a short struggle might be in the interests of capital in general, but those conditions are extremely rare. The uncertainty of the outcome of *any* conflict is usually sufficient to frighten a capitalist who might be tempted to push his country into war. A long struggle cannot be in the interests of capital in general, because the available supplies of capital as they accrue are absorbed by the public treasuries in the form of loans, while the more or less compulsory sale of general securities in order to provide funds for subscription to the public loans must lead to a shrinkage in the value of such securities. Moreover, the net income from invested capital must be diminished by increased taxation. High prices which are usually experienced during a war, apply only to certain commodities. They are also temporary. In any case they do not necessarily mean high net returns to capital.

The question of the reactions of the war upon the accumulation of capital and upon the returns to capital is very complicated, and need not be discussed in this place further than to say that not the slightest light has been thrown upon it by anything that has been written or spoken by Lenin. Indeed, Lenin betrayed no knowledge whatever of the realities of the functions of capital or of capitalism considered as an economic system. Yet his ill-considered and superficial pronouncements upon the subject, and his dogmatic statements of the *rôle* played by capital before, during, and after the war, were accepted by the Russian workmen and peasants, who were unable to subject them to critical examination. Even less uncritical minds accepted, without question, many dogmatic utterances made with an air of conviction and wisdom during the turmoil of the Revolution.

It may be questioned, however, whether the anti-capitalist propaganda of Lenin had any real influence upon the town proletariat, the peasantry, or the troops. The workmen and the peasants

## THE RUSSIAN REVOLUTION

had shown in 1905–1907 a predilection for " direct action." During these revolutionary years they had seized lands, forests, and factories. While any kind of riotous seizure was blessed by Lenin before his party was able to seize political power, individual direct seizure of property was not consistent with any of the forms of communism or state collectivism to which Lenin and his fellow-Bolsheviks adhered. Such seizures of land and other property as were made by peasants and workmen in the summer and autumn of 1917 were not due to the propaganda of Lenin, but to spontaneous action by the peasants and the workmen, who, the restraining hand of government having suddenly been withdrawn, simply seized what they could lay their hands upon. Meanwhile, the classes previously in possession were taken by surprise by the sudden collapse of the Government. They were widely scattered over the immense area of Russia, and were few in number in proportion to the remainder of the population. These circumstances rendered rapid organization impossible, and the possessing classes were thus unable to defend themselves or to retain their property.

No evidence is available from which the conclusion could fairly be drawn that the uprising of peasants and working men was due " to misery and oppression " either in the period immediately preceding it or in the remote past. The facts are that the economic position of the peasant had immensely improved between the years 1907 and 1914, due partly to the land legislation of the Imperial Government, partly to the concerted action of the peasantry and the working men, and also partly to the development of Russian industry, which drew recruits from the peasantry and thus reacted upon peasant economy. There were, since the Emancipation in 1861, benevolent and intelligent as well as oppressive and unskilful landowners in Russia. The fact that the seizures of land were universal showed that local oppression or the reverse had nothing to do with the matter. They were due to the sudden relaxation of the restraining hand of law. When the grasp of law became nerveless, the predatory impulses, latent probably in all peoples, were let loose, and everyone seized what his neighbours would allow him to take. Lenin and his party had no intention of permitting either the land to fall into the hands of the peasants or the factories to fall into the hands of the workmen. So soon as the Bolsheviks succeeded in placing themselves at the head of affairs, they proceeded to nationalize land and factories alike, dispossessing gradually—because any other method was impracticable—those proprietors who had not already been ejected by " direct action."

The Bolsheviks thus took advantage of the Revolution and, as it were, rode at its head. In no sense was it due to their propaganda

## DEMORALIZATION OF PEOPLE AND ARMY 105

or to their political manœuvres, though these resulted in placing the Bolshevik faction of the Social-Democratic party in supreme command of the greater part of the dominions of the former Imperial Government.

In the summer of 1917 Kerensky attempted to restore discipline to the army. He succeeded so well, especially with the southern divisions on the Austro-Hungarian frontier, that he determined to attempt an offensive movement in July. The preparations for this offensive were observed by the German High Command, and it is quite evident that von Hindenburg was in no mood to disparage Kerensky or to underestimate the importance of preventing, if possible, the reinvigoration of the *morale* of the Russian army. Von Hindenburg therefore did what he had done the previous year. He withdrew troops from the western front, though he could ill afford to do so, and sent them eastwards. " It was a question of six divisions." (11)

Marshal von Hindenburg remarks that it is difficult to say if Kerensky adopted the idea of an offensive of his own free will, or if he was induced or compelled to adopt it by the *Entente*. The materials for a judgment on this point are not yet available. In either case, he adds, " it was entirely to the interest of the *Entente* that Russia should be driven into an offensive once more. In the west they (the *Entente*) had already offered up in vain a good half of their best fighting troops ; perhaps more than half. What other alternative had they but to send in what they had left ? . . . German troops must be held in the east, and for that reason Kerensky must send Russia's last armies to the attack. It was a venturesome game, and for Russia most venturesome of all ! Yet the calculation upon which it was based was an accurate one, for if the game succeeded, not only would the *Entente* be saved, but a dictatorship in Russia could be created and maintained. Without such a dictatorship Russia would lapse into chaos." (12)

Writing in July 1916, Albert Ballin evidently entertained precisely similar views :—

" We . . . have only one choice left : we must force Russia, our second chief enemy, to her knees. Russia has been badly hit through the loss of the industrial regions of Poland. If we had exerted all our strength in that direction, and if we had taken Kiev, the economic key to Russia, the Tsar would have had no alternative but to conclude a separate peace, and this would have settled the Roumanian question at the same time. With less certainty, but also perhaps with less exertion, it might have proved possible to make peace *via* Petrograd. . . . If we were to arrive at an understanding with Russia to-day, we should be able to go on with the war against Great Britain for a

## THE RUSSIAN REVOLUTION

long time to come, and, by means of unimpeded submarine activity, to carry it to a successful issue." (13)

Whether Kerensky's plan of campaign was his own or derived from some of his subordinates, it was not destitute of sagacity. It involved pinning the Germans down by means of local attacks in the north, while the main force of the attack was directed against the weakest point in the defences of the Central Empires, viz. the Austro-Hungarian front. That front had indeed been subjected to a process of crumbling analogous to that which had infected the Russian army. (14) Kerensky's plan, however, was betrayed to the enemy by deserters. (15) The German reinforcements were sent to the Austrian lines instead of to their own. Wherever the Austrian lines were not " stiffened " by Germans, they gave way, as they did at Stanislau, so the Germans concentrated a strong force at Brody, and on July 19th attacked in the direction of Tarnopol. The Russians had not had time to recover from the exhaustion of their own attack, and under German pressure " Kerensky's whole offensive collapsed at a blow." Yet Kerensky, or his generals, contrived to withdraw the Russian army, and even to damage the lines of communication so effectively as to put a stop to the advance of the pursuing Germans.

Notwithstanding the defeat of Kerensky, there remained elements of danger for Germany in the military situation on the eastern front. The Russian army, defeated as it was, was still in being, and if any weakness in the German lines developed in consequence of the withdrawal of troops, the Russians might return to the attack. The German High Command decided therefore to strike a blow in the north, which was held, not by the reinvigorated troops of Kerensky, but by others. An outcome of this design was the attack of September 1st upon Riga, with consequent panic in Petrograd.

It is necessary now to turn to Petrograd in order to ascertain the nature of the impact upon Russian society of Kerensky's attempt and its failure.

The endeavour to restore discipline and to infuse energy into the conduct of the hostilities was employed as a weapon of agitation against the Provisional Government and against the war itself, and the very vigour with which Kerensky was carrying on the campaign was made a ground of discontent.

About six o'clock in the morning of July 16, 1917, the streets of Petrograd began to be occupied by soldiers with machine guns. At a quarter past nine a procession of armed workmen, together with three regiments of troops, crossed the Nicholas bridge, carrying banners inscribed " Down with the capitalist ministers," " Down with the war," " Give us bread." Kerensky left for the front on the evening of the 16th, and on the following day in Petrograd there were

## DEMORALIZATION OF PEOPLE AND ARMY 107

more processions, and rifle and machine-gun firing was heard in many parts of the city. (16) On the same day a meeting was held, at Helsingfors, of representatives of the central committee of the Baltic fleet, the Helsingfors executive committee of Socialist-Revolutionaries and Social-Democrats, and of other socialist bodies. This meeting passed the following resolution : " Discussing the question of power in the crisis, and having in view the events in Petrograd, we think that it is quite necessary that all the governmental power should be given into the hands of the All-Russian central executive committee of the Soviet of Soldiers', Labourers', and Peasants' Deputies." (17) The Bolsheviks were not yet ready for such a step. They did not have control of the Soviets, and the risk of giving power to them without some security that they would be able to exercise it was too dangerous to be contemplated ; moreover, the contact between the Bolsheviks and the army at the front was as yet imperfect. The rising seems to have been in the first instance a military affair. The Petrograd garrison was restive and impetuous, and the Helsingfors socialists of all parties, who were habitually more energetic than the Petrograd groups, threw themselves into the movement. Although the Bolsheviks probably acted on July 16th as a " brake," by the night of the 18th, Trotsky and Zinoviev were utilizing the situation as a test demonstration against the Government. At ten o'clock on the night of July 18th the square in front of the Taurida Palace (18) and the neighbouring streets were crowded with people, and amongst them were military units with red flags. The first machine-gun regiment carried a flag on which was the legend, " Down with the capitalist ministers." Behind this regiment were an automobile with machine guns and a Red Labour Guard. The tramway service was stopped, and members of the Soviet came out from the palace from time to time and spoke to the people and the soldiers. Chkheidze, the President of the Soviet, addressing the crowd, said that individual military units and individual groups of working men had no right to dictate to the central organ of the Russian democracy, and urged those who were demonstrating to lay down their arms and go away. Such speeches were received coldly ; but when Trotsky and Zinoviev (19) made their appearance and demanded that the power be transferred from the Provisional Government to the Soviets, they were greeted with applause. Throughout the night of July 18th–19th there was a continuous session of the Central Executive Committee of the All-Russian Soviet of Workers', Soldiers', and Peasants' Deputies, and reports came in from various parts of the city every few minutes. Shooting was going on in the principal streets, in the Nevsky Prospekt there were many wounded, and shops were looted. (20)

108 THE RUSSIAN REVOLUTION

On July 19, 1917, the Russian front began to crack at Tarnopol, (21) and on the same day Austro-German forces broke the Russian line at Zloczov, the retreat became a panic, whole regiments shot their officers and refused to fight, and thousands of prisoners fell into the hands of the Austrian and German armies. (22) The Bolsheviks had triumphed at the front, and Kerensky's offensive had collapsed.

On the same day the Finnish Diet, by a majority of 136 to 55 votes, declared the autonomy of Finland. (23) On this day also an attempt was made to assassinate Kerensky at Polotsk in the *gub* of Vitebsk, whilst Brussilov, who had swept through Bukovina, reaching the summit of the Carpathians, thereby threatening the plains of Hungary and relieving the pressure upon Italy, was dismissed by Kerensky (24) and Kornilov was appointed commander-in-chief in his place. As a condition of accepting the post, Kornilov demanded certain reforms in the army. " These reforms were acceptable in their essence ; . . . and were already being worked out by the Provisional Government before Kornilov's nomination ; but Kornilov presented his demands in an inadmissible form." Kornilov's " tone . . . compelled Kerensky to propose to the Provisional Government his immediate dismissal." (25) This was not at once enforced, but the quarrel between Kerensky and Kornilov rapidly became acute. The struggle for the capital which began on July 16th continued until early on Saturday morning (July 21st), when the last shots were fired. (26) Kerensky had telegraphed from the front in the middle of the week reproaching his colleagues for their weakness in refraining from taking active steps against the Bolsheviks, many of whom had been arrested and shortly afterwards released, whilst Kronstadt sailors who had assisted in the armed movement were disarmed but not punished. As for the Soviet, the attitude of its members and of its Executive Committee was of the same character. They were not on the side of the Bolsheviks—indeed, they had to be defended against them by the troops of the Provisional Government ; but the Soviet was not energetic enough to act decisively against the subversive elements. Had not the Cossacks and some other troops of the Petrograd garrison remained loyal to the Provisional Government, the Bolsheviks might have succeeded in establishing the Soviets in power, and in mastering them at that moment, instead of more than three months later. As it was, the military rising and the Bolsheviks were both defeated. The resignation of the Cabinet Ministers and the defeat of the Bolsheviks practically threw the direction of affairs into the hands of Kerensky, who, when Prince Lvov resigned on July 21st, became head of the Government. The new Ministry was composed predominantly of Socialist-Revolutionaries and Mensheviks

## DEMORALIZATION OF PEOPLE AND ARMY 109

(i.e. the Social-Democratic minority faction). Kerensky promptly ordered the dissolution of the central committee of the Baltic fleet and the arrest of the leaders of the disturbance at Kronstadt ; but on demand of the Soviet, these leaders were released. (27) On Sunday, July 22nd, the Germans took Tarnopol and the Russian line was broken. (28) How this came about is described by Generals Gourko (29) and Denikin. (30) *Order No. 1* issued by the Petrograd Soviet had done its work, and even more effective influence had been exercised by the " separate agitators who appeared at various parts of the front, and who incited the mass of soldiers at the meetings to destroy the internal order of their units, and called upon them to be insubordinate to their chiefs." (31)

Such was the confusion of impulses that on the same day (July 22nd) " the chief of staff of the south-eastern front, together with the commissars and committees, ordered all deserters at the front to be shot." (32) Yet events were hurrying towards a separate peace, and troops were already being withdrawn by the Germans to reinforce their front on the west. By July 24th Kerensky had completed his Cabinet. He was Prime Minister and Minister of War. The dark figure of Nekrassov was Vice-President of the Council and Kerensky's substitute in case of need, and Tseretelli was Minister of Interior.

On July 26, 1917, the Executive Committee of the Soviet passed resolutions demanding prosecution of those Bolsheviks who had incurred suspicion of receiving money from Germany, (33) but these resolutions had no consequences, probably because suspicion was so widespread that some prosecutions undesired by the opponents of the Bolsheviks might have been initiated. On the 27th the death penalty for offences against military law was re-established at the front for the duration of the war. (34)

On July 28th the Russians evacuated Czernovitz. On the same day the Cadets, formerly members of the Government, intimated that they might rejoin Kerensky's Cabinet provided the agrarian projects of Chernov were abandoned. (35) On the 29th the Austro-German army, in face of active resistance, crossed the Russian frontier at Zbrucz and began the invasion of Russia on the Russian south-western front. Famine in Lithuania threatened to exterminate the population, and Germany offered to relieve the people provided Lithuanian workmen went into the German factories and fields. Kerensky required the Russian generals to reintroduce discipline into the army gradually, (36) and on August 2nd he prohibited meetings of soldiers' deputies and of regimental committees, whilst the Russian Government, ignoring the declaration of autonomy by Finland, issued an edict dissolving the Finnish Diet and fixing the

# THE RUSSIAN REVOLUTION

date of new elections. (37) On August 3rd the Russian armies retired in the Carpathians and also across the rivers Pruth and Düna, blowing up the bridges. The Ministry of Justice decided to prosecute Lenin and " his accomplices for high treason," and Bolshevik leaders in Helsingfors were arrested and their journals suspended. (38) On August 4th Kerensky ordered the arrest of General Gourko, (39) and General Kornilov accepted the chief command on condition that no one should interfere with his orders and appointments. Events moved rapidly : a committee of sailors demanded dissolution of the Duma, describing it as " a living corpse of counter-revolution " ; the former Minister of Interior, Kvostov, was arrested, being accused of stealing more than a million roubles intended for election preparations ; the Russian liberty loan was subscribed for to the amount of three and a half millions of roubles ; Lenin and Zinoviev disappeared. The criminal action against them involved charges of " high treason," " organization of revolt," and " illicit relations with agents of enemy countries for the disorganization of the army," and the public prosecutor affirmed the existence in Russia of a vast organization of German *espionage*. (40)

Every day during this period a large number of members of the Duma met at the house of the President, Rodzianko. The labour members did not go to these meetings, and the Cossacks sent an expression of their devotion to the Executive Committee of the Duma, which they regarded as the " true vehicle of the aspirations of the Russian people." (41)

During the night of August 3rd–4th a conference presided over by Nekrassov was held at Petrograd. Tseretelli urged the union of all parties. Nekrassov said to the representatives of the Soviet, " Either take power, or let the Government alone." To this Chkheidze answered that the Soviet would not govern by itself. In spite of protests by the Bolsheviks, the Executive Committee of the Soviet and the delegates of the peasants voted, by 147 to 46, with 42 abstentions, a resolution confiding to Kerensky the formation of a Cabinet of " concentration." (42)

On August 6th two regiments quitted their position at Bistritz, and the entire Russian line at that point was obliged to withdraw. On this same day the Minister of Justice ordered the arrest of Trotsky and Lunarchasky, (43) and on August 7th there was a discussion among members of the Duma and especially among Cadets about the legality of the Soviet, for they were of opinion that this body was responsible for the misfortunes of Russia. (44) General Kornilov declared that Russia had ten millions of soldiers, of whom few were trained, and he called upon French and English officers for co-operation in training these troops. By a decree of August 8th

## DEMORALIZATION OF PEOPLE AND ARMY

the Russian Government abolished the restrictions as to profession of the Roman Catholic religion, and also those which had applied to the Uniats. At a meeting of Bolsheviks at Petrograd, Lenin and Trotsky were elected honorary presidents. Municipal elections held on this date showed that the socialists had a majority in practically all the communes, and the Russian Government gave the right of voting to both sexes, criminals and deserters being alone excluded.(45) On August 11th Kornilov telegraphed to Foch that he was convinced that the reorganized Russian army would be able to assure the Allies of its complete co-operation.(46) The Polish congress at Moscow, which had been in session for several days, concluded on August 11th by " demanding the autonomy of Poland, cession of the mouth of the Vistula, and the defeat of Prussian militarism." (47) On August 13th railway workers in Russia struck, insisting on the separation of the railways from the State.(48) The Cossacks, assembled in congress, demanded a government responsible to a constitution and repudiated anarchy in any form.(49) On August 15th a general strike was declared in Finland.(50) The next day Chernov urged before the Petrograd Soviet that the immediate carrying out of the agrarian reforms proposed by him was the only means of preventing destruction of property by pillage.(51) The Finnish socialists proposed that the Russian Government should at once call a session of the Diet and should transfer to it all Finnish affairs.(52) On August 17th Kornilov said that the Russian army had now been rehabilitated, and that he looked forward to a new campaign in the winter.(53) Kerensky presented himself at the Soviet, but he was coldly received. On August 22nd, towards Riga, the Russian army exhibited fresh symptoms of demoralization, and the demands by Kornilov for powers to enable him to re-establish discipline were refused by the Government.(54) The prosecution of the ex-minister of war, Sukhomlinov, and his wife began before the Senate at Petrograd on August 23rd,(55) and Kamenev,(56) one of the Bolshevik leaders, was arrested on the following day.

An All-Russian Conference was convened at Moscow by the Provisional Government, at which there were 2,500 delegates, including 488 members of the State Duma. The Cossack representatives requested that the seat of government be transferred to Moscow. On the opening day, August 25, 1917, Kerensky delivered a speech in which he spoke of the " shame of the front," the defeatist tendencies in Russia, and the rejection by the Allies of the peace offers of Germany, the last mentioned being a course which he approved. Kornilov addressed the conference on the same day and gave a pessimistic account of the situation of the army, declaring the fall of Riga to be imminent.(57) " The Ukrainian *Rada*" refused to

## THE RUSSIAN REVOLUTION

take part in the conference convoked at Moscow by the Provisional Government. (58) This *Rada*, or assembly, " convened by no one, and of which the members had not been elected by anyone, assembled at Kieff and set itself up as the autonomous Government of the whole of south Russia." (59)

At Moscow on August 26th the various political groups held incessant conferences. The Cadets represented by Miliukov pleaded for a national programme, without which Russia would be lost ; the Internationalists urged the abolition of the death penalty and the abandonment of all measures against Finland and the Ukraine (60) ; the Bolsheviks demanded " all power to the Soviets," (61) but finding themselves outnumbered, published a manifesto (August 27th) denouncing the conference as a counter-revolutionary manœuvre. The Union of Cossacks telegraphed to Moscow to the effect that the Soviets had no right to meddle in military affairs, and that if Kornilov was compelled to resign, the Cossacks would act. (62) Meanwhile on the southern front at Czernovitz the Russian army suffered further demoralization, infantry having abandoned positions and reserves dispersed themselves, whilst Austrian forces penetrated Russian territory. (63) At Kazan there was a great fire, and the inhabitants were plundered by bands of robbers. (64)

The militia of Petrograd chose this moment to strike for higher wages, whilst in Moscow there was (August 28th) a strike of tramway employees. The Roumanian army found itself seriously menaced owing to the abandonment by the Russian army of positions in the Carpathians (65) on the recurrence of demoralization at the front. The Moscow conference closed (August 29th) with an impassioned speech by Kerensky, but no progress towards a peace between the Bolsheviks and the other parties had been made. (66) Russian troops having occupied the palace of the Finnish Diet, 79 members of the Diet, all Social-Democrats, met elsewhere on August 30th. (67) At Tomsk a conference of representatives of Siberia demanded federal autonomy of the region. (68) In Bessarabia, Volhynia, and Podolia, Black Hundred bands (69) engaged (August 31st) in counter-revolutionary movements. (70) On September 1st the Germans effected the passage of the Dvina without serious resistance and commenced the bombardment of Riga. (71) The Petrograd Soviet demanded the annulment of the decree re-establishing capital punishment for offences at the front. (72) On September 2nd the large factory of Prokhorov at Moscow was destroyed by incendiaries. (73) Riga was evacuated by the Russians, and the fortifications, together with the bridge over the Dvina, were blown up on the following morning, and the Russian forces withdrew in a north-westerly

## DEMORALIZATION OF PEOPLE AND ARMY 113

direction, destroying the villages as they went. (74) The capture of Riga by the Germans facilitated the clearing from mines not merely of the Gulf of Riga, but also of a portion of the Gulf of Finland, (75) thus opening a route to other Russian ports on the Baltic. The Emperor William II entered Riga on September 8th, and it became evident that the collapse of Russia had infused fresh spirit into the German people and made them more hopeful than hitherto of a favourable peace. At many places on the front fraternization of a spasmodic character was going on. Propagandist literature intended to demoralize the Russian troops was being passed over the lines. Prince Ludwig Windischgraetz gives a lively account of his experiences with the Russians on the Roumanian front in the early summer of 1917. (76)

The specific causes of the demoralization of the Russian army in the summer of 1917 may be set forth as follows :—

(a) Previous demoralization and depression remaining over from the northern defeats of 1915 and enhanced by the retreat from the summit of the Carpathians.

(b) The effect upon the *morale* of the army of the heavy losses of experienced and respected officers in the costly advances of the early stages of the war, and the replacement of these officers by others less experienced and less respected.

(c) War-weariness in the rear of the army owing to the heavy casualty lists and the waning enthusiasm for the war, accompanied by doubts regarding its purpose and meaning.

(d) Desire on the part of the troops from the villages not to miss any distribution of land. If this distribution took place in their absence, their interests might be overlooked.

(e) Increasing lack of faith, on the part of the masses of the people, in the competence of the Government, beginning in the second year of the war and continuing even after the Revolution of March 1917.

(f) Propaganda, which was at once defeatist and destructive of discipline, conducted by various socialist elements, but principally by the Bolsheviks, as well as by the troops of the enemy.

As regards the *first* of these causes, the Russian army was by no means the only one suffering from demoralization in 1917. It was the same to a greater or less degree with the armies of the Central Powers. The superior authorities at Berlin had made up their minds early in 1917 that the war could not be continued by them for another year with any prospect of success. (77) The troops of the Central Powers were apprehensive of a formidable offensive

114 THE RUSSIAN REVOLUTION

on the western front on the part of the *Entente*. (78)   In the summer of 1917 there were even evidences of war-weariness and demoralization amongst some sections of the *Entente* forces.

As regards the *second* cause, the early battles of the war had involved, in the case of every one of the belligerents, heavy sacrifices of experienced officers.   In almost all other countries the fallen were quickly replaced by men of the same or of superior education and ability, even though less experienced, and the new armies were at least as well disciplined as the old.   In Russia it was otherwise : there was no large educated middle class from which a fresh supply of competent officers might be drawn, and thus the places of the fallen had, in many instances, to be filled by those who were not only inexperienced in a military sense, but were also unfitted for the control of men.   The vast numbers of troops mobilized by Russia, if they were to be competently commanded, would have required a larger reserve of officers than she possessed, or could produce ; thus the new armies of Russia were from the beginning deficient in *morale*.

The *third* cause of demoralization, viz. war-weariness in the rear of the army, affected Russia especially, not merely on account of the partial blockade, which was experienced in common with Germany and Austria-Hungary, but on account of deficient hospital and medical services.   Because of the grave defects in these, the wounded were returned to their villages almost direct from the battlefields, and in addition to the influence of so immediate a contact with the horrors of war, the villages felt the economic strain of supporting large numbers of disabled soldiers.   In spite of much speeding up of industries, the factory system had been insufficiently developed in Russia ;  and although, when there was an unprecedented demand for munitions in 1917, immense quantities were placed at the disposal of Russia by the *Entente* Powers, these munitions, owing to the absence of adequate military organization, were not used to the best advantage.   Thus in spite of tremendous efforts and incalculable sacrifices, the people in general thought that the war was lost, and that the sooner it was brought to an end the better.

The *fourth* cause, viz. desertion from the front of soldiers who wished to return to their villages in order to take part in the distribution of land, undoubtedly played a considerable part, as also did the *fifth* cause, the progressive loss of faith in the competence of the Government.   In a country where an extremely centralized administration exists, the Government assumes universal control, and the responsibility attaching to that control inevitably falls upon it.   Thus blame for every adventure, every blow of fate, is laid to its charge.

## DEMORALIZATION OF PEOPLE AND ARMY 115

The *sixth* cause, socialist propaganda, has been regarded by some as solely responsible for the demoralization of the army. This is an obvious error, for in the absence of those potent causes which have been just noticed, propaganda would have passed unheeded. The Bolshevization of the army made the October 1917 Revolution possible ; yet the Bolshevistic frame of mind of the troops was undoubtedly due not only to propaganda but also to the impact upon the minds of the soldiers of the various causes which have been here enumerated.

The specific causes of the dissolution of the Russian Empire, beginning with the separation from Central Russia of Finland, Poland, and the Baltic Provinces, and for a time of the Ukraine, Siberia, the Caucasus, and other regions, were as follows :—

(1) The collapse of the dynasty, which removed the most important unifying influence and left unrestrained the previous tendencies in many parts toward particularism of the Empire. (79)

(2) Disinclination on the part of the various nationalities, other than Russia, to submit to the dictation of relatively small Russian, or even mixed Russian and alien groups in Petrograd or Moscow, whom the non-Russian peoples regarded as their inferiors in culture.

(3) Doubts regarding the advantages of the drastic political and social changes which appeared to be imminent in the Russian Revolutionary State, and regarding the permanence of the institutions which appeared likely to be the outcome of the Revolution.

(4) Reaction against centralized administration, which had delayed local development and had involved unwelcome Russification in respect to language.

(5) The foreign policy of the Central Empires and of France.

(6) Divergence of economic interests, especially in view of the prolonged economic crisis in Russia.

The *first* of these causes affected all the regions subject to the tendency towards dissolution of the Empire. The *second* cause affected especially Poland, Finland, and the Ukraine, (80) whilst the *third* had influence in these regions together with the Baltic Provinces. The *fourth* cause affected especially the Baltic Provinces, Finland, and the Caucasus, whilst the *fifth* became influential in respect of Finland, Poland, the Baltic States, and the Ukraine when separate treaties of peace were concluded between the Central Powers and Russia, and between the former and the Ukraine. Later, France recognized Poland and refused to recognize the Soviet Republic. (81)

# THE RUSSIAN REVOLUTION

The *sixth* cause influenced especially Finland, Poland, and the Ukraine. Each of these regions experienced under the old *régime* certain economic advantages ; but with the passing of that *régime*, and with the obviously approaching changes in the social character of the Russian population, these advantages were likely to dwindle. The burden of taxation to meet the expenses of the war was necessarily enormous. A fiscal policy which might suit the central government and some regions of Russia might be fatally injurious to the outlying regions, and for these reasons, while the central authority was too weak to resist, separation seemed expedient.

## NOTES

(1) It is probable that the Russian army had not, in 1914, fully recovered from the demoralization of 1905. Count Witte remarks : " J'ai l'impression que vers la fin de 1905, l'armée au front était profondément démoralisée et révolutionnée. Si cette connaissance ne fut pas répandue dans le public, la dissimulation de cette plaie qui rongeait le cœur même de l'armée doit être attribuée à la conduite des autorités militaires." (Witte, Count, *Mémoires du Comte Witte* (Paris, 1921), p. 258.)

(2) The losses of the Russian army during the course of the war (August 1914–November 1917) may never be known. Marshal von Hindenburg says that the German estimate was between five and eight millions. (Cf. von Hindenburg, Marshal, *Out of My Life* (London, 1920), p. 273.)

(3) Until the summer of 1918, even well-informed publicists like Miliukov, for example, believed in the overwhelming military superiority of Germany, and refused to believe in the possibility of a victory by the *Entente* Powers.

(4) The popular idea was that the *Entente* Powers desired to throw upon Russia an undue share of the burden of the war.

(5) Lenin, N., in *Pravda* (Petrograd), Nos. 14–15, March 21 and 22, 1917. Reprinted in *Collected Works* (Moscow, 1923), vol. xiv, p. 7.

(6) Cf. Lenin, N., op. cit., p. 12.

(7) Cf. Lenin, N., *Louis Blancovism* in *Pravda*, No. 27, April 8, 1917 ; reprinted in *Collected Works*, vol. xiv, p. 21.

(8) The attitude of the Bolsheviks, when they came into power, towards small nations is noticed later.

(9) Cf. importantly, Huldermann, Bernhard, *Albert Ballin* (London, 1922), passim.

(10) On this point see Huldermann, B., op. cit., pp. 221–22.

(11) von Hindenburg, Marshal, op. cit., p. 277.

(12) Ibid., op. cit., p. 274.

(13) Huldermann, Bernhard, op. cit., pp. 259–60. The letter from which these passages are extracted was written in May 1916. Within a year Ballin had altered his opinion about the success of the submarine campaign. (Cf. ibid., pp. 267–68.)

(14) Von Hindenburg, Marshal, op. cit., p. 275.

(15) Ibid.

(16) Buchanan, Sir George, op. cit., vol. ii, p. 153.

(17) *Izvestia* (Helsingfors), July 6–19, 1917.

(18) The Taurida Palace was built by Catherine II for Prince Potemkin after the conquest of the Crimea. It became the palace of the State Duma in 1905.

(19) Ovsei Gershon Aronovich Radomieslsky, also known as " Shatsky," " Zinoviev," " Apfelbaum," " Gregoriev," and " Gregory," born in 1883, of

# DEMORALIZATION OF PEOPLE AND ARMY 117

Jewish parents, in Novomirgorod. Arrested in 1908, placed under surveillance of police at Elizavetgrad (Spiridovich, A. E., op. cit., p. 179).

(20) *Izvestia* (Helsingsfors), July 19, 1917.

(21) Cf. von Hindenburg, Marshal, op. cit., p. 279.

(22) *Chroniques de la Guerre*, 7<sup>e</sup> vol., p. 37.

(23) Ibid., p. 39. According to Bernhard Huldermann (in *Reconstruction in Europe*; *Manchester Guardian*, May 18, 1922, Section II, p. 100), managing director of the Hamburg-American line, Germany is entitled to the credit of separating Finland from Russia. It is by no means clear that Germany had anything to do with the declaration of Finnish autonomy, although guarantees may have been given by Germany against attack upon a separated Finland. A. Ballin, in a *Memorandum* dated September 1917, protested against the policy of breaking up the Russian Empire. (See Huldermann, B., *Albert Ballin*, London, 1922, p. 278.)

(24) General Gourko (*Memories and Impressions of War and Revolution in Russia* (London, 1918), p. 322) ascribes to petty reasons, scarcely credible, the action of Kerensky in dismissing Brussilov. It seems more plausible to believe that, at that moment, Kerensky was in favour of allying himself with the energetic Kornilov.

(25) Kerensky, A. F., *The Prelude to Bolshevism*; *The Kornilov Rebellion* (London, 1919), pp. 9–10.

(26) Order in the capital was restored by the military governor of Petrograd, General Polovtsev. (He was dismissed four days later.) Lenin fled from Petrograd, but offered (July 22nd) to surrender to the authorities (*Chron. de la Guerre*, 7<sup>e</sup> vol., p. 44). Trotsky was not molested.

(27) *Chron. de la Guerre*, 7<sup>e</sup> vol., p. 42. Sir George Buchanan's opinion that the Bolsheviks could have been finally crushed in the July rising (*My Mission to Russia*, vol. ii, pp. 156–58) is not established by the evidence (cf. his more cautious conclusion, op. cit., p. 160). Kerensky had not the support of the army, while the peasants' one fear was a counter-revolution which might deprive them of the land they had appropriated or intended to appropriate. Even the most discriminating severity was not unlikely to result in his government being immediately upset by the Bolsheviks, who though in a minority were too numerous to annihilate.

(28) *Chron. de la Guerre*, 7<sup>e</sup> vol., p. 43.

(29) Gourko, General Basil, *Memories and Impressions of War and Revolution in Russia 1914–1917* (London, 1918).

(30) Denikin, General A. I., *The Russian Turmoil* (New York, 1923). The details given by Denikin are ghastly.

(31) Gourko, General Basil, op. cit., p. 281.

(32) *Izvestia* (Helsingfors), July 24, 1917. Telegram July 22nd.

(33) *Chron. de la Guerre*, 7<sup>e</sup> vol., p. 52.

(34) *Izvestia* (Helsingfors), July 28, 1917.

(35) *Chron. de la Guerre*, 7<sup>e</sup> vol., p. 56.

(36) Ibid., p. 57.

(37) Ibid., p. 64.

(38) Ibid., p. 66.

(39) Gourko, General Basil, op. cit.

(40) *Chron. de la Guerre*, 7<sup>e</sup> vol., p. 70.

(41) Ibid.

(42) Ibid.

(43) Ibid., p. 71. Anatole Vasilievich Lunarchasky, also known as " Galerk " and as " Voenov," was born in Poltava *gub* in 1876. His father was a landowner. He received his early education in Kiev and then went to the University of Zürich. He travelled or resided for the greater part of his life in Switzerland, France, and Italy. Although he visited Russia occasionally, he rarely resided there until after the Revolution. He suffered a short period of exile in Siberia, from which he escaped. As a dramatist and poet, Lunarchasky must be regarded as occupying a high place, however short he may have fallen as an educational administrator. See *Three Plays of A. V. Lunarchasky : Faust*

## 118 THE RUSSIAN REVOLUTION

*and the City ; Vasilisa the Wise ; and The Magi.* Translated by L. A. Magnus and K. Walter (London, 1924) ; see also Spiridovich, A. E., op. cit., pp. 54–55.

(44) *Chron. de la Guerre,* 7e vol., p. 73.

(45) Ibid., p. 78.

(46) Ibid., p. 79.

(47) Ibid., p. 80.

(48) Ibid., p. 82.

(49) Ibid.

(50) Ibid., p. 84.

(51) Ibid., p. 87.

(52) Ibid.

(53) Ibid., p. 89.

(54) Ibid., p. 97.

(55) Ibid., p. 98.

(56) Kamenev (real name Leo Borisovich Rosenfeld) is a brother-in-law of Trotsky. He was born of Jewish parents in 1883. He was arrested in Tver for taking part in a demonstration. He became a member of the Central Executive Committee of the Russian Social-Democratic organization in 1908 (Spiridovich, A. E., op. cit., p. 49).

(57) *Chron. de la Guerre,* 7e vol., p. 101.

(58) Ibid.

(59) Nekludov, A., *Diplomatic Reminiscences Before and During the World War, 1911–1917,* translated from the French (London, 1920), p. 511.

(60) The penalty of death did not exist in Russia excepting for offences at the front against military law ; and there it had just been re-established.

(61) *Chron. de la Guerre,* 7e vol., p. 103.

(62) Ibid.

(63) Ibid.

(64) Ibid., p. 104.

(65) Ibid., p. 107.

(66) Ibid., p. 108.

(67) Ibid., p. 110.

(68) Ibid.

(69) Cf. Mavor, J., op. cit., vol. ii, pp. 297 and 499.

(70) *Chron. de la Guerre,* 7e vol., p. 111.

(71) Ibid., p. 112.

(72) Ibid., p. 113.

(73) Ibid.

(74) Ibid., p. 114.

(75) German submarines made their appearance in the Gulf of Finland on September 9th (ibid., p. 123).

(76) Windischgraetz, Prince Ludwig, *My Memoirs,* translated by Constance Vesey (London, 1921), pp. 126–29.

(77) Cf., e.g., Baron Flotow's report, dated January 15, 1917, to Austrian Foreign Office in Czernin, Count Ottokar, *In the World War* (New York and London, 1920), p. 134.

(78) Ibid. Flotow, reflecting contemporary opinion in Berlin, considered that the United States would be unlikely to go farther in any case than breaking off diplomatic relations (ibid., p. 135).

(79) For these tendencies see Mavor, J., *An Economic History of Russia,* vol. i, pp. 572 et seq., and vol. ii, p. 5 and pp. 244-48.

(80) While the superior social groups in these countries were not upon a higher cultural level than similar groups in Russia, the proletariat of all of them looked down upon the Russian proletariat and peasantry as culturally inferior to themselves.

(81) France recognized the Soviet Republic in November 1924.

## CHAPTER II

# THE KERENSKY–KORNILOV AFFAIR AND THE CRUMBLING OF THE FRONT

DURING the first week of September 1917 the party composition of the Petrograd Soviet and of some of the provincial Soviets appeared to be changing. The Socialist-Revolutionaries found their influence declining as that of the Bolsheviks increased. The Bolsheviks became, on September 9th, dominant once more at Kronstadt, (1) the municipal elections having given them an enormous majority ; and, the sailors being already " Bolshevized," the fortress and town fell into their hands.

On September 10th there began that series of incidents which comprised the Kerensky–Kornilov affair. Politician and general had both given evidence of energy and ability ; but they seem to have been unable to co-operate with the self-effacing loyalty in the service of their country so necessary at that historical moment. Neither Kerensky nor Kornilov appears to have been judicious in his choice of messengers, and both appear to have acted impulsively. Allowance must be made for the rapidity with which events were moving, for the need of instant though far-reaching decisions, and for the strain of the unusual and unanticipated *rôle* which both men had to assume. The course of the Russo-German war and the course of the Revolution were alike influenced by the issue of the personal quarrel between Kerensky and Kornilov, who had been made commander of the south-western front, and later, on the very eve of the quarrel, commander-in-chief of the Russian army. Kerensky's account of the Kornilov affair may be abbreviated as follows :— (2)

After the fall of Riga (September 3, 1917), owing to the approach of the battle front to the capital, it became necessary to declare Petrograd under martial law, to transfer some of the troops of the garrison to Kornilov's command, and to draft other troops into the city to take their places. Savenkov, (3) deputy Minister of War, was sent to Kornilov's headquarters (September 6th) for the purpose of transmitting to him the orders of the Provisional Government. In doing so, Savenkov was instructed to say that the Caucasian " Savage division " should not be included in the troops to be sent to Petrograd. Notwithstanding these orders, and in spite of a promise on the part of Kornilov to obey them, the " Savage division " was despatched

## THE RUSSIAN REVOLUTION

to Petrograd on " the following day " (September 7th), under the command of General Krymov. (4) While this and other forces under Krymov were approaching the capital, V. Lvov presented (September 8th) on behalf of Kornilov " an ultimatum " to Kerensky, in which he was ordered to transfer the power of the Provisional Government to Kornilov, who would give posts in the new Government to Kerensky and Savenkov. Kerensky called Kornilov to the telephone and apparently, without repeating to him exactly what Lvov had reported, received from him confirmation of Lvov's " authority " and " indirect " confirmation of " all that had been said by the latter." Kerensky " promised Kornilov to come to headquarters, and at the same time immediately took all steps to cope with the rebellion at its very beginning."

Kornilov, for his part, convened at headquarters the opponents of the Government, and " the ultimate form of the dictatorship was finally settled and the composition of the Government agreed upon." (5) On September 10th Kerensky dismissed Kornilov and summoned him to Petrograd, appointing Klembovsky commander-in-chief, (6) and he also ordered the arrest of V. Lvov and eighty others. (7) On the next day (September 11th) Kaledin, *Ataman* of the Cossacks, urged the Provisional Government to agree to Kornilov's conditions, and Kornilov continued to advance on Petrograd. The Soviet meanwhile issued a proclamation in favour of Kerensky. (8)

General Gourko interprets the Kornilov affair in a somewhat different manner. He says that it was Kerensky's idea to occupy Petrograd by troops faithful to the Provisional Government, that instructions for the occupation were given by him, and that they were no secret to the Petrograd Soviet. Members of the Soviet, however, were uneasy and interrogated Kerensky, who became afraid, ordered the troops not to enter Petrograd, (9) and dismissed Kornilov, thus placing upon Kornilov the onus of failure. The two explanations are not altogether inconsistent. The main point is : what use did Kerensky intend to make of Kornilov's troops when they reached Petrograd ? Kornilov seemed not to have any doubt that Kerensky intended to take vigorous action against the Bolsheviks and then to diminish or destroy the influence of the Soviets over the Government. It is doubtful if either Kerensky or Kornilov intended to treat one another fairly ; the evidence would seem rather to point the other way. Kerensky lays a large part of the blame for the subsequent calamities of Russia upon Kornilov. He says that " the adventure of a small group was transformed, in the inflamed imagination of the masses, to a conspiracy of the whole of the *bourgeoisie* and of all the upper classes against democracy

# THE KERENSKY-KORNILOV AFFAIR

and the working masses. . . . Nobody will ever succeed in breaking the fatal link between September 9th and November 7, 1917." (10)

The quarrel between Kornilov and Kerensky was probably inevitable because their ambitions were irreconcilable ; but it proved fatal to both. Kerensky defeated Kornilov, but found himself alone in his struggle against the Bolsheviks and unable to defeat them ; whilst shortly afterwards Kornilov lost his life in the civil war. Undoubtedly both were to blame—Kerensky for initiating the idea of bringing troops from the front to the capital, and then for changing his plans after the moment had passed when this could be done with safety ; and Kornilov for a fatal want of foresight in allying himself with a confederate so irresponsible as Kerensky. In a proclamation to the troops, Kerensky denounced Kornilov as a traitor, (11) and in so doing cut himself off from the support of the sole remaining disciplined elements in the army. The episode became in Kerensky's hands a real " prelude to Bolshevism."

Up to the beginning of September 1917 the Bolsheviks, being in a minority, had little power or influence in the Petrograd Soviet ; after that date they were able to utilize the situation created by Kerensky for the undoing of Kerensky himself. They had assiduously cultivated the Petrograd reservists, but they had not hitherto been able to make any general impression upon the army in the field ; now, however, they were in a position to take advantage of the fresh disorganization of the army due to the abortive Kerensky-Kornilov affair. It was necessary for the Bolsheviks to find support outside Petrograd, for the garrison of the capital was not in favour with the army at the front ; and with the rise of prices and the decline of employment the numbers of workmen in the capital were dwindling.

On September 12, 1917, Kerensky appointed himself dictator and generalissimo. " Finally, to crown everything, he and four of his colleagues—a kind of council of five—on their own authority and initiative, proclaimed the Republic, of which the generalissimo naturally became President. This was announced throughout the country (September 14th) by means of government circulars and posters, whereas Russian representatives abroad received instructions to defer the notification of this important change to the governments to which they were accredited." (12) In the confusion of the time, in the atmosphere of universal suspicion, (13) and in the intentional ambiguity of many of the essential documents, it is hard to discover the truth in detail. The conclusion, however, is clear, that neither Kerensky nor Kornilov was astute enough or strong enough to deal with the crisis. Their opponents, the leading Bolsheviks, probably with the occasional alliance of reactionary

## THE RUSSIAN REVOLUTION

Monarchists, knew no scruple, and had already acquired so much influence over the minds of the city working men that they could induce them to believe anything. Thus the Bolsheviks propagated the idea that Kornilov, " for the sake of his criminal aims, was ready to open the front to the enemy and to betray the fatherland," while they must have known all the time that he had been doing his best to restore discipline in the army for the purpose of preventing a dishonourable and disadvantageous peace.

At the time when the Kerensky–Kornilov affair was in progress, the case of Russia was probably already beyond redemption. The moment for action was in February 1917, when the dynasty fell, and before the social revolutionary forces had had time to organize their subversive and destructive campaign. A vigorous policy at that moment might have saved Russia ; but the tragic fact was that, although there were plenty of able Russians, there was not one of sufficient political sagacity, and at the same time of accredited public prestige, to take and to keep effective control. The conditions of the previous time had rendered this combination of virtues impossible, and that was the nemesis of the previous three centuries of autocratic rule. (14) Till the close of the Kerensky–Kornilov episode, Kerensky had a greater influence and a larger following than anyone else. He had behind him not only the Socialist-Revolutionaries and the Mensheviks, but also the army at the front. " The soldiers and a majority of the officers hailed him as their idol. In his person were concentrated all the prayers for the Revolution. On him there were placed such hopes as were quite unrealizable. The other heads of the revolutionary democracy, such as Chernov, Zenzinov, Tseretelli, etc., dwindled altogether before the personality of Kerensky. . . . Even the June advance, which led to the collapse of the idealistic revolution, was forgiven him because, as they said at the front, " he did it out of his great honesty." (15)

After the Kornilov affair, Kerensky lost the good opinion and support of the army, which began to distrust him as the betrayer of Kornilov's confidence ; Kornilov, on the other hand, disciplinarian as he was, enjoyed the confidence of soldiers and officers alike.

From the middle of September there were food riots in many places, as for example from September 15th in Jitomir, from the 23rd at Tashkent, from the 24th in Kharkov, and from the 25th in Tambov, Ufa, and Astrakhan. (16) On September 12th Guchkov, former minister, was arrested at Petrograd. On the 12th and 13th the Russian armies made small gains in the northern sector of the front, and on the 13th Kerensky named himself, commander-in-chief, with General Alekseiev as his chief-of-staff, and left Petrograd with a strong guard, whilst Kornilov announced that he was willing to

# THE KERENSKY-KORNILOV AFFAIR 123

give himself up. General Dragomirov was appointed commander of the south-west front, and General Russky was put in command in the north. General Kaledin and his Cossacks arrested the Soviet of Rostov-on-Don. The troops of Kerensky and those of Kornilov fraternized. On September 14th the Petrograd Soviet, by a majority of 279 votes to 115, passed a Bolshevik resolution (the mover of which was Kamenev) (17) containing the following : (1) Exclusion from power of the Cadets and the middle classes ; (2) Proclamation of a Democratic Republic ; (3) Immediate handing over of landowners' lands without compensation to committees of the peasants ; (4) Nationalization of industry ; (5) Declaration that *all* past treaties are null and void, and immediate offer of a general democratic peace ; (6) Abolition of the death penalty at the front; absolute liberty of propaganda ; (7) Dissolution of the Duma and of the Council of the Empire ; (8) Immediate convocation of the Constituent Assembly. (18)

In the middle of September the Russians recovered somewhat their positions in the sector of Riga, and the Russian fleet continued to manœuvre in the Gulf of Finland in spite of the presence there of German submarines. (19) Meanwhile the Petrograd Soviet demanded the formation of a strong power, and at the same time condemned all arbitrary and illegal acts. It decided to convoke at Petrograd, on September 25th, a general conference of representatives of organized democracy, but the Russian co-operative societies refused to participate in it. The municipal elections throughout Russia favoured a socialist *bloc* and proved disastrous to the Cadets. (20) On September 17th Kerensky appealed to the Kronstadt sailors, exhorting them to cease murdering their officers and committing other acts of violence. (21) The Russian forces in Bukovina returned to the attack, (22) and General Alekseiev resigned his position as chief-of-staff to Kerensky. (23) The president of the Executive Committee of the Petrograd Soviet, Chkheidze, resigned because of a Bolshevist majority which voted " all power to the Soviets." (24) At Pskov thirty-eight soldiers were condemned to forced labour for having fraternized with the enemy, (25) the Soviet insisted on the liberation of Trotsky, and an order of the day enjoined the punishment of those soldiers who murdered their officers. Near Pskov, on September 23rd, the Russians made an attack and captured a German sector. On the 24th Victor Chernov, formerly Minister of Agriculture, passed over to the Bolsheviks, (26) and a new candidate for the dictatorship arose the following day in the person of General Verkhovsky. (27) On September 26th the Soviet held a stormy session. Kamenev insisted that the Soviets should seize all power, and Trotsky pointed to the example of the Jacobins " who

124 THE RUSSIAN REVOLUTION

reared the guillotine against the *bourgeoisie*." (28)   At the same time
Sukhomlinov, formerly Minister of War, was sentenced to hard
labour for life, but his wife was acquitted. (29)  On September 28th
the Russian land forces in Finland and the naval forces in the Gulf
refused to support the Russian Government in preventing a meeting
of the Finnish Diet, previously dissolved by decree. (30)

On September 26th there were food riots at Kiev, on the 27th
at Kazan, and from September 30th till October 2nd in Orel.
Riots took place on October 2nd in Ostrogorsk, Ekaterinburg, and
Bakhmut, and on the 4th at Odessa. (31)  During September
agrarian disturbances had occurred in the villages.  The peasants,
uncertain that the policy of the Government would be in accordance
with their wishes, resorted to " direct action " on their own account.
Agitators contributed to these uprisings, but in general the peasants
were disposed to take the nearest land without suggestion from
party propagandists.  The month of September 1917 marks a
distinct stage in the march of events, for then the peasants began
on a large scale to seize the lands of proprietors and to destroy the
inventories.   In Bessarabia, Tambov, Saratov, and Kherson *gubernie*,
i.e. in the south and east, the Government tried to adopt strong
measures ; but there was no sufficient administrative or military force
in the regions, and this action only increased the chaos. (32)   With
the growth of anarchy, dissatisfaction with the Government became
widespread, institutions crumbled, and much was destroyed that
had taken centuries to build, whilst nothing constructive was accomplished.  The army was pervaded by a spirit of disaffection.  " After
the close of the Kornilov affair, the last walls of discipline disappeared, and the number of deserters increased to an unimaginable
figure."(33)   It seemed as though all the soldiers were possessed
of an uncontrollable desire to go home.  Deserters walking from
the front reported themselves to Bolshevik leaders and to the Petrograd Soviet, saying that if peace were not signed before November
the remaining soldiers would leave the trenches. (34)

After the Kornilov affair, and the election of Trotsky to the chair
of the Petrograd Soviet, Kerensky was induced or compelled to
permit the enlistment by the Soviet of an armed force which was to
be under its own control.  For the equipment of this force the
Government promised 70,000 rifles.  When this should be arranged,
factory and workshop committees were instructed to select from the
workmen in their establishments those who were known to be
the most revolutionary.  These workmen were to form troops and be
given the old name of *drujēnē*. (35)  Each of these troops numbered
from 10 to 100 or more and they were organized by districts,
every district being placed under a commander.  Several districts

# THE KERENSKY–KORNILOV AFFAIR

were grouped together, and over this combined region there was a commander who with his staff was elected by the *drujēnē* of the region. The aggregate of the troops of all districts formed the Red Guard. By the end of September 1917 they numbered 10,000 men, and at a meeting of the Red Guard of Petrograd and its suburbs they adopted by-laws and regulations and elected a commander-in-chief. According to the contemporary remark of a communist, " a Red Guard is the symbol of the dictatorship of the working man who has taken a rifle in his hand and overthrown the *bourgeoisie*." (36)

In the summer of 1917 the German High Command observed with relief (37) the process of disintegration that had begun in the Russian State. " From the outset our plan was to leave this process alone. We had to take care, however, that it should leave us alone also, and not perhaps bring us with it to destruction." (38) The Russian army was still in being, although it had changed enormously since its onslaught on East Prussia in the early days of the war. The mood of the soldier at the front in October and November 1917, on the eve of, and immediately after, the October Revolution, may be gathered from the memoirs of Boris Sokolov, Socialist-Revolutionary and anti-Bolshevik.

" The soldiers were not fighting ; that is an undisputed fact. The soldiers did not want to advance ; and can one blame them ? On the other hand, there were in fact very few cases of ' sticking the bayonet in the ground,' leaving positions, and opening the front. What prevented them ? There was at that time no power over them. The apparatus of punishment existed no longer. Even in these October days, when demagogues were calling upon the soldiers to leave the front and to go home, the soldiers answered : ' But what about the front and what about the position ? ' Some of the aspects of life at the front need to be illuminated in order to help to refute the legends that the front ruined the Revolution. The Russian Revolution was ruined by idealism—the idealism of the Russian democracy, the idealism of the revolutionary leaders— that is the opinion of President Masaryk, and the same opinion appeared to be held at the front.

" Ninety-nine per cent. of the soldiers were peasants, illiterate or half-literate, tired of war, homesick, unacquainted even with elementary political doctrines. . . . The officers were also tired of war, often lacking the necessary power of resistance, discontented with the authorities and with the General Staff, living apart from the mass of the soldiers and without knowledge of their lives and moods. The General Staff, for its part, did not want to take up any new ideas. It fought by all permissible and unpermissible means for its privileges. The soldiers were blind and limited in their outlook.

## THE RUSSIAN REVOLUTION

To such people, set apart from the rest of the world, dispersed in trenches, in uncomfortable, extemporized bomb-proofs, or in dirty and half-ruined villages, living with gloomy forebodings, from month to month, from day to day—' To live or not to live ? ' ' Will it be to-day or to-morrow ? '—to these masses came the revolutionary leaders from the capital. It is hard to imagine a real understanding arising between the two groups—the revolutionary leaders filled with belief in their own watchwords (' Power to the people ! ' ' The People are masters ! ') and with a tendency to idealize the masses " ; and the peasant-soldier who simply wanted to escape from the sound and the danger of the enemy artillery and to get home on any reasonable terms. Sokolov remarks that the " protocols of the Special Army, very well known to me, are full of examples of misunderstanding," both on the part of the " idealistically attuned " revolutionary representatives and also of the tired soldiers and officers who were equally self-interested. The newly arrived revolutionaries looked upon the troops at the front " as a conglomerate of politically ripe people," as developed citizens of a Russian Republic to whom it is proper to talk, first about their rights, and last of all about the duties which arise out of these rights. The situation was intensified by the characteristic delusion of the peasant mind that when a thing is embodied in a watchword it is as good as done.

The soldiers were mystified by the confident tone of the revolutionaries. " ' We do not understand anything,' they said. ' They say we are all equal ; but officers receive much higher wages than we.(39) Can their rations and our rations be compared ? Look how the generals are living ! And from the villages we hear that there are still landlords, and that we ought soon to return home.' " At the very moment when the revolutionary leaders of the Socialist-Revolutionary and Menshevik parties were counselling care and moderation, this attitude of the soldiers produced sharp disagreement between them and the *intelligentsia* in general.

When equality became a watchword, everyone, from the peasant's point of view, must be equal with everyone else. There must be no discrimination in land, in rations, or indeed in anything. When they realized that phrases employed by revolutionaries were not immediately given the force of law, they looked upon these revolutionaries as hypocrites, while the revolutionaries looked upon the *naïveté* of the peasant soldiers as proof of their unfitness for political life.

This attitude of the soldiers led them in many cases to make demands for the equalization of rations and wages, for new boots, for leave out of their regularly appointed turn, and for the cessation of the "imperialistic" war. "What they heard from the revolutionary propagandists penetrated each man's mind. Primitive they were, but they were also energetic and definite, destitute of abstract idealism." Claims such as those indicated were made by the N—— regiment while it was in reserve near Kovel in Volhynia. The soldiers did not absolutely refuse to go to the front, but they required that their demands should be satisfied first. The commissar (40) of the Special Army at that time was Boris Moeseenko, "a very nice and civilized man." (41) Moeseenko arrived in an automobile, smartly dressed, wearing French gaiters. He collected the regiment and talked to the soldiers for two hours, telling them of his exile in Siberia and how he had suffered imprisonment under the old *régime*. After explaining the distinction between party cries and party action, he said that the demands they had made could not be met, and that they would be sent to the front without further discussion. At an earlier stage such a speech by a commissar might have been followed by submission, but now the moody soldiers had become dangerous. They listened with impatience, and the commissar as he proceeded was interrupted with cries of " Enough ! " " Lies ! " etc. A few pebbles were even thrown, and only the energy of the regimental committee enabled him to escape. Sokolov and Captain Basilevich were asked by Moeseenko to speak to these soldiers the next day. There was tremendous excitement. Soldiers filled with incredible hostility towards the commissar Moeseenko collected in groups talking about the massacres of officers and *intelligentsia* in general and refusing to obey orders.

"Just think what he has been saying, that we should bow to the officers. He himself is a real *barin*, gentleman, master, landlord. He arrived in an automobile and he speaks like a *barin*. . . . He wears gaiters too ! . . . He is a typical *barin* and an intelligent. . . .

"We want to live. We do not want to die, especially just now, when we are getting land and freedom. To attack would be very dangerous for us." The two last sentences were contained in a resolution of the 100th division.

"The national feeling—the feeling of duty on the part of the masses at the front—was just enough to prevent them from deserting. . . . 'We must not allow the Germans to enter our country. . . .' The soldiers were willing to hold the front till the time of the Brest-Litovsk peace, but they did not want to attack."

Sokolov says sharply, "It matters little how we regard the Provisional Government, critically or uncritically ; but we have to recognize the fact that, towards the real assistance of the front (the direct arm of the war), the Government and the High Command have done nothing." (42)

# 128 THE RUSSIAN REVOLUTION

## NOTES

(1) *Chron. de la Guerre*, 7e vol., p. 122.

(2) See Kerensky, A. F., op. cit., passim.

(3) B. V. Savenkov, Socialist-Revolutionary and former Terrorist

(4) For account of Krymov's force, see Voronovich, N., op. cit., pp. 77–88.

(5) The statement in the text is abbreviated from Kerensky, A. F., *The Prelude to Bolshevism* ; *The Kornilov Rebellion* (London, 1919).

(6) On the same day Kronstadt fell once more into the hands of the Bolsheviks (cf. *Chron. de la Guerre*, 7e vol., p. 122).

(7) Ibid., p. 124.

(8) Ibid., p. 125.

(9) A long account of the stoppage of General Krymov and a corps of Cossacks on their way to Petrograd is given by Voronovich, N. (op. cit., pp. 78–81). Krymov was stopped by Voronovich at Luga on the ground that his entry into Petrograd was in opposition to the Provisional Government. This conclusion was confirmed by communication with Petrograd. Krymov was arrested and was sent to Petrograd in charge of Colonel Samarin, Kerensky's adjutant. A report was circulated that after an interview with Kerensky, Krymov committed suicide. There is, however, a belief that in the course of a dispute with Kerensky, Krymov struck the Minister, and the adjutant shot Krymov. Kerensky alludes to the matter in the phrase, " When Krymov shot himself " (Kerensky, A. F., op. cit., London, 1919, p. 236).

(10) Kerensky, A. F., op. cit., pp. 19–20.

(11) August 29–September 11, 1917.

(12) Nekludov, A., op. cit., pp. 511–12. A. Nekludov was ambassador at Madrid.

(13) Kerensky seems to have suspected members of his own Cabinet of communicating with the German High Command (cf. Wilcox, E. H., *Russia's Ruin*, London, 1919, p. 256).

(14) A detailed account of the Kerensky–Kornilov episode is to be found in Wilcox, E. H., op. cit., pp. 250–76.

(15) Sokolov, Boris, *Defence of the Founders of the All-Russian Constituent Assembly* in *Archives of the Russian Revolution* (Berlin, 1924), vol. xiii, p. 14.

(16) Spiridovich, A. E., *History of Bolshevism in Russia* (Paris, 1922), pp. 370–71.

(17) Known also as Rosenfeld, brother-in-law of Trotsky.

(18) *Chron. de la Guerre*, 7e vol., p. 129.

(19) Ibid., p. 130.

(20) Ibid., p. 131. On September 16th Samuel Gompers telegraphed to Kerensky offering him the aid of the American Federation of Labour (ibid., p. 132).

(21) Ibid., p. 133.

(22) Ibid., p. 135.

(23) Ibid., p. 138.

(24) Ibid.

(25) Ibid., p. 139.

(26) According to a despatch in *The Times* (September 24, 1917) the Petrograd Soviet appropriated to itself 700,000 roubles per month, and the Provisional Government printed daily 50 millions in paper roubles. All labour by peasants and workmen was suspended. Transportation had ceased. A fuel famine was a question of weeks. Wheat, which was in abundance, could not be either transported or distributed.

(27) General Verkhovsky, who as a youth had been a member of the corps of pages, exhibited an early disposition towards liberal opinions. He distinguished himself in the Japanese war. After the March Revolution he had assisted in the organization of the central executive committee of the Black Sea fleet, where he appeared to have rendered important services in preserving discipline. In May 1917 Verkhovsky was promoted to be a colonel and was given a sector

# THE KERENSKY–KORNILOV AFFAIR 129

at the front. Shortly afterwards he was made commander of the Moscow military district, where he remained until after the Kornilov rebellion.

(28) *Chron. de la Guerre*, 7ᵉ vol., p. 147.

(29) Ibid.

(30) Ibid., p. 157. The policy of the Provisional Government which permitted a dispute with Finland while the Government was with difficulty clinging to power, was on the face of it a blunder.

(31) Spiridovich, A. E., op. cit., p. 370.

(32) Ibid., p. 371.

(33) Ibid.

(34) Ibid.

(35) Cf. Mavor, J., *An Economic History of Russia*, vol. ii, pp. 547 and 553.

(36) Spiridovich, A. E., op. cit., p. 383.

(37) Von Hindenburg, Marshal, op. cit., p. 270.

(38) Ibid., p. 271.

(39) This was under the Provisional Government.

(40) Appointed by the Soviet.

(41) He was killed at Omsk during the Koltchak campaign.

(42) Sokolov, Boris, op. cit., vol. xiii, p. 12.

# CHAPTER III

## " ALL POWER TO THE SOVIETS "

THE Provisional Government, now practically in the hands of Kerensky, appeared to the general mass of the educated population to be powerless to act in the military, political, and economical crises in which the country was involved. Local and central administration alike had suffered paralysis. The *Zemstvos* had been disorganized by the Imperial Government and had not been restored by its successors ; the Duma had been moribund for months and the Constituent Assembly was not yet in being. Men began, therefore, to turn towards the Soviet, that spontaneously organized institution, which, destitute as it was of any legal authority, had nevertheless made its influence felt in the daily conduct of administration. This institution had sprung up in 1905–1906 in obedience to an urgent demand for a body that might take the administrative power from the hands of a Government which at that time seemed too feeble to retain its authority. (1) The Soviet, or Council, was composed of persons elected by means of an elastic franchise. It was, in its early stages, a revolutionary committee, self-appointed, but related to other similarly appointed revolutionary committees, from which were sent delegates to a council of councils, and in this way, by means of a pyramid of councils, the Soviet system was formed. The organization was quite simple ; a Soviet could without difficulty or delay be brought into existence, altered in character, or united with other Soviets ; its peculiarity was that while the members were in general soldiers, working men, or peasants, its activities were not confined to the affairs of these particular groups, but included all governmental, administrative, and judicial affairs whatsoever. (2) The numerous functions which in reality devolved upon the Soviets in the summer of 1917, through the collapse of the system of local government, compelled them to co-opt, or elect by some means, persons who were supposed to be specially qualified. Flexibility was thus an advantage because it admitted into the Soviets, ostensibly of workmen, many professional persons who contributed their knowledge and experience, and it admitted also to the Petrograd Soviet, in particular, some persons who were not residents in Petrograd, thus giving to this council a character not exclusively local. Yet this very flexibility exposed it to manipulation by astute politicians who might by skilful manœuvring rapidly acquire

# "ALL POWER TO THE SOVIETS"

sufficient power within the Soviet to use the system for the promotion of their policy. Thus immediately after the Revolution of March 1917, and the revival of the Petrograd Soviet, which had been non-existent since 1906, that Soviet was stampeded into issuing *Order No. 1.*(3)

While the Petrograd Soviet, under the control of a Menshevik-Socialist-Revolutionary *bloc*, gave only a qualified support to the Provisional Government, it explicitly refrained, excepting in the premature attempt of July 1917, from making any effort to displace the Government and to assume the responsibility of office. The reason for this reluctance lay in the absence of close contact between the Petrograd Soviet and the army in the field.

As the idea of parliament was suggested by the ecclesiastical councils, so also the idea of the Soviet is directly related to the system of ecclesiastical bodies by means of which the Roman Catholic hierarchy maintains its hold upon the Church throughout the world. The frequent party congresses correspond to the Œcumenical Councils of the Church, and the small group of persons whose names are to be found on all the important committees is analogous to the College of Cardinals, by whose votes the Supreme Pontiff is elected. The Catholic Church is the Church universal, it oversteps all national boundaries, and it conceives itself as not merely entitled but bound by the most sacred obligation to carry its propaganda everywhere and against all opposition. In its system are mingled local responsibility and central authority. In the case of the Church there is a presumption in favour of the claim by that central authority that its office is exercised with a single eye to the glory of God and the good of the Church. The Soviet system also disregards national frontiers, and carries its propaganda with an avowal of fervour everywhere. For the dictatorship of the proletariat, the central idea of those who now control the Soviet system, it claims universal dominion. There the resemblance ceases. The spiritual force which gives the ecclesiastical Soviet its momentum, which makes all men equal before the Altar, and mitigates the motive of personal gain, advocates community of goods by cheerful surrender of excess, and obliterates distinction of class by emphasizing a common religious obligation.

It would be a mistake to suppose that all the changes in the economic system which took effect on the morrow of the Bolshevik Revolution were introduced by the Revolutionary Government. The most important of these changes were brought about by " seizure of freedom," otherwise " direct action." This method had been adopted by peasants and workmen alike in the revolutionary move-ment of 1905–1907. While quasi-provisional governments were

## THE RUSSIAN REVOLUTION

formed at that time in St. Petersburg and Moscow, and were known as the Councils of Workmen's Deputies, (4) and while both in St. Petersburg (November 20th–26th, 1905) and in Moscow (December 9th-19th, 1905) these Councils exercised certain of the functions of government, the most important and widespread action was taken spontaneously by the peasants who appropriated the property of the landowners, and by the workmen who seized the factories. So also in the autumn of 1917 the peasants seized the land, killed many of the landowners, drove others from their estates, and permitted some to remain in the position of simple peasants ; while the workmen spontaneously formed committees to manage the factories displacing their employers and driving them away or degrading them to subordinate positions. (5)

The Russian socialist *intelligentsia* had adopted the theory of the class war and had promised to give land to the landless and property to those who had none ; but they constantly deplored the inertia of the peasants and the apparent impossibility of revolutionizing them. Social-democratic and socialist-revolutionary agitation alike had slender influence over the peasant masses, who were not easily roused to revolt, when revolt meant risk to their village interests and disturbance of their normal life of labour and petty accumulation.

The political revolution was accomplished by the socialist *intelligentsia*, who seized the reins of power from the all too feeble hands of the Constitutional-Democrats ; but the social revolution was effected by the peasants and the peasant artisans themselves at the moment when the collapse of the autocratic power and the failure of the constitutionalists left Russia without a government. These events resulted in the explosion from beneath, dreaded by every Russian statesman for more than a hundred years.

During the summer of 1917 it became evident that behind the Government stood the Soviet, and before that body it was powerless. The subordination of the Government to the Soviet was manifest to working men, peasants, and soldiers alike. Power had been seized by the Soviet while responsibility rested upon the Government. Clearly the Provisional Cabinet was helpless ; yet it appeared to stand in the way of peace because it nominally exercised executive authority. If the Government were displaced and the power nominally exercised by it were in the hands of the Soviet, there would be immediate peace ; and since peace was supposed to be desired by the vast majority of the people, the conclusion was gradually forced upon them that the Provisional Government should be displaced, and power handed over to the Soviets in order that peace might be made without delay.

The Petrograd Soviet was by no means a united body during the period of the Provisional Government. There were in it at least three parties : the Socialist-Revolutionary party, which had been strong enough at the outbreak of the Revolution and the resuscitation of the Soviet to place one of its members, A. F. Kerensky, in a high position in the Provisional Government ; the Mensheviks, or minority faction ; and, lastly, the Bolsheviks, or majority faction, these latter having come into existence as a result of the division of the Social-Democratic party. (6)

Numerous historical disputes upon problems of principle and of practice had disrupted the socialist groups ; but these disputes invariably disclosed, as their real origin, fundamental differences in the character of the disputants. Arbitrary and domineering personalities gravitated towards one another and became involved in perpetual quarrels, while the milder personalities inclined to each other for mutual protection. Opinions and parties frequently changed, the only constant element being the character of the personalities. During the early part of the summer of 1917 the Soviets appear to have performed many useful functions. The Committees of the Councils of Soldiers' Deputies were, for example, not always engaged in disintegrating activities. Some of them raised funds from civilians and soldiers, and expended this money in providing for the troops newspapers, libraries, cheap restaurants, etc. Peasants contributed by bringing supplies for which they received, in exchange, books and pamphlets. (7)

The Soviets deteriorated rapidly as soon as Bolshevik agents obtained a footing in them. Up to that time the members of the Soviets of various parties felt that they had work to do, and did it conscientiously, no matter how irksome and unusual it was. (8) When the Bolsheviks acquired influence, their ostensible aim was to make the worst rather than the best of a difficult situation ; in fact the most speedy way of overcoming the Provisional Government seemed to them to lie in making the process of administration as unworkable as possible. They were astute enough to recognize that the issue of the moment was peace at any price versus the war policy of the Provisional Government. Peace being unquestionably the popular policy, the Bolsheviks easily rode into power upon it. Like many another political party, they gained office upon one issue, and subsequently carried out a policy for which they had received no mandate from the people.

The growth of the power of the Petrograd Soviet, together with the formation of numerous Soviets of similar character throughout European Russia, led to many regulations which were sent at their instance to the army at the front. The dictation implied in these proceedings was resented by the soldiers of the active army, and

## THE RUSSIAN REVOLUTION

relations were very strained (in April 1917) between the soldiers' Soviets and those of the capital and the towns of the interior. (9) When reinforcements were demanded by the committees at the front, elected according to *Order No. 1*, and by the soldiers' Soviets, these reinforcements were often refused on various grounds by the Soviets of the interior cities. There thus grew up a feeling of hostility between the front and the rear.

Difficulties notwithstanding, the Soviets had much influence at a time when there was no accepted representative assembly, and the cry " All power to the Soviets " became popular. The Bolsheviks were reluctant to use this cry until they felt certain that the Soviets would be controlled by them, and their real reason for adopting it finally was because it was brief and intelligible, and because they hoped that, time telling in their favour, their control over the Soviets would not be long delayed.

During September 1917 meetings of workers in the following establishments in Petrograd decided that the governmental powers should be transferred to the Soviets : The Arsenal, Old Parvian factory, Petrograd tobacco-pipe factory, labourers on Vasili Ostrov, Vulcan factory, the Mint, Rasteryaev factory, Ziegel company (optical factory), Leather production company, Weiss's shoe factory, Neva shipbuilders, Ijorsky factory, Russo-Baltic mechanical works, Sestroryetsky factory, and some others. (10) The growing belief in the ability of Soviet government to prevent the social and political disintegration of Russia had no necessary connection with Bolshevism. There had been some Bolsheviks in the Soviets from the beginning (in March 1917), as there had been Bolsheviks in the St. Petersburg and Moscow Soviets in 1905–1906, but the Bolshevik party did not dominate the Soviets. Not until September 1917 were they strong enough to control the Petrograd Soviet, and even then there were many local Soviets over which they had no control. Sovietism is thus one thing and Bolshevism quite another.

Yet towards September 1917 the Bolsheviks were gradually improving their position in the Soviets, very largely through their increasing influence in the army at the front. They astutely discerned that by a Cabinet formed after the manner of western European Cabinets, i.e. by means of compromises and accommodations, their drastic social projects could never be realized. They were therefore inevitably hostile to coalition government and even to parliamentary government in any form. The only governmental body that could be utilized by them was one which should be absolutely subservient to them, and might be employed for the purpose of annihilating opposition by acquiescence in the use of force irrespective of law or precedent. Such a body the Bolsheviks saw in

## "ALL POWER TO THE SOVIETS" 135

the Soviet, and it was elastic enough to be twisted by them into any shape they desired. An alternative was a government by a coalition which would admit into the Provisional Government an increased number of socialists. There was no unanimity upon this question even among those who entertained no sympathy for the Bolshevik attitude. The peasants, for example, were divided. Towards the end of September 1917 meetings of regional peasant Soviets were held at Petrograd. For a coalition government, the Cadets being excluded, (11) there voted the executive committees of the Peasants' Soviets of Vladimir, Riazan, and Chernigov *gubernie*, and also the deputies of the 11th and 12th armies. Against any kind of coalition, there voted the committee of peasant deputies of Bessarabia, Voronezh, Kaluga, Kuban, Minsk, Pskov, Saratov, Sirdarin, Tobolsk, Kherson, Jaroslav, Penza, Petersburg, Podolia, Smolensk, Ufa, and Kharkov *gubernie*, part of the Don region, and the 4th, 5th, 6th, and 8th armies, as well as the executive committee of the Sevastopol Soviet of Peasant Deputies from army and fleet, the Finland Soviets, and the Caucasian central peasant organization. At a meeting of the Social-Democratic Congress held on October 1st, 1917, the majority of the representatives of regional workmen's and soldiers' Soviets passed a resolution of a strongly Bolshevist character of which the conclusion was as follows : " Only by union between the town and the village democracy, between the proletariat and the army, in the struggle against all counter-revolutionary forces, will those high problems be successfully solved which all Russia is encountering."(12) So great was the confusion of the time that events with contradictory tendencies occurred simultaneously. The Executive Committee of the Soviet telegraphed (October 2nd) to French socialists who were meeting at Bordeaux, protesting against any idea of a separate peace (13) ; a democratic conference at Petrograd voted confidence in Kerensky by 139 to 106 votes ; the Petrograd Soviet voted a resolution challenging the authority of the Social-Democratic Congress (14) ; General Alekseiev said that the officers who had been " struck down as counter-revolutionaries were true patriots and defenders of liberty "(15) ; General Kornilov insisted that he had been deceived and that his innocence would be proved before a tribunal ; (16) on October 5th part of the estate of Yasnaya Polyana, which had been handed over to the peasants by the Countess Sasha Tolstoy after her father's death, was pillaged, (17) and on the same day there was extensive incendiarism at Baku. (18)

A new institution called the Pre-Parliament was constituted (October 6th) under the presidency of Chkheidze, who had been president of the Soviet. In Tashkent the food riot of September 23rd (19) developed into a revolt, and a newly elected Soviet of

## 136 THE RUSSIAN REVOLUTION

labourers' and soldiers' deputies formed an executive committee and decided to take all power into their hands. An attempt by the military commandant of the district to arrest the committee led to the arrest of the commandant himself as well as other members of the local government, so in order to put an end to the regional Soviet power the Government at Petrograd had to send troops to Tashkent, and these on October 9th put down the disturbance. (20)

Food riots occurred on October 7th in Kishenev and on the 8th and 9th in Bender. (21)  On October 9th the Germans made a descent with sea and land forces upon the islands of Dago and Oesel to the north of the Gulf of Riga, the Russian batteries being blown up by shells from the German dreadnoughts. (22)  The Government and the inhabitants of Petrograd became alarmed, for the Germans were rapidly approaching the city ; accordingly plans were hastily laid to transfer the seat of government to Moscow. On or about this date a meeting of the Central Committee of the Bolshevik faction took place in Petrograd, presided over by Lenin. The question of the seizure of power was discussed, but though there was no unanimity, the Bolsheviks were alert in taking advantage of every change in the situation that might favour a *coup d'état*. They agitated for a Constituent Assembly ; they agitated for the retention of the Government in Petrograd—for anything indeed which gave excuse for street demonstrations.

At this moment, that is towards the middle of October, the population of the capital was in a highly nervous condition.  The Germans were drawing nearer, soon they might be throwing shells into Petrograd.  The Provisional Government had been unable to protect the country against the external enemy, and it was hourly showing its incapacity to maintain internal order.  The masses of the people were easily swayed to one side or the other, and either by superior tactical skill or by promises more ample than the Government chose to offer, the movement of the Bolsheviks gained steadily in momentum.

The Executive Committee of the Petrograd Soviet decided to convoke a General Congress of Soviets in November.  Finland on October 6th proclaimed itself a Republic, and the Russian Government next day advised all Russian families living in Finland to leave that country. (23)  On October 8th a new Russian Ministry was announced—Kerensky became President of the Council and Generalissimo of the Army, Konovalov Minister of Commerce and Industry and Vice-President of the Council, whilst Tereshtchenko remained Minister of Foreign Affairs.  On the same day Trotsky was elected President of the Petrograd Soviet. (24)

On October 9th both the Kronstadt Soviet of Labourers and the

## "ALL POWER TO THE SOVIETS" 137

garrison absolutely refused any kind of support to "the treacherous Government," and declared that "only through the Soviet can the power of the Revolution be organized." The Helsingfors Soviet of Workmen's and Soldiers' Deputies, the regional committee, and the central Soviet of the fleet likewise passed a resolution that they would not support the Government. (25)

On October 13th food riots occurred on the River Don and in the Militopolsky and Neprovsky regions of Simferopol *gub* and elsewhere. (26) On the same day, from the general headquarters at Mohilev, Kerensky issued a manifesto to the Russian navy, urging the sailors to serve their country. The Government meanwhile formed special committees for the struggle against Bolshevism, and the Cossacks of the Kuban offered to put an end to the Soviets. (27)

During the first fortnight of October 1917 the working people in the provinces and the general mass of the soldiers in reserve, in the garrisons, and at the front, were inclining towards Sovietism. The Bolsheviks had not invented the Soviet, they had found it in existence. Unless they could control it in the interests of their party, they were indifferent to it. They had had difficulty in mastering it, yet in the eyes of the workers and the troops Sovietism and Bolshevism were indistinguishable.

Although the Government had formed in the middle of October special committees for the struggle against Bolshevism, they had not even then grasped the serious nature of that struggle. Legal proceedings against the Bolshevik leaders were not pressed. The Minister of Justice, S. D. Milyantovich, seemed to be more anxious to make himself popular with the sailors and workers who were members of the Soviet than to engage in any struggles. Kerensky was himself inactive, (28) and the newspapers in general applauded Milyantovich for his "liberal tendencies." The only person who gave signs of realizing the gulf to which events were hurrying the country was V. Burtsev (29), who on October 13th published an article, "*The Enemy who is forcing his way into our homes.*" "Let the Government understand first of all that the Helsingfors Tovaristchi (Comrades), Trotsky, Riazonov, Kamenev, and Lenin, with their efforts to overthrow the Government and to take by force the power from their hands at a critical moment, are traitors to their country. The Provisional Government should collect about it all to whom the rescue of their country is dear, and at the same time immediately put all the traitors out of the country. If the present Provisional Government is not able to do that, then it should go. It should not wait until it is put out." (30) The Government of Kerensky took no notice of this appeal. The difficulty of the

## THE RUSSIAN REVOLUTION

situation lay in the fact that no authority competent to " dismiss " the Government existed, and no party or combination of parties had developed sufficient energy to deal decisively with a situation complicated by an external war in progress and a civil war hourly threatened.

In Bessarabia (October 14th) there were grave disorders, fires at Tiraspol and at Kharkov, and mutinies in Astrakhan. The Government (October 14th) opened administrative careers to women on the same conditions as to men. (31) On the 16th the Russians began to evacuate Reval, (32) and the following day there was a naval engagement between Russians and Germans in the Gulf of Riga, in which the dreadnoughts at Kronstadt took no part. (33)

After long preliminary discussions, the representatives of various socialist organizations made ready in the third week of October to assemble at Stockholm for a conference, the design of which appeared to be to bring the war to a conclusion. There was strong reason for believing that the conference was convened in the interests of Germany, (34) other attempts to secure discussion of peace terms favourable to that country having failed. On August 9th the sailors on the vessels crossing from Great Britain to Norway for Sweden refused to permit the conveyance of British socialist delegates to the Stockholm Conference, (35) yet on August 10th, by a majority of more than three to one, (36) the British Labour Party decided to send representatives on condition that the conference was purely consultative. Arthur Henderson argued that if none but Russian socialists met the Germans at Stockholm, danger would lie in that fact, and Branting sent a message to the socialists of the *Entente* pointing out that the Russians had decided to ally themselves with the Austro-German socialists. (37) On August 11th the French socialists, in spite of the advice of some of their leaders, decided to send representatives to the conference, (38) but Gompers, on behalf of the American Federation of Labour, refused to participate. (39) The German Government also refused to send delegates excepting under the condition that responsibility for the war would not be discussed, and on August 13th the House of Commons approved the refusal of passports for Stockholm. The Russian Government, however, declared (August 15th) that passports would not be refused, but that the resolutions of the conference would not place the Government under any obligation to give effect to them. At a socialist congress held in London a resolution approving of the proposed conference at Stockholm was brought forward. Vandervelde and Hyndman moved an amendment, arguing that such a conference was impossible so long as Allied territory was occupied by Germany. (40) On October 19th the

## "ALL POWER TO THE SOVIETS" 139

committee of the projected conference published a peace programme
—Neither victor nor vanquished ; law to be substituted for force ;
neither annexations nor indemnities ; safeguards for the principle
of nationality under international control ; and a plebiscite in
Alsace-Lorraine. Opposition, not only on the part of many Governments, but also on the part of many leading socialists, rendered the
project of a conference at Stockholm abortive. The Pre-Parliament
met (October 20th) at the Marie Palace, and the presidency was
offered to Madame Breschkovskaya. (41) In his speech Kerensky
praised the navy, but said he could not praise the army, whereupon
the Bolsheviks marched out of the hall.

A rumour having been circulated on October 19th that the
Government was preparing to leave Petrograd for Moscow, the
Soviet, on the initiative of Trotsky, declared itself next day against
the proposed transference. The Workers' Central Committee
called a new All-Russian Congress of Workers, and this was regarded
as a manœuvre of the Bolsheviks against the Government. (42)
There was at this time observable an increase of crime in Odessa ;
in the Caucasus (October 20th) a train was attacked by brigands
and 100 passengers killed. (43) The Union of Cossacks called upon
Kerensky to make clear his position regarding Kornilov, " of whose
loyalty and patriotism there could be no suspicion." (44) On
October 21st German dirigible aircraft dropped bombs over Finland
and Riga, causing numerous casualties, (45) and the State Duma,
which had nominally continued its functions, was declared to be
dissolved directly the date of November 25th had been fixed for
the elections to the Constituent Assembly. (46)

The working men in the Petrograd district were becoming
gradually Bolshevized during 1917 and 1918 ; but the *intelligentsia*,
of course, remained hostile to Bolshevism, as also were the other
classes of Petrograd society, the nobility, manufacturers, merchants,
shopkeepers, and clerks—in short, the general mass of the inhabitants
of the capital apart from the working men, troops, and professional
groups. This anti-Bolshevism might have afforded ground for
political parties in opposition to the Bolsheviks to build a combined
oppositional movement. Yet here again were manifest those characteristics which have already been noticed in relation to the army,
a natural passivity, and a reluctance to undertake responsibility
and trouble. Those who were opposed to Bolshevism were displeased with the Provisional Government because of its concessions
to the Left ; and they were equally displeased with the Soviet because
of its excessive benefactions to the proletariat. (47) Yet they wore
an air of indifference. " Let other people fight the Bolsheviks,"
" Let us see how they will cope with the Bolsheviks." This indo-

## 140 THE RUSSIAN REVOLUTION

lence was fatal, for they were speedily swept into the *maëlstrom* of the Revolution, and it is no exaggeration to say that few survived who did not escape to foreign countries.

Boris Sokolov, Socialist-Revolutionary, remarks that his own party and the Mensheviks committed a great political blunder in not exploiting and fostering the anti-Bolshevist feeling which underlay the passivity of a great number of the inhabitants of Petrograd. Some concession to conservatism might have been made, some qualification of the socialist attack upon the *bourgeoisie* might have won over the *bourgeois* inhabitant, and under the guidance of the Socialist-Revolutionaries and the Mensheviks the combined force might have defeated the Bolsheviks. (48) The course of events was otherwise, the inhabitants were taken by surprise in October 1917, and although they made street demonstrations on January 5, 1918, they could make no effective combination nor any determined isolated resistance.

---

### NOTES

(1) According to a report drawn up by the Chief of the Political Police (Petrograd branch) and presented to the Minister of the Interior in August 1915, Kerensky, then a member of the Toil Group in the Duma, suggested that the working men should organize factory groups for the election of workmen's and soldiers' Deputies, as had been done in 1905. The report stated also that Kerensky was circulating rumours to the effect that he was receiving " numerous letters demanding that he should overthrow the Romanov dynasty " and take its power into his own hands. If this police report is true, the revival of the Soviets may have been due at least as much to Kerensky as to the Bolsheviks, although it does not appear that any immediate effect was given to his suggestions. (Cf. Wilcox, E. H., *Russia's Ruin*, London, 1919, p. 192.)

(2) Cf., e.g., the case of the Soviet of Luga, supra, p. 88.

(3) Cf. supra, p. 94.

(4) These Councils (Soviets) continued to exist, and their name was applied to the system of government which was adopted by the Revolutionists of October 25, 1917.

(5) Cf. Antonelli, Étienne, *Bolshevik Russia*, translated from the French by Charles A. Carroll (New York, 1920), pp. 227–30.

(6) The division occurred in 1903 at the second Congress of the Russian Social-Democratic-Labour party. The Bolsheviks, for some time after the resuscitation of the Petrograd Soviet, were in a decided minority.

(7) Voronovich, N., op. cit., p. 55.

(8) This is very evident from the candid narrative of Voronovich.

(9) Voronovich, N., op. cit., p. 56.

(10) Spiridovich, A. E., op. cit., p. 372.

(11) Exclusion of the Cadet party would have left the Government wholly socialist.

(12) Spiridovich, A. E., op. cit., p. 372.

(13) *Chron. de la Guerre*, 7ᵉ vol., p. 155.

(14) Ibid., p. 157.

(15) Ibid., p. 158.

# " ALL POWER TO THE SOVIETS "

(16) *Chron. de la Guerre*, 7<sup>e</sup> vol., p. 155.

(17) Ibid.

(18) Ibid.

(19) Cf. supra, p. 122.

(20) Spiridovich, A. E., op. cit., p. 370.

(21) Ibid., p. 372.

(22) Ibid., p. 374.

(23) *Chron. de la Guerre*, 7<sup>e</sup> vol., p. 160. On October 7th the United States Government approved of the formation in the U.S. of a Polish army, following an appeal by Paderewski. An army was equipped, drilled, and sent to Europe.

(24) Ibid., p. 161.

(25) Spiridovich, A. E., op. cit., p. 372.

(26) Ibid., p. 370.

(27) *Chron. de la Guerre*, 7<sup>e</sup> vol., p. 168.

(28) Spiridovich, A. E., op. cit., p. 373.

(29) Vladimir Burtsev, Socialist-Revolutionary (cf. supra, vol. ii, pp. 581, 582 n.). After the March Revolution, he supported the Provisional Government and opposed the Bolsheviks. After the October Revolution, he resided in Paris, publishing for a time *La Cause Commune* (*Obshoyé Dielo*).

(30) *Obshoyé Dielo* (*La Cause Commune*), Petrograd, September 30th, O.S.–October 13th, N.S., 1917.

(31) *Chron. de la Guerre*, 7<sup>e</sup> vol., p. 169.

(32) Ibid., p. 170.

(33) Ibid., p. 172.

(34) This was H. M. Hyndman's view. On August 8th he protested against the participation in the conference of socialists of the Allied countries on the ground that the conference was organized for the advantage of Germany. He urged the British Government to refuse passports to British socialists (*Chron. de la Guerre*, 7<sup>e</sup> vol., p. 74).

(35) Ibid., p. 75.

(36) The majority was 846,000 against 550,000 (*Chron. de la Guerre*, 7<sup>e</sup> vol., p. 77). Eleven days later another vote was taken. The majority then was only 3,000 (ibid., p. 94).

(37) Ibid.

(38) Albert Thomas urged that representatives should be sent to Stockholm in order to declare " the right " (*Chron. de la Guerre*, 7<sup>e</sup> vol., p. 80).

(39) Ibid., loc. cit.

(40) Ibid., 7<sup>e</sup> vol., p. 107.

(41) Well known as the " grandmother " of the Revolution.

(42) *Chron. de la Guerre*, 7<sup>e</sup> vol., p. 177.

(43) Ibid

(44) Ibid.

(45) Ibid., p. 178.

(46) Ibid., p. 179.

(47) Sokolov, Boris, op. cit., p. 27.

(48) Ibid., op. cit., p. 28.

## CHAPTER IV

## " RED OCTOBER." THE PREPARATION

THE Government of Russia during the summer of 1917 was, as it were, at the disposal of the highest political bidder, who must be the party who could demonstrate most decisively possession of the greatest capacity for implementing the most magnificent promises. The struggle was now narrowed between two antagonists. " Rights " had disappeared ; Constitutional-Democrats and Octobrists had either joined one of the socialist parties or had ceased to influence the movement of public life. On one side was Kerensky, who had isolated himself from all parties with the exception of the Mensheviks (the Social-Democratic minority) and the Socialist-Revolutionaries. These parties contained the best personal elements in the socialist groups, but they were intellectually aloof from the masses of the workmen and peasants, and they had little influence over them. As parties they were not very cohesive. On June 17, 1917, a meeting of the Menshevik faction of the Social-Democratic party was held in which three groups were distinguishable (1) : (a) Defencists, 86 ; (b) Internationalists, 12 ; (c) Undecided, 39. All of these 137 persons were members of the Union of Soviets, with their meeting in Petrograd. The Socialist-Revolutionaries had been similarly divided into " Zimmerwalders," who, with the Menshevik Internationalists above mentioned, adhered to the Zimmerwald programme of peace as soon as possible without annexations or indemnities, and " Defencists," who, with the Menshevik " Defencists," (2) recognized the danger of capitulation to Germany and desired to maintain the defence of their country at all costs ; this group was led by Plekhanov. (3) The Mensheviks and the Socialist-Revolutionaries were thus divided into three groups, " Defencists," " Pacifists," and " Undecided." Kerensky could rely only upon the Defencists, although neither of the other two groups took active measures against him. Besides the above-mentioned socialist parties he had practically no support ; the Cadets had gone out of the Government ; the landowners were afraid of both Chernov and Kerensky ; the peasants were doubtful whether Kerensky's Government would carry out Chernov's agrarian scheme ; and the working men and employers found little in Kerensky's programme to interest them. Monarchists and Octobrists both held aloof. Kerensky was committed to the prosecution of

## "RED OCTOBER." THE PREPARATION 143

the war, but the army was already demoralized. He had quarrelled with the most popular Cossack officer, and the Cossacks were accordingly dissatisfied. A large proportion of the army was Bolshevized, partly by spontaneous tendency and partly by propaganda. How then could Kerensky, without sufficient power, carry out his programme?

On the other side were Lenin, Zinoviev, and the Bolsheviks—"Defeatists" all, demanding immediate cessation of the war. They proposed that Russia should offer peace, as if Russia had overcome Germany and Austria, and they graciously proposed to grant peace without annexations and without indemnities.

There was little disguise on the part of the Bolsheviks that they were acting in the interests of Germany. Their answer to such an accusation was to the effect that they were "internationalists," and as such were not concerned with national interests. In October 1917 the Bolshevik leaders were under threat of prosecution. Some of them were in hiding, and everyone knew of the charges of treason laid against them. Yet by assiduous labour on their part they had secured the sympathetic support of the army to their peace programme, and notwithstanding the charges against them, they managed to retain that support. They proposed, on the one hand, to put an immediate stop to the external war, and, on the other, to begin at once an internal struggle against capitalists and landowners, by taking away all industrial enterprises from the one and all land from the other. Both the workmen and the peasants wanted factories and land for themselves ; but if the Bolsheviks assisted them in dispossessing the owners, the Bolsheviks might be compelled later to hand the "instruments of production" in each case to those who were using them. Thus, although the workmen and the peasants were not Bolsheviks, although they knew nothing about the meaning of "imperiocratism" or the other recondite topics of discussion with which the party leaders had been wont to exercise themselves, they were not unwilling to permit the Bolsheviks to organize a victory over the classes above them. One day the Bolsheviks might have to be reckoned with ; but the workers need not trouble about that yet. Meanwhile, with the army behind them, the Bolsheviks were stronger than Kerensky and his small group. Such were the feelings with which, in general, working men and peasants watched, and indeed facilitated, the rise of the Bolsheviks to power. The slender hold which the Government of Kerensky retained upon the people, and the obvious decline of his influence, weakened the sense of public order in the capitals, induced more frequent acts of violence in Petrograd, and made rioting an easy matter.

# THE RUSSIAN REVOLUTION

While Kerensky, handicapped by the unfavourable conditions of the time and the limitations of his own personality, was doing his utmost to raise the *morale* of the army, which was no longer suffering from inadequate equipment, his efforts met with slender response and were being skilfully counteracted by Bolshevist propaganda in the ranks of both army and fleet. At the same time, the Bolsheviks were conducting open hostilities against him in the capital, losing no opportunity to discredit him, and taking advantage of any and every cry—" Constituent Assembly ! " " Petrograd the capital, not Moscow ! " " Stop the war ! " " Land and bread ! " etc., etc. The subsequent career of the Bolsheviks showed that they cared less than nothing for the Constituent Assembly, and that they took the earliest occasion to remove the seat of government from Petrograd to Moscow.

The municipal elections in Moscow (October 21st) resulted in the return of 500 Bolsheviks, 168 Cadets, and 80 Socialist-Revolutionaries. (4)

The Petrograd Soviet (October 22nd) passed a vote of no-confidence in the Provisional Government, and the Executive Committee discussed the formation of an independent Soviet revolutionary staff. The Mensheviks and Socialist-Revolutionaries opposed this measure, and their opposition was strong enough to defeat the Bolsheviks in the Executive Committee ; but when the question came before the Soviet, the independent staff was realized in effect by the formation (October 25th) of the War-Revolutionary Committee. (5) Trotsky became chairman of this committee, and under his guidance it became the staff by which the October Revolution was engineered. The Mensheviks immediately recognized the purpose and probable *rôle* of the War-Revolutionary Committee. They described it as " a staff for seizing power," and the Bolsheviks did not deny the imputation. The membership of the committee was arranged in such a way that, while it was primarily an organ of the Petrograd Soviet, its membership included representatives of the Presidium of the Soviet, the soldiers' section of the Soviet, the Central Committee of the fleet, the Finnish Regional Committee, the Railway Union, Post and Telegraph Union, the Soviet of factory committees, the Soviet of Trade Unions, party military organizations, Union of Socialists of the People's Army, the military branch of the Petrograd section of Peasants' Deputies and the military department of the Central Executive of the Labourers' Militia, and, in addition, several persons specially appointed. (6) Through these representatives the War-Revolutionary Committee was in a position to maintain contact with the navy, the army at the front, and every military or semi-military unit—in short, with every force which

## "RED OCTOBER." THE PREPARATION 145

might in any way be used when the opportune moment should arrive for the overthrow of the Provisional Government. The committee was organized in seven sections for the systematic collection of information and for the rapid dissemination of orders. On October 26th the soldiers' section of the Soviet approved the project, and on October 29th the Soviet confirmed it in a plenary session.

The mechanism of the coming Bolshevik Revolution was now complete. The War-Revolutionary Committee was charged by the Petrograd Soviet with the arming and provisioning of the garrison of the capital and its surrounding suburbs, with the defence of Petrograd, and with the questions of *pogroms* (in this case " counter-revolutionary " attacks), deserters, and revolutionary discipline.

The arrangements which have been described gave the Bolsheviks control of the artillery, machine guns, rifles, armoured cars, and ammunition in the Petrograd military district. Thus by means of the formidable organ of the War-Revolutionary Committee, with Trotsky as chairman, the Bolsheviks had every reason to believe that they could make a speedy end of the Provisional Government whenever the time should be ripe.

At an assembly of Soviets of the region of the north (October 27th) the peasants were called upon to seize the property of the landowners. Plekhanov declared (October 27th) that the Soviet programme was the same as that of German imperialism, and Brussilov and Russky protested against the actions of the commissars sent to the army.(7) Kerensky's adherents issued an appeal that in the elections for the Constituent Assembly votes should not be recorded for candidates who had returned to Russia through Germany ; this was intended to strike chiefly at Lenin.(8) On October 31st there was a report that Lenin had returned to Petrograd and was in hiding there. (9) That report was true ; Lenin had evidently made up his mind that the time to strike was at hand. He arrived in Petrograd before the beginning of November, and immediately convened fifteen or twenty leading Bolsheviks and others, some of them coming from Moscow. They met twice, once in the house of Kalinin and once in the house of Sukhanov, neither being important members of the party. Lenin is described as having been disguised, and as being unrecognizable under the mask of a heavy beard. He urged " categorically " the " necessity " of riot, and for that purpose the need of organization. He also urged that preparations should be made for an uprising in the near future. Those who were assembled by Lenin agreed with him, and five persons were elected to guide the " riot "—Lenin, Trotsky,

K

146    THE RUSSIAN REVOLUTION

Kamenev, Stalin, and Dzerjensky. The leadership of the enterprise was given to the War-Revolutionary Committee, of which Trotsky was chairman. (10)

The Russian co-operative societies resolved (November 1st) to combat anarchy. (11) At a session of the Pre-Parliament (November 2nd) Miliukov, in spite of interruptions from the extreme Left, delivered a speech in which he criticized the Utopian schemes of the Soviet and the peace proposals of Skobelov. (12) The majority of the Pre-Parliament approved of the news that Brussilov and Russky had just been appointed to high commands. Goldstein in a speech to the Pre-Parliament (November 3rd) insisted that the Russian Jews were loyal to their country, but that the internationalist Jews were renegades. (13) On November 5th the Cossacks of the Don intimated to the Government that they withdrew their support because of the submission of the Government to the Soviet. (14)

The War-Revolutionary Committee had among its members the most energetic workers in the Bolshevik ranks—Sverdlov, Uritsky, (15) Podvoësky, Chudnovsky, Ioffé, Antonov, Eremiev, Mekhanoshchin, Karakhan, Lashchevich, etc., and it established itself in the Smolny Institute. (16)

One of its first acts was to appoint commissars to all the units of the Petrograd garrison and to all the important establishments in Petrograd and the suburbs. One was appointed to each arsenal and magazine where arms were stored. These commissars quickly took control, displacing the commissars previously nominated by the Central Executive Committee of the Soviet. Through the War-Revolutionary Committee the Bolsheviks had thus complete control of all reserves of arms and ammunition within the Petrograd military district. The commissars who were appointed for this service were drawn chiefly from those members of the Bolshevik group who were involved in the rising of July. (17) Almost all of them had been arrested at that time, but they had since been liberated.

The second important act of the committee was to obtain endorsement from the Petrograd garrison. At a meeting of regimental committees of the garrison a resolution approving of the formation of the War-Revolutionary Committee, and offering it the fullest support, was passed at the instance of Trotsky. (18) This endorsement placed the War-Revolutionary Committee in an authorized and accepted position of control over the Petrograd military units. In other quarters, too, the Bolsheviks were exceedingly active. Meetings were held incessantly in barracks, halls, factories, and in the two large circuses, the *Moderne* and Chinizelly, and were

## "RED OCTOBER." THE PREPARATION 147

addressed by all the best speakers of the Bolshevik party. There was no concealment about their aim ; the attack upon the Government was open and avowed, and only the date of the final assault was unrevealed. Perhaps it had not been precisely determined ; but many people began to talk about a date a fortnight before November 2nd, and of something which was going to happen on that date. At one of the meetings in the *Cirque Moderne*, while Kollontay was speaking, someone shouted, "What is going to happen on October 20th ?" (19) Kollontay answered, "An uprising will take place, the Provisional Government will be overthrown. All power will be transferred to the Soviets." This reply was greeted with applause. (20)

On October 25th a large military meeting was held at the Smolny Institute, comprising representatives of the northern district, and all the speakers demanded that the Government be overthrown and that power be transferred to the Soviets. The chairman of this meeting was Krilenko. (21) Every day the newspapers printed notices about the coming uprising. Proclamations by the Bolsheviks were distributed everywhere, whilst in factories, workshops, and barracks it was the universal topic of conversation. In his newspaper Burtsev sounded daily warnings. On October 25th, e.g. :—

"Lenin, Zinoviev, Trotsky, Riazanov, Kollontay, Nakhanikess, and their Bolshevik comrades are threatening us with a new uprising against liberty, the right, and the Republic. They are even fixing the date. They are deriving their main strength from the weakness of the Government. They are strong only because they are permitted to be so by the Kerensky, Milyantovich, Verkhovsky, Polkovenekov group—because of their cowardice and the passive exercise of authority against them. Because of the criminal agitation of the Bolsheviks, the course of life in Petersburg is destroyed, and that hungry, sick, and suffering city will have to pay a high price for the rest of its days for the criminal activity of Trotsky and Co." (22)

November 2nd passed ; clearly the time had not yet come. Then November 4th was announced as the day of the Petrograd Soviet, when a collection was to be taken in the streets for the official organ, *Izvestia*, and on that day meetings took place all over the city. Trotsky describes the scene :—

"Tens of thousands of people thronged the building of the People's House. They moved along the corridors, filling up the halls. On the iron pillars there hung garlands, like grapes, of human heads, hands, and feet. In the air there vibrated an electric force which indicated the most critical moment of the Revolution.

## 148 THE RUSSIAN REVOLUTION

Down with the Kerensky Government! Down with war! All power to the Soviets!" (23)

At this meeting in the People's House public feeling reached a high pitch of excitement. Trotsky, in a state of ecstasy, (24) called upon the audience to swear that they would fight for power until the last drop of blood had been shed. Thousands of hands were raised, for the audience was electrified and not less excited than the speaker. Trotsky afterwards described this moment. "The campaign was already won. It still remained to give the final military blow to a shadowy authority." (25) Certainly with complete control of the Petrograd garrison, and with the keys of the military storehouses in his pocket, Trotsky might very well regard the authority of Kerensky's Government as "shadowy."

On the night of November 4th representatives of the War-Revolutionary Committee walked into the offices of the Petrograd military district and demanded the right of censoring all orders of the staff. They met with a decisive refusal from Colonel Polkovenekov, chief of the military district. The representatives withdrew; but their visit was followed immediately by imperative instructions from the Executive Committee of the Soviet, the chairman of which was Trotsky, that no orders which were not signed by the Executive Committee of the War-Revolutionary Committee were to be executed. This meant really that only orders signed by Trotsky or under his direction were valid. (26)

On the following day, November 5th, the Executive Committee of the Petrograd Soviet made the following announcement :—

### "To the Population of Petrograd.

"For the information of the workers, soldiers, and all citizens, we announce :—

"In the interests of the defence of the Revolution and its gains against the attacks of counter-revolution, we have appointed commissars in the military units and in important places in the capital and its suburbs. Orders and instructions which are destined for those places are to be executed only after they are confirmed by the commissars who are appointed by us. The commissars as representatives of the Soviet are unimpeachable. Action counter to the commissars is action against the Soviet of Workmen's and Soldiers' Deputies. The Soviet has taken all measures for maintaining revolutionary order against counter-revolutionary and *pogrom* attacks. All citizens are invited to render full support to our commissars.

## "RED OCTOBER." THE PREPARATION   149

In case of disorder they must address themselves to the commissars of the War-Revolutionary Committee in the nearest military unit of the War-Revolutionary Committee of the Petersburg Soviet of Workmen's and Soldiers' Deputies." (27)

On the same night (November 5th) another decisive step was successfully taken.   The commissar (28) allotted to the fortress of St. Peter and St. Paul reported to the War-Revolutionary Committee that the commandant of the fortress had refused to recognize him and had threatened to arrest him.   Either the garrison of the fortress was insufficiently Bolshevized, or the War-Revolutionary Committee was doubtful about its attitude, for one member suggested that two companies of the most Bolshevik regiment in the garrison should be introduced into it (as though in the ordinary course of moving troops), and in that way the fortress might in effect be captured before the uprising.   This expedient, however, was rejected.   It was then proposed to call a meeting of the fortress garrison and to make an attempt by means of " persuasion and argument " to win it over to Bolshevism.   This plan was adopted and the arrangements were confided to Trotsky and Lashchevich. These emissaries performed their mission brilliantly.   The garrison of the fortress joined the Bolsheviks, a resolution to that effect being passed by the meeting. (29)

Further measures which were taken with regard to other military units, and involving appeals to the Cossacks and to the Semenovsky regiment, were also successful.   Then came a joint meeting at the Smolny Institute of representatives of the army at the front and of the Petrograd garrison, on the night of November 5th.   All the speakers demanded the overthrow of the Government and the transference of power to the Soviets.   At a meeting of the Petrograd Soviet held that evening, the same note was struck.   Trotsky spoke quite frankly :—

" If the Government during the twenty-four or forty-eight hours which remain at its disposal should try to use these hours in order to put a knife in the back of the Revolution, we, the advance guard, announce that we will return blow for blow ; we will answer iron by steel." (30)

The War-Revolutionary Committee headed by Trotsky were confident that their attack would succeed.   They were evidently convinced that the Government were doing nothing, and indeed were powerless to check the uprising ; but they knew that success could only be made certain by deliberate and skilful preparation.

Such preparation might be accomplished partially by utilizing the governmental military machinery, which, through the anomalous

## THE RUSSIAN REVOLUTION

relation of the Soviet to the Government, was available for the War-Revolutionary Committee. Still more could be done through the sympathy of the army with Bolshevism, and all this could be accomplished without cost to the War-Revolutionary Committee. Yet for further preparations, also deemed necessary, money must somehow be forthcoming, and not only money, but men who had not been infected by that decay of discipline in the army which had at one time been fomented purposely by the Bolsheviks, but was becoming very inconvenient now that they were trying to acquire control of the troops. Both money and men were necessary, and both were procured. (31)

The preparations were systematic and complete. On the night of November 5th, two days before the actual moment of the uprising, as precisely stated by Trotsky, commissars were sent to all railway stations, with instructions to watch the incoming and outgoing trains in order to keep in touch with the movements of the Government forces. Connection between the capital and the suburbs was established by means of automobiles and telephones. The Soviets of the suburbs were charged to report to the War-Revolutionary Committee any movement of troops towards Petrograd. The Red Guard which had been mobilized a few days earlier was utilized for the provision of posts and pickets for the watching and guarding of bridges, factories, and party and Soviet institutions. All these measures were organized by, and were under the control of, the War-Revolutionary Committee, whose chairman sat in Smolny with the other members in continuous session. They practically lived in a small room on the third floor of the building. Trotsky was without intermission at the telephone, receiving information, or expounding, prohibiting, and instructing. To this small room came also all the communications by post, telegraph, and messenger. One of the secretaries of the War-Revolutionary Committee describes the scene :—

" In the War-Revolutionary Committee life was at boiling-point day and night. Sometimes for two or three days people did not wash themselves or comb their hair. I recollect Comrade Lenin in his working dress with torn trousers, as a real smith of the proletarian State. Comrade Trotsky appeared one morning without a necktie, as a model of the proletarian military commander on the field of battle. On the third floor (of the Smolny) were also to be found the military branch of the Petersburg Soviet and the staff of the Red Guard." (32)

The Smolny Institute was transformed into a real fortress. Its commander was a sailor called Mankov. " In the windows along the front of the main building and on its left wing, where a

## "RED OCTOBER." THE PREPARATION 151

governess used to live . . . machine guns were stationed, and the main entrance was defended by artillery. Later, artillery was also placed to command the approaches from Suvorovsky Prospekt and Shpalernoy Street." (33) The Smolny fortress was victualled as if for a siege. A supply of food was stored within its walls, and for several days cartloads of potatoes, vegetables, and fruit were taken into the building. The teachers and pupils who watched these proceedings with amazement wondered for what purpose these formidable stores were being accumulated. In the neighbourhood of the Smolny was a barracks for the battalion of women, who remained loyal to the Government.

On the night of November 5th–6th Lenin took up his residence in Smolny and joined the other members of the Bolshevik staff in their continuous session.

Meanwhile the Government of Kerensky began to act. The events of November 4th had roused it, yet even at that late date it underestimated the strength, skill, and activity of its Bolshevik rival. It seemed to be labouring under the delusion that the Bolshevik leaders entertained opinions so fantastic that they would not be accepted by a sufficient number of people to enable them to attain power, and that the charges still hanging over their heads in respect of connivance with, and the receipt of money from, the enemy would prevent the people from trusting them.

On November 5th Sir George Buchanan entertained to luncheon three members of Kerensky's Government—Tereshtchenko, Konovalov, and Tretiakov. They "arrived quite unmoved"; they said that the reports about the uprising were premature, and that "the Government had sufficient force behind it to deal with the situation." (34)

On the afternoon of the same day there was a meeting of the Provisional Council, corresponding to the former Council of State. Here there was a majority against the Government, an ominous sign under the circumstances. The Council threw the responsibility for the crisis upon the Government, although it condemned the Bolshevik rising, and it came to the conclusion that the control of the land must be transferred to the land committees [a resolution which clearly indicated that the Council did not grasp the real meaning of the projected uprising], and that the Allies must be induced to publish their conditions and to commence negotiations for peace [an indication that they did not understand the real meaning of the war or the stage at which it had then arrived]. The Council also proposed to form a committee of public safety and to call the revolutionary democracy to the aid of the Government. (35)

## THE RUSSIAN REVOLUTION

Kerensky had, on November 4th, demanded that the disorganizing *Order No. 1* be withdrawn by the Soviet. The Committee of the Soviet at once acquiesced ; the purpose of *Order No. 1* had been served ; why trouble about it ? Kerensky was not, however, deceived by this prompt obedience. On the night of November 6th he pounced upon two unimportant newspapers, (36) closed their printing offices, and prosecuted their editors for inciting to an uprising. He also ordered the re-arrest of the Bolsheviks who had been imprisoned for complicity in the July disturbances and since liberated. The commander of the Petrograd military district ordered certain military units to keep to their barracks and to expel the commissars from them. Artillery, some battalions from Tsarskoë Selo, cadets, etc., were ordered to hold themselves in readiness, and the bridges over the Neva, with one exception, were broken. For the defence of the Winter Palace, four guns, the battalion of women, and some military cadets were requisitioned and the telephone wires to the Smolny Institute were cut.

On the night of November 6th Kerensky appeared before the Pre-Parliament and asked the question, " Is the Government empowered to take the measures which it thinks proper, and does it enjoy the confidence of the Pre-Parliament ? " The Pre-Parliament refused the vote of confidence for which he asked, and from that moment the Kerensky Government was doomed. But the Provisional Council and the Pre-Parliament were to share the same fate, for the whole structure of the State and the fabric of society were to fall. What Russia was about to experience was not a change of government in the sense accepted by countries possessing a parliamentary system ; it was not even a change in the form of government ; it was the cessation of government altogether by any legally recognized group of persons. The country, in fact, was plunged for a time into an anarchic condition. Neither the Provisional Council nor the Pre-Parliament could without blame lightly throw off their responsibilities to the Russian people, but by November 7th the case was hopeless and Kerensky's Government had become impossible. The measures he had taken and those he was about to take against the Bolshevik uprising were ridiculously inadequate. Probably only a foreign army of considerable dimensions could have dealt with the situation at that stage, certainly the Russian army was beyond any governmental influence ; the Provisional Council and the Pre-Parliament might, however, have acted earlier, and in any case should have made some attempt to save the Russian people from the misfortunes which overwhelmed them.

Members of the Provisional Government, and many others, including foreign observers, seem to have satisfied themselves that

## "RED OCTOBER." THE PREPARATION 153

no Bolshevik Government could endure. Lapse of time has shown that this anticipation was quite unfounded, and that Lenin's diagnosis of the situation in 1917 was sounder than his critics had conceded.

---

### NOTES

(1) *Izvestia* (Helsingfors), June 17, 1917.

(2) Cf. Antonelli, Étienne, *Bolshevik Russia,* translated from the French by Charles A. Carroll (New York, 1920), p. 65.

(3) Prince Peter Kropotkin was a member of this group.

(4) *Chron. de la Guerre,* 7e vol., p. 179.

(5) Spiridovich, A. E., op. cit., p. 375.

(6) Ibid., pp. 375–76.

(7) *Chron. de la Guerre,* 7e vol., p. 189.

(8) Ibid., p. 190.

(9) Ibid., p. 194.

(10) Spiridovich, A. E., op. cit., p. 376.

(11) *Chron. de la Guerre,* 7e vol., p. 196. The Cossacks, through their new organ *Volnost,* edited by Amfitreatov, spoke (November 1st) of a coming merciless struggle against the Bolsheviks.

(12) Ibid., p. 197.

(13) Ibid., p. 198.

(14) Ibid., p. 199.

(15) Uritsky was assassinated in July 1918.

(16) On November 5th the chief Bolshevik organizations were transferred to the Smolny Institute (a school for girls). The Petrograd Soviet had already made the Smolny its headquarters. The ordinary functions of the building were not interrupted.

(17) Trotsky says, " All of these put themselves into the hands of the War-Revolutionary Committee. They were appointed to the most responsible military posts." Trotsky, L. D., *The October Revolution,* quoted by Spiridovich, A. E., op. cit., p. 378.

(18) Trotsky, L. D., *The October Revolution* in *Archives of the Russian Revolution* (1917), p. 159, cited by Spiridovich, A. E., op, cit., p. 378.

(19) I.e. November 2nd, (N.S).

(20) These details are from Spiridovich, A. E., op. cit., pp. 378–79.

(21) Who afterwards became commander-in-chief.

(22) *Obshoyé Dielo* (*La Cause Commune*), No. 20, October 31, 1917. Article, " Bolsheviks are threatening to commit a new crime."

(23) Trotsky, L. D., *The October Revolution* in *Archives of the Russian Revolution* (1917), p. 65.

(24) He had probably been working without intermission for the preceding two days at least, and was in a highly nervous condition.

(25) Trotsky, L. D., loc. cit.

(26) Spiridovich, A. E., op. cit., p. 380, and other sources.

(27) Ibid., p. 381. From original proclamation.

(28) The name of the commissar was Ter-Arutenyants.

(29) Spiridovich, A. E., op. cit., p. 381.

(30) Trotsky, L. D., *The October Revolution* in *Archives of the Russian Revolution* (1917), p. 164, and Spiridovich, A. E., op. cit., p. 382.

(31) Under the old *régime* there were not a few rich men who sympathized with even the most extreme revolutionists and contributed to their funds. From some of these it is conceivable that the Bolsheviks obtained a portion of their

# THE RUSSIAN REVOLUTION

resources. It seems certain, however, that they were indebted for a not inconsiderable part of their funds to Germany—how much may never be known. The Provisional Government at the time of its fall was inquiring into this matter. If the evidence was in the hands of the Political Police, it was probably destroyed with the premises of the police department in the October Revolution ; if it was in the Ministry of Justice, it has probably been destroyed by the Soviet Government. There is no doubt that immediately after the October Revolution the Soviet Government utilized German, Austrian, and Hungarian prisoners of war in the Red Army (on this point see, e.g., Mrs. A. Tyrkova-Williams. *From Liberty to Brest-Litovsk*, London, 1919, pp. 292, etc). German officers were also employed in the campaign against Kaledin and the Cossacks.

(32) Akhmanov, *Red Sketches*, quoted by Spiridovich, A. E., op. cit., p. 383.

(33) Spiridovich, A. E., op. cit., p. 383.

(34) Buchanan, Sir George, *My Mission to Russia* (London, 1923), vol. ii. p. 203.

(35) Ibid., p. 204.

(36) *Rabochi Put* (*The Workers' Way*), and *Soldat* (*The Soldier*)

## CHAPTER V

## " RED OCTOBER." THE EXPLOSION

On the morning of October 24th, (O.S.), November 6th, (N.S.), the War-Revolutionary Committee of the Petrograd Soviet, which was, in effect, the Bolshevik General Staff, became aware of the steps taken overnight by the Provisional Government. The printing-presses which had been stopped by the Provisional Government were immediately set going again under a guard consisting of pickets from the Litovsky regiment and from the 6th sapper battalion. At the Smolny Institute the guard was reinforced, and the garrison troops were told not to leave their barracks—an order which meant that they were to refuse to obey the Government. In the evening of November 6th a company of the Litovsky regiment was held in readiness as well as a company of machine gunners. At the same time members of the Petrograd Soviet, as well as district Soviets, were called to a special meeting. The cruiser *Aurora*, the crew of which was inclined to Bolshevism, was brought up the Neva, and the presence of this ship had an important influence both upon the Bolsheviks, whose audacity it increased, and upon the Government, whose fears it enhanced. The War-Revolutionary Committee called upon Kronstadt to furnish sailors and torpedo boats, whilst pickets from the Pavlovsky regiment were placed about the Winter Palace.

In view of these energetic measures, the feebleness of the Government became the more apparent. The Winter Palace, its headquarters, was covered by the guns of the *Aurora* and of the fortress of St. Peter and St. Paul, and these were under Bolshevik control. Some of the cadets who were guarding the Winter Palace were disarmed late in the evening of November 6th, by pickets of the Pavlovsky regiment, and persons going to and from the palace were arrested. Among these was Kartachov, a member of the Provisional Government ; but his arrest being censured by the Committee at the Smolny, he was released. Apparently the Committee desired to wait until the Government took some aggressive action against it or against the Soviet. This it could afford to do in view of its greatly superior strength.

In the evening of November 6th a proclamation was issued in the following terms : " The counter-revolution has raised its criminal head. The Kornilovists are mobilizing forces in order

## THE RUSSIAN REVOLUTION

to annihilate the All-Russian Assembly of Soviets and the Constituent Assembly." The population was warned that the "*pogrom* men*" might try to produce in the Petrograd streets disorder and bloodshed, and therefore the inhabitants were requested to arrest all " hooligans (1) and Black Hundred (2) agitators " and deliver them to the commissariat. They were also told to keep quiet.

At two o'clock in the morning, November 7th, Bolshevik troops, under the orders of the War-Revolutionary Committee, silently occupied the railway stations, bridges, power plants, and telegraph offices. The Bank of Russia was also occupied, although it was guarded by Government forces in armoured cars. At seven o'clock in the morning the telephone offices were seized, and from that moment the Bolsheviks were in command of the capital. At ten o'clock in the forenoon of November 7th the following proclamation was issued :—

### " TO THE CITIZENS OF RUSSIA.

" The Provisional Government is overthrown. The authority of the State has been transferred to the hands of the organ of the Petersburg (3) Soviet of the Workmen's and Soldiers' Deputies— the War-Revolutionary Committee, which is at the head of the Petersburg proletariat and garrison. The cause for which the people have struggled, viz. the immediate offer of a democratic peace, the withdrawal of the landowners' property in land, the workers' control over production, the erection of the Soviet Government—this cause has been secured. *Vive* the Revolution of the workers, soldiers, and peasants !

> War-Revolutionary Committee of
> the Petersburg Soviet of Workers'
> and Soldiers' Deputies.

> October 25th, 1917 (O.S.).
> Ten o'clock in the morning."

At the same hour the following was broadcast by radio :—

" Petrograd is in the power of the War-Revolutionary Committee of the Petrograd (4) Soviet. Soldiers and workers uprising unanimously have conquered without any bloodshed. Kerensky's Government is overthrown. The Committee asks the front and the rear not to give way to provocation, but to support the Petrograd Soviet and the new Revolutionary authority, which is going at once to offer a just peace, to transfer the land to the peasants, and to

## " RED OCTOBER." THE EXPLOSION 157

summon the Constituent Assembly. Local authority is being transferred into the hands of the Soviets of the Workers', Soldiers', and Peasants' Deputies.

The War-Revolutionary Committee
of the Petrograd Soviet." (5)

Sir George Buchanan's account of the events of the morning of November 7th is as follows :—

" November 7th. Yesterday evening the Executive Committee of the Soviet decided to arrest the Ministers and to form a Government themselves. . . . I heard that all the troops of the garrison had obeyed the summons of the Bolsheviks, and that the whole town, including the State bank, stations, post and telegraph offices, were in their hands.

" All the ministers are at the Winter Palace, and their motors, which had been left unguarded in the adjoining square, have been either damaged or seized by the soldiers. About ten in the morning Kerensky sent out an officer to try to get another motor for him. The officer found Whitehouse, one of the secretaries of the United States embassy, and persuaded him to lend Kerensky his car with the American flag. They drove back together to the Winter Palace. After telling Whitehouse that he (Kerensky) proposed driving to Luga to join the troops which had been summoned from the front, he begged him to ask the Allied ambassadors not to recognize the Bolshevik Government, as he hoped to return on the 12th with sufficient troops to re-establish the situation." (6)

Thus Kerensky ignominiously faded away. At four o'clock in the morning of November 7th he had had a meeting of the staff of the military district. After this meeting he had ordered three Cossack regiments to come to Petrograd ; but with the exception of two infantry companies they refused. The Government found itself guarded by about two hundred Cossack infantry, a thousand young cadets, the women's battalion, and four guns from the Michael artillery college. Kerensky left the Palace about seven o'clock in the morning, ostensibly to procure troops to defend the Government. He transferred his authority to his colleague, Konovalov, who with Keshken, Milyantovich, and other ministers remained to face their fate. Milyantovich, Minister of Justice, who had refrained from pressing the criminal suits against Lenin, etc., " said nothing, but only listened. His eyes glowed sorrowfully." (7)

Meanwhile the Bolshevik troops were divided into three parties. The first surrounded the Winter Palace, from the morning of

**158**      THE RUSSIAN REVOLUTION

November 7th; the second defended the Smolny Institute, where the Bolshevik staff were superintending operations; and the third guarded the approaches to Petrograd.

Sailors from Kronstadt were ordered to dissolve the Pre-Parliament, and about noon these sailors surrounded the Marie Palace and ordered everybody in it to leave the building. In this way the Pre-Parliament was dissolved. At three o'clock in the afternoon there was a discussion at the Smolny Institute among the members of the War-Revolutionary Committee, during which there came a report that the Government had no troops in the capitals upon which it could rely. On the strength of this, the Committee decided to go on with the attack on the Winter Palace, and if necessary to use the guns of the fortress and those of the *Aurora*. The palace was attacked by the Pavlovsky and Kexholm regiments, two companies of the Preobrashensky regiment, 800 Red Guards with a sanitary detachment, two armoured cars, and two guns. About five o'clock these troops began the attack. Barricades of wood had been built by the military cadets in front of the entrances, and these were defended. Before the main entrance the four guns of the Michael artillery college were planted. At six o'clock the War-Revolutionary Committee telephoned to the Winter Palace from the Smolny Institute demanding its surrender, but the members of the Government confined within it refused. At half-past six a group of *parlementaires* from the fortress of St. Peter and St. Paul went to the General Staff headquarters opposite the Winter Palace, where were Keshken and his assistants, and demanded the surrender of the staff, with the threat that if they refused, the guns of the fortress would open fire upon the Winter Palace. The cadets retreated into the palace and the quartermaster-general, Paradeilov, surrendered. Meanwhile the Bolsheviks had been fraternizing with the two companies of Cossack infantry, with the result that about seven o'clock the Cossacks were induced to abandon the Government, and were conducted to their barracks by a Bolshevik armoured car.

At eight-thirty Bolshevik *parlementaires*, headed by Chudnovsky, were admitted to the palace. They handed the members of the Government an ultimatum demanding immediate surrender, but they met with another refusal. At nine o'clock some blank rounds were fired from the fortress and from the cruiser *Aurora*. Then began a bombardment which continued for an hour. During the bombardment " the commissar of the Provincial Government, an anarchist by conviction, who was attached to the Michael artillery college, and had commanded a battery there, spoke to the gunners, and took the guns at the trot through the arch at the staff head-

## RED OCTOBER." THE EXPLOSION

quarters and farther on to the Police bridge, where he surrendered the battery to the Bolsheviks. The cadets who were with him were disarmed and sent back to their college. Two of the guns were placed within the arch and the bombardment of the palace on that side began." (8) This treacherous abstraction of the guns upon which the defenders had relied demoralized their slender forces. At eleven o'clock the attacking force began to close in upon the palace. The crews of sailors from Kronstadt were brought into action, and the front of the palace was swept by machine-gun fire, while the river front was struck by shrapnel in at least three places. (9) The besieged were caught like rats in a trap, which, large and luxurious though it was, was not fitted to resist artillery bombardment. Desertions began ; the women's battalion melted away, till at length the entrance was taken, and the Bolsheviks, headed by Chudnovsky and Antonov, (10) poured into the halls. A struggle followed from room to room. The members of the Government with a few cadets, encouraged by Palchensky and Rutenberg, continued to defend themselves. In close quarters the cadets for a time succeeded ; but they were heavily outnumbered, though many of them stood their ground to the end, and some of them defended themselves valiantly in the cellars. About two o'clock in the morning Antonov found in one of the rooms a group of sixteen ministers, and declared that they were under arrest. An excited group of soldiers, sailors, and Red Guards surrounded the ministers, shouting for Kerensky, and when they were told that he had gone, they were furious and wanted to lynch those who remained, proposing to shoot them at once. Antonov and Chudnovsky, assisted by some of the sailors, protected their prisoners, who, under a heavy guard and accompanied by a yelling mob, were taken to the fortress. Grozden, Milyantovich, and Nikitin, the three socialist ministers, were soon released. That same evening Prince Tumanov, the deputy War Minister, was lynched by sailors. Arrested with the commanding officer of the district, General Bagratin, he was first beaten and then bayoneted near the barracks of the 2nd naval equipage. (11) Many of the cadets who were captured were ill-treated by the Bolsheviks, as were some of the women of the women's battalion. (12) The mob began to loot the palace, but the Red Guards and the sailors put a stop to this. In the grey dawn the Bolshevik units paraded in the great square, and the War-Revolutionary Committee complimented them. Sir George Buchanan, who went into the Winter Palace next day to investigate the extent of the damage, says that on the entrance front of the palace the walls were riddled with thousands of bullets, but there was no sign of a shot from a field gun, although shots had been

## THE RUSSIAN REVOLUTION

fired. In the interior " very considerable damage was done by soldiers and workmen, who looted or smashed whatever they could lay hands upon." (13) There was no organized defence of the palace, and the casualties on either side were but few in number. (14)

At two thirty-five in the morning of November 8th the Petrograd Soviet met under the presidency of Trotsky, who announced the dissolution of the Pre-Parliament, the arrest of some of the ministers, the approaching capture of the Winter Palace, and the fall of the Provisional Government. Then Lenin spoke on the programme of the new Government.

" Comrades, the workers' and peasants' Revolution, the necessity of which has all along been urged by the Bolsheviks, has been accomplished. What does the workers' and peasants' Revolution mean ? First of all, the meaning of the overthrow is that we are going to have a Soviet government. We will have our own organ of authority without any participation of the *bourgeoisie*. The depressed masses will build up an authority for themselves. The old state apparatus is going to be broken up, and a new apparatus of administration, in the form of the Soviet organization, is going to be built up. From to-day a new phase in the history of Russia begins, and this *third* Russian Revolution (15), as a final result, is to bring the victory of socialism. Our next task is the immediate liquidation of the war ; but in order to dispose of that war, which is firmly bound up with the present capitalistic order, as all understand, it is necessary to vanquish capital itself. In that case we shall be helped by the All-the-World Workers' movement, which has already begun to inspire—in Italy, England, and Germany—a desire for a just and immediate peace. This has been offered to us by international democracy. Everywhere this is going to meet with a warm welcome on the part of the international proletarian masses. In order to strengthen the confidence of the proletariat, it is necessary to publish at once all secret treaties.

" In the interior of Russia a great part of the peasantry has said, ' We are finished with the game of the capitalists, let us go with the workers.' We will gain the confidence of the peasants by a decree which is to abolish the ownership of land. The peasants will understand that their only salvation is a union with the workers. We are going to establish real workers' control over production. We have already learned to work in a friendly way, as is proved by the Revolution which has just now been accomplished. We are in possession of that power of organization of the masses which is going to vanquish everything, and by it the proletariat will be brought to the World Revolution. In Russia now we have to

## " RED OCTOBER." THE EXPLOSION 161

begin the building up of the proletarian socialist State. *Vive* the All-World Socialist Revolution ! " (16)

After speeches by Lunarchasky and Zinoviev, a resolution was passed approving the action of the War-Revolutionary Committee and acknowledging its authority until a Soviet Government could be established. The resolution went on to appeal to revolutionary soldiers to watch their officers, and, if they did not at once accept the Revolution, to have them arrested as enemies.

The second All-Russian Congress of Soviets met at ten forty-five on the night of November 7th. The Bolshevik leaders had been anxious to have this meeting earlier and to secure from it, before the event, approval of their campaign against the Provisional Government. The composition of the congress was varied, but the Bolsheviks had a majority over all other parties combined. (17) The fight at the Winter Palace had been in progress for some time. All parties were in a condition of high tension, and the Bolsheviks were very anxious. At last, during the night, Antonov rushed into the congress and announced that the palace had been taken, and that the ministers had been arrested and lodged in the fortress. The anxiety of the conspirators assumed a new phase. The Revolution was accomplished, power had been given to the Soviets, yet there were over one hundred members of the congress whose constituents did not approve of the proceedings of the Petrograd Soviet. The Mensheviks, the Socialist-Revolutionaries, and some of the others who were hostile, protested and left the congress, including a large number of the army representatives. Besides the Bolsheviks, only the Left Socialist-Revolutionaries, the United Internationalists, and a few others remained, but these made altogether about 500 members, or 90 per cent. of the whole. Those who remained passed a resolution formally taking over the government, which thereupon became the Soviet Government. The resolution declared that " the authority of the Soviet gives peace, land, the right to soldiers' and workers' control, bread and necessities, the Constituent Assembly, and self-development of the nations included in Russia, authority in local affairs being transferred to the Soviets." This resolution warned the soldiers against Kerensky and Kornilov. The session closed at six in the morning of November 8th. (18)

In the afternoon of the same day there was a joint meeting of the All-Russian Congress of Soviets, the Petrograd Soviet, members of the conference of the garrison, and many people of the Bolshevik party. This was the first large audience in Russia at which Lenin made his appearance, and he came before it as the prospective head of the new State. He was received with " tempestuous and ecstatic

L

## 162 THE RUSSIAN REVOLUTION

applause," as also was Zinoviev. At nine o'clock the same evening (November 8th) the second session of the Congress of Soviets was held. This was an important session, for in it the character of the future government of Russia was determined, and elections were made to the higher offices of state. The congress was asked to confirm the address to the belligerent nations, and the decree about the land, these having been the work of the Petrograd Soviet. Lenin expounded the address, and it was confirmed unanimously without discussion. The question of the land was not so simple. The congress discussed it until two o'clock in the morning, and then confirmed the project of the Petrograd Soviet, one member voting against it and eight abstaining. (19)

The congress abolished capital punishment, and passed a decree to provide for the formation in all the divisions of the army of War-Revolutionary Committees, the commanders-in-chief to be under their orders. The congress also invited the Cossacks to form Soviets of their own and to ally themselves to the Soviets already formed. It then passed what became the fundamental law of the Russian Federated Soviet Republics :—

" The All-Russian Congress of the Workers', Soldiers', and Peasants' Deputies decrees :—

" To establish for the administration of the country, until the Constituent Assembly provides otherwise, a Provisional Workers' and Peasants' Government, which is to be named ' The Soviet of the Peoples' Commissars.' The management of the different branches of the life of the State is entrusted to commissions, the personnel of which secures the accomplishment of the programme announced by the congress, in close contact with the mass organizations of the working men, working women, sailors, soldiers, peasants, and employees. The governmental authority rests with the *collegia* of the chairmen of these commissions, viz. with the Soviet of the People's Commissars.

" Control over the activity of the people's commissars and the right to recall them belongs to the All-Russian Congress of the Soviets of the Workers', Soldiers', and Peasants' Deputies and its central Executive Committee.

" For the present the personnel of the Soviet of the People's Commissars is as follows :—

Chairman of the Soviet, Vladimir Ulianov (Lenin).
People's Commissar of the Interior, A. J. Rykov. (20)
People's Commissar of Agriculture, D. P. Melyutin.
People's Commissar of Labour, A. R. Schlaknikov.
War and Navy Committee, V. E. Ovceĕnko (Antonov), N. V. Krilenko, and Dibenko.

## "RED OCTOBER." THE EXPLOSION 163

People's Commissar of Commerce and Industry, V. P. Nogen.
People's Commissar of Education, A. V. Lunarchasky.
People's Commissar of Finance, I. I. Squartsov.
People's Commissar of External Affairs, L. D. Bronstein (Trotsky).
People's Commissar of Justice, G. E. Oppokov (A. A. Lomov). (21)
People's Commissar of Supply, I. F. Theodorovich.
Post and Telegraph, N. P. Idelov (Glyebov).
Chairman of National Affairs, J. B. Jugashbeli (Stalin).
Chairman of Railway Affairs, no appointment.

The Congress elected the Central Executive Committee, numbering one hundred persons, of whom seventy were Bolsheviks, and adjourned at five o'clock in the morning. (22)

Thus the Government with a double name, " The Provisional Workers' and Peasants' Government," or " The Soviet of the People's Commissars," began to function.

On November 7th, the day of the seizure of power by the Bolsheviks, the following letter is alleged to have been sent by one of the branches of the German General Staff to the " Council of the People's Commissars " :—

" As per agreement made in Kronstadt in July 1917, between members of our general staff and the leaders of the Russian revolutionary army and democracy, Messrs. Lenin, Trotsky, Raskolnikov, and Dibenko, the Russian branch of our general staff in Finland commandeered officers to Petersburg for the formation of the intelligence branch of the staff. At the head of the Petersburg branch are to be the following officers who know the Russian language perfectly and who are conversant with Russian conditions : Major Leobertz, to be known as ' Major ' ; von Belke, to be known as ' Schott ' ; Major Bauermeister, to be known as ' Bear ' ; Lieutenant Hartvin, to be known as ' Heinrich.' The intelligence branch, as per agreement with Messrs. Lenin, Trotsky, and Zinoviev, will have to watch the foreign missions and military delegations and the counter-revolutionary movement, and will also do the intelligence and counter-intelligence work in the interior of their fronts. For this purpose agents are to be sent to different cities. At the same time we inform you that the following advisers to the Government of the People's Commissars have been appointed : to the Ministry of Foreign Affairs, Herr von Schenemann ; and to the Ministry of Finance, Herr von Poll.

The chief of the Russian branch of
the German General Staff,
O. RAUSCH.
N. WOLFF, Adjutant." (23)

164 THE RUSSIAN REVOLUTION

The authenticity of this letter would be difficult to prove or to disprove. There can, however, be no doubt that during the winter of 1916–1917 the political authorities of Germany were eagerly watching for signs of revolution in Russia. Whenever these made their appearance, the policy of Germany was directed towards disintegration of the imperial system and towards avoiding anything which might contribute to maintain a united Russia. Vigorous military attacks were therefore avoided, and every means taken to conciliate the Russians and thus bring about a speedy separate peace. This policy was accepted by von Hindenburg, but his after-reflections seem not to have been favourable to it. " Ought we not to have attacked when the first cracks of the Russian edifice began to be revealed ? May it not be that political considerations robbed us of the finest fruits of all our great victories ? " (24) On the other hand, the effect of an attack in the early stages of disintegration might have been to reunite the demoralized forces of Russia. Von Hindenburg remarks upon the fluctuations of mood among the Russian troops and upon the difference in spirit between the artillery and the infantry, (25) and he observes that at any moment the Russian troops might have dropped their sullen inertia and turned upon the German lines.

Power had been seized in the name of the Soviets. Lenin, Zinoviev, and Trotsky had placed themselves " in the seats of the mighty." The command of the army which had been secured by the Bolsheviks gave them an immense advantage, yet they could only be really certain of the loyalty of the Petrograd garrison. They were in close contact with the garrison ; but the fluctuations of opinion at the front and in the provinces could not be controlled and could be followed only with difficulty. The disappearance of Kerensky was a source of uneasiness, for he might return to Petrograd with hordes of Cossacks. There was an actual counter-revolt nearer home. On the night of November 8th, while the All-Russian Congress of Soviets was " bowing " to the Bolsheviks, and confirming their governmental " list," another group was meeting under the chairmanship of the mayor of Petrograd (Shreider). At this meeting there was formed " The Committee for the Saving of the Homeland and the Revolution." The chief supporters of the movement were the municipal councillors of the capital. It was more widely representative than the circumstances of its formation would imply. There were three representatives from each of the following bodies : Petrograd Municipal Council, Peasants' Soviet, the Executive Committee of the Peasants' Soviet, Socialist-Revolutionaries, Social-Democrats (these last being appointed at the second session of the Congress of Soviets), Co-operative Societies, and the Railway

## " RED OCTOBER." THE EXPLOSION 165

Union. This was undoubtedly a widely representative committee, yet in the confusion of the time it effected nothing.

Three days after its formation (i.e. on November 11th) this committee seems to have encouraged the students of the Paul and Vladimir colleges and of the engineering college to make an armed uprising. The students seized the Michaelovsky stables and with armoured cars captured the telephone office. They do not appear to have extended their insurgency any farther.

Against the War-Revolutionary Committee, with its experience and its methodical habits, such a revolt was an affair of amateurs. The Committee at once took energetic measures. The colleges which were the centres of the new insurgents were surrounded by Bolshevik troops with machine guns and artillery. The Vladimir college offered resistance and was bombarded, and there were numerous casualties on both sides. It, however, was captured, as were also the Michaelovsky stables and the telephone office. Many of the insurgent students were taken to Kronstadt, but " their fate is unknown." (26) The suppression of this unimportant rising was ruthless. The captured students were beaten, bayoneted, raised on bayonets and shot. They were the first victims of unchained ferocity.

" The Committee for the Saving of the Homeland and the Revolution " attempted also to organize a democratic movement in the rural districts by the circulation of broadsheets, etc. ; but within a few days of the students' rising its proceedings were officially arrested by the Soviet Government. (27)

Meanwhile Kerensky, who had left Petrograd early in the morning of October 25th (O.S.), made his appearance at Pskov. There, by accident, General Krassnov learned of his arrival. Kerensky now became aware that his order for the movement of troops to Petrograd had been ignored by General Cheremesov, on the ground that the Provisional Government, headed by Kerensky, had ceased to exist, and that its place was taken by another government. Kerensky was also told that the administration of the railways had declared their adhesion to the new government, viz. the War-Revolutionary Committee. Notwithstanding this information, General Krassnov, who was commander of the 3rd army corps, decided to move towards Petrograd. Kerensky asked to be given an opportunity to address the troops ; accordingly the soldiers were drawn up in order and ladies brought flowers with which to greet him. From the beginning an atmosphere of hostility could be felt. Kerensky's accusations against the Bolsheviks were received with shouts of " Falsehood ! " A Cossack shouted, " Too little have they drunk of our soldiers' blood ! Comrades, a new *Kornilovstchina* is before us !

**166** THE RUSSIAN REVOLUTION

Landowners and capitalists! . . . Comrades, you are going to be deceived! . . . This affair is being undertaken against the people!" (28)

In spite of these manifestations, unfriendly to the Provisional Government and clearly sympathetic with the Bolsheviks, General Krassnov moved with a small force towards Petrograd. He arrived at Tsarskoë Selo on the evening of October 29th with 630 mounted Cossacks, eighteen guns, one armoured car, and an armoured train. Although they had gone so far, the Cossacks refused to go farther without the support of infantry, which indeed was non-existent. Instead of troops there were groups of politicians, and, according to General Krassnov, there were ladies in a motor car with Kerensky within a short distance of the spot where an engagement with the Bolsheviks was already in progress. The Bolsheviks had moved rapidly. Petrograd was now completely in their hands, and a large force of sailors, infantry, and Red Guards was speedily detached to deal with any force that Kerensky might be able to procure. The first contact between the two forces took place at Pulkov, (29) near Tsarskoë Selo. Krassnov and his Cossacks were defeated and compelled to retire upon Gatchina.

At Gatchina the demoralization of this small force set in. The Cossacks began to talk about an armistice and even about peace with the Bolsheviks. Soon the Bolshevik troops approached, and before long they were fraternizing with the Cossacks. Kerensky, being urged to enter into negotiations with the Bolshevik leaders, insisted on referring the question to his colleagues in Petrograd. Evidently he did not know that his colleagues were already in the fortress. He caused Stankevich, who with Savenkov had accompanied Kerensky from Petrograd, to return to the capital for consultation with the ministers and with the Bolshevik leaders. The discussions between the Cossacks and the Bolsheviks assumed a sinister tone. The Cossacks debated among themselves whether they should hand over Kerensky to the Bolsheviks in exchange for Lenin, or simply shoot him. When Kerensky realized their hostile intentions, he betook himself again to his motor and disappeared.

Shortly after Kerensky's departure, Trotsky, Muraviev, Dibenko, and Rochal, representing the War-Revolutionary Committee, accompanied by a large Bolshevik force, entered Gatchina and made peace with the Cossacks. General Krassnov was arrested and sent to the Smolny Institute, but on account of his popularity with the Cossacks he was afterwards liberated.

Immediately after the conclusion of these negotiations, Trotsky went to Tsarskoë Selo, where he seized the powerful radio station,

# "RED OCTOBER." THE EXPLOSION 167

which had been installed there under the old *régime*, and broadcast from it a bombastic radiogram in which with great fervour he announced his victory over Kerensky and the Cossacks.

The high hopes which had been quite unwarrantably fostered in Petrograd by many who anxiously waited for the return of Kerensky and the Cossacks to relieve them from the tyranny of the Bolsheviks were thus doomed to disappointment. On November 14th Trotsky telegraphed, " Gatchina has been occupied by the Finland regiment. The Cossacks have fled in disorder. . . . Kerensky fled in a motor car." (30)

Petrograd was not the only city to fall with comparative ease into the hands of the Bolsheviks. As soon as the events of November 7th were known in Moscow, the Moscow Soviet of Workers' Deputies assembled and decided to sustain the Revolution proclaimed by the Petrograd Bolsheviks. Here also plans had been made for the occupation of important places in the city. A part of the garrison had been won over to the Bolshevik interest. The mayor of Moscow (Rudnev) formed a " Committee of Public Safety," and around this body there were collected military and civilians who were desirous of maintaining public order and of supporting the Provisional Government. But in three days the forces of this committee were defeated and the city was in the hands of the Soviet. In Kiev and elsewhere there were armed conflicts, but everywhere the Bolsheviks defeated their opponents. Only one centre held out. This was the headquarters of the army at the front, which was at Mohilev, under the orders of the Chief of Staff, General Dukhonin. On November 10th, three days after the beginning of the Revolution, he wired to Petrograd :—

" On behalf of the army at the front, we demand immediate stoppage of the violent actions of the Bolsheviks, and the armed seizure of power, and an unconditional surrender to the Provisional Government, which is acting in full accord with the authorized organs of the democracy, and alone is able to give the country a Constituent Assembly, the only master of Russia. The active army is going to sustain this demand by force.

> The Chief-of-Staff of the Commander-in-Chief, DUKHONIN.
>
> Deputy Chief-of-Staff for Civil Affairs, VIRUBOV.
>
> Chairman of the All Army Committee, PEREKRESTOV." (31)

# 168 THE RUSSIAN REVOLUTION

Under the pressure of the times, Mohilev became the centre of opposition to the Bolsheviks, and there the headquarters staff offered the nucleus of a new governmental organization.

The Finnish Diet, on the ground that the Provisional Government of Russia had ceased to exist, formed (November 10th) a directory of three persons for the government of the country. The post of Governor-General of Finland was abolished. (32) On November 15th there was a strike on the Finnish railways. (33) On November 16th the Finnish socialists dispersed the Senate and the Diet, and there was a general strike of workmen. On November 10th the Congress of Soviets declared that the right of proprietors to the ownership of their lands was abolished. The civil servants in nearly all the ministries of the capital struck. The Soviet of Moscow seized the Kremlin, and General Kaledin assumed the government of the Cossack regions. (34)

On November 13th street fighting took place in Moscow between students in the military schools and the Bolsheviks. Gradually all the troops in that city, with the exception of the Cossacks, who remained undecided, passed over to the Bolsheviks, (35) and on the 14th there was again violent fighting in Moscow, and Kiev was bombarded. At Moscow the Bolsheviks agreed to a peace advantageous to themselves. (36) On November 21st the committee of the Soviet of Peasants protested against the pretension of the Petrograd Soviet to assume the government of Russia, (37) and the Russian Senate refused to promulgate Bolshevik decrees. (38) At Petrograd the offices of the Ministry of Finance were pillaged by an armed band. (39) Meanwhile, on the Austro-German fronts, the Russian soldiers were fraternizing with the enemy, but in the Caucasus they defeated the Turks and took 1,600 prisoners. (40)

---

### NOTES

(1) The word " hooligan " has been adopted into Russian under the guise of " khulēgan."

(2) Cf. Mavor, J., *An Economic History of Russia*, vol. ii, pp. 297 and 499.

(3) The names " Petersburg " and " Petrograd " were both used at this time in public documents.

(4) See last preceding note.

(5) Spiridovich, A. E., op. cit., pp. 387–88.

(6) Buchanan, Sir George, op. cit., vol. ii, pp. 205–06.

(7) Stankevich, V. B., *Memoirs*, p. 265, cited by Spiridovich, A. E., op. cit., p. 389.

(8) Spiridovich, A. E., op. cit., p. 391.

(9) Buchanan, Sir George, op. cit., vol. ii, p. 207.

(10) Otherwise Ovceĕnko.

# "RED OCTOBER." THE EXPLOSION 169

(11) Spiridovich, A. E., op. cit., p. 392 n.

(12) Buchanan, Sir George, op. cit., p. 207.

(13) Ibid., p. 208.

(14) Ibid., p. 207.

(15) The *first* according to Lenin's reckoning was in 1905–1906, and the *second* in February-March 1917.

(16) Spiridovich, A. E., op. cit., pp. 394–95.

(17) The number of delegates attending the congress was 562. These were distributed as follows : Bolsheviks 323, non-party but sympathetic to the Bolsheviks 31, Left Social-Revolutionaries 70, Anarchists 5, United Internationalists 15, Menshevik-Internationalists 30, Menshevik-Defencists 26, National Social-Democrats 7, Socialist-Revolutionaries of the Centre 36, Right Socialist-Revolutionaries 16, Socialist-Revolutionary Nationalists 3. The Bolsheviks seem to have commanded a vote of 382. (Cf. Spiridovich, A. E., op. cit., p. 396 n.)

(18) Spiridovich, A. E., op. cit., p. 396. Nothing is said in this resolution of the abolition of private property. Subsequent events showed that the Soviet Government abruptly closed the Constituent Assembly, restricted local self-government, and did its utmost to control from the capital the new nations which had been formed within the Russian area.

(19) Ibid., op. cit., p. 397.

(20) On the death of Lenin, A. J. Rykov succeeded.

(21) Oppokov occupied his office for a few days only.

(22) Trotsky, L. D., *The October Revolution* in *Archives of the Russian Revolution* (1917), p. 219.

(23) *Le Complot Germano-Bolshevist*, Document No. 5, p. 35. See also Simeonev, *German Money and Lenin* in *The Last Information*, No. 299, April 10, 1921 ; and Spiridovich, A. E., op. cit., pp. 399–400. The discrepancy between the date of the letter (November 7th) and that of the formation of the " Council of the People's Commissars " (November 9th) requires explanation. The authenticity of the letter does not appear to have been challenged.

(24) Von Hindenburg, Marshal, *Out of My Life*, p. 272.

(25) Ibid., p. 273.

(26) Spiridovich, A. E., op. cit., p. 401.

(27) Ibid., op. cit., p. 400.

(28) Krassnov, P. N., *The Internal Front* in *Archives of the Russian Revolution* (Berlin, 1921), vol. i, p. 153.

(29) For an account of this engagement see Krassnov, P. N., op. cit., pp. 165–68.

(30) Trotsky, L. D., *The October Revolution* in *Archives of the Russian Revolution* (1917), quoted by Spiridovich, A. E., op. cit., p. 404.

(31) *Archives of the Russian Revolution* (1917), p. 360, and Spiridovich, A. E., op. cit., pp. 406–07.

(32) *Chron. de la Guerre*, 7ᵉ vol., p. 203.

(33) Ibid., p. 210.

(34) Ibid., p. 205.

(35) *Journal de Genève* (13 janvier, 1918). The same journal adds that on November 13th there were incendiarism and pillage in Moscow.

(36) *Chron. de la Guerre*, 7ᵉ vol., p. 209.

(37) Ibid., p. 216.

(38) Ibid.

(39) Ibid.

(40) Ibid.

## CHAPTER VI

## THE SEPARATE ARMISTICE

GREAT BRITAIN and France had made enormous efforts to keep Russia in the war. They had sent munitions, military missions, statesmen, politicians, and socialists to aid and encourage the Russians, and the success of these efforts was indubitable. This is shown by the accusations of the " Defeatists " in Russia, who were constantly saying, " England and France are keeping Russia in the war for their own purposes." They were ; and their purpose was to win the war. They had to keep Russia against her will from contributing to the defeat of herself and her allies, and the German High Command was well aware of that fact.

" Russia had to remain in the war, at least until the new armies of America were on French soil ; otherwise the military and moral defeat of France was certain. For this reason the *Entente* sent politicians, agitators, and officers to Russia in the hope of bolstering up the shattered Russian front. Nor did these missions forget to take money with them, for in many parts of Russia money is more effectual than political arguments.

" Once more we were robbed of the brightest prospect of victory by these counter measures. The Russian front was kept in being, not through its own strength, but mainly through the work of the agitators whom our enemies sent there, and who achieved their purpose even against the will of the Russian masses." (1)

Thus, during the spring and summer of 1917, Russia was kept in the war, and time was gained for new British and American forces and equipment to be made ready for the decisive campaign of 1918.

The wireless station of the Russian Government at Tsarskoë Selo, which had been seized by the Bolsheviks when General Krassnov and his Cossacks were defeated at Pulkov, gave publicity on November 21, 1917, to a note signed by Lenin, Trotsky, Krilenko, and Bonch-Bruyevich, (2) in the name of the All-Russian Congress of Workmen's and Soldiers' Deputies. This note, dated the previous day, was addressed to General Dukhonin, who as chief-of-staff to the commander-in-chief became, after the flight of Kerensky, the effective head of the Russian army. The new authorities announced that they had taken power into their hands, and that it was their intention " to propose to all peoples and their respective governments an immediate armistice on all fronts, with the purpose of

# THE SEPARATE ARMISTICE

immediately opening *pourparlers* for the conclusion of a democratic peace." (3)  On November 22nd a note similar in effect was sent by Trotsky to those diplomatic representatives who had remained in Petrograd. (4)

General Dukhonin, who was at Mohilev, did not obey the instructions of the new Government.  Evidently he considered, as he says in his despatch of November 10th, that the Petrograd Soviet was unjustifiably assuming an authority with which it had not been endowed by any body representing the Russian people.  When summoned to a telephone conversation with Lenin, Djugashvele, (5) and Krilenko, (6) who asked him why he had not obeyed orders, he replied, " The peace which is necessary for Russia can only be arranged by a central government." (7)  This was in formal terms a correct view.  Even the Germans, anxious as they were for peace, were embarrassed by the idea of having an armistice concluded at one part of their line and not at another, according to the action of the local commanders, or of having an armistice with Petrograd and not with Kiev.  The new Soviet Government disregarded all such considerations.  On November 22nd Trotsky gave notice to the foreign embassies remaining in Petrograd that on November 21st a new " Government of the Republic of All the Russias " had been instituted by the " Congress of Councils of Workmen's, Soldiers', and Peasants' Deputies of All the Russias." (8)  Trotsky also proposed to all governments an immediate armistice and commencement of preliminaries of peace, and declared that hostilities had been suspended.  On the same day Dukhonin was dismissed, (9) and the Soviet Government issued the following address to the army.  This address was the signal for the civil war which during the following years, in a series of struggles, tore Russia in pieces.

" Soldiers !  Peace is in your hands.  You are not going to allow the counter-revolutionary generals to tear away from you the great cause of peace.  You will surround them by a guard in order to avoid the lynchers who are unworthy of the revolutionary army, and in order to prevent those generals from escaping trial. Let the regiments at the front at once elect representatives for an armistice with the enemy.  Soldiers ! the keys of peace are in your hands.  Watchfulness, restraint, and energy, and the cause of peace will prevail." (10)

On November 24th Lenin issued a proclamation authorizing the various nationalities of Russia to constitute themselves independent states. (11)  The Bolshevik newspapers began to print the secret treaties between Russia and the Allies found by them in the Russian department of foreign affairs. (12)  On November 25th the Ukrainian *Rada* proclaimed the Ukrainian Republic federated

## 172 THE RUSSIAN REVOLUTION

to the Russian Republic, the Ukrainian soldiers were at the same time recalled from the front. (13) Towards the end of November difficulties were experienced in provisioning the army. " Hordes of famished soldiers invaded the villages and committed depredations." (14) Pillage and *pogroms* took place in the Ukraine. The Allies protested to General Dukhonin that the Treaty of London was being violated, but Trotsky took occasion to state that in his opinion the treaty was not valid. The Spanish ambassador alone replied to the circular letter of Trotsky, by intimating that he had forwarded that document to his Government. The Cadet party published a manifesto in opposition to any peace negotiations by the Bolsheviks ; the higher functionaries of the Ministry of Marine were dismissed, and Bessarabia and Caucasus declared their independence. (15) On November 28th Lenin and Trotsky appealed to the belligerent countries to conclude " a white peace," and fixed December 2nd as the date for the commencement of *pourparlers*. Should the *Entente* Powers refrain from availing themselves of this invitation, they were informed that, since the treaties concluded with Tsarist Russia were not regarded as binding upon the Russian people, the Russian Government would proceed forthwith towards a separate peace with Germany.

The Peasant Conference gave a hostile reception to Lenin and refused to felicitate him upon the conclusion of an armistice ; and the elections for the Constituent Assembly, up to November 28th, gave a majority of 77,600 votes against the Bolsheviks. (16)

On November 28th Trotsky sent a note to Sir George Buchanan demanding the release of Chicherin and Petrov, who had been interned in England on account of the anti-war propaganda in which they had been engaged. (17)

Up to November 29th only three Russian armies out of fifteen recognized the power of the Bolsheviks. The General Assembly of the representatives of all the state institutions at Petrograd passed a resolution calling for a general strike against the dictatorship of Lenin, and the central committee of the Constitutional-Democratic Party (the Cadets) announced that no project or declaration emanating from the Bolsheviks represented the will of the Russian people. Sir George Buchanan refused to reply to the notes of the new government on the ground that it was not recognized by Great Britain. (18) From many different quarters there were protests against the assumption of power by the Bolsheviks. The generals commanding in the Caucasus and on the south-western front declared themselves in sympathy with General Dukhonin, whilst the municipal council of Petrograd repudiated any attempt at a separate peace, and declared that a shameful peace would degrade Russia to the level of a German

# THE SEPARATE ARMISTICE

colony. The municipal council of Moscow protested against " a peace imposed by German spies and usurpers "; the former ministers in the Kerensky Government objected to the usurpation of Lenin, (19) and Prince Kropotkin and other veterans of the revolutionary movement, who feared a Prussianized Russia, protested against a " Leninist peace."

From November 23rd till December 1st there was a week of protests and of more or less feeble and spasmodic attempts to shake the position of the Bolsheviks. All was useless. The ingenuity and activity with which they had enlisted the support and interest of the army rendered the Bolshevik position impregnable. Nevertheless the Soviet Government had to abandon the naïve idea of arriving at an armistice by fraternization of soldiers. Attempts at fraternization on the Russo-Roumanian front were received with fusillades. (20) On November 27th three *parlementaires* despatched from Petrograd crossed the German lines at Pritalensky, between Dvinsk and Vilna, and negotiations for an armistice began. On this day also Sir George Buchanan sent a despatch to the Foreign Office, in which he suggested that Russia should be voluntarily informed by Great Britain that, on account of the exhaustion of Russia by the war and the disorganization inseparable from a great revolution, she would not be expected to implement the agreement affecting a separate peace, although so far as the Allies were concerned they were determined to prosecute the war to a conclusion, in which " binding guarantees of the peace of the world would be secured." Sir George added, " one cannot force an exhausted nation to fight against its will." (21)

The only possible comment upon this despatch is that, coming as it did when Trotsky's *parlementaires* were already crossing the German lines, the advice, however sound, was too late. If it had been given at the time of the accession of the Provisional Government, or even when the question of an immediate peace began to exercise every grade of Russian society, and thus to give the Bolsheviks (who were the only political group to advocate an immediate peace) a political influence which eventually became paramount, such advice might have been useful, although unwelcome and quite possibly ignored.

On December 1st the municipal council of Petrograd was dissolved by decree, and new elections were ordered for December 9th. The mayor and five councillors were arrested. The council continued its sittings until December 3rd, when it was dispersed by sailors and by the Red Guard. (22)

During the last week of November, the opposition to the Soviet Government, and especially to the appointment of Krilenko as

## THE RUSSIAN REVOLUTION

commander-in-chief, continued at the headquarters of the staff at Mohilev. The staff protested also against Krilenko making his appearance, as seemed likely, at Mohilev with an armed force. Notwithstanding these protests, however, the headquarters staff and its immediate *entourage* were by no means united. Bolshevik influence had been at work among them. The army committees were already carrying on conversations with Smolny, and at a meeting held in the night of December 1st–2nd they decided that headquarters must not be defended against Krilenko in any event. Early in the morning of December 3rd a War-Revolutionary Committee was formed at Mohilev, and decided that none of the chief commanders should be permitted to leave until the arrival of Krilenko. On December 3rd Krilenko reached Mohilev with a punitive detachment of sailors. He met with no resistance; the War-Revolutionary Committee, together with numerous deputations, greeted him with respect, the bands played the *Marseillaise*, headquarters with its generals had been captured without a shot. At that moment there was no effective group of persons with any force at its disposal to question the authority of the Soviet—or even the personal dictatorship of Lenin. Not merely had the citadel of Tsardom fallen, but almost without a struggle the hastily constructed defences of a democratic state had fallen also.

Next day, December 4th, Krilenko sent for General Dukhonin, who had openly disobeyed the Soviet Government, and had therefore, from its point of view, incurred dismissal. Dukhonin went, and under the eyes of Krilenko, although not necessarily by his express orders, he was brutally murdered by the sailors whom Krilenko had brought with him, and his savagely mutilated body was left for some time in the streets of Mohilev. (23)

The Armistice negotiations began on November 27th, and within a week German officers and private soldiers made their appearance in the streets of Petrograd.

Trotsky dismissed 160 Russian diplomatists who refused to recognize the Soviet Government. In a note supplementary to that of November 27th he employed the argument that his Government never desired a separate peace, but on the contrary proposed a general peace. If the Allies refused to act along with Russia, it would be their fault if Russia had to act separately. (24)

While the Soviet Government had now, after a fashion, all central and all northern Russia under its control, the Ukraine and all southern Russia had not yet given adhesion to the new *régime*. Finland had already declared its independence; Poland was in the hands of Germany.

A Ukrainian *Rada* had formed a Government; and now the

# THE SEPARATE ARMISTICE

Ukrainian Minister of War called upon his troops to refrain from giving support to the Bolsheviks on the ground that to do so would lead to an invasion of the Ukraine by the Germans. This was undoubtedly a sound idea. Although the release of the large army which was holding the eastern front and its transference to the west were the chief reasons for concluding a speedy peace with Russia, there was the additional advantage that the Ukraine was understood to have large reserves of grain which might be obtained, so soon as peace was concluded, for the victualling of Austria and Germany. The Ukrainian Government was not unnaturally apprehensive that the terms of peace which the Germans might be expected to impose would involve payments of grain, and that the Germans would go to the Ukraine to see that they got it. The north had no grain to give, or anything likely to be useful. Agricultural products, mineral resources, etc., were all in the south.

Great Britain having liberated Chicherin and Petrov from internment, a hundred and fifty British subjects were allowed to leave Russia (December 12th). The new municipal council of Petrograd was returned wholly Bolshevik, the electors who were not Bolshevik having refrained from voting. (25)

On December 14th there was organized at Kishinev an independent government of Bessarabia, and also in the Caucasus. (26)

---

## NOTES

(1) Von Hindenburg, Marshal, *Out of My Life*, pp. 271–72.

(2) Vladimir Bonch-Bruyevich, under the old *régime*, had not been publicly identified with any party. He was known for his researches into the history and beliefs of dissenting religious sects in Russia. He wrote in particular upon the Doukhobors.

(3) This document and others relating to the armistice of November 1917 and Brest-Litovsk are to be found in the *Daily Review of the Foreign Press* (London), November 23, 1917, till March 12, 1918, and in *Proceedings of the Brest-Litovsk Peace Conference* (Washington, 1918), and *Texts of the Russian Peace* (Washington, 1918). For a narrative, etc., with valuable references to sources, see Dennis, A. L. P., *The Foreign Policies of Soviet Russia* (New York, 1924), pp. 21–55. Cf. also Czernin, Count Ottokar, *In the World War* (New York and London, 1920).

(4) Sir George Buchanan says he received the note "nineteen hours after General Dukhonin had received the order to open *pourparlers* with the enemy." *My Mission to Russia*, vol. ii, p. 229.

(5) Joseph Bessarionovich Djugashvele, also known as "Koba" and "Stalin," was a Georgian peasant of the *gub* of Tiflis. He joined the Labour Party in 1908. In 1912 he was arrested and sentenced to three years' banishment to Narimsk (Spiridovich, A. E., op. cit., p. 239).

(6) Nikolai Vasilievich Krilenko was born at Belye, *gub* of Smolensk, in 1885. He completed a course at Lublin gymnasium and studied at the university of St. Petersburg. In January 1905 he joined the Bolshevik party organization at St. Petersburg, where he was known as "Comrade Abram." In 1906 he worked

## 176 THE RUSSIAN REVOLUTION

in the military organization. Searched for, but successfully eluding capture, he lived at large in an illegal position. He subsequently removed to Moscow. Soon afterwards he was arrested in St. Petersburg and accused in the case of " the 51 Bolsheviks," but was discharged. In December 1913 he was arrested again and sent to Kharkov. There he passed the state examination whilst working in a local organization. He was on the point of being arrested when he succeeded in escaping to Switzerland. In 1915 he was again arrested in Moscow and taken to Kharkov. During the rule of the Provisional Government he was arrested for agitation in the army and for distributing Bolshevik proclamations. He was flogged with a *nagaïka* and sent to Petrograd, where he was liberated by order of Kerensky. (Cf. Spiridovich, A. E., op. cit., pp. 406–07.)

(7) *Izvestia* (Petrograd), No. 221, November 23, 1917.

(8) *Daily Review of the Foreign Press* (London), November 26, 1917, and *The Peace Negotiations between Russia and the Central Powers* (Washington, 1918), p. 8.

(9) *Izvestia* (Petrograd), No. 221, November 23, 1917.

(10) Ibid.

(11) *Chron. de la Guerre*, 7ᵉ vol., p. 216. Notwithstanding this proclamation, the Soviet Government refused to acknowledge the various States unless they were controlled by Bolshevik elements.

(12) Ibid. An analysis of the diplomatic documents published in Petrograd at this time was printed in the *Débats* (Paris), November 27, 1917.

(13) *Chron. de la Guerre*, 7ᵉ vol., p. 220.

(14) Ibid., p. 221.

(15) Ibid.

(16) Ibid., p. 223.

(17) Buchanan, Sir George, op. cit., p. 226.

(18) *Chron. de la Guerre*, 7ᵉ vol., p. 225.

(19) Ibid., p. 226.

(20) Ibid., p. 227.

(21) Buchanan, Sir George, op. cit., vol. ii, p. 225.

(22) *Chron. de la Guerre*, 7ᵉ vol., pp. 228–30.

(23) Spiridovich, A. E., op. cit., pp. 407–08.

(24) Buchanan, Sir George, op. cit., vol. ii, p. 225, and also *Proceedings*, etc., pp. 34 and 52.

(25) *Chron. de la Guerre*, 7ᵉ vol., p. 242.

(26) Ibid., p. 244.

# CHAPTER VII

## THE CONSTITUENT ASSEMBLY

DURING the revolutionary years 1905–1907 insistent cries arose in many quarters for the convening of a Constituent Assembly by which " the will of the people " should be revealed. (1) Although this Assembly was to be called by the historical Russian name *Sobranje*, its model was to be the *Assemblée Constituante* (2) of the French Revolution. It was anticipated that nine-tenths of such an Assembly, if it were really representative of the people, would be composed of peasantry. Thus the outcome must be " a complete revolution of all economic and state relations." (3) This was the opinion of Marx, who suggested two courses of action for the Russian revolutionists—either to compel the Tsar to convene a Constituent Assembly, or to frighten him with disturbances which would provoke him to do so. (4) None of the revolutionary parties had any doubt that a Constituent Assembly would lead inevitably to drastic social changes. The *intelligentsia* in general regarded it as their own particular " offspring," in which their interest and hopes centred. An assembly of the people, where their freely elected representatives would be entitled to freedom of speech and of deed, was for the *intelligentsia* " a fairy kingdom " (5) to which the Russian people would be called by the Revolution.

In 1917, however, when they realized the political immaturity of the workers and their readiness to allow themselves to be influenced by " every wind of doctrine," the high hopes they had entertained of a people's assembly began to seem illusive, and soon the idea actually became unpopular among the *intelligentsia*. By this new attitude they confessed their lack of perspicacity in advocating, for at least twenty years, a scheme which they now contemplated with misgiving. They even admitted that they had idealized the peasant and the working man, for when the moment came they evidently felt afraid to trust political affairs in the hands of those who were engaged in manual labour. Here again is evidence of the fatalistic and passive spirit which infected the *intelligentsia* at this time. Notwithstanding their new distrust of the people, they appear to have thought that the Constituent Assembly should meet ; and in spite of their dislike of the Bolsheviks, and their justifiable dread of the thoroughness with which they always pursued

## THE RUSSIAN REVOLUTION

their aims, the majority of the *intelligentsia* were of opinion that the Bolsheviks would not dare to lay hands upon the sacred Ark of the Assembly which had been worshipped by the educated classes for so many years ; would not any other supposition be incredible ? The Russian people had dreamed of this Assembly ; would they allow it to be crushed before their eyes by any political group ? Surely they would never permit such a profanation. Sokolov's diagnosis of the position is contained in the following passage :—

"Fatalism held in its strong hands the vital organs of all the political parties. It dominated all their resolutions and decisions. It paralysed all the actions and organizations aimed against the activities of the Bolsheviks. This uncommon (6) psychological attitude was rarely felt or recognized by us, but the result was very obvious. It was this pacifism that, in addition to the chronic Russian inertia, brought about Bolshevism and gave it its full victory, a victory which did not arise from the strength of the Bolsheviks, and still less from the support, however extensive, which they received in the country." (7)

Thus the Bolsheviks owed their victory to the activity of their small force, opposed as it was by passivity on the part of the majority of the people and blind indifference on the part of the educated and middle classes. The assistance, if any, which the Bolsheviks received either from the Monarchists or the Germans cannot be regarded as having been a determining factor.

The manner of election occupied a large part of the time devoted to discussion. The method adopted, that of selecting the candidates by central committees of the respective parties, was much criticized. Opponents of this method pointed out that in many districts candidates must be unknown to electors, and that therefore such candidates must be equally ignorant of their constituents. The answer to this criticism was that "X and Y," being party leaders, were so widely known that the particular constituency they represented was unimportant. In response to this, it was argued that the reputation, even of well-known party leaders, was superficial, and that electors in general were either wholly ignorant of them or were aware of them only by hearsay ; in either case electors were indifferent to unknown candidates and careless of the manner in which they were treated. (8) These discussions show conclusively how slender was the preparation even among the *intelligentsia* for effective use of representative institutions. The technique of popular government, familiar enough to western Europeans and to Americans, was to them a strange and novel affair.

The Peasants' Congress, by 360 votes to 321, declared in favour of the Constituent Assembly. (9) During December 1917 the

# THE CONSTITUENT ASSEMBLY

dispute between the Ukraine and Petrograd became more and more acute. The troops of the Ukrainian *Rada* occupied the headquarters of the south-western and Roumanian fronts, and the Ukrainian soldiers had been instructed to refuse to obey the orders of Krilenko ; the Bolsheviks meanwhile addressed an ultimatum to the *Rada*. Already the movement of food-stuffs had begun from the Ukraine to Germany, at the moment when food became scarce in the north of Russia.

After repeated postponements, the date for the opening of the Constituent Assembly was fixed for January 18, 1918. Ten days before, on the 8th, the Grand Duke Michael declared that, even if he were offered the throne by the Constituent Assembly, he would refuse to accept it. As the day approached, the Bolsheviks became aware that they would be in a minority, and only small groups of members of the other parties—principally the Socialist-Revolutionaries—properly grasped that this very fact meant danger to the Assembly. They realized that the characteristic thing for the Bolsheviks to do was to threaten with dispersal an assembly in which they found themselves in a minority, or even to disperse it without warning. Indeed, some of the Socialist-Revolutionaries decided that the Assembly stood urgently in need of an armed force to defend it against such a possible attack, and defence measures were secretly organized, though very few of the members were willing to admit the necessity of these precautions.

Boris Sokolov, Socialist-Revolutionary and partisan of the Constituent Assembly, gives an account of his experiences in trying to defend it, and from this account the greater part of the following narrative is drawn :—

" The soldiers of a Petrograd regiment asked me [Sokolov] to read a paper on ' Should the Constituent Assembly meet or not ? ' I read it in one of the barracks." Sokolov found himself in the presence of two mutually hostile groups, " one of which consisted of Bolsheviks and the other of the great mass of soldiers, intelligents and otherwise. The intelligent soldiers argued with the Bolsheviks, who answered in choice revolutionary expressions which have unfortunately become part of the Russian language, and the mass of the soldiers applauded both of them. It was very hard to find out on which side their sympathy really lay.

" ' The Constituent Assembly is our very own. [Literally, flesh of our flesh].'

" ' That is right.'

" ' The Constituent Assembly is filled with social traitors. It should be dispersed by force.'

## THE RUSSIAN REVOLUTION

" ' Comrade soldiers, are you going to disperse the Constituent Assembly ? '

" ' No, we won't. We swear.'

" ' But will you defend the Constituent Assembly ? ' (Confused and very indistinct shouting.)

" From individual conversation, I found that the majority of the soldiers were very friendly, not only to the Constituent Assembly, but also to the Provisional Government." Neither the passivity of the *intelligentsia* nor the energy of the Bolsheviks had any influence upon this friendly attitude, neither was it affected by the unfavourable political situation. The soldiers were merely passive and did not profess any active desire to defend either the Constituent Assembly or the Provisional Government.

The mood of the workers in the Petrograd region was " more or less the same " as that of the garrison. The labour masses, however, had been subjected to a greater amount of propaganda by the Bolsheviks than had the troops. The attitude of labour, though friendly to both the Constituent Assembly and the Provisional Government, was rather inclined " towards scepticism and indifference." The large majority of the Petrograd working men were neutral, but they were not Bolshevik. According to the statistics of the factory committee, not more than 15 per cent. voted for Bolshevik candidates in factory organizations. The workers of the Franco-Russian factory were very friendly to Sokolov, who had a specially intimate acquaintance with them on the Admiralty and Galerny Islands, and they were visited by various groups of workers from other places. Through them it was possible to obtain valuable notes on the real mood of the labour masses.

" Here, as well as in the regiments," Sokolov writes, " I met with the passive mood. The people affected by it seemed to be disillusioned and even lost, having no courage and being equally unwilling to go to the help of the Provisional Government or to join the Bolsheviks." The masses of Petrograd labour were at once passive and pacifist. The numbers of the Bolsheviks were small, even minute ; but the party was compact and well organized, and could easily withstand the Socialist-Revolutionary and Menshevik parties, whose energies were insufficiently combined and concentrated. The Bolsheviks knew how to agitate and how to hypnotize the labouring people. Up to the beginning of 1918 they had drawn into their net only a minority of the Petrograd working men, but about that time their strenuous efforts were beginning to bear fruit. " We have to recognize that the labour masses of Petrograd went away from us [the Socialist-Revolutionaries] and also from the Menshevist influence. Why did this happen ? Chiefly

# THE CONSTITUENT ASSEMBLY 181

because of the lack of well-organized work in the region. Most of the active party workers ceased to adhere to us or to the Menshevik influence, and went to the centre or to the municipality." The Provisional Government was not approved by the working people, who found it " guilty of indecision, indefiniteness, and endless hesitation." (10) This does not prove that in 1917 the workers were Bolshevist or that they were even inclined that way ; at the same time, none of this evidence is inconsistent with the idea that in their general course of action, apart from the Bolshevik doctrines which were not closely adhered to, and were only dimly understood by themselves, or by others, both working men and peasants found that they were quite often in accord with the Bolsheviks, and that sometimes they would willingly have gone even farther than they in the path of destruction and disorganization.

In the struggle of the Provisional Government against the Bolsheviks, the Socialist-Revolutionaries regarded as an open secret the fact that monarchists, even of the most reactionary groups, assisted the Bolsheviks against the Government. (11) Such action might be defensible on the principle that one revolutionary body may be used to overthrow another. The monarchists probably thought that harm was unlikely to come of supporting the Bolsheviks because they were even less likely to achieve a stable government than any other revolutionary body. Their motives are obscure ; but if, as has been alleged, some of the reactionary monarchists did fight in the streets for, rather than against, the Bolsheviks, they were guilty at least of fatal miscalculation.

When the Assembly had arrived at Petrograd, and was about to begin sessions, Sokolov asked one of the members who was a prominent leader in one of the factions opposed to the Bolsheviks : " ' How shall we defend the Constituent Assembly and how shall we defend ourselves ? ' The member was very much surprised. ' Defend ! Self-defence ! How absurd ! Do you forget that we are the representatives of the people ? We have to give the people new life, new laws ; but to defend the Constituent Assembly, that is the affair of the people who elected us.' " (12) To understand this attitude on the part of a Socialist-Revolutionary, it is necessary to realize the change which had taken place in the temper and character of that party since the February-March 1917 Revolution. So long as the autocracy continued, the Socialist-Revolutionaries were implacably opposed to the Government. Their political programme had in effect been " Down with the autocracy ; let the people govern, and trust them." But towards the end of 1917 they had reached a somewhat different point of view. They had seen the Provisional Government assume office and they had

## THE RUSSIAN REVOLUTION

supported it on principle until a Constituent Assembly could be convened and a permanent form of government evolved by that Assembly. Any attempt to dictate by force to the people was very repugnant to them, and on this ground they opposed the Bolsheviks. But they found that the Bolsheviks were swept into power in consequence of the inertia of the people. From the Socialist-Revolutionary point of view, the people were deceived by the Bolsheviks ; but they would not always be so deceived. " Wait for the Constituent Assembly, and then we shall see what the people in their might will choose ! " That was their idea. The Socialist-Revolutionary party had always been divided into two groups, those who advocated individual terror and those who did not. The party as a whole was hostile to the autocracy, but it was not hostile to the *bourgeois* class as such. The class war was thus not their affair. When the autocracy disappeared, there was no logical reason for the application of individual terror. Hence the reluctance of the party in general to engage in violent measures for any reason whatever while the Constituent Assembly for which they had ardently longed was on the point of meeting. The Socialist-Revolutionaries had become political pacifists, who had learned to resort to parliamentary methods.

The fact that one of their party men, Kerensky, was placed in an important position in the Provisional Government at the commencement of its career, and that other members had been added to the Government subsequently, gave the Socialist-Revolutionaries a sense of the responsibility of power. Since the Socialist members of the Government were co-operating with persons experienced in the tasks of administration, they learned something of the perplexities and difficulties which administrative duties entail. These circumstances at once caused and enabled them to cut themselves off from their terrorist and conspiratorial past and to desire to proceed for the future along the path of order. Thus, as Sokolov puts it, " Between the S.R.s of the beginning of 1917 and the S.R.s. of the end of 1917 there is a precipice." (13) Naturally this evolution applies especially, and perhaps in its full sense exclusively, to the leaders, to those who came to be called the Right Socialist-Revolutionaries.

The other socialist parties were also subject to evolution ; but they did not evolve after the same manner. The Social-Democrats had never been implicated in individual terrorism ; only in 1905-1907 had they as a party countenanced expropriations and other violent actions. (14) The Bolshevik faction of that party, when it came into power, ceased to employ the pacific parliamentary methods which had in general been adopted by the Social-Democrats in the

# THE CONSTITUENT ASSEMBLY                     183

past ; and, imitating its autocratic predecessors, adopted a systematic and continuous policy of ruthless suppression of the *bourgeois* class.

The small group of active spirits among the Socialist-Revolutionaries consisted chiefly of soldier deputies from the front.(15) The members of this group had not been in the " upper layers of the party, and therefore were not influenced by the evolutionary process, but had maintained practically the old point of view, and revolutionary acts and movements continued to form the atmosphere in which they lived. They did not quarrel with the party leaders, but, in a large measure, separated themselves from them, and thus relieved the leaders of responsibility for what they did. Their hostility to the Bolsheviks was determined, effective, and continuous. This accounts for the equally determined hostility of the Bolsheviks towards them. Many were shot, imprisoned, or sent to outlying places, and they had often to be hidden." (16)  At one time anti-Tsarist, their attitude was now anti-Bolshevist ; the positive side of political or social action did not appeal to them.

During the month of December the Socialist-Revolutionary and Menshevik party leaders devoted themselves to preparations for the opening of the Constituent Assembly. They drew up many projects of new laws, and formulated policies upon the land question, popular education, and foreign affairs, as well as programmes for the daily debates. There were committees for all these subjects and many more. " What committees were there not ? " asks Sokolov, who shared in these proceedings. (17)  Mark Vishnyak, a young and ardent parliamentarian, was especially concerned that none of the sides of governmental construction should be neglected. There were numerous meetings at which there took place serious discussions, in which experts, specially invited, took part and read prepared reports. The meetings were very interesting, yet everything was going on in an atmosphere of unreality. Several assumptions contributed to this—e.g., that there was no such organ as the Bolshevist Government ; that there was no chance whatever of the dissolution of the Assembly ; that the Assembly could alone dissolve or prorogue itself ; and that parliamentary life would flow on noiselessly and without friction immediately after the opening ceremony.

The arrangements for this opening had been well thought out. Who should address the Assembly, and on what topics they should speak, who should guide the respective factions—these and kindred problems had already been debated. " Everything was provided for except—the bands of drunken soldiers who filled the galleries of the Taurida Palace, and the non-parliamentary cynicism of the Bolsheviks." (18)  These were not on the agenda, but they were

## THE RUSSIAN REVOLUTION

observable in the proceedings. Immediately before the opening the active spirits remonstrated with the leaders for spending so much time and energy upon preparations, while the opening of the Assembly was still uncertain. "We do not know exactly the intentions of the Bolsheviks ; but we are sure that they will not dare to interfere with the prerogatives of so high an organization [as the Constituent Assembly], elected by the people ; but if they do . . . then we shall arrive armed with our political experience, with the full understanding of the seriousness of the problems placed on our shoulders by the Russian people."

The idea was tenaciously held, even in the Socialist-Revolutionary party, that the Bolsheviks must be met in the Assembly and nowhere else, that the people must defend the Assembly which they had elected, and that any struggle which might ensue must be fought out between the Bolsheviks and the people, on whom the responsibility rested. The question was discussed throughout December 1917, and the party adhered rigidly to this standpoint.

The chairman of the *Plenum*, or all-parties committee of the Socialist-Revolutionaries, V. V. Rudnyeb, anticipated any struggle with the Bolsheviks by denouncing an armed attack on their part as "adventurism," and as being likely to have evil consequences beyond the parliamentary contest. When, late in December, the All Russian Union of Service sent a delegation to one of the factions of the S.R.s, they reported that they were prepared to bring all their forces to protect the Constituent Assembly, proposing as a measure of war the threat of a general strike ; they were told at once that the suggested procedure was quite undesirable, and that the S.R.s would dissociate themselves from any such movement. The same answer was given to other deputations on the same subject.

Meanwhile the Bolsheviks were conducting a very skilful campaign against the S.R.s. They were evidently trying to foster a feeling against them in the minds of the working people. The same astuteness and thoroughness exhibited by the Bolsheviks in their preparation for the October Revolution was exhibited now in their plans for the dissolution of the Constituent Assembly. They left nothing to chance. As before they had prepared the army, so now by assiduous cultivation of a number of regiments of the Petrograd garrison they secured military support for a fresh attack upon public institutions. To gain the friendly assistance of the workmen was important enough, but the support of a few regiments was absolutely indispensable to overawe thoroughly the Socialist-Revolutionaries—even the Red Guard and the sailors from Kronstadt might not stand an attack. It was necessary to make sure by winning over some regiments of the regular guard, disorganized

# THE CONSTITUENT ASSEMBLY 185

and demoralized as they were. The Bolsheviks started with the great advantage of position. Theirs was the only party organization among the soldiers which had survived the October Revolution. Though the adherence they gave was only passive, it was none the less important. There was no tendency towards armed operations. For this reason some of the military people who were watching the situation conceived the idea that the military force of the Petrograd garrison had sunk to nothing at all and that one or two regiments of disciplined troops might have overwhelmed them. Probably they might, but there remained the question, could they hold the position afterwards ?

The Petrograd garrisons were rendered more formidable owing to the absence of any organized force on the side of the opponents of the Bolsheviks. Yet a large number of soldiers and sailors were neutral, and none of them wanted to fight. The number upon which the Bolsheviks could actually rely on January 18th, after they had been in power for two months, was, according to the statement of Kuzmin, not more than 3,000 to 4,000 men—that is, one regiment. (19) They had, in addition, the Red Guard, numbering at that time about 5,000, but Kuzmin did not regard the strength of this force as very formidable. Many of them had had no military training ; and, in general, most of the Red Army is represented as being " not heroic." (20)

These facts gave the self-appointed " war committee " (21) of the Socialist-Revolutionaries their opportunity. The attempt to carry on a struggle with the Bolsheviks outside the Taurida Palace, where it was to meet on January 18, 1918, was not approved of by the leaders of the Socialist-Revolutionary party, and only a few of the deputies of the Assembly were in touch with the committee. The problem was to select from the Petrograd garrison those who were efficient in a military sense and at the same time anti-Bolshevist, and so the members of the committee distributed themselves over the regiments stationed in Petrograd, for the purpose of discovering the mood of the soldiers. The Pavlovsky regiment and the Jägers, as well as some others, were quite hopeless. In the Ismaelovsky regiment and in many technical and artillery units there were found some encouraging signs ; but in only three were the indispensable conditions found together, viz. military strength, discipline, and anti-Bolshevism. These were the Semenovsky and Preobrashensky regiments and the tank division stationed in the grounds of the Ismaelovsky regiment. The regimental committees as well as the company committees of the two first-mentioned consisted chiefly of non-party persons, who were, however, sharply and openly anti-Bolshevik. There were many, wearing the decoration of

## 186 THE RUSSIAN REVOLUTION

chevaliers of St. George, who had been wounded in the war, and who were disgusted with the Bolshevik chaos. The relations in these three units between the commanding officers and the troops were very friendly, and they were selected as the nucleus of the anti-Bolshevik forces. In addition, the S.R. war committee was able to bring from the front 600 officers and men who were hostile to Bolshevism. These were divided among the companies of the Semenovsky and Preobrashensky regiments in the proportion of two-thirds to the first and one-third to the second. Some of the new arrivals, chiefly ex-students who were technical experts, were put into the tank division, and some of those from the front were introduced into the company and regimental committees. Towards the end of December these plans had been carried far enough to increase alike anti-Bolshevik forces and feeling. The war committee decided to publish a daily newspaper in order to propagate an impression of the iniquities of Bolshevism by a re-cital of the daily doings of the Government. This newspaper was called *Sieraya Shinel, The Grey Cloak*, and was published by a committee of the soldiers of the Semenovsky and Preobrashensky regiments. Most of the money was subscribed by the former, but other regiments were to guarantee the necessary funds. The editorial committee consisted of volunteers : B. Petrov, who was shot by the Bolsheviks during the advance of Yodyenich ; G—sky, of the Preobrashensky regiment ; K.,(22) of the Semenovsky regiment ; and Boris Sokolov.

The first number of *The Grey Cloak* was written in a warlike and strictly anti-Bolshevist tone. It contained caricatures of Lenin and the Red Guards. Of this 10,000 copies were published, and the whole issue was sold in two or three hours, for at that moment, at the end of December 1917, all the newspapers opposed to the Bolsheviks had been suppressed. The appearance of *The Grey Cloak* produced great excitement in the Smolny Institute. The paper was denounced in *Pravda*, and the Semenovsky were accused of accepting bribes from the *bourgeoisie*. The second number had a like success and produced a like impression. There was no third issue, for, at two o'clock in the morning when the paper was about to appear, the printing-office was raided by a company of the Red Guard upon an order by signed Lenin, requiring the arrest, on the ground of counter-revolution, of B. Petrov and B. Soko-lov ; the editors, however, did not surrender. On January 15th the printing-office was guarded by a number of soldiers from both regiments with two machine guns, and a new periodical, *The Grey Cloak Shot Through*, was printed and issued without interference. On the same evening the Preobrashensky and the

# THE CONSTITUENT ASSEMBLY 187

Semenovsky regiments were visited by Krilenko, who demanded a general meeting. In a speech lasting for an hour he tried to persuade the soldiers to refuse sympathy with the *bourgeoisie* and to stop issuing *The Grey Cloak Shot Through*, because such a newspaper was very injurious to the Revolution. The soldiers treated Krilenko " very dryly." The regimental committee of the Semenovsky promised " diplomatically " to obey the orders from Smolny. In spite of this promise the newspaper appeared on January 16th and 17th, and both issues had an even greater circulation than those that preceded them. The humorous tone of the paper partly accounts for its popularity, for it contained many jibes against the leading Bolsheviks and the Red Guard.(23) On the 17th the Socialist-Revolutionary party issued a manifesto calling upon the people to defend the Constituent Assembly on the ground that it alone had the right to speak in the name of the country, and to conclude a democratic peace.(24) On the same day a second Ukrainian *Rada* was formed at Kharkov under the auspices of the Petrograd Bolsheviks. (25)

On that same night the printing-office of *The Grey Cloak Shot Through* was surrounded by the Red Guard. Finding, however, that it was defended by two regiments, the Red Guard retired without attempting to carry out the orders from Smolny for the arrest of the editors. The newspaper was printed that night and issued next morning ; its sole topic was the Constituent Assembly, and the intention of the Bolsheviks to break up the meeting was fully disclosed.

The advantage enjoyed by the Bolsheviks of having access to stores of arms, while the S.R.s, excepting those who were in the army, were wholly deprived of them, rendered successful opposition to the Government almost hopeless. Yet the war committee of the S.R.s attempted to accumulate arms for their adherents. At that time Petrograd had plenty of military equipment, but the Bolsheviks took great pains to control its distribution. Thus, while arms were furnished without stint to extemporized sections of the Red Guard, the S.R.s were able to secure only a limited quantity, and even competent volunteers were insufficiently provided with rifles and ammunition, and in some instances had none at all.

The workmen who were enlisted by the S.R.s were, Sokolov admits, not infected by any special enthusiasm for fighting. For example, at a meeting of the workmen of the Franco-Russian factory, when Sokolov was explaining that from his point of view the only way of defending the Constituent Assembly against the Bolsheviks was by means of armed bands, the workmen were very dubious,

## 188 THE RUSSIAN REVOLUTION

and asked, " Has not enough blood been shed ? Four years of war ; all the time blood, blood ! The Bolsheviks are really swindlers ! They will not dare to do anything to the Constituent Assembly."

One young workman said, " I think, comrades, we need not talk about quarrelling with the Bolsheviks, but rather about how we may come to an agreement with them. After all, they are defending the interests of the proletariat. . . ."

Delusions about the Bolsheviks, their methods, and their aims, were very prevalent among the workmen, even among those who were inclined towards anti-Bolshevism. Sokolov states that after his appeal only fifteen men came forward, the Bolsheviks having already secured two or three times that number. (26)

The activities of the war committee of the S.R.s resulted in the enlistment of about 2,000 volunteers from among the Petrograd working men, but of these a minority only were armed, whilst many of them did not appear at the meetings where alone they could learn of the progress of events, and not a few were influenced by neutral feelings and by the prevalent and depressing passivity. The Bolsheviks were in a similar position, they had to endure the inertia of even their own volunteers, armed though they were. The most promising side of the work of the S.R. war committee seemed to be the organization of volunteers from the army in the field. The S.R. propaganda in general had been fairly successful among the soldiers, especially on the south-eastern and Roumanian fronts. If a number could be transferred to Petrograd, well armed and reliable, they would at once reinforce and stiffen the all too small group of defenders of the Assembly. In order to account for the continued presence of these selected soldiers in Petrograd without incurring the suspicion of the Bolsheviks, it was necessary to devise some plan. To this end the war committee inaugurated a soldiers' university, and in the middle of December this institution was opened in one of the high-school buildings. The ceremony was public and sanctioned by the Government, and among the lecturers there were some Bolsheviks who were loyal to their party. The idea was ingenious. The volunteers were concentrated ; they could defend themselves if attacked ; and they were ready if required for use in offensive ; while their presence did not arouse suspicion. They were housed, to the number of two hundred, in the Red Cross building in Fontanka Street. So far the plan was successful ; but the central committee of the Socialist-Revolutionary party became timorous. They thought the adventure too risky, and though the small force remained it was not increased, not was it employed for the purpose for which it was formed.

# THE CONSTITUENT ASSEMBLY 189

The soldiers who volunteered from the front seemed to be at a loss to understand the inertia of the *intelligentsia*. " The Bolsheviks," they said, " are using armed force without compunction. Why cannot we do that ? " They understood quite well, although they were politically uneducated, the meaning of the dissolution of the Constituent Assembly. On this subject they remarked, " There is much unripeness in the Assembly ; but if it did not exist, our case would be still harder. Destruction will begin, and God knows what will happen to us." (27)

In the early days of January 1918 a meeting of the workers in the government paper-money factory was held. About 4,000 were present. They were addressed by representatives of the various parties, and they discussed Bolshevism and the defence of the Constituent Assembly. The general feeling was anti-Bolshevik, and the audience would not listen to the Bolshevik speakers. The workmen shouted to them, " You dissolved the Provisional Government ; now you want to insult the Constituent Assembly. How many years have we been waiting for it and we only have it now ! You have somehow got into power, and it seems that you like power. Long live the Constituent Assembly ! Long live the Soviet ! " (The latter cry referred, of course, not to the Bolshevik Soviet, but to their own.) (28)

Another meeting was held about the same time at which most of the workers in the Franco-Russian factory were present. The chairman was Smirnov, (29) a well-known Bolshevik.

" Comrades," he said, " we are facing a crisis, facing the possibility of dissolving the Constituent Assembly, because it is obvious already that it is full of *bourgeois* superstition and that it has a counter-revolutionary tendency."

Smirnov was answered by a workman, Shmakov :—

" No, comrade Bolsheviks, you should not do that : it is not right. You are ruining the prerogatives of all who elected this Constituent Assembly. If you do that, then you must remember that this forcible dissolution will never be forgotten or forgiven by the Russian people, by the Russian proletariat."

The majority of the workers present seemed to support Shmakov and to disapprove of the Bolshevik attitude towards the Assembly, although they looked upon themselves as Bolsheviks and as being opposed to the Provisional Government. (30)

At a meeting held on January 18th at the Franco-Russian factory Zinoviev made his appearance and spoke contemptuously of " the small *bourgeois* Assembly " and of the power of the proletariat to dissolve it, and he was enthusiastically received by the workers. (31)

## THE RUSSIAN REVOLUTION

The Ismaelovsky regiment was one of those which hesitated for a long time before deciding upon which side to range itself. The Bolsheviks conducted a vigorous canvass of the soldiers, and a large meeting was held early in January in the cinema theatre of the regiment. Krilenko and Pyatakov spoke for the Bolsheviks, Fortunatov and Sokolov for the Socialist-Revolutionaries. Krilenko and Pyatakov delivered the customary onslaught upon the " imperialistic war," and attacked the *Entente*, Clemenceau, the " *bourgeois* " Provisional Government, etc. Then they spoke of the Constituent Assembly. Immediately the soldiers shouted, " Don't dare to touch it. Let there be a Soviet and a Constituent Assembly. Do you think we elected our deputies for nothing ? "

On January 16th Krilenko went to the Semenovsky regiment in order to prepare the ground for the dissolution of the Constituent Assembly by " clearing away," as he said, " the heavy atmosphere of counter-revolution which filled the barracks." He was not favourably received, and was advised to be very careful in what he said, otherwise the soldiers might not listen to him. Shouts were raised by the audience. " It would not be a bad thing to beat that fellow. He is getting too conceited."

Krilenko began, " Comrades, I have come to talk to you in the name of the labour-peasant government "—(" What is that government ? " the soldiers shouted ; " we do not recognize it.")—" which is very much troubled by the feeling in this regiment. We are advised that the hydra of counter-revolution has a nest here "—(" You are a hydra yourself ! You are a *bourgeois* yourself ! Down with him ! ")—" I come to you to speak to you about the so-called Constituent Assembly. Because of its *bourgeois* and counter-revolutionary past, it decided to dissolve the Soviet Government "—(" Long live the Constituent Assembly ! Down with the Bolsheviks ! ") —" I advise you—remember—in the name of the Soviet Government that if you dare to disobey, you will be punished very severely and without mercy." (" Your hands are too short. We are not Dukhonins for you. In Semenovsky it is not so easy to threaten." " Enough ! ")

Krilenko's final words were lost in the clamour that arose from every part of the room. Going to the regimental committee, he made the following threat :—

" If the Semenovsky dare to come out [i.e. to defend the Assembly], you will be responsible. It is very dangerous to jest with me."

After Krilenko had left the meeting, a soldier spoke, amid cheers, of the necessity for the Constituent Assembly.

The S.R. war committee became aware that the Bolsheviks

# THE CONSTITUENT ASSEMBLY

intended to utilize the sailors of the 1st and 2nd Baltic squadrons in the demonstration against the Constituent Assembly. The S.R.s had a small organization among the sailors of the 2nd squadron, the chairman of the squadron committee, an intelligent sailor called Safranov, being on the side of the S.R.s. A meeting was held on January 16th, and after speeches by Safranov and others, an enthusiastic sailor leaped on to the platform and shouted :—

" Brothers, comrades, let us swear that we will not go against the people's Assembly."

" We swear ! "

" On your knees, comrades, on your knees ! "

And all these thousands of sailors knelt and shouted :—

" We swear not to go against the Constituent Assembly." (32)

This hysterical enthusiasm notwithstanding, nothing further happened. The sailors swore not to go against it—as for defending it, that was another question altogether. (33)

Among the soldiers at the front who were influenced by the S.R.s, although they were not brought to Petrograd, was the garrison of Luzhof in Kovno. Many groups in this garrison, especially the artillery, had become very anti-Bolshevik and had volunteered for the defence of the Constituent Assembly. There were two reasons why this available force was not employed. The central committee of the S.R. party had so unconquerable an aversion to the employment of force that they forbade the use of these troops (34) ; and the central committee of the Railway Workers' Union, though not in sympathy with the Bolsheviks, made difficulties about conveying the troops, on January 20th, to Petrograd for the opening of the Assembly.

Besides these activities on the part of members of the Socialist-Revolutionary party there was another form of activity more in keeping with its past history. Onepko, a courageous and venturesome man, conceived the idea in December 1917 of cutting off the leading Bolsheviks one by one. For the carrying out of his plan, he selected a small number of men who could be relied upon, not members of any one party, but all anti-Bolsheviks. On the principle that the Bolsheviks must be fought with their own weapons and that any weapon was permissible, they decided as a first step that Lenin and Trotsky should be captured, but should not be killed unless necessity arose.

At that moment the Smolny Institute was in a state of confusion, and it was easy to utilize this confusion for the furtherance of their scheme. Two of the conspirators found work in Smolny, the Bolshevik headquarters, and two others obtained employment as chauffeurs of Bolshevik motor cars. Another became *concierge*

## THE RUSSIAN REVOLUTION

of the house occupied by Lenin's sister, who was visited by Lenin nearly every day. A sixth conspirator was fortunate enough to be selected as Lenin's personal chauffeur. A similarly close web was woven around Trotsky.

The conspirators did not exaggerate the importance of the capture of a few of the leaders; they seem to have thought that the attempt would show that there were still " some people who were able to offer resistance to the conceited Bolsheviks." The plot was worked out in great detail, and it might have succeeded, had not word of it reached the ears of the central S.R. committee, and so rendered the whole affair abortive.

The point of view of the majority of the committee was that the arrest of Lenin and Trotsky would precipitate a Bolshevik reign of terror, and that, outside the Bolshevik ranks, their arrest would produce such agitation among the workmen and the soldiers that a general *pogrom* against the *intelligentsia* might follow. (35) Those who held this view pointed out that to many people Lenin and Trotsky were great popular leaders. At the election held shortly before in Petrograd, Lenin had received thousands of votes. Those members of the committee who had been subject to the process of evolution already mentioned argued that " terroristic acts are foolish; they are committed only by idiots. In Russia, now, there is no autocracy, no autocratic police force. If we allow terror against the Bolsheviks, this will be a crime—a crime which will not be forgiven for generations. It would be madness." (36)

The opposite view, that of the minority, was that they knew the Bolsheviks thoroughly, that their revolutionism and their devotion to the proletariat were mere myths. What they wanted was power at any price; they were even now making arrests right and left, and no compromise with them was possible. In the struggle " fists, feet, and teeth must be used." All means must be employed, otherwise they will win. (37)

After two months of Bolshevism, the people of Petrograd— merchants, manufacturers, financiers, working men, with all that remained of the professional classes and of the landowning aristocracy —found themselves face to face with the contingency of prolonged or permanent submission to a rule which nearly all of them loathed. The autocracy had been overthrown in February 1917; the resistance it offered was inexpressibly feeble, but the people had been united. Now, instead of combining, they argued among themselves—argued endlessly. This argumentation was most conspicuous within the political parties. Some were engaged in exhaustive studies of various kinds of constitutions, seeking to find some formula which might be adapted to the case of Russia;

# THE CONSTITUENT ASSEMBLY

others were busying themselves with conspiratorial plots for the overthrow of the Bolsheviks; one and all were talking. During the days before the opening of the Constituent Assembly, the people grew every day more and more excited, and from early morning they thronged the headquarters of the various parties. The Bolsheviks went to the Smolny Institute and the Socialist-Revolutionaries to the Litany Prospekt or to Galernya Street.

The war committee of the S.R.s arranged a programme for January 18th, when the Constituent Assembly was to open. At eight in the morning the workers in the government paper-money factory, who were extremely anti-Bolshevik, were to meet at their premises in Fontanka Street. Forces were to be mobilized and brought from the districts surrounding Petrograd by the war committee, and these people, expected to number from 8,000 to 10,000, were to march to the premises of the armoured car section of the Ismael-ovsky regiment, which was entirely in the hands of the S.R.s, the doubtful elements having been sent on holiday by the committee. There were eight or nine armoured cars available. These demonstrators were to be joined at the technological institute by a body of students, by groups from the country districts round Petrograd, and by workers from Moscow. The crowd was then to go in procession to the Semenovsky barracks, where it was to be joined by 3,000 men of the regiment with machine guns. To this company was to be added later another group of demonstrators from Vasili Island and from Viborg, who were to pass by the Preobrashensky barracks and be joined by soldiers from that regiment.

All the arrangements were made. Some of the S.R.s had high hopes of a successful issue; but others realized the difficulty of inducing the soldiers and the people to defend anything: witness the fall of the Imperial Government in February and of the Provisional Government in October. This was a case of defending the Constituent Assembly, not of attacking the Bolsheviks. The critics also urged that the two guard regiments had deteriorated, and that those who composed them had become mere adventurers.

From early morning of January 18, 1918, the streets of Petrograd were filled with people—civil servants, working men, students, and others. There was no disorder, yet an atmosphere of dissatisfaction, sullen and passive, seemed to pervade everything. One group of working people, men, women, and some children, were singing revolutionary songs, carrying red flags and banners inscribed with legends such as " Long live the Constituent Assembly," " Long live the Rights of the People." " Land and Freedom," etc. The people who were demonstrating were unarmed, for they knew that armed demonstrations were forbidden by the Bolshevik Government, and

194 THE RUSSIAN REVOLUTION

when occasionally they met a solitary Red Guard soldier, armed from head to foot, they shouted to him, " Traitor ! " The Red Guards took refuge in side streets. Near the barracks of the Petrograd regiment there was a large group of soldiers, who, rendered bold by numbers, shouted opprobrious epithets to the marching people : " You damned *bourgeois* ! " " You will catch it from Lenin ! " " You counter-revolutionaries and slaves of the *Entente* ! " and some of them threatened to fire upon the mob, but were restrained by their comrades. Except for this incident, the crowd moved quietly into the Nevsky Prospekt. Two or three patrols of the Red Guard passed without taking notice, but when the demonstration reached the Semenovsky barracks, several hundred soldiers poured out, unarmed and many of them only partially dressed. They shouted, " God help you to beat the Bolsheviks ! " " Imprison Lenin ! " " See that you defend the Constituent Assembly ! " These shouts were obviously ironical, for when the crowd appealed to the soldiers to join them, they cried, " Not allowed," nevertheless a few did fall in. When the crowd reached Litany Prospekt, it numbered about 10,000 demonstrators, with, in addition, some spectators. At this point Red Guard patrols prevented them from entering and this resistance seemed to have a bad effect on the temper of the mob. The people began to shout angrily, " Down with the Bolsheviks ! " " Down with the Soviet Government ! " " Long live the Constituent Assembly ! " Those in the rear pressed on the ranks in front of them till, the Red Guard being forced to retreat, they were enabled to surge into Litany Prospekt. A few shots were fired, and the crowd, now frightened, ran back, leaving dead and wounded on the pavement. The Red Guards who fired the shots were evidently as frightened as the mob, which, regaining courage, rushed forward, shouting, " Down with the Bolsheviks ! " " The Red patrol, formed of Red Guards, in green untidy overcoats swathed in cartridges, bristling like hedgehogs," (38) stood with a group of sailors from Kronstadt and kept back the people. They were only a few, but they had the advantage of being armed, and consequently the demonstration came to nothing.

Sokolov describes how he tried to pass to the Taurida Palace, where the Constituent Assembly was to meet. On showing his card as a member, he was allowed to go through, and when he reached the palace, he found many groups of the Red Guards, but only a few civilians in its neighbourhood.

Analysing the crowd of demonstrators and their varying moods during the forenoon of January 18, 1918, Sokolov finds it is " more than possible that only a small minority was really interested in

# THE CONSTITUENT ASSEMBLY

the Constituent Assembly. Another feeling besides favour for a democratic constitutional body dominated the crowd—that was, hatred of the Bolsheviks. This hatred had grown during the two months in which they had governed the country. The inhabitants of Petrograd, in the broad meaning of this word, were willing to abandon pacifism and to march with the Constituent Assembly, provided it could find in itself enough power to dissolve the Bolshevist Government. At that time they had hopes of democracy and were ready to follow the democrats so far as might be convenient for them, sustained by extravagant notions about the power of the Constituent Assembly. We (the Socialist-Revolutionaries) could not utilize the attitude of the people of Petrograd. We could not drive them against the Bolshevist movement." (39)

At noon the Bolsheviks attacked a group formed for the defence of the Assembly, and many persons were killed. Thus, before the meetings began, they had evidently made up their minds to deal with the Assembly by force, and to run no risk of incurring popular disapproval, through criticism of its proceedings in a public body not directly under Bolshevik control.

At four o'clock of the same afternoon the Assembly met at the Taurida Palace. (40) There were two candidates for the presidency, Victor Chernov, the Socialist-Revolutionary who had been a member of the Provisional Government, a well-known writer upon agrarian questions and author of the legislation which in effect confirmed the seizures of land by the peasants, and Marie Spiridovna, the Bolshevik candidate.

Chernov was elected by a large majority. In his opening address he said that at Brest-Litovsk the Germans attempted to conclude a peace at the expense of Russia. The Bolsheviks moved a resolution to the effect that the working classes should be armed and all other classes disarmed. This resolution was rejected, and after violent scenes the Bolshevik members of the Assembly left the hall. (41) Defeated in the election of the president and in their test resolution, the Bolsheviks evidently made up their minds that since in every important vote they would be in a minority, they would best serve their own interests by putting an end to the Assembly.

The character of the Assembly had now become apparent. It was dominated by the Right Socialist-Revolutionaries, who had become parliamentarists. They were joined by the *Chernovtsi*, or adherents of Chernov, who, although they leaned to the Left, especially on agrarian questions, owing to their having undergone a process of evolution similar to that of the Right faction, had also become parliamentarists. The majority of the deputies shared the parliamentary views of these two groups about the functions

## THE RUSSIAN REVOLUTION

of the Constituent Assembly. They all regarded it as the single and appropriate arena in which the difference between the Bolshevik and the other parties could be threshed out. Any method in which violence interfered with the freedom of decision by the representatives of the people was inconceivable to them. At the same time there seems to have grown up in the minds of the parties hostile to Bolshevism a repugnance to " adventurism," it being regarded as a crime against the people of which the Bolsheviks were held guilty. All that savoured of " adventurism " must therefore be avoided. The Bolsheviks had seized power and had overthrown the Provisional Government, but power ought now to be taken from them, because they had shown themselves unworthy of its exercise ; but not by the same methods as they had employed to acquire it ; the process must be absolutely lawful. Some of the deputies put the case in this way : " We must defend the right by the only way permissible to the representatives of the people—the way of parliament. . . . We have had enough of blood, enough of adventurism." (42)

Victor Chernov seems to have imagined that not only was it impossible for the Bolsheviks to refuse the forms and the decisions of the Constituent Assembly, but that they would embrace the opportunity of advancing at least a plausible plea for their retention in power by the people. He may even have thought that they could make out so good a case that their seizure of power might have been homologated by the Assembly. Chernov was strongly opposed to civil war, and for that reason refused to take part in active measures for the defence of the Assembly. A small group, an insignificant minority, had other views : they looked upon the " strict parliamentarists " as occupying the same naïve position as the Bolsheviks when *vis-à-vis* with the Germans at Brest-Litovsk. The Germans had no intention of abandoning any advantages that the campaign had given them : and the Soviet Government had no alternative but to accept the peace given them by the conquerors. The Assembly was so situated that without an armed force to give it a position of military supremacy there was not the slightest hope of inducing the Bolsheviks to abandon their strategic advantage and to accept a subordinate *rôle*.

About four o'clock in the afternoon of January 18th the elected members made their way to the Taurida Palace. At the doors of the white salon there were armed sailors on guard. The members who had arrived had already passed to the floor of the hall, and the gallery was full of the " invited," who were admitted by cards issued by the Bolshevik commander. These consisted of workmen, sailors from Kronstadt, soldiers from different regiments, and some of the Red Guard. They occupied a position which com-

# THE CONSTITUENT ASSEMBLY

manded the rest of the hall and they were all armed. But the " invited " were not only in the gallery, they swarmed over the building, passing from one buffet to another, drinking, or sleeping off their carousal on sofas. This miscellaneous crowd cannot be supposed to have had any serious interest in constitutional questions, yet their presence there was a determining factor in the course of events. They had been promised food, drink, and perhaps money. The Socialist-Revolutionaries say that they were also promised an opportunity to " play with " the elected members of the Assembly—in plain language, to massacre them. To prove this would be difficult ; anyway, there was no massacre, although the members evidently expected to be fired upon from the gallery.

All the afternoon the Bolshevik members held a separate preliminary conference in another room, and the five hundred odd anti-Bolshevik members were kept waiting. Meanwhile there were jeers from the " invited " in the gallery.

" Lenin will send his orders. Till then sit down quietly." (43) It became apparent that the Bolsheviks were endeavouring to gain time. The demonstration in the streets had been successfully diverted ; the regiments did not join the demonstrators ; and the inhabitants in general went peacefully about their business. Only a few were killed or wounded, there was no public excitement, and as no force existed adequate to defend the Constituent Assembly, there need be no disguise or delay in putting an end to it.

The All-Russian Constituent Assembly at last opened its first and only sitting. The noise from the gallery was so insistent and continuous that little could be heard when the speakers mounted the tribune. Tseretelli, Victor Chernov, and others spoke, but what they said was lost in a clamour of inarticulate noise, while rifles were aimed from the gallery, threatening at any moment a fusillade—like a chorus in a savage drama.

Chernov, the president, read fast and indistinctly a prepared declaration or manifesto ; Lenin, who had been present, had gone, and the Bolshevik faction left their seats, and from the gallery there poured down the " invited," who took the vacant places without ceremony. Somehow or other, in this chaos and hubbub, resolutions were made and passed, important steps were apparently taken, carefully prepared drafts of laws were read, but there could be no real discussion or argument of any kind.

Then came a sinister rumour that the " invited " were going to " put out the lights and kill." Murmurs were heard : " How soon ? It is time to dissolve these *bourgeois*." " Patience, comrades ! Wait for orders."

A sailor approached Victor Chernov and spoke to him in a

## THE RUSSIAN REVOLUTION

whisper; no one else heard, but Chernov was visibly perturbed. A feeling of tension diffused itself quickly, and the members rose in their places. The hour was five o'clock in the morning of January 19th. Soldiers and sailors rapidly filled the great hall, clearly all was over, and the members marched out of the white salon in a body to the accompaniment of derisive jeers from drunken sailors. (44) The brief career of the long-desired Constituent Assembly had come to an ignominious conclusion.

On the night of January 18th the two regiments which had taken upon themselves the responsibility of publishing *The Grey Cloak* refused to act, (45) and at daybreak the printing-office was occupied by a strong force of sailors at the same moment as a similar force was putting an end to the Constituent Assembly. During the following days many meetings were held in the factories and barracks. These meetings were promoted by the Bolsheviks, and, with rare exceptions, none but Bolsheviks were permitted to address them. At the Franco-Russian factory, whilst Zinoviev was speaking, Sokolov ventured to dispute with him, and although Sokolov was well known to the workers, they listened to him with reluctance and gave him little attention.

On January 19th the Ismaelovsky regiment held a meeting. The Bolsheviks were received with loud and continuous applause, and no others attempted to speak. Had they done so, they would not have been given a hearing. On the same day there was a meeting of the Preobrashensky regiment, and there also the soldiers listened patiently to long, plausible speeches by Bolsheviks, to whom previously they would not have paid attention. The regimental committee was at a loss what to do. " Who will now give peace to the people ? "  " Who will give the soil to the people ? "  " Why did nobody defend the Constituent Assembly ? "

At a meeting in the Franco-Russian factory, held on the same day, and organized by the Bolsheviks, a resolution was passed approving of the dissolution of the Assembly, and only two of the Socialist-Revolutionary deputies who were present thought it necessary to interpose objections. (46)

On January 19th, in the government paper-money factory, (47) a meeting was held in which the workers were present in the same numbers as at the meeting of three or four days earlier. Then the Bolsheviks had regarded the factory as " a nest of small *bourgeois* and counter-revolutionaries," while the workers had regarded the Bolsheviks with distrust and dislike. The temper of the workers had changed since then. The Constituent Assembly had not been able to defend itself against the Bolsheviks, and the defenders had been shot down, although they knew that the Constituent Assembly

# THE CONSTITUENT ASSEMBLY 199

had been elected by the people by means of a popular vote. Thus the workmen realized that the Bolsheviks were to be reckoned with, and they listened silently and morosely to what they had to say. The minds of these workers seemed to change quickly. Formerly they hated the Bolsheviks and their methods, and worshipped democracy, regarding the Constituent Assembly, elected by popular suffrage, as the ideal political mechanism for discovering the people's will. Now all these enthusiasms were abandoned. (48) Many workmen had taken service under the Bolshevik Government after the October Revolution, and even before the European War the state paper-money factory was looked upon as a nest of Bolshevism. The Bolsheviks had thus a hold of long standing upon certain important groups of workmen. When the workers in general realized that the Bolsheviks were victorious, they argued that there must be a solid foundation to their political and economic position, otherwise they would not have conquered so easily.

Soon after the dissolution of the Assembly a regiment of Red Guards surrounded the high school in which the soldiers' university was installed, and also the Red Cross building in Fontanka Street where the soldier-students lived. They arrested them all and had them disarmed and imprisoned. (49) So rapidly did opinion change during the confusion of the winter of 1917–1918, that some of the volunteers from the front who had joined the force raised by the Socialist-Revolutionaries for the defence of the Constituent Assembly, and who had lived in this soldiers' university, afterwards enlisted in the Red Army and came to be among its most active officers. The dissolution of the Assembly had a peculiar reaction upon them. They blamed, not the Bolsheviks who dissolved it, but the Socialist-Revolutionaries who had permitted them to dissolve it, and it was in this mood that many of them became Bolsheviks. (50)

At the meetings of which an account has been given, even those who had been favourable to the Constituent Assembly were inclined to blame the defenders of it for their want of success. The Bolsheviks must be right because they were victorious. The inhabitants of Petrograd in general seemed to look upon the Constituent Assembly as a savage looks upon his fetish. He worships it so long as he attributes power to it ; but no sooner does it appear to lack that power than the savage destroys and tramples upon his former idol. This primitive attitude seemed to be characteristic of the Russian people at that time. To them the Constituent Assembly had been long anticipated, and they attributed to it miraculous powers. When it met, all the difficult political and social problems which had arisen in acute forms would forthwith be settled. The will of the people was to be announced in the speeches of persons delegated by the

## 200 THE RUSSIAN REVOLUTION

whole population from every part of Russia. The Bolshevik Government with its passion for Soviets was a temporary affair. The Constituent Assembly would decide how many, if any, of its projects should be carried into effect, and who, if any, of its leaders should be permitted to form part of the new government. To them the Assembly was an objective, autonomous body, which had to vindicate its existence and justify their confidence. Although they wished it well, and wanted no one to interfere with it, its defence was not their affair ; it must be powerful enough to look after itself ; if not, it was not strong enough to be of any service to them. Thus the Assembly was to blame for its own downfall, and those who attempted to defend it were people of inferior judgment, who had been defeated.

Until the night of January 18, 1918, the Bolsheviks were insecure in the saddle. They were afraid to do many things lest their seat should be upset. With the dawn of January 19th the sky brightened for them. Henceforth they felt themselves safely established, and realized that they could go back to Brest-Litovsk and make what kind of peace they liked : no one in Russia would blame them or dispute with them ; if anyone presumed to do so, they were in every respect sufficiently powerful to ignore or deal with such opposition.

---

### NOTES

(1) Cf. Mavor, J., *An Economic History of Russia*, vol. ii, p. 19.

(2) An elected body analogous to a parliament.

(3) *Narodnaya Volya*, No. 2 (1879), reprinted in *Literature of the Social-Revolutionary Party : Narodnoe Vole* (Paris, 1905), (in Russian). (Cf. Mavor, J., *An Economic History of Russia*, vol. ii, p. 117.

(4) Mavor, J., op. cit., vol. ii, p. 185.

(5) Sokolov, Boris, op. cit., p. 28.

(6) Not so very uncommon in Russia.

(7) Sokolov, Boris, op. cit., p. 29.

(8) Voronovich, N., op. cit., p. 72. Voronovich goes on to point out that when the Bolsheviks dissolved the Constituent Assembly the party leaders " X and Y " were arrested and ill-treated, and no public interest was excited about them.

(9) On December 16, 1917 (*Chron. de la Guerre*, 7e vol., p. 246).

(10) Sokolov, Boris, op. cit., pp. 26–27.

(11) Ibid., op. cit., p. 28.

(12) Ibid., loc. cit.

(13) Ibid., op. cit., p. 32.

(14) For an account of the Social Democratic party in 1905–1907, see Mavor, J., op. cit., vol. ii, book vii, passim.

(15) None of this group had been very prominent in party circles. The names of some of them were D. Surguchev (later shot by the Bolsheviks), Fortunatov, Sergius Maslov (a member of the Central Communist party), Onepko, and Boris Sokolov. (Cf. Sokolov, Boris, op. cit., p. 33.)

(16) They called it after the revolutionary fashion " going on the floor " (Sokolov, Boris, loc. cit.).

(17) Sokolov, Boris, op. cit., p. 33.

# THE CONSTITUENT ASSEMBLY

(18) Ibid., op. cit., p. 34, and cf. infra, p. 197.

(19) Kuzmin's statement was made "much later" to Sokolov (cf. Sokolov, Boris, op. cit., 41).

(20) Sokolov, Boris, op. cit., p. 41.

(21) For the names of some of the members of this committee, see above, p. 137.

(22) Thought to have been shot by the Bolsheviks.

(23) The above details are from Sokolov, Boris, op. cit., pp. 42–43.

(24) *Chron. de la Guerre*, 8e vol., p. 27.

(25) Ibid.

(26) Sokolov, Boris, op. cit., p. 44. The number of workmen in the factory at this time is not stated. There were probably several hundred.

(27) Sokolov, Boris, op. cit., p. 45.

(28) Ibid., op. cit., p. 51.

(29) Alexander Peterson Smirnov (otherwise known as "Thomas" and as "Isbetkow") was a peasant of the *gub* of Tver. In 1899 he joined the revolutionary labour movements in St. Petersburg, afterwards moving to Nijni Novgorod, and subsequently returning to Tver. In 1910 he was in the Moscow organization, and at the end of that year he was arrested and sentenced to three years' banishment from Moscow (Spiridovich, A. E., op. cit., p. 239).

(30) Sokolov, Boris, op. cit., p. 51.

(31) Afterwards these workers said "nobody dissolved the Constituent Assembly ! It dissolved itself. The Bolsheviks did not need to do it" (Sokolov, Boris, op. cit., p. 52).

(32) Sokolov, Boris, op. cit., p. 54.

(33) These sailors kept their word and did not join with those who afterwards attacked the Assembly (cf. Sokolov, Boris, loc. cit.). " Soon moved to be moody, and as soon moody at being moved."

(34) Sokolov says that he cannot explain the precise motives for this attitude of the central S.R. committee. He suggests that the desire to keep the army out of politics, and to avoid bloodshed, and doubt of the success of the " adventure " may have impelled the opposition to the enterprise (cf. Sokolov, Boris, op. cit., p. 46).

(35) Notwithstanding the abandonment of the plot, the general *pogrom* against the *intelligentsia* followed in due course.

(36) Sokolov, Boris, op. cit., p. 48.

(37) Ibid.

(38) The above description is from Sokolov, Boris, op. cit., pp. 62–65.

(39) Sokolov, Boris, op. cit., pp. 65–66.

(40) The election had taken place in November. The total vote cast was 36,357,960. The Socialist-Revolutionaries polled 20,893,734, the Bolsheviks 9,023,963, and other parties 6,340,263. The elected members were Bolsheviks 168 ; anti-Bolsheviks 535.

(41) For a description of these scenes, see L. Naudeau in *Le Temps* (Paris), April 14, 1918.

(42) Sokolov, Boris, op. cit., p. 32.

(43) Ibid., op. cit., p. 67.

(44) Descriptions of the scene by participants and eyewitnesses are to be found, e.g., in the account by L. Naudeau in *Le Temps* (Paris), April 14, 1918 ; and in the account of Sokolov, Boris, in *Archives of the Russian Revolution* (Berlin, 1924), vol. xiii, pp. 66–68. The description in the text is chiefly drawn from the account of Sokolov.

(45) Sokolov, Boris, op. cit., p. 35.

(46) The motives of this inaction have not yet been explained (cf. Sokolov, Boris, op. cit., p. 43).

(47) About 10,000 persons were employed in this factory at the time.

(48) Sokolov, Boris, op. cit., p. 51.

(49) Ibid., op. cit., p. 45.

(50) Ibid.

# CHAPTER VIII

## BREST-LITOVSK

THE negotiations at Brest-Litovsk opened on December 3rd. After a formal reception by Prince Leopold of Bavaria, commander-in-chief of the eastern front, the following remained for the discussion of peace terms : for Germany, General Hoffmann, chief-of-staff on the eastern front, with five other officers ; for Austria-Hungary, Lt.-Col. Hermann Pokorny with three other officers ; for Bulgaria, Col. Gantchev and a legal assistant ; and for Turkey, General Tsekki Pasha, with both an *aide-de-camp* and a legal assistant. Representing Russia there were nine civil-military delegates and nine others, including one sailor, one soldier, one peasant, and one workman, with three legal and seven other assistants, (1) and the delegation was headed by A. A. Ioffé.

The Russians opened with their formula, " Peace without annexations or indemnities and the right to national self-determination." They also proposed to negotiate an armistice " on all fronts " and " for all armies," irrespective of the representation or otherwise of these armies at the conference. The purport of the German reply is contained in a semi-official telegram : (2) " We could not accept this proposal, as neither were Russia's allies represented nor had the Russian delegates been empowered to speak on their behalf. We therefore agreed to restrict the negotiations to the conclusion of an armistice between the allied armies of the Central Powers and the Russian army. The Russians then expressly emphasized that the object of the armistice should be an immediate entry into nogotiations for a general peace between all the belligerents. The allied [Central Powers] plenipotentiaries took cognizance of this statement with satisfaction, but it was impossible immediately to enter upon the discussion of peace terms, as the credentials of neither party sufficed for that purpose."

After a long discussion, the Russians were compelled to confine the negotiations to purely military questions. Next day (December 4th) they produced their project of an armistice. In effect this amounted to a suspension of hostilities for six months with seventy-two hours' notice of resumption, prevention of the movement of troops to or from the front, and evacuation of the islands in the Baltic which had been occupied by the German navy. In exchange the Russians offered nothing.

# BREST-LITOVSK

This peculiarly oriental style of bargaining did not deceive the Germans. The German account remarks that the Russian " conditions were in part quite astonishingly extravagant in view of their military situation." (3) A truce of ten days from December 7th was arranged however by mutual consent as a preliminary. On December 5th the Russians, in addition to the evacuation of the islands in the Moon Sound, (4) proposed that the Central Powers be interdicted from sending forces from the Russian front to other fronts. The Germans very naturally declared " that such demands could be addressed only to a conquered country." (5) The Russians replied that their task consisted in drawing all belligerent countries into the negotiations for the purpose of securing a general peace. The Germans on their part refused to negotiate, and the proceedings accordingly came to a deadlock, and were temporarily suspended for a week, during which some of the Russians were to return to Petrograd for consultation. On December 6th Trotsky sent a note to all the allied embassies and legations calling upon the allied governments to define their attitude towards " the peace negotiations. . . . In case of a refusal, they must declare clearly and definitely, before all mankind, the aims for which the peoples of Europe may have to shed their blood during a fourth year of war." (6) Plenary sittings of the commission were resumed on December 13th, and on December 15th an armistice was signed. By one of the clauses (clause 9) of this treaty, negotiations for peace were to begin immediately after the signing of the armistice.

On December 22nd Baron von Kühlmann, German secretary of state for foreign affairs, Count Czernin, Austro-Hungarian minister of foreign affairs, M. Popoff, Bulgarian minister of justice, with numerous staffs, arrived at Brest-Litovsk. Representing Russia there were A. A. Ioffé, Kamenev, (7) Mme. Bitsenko, (8) Pokrovsky, (9) Karakhan, and others, whilst Nessimy Bey, minister of foreign affairs, appeared for Turkey.

The first Peace Conference, which was destined to bring the war on one front to a conclusion, had at last met to consider the terms of a treaty. There could be no doubt of the necessity of peace for Russia ; her people were thoroughly beaten and they would fight no more, so at least they and everyone else thought in December 1917.

On the other hand, Austria-Hungary was exhausted. Hunger riots were occurring in Vienna, (10) and unless supplies of grain were quickly forthcoming, the prosecution of the war appeared to be impossible. The increasing weakness of Austria rendered an immediate cessation of hostilities scarcely less necessary for Germany, for Austria might throw herself at any moment upon the mercy of the *Entente* and sue for a separate peace.

## THE RUSSIAN REVOLUTION

The U-boat campaign had reached the height of its success and had begun to decline, and the pressure of the blockade was beginning to strangle the German people. To make peace with Russia, throw a hundred and fifty or more additional German divisions on to the lines in France, seize Paris and Calais, force a decision, and end the war victoriously—that was the plan. (11) As Hindenburg says, " Could any notion be more obvious than that of bringing all our effective troops from the east to the west and then taking the offensive ? " (12) And Czernin remarks, " The end of the war in the east was within sight, and the possibility of being able to fling the enormous masses of troops from the east into the line in the west, and at least break through there, greatly improved the situation." (13)

But this great improvement depended first upon " the end of the war in the east." From the Austrian point of view, " Peace at the earliest moment is necessary for our own salvation, and we cannot obtain peace unless the Germans get to Paris—and they cannot get to Paris unless their eastern front is freed. That is the circle complete." (14)

Inexperienced as they were in international affairs except from their own sectarian point of view, the Bolshevik leaders were not unaware of the broad facts of the military and political situation of the Central Powers at that moment. Therefore, although Russia herself was in an even more parlous state, they astutely determined to assume a truculent demeanour instead of suing abjectly for peace. (15) They went to Brest-Litovsk with an ostentatious air of conferring an inestimable benefit upon all mankind, and presented a catalogue of demands, sufficiently formidable for a people not only beaten in the field, but dispirited and demoralized, politically, socially, and economically :—

1. Union by violence of territories conquered during the war will not be tolerated. Troops in occupied territories to evacuate them within a short time.
2. Restoration of political independence of people who have been deprived of their independence during the war.
3. Groups of different nationalities which did not enjoy independence before the war, shall have guaranteed to them the right of deciding by means of a referendum the question of whether they shall belong to one State or another, or shall enjoy national independence. . . .
4. In territories inhabited by different nationalities, the rights of minorities shall be guaranteed, with special rights of national independence regarding culture and administrative autonomy.

# BREST-LITOVSK

5. No belligerent country shall pay an indemnity. In regard to so-called costs of war, payments already made shall be returned. As for indemnities levied upon private persons, special funds shall be constituted by proportional payments from all belligerent countries.

6. Colonial questions shall be settled in conformity with the first, second, and fourth clauses.

The Russian delegation also denounced as " intolerable " any restriction of the liberty of weaker by stronger nations, as, for instance, by an economic boycott, by the subjection of one country to another by means of commercial treaties, or by separate customs conventions hindering freedom of commerce with a third country.

The gist of the matter was the project of a general peace, with behind it, the design of a series of civil wars to eliminate nationalism, and to establish some form of universal communism.

It soon became evident that the Bolsheviks intended to exploit the Peace Conference and to utilize Brest-Litovsk as a conspicuous platform by means of which they might draw to themselves and their ultimate plans the attention of the workers of the world.

A project of a general peace, by whomsoever it was advanced, and by whatsoever fantastic arguments it was supported, might, by means of skilful diplomacy, be manœuvred into an attractive form. The experiment was worth trying; Trotsky might succeed where the Pope had failed;(16) in any case there was the publicity.

Count Czernin, who had been for some time coquetting with peace manœuvres to the embarrassment of the German General Staff,(17) went to Brest-Litovsk with the definite intention of supporting the Russian proposal. (18) But his chief anxiety was for such a peace as would most certainly enable Austria to get from the Ukraine the grain of which she stood in such sore need, the Hungarian supplies being insufficient. (19) At the session held on Christmas Day 1917, Count Czernin spoke in the name of the Quadruple Alliance.(20) He said that the Powers he represented had already clearly expressed their desire to reach as soon as possible a general and just peace, without forcible acquisitions of territory and without indemnities. When the Russian delegation condemned a war prosecuted only for purposes of conquest, the delegations of the Allies (the Central Powers) were in accord with this view. The statesmen of the Allies had repeatedly emphasized that they would not prolong the war a single day in order to make conquests. He declared that the Quadruple Alliance was willing to end the war on such a basis with the same " just conditions " for all the belligerent Powers. But he pointed out expressly that, if

## THE RUSSIAN REVOLUTION

the expectations of the Russian *exposé* were to be fulfilled, all the Powers now participating in the war must within a suitable period, without exception and without any reserve, guarantee their strict adherence to conditions binding all nations in the same manner.

Count Czernin then went on to deal with the six points elaborated by the Russian delegation. He disclaimed any intention on the part of the Quadruple Alliance to appropriate forcibly occupied territories, or to deprive of independence any State which had lost its independence temporarily during the war. The question of state allegiance of national groups must, he said, be regulated as between States, the rights of minorities must be respected, neither war indemnities nor war damages should be imposed, and colonies which had been taken in the war must be returned.

The Russian delegation noticed the reservation on the third point, i.e. the question of States not now independent, but members of groups of States ; and it emphasized the need of indemnification for the support of prisoners of war, and for the creation of an international fund for the compensation of private persons who had suffered from acts of war. (21)

In the session of December 28th the German delegation proposed to give the following form to the two first articles of the preliminary treaty :—

(1) Russia and Germany are to declare the state of war at an end. Both nations are resolved to live together in peace and friendship. On the condition of complete reciprocity *vis-à-vis* her allies, Germany would be ready, as soon as peace is concluded with Russia and the demobilization of the Russian armies has been accomplished, to evacuate her present positions and occupied Russian territory, in so far as no different inferences result from Art. 2.

(2) The Russian Government, having in accordance with its principles proclaimed for all peoples, without exception, living within the Russian Empire the right of self-determination, including complete separation, takes cognizance of the decision which expresses the will of the people, who demand full state independence and separation from the Russian Empire for Poland, Lithuania, Courland and portions of Esthonia, and Livonia. The Russian Government recognizes that in the present circumstances these manifestations must be regarded as the expression of the will of the people, and is ready to draw conclusions therefrom. As in those districts to which the foregoing stipula-

## BREST-LITOVSK

tions apply, the question of evacuation is not such as is provided for in Art. 1, a special commission shall discuss the already existing proclamations of separation, and fix the time and other details in conformity with the Russian idea of the necessary ratification by plebiscite, on broad lines, and without any military pressure whatever.

The intention of these provisions is obvious. Germany held Poland and the Baltic Provinces of Russia, and had her hand also on Finland. In the strict interpretation of the Russian conditions, these regions would be simply handed back forthwith to Soviet Russia. Such an arrangement was out of the question ; but Germany wished to prepare the way for an eventual demand for the restitution of her colonies, and therefore by some means the principle of no annexations must be adhered to in the case of the Russian territories. If the clearly expressed opinions of the people of the countries in question could be relied upon, reunion with Russia seemed unlikely. There was therefore small risk in leaving the occupied regions to determine their own destiny.

Radoslavov announced (December 27th) in the Bulgarian *Sobranje* that peace had been concluded between Russia and Bulgaria on the basis of the *status quo ante*. (22)

The Bolsheviks having occupied all the banks in Petrograd (December 28th), combined these into one—the Bank of the Russian People. (23)

The Moldavian Republic was proclaimed by Bessarabia (December 29th). Turkestan proclaimed itself autonomous. A Siberian Confederation was proclaimed at Tomsk. (24) A decree was issued at Moscow declaring the municipalization of all immovable property. (25)

During December 1917 the Russian front had been preserved after a fashion. There were desertions and much fraternization, but the lines were still formally held. The Germans withdrew troops from time to time and held their lines in a similarly formal fashion. In the last days of December the Russian troops on the Riga front disbanded themselves *en masse*. (26)

Trotsky showed a keen appreciation of the fact that unless the Bolsheviks acquired control of Poland and the Baltic Provinces, these regions would be politically a menace to any Soviet Government. The standard of education and of political development in the Baltic Provinces was so much higher than in Russia in general that, under the circumstances of the time, had the former political unity been maintained, All-Russia must have been dominated by Poland, Finland, the Baltic Provinces of Courland, Esthonia, and

## THE RUSSIAN REVOLUTION

Latvia, and perhaps also to some extent by Georgia. Thus, although Trotsky was not himself a Russian, he was fighting for what he considered the interest of the *mujik*—viz. the unity of the Russian system, but the subordination of the intelligent elements of the westernized regions in case these should overwhelm the east.

The discussions at Brest-Litovsk have an air of unreality. If on one side there were experienced diplomatists like Count Czernin, on the other hand inexperienced negotiators like Ioffé were not less skilful in masking their designs with plausible phrases. Germany had no idea of giving up Belgium unless she could bargain, with it in hand, for the return of her colonies. Austria had the nightmare of the resolutions of the London Conference (27) always looming before her eyes, yet neither was willing to give back a foot of territory to Soviet Russia and thus so far admit a principle. The Russian habit of laying down principles and of insisting that their opponents should adhere to them was extremely inconvenient, and was not mitigated by the fact that there was from the beginning a very reasonable doubt that the Russians would abide by their own principles, or that there was any feasible method of compelling them to do so. Later events showed that the Bolsheviks cared nothing for self-determination except in so far as they themselves were concerned, and that for them the rights of minorities had no existence.

The sessions of the conference were adjourned until January 4, 1918. Meanwhile the Russians, pursuing the policy of making a sort of peace offensive, proposed to transfer the *locus* of the conference to Stockholm. The object of this manœuvre seems to have been to obtain a more public platform and to ensure that wider interest should be taken in the proceedings by the international press, so that the tenets of Bolshevism might be promulgated more effectively than was possible from Brest-Litovsk. The German and Austrian diplomatists cared nothing for publicity, and the dread that the *Entente* Powers might in some manner interfere led them to insist that the sessions be resumed at Brest-Litovsk. (28)

But the Russian delegation was reluctant to return to that place. Undoubtedly the delegates were convinced that they had made no progress whatever towards the conclusion of peace. They had probably expected the Germans and Austrians to debate their principles with them, and they were astonished at the polite acquiescence, without debate, of Count Czernin. They did not realize that acquiescence was a mere *façon de parler*.

Meanwhile an event occurred which had not apparently been anticipated by the Bolsheviks. The Ukrainian *Rada*, in spite of the prevailing doubt of its validity, had sent a delegation on

## BREST-LITOVSK

its own account to Brest-Litovsk to discuss terms of peace for the Ukraine, and this delegation had been welcomed by Germany and Austria.

The Ukrainian representatives arrived on January 3, 1918. On January 8th the Germans announced from Berlin that the negotiations with Soviet Russia had been " temporarily broken off." On January 5th the representatives of the Quadruple Alliance had returned to Brest-Litovsk and had telegraphed inviting the Soviet representatives to come there. They arrived two days later, to the great relief of the Germans. (29) The negotiations with the Ukrainians had been going on since January 4th. Either because he was dissatisfied with the conduct of affairs by Ioffé or for some other reason, Trotsky, commissar for foreign affairs, arrived as the new head of the delegation. A German officer, Captain Baron Lamezan, who had been sent to Dünaburg to escort Trotsky and his colleagues to Brest, reported that the trenches before Dünaburg were deserted, and that at many stations people were waiting for the delegates to demand that they should make peace. As they proceeded on their journey, Trotsky became more and more depressed. Lamezan thought that this was due to his conviction that there was no choice save that between a bad peace and no peace at all, and that in either case the Bolsheviks would be swept away. (30) If this was a correct diagnosis of Trotsky's state of mind at that time, and possibly it was, his fears were groundless, because the Bolsheviks survived even the bad peace. They might not have done so, however, had the *Entente* Powers not won the war and so nullified Brest-Litovsk.

Count Czernin's impression of Trotsky was as follows : " An interesting, clever fellow, and a very dangerous adversary. He is quite exceptionally gifted as a speaker, with a swiftness and adroitness in retort which I have rarely seen, and has, moreover, all the insolent boldness of his race." In general, Count Czernin calls the Bolsheviks " brutal tyrants, autocrats of the worst kind, a disgrace to the name of freedom." (31)

At the first session after the vacation, January 10th, Trotsky " made a great and, in its way, a really fine speech, calculated for the whole of Europe, in which he gave way entirely. He accepts, he says, the German-Austrian ' ultimatum ' . . . as he will not give us the satisfaction of being able to blame Russia for the continuation of the war." (32)

" We," Trotsky concluded, " think it our duty to the peoples and armies of all countries to make a fresh effort to establish clearly and distinctly here at the headquarters of the eastern front, whether immediate peace with the Quadruple Alliance is possible without

O

violence to the Poles, Lithuanians, Letts, Esthonians, Armenians, and other nationalities to whom the Russian Revolution assures on its side full right to free development without reservation, without restriction, without *arrière pensée*." (33)

In subsequent discussions Trotsky dilated at great length upon a puzzling topic—the means which a people, stripped bare of political institutions, should adopt in order to acquire others. Von Kühlmann made the obvious suggestion that there is no need to strip the people in the first instance, and that the new political institutions may be suffered to grow out of those that exist. But to Trotsky this was not the revolutionary way.

The appropriate revolutionary method, surely the obvious one under existing conditions, was to allow the community, whatever it might be, to find its own administrative organ, by taking a known form or inventing a new one. If it cannot do either, then its self-determination is a meaningless phrase. Trotsky, however, did not suggest this method. He proposed rather vaguely, although he may simply have had the Soviet in his mind, the formation of a provisional organ by which the process of election for the permanent administrative system might be devised. Von Kühlmann repeatedly inquired by whom this provisional organ should be appointed. Trotsky objected to appointment by an alien Power whose troops were in occupation, but he refrained from stating positively what was clearly in his mind, that the appointment of such a provisional organ should be practically in the hands of the Soviet Government. The discussion was for the most part in general terms, but the special application was to the cases of Esthonia and Courland.

In his references to questions of theory, Trotsky is rarely lucid and sometimes almost unintelligible. (34) Only when he descends to concrete cases is he really forcible. " Do you agree to evacuate Poland, Lithuania, and Courland and to leave the people freedom of decision ? Do you renounce the idea of tearing away these territories [i.e. from Soviet Russia], of imposing military and customs conventions upon them, and of establishing a monarchical government on the strength of the decision of little groups of exploiters ? (35) There must be self-determination," he said ; " but this principle applies to the peoples themselves and not to certain privileged parts of them." He therefore rejected the view that the will of " an occupied district has been expressed by *de facto* plenipotentiary bodies." (36) Baron von Kühlmann summed up the discussion thus :— (37)

" M. Trotsky proposed the establishment of representative bodies which should be entrusted with the organization and fixing of methods of procedure under which popular votes, or popular

## BREST-LITOVSK

manifestations, which were for the time being conceded by us only in theory, shall follow on a broad basis ; while we take, and must take, the standpoint that in the absence of other representative bodies, the existing bodies, which have become historical, are the presumptive expression of the people's will, especially in the vital question of a nation's will to be a nation." (38)

Trotsky's points were embodied in a memorandum which drew from General Hoffmann a sharp rebuke. " The Russian delegation talks to us as if it stood victorious in our countries and could dictate conditions to us. I would like to point out that the facts are just the reverse : that the victorious German army stands in your territory. . . . The Russian delegation demands for the occupied territories the application of a right of self-determination of peoples in a manner, and to an extent, which its government does not apply to its own country. Its government is founded purely on force, which ruthlessly suppresses all who think otherwise. Anyone with different views is simply declared an outlaw, as a counter-revolutionary and *bourgeois*. I will only substantiate my view by two examples. During the night of December 30th the first White Russian Congress at Minsk, which desired to put into force the right of self-determination of the White Russian people, was broken up by Maximalists [Bolsheviks] with bayonet and machine gun. Again, when the Ukrainians claimed their right of self-determination, the Petrograd government sent an ultimatum and endeavoured to carry out their will by force of arms. As far as I can make out from wireless messages here before me, civil war is still in progress. Thus do the Maximalists apply in practice the right of self-determination." (39)

Trotsky's reply to this outburst was to the effect that the White Russian Congress was composed of agrarians, and that " if it met with resistance, that resistance originated with the soldiers." He said also that the conflict between the Petrograd government and the Ukraine did not affect the question of self-determination, and this at least cannot be regarded as a candid statement.

In its formal reply to General Hoffmann's observation that the Russian Government was based on force, the Russian delegation remarked, " throughout the whole of history no other kind of government has been known." (40)

The note of the Central Powers, read at the sitting of January 14, 1918, by von Kühlmann, secretary of state, (41) in dealing with the question of the individuality of States, particularly in relation to those newly erected, which had formerly been portions of the Russian Empire, referred to a decision of the supreme court of the United States in the year 1808 regarding the date upon which

## THE RUSSIAN REVOLUTION

the independence of the constituent States became effective. This decision was that they became effective on the Declaration of Independence in 1776, not on the recognition of independence by Great Britain in 1782.

Trotsky, in replying to this, made the ingenious observation that "legal philosophy plays a very subordinate *rôle* in deciding the destiny of peoples." (42) He also pointed out that, in the present case, it was of greater importance to quote the opinions of the English jurists who deduced from English law "the right to keep the American colonies in their hands," i.e. in the hands of Great Britain, than to quote from the decisions of the supreme court which "has frequently modified the interpretation of its legal philosophy according to the necessity or otherwise of extending United States territory."

In his answer von Kühlmann very naturally drew attention to Trotsky's depreciation of the highest court of the United States. (43)

At the sitting of January 15th Trotsky proposed that representatives of the new States be allowed to participate in the negotiations—certainly a logical consequence of the principle of self-determination. Baron von Kühlmann at once agreed, "but only on condition that the appearance of the representatives should be regarded as indicating at least a presumptive recognition by the Russian Government of their position as States." Trotsky refused to recognize the representatives as being fitted to express the will of the entire population of the regions (44); the proposal thus came to nothing, and the affairs of the Baltic States were settled without reference to their inhabitants.

The importance attached by the Russian delegation to the status of "the occupied territories" can be readily understood. These territories were economically important, they contained large timbered areas, and Russia had drawn from the Baltic Provinces a large proportion of her civil servants as well as of her military leaders. To cut off Esthonia, Courland, and the other new Baltic States from the Moscow State was to disorganize the economic foundations of Moscow just as completely as if the Ukraine and the Lower Volga were separated from it.

Trotsky fought hard at Brest-Litovsk to prevent these States from falling under the influence of Germany. He was evidently under the impression that if the government in each of them could by some means be placed in the hands of working men and peasants, these governments would be more likely to take their instructions from Moscow than from Berlin. On the other hand, if the State organs were under the control of the landowners, the overlord was

# BREST-LITOVSK 213

very likely to be Germany. Thus the formal autonomy of these States was an unimportant affair.

The discussion on this point closed with Germany's refusal to evacuate the Baltic States until after the conclusion of a general peace and Russia's refusal to accept this arrangement. (45) After about three months of debate, practically no progress had been made. This circumstance was due partly to lack of skill on the part of the debaters—for neither Baron von Kühlmann nor Trotsky was an expert in international affairs, and neither of them was a distinguished expounder of the philosophy of the State. But the absence of progress was due chiefly to irreconcilable differences in the interests of the negotiating parties. The Germans had done their best to destroy Russia's will to fight by helping to promote the Revolution ; and the Revolution had thoroughly accomplished that purpose and a good deal besides, for it had become a real menace to Germany. Therefore it was necessary that the Revolutionary Government should be restricted in its power as much as possible, and that the area over which it ruled should be curtailed. On the other hand, it was urgent that the holding of the frontier should be simplified at once in order that some of the troops from this area might be sent to reinforce the armies on the western front.

Eventually the Germans decided to cease discussion and at all hazards to insist upon immediate submission to their terms. Trotsky was evidently ill at ease ; he feared the consequences of abject submission, and on February 10th he handed the Germans a note which was probably unique in its terms : " We are going out of the war ; but we feel ourselves compelled to refuse to sign the peace treaty." (46)

The Germans refused to allow so anomalous a submission. On the faith of a mere declaration that Russia was going out of the war, Germany could not withdraw her troops, for the moment their backs were turned to the eastern front Russia might change her mind. For that reason the German General Staff, on February 18th, resumed military operations, (47) with the result that Lenin and Trotsky capitulated the following day and agreed to sign the peace. Capitulation led to conditions of increased stringency— evacuation by Russia of Livonia and Esthonia, cessation of propaganda by Russia, acceptance of the Ukrainian Treaty (which had meanwhile been concluded), together with indemnities for civil damages and for prisoners of war.

Trotsky did not return to Brest-Litovsk ; he sent Sokolnikov, Petrovsky, and Chicherin as his representatives, and the treaties were signed by them on March 3, 1918. Before signing, however, G. J. Sokolnikov said that " the peace was not a peace by under-

## 214 THE RUSSIAN REVOLUTION

standing, and that, forced by the breaking of the armistice, Russia signed the peace treaty without deliberating on it, after her appeal to the German working classes had failed." (48) General Hoffmann repudiated the charge that Germany had violated the armistice treaty : he held that the rupture by Russia of the peace negotiations had automatically abrogated it, and Baron von Rosenberg with some heat denied that the German workman would take " his instructions from abroad." (49)

The episode ended with a manifesto addressed by wireless from the peace delegation to Paris, Vienna, Berlin, Sevastopol, Odessa, Kharkov, Nikolaiev, Tashkent, Archangel, Kazan, and Irkutsk. This manifesto denounces the peace " as an annexationist and imperialistic peace . . . dictated by force of arms. . . . This is a peace which gives back the land to the landlords, and again drives the workers into the serfdom of the factory owners. . . . This is a peace which imposes upon the workers of Russia, in a still more aggravated form, the old commercial treaty which was concluded in 1904 in the interests of German agrarians, and which is at the same time guaranteeing, to German and Austro-Hungarian capitalists, interest on the debts of the Tsarist Government, which have been repudiated by Revolutionary Russia. Finally, as if it was the purpose explicitly to emphasize the character of the German armed offensive, the German ultimatum is attempting to muzzle the Russian Revolution by forbidding all agitation directed against the Governments of the Quadruple Alliance and their military authorities." The manifesto then refers to the annexation to Turkey of Ardahan, Kars, and Batum, and to the presence of German troops in Ukrainia. It concludes by saying that " Germany has taken the offensive under the pretence of re-establishing order, but in reality with the purpose of strangling the Russian Workers' and Peasants' Revolution. . . . We declare openly before the workmen, peasants, and soldiers of Russia and Germany, and before the labouring and exploited masses of the whole world, that we are forced to accept the peace dictated by those who at the moment are the more powerful, and that though we are going to sign immediately the treaty presented to us as an ultimatum, we refuse to enter into any discussion of these terms." (50)

---

### NOTES

(1) The Russian delegation numbered eighteen members plus ten assistants, secretaries, etc. The delegations of the four allied Central Powers numbered seven members, with eight consultative members, assistants, secretaries, etc.

# BREST-LITOVSK

(2) *Proceedings of the Brest-Litovsk Peace Conference* (Washington, 1918), p. 29.

(3) Ibid.

(4) To the north of the Gulf of Riga.

(5) Russian account. *Wireless* (December 6th). See *Proceedings*, etc., p. 31.

(6) *Wireless* (December 6th), *Proceedings*, etc., p. 34.

(7) Real name Leon Borisovich Rosenfeld.

(8) Anastasia Alexandrovna Bitsenko, the only woman member of the Delegation. She had shot and killed General Sakharov (Czernin, Count Ottokar, *In the World War* (New York and London, 1920), p. 244).

(9) Michael Nikolaevich Pokrovsky, otherwise known as " Domov."

(10) Cf. Czernin, Count, op. cit., pp. 231 and 271.

(11) This is made perfectly clear from Count Czernin's candid memoirs.

(12) Von Hindenburg, Marshal, *Out of My Life*, English translation by F. A. Holt (London, 1920), p. 271.

(13) Czernin, Count Ottokar, op. cit., p. 199.

(14) Count Czernin in a letter to a friend, dated November 17, 1917. Ibid., p. 241.

(15) " It seemed to me that Lenin and Trotsky behaved more like the victors than the vanquished " (von Hindenburg, Marshal, op. cit., p. 334). Lenin and Trotsky were adopting a rule sound enough under certain conditions—" When you are completely cornered and nothing more can be lost, strike as hard as possible without regard to consequences."

(16) In the summer of 1917 the Pope had made a *démarche* for peace.

(17) See von Hindenburg, Marshal, op. cit., p. 422.

(18) Czernin, Count Ottokar, op. cit., p. 243.

(19) Von Hindenburg, Marshal, op. cit., p. 423.

(20) Germany, Austria-Hungary, Turkey, and Bulgaria.

(21) Since private property had been formally abolished, the effect of such a provision would be that the Soviet Government could collect private claims from the international fund, to which it would of course also have to contribute. It could retain for its own purposes the funds collected on account of private claims.

(22) *Chron. de la Guerre*, 7e vol., p. 256.

(23) Ibid., p. 258.

(24) Ibid., p. 259.

(25) Ibid. Immovables had previously been declared national property.

(26) Ibid., p. 261.

(27) The Resolutions of the London Conference (April 26, 1915) were published in Russian by *Izvestia* (St. Petersburg), February 28–March 12, 1915. An English translation of the German text is given in Count Czernin's *In the World War*, pp. 307–11.

(28) *Proceedings*, etc., p. 53.

(29) Cf. Czernin, Count Ottokar, op. cit., p. 257.

(30) Baron von Kühlmann, the head of the German delegation, said to Count Czernin, " *Ils n'ont que le choix à quelle sauce ils se feront manger.*" Czernin answered, " *Tout comme chez nous.*" (Ibid., p. 259.)

(31) Czernin, Count O., op. cit., p. 261.

(32) Ibid.

(33) *Proceedings*, etc., p. 63. These may have been sincere protestations at the time ; but ere long the Red Army was making havoc in Poland and the Ukraine, as well as in the Crimea and the Caucasus, where a reign of terror was established in defiance of the wishes of the population.

(34) Lenin reproaches Trotsky for his want of aptitude for study or discussion of problems in theory (cf. Lenin, *Collected Works*, Moscow, 1923, vol. xviii, part 1, p. 9).

(35) *Proceedings*, etc., p. 55.

(36) Ibid., p. 67.

(37) This discussion is not fully reported in the *Proceedings*. The portions of it which are reported are not very systematic. Neither of the disputants was an expert on the theory of the State.

## 216 THE RUSSIAN REVOLUTION

(38) *Proceedings*, etc., p. 68.

(39) Ibid., p. 82.

(40) Ibid., p. 94. The obvious retort is that, while a government may and must employ force, no government can rely for support exclusively upon force. " Bayonets cannot be sat on."

(41) For the text of the note see *Proceedings*, etc., pp. 91–94.

(42) The same may probably be said of " social philosophy."

(43) *Proceedings*, etc., pp. 93–94.

(44) Ibid., p. 97. It is to be observed that the Moscow Government cannot be said to have ceased interference with the internal affairs of all these new States.

(45) Ibid., p. 104.

(46) Ibid., p. 172.

(47) The German army report of February 18th announces that the German troops have advanced across the Dvina and from Kovel eastwards (*Proceedings*, etc., p. 174).

(48) Ibid., p. 183.

(49) Ibid., p. 184.

(50) Ibid., pp. 186 and 187.

## CHAPTER IX

## THE LABOUR ARMY

THE fatal mistake of the leaders of the anti-Bolshevik forces of neglecting during the Civil War (1) the civil organization of the country, in so far as it came under their control, was not committed by the Bolsheviks. Clumsy and inadequate as their measures were, the Bolsheviks nevertheless wrought strenuously at political and economic construction, sometimes in accordance with their previously conceived doctrines, and sometimes in opportunist contradiction to them. The consequences of the neglect of such measures were disastrous to the forces of Denikin and Wrangel ; while their adoption by the Bolsheviks consolidated their power even over those elements in the population to which the main communist programme was repugnant.

As soon as the Civil War was over, the Soviet Government encountered the problem of demobilization of the military forces and the immediate absorption of the Red Army in industrial employment. The military units had to be speedily transformed into groups of workers upon the railways, and in factories, mines, etc. ; in short, a labour army had to be created out of the fighting army.

At the end of the year 1919 the War-Revolutionary Committee was instructed by the Council of the People's Commissars to organize without delay four labour armies. The following were the principal *desiderata* : increase of the output of fuel and of the most urgently required raw materials, provision of food, supply of labour to the various enterprises of the State, establishment of labour discipline, and finally, the application of military precision to industrial establishments.

The territory of the Federation of Soviet Republics was divided among the labour armies in accordance with the varied character of the productive regions, and a labour and defence committee was entrusted with the distribution of this labour force.

The four labour armies almost simultaneously began operations in February 1920. The first step was the organization of labour for the Donetz mineral field, for without an adequate supply of fuel it was impossible to restore activity in the most vitally important railways and factories, especially in south Russia. The task of organizing labour in the Donetz basin was entrusted to the Ukrainian army. Hitherto the civil administration had been so ineffective

**218**  THE RUSSIAN REVOLUTION

that one-third of the enterprises were idle; now, within four months, the labour army had repaired 120 large and many small bridges which had been damaged or destroyed in the Civil War, and it had materially increased the output of coal. The output of coal per work-soldier in May 1920 was 181·5 *pùdi*; in June, 278·8 *pùdi*; and in July the minimum was 299·4 *pùdi* and maximum (by the 5th labour regiment) 788·6 *pùdi*. At the same time the soldiers guarded the stores, accompanied the cargoes (to prevent plundering), and built and repaired houses in workers' villages. They fought with many disorderly bands and, in addition, assisted the civil authorities and the political sections of the labour army ; they organized production technically, and endeavoured to create a general atmosphere of enthusiasm for industry by means of meetings with the proletariat of the Don, by the foundation of elementary schools, reading-rooms, communist clubs, etc., and by the distribution of literature. (2)

On February 20, 1920, an *Order*, of which the following is an abstract, was issued to the Petrograd labour army :— (3)

1, 2. The seventh army is converted into the Petrograd revolutionary labour army. Its military efficiency is nevertheless to remain on its previous scale.

8. Within ten days [from the date of the *Order*] an inquiry must be made into the trade of every member of the labour army. All technicians and trained workmen are to remain in the army and to carry on work. We are going to use all the best forces for the repair of locomotives and cars. Individual specialists will be allowed to go to plants and factories under exceptional circumstances only.

9. Commanders and commissars are to be held even more responsible than formerly for discipline in their units, for carrying out industrial tasks, for the maintenance of military authority, for diligence and accuracy in work, for correct accounting, for delivery in good time of the work-tables (periodical instructions regarding work to be done), and for the facilitation of service to associated plants, after the same manner as they were formerly responsible for the execution of military orders.

The council of the People's Economy was able to report in July 1920 that, owing to improvement in the supply of food to labour, to the working of the premium system, and to increased regularity in the fuel supply, the output of the Putilov ironworks on the Neva near Petrograd had exceeded the programme by 15 per cent. (4) Since the industries especially affected were those associated with

# THE LABOUR ARMY

locomotives and cars, the activity represented by this increase was extremely important to the railways.

Uncertainty of life in the industrial centres, inadequacy of the normal ration, with loss of time in getting delivery, impossibility of obtaining supplementary food except by means of illegal trade with its consequent risks, weariness of demonstrations and agitation on the one hand, and on the other the relative peacefulness and security of village life with sufficient land to obtain a fair livelihood by reasonable cultivation, all these circumstances combined to cause the dispersal to the villages of the urban proletariat which had worked temporarily or permanently in the towns.

Thus, during the first three years of dictatorship, the proletariat as a class was greatly diminished. Indeed, the " great problem of the nineteenth century, the abolition of the proletariat " (according to Marx) (5) seemed to have been solved by Soviet Russia. Setting out to destroy the *bourgeois* class, the Bolsheviks had succeeded in partially abolishing the proletariat. The dispersal of the working men embarrassed the Soviet Government. A surplus of submissive labour was even more necessary for the maintenance of operations in the state factories than it was for individual capitalist enterprises, because the former possessed less flexibility in their methods of attracting labour than the latter ; they had a narrower field, and therefore relied to a greater extent upon external pressure to force workers to seek employment.

The labour army with its four divisions had been mobilized at the beginning of the year 1920. Yet the results had not been adequate, and the labour crisis continued. While the shortage of labour varied in different trades, it was noticeable throughout the year 1920 in the most important branches. This condition led the central committee of the Russian Communist party, in other words, the Bolshevik leaders, to issue a manifesto on October 10, 1920, addressed to the provincial committees of the Communist party, urging them to take measures to secure workmen for the state enterprises.

" The need of labour in the most important branches of industry is very great. The lack of workers is felt with particular acuteness in the military plants, in the special transport group, and on the railways. Our army needs recruiting, and yet we have to retain thousands of young people in different enterprises, in timber supply, in loading fuel, etc., because of the impossibility of replacing them by older workers.

" The position of the Republic with regard to provisions is somewhat better. Our industry is secured, so far as fuel and raw materials are concerned, to a much greater extent than in the past year. Productivity of labour in the factories is increasing,

## THE RUSSIAN REVOLUTION

yet the carrying out of the programme of production is being especially handicapped by the lack of labour.

" At the present moment the council of the People's Economy and the People's Commissariat of communications require an additional force of 160,000 skilled and 300,000 unskilled workers. That labour must be supplied to our industry for next winter.

" To that end the council of People's Commissars and the council of Labour and Defence, after having heard the report of the labour commissar, resolved :—

" 1. To mobilize for labour citizens born in 1886, 1887, and 1888.
" 2. To undertake the systematic withdrawal from the villages of trained workers living there.

The mobilization of these three ages ought to be carried out throughout almost the whole of Russia during October. Mobilization of skilled workmen not already engaged in the enterprises of the State must be carried out by the end of October in the following *gubernie* : Petrograd, Moscow, Vladimir, Yaroslav, Novgorod, Smolensk, Tula, Kostroma, Kaluga, Ryazan, Nijni Novgorod, Ekaterinburg.

" Your especial attention is required to this mobilization as well as to the work of supply.

" 1. You must start a widespread propaganda in order to make clear to the masses the importance of this mobilization of labour to the welfare of the country and to the development of socially organized economy.

" 2. You must assist in reinforcing the apparatus of the labour commissariat which conducts these mobilizations.

" 3. You must encourage all organs of Soviet activity to assist these mobilizations with energy.

" 4. You must sustain in the enterprises a courageous labour discipline in order that the mobilized workers may enter at once upon a course of solidly organized production.

" 5. You must see that those who are to be mobilized are not required to put up with worse conditions of living and provisions than those already working in the enterprises.

" 6. You must organize the sending-off, escort, and reception of the mobilized workers in such a way that the mobilization be carried out with revolutionary animation and that it bear the character of a demonstration for the socialist economy.

" With regard to the mobilization itself, it is especially necessary to make sure of the following :—

" (*a*) An exact census must be made of all workers and employees not engaged in work for the State.

# THE LABOUR ARMY

" (*b*) No abuse of the regulations, by exemption or delay on the ground of illness, must be permitted.

" (*c*) The orders of the administrative centre must be carried out with firmness, and no local abuses allowed. Mobilization must be conducted promptly and carefully . . . and in accordance with the resolutions of the council of the People's Commissars, the council of Labour and Defence, and the instructions of the main labour committee and the All-Russian main staff." (6)

The arrangements for the distribution in Petrograd of the new labour army were made by the supreme court of the People's Economy. The first sections were sent to the following plants :

| | | |
|---|---|---|
| Rosencrantz Plant | .. | 220 men housed in barracks. |
| Baltic Works .. | .. | 550 men housed in barracks. |
| Obuhor Plant.. | .. | 350 men housed in bungalows, etc. |
| Radio-Telegraph Plant | | 100 men housed in a mess-house. |
| Tjor Plant | .. | 300 men ⎫ |
| Pipe Plant | .. | 50 men ⎬ to be housed in apartments to be built for their accommodation. (7) |
| Admiralty Plant | .. | 100 men ⎭ |

The Commission in charge of the reception of the mobilized men furnished each man through the Petrograd commune with warm clothing, shoes, two linen sheets, towel, napkin, mattress, pillow, bed-cover, soap, and utensils. (8)

In consequence of the difficulty of obtaining from the army-clothing factories a sufficient supply of linen garments for the army, the council of People's Commissars commandeered the services of all " citizenesses of the Republic between the ages of 15 and 45 ' for " the compulsory sewing of linen for the Red Army." Local executive committees were instructed to see that this order was carried out with " maximum energy." (9)

Such measures had not been employed in Russia since the time of Peter the Great. By means such as these St. Petersburg had been built and many of the State industrial enterprises had been founded. (10) Precisely such measures produced the state of mind among the peasants in the reign of Peter and in succeeding reigns that led to frequent serious uprisings, culminating in the reign of Catherine II, in the revolutionary movement of Pugachev. It is small wonder that in carrying out their policy the Bolsheviks met with sullen resistance from the peasantry, and that their whole-sale mobilization yielded but slender results.

# THE RUSSIAN REVOLUTION

## NOTES

(1) The Civil Wars are discussed in Book IV, Ch. IX.

(2) Cf. *The Communist Calendar* (Moscow, 1924).

(3) *Order No. 1 to the Petrograd Labour Army.* *Pravda* (Petrograd), No. 39, February 20, 1920.

(4) *Pravda* (Petrograd), No. 154, July 14, 1920.

(5) Marx, Karl, *Revolution and Counter-Revolution* (Chicago, 1907), p. 23.

(6) *Labour Mobilization* in *Pravda* (Petrograd), No. 227, October 10, 1920. The manifesto is expressed in language even more redundant than the above translation shows. It is signed by the central committee of the Russian Communist party.

(7) *Pravda* (Petrograd), No. 240, October 26, 1920.

(8) Ibid.

(9) Ibid., No. 255, November 2, 1920.

(10) Cf. Mavor, J., *An Economic History of Russia*, vol. i, pp. 130–32.

## CHAPTER X

## THE RUSSIAN PEOPLE AND THE REVOLUTION

THE Russian people were from time immemorial divided sharply into social classes, each with its separate traditions, manners, and, to a large extent, language. These classes were subject to changes in the course of their history, alike in relation to one another and in their interior character ; but in general there remained sharp divisions between the gentry and the peasantry, and between these and the merchants. Each class had its own interests and its own class property, and any passing from one to another was regulated by interior class laws. The class property consisted chiefly of estates which had been escheated to the order to which the owner belonged, and they were generally kept intact, the revenues being treated as income of the class, and expended primarily upon education ; many important institutions were thus maintained by each of the social orders. When the Revolution of October 1917 occurred, the remaining class distinctions of the old order were inverted. All the privileges, such as they were,(1) which remained to the gentry and the merchant class were abolished while fresh privileges in respect to rations, etc., were bestowed upon manual workers, those who did not belong to this category being subjected to obligatory labour. Later the children of manual workers only were admitted to the universities. Thus class distinctions were not abolished— the classes were simply inverted, obligatory labour being imposed upon the once superior class, although such labour had not been imposed upon the peasantry since the Emancipation in 1861.

In the first days of the Revolution of February 1917 many Russians who had been living abroad, either because they had exposed themselves to prosecution under the Imperial Government, or because they disliked the political atmosphere of Imperial Russia, returned to their own country full of enthusiasm for the new spirit which seemed to inspire the people. Among these returned *émigrés* there were revolutionists of all parties, together with many who did not entertain revolutionary opinions. Some of these were in the prime of life ; but there were many old men who had spent the greater part of their lives abroad and had thus lost intimate touch with their country. All had imbibed the political atmosphere of western Europe ; and without realizing the difference in conditions between Russia and Great Britain or France, for instance, they

## THE RUSSIAN REVOLUTION

appeared to think that democratic institutions which had been productive of social progress elsewhere might have similar results in Russia.

When these *émigrés* arrived in their own country and met, in many cases for the first time, representatives of the Russian *intelligentsia* who had not left Russia, the copious discussions which ensued, after the Russian manner, revealed important differences, accentuated by the intense feeling within the party groups of the time. During the period between the Revolution of February 1917 and that of October, the disputes between and within the socialist groups became more and more violent. After the Revolution of October, it was therefore not surprising that professed socialists of different parties were shooting one another in the streets of Petrograd.

So soon as peasant risings, increasing demands by the workers, and other signs of the coming Revolution made their appearance, an exodus of Russians of the superior orders began. When the Revolution occurred, large numbers made their escape by Finland and Siberia. When south Russia fell into the hands of the Bolsheviks, further emigrations took place to Constantinople and to the Danubian countries, and colonies of Russian refugees sprang up everywhere. Their numbers are variously stated ; but after the main exodus was over, they probably numbered between two and a half to three millions. The influence of this large migration upon the countries in which refuge was found, and the reactions upon the *émigrés* themselves, can only be disclosed by time, but the effect upon Russia could not be otherwise than disastrous. No matter how justly the past administration of Russia may be criticized, the abrupt withdrawal of probably one-half of the educated people imposed a strain which few countries could have endured. The administration unquestionably suffered from the absence of experienced and educated men, and the substitution of officials who were totally unacquainted with the nature of public business.

The *bourgeoisie* (which, in revolutionary phraseology, includes everyone not a manual worker or a communist) having been crushed and reduced to the status of proletarians, the dominant classes in Russia came to be the peasants and working men, the latter being also mainly of peasant origin. Merchants and factory owners, Russian and foreign, shopkeepers and professional classes, were annihilated. The necessity of keeping the people amused led the Soviet Government to subsidize the theatres and to offer special privileges to actors and musicians. (2) Apart from the Jews, who occupied a large number of the administrative posts, and the clergy, who were variously treated by the Government, the peasants and the working men were the conspicuous elements in Russian society.

# THE RUSSIAN PEOPLE AND THE REVOLUTION

The character of the Russian peasant has been described elsewhere. (3) His is not a simple nature ; rather is it highly complex. The peasant can be amazingly kind and he can be also amazingly cruel. Russian literature is saturated with peasant psychology, with the tortuous reasoning of the peasant mind when he wants to defend himself against himself, his capacity for intimate and exhaustive confession, his suspiciousness and proneness to lay blame upon hereditary and external influences, and his persistent conviction that when he is acting weakly or wickedly he is doing so in a peculiarly Russian manner for which he cannot be held responsible.

Dostoevsky puts these words in the confession of Ivan Karamazov :—

" Our time-honoured pastime is the immediate satisfaction of inflicting pain. There are lines in Nekrassov describing how a peasant lashes a horse in the eyes, ' on its meek eyes ' ; everyone must have seen it. It is peculiarly Russian." (4)

Foreign observers have for centuries noticed the cruel strain in the Russian character. Fletcher, an acute and intelligent traveller, attributes peasant cruelty to the harshness of the government. " For as they themselves are very hardly and cruelly dealt with by all their chief magistrates and other superiors, so are they as cruel one towards another, especially over their inferiors, and such as are under them. So that the basest and wretchedest *Christianoë* (as they call him) that stoopeth and croucheth like a dog to the gentleman, and licketh up the dust that lieth at his feet, is an intolerable tyrant where he hath the advantage. By this means the whole country is filled with rapine and murder. They take no account of the life of a man." (5)

A recent writer quotes a portion of this passage and remarks, " The whole Bolshevist-Social Revolution is contained in that sentence." (6) This is, however, too facile a conclusion. There is as much reason to believe that the Government was cruel because the peasant was cruel, as the converse. Moreover, cruelty is no monopoly of Slavic governments or Slavic peoples. The Revolution was brought about, not by the cruelty of the Government of the Tsar, but by the whole complex of the previous history of the people. It was not the socialist *intelligentsia*, nor the Jewish element within that group, nor the Bolsheviks, and the Socialist-Revolutionaries as socio-political parties, who made the Revolution or determined its character, neither was it the proletarian working men, nor the peasants ; the upheaval was the outcome of the nature of the people as a whole, now one influence and now another making itself felt in the swift course of events.

## 226 THE RUSSIAN REVOLUTION

The difficulties arising from the reactions of the Stolypin agrarian legislation of 1906 and its subsequent amendments (which have already been noticed) became accentuated during the war. In the year 1916, for example, there was heard before a military district court in Stavropolsky *gub* a case in which sixty-seven peasants and two wounded soldiers were accused of contravention of the military code. (7) The hearing of the case occupied a month. The evidence disclosed an extraordinary state of affairs in the village of Blagodarn and in other villages in the district. Shops had been looted, the apartment of a member of the municipality had been destroyed, the *zemstvo* schools had been burned, and the *Starshina* (village elder) had been tortured by the crowd.

This affair surprised alike the local and the central authorities. A *Zemstvo* had been established immediately before the war, efforts were being made to improve the life of the peasants—and then in two years there were riots and destruction of those very schools for which they were reported to have been pining.

The intention of the legislation seems to have been to promote the welfare of the peasants ; but the effect was rather to irritate them. The peasants had been given to understand that they were to be endowed with a large share in the local administration, but the relatively high land-qualification for membership of the *Zemstvo* disqualified all but rich peasants and landowners. Some of those who were elected seem to have conducted themselves in a foolish fashion. They provided, at the public expense, a carriage for the use of the members, put cockades in their caps, required that they should be addressed as " Excellency," and the like. The chairman of the *Zemstvo*, who had been a public official in a minor office, had begun immediately after his assumption of authority to issue orders, both written and oral, with respect to peasants and others. The new *Zemstvo* multiplied the rate of taxation tenfold at one stroke, whereas in other *Zemstvos* the taxes had been increased gradually. When this occurred the peasants protested, asking, " Where does this *Zemstvo* come from ? " In the village of Alexandria, where the main revolt had its origin, the *Zemstvo* had decided to build a school, but it was not built where the people of the village in general wished, but on a site near the house of one of the members, for the convenience of whose family a stone bridge was erected across the road.

The war was meanwhile making increasing demands upon the villages, the peasant workers were being drawn into the army, and those who remained had proportionately increasing burdens laid upon them. They found the payment of taxes more and more difficult, and the authorities found the collection of them harder.

# THE RUSSIAN PEOPLE AND THE REVOLUTION 227

Force was employed in some cases, and when such rough methods were applied to the families of soldiers who were absent at the front, the soldiers' wives fought with the police in their attempts to keep possession of animals which were being taken from them, and threatened to " let the front know " about what was being done ; but the women were beaten by the police and put in prison. The most outrageous irregularities were perpetrated. In one instance, for a tax due of seven roubles the collectors appropriated a pair of horses, a cow, and a sewing-machine, and these were added to the stock of one of the members of the *Zemstvo*, who probably paid the amount due into the treasury. The peasants appealed to the president, a local proprietor, who replied, " I understand as much about *Zemstvos* as an archbishop about sheep."

On one occasion an inspector of police was asked by the peasants, " Did the *Zemstvo* come from the Tsar ? Can anything be done ? " The policeman said, " I will hang every one of you on telegraph poles, then you will know all about the *Zemstvo*."

Another day there came from the front to the village of Alexandria two wounded soldiers. Their wives told them what had been happening and asked them :

" Is there a law that the *Zemstvo* can take animals from soldiers' houses ? "

" No, there is no such law," replied the men. " The Grand Duke [Nicholas] himself has promised that nothing should be touched that belonged to the soldiers."

" Is there a law to hang people on telegraph poles ? "

" Yes, there is such a law. We have seen it ourselves. But what is the news about the *Zemstvo* ? Is it from the Tsar or from the *tavrĕches* ? (8) The Don Cossacks told us that they did not want the *Zemstvo* and that the Tsar had undertaken that the *Zemstvo* would not be imposed upon them." A village meeting was held to discuss the question, but nothing happened except that everyone shouted, " We don't want the *Zemstvo* ! " and the meeting broke up in confusion.

This was a case which an intelligent official might have settled by requiring the *zemstvo* members and officials to proceed according to *zemstvo* law and not otherwise, and by explaining its functions to the people. The root of the difficulty, however, lay in the character of the people from whom the members were obliged to be drawn in that locality. The introduction into the *Zemstvo* of a few poor peasants would not necessarily have made any difference.

Instead of sending down an intelligent official, the district authorities sent police, who in the night made a number of arrests and told their captives that they were to be imprisoned for a month

## 228 THE RUSSIAN REVOLUTION

by administrative order under the war emergency regulations. The police force, however, proved inadequate, the village firebell was struck by somebody, and this brought the whole population out of doors. They overpowered the police and rescued the prisoners, after which they destroyed the school and the neighbouring house of that member of the *Zemstvo* who had used his position for his individual advantage. Some hours afterwards, however, the police re-entered the village with reinforcements, and fired into the house-yards, killing seven peasants and wounding twenty.

When the case of the sixty-seven prisoners came before the military court, the prosecutor demanded a death penalty for all, but eventually three only were sentenced to be hanged, and forty were sent for varying periods to Siberia or to prisons in European Russia.

The reforms of Stolypin and the growth of peasant proprietorship had thrown the control of local affairs more and more into the hands of the active large and middle proprietors—gentry and peasantry—while the poorer peasants, ill-educated and unprogressive as they were, had little interest or weight in the councils. Any increase of influence among local landowners had been opposed by the autocracy because local autonomy and central bureaucracy were mutually exclusive. The effect of this hostility has been already noticed ; to it was due the loss to the dynasty of one of the main props of the throne.

The correspondent from the *gub* of Tver already quoted reports : " It was in 1918 that the worst began, and I think it is safe to say that in most parts of Russia that was the hardest period for landowners (so far as the peasants were concerned). In our immediate vicinity the agrarian question was not so acute as it would have been had the peasants possessed more seed. We had a partial failure of crops, and in most cases the peasant had hardly sufficient seed for his own strip of land." (9)

Between the spring of 1917 and the year 1923 all the land of Russia had passed under the control either of the peasants or of the Government, the proprietors being formally or informally dispossessed. In some cases the owners were permitted to remain upon their estates, but only by sufferance of the peasants or as managers for the Government. Their position depended upon their conscientious or assumed political and social convictions. In some cases the peasants besought the proprietors to remain in order to organize their labour for them, and they brought them supplies over and above the allowances to which they were legally entitled according to their category.

When the new communist bureaucracy came into relations with

# THE RUSSIAN PEOPLE AND THE REVOLUTION 229

the peasantry, it found with dismay, as may be gathered from the speeches of Lenin, that it was impossible to found a communist-collectivist-proletarian State which was dependent for food upon a locally autonomous peasant community. The communist Government therefore resolved to undermine local autonomy by forcibly removing all the well-to-do and energetic peasants from the local institutions, and filling their places with the poorest class, who might be relied upon to be subservient to the central authority. This anticipation was not wholly realized. The poorest peasants found themselves becoming less poor ; they began to acquire a taste for power within their restricted sphere, and to manifest a sullen opposition to the dictatorial methods of the central government. They were extremely unwilling to accept arbitrary prices from the government purchasing-department to which they were obliged to send all their surplus produce, and they were by no means reluctant to receive substantial returns by means of illicit trade even with the depressed *bourgeoisie*. Punitive expeditions were sent into the villages to coerce recalcitrant taxpayers and to prevent illegal commerce. The Soviet Republic, like the autocracy, in order to vindicate the authority of the central government, adopted an attitude of hostility towards local autonomy. The result was the same in both cases—decline of local initiative and organization, with diminution of agricultural production. But under the Soviet Government the decline was more marked than under the old autocracy, for with the fall of the system of local self-government, there came also the decline of spontaneous movements such as co-operative societies, which were seized by the Government and the spirit rapidly crushed out of them.

The motives for these activities on the part of the Soviet Republic can readily be understood and have already been noted. An individualistic peasantry and a communistic or state-collectivist urban proletariat could not exist side by side.

" The Revolution gave the peasant what he wanted, the landlord's land and the church land. In European Russia, the peasant [before the Revolution] owned only 76·3 per cent., and the landlords 23·7 per cent. In the Ukraine the peasant owned 65·4 per cent., the landlords 44·6 per cent." (*sic*). (These last figures should be 65·4 per cent. and 34·6 per cent. respectively.) " Speaking generally, the peasants got 40 million *desiatines* of land." (10) It is obvious that the transference of property from the landowners to the peasants resulted in less sowing and greatly diminished production, even in years of favourable climatic conditions.

The status of the peasant as occupant of land, the ownership of which is vested in the State, seems to differ little from that of the

## 230 THE RUSSIAN REVOLUTION

former state peasant. (11) Under the Soviet State the peasant might leave his land, but so long as no private employment could be obtained, he was obliged to apply to the State for work. His neighbours being as poor as himself, he could not find employment with them, so that, if there was no state enterprise within reach, the peasant was practically as much bound to the soil as were his fathers under serfdom. He, however, suffered from the disadvantage that on one excuse or another he might be removed from his land. An accusation that he was not a " firm communist," or that he was a " *kulak*," might be sufficient to send him to Siberia, thus forfeiting his land to a more favoured peasant.

The peasants have never, formally or in fact, accepted the dogma of the Soviet Government that their lands have been nationalized. About 75 per cent. had been bought and paid for by them under the old *régime*, for the redemption payment represented for them the purchase price of part of their land, and more had been paid for under various Land Purchase Acts of the Imperial Government. The peasants had no objection to the Soviet Republic taking such of the landowners' estates as they themselves did not want, but they strongly objected when it claimed the ownership of their own property.

The Russian peasants are not clear upon the rights of property as these are understood in western Europe ; but they are quite convinced that if the peasant has no legal right in his land, that right cannot be vested in anyone else. (12)

There is, however, one important consequence of the nominal nationalization of the peasants' lands. This condition effectually prevents the peasant from using his strip as security for borrowing. If he had the power to do this, his land would speedily pass by means of foreclosed mortgages into the possession of the lender. The attitude of the peasantry to the Soviet Government ultimately depends upon the amount of the land tax levied by the State, and upon the form of distraint employed to collect that tax in the event of delay or refusal to pay.

---

### NOTES

(1) " Of class inequality in taxation, at the moment of the Revolution, it would be ridiculous to speak " (Struvë, P. B., article *Russia* in *The Slavonic Review*, vol. i, p. 35).

(2) During the winter of 1924–1925 two opera houses were opened simultaneously in Moscow, where Russian, Italian, French, and German operas were performed.

3) Cf. Mavor, J., *An Economic History of Russia*, Book IV, Chs. 2 and 10 ; Book V, Chs. 1, 2, 7, 8, and 10 : and Book VI, Chs. 2 and 12.

# THE RUSSIAN PEOPLE AND THE REVOLUTION 231

(4) Dostoevsky, F., *The Brothers Karamazov*, translated from the Russian by Constance Garnett (London and New York, 1917), p. 253.

(5) Fletcher, G., *The History of Russia, or the Government of the Emperour of Muscovia with the manners and fashions of the People of that Country* (1643 ; originally published in 1591), p. 280.

(6) Antonelli, Étienne, *Bolshevik Russia* (translated from the French by Charles A. Carroll, New York, 1920), p. 280.

(7) The particular clause under which the accused were prosecuted was the 279th of the military code, the punishment for the contravention of which is death.

(8) An expression meaning land-grabber, derived from the name of Count Tavrech, who lived in the time of Catherine II.

(9) Therefore the peasant did not feel the want of land. (From a private correspondent, formerly a large landowner in the *gub* of Tver.)

(10) All the statements in inverted commas are from *The Communist Calendar* (Moscow, 1924), pp. 549–50.

(11) Cf. Mavor, J., op. cit., vol. i, p. 267 et seq.

(12) In March 1917 the Russian newspapers alleged that French and Russian adventurers were buying land in the *gub* of Saratov.

*BOOK IV*

# THE SOCIAL REVOLUTION AND ITS PROBLEMS

## CHAPTER I

## THE CHARACTERS AND IDEOLOGY OF THE BOLSHEVIKS AND THE DEVELOPMENT OF THEIR POLICY

THE leaders of the Bolshevik faction of the Social-Democratic party differed in character, intellectual ability, and political sagacity, both from the conspicuous figures in the revolutionary movements of former epochs, and from the leaders of the several political parties by whom the struggle for power in 1917 was waged.

The heroic figures of the Dekabrists have no modern counterpart, nor have those of the group of Slavophils who threw themselves into the anti-governmental movement preceding the emancipation of the serfs in 1861. Among revolutionary leaders of recent times, Lavrov (1) and Mikhaelovsky (2) may be regarded as the descendants of the philosophical socialists, as contrasted with Lenin and Bukharin, who, skilful enough in party management and political tactics, are merely philosophical speculators of undeniably inferior intellectual ability.

The parties of the Right (3)—Octobrists, Constitutional-Democrats, Socialist-Revolutionaries, and minor groups—all of which were in opposition to the Bolsheviks, were composed of men of ability somewhat above the general average of the *intelligentsia*, while some of the members of each of the parties had either superior intellectual qualifications, or long experience in central or local administration. A few had occupied important academic positions, most of them belonged to superior social strata, though some were of humble origin, and all comprised men of irreproachable integrity ; the discreditable elements in the extreme Right had ceased to have any position or influence.

The Bolshevik leaders may be divided into distinctive intellectual groups. Probably the only Bolshevik of outstanding intellectual capacity was Lunarchasky, whose dramas disclose ability of the first order. Although Lenin assumed a contemptuous attitude towards his colleagues when they discussed questions of principle, his own excursions into the field of economics or social philosophy are generally neither original nor illuminating. It is clear from his essays on these subjects that, while he was an omnivorous reader, the absence of systematic training induced in him an essentially noncritical attitude and a lack of proportion, though had he possessed

## THE RUSSIAN REVOLUTION

first-rate abilities he would probably have risen above his disadvantages. While positive evidence of intellectual capacity of a high order is certainly wanting in the case of Lenin, a large measure of tactical sagacity must be allowed him. Evidently this quality was absent in his colleagues, for his influence over them arose from their having constantly to refer to him at critical moments ; indeed, his reputation for sagacity was mainly due to the shrewdness of the advice he gave them. Lenin's power over an audience seems to have been directly attributable to his ringing voice and habit of demagogic denunciation, always energetic, generally clear, though often verbose, and sometimes vulgar. Trotsky appears as a clever, quick-witted, but vain person, who, as the Brest-Litovsk negotiations show, was easily imposed upon. He organized the Red Army with energy and skill, but otherwise his influence upon the course of events does not seem to have been very great. For some reason not yet clear, he fell out with his colleagues, and in 1924 they got rid of him for a time. The writings of Trotsky are those of a vivacious journalist, whose thesis is the dullness and selfishness of all who engage in politics, commerce, industry, or agriculture. Although he had not a highly developed talent for literary criticism, and the absence of positive standards renders such as he had spasmodic and rhapsodical, the essays which comprise his book *Literature and the Revolution* are interesting and suggestive, and are probably the only products of his pen which are destined to survive.

There is no evidence that any of the other leading Bolsheviks possessed exceptional intellectual gifts. Some of them, Rykov, for example, were men without education or ability, but who showed that they possessed energy, courage, swift power of decision, and unyielding obstinacy. That they were ruthless, unscrupulous, and on the whole extremely short-sighted, there seems no doubt. Their incompetence as administrators is proved by their own reports and admissions. There have been in all countries incompetent members of governments ; but, in democratic nations, these governments have been chosen by the people from such candidates as were available, and when their incompetence manifested itself with sufficient clearness, they have been quietly and without violence replaced. The Bolsheviks were not chosen by the people ; they thrust themselves into power, and coerced the people into obeying their orders ; they therefore stand upon a wholly different footing, and for that reason their deficiencies cannot be excused on the plea that all governments are more or less incompetent. There was among them an ostentatious contempt for and disregard of *bourgeois* standards of conduct and morals ; indeed, it is not too much to say that many Bolsheviks had " a dark past."

## CHARACTERS AND IDEOLOGY OF BOLSHEVIKS 237

In February, and even as late as July, 1917, the anti-Bolshevik parties were acting together, and were collectively much stronger and more numerous than their opponents. They had power in their hands, but they allowed it to slip through their fingers, and cannot therefore be acquitted of the charges of inertia and of fatuous optimism which have been brought against them. They grossly under-estimated the energy, strength, and unscrupulousness of the Bolsheviks, and by so doing brought about their own downfall. (4) They may be regarded in fact as victims of their own good-nature and lack of perspicacity.

On the other hand, when the Bolsheviks found themselves in the saddle, they made no such mistake. They accused their opponents of promoting a counter-revolution, the very offence which they were themselves committing, and without hesitation, scruple, or mercy, they hunted down the members of all the other parties, shot them without form of law, or frightened them into the dangerous expedient of trying to escape from the country, whereby many were killed by the frontier guards. The Bolsheviks hypnotized their antagonists by sheer terror. (5) By so doing they imitated the Government of the Tsar, which in 1882, after the assassination of Alexander II, and in 1907, after the revolutionary episodes of 1905–1907, instituted a reign of terror that depressed and took the heart out of its opponents. The inertia and despair, which characterized the *intelligentsia* in the periods immediately succeeding both 1882 and 1907, made their appearance again during and after the Bolshevik terror of 1918 and succeeding years, with the result that the *intelligentsia* in general lapsed into helplessness, while those of the educated classes who were socialists, after suffering the loss of their illusions, exhibited a tendency towards mere reaction. They had seen the magnificent edifice of their dreams crumble before their eyes ; this new socialist *régime* was like the old Tsardom, only worse, more brutal and degrading, and with less regard for human life ; but the power with which to combat it was no longer forthcoming.

This decline of spirit among the *intelligentsia* appears in many recent memoirs, and may be supposed not merely to have unfitted the Constitutional-Democrats and the Socialist-Revolutionaries for effective opposition to the Bolsheviks, but also for the task of establishing a government either of a moderate socialist or of a democratic character. After three years of unsuccessful struggle they gave up the effort, and the way was thus left clear for the Bolsheviks. The dispersal of the intellectuals contributed further towards this depression and inertia. The hardships endured by professional men, writers, and artists in foreign countries, where

238 THE RUSSIAN REVOLUTION

their special talents could rarely be employed to advantage, exhausted the spirit of those who escaped abroad; albeit greater trials were undoubtedly experienced by those who remained in Russia. (6)

While impartial judgment must impute guilt to the Bolsheviks for the methods adopted by them in seizing and retaining power, it must not be forgotten that, while some of the intellectuals had the courage to withstand Bolshevism and suffered death in consequence, in general they lacked the energy and political and strategic sagacity to contend successfully. Thus, although the political parties in opposition to the Bolsheviks greatly exceeded them in number, they were defeated by the superior adroitness, activity, and political sense of the Bolshevik leaders.

Numerous memoirs show that neither working men nor peasants fully grasped the meaning of Bolshevism or believed in it in so far as they did grasp it, while the peasants certainly rejected wholesale what little they knew of it. The attitude of the leading Bolsheviks was from the beginning hostile to them, and this hostility was not lessened by their increasing resistance. In fact the conquest of power by the Bolsheviks was not in any sense due to their doctrine, but rather to the skill with which they took advantage of the revolutionary state of mind of both working men and peasants.

So soon as the pressure of the police was removed by the collapse of the Imperial Government, the peasants knew very well what to do. They needed no guidance and wanted no other government, until they had fully satisfied their craving for land; anarchy suited them perfectly, for it enabled them with impunity to take what they wanted and to destroy what they did not want. A similarly covetous state of mind impelled the workmen to seize the factories.

Any government would have found grave difficulty in dealing with revolutionary workers. The Bolsheviks, previous to their accession to power, encouraged this revolutionary spirit as subversive of the Provisional Government; but when they were established in authority they turned upon proletarian and peasant alike, and soon obtained mastery over them. Such was the effect of their political acumen, energy, ingenious and well-organized propaganda, and by no means least of all, the terror.

They talked glibly about "the materialistic interpretation of history," "the inevitable course of the class struggle," "the dictatorship of the proletariat," "the bankruptcy of capitalism and of imperiocratism," and "the leadership of Russia in the world revolution," but their opinions on such subjects had little to do with their political advancement. Although intellectually and morally less worthy of public confidence, the Bolsheviks possessed

## CHARACTERS AND IDEOLOGY OF BOLSHEVIKS 239

to a greater degree than the opposing parties the lust for power, and the skill and courage indispensable for its satisfaction. Their ascendancy did not depend upon their social doctrines, nor upon their methods of carrying these into effect, for their doctrines and their methods were alike fluctuating and inconsequent, and were often repugnant to the mass of the people : their position depended rather upon their strategic skill in politics, upon the relative weakness in this respect of their opponents, and upon the primitive stage of culture of the people. Their ability enabled them to take advantage of the opportunity afforded by a revolution which they had a very slender share in bringing about, and this same ability also helped them afterwards to master the unquiet elements, and to bring order of a kind out of chaos. (7)

In these facts lay the reasons for their successful seizure of power. In their own phrase they dealt with " realities " ; and they adapted themselves to every change which came with the swift progress of events. They cherished certain doctrines which they could make much of on occasion ; but their most conspicuous characteristic was the facility with which they executed dialectical manœuvres, when these were necessary to reconcile their dogmas with their practice. They were not even above taking over the plans and schemes of those whom they were hounding to death, as, for example, when they destroyed the Socialist-Revolutionaries, and then appropriated to themselves, and subsequently applied, the agrarian policy of that party. (8)

The Bolsheviks fully recognized their numerical inferiority. Even in the Soviets they were outnumbered by the Socialist-Revolutionaries, as they were also in the Constituent Assembly. They saw clearly that, if they were to gain power, they must first hypnotize the garrison of Petrograd, and then the plastic mass of the working men of the capital. They also knew that by different methods they must if possible obtain the acquiescence of the peasants, and if this acquiescence was not forthcoming, the peasants would probably yield to pressure from the army and the working men.

While the Bolsheviks neither obtained nor retained their power by virtue of doctrine, they have with much insistence expounded a policy by which they allege themselves to be usually guided ; it is expedient therefore to examine the character and origin of their tenets.

The leading ideas in the programme of the Bolsheviks, (9) viz. " liberation from the yoke of capital," and " dictatorship of the proletariat," or " the taking possession by the working classes of the political power in any given country," are to be found in the programme, issued in 1885, of the first definite social democratic

## 240    THE RUSSIAN REVOLUTION

organization in Russia, *Osvobojdenie Truda* (Emancipation of Labour). (10) This document was drawn up by G. V. Plekhanov, (11) who recognized the organic character of the process by means of which alone he considered the working class could not only acquire power, but also adopt such methods of administration as would ultimately result in an ideal commonwealth. (12)  It was obvious that since this process was composed of a series of organic changes, violent action might produce developments quite other than those which would have naturally occurred, a consideration which implied doubt of the efficacy of violent revolutions.  Such an implication was fully accepted by Plekhanov, who, while retaining his belief in the eventual emergence of a state administration and social conditions approximating to the ideals of the Marxists, was of opinion that premature revolutionary steps might retard rather than promote the ideal commonwealth.  Plekhanov remained of this opinion, and when, in 1917, thirty-four years later, Bolshevism emerged as an active doctrine urging an immediate dictatorship of the proletariat, Plekhanov stoutly opposed the movement.

An incident, of little account at the time, but nevertheless indicative of the reaction of the doctrines of the *émigrés* upon certain groups of working men, took place in 1885.  This was the publication at St. Petersburg, by a small social democratic group formed by a Bulgarian named Blagoev, of a newspaper, *Rabochaya Gazeta* (Workmen's Gazette), but only two numbers appeared before the group was arrested.

Their programme contained a mixture of Marxism and Lavrism. (13)

" The aim of the group was to separate the working class and to form it into an independent political party, the final object of which was to be the reorganization of society upon a socialist basis—viz. the collective use of the means of production.  In order to achieve that object, the working men's party must struggle for a constitution ; but a constitution would be a dream unless this party had aims independent of those of the *bourgeoisie*."  Plekhanov contributed an article to the second number [of the *Rabochaya Gazeta*], in which he called the Social Democratic party " an exclusively working-men's party . . . our revolutionary *intelligentsia* must go with the working men, and the peasantry must follow them."  This blunt statement of the determinism of undiluted Marxism probably represents fairly the view of the few Russian Marxists of that time. (14)

The moment came when the working men, encouraged no doubt by propaganda, discovered that the Social-Democratic party was overloaded with *intelligentsia*, and that its movements were hampered

# CHARACTERS AND IDEOLOGY OF BOLSHEVIKS 241

by their cautious attitude. The peasants also grew suspicious of them and began to denounce them as *bourgeois*.

The programme of the *Rabochaya Gazeta* is significant because it contains the germ of Bolshevism, and further indicates the process by which Bolshevism acquired power.

The next important stage in the development of Russian social democracy occurred in March 1898, at the congress of the party at Minsk. (15) This congress was held in the strictest secrecy. Although no account of the proceedings as a whole seems to have been issued, the course of events afterwards proved how momentous in their consequences these proceedings were. Two events of first-rate importance took place—first, the formation of the Russian Social-Democratic Working Men's party ; and, secondly, the practical adoption by the congress of the ideas of Nicholas Lenin, as embodied in a pamphlet written by him and issued immediately before the meeting was held. Lenin was not present himself, but his views received general acceptance.

Three distinct points of view were presented to the congress : first, that of the adherents of the *Osvobojdenie Truda*, referred to above, which was expounded by G. V. Plekhanov ; second, the view of local organization (practically regional trade-unionism), with its policy of promoting " the immediate improvement of every working man " ; and third, the standpoint of limited centralization, involving the preservation of the secret, conspiratorial character of the " general staff " or central organization, by gradually enlarging its structure in such a way as to bring it into more direct contact with locally organized groups. According to this idea, the organized mass should have no control over the party. The business of the party was to discipline the masses through " continuous agitation," strikes should be steadily " developed," and the party should bear a share in " propaganda circles " and " in managing the strike funds." In effect, the party was to be dominant, acting as it thought in the interests of the working classes, but not in any way suffering itself to be directed or controlled by the working man or the peasant. The third point of view, which was that of Lenin, appeared to carry all before it. The pamphlet in which he expressed his views follows in general the manifesto issued by Karl Marx in 1849. Lenin begins by drawing a comparison between the French Revolution of 1848 and the coming Russian Revolution. (16) The manifesto insists that a political revolution must precede the social revolution, but this political revolution must be achieved by the proletariat without the aid of the *bourgeoisie*. " All the organization (the Russian Social-Democratic Working Men's party) must act according to one plan, and must obey the directors." That is to say, the centrali-

Q

## 242 THE RUSSIAN REVOLUTION

zation of power, at all events in the active revolutionary stage, must be absolute. (17) There is no reference in the manifesto to the agrarian question. The resolution which embodied the policy outlined in the manifesto was drawn up by P. Struvë, who seems to have expressed in it, not his personal opinions, but those which had been accepted by the congress. The *Osvobojdenie* group apparently agreed with Lenin at this time, for it attempted unsuccessfully to win over to his policy the unions of working men, who held a congress in the autumn of 1898. Other elements hostile to the plans of Lenin now made their appearance. The principal objection to these plans was that they laid too much emphasis upon centralization, and the soundness of the objection was immediately demonstrated by the arrest of the central committee of the Social-Democratic party and the seizure of the office of the *Working Men's Gazette*, which was the party newspaper. (18) This arrest, together with discussions inside the party, led gradually to wider adoption of Lenin's views, and this became apparent during the succeeding years.

The third important stage in the development of the Social-Democratic movement in Russia was marked by the congress held in London in 1903. At that congress the party was divided into the Bolshevik or majority faction led by Lenin, and the Menshevik or minority faction led by L. Martov. The point of difference was the question of admission to membership of the party. The Mensheviks were desirous of admitting anyone who subscribed to the party programme and supported its activities; the Bolsheviks, on the other hand, looked upon the party as a fighting organization, the membership of which should be confined to those who were prepared to take part in the struggle. The Mensheviks, in short, were willing to ally themselves with the *bourgeois* parties, so far as these could be induced to go with them, while the Bolsheviks looked upon the *bourgeois* parties as their chief antagonists.

The fourth important stage in the evolution of Bolshevism occurred at the so-called Zimmerwald-Kienthal Conference. (19) The series of incidents connected with this conference may be said to begin after the failure of the German armies to break through the French and British defences in the beginning of September 1914. (20) Shortly after the battle of the Marne, the German Social-Democrats attempted to organize international socialist peace meetings, the terms of peace proposed being the *status quo ante bellum*. These attempts were not successful; but at a congress of Swiss and Italian socialists, both belonging to countries neutral at that time, a peace proposal was brought forward at Lugano on September 27, 1914. (21) When the Germans occupied Brussels, they approved

## CHARACTERS AND IDEOLOGY OF BOLSHEVIKS 243

of the transference of the international socialist bureau from that city to Amsterdam, and the bureau shortly afterwards proposed to call an international socialist congress at The Hague. This congress did not meet. At the same time the revolutionary syndicalists of France proposed the removal of the trade union International from Berlin to Switzerland, and the president of the Geneva centre, after its removal there, proposed an international congress of trades unions in Amsterdam ; but the English unions refused to participate. A conference of socialists of the neutral countries met, however, on January 12, 1915, at Copenhagen, and resolutions were passed of an extreme nature, but no alteration in party tactics was made. Then the Swiss socialists attempted to convene a meeting of the international socialist bureau to be held at Zürich on May 30, 1915, but the majority of the socialist parties either refrained from replying or refused to attend. On May 15, 1915, the central committee of the Italian socialist party had addressed itself only to the known adherents of extreme internationalism who might be willing " to oppose the policy of internal peace and to promote a combined and simultaneous movement of the socialists of different countries against the war, on the basis of the proletarian class war." A preliminary meeting was held at Berne on July 11. The *Labour Leader* (London), August 12, 1915, remarked about the projected international conference : " We should prefer by far to see the old International reconstituted ; but if it is impossible, we agree with the Italian comrades that direct efforts must be tried in order to build a new International representing neutral parties and anti-war socialists of belligerent countries." (22)

The next step was the conference held September 5th–8th, 1915, at Zimmerwald, a small village near Berne. The Italian and Roumanian socialist parties alone were able to send official delegates, although many persons attended as individuals, whilst the representatives of the Independent Labour party and of the British socialist party were refused passports by their Government. The French, German, and Belgian socialists were not asked to participate, although individual French and German socialists were present, and issued a manifesto declaring their disapproval of the war and demanding " peace without annexations on the basis of self-determination of peoples." Professor Miliukov says that this is the first appearance of a formula which played a great *rôle* in later discussions, and adds that the chief feature of the Zimmerwald Conference was the predominance of eastern European socialists : Russians, Poles, Letts, Roumanians, and Bulgarians, (23) who formed the Left or extreme wing. The following are the names of the Russian

## 244 THE RUSSIAN REVOLUTION

delegates, with the names of the organizations by which they were appointed :—

Ulianov (Lenin) and Goldendakh (Ryazanov), by the Central Committee of the Russian Social-Democratic Working Men's party ; Akselrode, Tsederbaum (Martov), Pekker (Martinov), by the organization of the committee of the Menshevik faction of the Russian Social-Democratic Working Men's party ; Levensohn (Lapinsky), by Social-Democrats of Poland and Livland ; Berzine, by Lettish Social-Democrats ; Lepnik (Vladimirov), by the Jewish *Bund* ; Varsky and Gankevich, by the Polish Socialist party ; Victor Chernov (Gardenine) and Mark Nathanson (Bobrov), by the Socialist-Revolutionary party. (24)

The manifesto which was agreed upon at the Zimmerwald Conference created a sensation in Russia out of all proportion to its terms, which amounted simply to an exploitation of the war in the interests of international socialism. According to the manifesto, " the war is the fruit of imperialism," and imperialism is " the aim of the capitalist class in every nation, in order to slake its thirst for profit by the exploitation of human labour, and of the natural wealth of the whole world. Economically backward or politically weak nations are getting into the hands of great nations which are able through the war, by means of blood and iron, to recast, in their own interests, the map of Europe. . . . The capitalists of all the countries, who are minting gold from the blood of the people, are saying that the war is for the defence of the country, for democracy, and for the freedom of nations. . . . In the beginning of the war they said that it was for the benefit of the people ; but poverty, unemployment, high prices, famine, and epidemics are the real results of it. The war is disclosing the real meaning of the new capitalism, which is absolutely inconsistent, not only with the interests of the labouring masses, not only with the requirements of historical development, but with the elementary demands of human life. The ruling powers are the capitalist society, in the hands of which are the fates of the people in monarchical as well as in republican governments. Secret diplomacy, the strong organization of the *bourgeois* class, the capitalist press, the church—all carry upon themselves the heavy responsibility of this war, which sprang from the social structure which is fed by them, defended by them, and carried on by them in their own interests."

Addressing the workers, the manifesto says : " You, the exploited, you who are poor and without rights, at the beginning of the war, when it was necessary to send you to slaughter . . . they called you comrades and brothers ; but when militarism has disabled you, they destroy you ; and the ruling powers ask you to

## CHARACTERS AND IDEOLOGY OF BOLSHEVIKS 245

discard your own interests, your aims, your ideas, and they demand servile obedience in the interests of so-called national unity. . . . The press is suppressed, political rights and freedom are trodden down. Military dictatorship rules with armed fist. . . .

"The socialist parties and labourers' organizations in different countries . . . set aside, at the beginning of the war, all their projects. Their representatives asked the labourers to stop the class struggle which is the only possible and real measure for [securing] the freedom of the proletariat. They gave their votes for the war credits to the ruling classes."

Many of them became ministers and plenipotentiaries. "In that way they became responsible to our labouring classes, responsible for the present and the future, responsible for the war." Under these circumstances, the manifesto adds, the "international labour class . . . did not find any way or means to begin a final battle for peace simultaneously in all countries. In such an urgent situation we, the representatives of all the socialist parties and trade unions, as well as of the minority parties ; we, Germans, French, Italians, Russians, Poles, Letts, Roumanians, Bulgarians, Swedes, Norwegians, Dutch, and Swiss ; we, who are standing, not on the ground of national unity with the classes of the exploiters, but on the ground of international agreement of the proletariat and the class struggle ; we, gathered for the purpose of mending the broken connections, ask the labouring class to remember its duty and to begin the struggle for peace. . . .

"It is necessary to start a war for peace without annexations or indemnities. Such a peace is possible only if we drop all ideas of conquering the rights and freedom of peoples. . . . The independence of the nations should be the impregnable foundation of national relationship.

"From the beginning of the war, you, the proletariat, gave your strength, your bravery, your endurance for the service of the ruling classes. Now you should begin the war and the struggle for your own interests, for the sacred cause of socialism, by means of an implacable proletarian class struggle. It is the task and the duty of the socialists of fighting countries to start with all their might upon this struggle [with the support of the socialists of neutral countries] against blood barbarism. There has never been in the history of the world such an honourable task. . . . No sacrifices would be too great to make for this end. Peace between the nations ! Workmen and workwomen, mothers and fathers, widows and orphans, wounded and crippled—all who suffer from the war and through the war—we address you all across the frontiers,

246          THE RUSSIAN REVOLUTION

through the smoking battlefields, through the ruined towns and villages. Proletariats of all countries, unite ! " (25)

The following are the signatories of the manifesto :—

For Germany, Georg Ledeburg and Adolf Hoffman ; for France, A. Bourderon and A. Marrheim ; for Italy, G. E. Modeliani and Constantino Lazari ; for Russia, Lenin, Akselrode, and M. Bobrov ; for Poland, Lapinsky, Varsky, and Chanetsky ; for the Balkan Social-Democratic Federation, the Roumanian delegate Rakovsky (26) and the Bulgarian delegate Basil Koldrov ; for the Swedish and Norwegian delegation, Heglund and Ture-Nermann ; for Holland, Roland Holst ; for Switzerland, Robert Grimm and Charles Nenn. (27)

There was no unanimity in the project for a new International, and the conference adjourned without any progress being made in this respect. A new organization was, however, formed—" The International Socialist Commission." This body was to have its bureau at Berne, and the president of it was to be Robert Grimm, (28) assisted by Angelica Balabanova. (29)

The manifesto which was agreed upon at the Zimmerwald Conference in September 1915 was immediately circulated in Russia, and created a great sensation. Some regarded it as a notable humanitarian effort to put a stop to bloodshed, others looked upon it as insidious German propaganda seeking to diminish the war spirit among the nations of the *Entente*, while at the same time fostering it in Germany. Many of the socialist groups, however, were indifferent to its character and its origin so long as it served their party purposes.

The second Zimmerwald Conference was held (April 27–30, 1916) at Kienthal, another village near Berne, and the manifesto of that conference was issued on May 1, 1916. The terms were similar to those of the first conference, with the addition of such statements as the following : " Behind the front you see rich people and their adherents, who are hiding in safety ; for them the war means the death of others. . . . Before the war the capitalist system took all the pleasure out of life for the labourer ; during the war it is taking from him even life itself. . . . To-morrow new taxes will be on your shoulders ; let us arise and fight for immediate peace without annexations. . . . The duty of the labouring class is to utilize all its forces and to end the war quickly. Put every pressure upon your deputies, upon your members of parliament, upon your governments. . . . Demand the stoppage of the war. . . . Rise up for the struggle of the ruined and dying peoples." (30)

Since the close of the war several German writers have admitted

# CHARACTERS AND IDEOLOGY OF BOLSHEVIKS 247

that the fomentation of subversive revolutionary movements within the enemy countries was a military measure, which some critics now think was unwisely adopted ; it must, however, be admitted that very little stimulation on the part of Germany was needed to arouse these movements. While the majority of the socialists in Germany and in France placed the interests of their respective countries before those of international socialism, there were many who took a contrary view ; and these persons needed little encouragement to write manifestos accusing the financial, mercantile, and manufacturing groups in various countries of having brought about the war. (31)

So far, the propaganda peculiar to the Bolsheviks was concerned chiefly with methods of revolutionary agitation and of class war, and very little with the organization of a possible Bolshevik government. Their ideas as to what state collectivism or communism really meant were evidently vague, and they obviously had no idea what kind of government the proletariat would want if it had the power to choose.

On January 23, 1919, Lenin issued by wireless an invitation to the communists, Left socialists, and other revolutionaries throughout the world to meet at Moscow. (32) This congress sat from March 2 to 6, 1919, and seventeen groups sent appointed delegates, whilst a similar number were unofficially represented. This meeting was the first congress of the Third, or Communist, International. The Second met in July 1920, and thirty-one countries were represented : these were Great Britain, German Austria, Germany, France, United States, Italy, Norway, Switzerland, Denmark, Holland, Belgium, Spain, Sweden, Hungary, Galicia, Poland, Latvia, Czecho-Slovakia, Esthonia, Finland, Bulgaria, Jugo-Slavia, Georgia, Armenia, Turkey, Persia, India, Dutch India, China, Korea, and Mexico. (33)

During the year there had been some defections from the Second International and adhesions to the Third. But the Second International was not yet dead. It held a congress at Berne, February 3–8, 1919, (34) when a resolution which appears to express the sense of this congress was drawn up by Hjalmar Branting. (35) This resolution condemns revolutionary syndicalism, emphasizes the " constructive character of the socialist programme, . . . stands immovably upon the ground of democracy, . . . and upon the principles of freedom," and urges " the elimination of all methods of socialization which can have no chance of winning the adherence of the majority of the people." It points out the danger of a dictatorship which leans " upon only a part of the proletariat," and that in the end must be " a dictatorship of reaction." The

## 248 THE RUSSIAN REVOLUTION

resolution concludes with a similar warning against imperialism and the military and economic enslavement of peoples, culminating in a final plea for " socialism and democracy."

Fritz Adler and Longuet moved a counter-resolution which demanded the restoration of the international front by including the " revolutionary and conscious proletariat " (the Zimmerwaldians, including the Bolsheviks). They were not able, they said, with the information they had, to take a view hostile to the Soviet Government. They wished to hear the other side. In the vote, the German, German Austrian, and French delegates were divided ; Spain, Greece, Holland, and Norway voted against Branting's resolution ; the delegates of other nations voted for it. There were ninety-seven delegates in all. Miliukov criticizes the main resolution on the ground that, while it is clear and forcible in stating the negative attitude towards Bolshevism, its positive statements as to the policy and doctrine of international socialism are characterized by confusion and internal contradictions. (36) Certainly, to an audience of working men and peasants, Lenin's speeches made a more direct and effective appeal.

The mere fact, however, that representatives of the socialist parties of almost all countries in Europe, including Russia, the Ukraine, and Finland, had voted against the Bolshevik doctrines and methods was extremely important, and embarrassed the Bolsheviks much more than if the criticism had come from any other quarter.

One of the most illuminating statements showing the Bolshevik ideology as it had developed after the Soviet Government came into power was made by Lenin at the 8th All-Russian Soviet congress held on December 30, 1920. (37) In this speech he addressed himself to a criticism of a pamphlet by Trotsky (*Rôles and Problems of Trade Unions*) and of the theses submitted by Trotsky to the central committee of the 8th congress. Lenin argued that trade unions are not merely historically necessary, as Trotsky had assumed, but are " inevitable organizations of the proletariat." In the dictatorship of the proletariat, the *rôle* of trade unions is indispensable, it is unique. In organizing industrial labour, the trade union is the ruling organization of that class which creates the dictatorship, and which makes also the structure of the organization. This, however, is not the organization of action, but of education. The trade union is thus the school—the managing school of communism. The advance guard, or organization of action, comes from the revolutionary proletariat, and " to talk about trade unions without considering that fact obviously leads to many mistakes. The trade unions, if I may say so, are the links between the parties and the

# CHARACTERS AND IDEOLOGY OF BOLSHEVIKS 249

government. Progress towards socialism involves the dictatorship of the proletariat, but organization of labour does not constitute dictatorship." Lenin goes on to illustrate his point: " The party is chosen from the advance guard of the proletariat, and this advance guard constitutes the dictatorship of the proletariat. Without the foundation of the trade unions we should not have been able to have the dictatorship. We should not have been able to organize the functions of government. In order to organize these, we have to pass through new types of organization as (for example) through the apparatus of Soviets. What are the practical conclusions ? The trade unions connect the advance guard with the masses. The trade unions in their everyday work are teaching the masses—the masses of that class which is in the position of transferring us from capitalism to communism.

" On the other hand, trade unions are the ' reservoir ' of the powers of the government. That is what the trade unions are in this period while the change is going on from capitalism to communism. This change cannot be successfully accomplished without the services of the trade unions, which constitute the only class educated by the capitalism of great production, and the only one which is separated from the interests of small owners.

" But the dictatorship of the proletariat through the organization [of labour] as a whole cannot be accomplished, because, not only here in one of the capitalistically backward countries, but in the other capitalistic countries, the proletariat is so much split up, is so bribed by imperialism in different countries, that the organization of the proletarian dictatorship as a whole could not fulfil its mission. Dictatorship can be fulfilled only by that advance guard which has in it the revolutionary energy of the masses and therefore is something like a cog-wheel. That is the mechanism of the foundation of the dictatorship of the proletariat during the steps taken in passing from capitalism to communism." (38)

Nothing stands out more vividly in Lenin's speeches and writings than his utterly unsympathetic attitude to the peasants. In this he discloses the frame of mind of the petty *pomyeshchik* class from which he sprang, and he also betrays a certain idolatry of industry on the large scale, which is not uncommon among men of his type—men with one idea, whose knowledge is not the outcome of experience of life, but of unguided study of a restricted range of literature.

Having eliminated the *bourgeoisie* and the intellectuals, Lenin finds remaining two opposing classes—the proletarian artisan and labouring man on the one hand, and the peasant on the other. He considers that the proletariat is the only revolutionary class,

## 250 THE RUSSIAN REVOLUTION

and that, having made the revolution and appropriated factories, workshops, railways, and shipping, everything belongs to it. It is therefore " quite obvious " that the proletarait should bring its products to the peasant and should receive from the peasant " the surplus of farm products." (39) " The surplus products of the peasant should come to the labour government, not as a tax, not as surplus, but in exchange for all the necessary manufactured products which are brought to the peasantry by means of transport. That is to say, if the peasant economy can be developed, the economy of the country which becomes socialistic can be built up. We should vigorously attempt a further change which would involve the absorption of the less beneficial and most backward small peasants' economy by a great agronomical economy. . . . That is how our communist party looks at it." (40)

This means that all industry should be conducted in great factories owned and managed by the State, that the small peasant industries should be absorbed in these, and that the labour of the peasants should be organized in state gangs working upon estates belonging to the government. The inevitable outcome of such a policy must be the uprooting of village life, with complete subservience of the agricultural labourer to the proletariat of the towns. Having rid himself of the capitalist, Lenin found himself face to face with the farmer.

Perhaps the peasants did not see to the end of Lenin's scheme ; but they certainly saw far enough to realize that during the civil war they were getting no return for their produce, and after the civil war, only such return as the proletariat government chose to give them. Under these circumstances, concealment of their produce and sale of it, not to the government, but to private persons, sometimes at extortionate prices, was a very natural and obvious expedient.

In a sense, Lenin emulated Peter the Great, alike in the roughness of his methods, in the ruthlessness with which he crushed those who opposed his plans, and in his desire to make Russia a huge state-industrial enterprise. Lenin, however, lacked both Peter's practical sagacity and his patriotic enthusiasm, (41) and without his genius he was dealing with a population ten times as large as it was in that Emperor's time.

---

### NOTES

(1) Peter Lavrov (1823-1901), mathematician, anthropologist, and philosopher, author of *The Mechanical Theory of the Universe, The History of Modern Thought,* and *Historical Letters.* (Cf. Kropotkin, P., op. cit., 276-77 ; Mavor, J., *An*

# CHARACTERS AND IDEOLOGY OF BOLSHEVIKS 251

*Economic History of Russia*, vol. ii, pp. 101, etc. ; and Masaryk, T. G., *The Spirit of Russia* (London, 1919), vol. ii, pp. 181, etc.)

(2) Mikhaelovsky, N. K. (1842–1904), author of *Individualism, Heroes and the Crowd, Happiness*, etc., critic of Herbert Spencer. (Cf. Kropotkin, P., op. cit., pp. 131–32 and 294–95 ; Kovarsky, B., *N. K. Mikhaelovsky and the Social Movements of the Seventies*, St. Petersburg, 1909 ; and Masaryk, T. G., op. cit., vol. i, pp. 148, etc.)

(3) The extreme Right had disappeared.

(4) Kerensky's demand upon the British Government that Trotsky be released, and the feebleness of the Provisional Government in July 1917, illustrate the passivity with which it seemed to be obsessed. Even among the Socialist-Revolutionaries there was the same passivity. (See, e.g., Sokolov, Boris, in *Archives of the Russian Revolution*, Berlin, 1924, vol. xiii, pp. 46–48, and infra, p. 259.)

(5) Trotsky expounds the *rationale* of the terror in his *Defence of Terrorism* (London, 1921).

(6) Many deplorable cases have come to the knowledge of the writer. They cannot be narrated without risk to persons now living in Russia.

(7) The only other party which might have succeeded to power in October 1917 was the Socialist-Revolutionary. What kind of government they would have attempted to establish can only be conjectured. Their programme was subject to frequent fluctuations.

(8) Cf. Manifesto of August 13, 1917, appended to this chapter.

(9) The expression Bolsheviks has come to be accepted in English, and it is therefore used in this volume in preference to Bolskeveke. (See Mavor, J., *An Economic History of Russia*, vol. ii, pp. 541–43. For the origin of the party see supra, p. 133.

(10) Cf. Mavor, J., op. cit., vol. ii, p. 143. The *Osvobojdenie Truda* united with the Constitutional Democrats in 1905. After the adoption of the New Economic Policy the name Bolshevik was gradually dropped, until in 1925 it passed wholly out of use.

(11) G. V. Plekhanov was born in 1850 in the *gub* of Tambov. In 1878 he joined the *Zemlya e Volya* party (cf. Mavor, J., op. cit., vol. ii, pp. 73, 112, etc.). He afterwards associated himself with the *Chornie Peredyeltsi* (cf. ibid., pp. 111, etc.). He spent a large part of his life in Switzerland. His influence was thrown against the Bolsheviks in the summer of 1917. He died at Petrograd in 1918.

(12) Cf. Mavor, J., op. cit., vol. ii, pp. 145–46, and Lyadov, *History of the Russian Social-Democratic Working Men's Party* (St. Petersburg, 1906), vol. i, p. 46.

(13) For Peter Lavrov, see supra, p. 235.

(14) Mavor, J., op. cit., vol. ii, pp. 145–46.

(15) For the history of the social-democratic movement between 1885 and 1898, see Mavor, J., op. cit., vol. ii, pp. 146–60. The important feature of this period was the emergence for the first time, between 1892 and 1896, of a spontaneous working-class movement in Russia (cf. op. cit., p. 149). For an account of the congress of 1898 at Minsk, see op. cit., vol. ii, pp. 160–64, and Lyadov, op. cit., vol. ii, pp. 67–72.

(16) Lenin long afterwards published a criticism of the French Revolution of 1848, in two short articles, *Louis Blancovism* in *Pravda* (Petrograd), April 8 and 9, 1917. These articles were republished in *Collected Works* (Moscow, 1923), vol. xiv, pp. 21–26.

(17) The Jewish *Bund*, which was already a centralized organization within the Social-Democratic party, was given full autonomy. The reasons for this are given in Mavor, J., op. cit., vol. ii, p. 162.

(18) No doubt there had been a spy at the centre (cf. Mavor, J., op. cit., vol. ii, p. 163).

(19) The best general account of the Zimmerwald-Kienthal Conference and related episodes is to be found in Miliukov, Paul, *Bolshevism : An International Danger, Its Doctrine and Its Practice through War and Revolution* (London, 1920), pp. 49–63.

(20) Pointed out by Professor Miliukov, op. cit., p. 51.

# THE RUSSIAN REVOLUTION

(21) Spiridovich, A. E., op. cit., p. 270.

(22) Quoted by Miliukov, P., op. cit., p. 53.

(23) Ibid., op. cit., p. 54.

(24) Spiridovich, A. E., op. cit., p. 274.

(25) Dated Zimmerwald, September 1915. Translated from text in Spiridovich, A. E., op. cit., pp. 275–78.

(26) Now Soviet Russian Minister in London.

(27) Spiridovich, A. E., op. cit., p. 279. The names are transliterated from the Russian text.

(28) " Robert Grimm was working for Germany. He is married to a Russian emigrant from whom he gets his information about Russian affairs. Balabanova was also working for Germany. In an Italian newspaper, *Messagero*, there appeared a letter from an Italian socialist organization to its central committee accusing Balabanova of close relations with German spies, and of having introduced one of these into a socialist organization " (*Obshoyé Dielo*, Paris, October 12, 1917, cited by Spiridovich, A. E., op. cit., p. 279).

(29) Professor Miliukov speaks of Angelica Balabanova as an " Italian " of Russian descent (Miliukov, P., op. cit., p. 57).

(30) Extracted from the text in Spiridovich, A. E., op. cit., pp. 284–86.

(31) Undoubtedly this propaganda had a wide influence, not only in Russia, but also in other countries, especially France. The international character of the movement cannot be adequately treated in this place.

(32) For a list of the thirty-nine invitations issued by Lenin, and for the text of the basis of the proposed Third International, see Miliukov, P., op. cit., pp. 119–21. The documents are taken from *Écho de Paris*, January 25, 1919.

(33) The list of countries is taken from *The Proletarian* (Detroit, Mich.), vol. iii, No. 4, January 1921.

(34) The text of this resolution is given by Miliukov, P., op. cit., pp. 121–23.

(35) Hjalmar Branting was for a time Prime Minister of Sweden. He died in February 1925.

(36) Miliukov, P., op. cit., p. 126.

(37) An address to the communist party at the 8th All-Russian Soviet Congress (Lenin, N., *Collected Works*, Moscow, 1923, vol. xviii, part 1, pp. 7–18).

(38) Ibid., p. 9.

(39) Lenin's statements are quite explicit (see Lenin, N., *Collected Works*, vol. xviii, p. 188.)

(40) Lenin, N., op. cit., p. 189.

(41) Mavor, J., *An Economic History of Russia*, vol. i, pp. 124–63.

# APPENDIX D

### Manifesto of the Russian Social-Democratic Workers' Party, August 13, 1917.

Five months have elapsed since the revolutionary proletariat over-threw and locked up Nicholas Romanov. Peace and fraternity to the people. But an international uprising is necessary. Capital understands that motto, and has conspired to destroy the Russian Revolution. The Russian *bourgeoisie* who had nothing against the overthrowal of the Tsar was frightened by the further course of the Revolution because the Revolution threatened to take the land and the capital and to arm the workers. Therefore the Russian *bourgeoisie* united with the capital of Europe and America. In London and New York there was established a capitalistic *bloc* against the Revolution. The small *bourgeoisie* of Russia and the upper layers of the peasantry did not understand the danger of the capitalistic plot ; and therefore their parties—the Mensheviks and the Socialist-Revolutionaries—followed the *bourgeoisie*. They did not under-stand that the *bourgeoisie* of all countries deceived [literally, fooled] the workers. Only the revolutionary proletariat and its party understood the situation. They demand transference of the land to the peasants, mastery of the workers over production, and uni-versal peace. (1)

(1) Extracted from copy in Spiridovich, A. E., *History of Bolshevism in Russia* (in Russian ; Paris, 1922), pp. 453–59.

## CHAPTER II

## PROBLEMS OF POWER

THE uprising of October 1917 was a sign that the foundations of the social life of the Russian people had crumbled. The Revolution had swept over the country like a tidal wave, carrying everything before it, and on its crest the communist party was borne into power. As soon, however, as that party had reached a fixed position, it encountered an immense task—nothing less than the organization, speedy, even instantaneous if that were possible, of the corporate life of the Russian people in all its social, economical, and political relations.

The members of the communist party had been proscribed, prosecuted, imprisoned, and dispersed under the old *régime* : all of them had been inimical to the government of the Tsar, and many of them had been hostile to other governments with which they had come in contact. They knew nothing of power excepting as an agency to which they were implacably opposed, and they knew little of the technique of government, in fact only what they had learned in the numerous legal processes to which they had been subjected. They had no experience of administration except through their contact with the police of Imperial Russia, or those of other countries where they were occasionally arrested and imprisoned, or from which they were deported as undesirables. A few of them had been educated at universities or technical colleges, but in many cases this education was fragmentary because the students had been dismissed for political agitation before their studies were completed. Others were self-educated or were wholly without intellectual equipment, and the youth of all had been spent in an atmosphere of demonstration and agitation, until their customary frame of mind was a chronic repugnance to public order. Upon the shoulders of these people there was suddenly imposed the burdens and responsibilities of power.

The first and most imperative of the urgent tasks awaiting them was the organization of supplies of food and fuel. Performance was rendered the more difficult because the apparatus of social production had already begun to deteriorate before the Revolution began, and the chief difficulty lay in the absence of any means of effecting an immediate exchange of commodities in order to induce the agricultural peasants to part with their surplus grain.

# PROBLEMS OF POWER

Factories were closed because the demands of the workmen could not be met, or because fuel and the raw materials of manufacture could not be procured. Stocks in the warehouses might of course be seized, but when these were exhausted there were no other goods to exchange for food. Everything possible was hidden to avoid confiscation. The Government seized the banks and confiscated gold wherever it could be found; it controlled the printing-presses and produced enormous quantities of paper money; but the peasants were reluctant to exchange food-stuffs for a circulating medium which was daily increasing in quantity and diminishing in purchasing power, and in spite of a general stampede of people from both capitals, life continued to grow daily more and more precarious.

Those who profited by the Revolution and obtained authority by its means found themselves in a dilemma. Either they had to solve without delay the problem of maintaining life in the capitals, or they had to abandon them altogether, and in so doing relinquish power. Food, fuel, and clothing had to be procured by organized effort, but the customary organization had been, if not altogether smashed, at least seriously impaired, and no new scheme had been devised to take its place.

Meanwhile the victorious communists had been busy proclaiming that the advent of communism meant the dawn of a new era of universal and equal well-being, that poverty had been an incident of capitalism, and would vanish when the capitalists were dead, or under lock and key, and that the goods of the wealthy, their houses, and their property, would now be made available for the use of those who had been previously poor.

To the problems of power the Bolsheviks had paid little heed. They had imagined, no doubt quite sincerely, that the chief difficulties of government were due to the fact that it was in the hands of the *bourgeoisie*, who they thought had purposely exaggerated the difficulties, in order to frighten the inexperienced from trying their hand. If the world were rid of the *bourgeoisie*, with their conceptions of morals, law, rights of property and person, social and political conventions—in short, their standards of life in general—the government of the people would be a very simple affair. Inquiry into the history of the Soviets during the preceding six months, without researches into more remote periods, would of itself have dispelled any such illusion, for many social difficulties had emerged in acute forms and had puzzled the overworked committees.

The tendency towards an increasing complexity of life seems to be inherent in all communities, but government and spontaneous social co-operation are devices to simplify life for the individual;

## THE RUSSIAN REVOLUTION

when, in Russia, these devices ceased to function because the appropriate administrative organs had been destroyed, the Soviets were perplexed by problems of which naturally they did not know the simplest, much less the best, solution.

The exaggerated importance attached by them to the mechanical aspect of social relations, led the Bolsheviks to suppose that they could smash society in pieces, and then take their own time about putting together such of its elements as they might wish to preserve. Perhaps they even thought that new elements for the composition of the new society might, by some miraculous intervention, make their appearance. They found, however, after a time that they were encountering opposition, not merely from individuals and social classes whose existence they might be able to obliterate, degrade, or disperse, but from life itself, and that, ruthless as they were, the obliteration of life was beyond their power.

The Bolshevik leaders thought that when the banks were nationalized and when large numbers of capitalists were arrested or forced to flee the country, the power of the *bourgeoisie* would be broken, and the proletariat would then become simple, faithful workers acting in the interests of their own class.

The bureaucrats of the old *régime* had been dispersed; the *intelligentsia* (with the exception of the small number of educated Bolsheviks) were not rigid enough in their adherence to the sacred doctrines; accordingly the Bolshevik leaders thought that it was at once advisable and necessary to substitute for the former bureaucrats " firm communists," simple, faithful workers drawn from the ranks of the proletariat. Thus the revolutionary leaders placed in responsible positions men who had been artisans and peasants, and then expected them to perform the functions of specially trained and more or less carefully selected officials. If it should turn out that the new-comers could not fulfil these necessary functions at once, the leaders reckoned that it would not take them very long to learn.

There was another reason for such appointments. When the October Revolution occurred and the *bouleversement* of society began, the *intelligentsia* in general believed that the Soviet Government could only last a very short time. They therefore declined to assist in the administration, even after the Bolsheviks had made the discovery that their " assistance " was essential for the survival of Bolshevik rule. The so-called *sabotage* of the *intelligentsia* was welcomed in some of the more extreme circles because it gave an excuse for severe measures against them, and made more easy the problem of radical administrative revolution. (1)

In the very early days of the upheaval, some *intelligentsia* who

## PROBLEMS OF POWER

joined the Bolshevik ranks for one reason or another were admitted to public offices. The proletarian officials accounted for the presence among them of these *bourgeois* by saying that they were employed, not because their services were needed, but because " the kind-hearted proletariat " did not want to refuse employment to those who, having been blind, had recovered their sight and wished to serve " the great historical affair." There were, however, only a few of these in the public offices, which were later, in 1918, largely occupied by proletarians. During the first days of the Revolution, confidence in the latent administrative talent of the proletariat was unbounded, (2) but only a few weeks elapsed before there were heard " in the higher spheres " voices, " in the beginning rather shy . . . but later more confident . . . which suggested that without broad utilization of the forces of intelligence the administration could not survive." (3)

Thus, about the time that the seat of government was transferred from Petrograd to Moscow, there was manifest a tendency towards appointing, to the more important positions, *intelligentsia* if not technical experts. (4) At the same time, the idea prevalent among the *intelligentsia* that Bolshevism was a passing phase rather hindered such appointments.

The nationalization of commerce and industry could not be accomplished at a stroke ; thus there remained in the employment of private enterprises a large number of educated people. Through the gradual closing down or absorption by the State of the larger private enterprises, the most efficient employees, whose services had been retained to the end, were eventually obliged to leave the country, to resort to manual labour, or to offer their services to the Soviet Government.

Three categories of *intelligentsia* were employed in the public offices and in the nationalized establishments : firstly, those who were not communists, but were willing to conform to communism for the sake of their country, realizing that to leave Russia was to lose touch with the people at a time when conscientious work might still be done, though under very unfavourable conditions ; secondly, those who thought that they could more effectively combat and weaken the Bolsheviks from the inside ; and thirdly, those who had a liking for fishing in troubled waters.

The Bolshevik leaders were not lacking in shrewdness. They quickly observed and distinguished between these three categories and made vigorous efforts to increase the numbers of the first, both by fresh appointments and by endeavouring to transfer individuals from the second category ; they paid but little attention to the third.

## 258 THE RUSSIAN REVOLUTION

The following dialogue between two brothers illustrates the attitude of different groups of *intelligentsia* towards the question of service under the Soviet Government and towards the Soviet Republic in general. Smelg-Benario had taken service with the Soviet ; his brother, on the other hand, had not.

" ' You should understand,' said my brother, ' that the Bolsheviks have ruined Russia. Is it not clear to you that what is going on now has nothing to do with socialism ? The Bolsheviks have brought our country to absolute barbarism and have systematically destroyed its economic life. Factories have stopped working, the towns are practically dead, and the starving proletariat have run away to the villages or have become soldiers in the Red Army, which by the aid of the rifle is forcing socialism on Russia. How can you work side by side with the criminal elements who are now in a majority in the Soviet ? And how can you take part in the crime which is now being committed in Russia ? '

" ' I know very well that the Bolshevik reign has brought with it great sorrow ; I know that the economic life of the country is ruined ; I know that Bolshevism is little by little changing into ownership of property by individual commissars ; I know also that many of the commissars have dark pasts ; I certainly see that everywhere there is a reign of terror, sadness, and evil ; but that is why I am sure that we *intelligentsia* and socialists should work together with the Bolsheviks, because only in this way shall we be able to clear from the Revolution the filth that has stuck to it.' " (5)

Smelg-Benario, after having worked for six months in the people's commissariat of jurisprudence in the department of law in Moscow, returned to Petrograd in the middle of August 1918, and decided to offer his services there to the war commissar, who at that time was comrade Pozern. Smelg-Benario, armed with favourable recommendations from Moscow, obtained immediate employment in the Bolshevik war office. He says : " I found myself in the centre of Red Army life in the Petrograd war region. In spite of disagreements which I had with him later, I have a very kindly feeling towards Pozern. He resembled the Tsar very closely—the same facial features, the same beard, and the same pleasant smile. When Pozern in his full military uniform was taking parade, he seemed to me the double of the murdered Emperor. He is undoubtedly one of the most sympathetic persons among the Bolshevik leaders. A man with an iron will, he began to work with all his strength for the organization of the Red Army of the northern provinces. From morning till late at night, without rest, he worked in the war commissariat. With his good nature and pleasant manners he was quite different from other Bolsheviks. I was loyal

## PROBLEMS OF POWER

to him with all my soul, and I must admit that when I began to doubt Bolshevism, the fact that Pozern was a Bolshevik influenced me greatly, because I argued with myself that the cause for which such a man was fighting could not be criminal and wrong.

" But as I worked in the war commissariat I became more and more doubtful. I began to feel that my brother was right, (6) and if this doubt did not affect me very deeply, it was only because I had no time for my own thoughts. Meetings, parades, inquiries, revisions, and service journeys took up all my days, and when I returned home in the evenings I was so tired that I had no time to think about the rights and wrongs of Bolshevik methods. At other moments it really seemed that fate was determined to prove to me that the great crime which is being committed in Russia lies partly at my door. I had by force of circumstances to witness the wild doings of the Bolshevik *régime*." (7)

N. Mayer, who was procureur in the department of justice during the war (1914–1917), served the Soviet Government from different motives.

" The anger," he says, " of the lower classes of the population against everyone who resembled the upper classes was rising to such heights that it was impossible, for instance, to ride in street tramways, to be present at meetings, or to criticize the Bolsheviks without being insulted. A rough stream of soldiers was flooding Russia, and stealing and selling the property of the government. Estates and manor houses were being burnt. . . . On February 18 [1918] I entered the service of the Bolsheviks. Of the numerous causes which induced me to do so, the chief was that I might understand. For some time I could comprehend nothing. I could not see why the *Kerenskchina* [the dictatorship of Kerensky] had collapsed, why the small group of Bolsheviks had kidnapped the government as easily as Ivan Tsarevich [in the story of the Sleeping Beauty]. On what grey wolf are they riding, and towards what other Tsardom ? Later I began to think it was owing to the fact that Kerensky did not arrest Lenin and Trotsky in time, that the Soviet of Workmen's and Soldiers' Deputies was not liquidated, and that the poor selection of people in the Provisional Government had left it without international strength and authority." These he found to be not the real but only the apparent causes. The real cause of the success of the Bolsheviks in seizing power was, he thought, the support received by them from " the Bolshevik soldiers in the army, and from the mass of the people (including the peasantry) whom they had successfully deceived." (8)

While some of the Bolshevik leaders had more or less clear notions of the practical measures which must be taken on the morrow

## THE RUSSIAN REVOLUTION

of the Social Revolution, they had not prepared the mechanism for carrying them into effect. They had been in the habit of scoffing at bureaucratic incompetence; but they had neglected to observe that governmental organs did, more or less, perform their proper functions, and that these were necessary to the continuance of the life of the community. Although the Bolsheviks had smashed the government together with its administrative organs, they probably did this more completely than they at first intended. It is reasonable to suppose that they thought that the government officials would remain at their posts, until " firm communists " who had received the small amount of training considered necessary were ready to replace them. In any case they appear to have believed that, somehow or other, the daily needs of the population would be satisfied pending the completion of the Revolution. But the work of the Bolsheviks was too thorough and too crude. They inherited from the old *régime* and from the Provisional Government a disorganized State and an impoverished people, thus their obvious task should have been to set about organization without delay. Instead of doing this, and with the fixed idea in their minds that they must utilize the opportunity afforded by the political revolution to carry out a complete social *bouleversement*, they reversed the positions of the proletariat and the former property-owning classes. There may have been examples here and there of rough and ready justice, but mere change in ownership of property and goods does not necessarily imply a step forward in social progress. In no country to-day is there evidence that those who are now poor would, if they became rich, make more unselfish and more socially beneficial use of their wealth than those who now possess it; nor is there any evidence that those who are already wealthy, if they were suddenly deprived of their means by some cataclysm, would remain impoverished, no matter under what laws they might temporarily be placed. Should the *régime* be too oppressive, the active though impoverished persons would inevitably make their way to some place where the laws against accumulation of property were less stringent. (9) In short, it cannot be shown conclusively that the transference of private property to public ownership would increase in the least the sum of human happiness.

Within the ranks of the *intelligentsia* changes of opinion began to take place. Many realized that the Bolshevik *régime* had come to stay, and that, if educated people kept themselves aloof, the public administration would fall into the hands of ignorant persons, with consequences even worse than those that might be expected to result from the adoption of a policy of communism. (10)

A. Yurovich, who, in the last days of the old *régime*, was secretary

## PROBLEMS OF POWER

to the main committee of the All-Russian Union of Municipalities, describes in detail how he was urged to enter the public service by two heads of departments of the Soviet Government, although they knew that he was not a Bolshevik. The first incident (11) was an unsuccessful attempt on the part of " comrade " Kuskov to enlist his services for the department of finance. Kuskov said that he was aware that Yurovich had belonged to the Cadet party, but the reasons for applying to political opponents for assistance were that the business of finance generally (and especially the section of the department for which he sought assistance, viz. the valuation of industrial and commercial establishments and the assessments of profits of trade and industry in Moscow), was very important, while the total incompetence of his existing staff for the required services had been fully demonstrated.

" You simply cannot understand," he said, " the ludicrousness of my position. My assistants, all of them, are absolutely ignorant, or are selling themselves right and left." Kuskov went on to develop his political theories. " It is impossible to rule if the citizens are not afraid of authority and do not believe in its omnipotence. They believed in the Tsarist *régime* because it was their habit so to believe, and therefore the Soviet Government should openly demonstrate its omnipotence before the *bourgeoisie.*"

Kuskov was at that moment at the head of two sections of the Moscow executive committee—the finance and the housing departments.

The nationalization of industrial and commerical enterprises was proceeding slowly. Many of the Bolshevik leaders did not desire the process to be rapid because of the difficulty of getting managers and foremen to replace the *bourgeois* technicians whom they wanted to dismiss. Their policy therefore lay in taxing these enterprises highly, but not so highly as to lead the owners and organizers to abandon them to the municipality or to the government. In the housing department the homes of the *bourgeoisie* were taken and used for public purposes, or allotted to the servants of the government. In both these departments there was opportunity for either concession or severity. Kuskov, who had been in earlier days a Left Social-Democrat internationalist, was nevertheless as ardent an antagonist of the *bourgeoisie* as any Bolshevik. He told Yurovich explicitly that he wanted " to discipline the *bourgeoisie*, to make them realize that their past life is ended." (12) In levying " income tax," amounting to more than the capital value of an undertaking, Kuskov did not concern himself with the circumstance that such a tax could not be collected. After the *bourgeoisie* had been convinced of the power of the Soviet to impose

## THE RUSSIAN REVOLUTION

even an economically impossible levy, the tax might be modified by favour. In the housing department Kuskov's policy was the same. It did not matter that houses from which *bourgeoisie* had been expelled, or in which they occupied only the cellars or garrets, remained otherwise untenanted, so long as these former tenants were subjected to discipline.

Yurovich declined service in either of the departments presided over by Kuskov, but the latter was not in the least disturbed. " In that case," he said airily, " we shall have to find something for you to do in another department. I shall ask my friend, ' comrade ' Pyategorsky, to try to induce you to take service under him. He is looking for a specialist for the organization of central control."

The plain fact was that the Bolshevik leaders found themselves confronted by slaves, submissive indeed, but whose labour was rendered useless for want of the direction which the Bolshevik ranks were incapable of supplying. The necessary intelligence might in time be developed in the proletariat and among the peasantry, but it would be altogether too slow a process to keep pace with the onward march of events.

A few days after his interview with Kuskov, Yurovich received a communication from Pyategorsky, to the effect that he, Yurovich, should organize a kind of inspectorate of the activities of the All-Russian Soviet of People's Economy. Yurovich throws the interview into the form of a dialogue which, he says, is a precise and accurate account of the proposition.

" *Pyategorsky.* ' You understand, no doubt, that the position I speak of is a very responsible one, and that we want anyone who occupies it to be more or less Bolshevistic.'

" *Yurovich.* ' I recognize that the Soviet Government exists ; but my opinion about it is absolutely negative.'

" *Pyategorsky.* ' Negative, is it ? That doesn't matter. We are not doctrinaires. I myself, for instance, am not a communist. I am a Left Socialist-Revolutionary ; but in any case one thing is essential, although we do not stand for uniformity. The man who is working in the All-Russian Soviet of People's Economy should give his whole time to this work. You agree to that ? '

" *Yurovich.* ' No, I don't ! I will not leave the union of municipalities so long as it exists.'

" *Pyategorsky.* ' Is that so ? But, as a matter of fact, that is a secondary question. Only try to organize control, and then you will see for yourself whether or not it is worth your while to stay there.' " (13)

Beginning with all sorts of indispensable conditions, Pyategorsky at last reached the point of beseeching Yurovich to undertake

## PROBLEMS OF POWER 263

the task of reducing the All-Russian Soviet of People's Economy to something like order. There were many such cases. What would have happened if the Bolsheviks had been unable to induce at least some of the *intelligentsia* to enter the public service, or to remain in it, is difficult to imagine. Appalling inefficiency, such as (without a revolution) would have brought to a speedy end any government in a democratic country, scarcely affected the stability of the group which composed the Soviet of the People's Commissars.

Yurovich yielded to persuasion and entered the service of the All-Russian Soviet of People's Economy, thinking that by so doing he might contrive " to save some valuable items in commerce and to diminish the severity of the *régime*." At that time (early in May 1918) the High Soviet, as it was called, was a very large department, with many subdivisions and committees, both principal and subordinate. It had grown very rapidly. In November 1917, six months earlier, it had consisted of two persons—V. Obolensky (14) and the economist Larin. (15) Each of these formulated decrees according to his own opinion, and they were adopted without question because disobedience meant arrest. In May 1918 this body had a much larger staff, but its proceedings were still conducted in the same haphazard manner. The business of the High Soviet of People's Economy consisted at that time chiefly in giving advances to organizations and to various persons, on account of work which had to be done for the Government. A certain amount was expended directly by the High Soviet, and this could be controlled, but advances came into another category, and control over the outlay with regard to them was very difficult. They constituted nine-tenths of the enormous turnover of the High Soviet, and therefore questions concerning them were frequent, although inquiry after the expenses were incurred was fruitless. There were numerous committees, meetings, and reports in the preparation of which hundreds of persons were employed. There was in fact a huge governmental apparatus and an air of business-like activity, yet much of this was obviously futile, and instead of removing, only served to intensify and foster the economic chaos. In a week Yurovich was sick of it, and asked to be transferred to a juridical office where he might be of some real service. (16)

If it was hard to find competent functionaries in the state departments in the capital, it was still more difficult to find efficient persons to occupy regional and rural positions.

" The presidents of the regional committees were, in the majority of cases, hard, very ignorant people, who could not even sign their names, and who had not the slightest idea how to organize work.

## THE RUSSIAN REVOLUTION

I remember very well the president of the Viborg region—Comrade Abrahamov. This man had the face of a typical drunkard and criminal. People in whom I had absolute faith told me that Abrahamov was always drunk while at work. Later, after my departure, he was made president of the central committee. It seems to me that Zinoviev was of the same opinion as Koslovsky—that for such work only criminals are suitable." (17)

The problems of government as the Bolshevik leaders conceived them after seven years of power, and at least four years of undisputed authority, are shown in various writings, and especially in the resolutions of congresses. For example, at the Twelfth Congress of the Russian Communist party held in 1923, the question of the division of work between the party and the Soviet organizations was subjected to serious discussion.

It appears that the communist party was expected to continue to lead " all the political and cultural work of the organs of the State, and to continue to direct the activities of all the economic organs of the Republic. The task of the party is not merely to distribute its workers properly among the different branches of the state administration, but also to control the very course of work in all essentials." (18) The party must not confine its activities to general propaganda and agitation, but must be looked upon as the advance guard of the working class in its *rôle* as dictator. While it must attract systematically to the work of the State all useful non-party workers and peasants, it should not forget that the chief responsibility for the working of the political and economic organs rests upon the Russian communist party because it alone has been called by history to be the real guide in the dictatorship of the working class. Thus, without forgetting its constant revolutionary tasks, the party must regard leadership in the constructive period of the Revolution as its fundamental duty. Only when its experience in economics grows side by side with the increasing complexity of the economical tasks of Soviet authority does the party fulfil its historical mission. This leadership is essential, especially under the circumstances brought about by the New Economic Policy, for this policy creates a danger of internal degeneration on the part of the bodies of workers and administrators, and a danger also of the distraction of proletarian forces from economical reconstruction. But leadership must not degenerate into interference with the routine of the economic organs, or into attempts at direct administration through appointments, dismissals, and the like.

The only firm basis of proletarian dictatorship is manufacturing industry. " The party, trade unions, unions of youth, our schools, etc., have the task of educating and preparing new generations of the working class ; but all will be found to be built on sand unless they have a growing industrial foundation. . . . (19)

" Agriculture, notwithstanding its present low technical level, has great importance for the whole economy of Soviet Russia." Yet a change in " the centre of gravity of the economic system " is possible ; the peasants' economy may be replaced by industry ; but this can only be done in proportion to " real success in manufacturing," to " restoration of the heavy industries " and to " the coming accomplishment of the work of electrification. . . . The party must work systematically and insistently, without shrinking from making victims, sparing no efforts to accelerate the process of the rapid restoration of industry, including heavy industry." (20)

This document bears the impress of the hand of Lenin, in its general tenor and in its reference to " electrification." He seems to have thought that electrical power, owing to the great advances which have been made in applied science, can be transmitted for immense distances at a cost lower than that of other forms of energy. The economic limits of the transmission of electrical power vary with the comparative costs of prime movers, such as coal, oil, and other fuel, and with the expense of the electrical installation by water power or otherwise. For the supply of power to a region remote from coal or oil deposits, but within reach of water power susceptible of being converted into electricity, (21) the utmost limit of the economical supply of electrical power in competition with other forms of power is probably not more than two hundred miles from the source of the power, and in many regions is not more than half that distance. (22) It is a fantastic dream, therefore, to suppose that the vast plain of European Russia, with its sluggish river systems and infrequent sharp changes in level, could under the present electro-technical conditions be economically furnished with electrical power excepting over a very limited area.

Scarcely less fantastic is the idea that the centre of gravity of Russian economic life can be more or less easily shifted ; in other words, that the peasant can readily be induced or compelled to become an artisan. The enthusiastic phrases of the resolution of the congress of 1923 bear a close resemblance to the utterances of enthusiasts for the promotion of factory industry in Russia in the eighteenth and nineteenth centuries. (23) During a century and a half, it is true, industry was developed under bondage, and for half a century under capitalism, while now the project is to develop industry under collectivism ; but the peasant is not any more easily convinced of the desirability of abandoning the land for which he has an almost superstitious attachment. Relatively high wages may induce migration to the industrial centres ; but the low technical

266 THE RUSSIAN REVOLUTION

ability of the new workers, inevitable under existing conditions, must result in high labour costs when these are compared with the costs in similar industries in central and western Europe. Export would thus be checked and the absence of domestic demand would result in decline of wages, and consequent diminution of inducement to the peasants to be drawn into industry.

The Provisional Government, containing as it did several persons, notably Prince Lvov, who were accustomed to deal with the complicated problems arising out of the historical relations of the central authority with local administrative bodies, had been reluctant for that very reason to legislate in a hurry, even although many of the local grievances had been of long standing and some of the people were clamouring for immediate action. The Soviet Government was not embarrassed by any consideration of historical conditions or local prejudices. It did not owe its existence to the will of the Russian people, and its continuance in power was not subject to popular approval; the principle of its action was not devolution, but centralization of authority.

Immediate measures, however, were necessary because of the dissolution of the imperial system. Poland, Finland, and the Baltic Provinces had long enjoyed a certain measure of autonomy, and these countries were now independent States, in spite of the attempts of the Soviet Republic of Russia to retain control over them. But there were other regions over which it had been able to maintain its influence, and the form of the relations between these and the central authority had to be defined, even although in some cases the peoples had declared their independence. Among such regions were those occupied by the Ukrainians, the White Russians, the Kalmucks, Kirghiz, Crimean, and other Tartars, the Bashkirs, Zirianes, Votjaks, Chuvashi, Turcomans, Yakuts, Georgians, Armenians, Cherkesi, and some others. (24) There were, moreover, other regions which formed the Soviet Republic of Russia properly so-called, and in these the *zemstvo* organization, built as it was upon a system of estate ownership, had crumbled, and Soviets of peasants, working men, and soldiers had sprung up everywhere, loosely organized and without definite relation to the central power.

The combination of which the All-Russian Congress of Soviets was the more or less representative body consisted of a union of four federated and eleven autonomous Soviet republics. The four were called collectively, in the first instance, the Union of Soviet Republics, and later the Union of Socialist Soviet Republics. The initial letters of the Russian words, C.C.C.P. (or in Latin characters, S.S.S.R.), were customarily employed, the name Russia being sup-

## PROBLEMS OF POWER

pressed. (25) These nuclear republics were, first, the Russian Union of Federated Republics; second, the Caucasian Union of Federated Republics (including the Azerbaijan, Armenian, and Georgian), third, the Ukrainian Socialist Soviet Republic; and fourth, the White Russian Socialist Soviet Republic. The whole system was divided into 11 "autonomous" republics, 14 "autonomous" provinces, 76 *gubernie*, 715 *uezds* (districts), and 11,887 *volosts* (parishes or groups of villages).

During the revolutionary year 1917, and again in 1918, there was a heavy movement of population from one part of Russia to another, and for this and other reasons it seemed necessary to initiate at once a study of the problems of local government. The Soviet authorities proposed to reject altogether the customary division of administrative areas on the basis of fiscal convenience, and to attempt to arrange this division on broader economic grounds, as, for example, with respect to roads or other facilities for communication, the economic resources of the regions, the economic tendencies of the population, and the like. "The problem will be rightly decided if the new division is made on the ground of an understanding with the leaders at the centre."

Since the local Soviets were selected mainly from the poorest peasants and were in general dominated by commissars appointed by the centre, the "understanding with the leaders at the centre" would be a foregone conclusion, the result being that the chief consideration in local government arrangements would be the facility with which control from the centre might be applied. The first region which transformed its system of local government was not the Moscow or Russian Republic, but the Ukrainian. The plan adopted was to arrange the administrative divisions of the country " on the basis of their economic character and their adaptability to the Soviet apparatus, with the object of bringing the centre closer to the population." (26) The last clause indicates the intention of the changes, which was clearly to enable the central power to obtain a firm grip upon all the local authorities.

Under the old *régime* the Ukraine was divided into 102 districts, now reduced to 52, and the number of *volosts* (approximately parishes) once 1,989, was now 706. In addition there was organized one Soviet or council for every 1,000 persons. (27)

---

### NOTES

(1) This point of view was stated by V. G. Smithovich, president of the Moscow Soviet of Labour Deputies, and by V. N. Nogen, another Bolshevik leader. (Cf. Yurovich, A., *The Highest Soviet of People's Economy* in *Archives of the Russian Revolution*, vol. vi, p. 305.)

## 268　THE RUSSIAN REVOLUTION

(2) Yurovich, A., op. cit., p. 305.

(3) Ibid. Cf. Krylov's fable, *Young Lion's Education*, translated by Sir Bernard Pares in *The Slavonic Review* (London), vol. ii, pp. 158–60.

(4) Yurovich, A., op. cit., p. 305.

(5) Smelg-Benario, *In the Service of the Soviet*, in *Archives of the Russian Revolution* (Berlin, 1921), vol. iii, p. 147.

(6) Cf. supra, p. 258.

(7) Smelg-Benario, op. cit., vol. iii, p. 148.

(8) Mayer, N., *Service in the Commissariat of Justice and the People's Court*, in *Archives of the Russian Revolution* (Berlin, 1923), vol. viii, pp. 56–60. This interpretation is not convincing. Cf. infra, p. 273.

(9) Some of the Russian musicians, e.g. those whom the Soviet Government attempted to placate by extraordinary allowances, preferred to go abroad as soon as they were able to escape.

(10) This new view was advocated, e.g., by E. D. Kuskov and N. M. Keshken (Yurovich, A., op. cit., p. 306).

(11) These incidents occurred in April 1918.

(12) Yurovich, A., op. cit., p. 307.

(13) Ibid., op. cit., pp. 308–09.

(14) V. Obolensky soon left the Bolshevik group and went to reside in Rome.

(15) Also known as " Lurye," etc.

(16) Yurovich, A., op. cit., p. 309.

(17) Smelg-Benario, op. cit., p. 166.

(18) *The Communist Calendar* (Moscow, 1924), p. 250.

(19) Ibid., p. 251.

(20) Ibid., pp. 249–51.

(21) These circumstances are granted here as being the most favourable for the supply of electrical power.

(22) Total disregard of labour costs, and unlimited resources in labour, might be used to carry electrical power to any distance.

(23) Cf. Mavor, J., *An Economic History of Russia*, vol. i, Book iii, *Industry under Bondage*, especially p. 563 ; and vol. ii, Book vi, *Industrial Development under Capitalism*.

(24) Cf. Mavor, J., op. cit., vol. i, Appendix II; *Sketch of the Ethnology of the People of Russia*, pp. 572–89.

(25) The avowed intention was to add other European and Asiatic States by agreement or by force and to suppress nationality.

(26) From the resolution of the 2nd Assembly of the All-Russian executive committee of the 7th Congress. (Cf. *The Communist Calendar* (Moscow, 1924), p. 483.)

(27) The *gubernie* Soviets were composed predominantly of persons having direct relations with the central government. The *gub* Soviet of Vladimir, e.g., was composed of five representatives of the control commission, one of the metallist union, and one of the land committee. (*Labour Control (Rabochi Kontrol)*, Moscow, May 1, 1918.)

---

For Author's note with reference to hydraulic power, see Appendix E, p. 305.

CHAPTER III

# THE ADMINISTRATION OF JUSTICE UNDER THE SOVIET REPUBLICS

THE Revolution of October 1917 immediately disorganized the course of justice. The Courts of Law, from the Senate, the highest court of appeal, downwards, were abolished; the codes, criminal and civil, ceased to be operative; judges functioned no longer; lawyers struck against the Government; (1) litigation in progress was arrested; and disputes of all kinds remained unsettled.

Yet even in a revolution the currents of human life continue to flow. People had their unsatisfied claims against one another in respect of personal services and possessions, notwithstanding the abolition of the rights of property. Criminals were arrested and held for trial, so also were many who were not criminals, but who were accused of offences against the new laws which in bewildering numbers, and in discordant terms, were being issued every day. Yet there were no courts, and people accordingly remained in prison without trial for long periods. The mechanism of justice under the old *régime* may have been faulty, and the principles of Russian jurisprudence indefensible, but at any rate they comprised a working system now brought suddenly by the Revolution to a complete stop.

The revolutionary tribunals set up for the purpose of trying persons accused of counter-revolutionary activities, and the executive committees of many Soviets, together with the new locally elected proletarian and peasant judiciary, were inundated with all kinds of business. Committees composed wholly of soldiers or peasants, now called upon to deal with divorce and other suits involving personal grievances, were embarrassed by the number of such cases, (2) and were even anxious that the judicial functions, which had devolved upon them without volition on their part, should be transferred to some more appropriate and better qualified tribunal. In the beginning of the year 1918 an effort was made to organize the Commissariat of Justice. As only a few clerks had come over or been brought over to the Bolshevik *régime* from the old judicial ministry, (3) a wholly new personnel had to be appointed. The head of the Commissariat was Steinberg, a Jew, who had been a Left Socialist-Revolutionary, and with him were two assistants, Schröder and Algasov, who belonged to the same group, the last

## THE RUSSIAN REVOLUTION

mentioned being a Tartar. In February 1917 these were joined by others, including Professor Reisner, who was of German extraction.

The Commissariat was now divided into three departments for civil, criminal, and administrative affairs. The head of the civil department (in February 1918) was Krasekov, a Bolshevik, who had been a lawyer practising in the criminal courts. (4) With him were a secretary, an assistant secretary, a consultant, N. Mayer, (5) and a chief consultant. This last was actually the head of the department, because Krasekov rarely put in an appearance, attending only the meetings of the collegium of consultants, though to him were sent the papers concerning projects of law. The work of the civil department was divided into two categories. Under the first were considered all such cases as had been sent in the days before the October Revolution to the former second department of the Ministry of Justice. These cases arose mainly on petitions for appeal to the Senate from decisions of the district courts, and were chiefly concerned with peasant affairs. Fully one-half related to disputes about property in land, (6) and they disappeared when the land was nominally nationalized. Since the Senate had been abolished and no other court of appeal had been established in its place, the Commissariat reserved to itself the hearing of appeals. Under the second category were grouped those cases which were being brought before the department by litigants who were " absolutely baffled by the closing of the courts, and who were bombarding the Commissariat of Justice with all sorts of questions." These litigants were received daily in rotation by a consultant, " who gave information based upon the decrees of the Soviet of the People's Commissariat." (7)

The closing of the courts threw the administration of justice into confusion all over the country. When a case reached the Commissariat, there was some prospect of its being considered by more or less qualified persons ; but when it was brought before the revolutionary tribunals or the elected judges in district or other new quasi-courts in the towns and rural areas, there was but slender chance of any justice being rendered. The persons before whom litigants had to appear were " soldiers and labourers—uneducated in the literal sense of the word." (8)

Even the Commissariat of Justice was not always able to enforce its authority. There was no penalty for disobedience to its decisions ; none of the decrees provided for such a contingency. The force of a verdict of the Commissariat depended upon the goodwill of the litigants. (9) It had no control over the new local courts, excepting in so far as the Government of which

## JUSTICE UNDER THE SOVIET REPUBLICS 271

it formed a part exercised control over all local life. There was no legal gradation of appeals. The decisions of the new local courts were not founded upon any principles of law (for the members of the courts were ignorant of these), or even upon any knowledge of the decrees of the Soviet of People's Commissars. They gave their decisions by the light of their " revolutionary state of mind." (10) Thus verdicts were often indefinite and unintelligible, and difficulties referred to the Commissariat were frequently insoluble.

This state of confusion was not confined to civil causes. Similar conditions obtained in respect of criminal procedure, excepting that as there were no consultants in the criminal department, important decisions, having immediate effect upon the freedom and even upon the life of individuals, were made by persons who were not qualified to weigh evidence. (11) The local revolutionary tribunals, the local Soviet committees, and the rudimentary courts presided over by elected judges—workmen or peasants—before whom were brought persons accused of offences against the Soviet Republic, were very varied in their character. In those cases where the chairman of the tribunal was an intelligent man, not unduly ambitious of a reputation for severity which might be to his advantage in the " higher spheres," if he was courageous enough to permit his personal conscience to impose a check upon his " revolutionary state of mind " and was not susceptible to corrupt influences, it is probable that substantial justice was rendered, irrespective of whether the chairman was familiar with the technique of judicial procedure or no. Where, however, he was unlettered, without knowledge or perspicacity, as was not unusual, or in cases where he was dishonest, grave injustice was frequently done.

The following case was narrated to the author by a participator in the events recorded. A. B. was summoned before a tribunal at X, charged with " speculation," in other words, with private trade for the sake of profit. The chairman of the tribunal was a lamplighter in the employment of the municipality of X. The accused brought with him a witness who gave evidence for the defence. The chairman, rightly or wrongly, conceived the idea that the witness was an accomplice of the accused, and in spite of the fact that the witness had come voluntarily to the court and had been neither accused nor arrested, the chairman sent both A. B. and his witness to jail. There was no lawyer present, as the local lawyers had decided not to plead before the tribunal. The relatives of the imprisoned, however, managed to procure one, but witness, after making a study of the legislation of the Soviet of People's Commissars in cases of " speculation," and also of the procedure before the new courts, this lawyer found that a sentence of imprisonment without indictment

## 272 THE RUSSIAN REVOLUTION

and without trial was explicitly forbidden; so, armed with this argument, he called on the lamplighter, who thought the plea very reasonable, and immediately ordered that the witness should be released.

In some provincial towns the police inspectors fled upon the outbreak of the Revolution of March 1917. During the Revolution of October 1917 a still greater number abandoned their posts, and many were dismissed, and their places filled by university students, boys from the elementary schools, or clerks unaccustomed to police duties, appointed by the Soviets. Such a force was extremely incompetent, and even unconscientious and indifferent. "Very often" an examining magistrate who had summoned a witness to appear before him was told by the police that as "the witness lived in a part of the town remote from the centre, and as the streets were very dirty, the policemen refused to carry out the order." (12) Occasionally, too, the examining magistrate received communications such as this :—

"The executive committee (of a village) wishes to let the citizen examining magistrate know that the notice summoning A. B. (a witness) was not delivered to that person, as the committee knows that he does not know anything about the case." (13)

The following statement was received by an examining magistrate : "I, C. D., revolutionary inspector of militia of E. region, examined on (such a date) citizen F. G. of H. village, who was accused of burglary. The latter did not plead guilty. Considering that the best proof of guilt is self-consciousness, and that as this was not shown by the accused person, I thought the best thing to do would be to make an assay. Therefore I ordered some straw to be brought and the soles of his feet to be burnt. (Signed) C. D., Head of the Militia. P.S.—The assay gave splendid results : the accused confessed." (14)

The last meetings of the legal profession in Petrograd were held in the beginning of the year 1918, when the principal topic of discussion was the "obligatory labour" which had been imposed upon everyone not already enrolled in the ranks of manual workers. Lawyers were not accustomed to work at handicrafts or to watch and direct the movements of machines. They had seen a sudden rupture of the old social life in October 1917, and after that "the clean sweep" of all the laws laboriously built up into a code during the previous three hundred years. (15) The courts of law, presided over and attended by persons who had had professional legal training, had been abolished, and the inferior courts were being replaced partly by workmen's and peasants' Soviets, partly by new tribunals whose presidents and members were elected by the peasants and the

## JUSTICE UNDER THE SOVIET REPUBLICS 273

workmen, partly again by the Commissariat of Justice, which functioned as a court of appeal, and finally by the local Soviets, to which disputants and suitors went because these bodies seemed to be in control of everything. (16) These new institutions might in course of time develop laws, and even, perhaps, a legal system ; but meanwhile all laws were in effect abrogated, and had disappeared because the people paid no further attention to them. The new law arose not merely through the mechanism of various decrees issued by bodies or individuals in a haphazard manner, but through the direct expression of the popular will. At the same time the people were in an anarchic mood and all laws were repugnant to them. A young lawyer named Entin remarked at one of the meetings referred to : " It cannot really be said that the Bolsheviks are not leaning on anything. They do not believe in themselves. They think that they are Caliphs for an hour. They are leaning on the bands of deserters and robbers." (17) This, however, was a very partial diagnosis. The Bolsheviks were depending by accident or design, or by a social miracle, not upon the criminal classes, but upon a mood now prevailing amongst the majority of the people. The people might change their mood, probably they would ; but meanwhile, so long as the Bolsheviks interpreted the popular trend and expressed it in a popular manner, and especially if they did not alter their expressed opinions too rapidly or too slowly, they were likely to remain Caliphs, not for an hour, but for years.

The outcome of these meetings in Petrograd already mentioned was that the lawyers in the capital struck and refused to attend the non-professional courts. Later, most of the lawyers throughout Russia either refrained from attending or carried on a precarious practice of advising clients on their own account and sometimes appearing for them ; the legal profession in Russia was, in effect, destroyed.

Probably the only man of real genius who has chosen to align himself with the Bolsheviks is Anatole V. Lunarchasky, the dramatist, who became Commissar of Education in the Soviet Republic. His account of the Soviet attitude towards law is exceedingly instructive, although undoubtedly it expresses his personal opinion rather than the general view of the communist party. (18)

He begins with the hypothesis that society is not a unit, for inside any social group there are classes whose psychology differs. These classes, in view of their opposed interests and varying conceptions of rights, are continually struggling amongst themselves. The dominant section, by means of its control of the State, secures for itself privileges and meets with equanimity attacks upon these in the courts, because it has itself made the laws which the courts

S

**274** THE RUSSIAN REVOLUTION

administer. Moreover, it endeavours to induce in the minds of the people the belief that this legal system and its contingent series of law courts are concerned with justice. Since the institution of the courts forms the basis of all social life, the shattering of this basis involves the downfall of the whole cultural structure.

" As a matter of fact, the new class, the proletariat in a capitalistic *régime*, carries with it a higher economic order, and struggles for a much higher system of law, than the frail, ossified system of the old *régime*, which appears as the watchdog of the oppressors and exploiters. That new class, so long as it is oppressed, and victimized by the application to it of the law of its masters, is naturally deprived of the possibility of formulating its conception of law. It cannot create in the air its ideal of justice, its ideal court, and its ideal code." (19) If some jurist, a specialist in such matters, were to devise a draft of the projected laws of the coming *régime*, this could be nothing more, at the best, than a fascinating scientific phantasy, as, for example, those that have been described in " novels by Wells and Bellamy." (20) " That kind of work has been done, for instance, by Anton Menger, half *bourgeois*, half socialist, who has acquired thereby a great though theoretical fame."

Every class builds up its system of law (*recht*) in reality, when it applies its power, when it builds up a social order in its " image and likeness "—that is to say, when it builds in accordance with fundamental class interests on the one hand and with real conditions on the other. But no class, even that which acquires political power by overthrowing (i.e. by revolution), can create its world at a stroke. In Marx's words, " this world is being born, enveloped in the material of the old social clothes." Therefore it is obvious that the revolutionary class cannot afford to delay, and dally ceremoniously with the old order ; on the contrary, its task is to destroy and to create. It must carry with it a new conception of law and anticipations of new juridical relations and forms, which are in close accord with the new economic conditions of life created by the Revolution. The revolutionary class also contains within itself a new judicial conscience and new conceptions of good and evil. The Revolution is, in fact, a new law in opposition to the old, it is an act in the mass-trial by the people of the hated order of the privileged classes.

The creation of a new civil and criminal law, a new State, and a new instrument of power, including judicial authority, is at once the confirmation and the fruition of the conception of law underlying the Revolution. This is the creation of a new class interest and a new economic plan. " On November 7 (1917) there was accomplished the greatest Revolution which the world had seen.

## JUSTICE UNDER THE SOVIET REPUBLICS 275

For the first time the toiling classes not merely conquered, but secured the fruits of their victory." They did not give way to timid hesitation as they did in March 1917. " Can we believe that having accomplished this overthrow, having become the political and military masters of the land, the proletariat and the peasantry " would acquiesce in the power of Kerensky and would regard everything " as all right," while the Senate, as if nothing had happened, continued to publish the last laws of the dethroned authority ?

The purpose of every Revolution is the creation of new law, and the giving reality to the new conception of law formed by the masses. That is why a victorious people should at once start to create new courts and a new code, working at first experimentally, groping their way, as it were, " being led by the revolutionary state of mind," (21) and " by degrees shaping the new law and crystallizing the new, beautiful, and solid forms of a really popular justice. To smash in pieces the old justice, the weapon of the enemy and our chains—that is the first duty of the revolutionary when guided by his natural military instinct.

" Afterwards he must plan roughly the foundation of a new justice, leaving the rest [the precise forms] to the creative power of the revolutionary people."

Lunarchasky goes on to remark that the European *bourgeoisie*, having penetrated by degrees into feudal society, was gradually able to replace the old conception of law by a slightly revised Roman law based upon the absolute acknowledgment of private property. The proletariat cannot now proceed after that manner. Its movement is forward and is in no respect backward. For the new proletarian law there are no historical precedents. While it was still within the shell of capitalism, the proletariat had no opportunity to create its new law ; it cannot do otherwise now than learn by practice. The proletariat must create a common law of its own, must draw it up out of the very source of that spiritual movement which brought it to victory, and which now reflects the class character of that revolution as well as the mighty growth of its influence in social life.

" The Soviet of People's Commissars, after abolishing the Tsar and also the *bourgeois* law, calls upon the toiling masses of the Russian people for that creation. . . . The *bourgeois* jurists need not say that what we are talking of, and what the people is going to make to-morrow, is incredible and, from the legal point of view, monstrous. This is not admissible from the point of view of that obdurate false science which is itself founded upon an artificial basis designed to sustain the inhuman law of mastery. Even the most honest and talented *bourgeois* scientific men who have tried

## THE RUSSIAN REVOLUTION

to build up their legal science on the foundation of the real sciences—biology, psychology, and sociology—long before our Revolution, were compelled, as if in anticipation of it, to use our language." (22)

In the street fighting of the Revolution, and in the war of words which accompanied the conflict in the streets, law was constantly in question, because it contains in its very essence a demand for the real force which is to secure the external law for the bearer of that force. The transformation of the inner conception of law into a mighty external code, through the transference of power to new classes, is the gist of the whole matter.

That is how it is put by Lunarchasky; but perhaps it might be more simply expressed in the formula that all statute laws do not meet with universal public approbation, and occasions arise when, in default of the amendment of such laws by competent authority, the law, or even the whole contemporary code, is abruptly abolished by means of a revolution.

Lunarchasky continues : " That is what happened on October 25 (1917), and if, after the Revolution, the ' positive law ' of the *bourgeoisie* had as though by a miracle remained, this would have been incomprehensible, since the victorious Revolution was brought about just to kill it."

Lunarchasky points out that Petradjetsky depicts in detail (23) how, under the influence of changing circumstances, there grows up a new law-ideal which is felt, not distinctly, but very warmly ; how the feeling of justice becomes angrier as it meets greater resistance ; and how it develops " into a fanatical hatred of the existing order and its laws, and finally produces explosion—revolution.

" Petradjetsky does not shrink even from such manifestations of new popular and revolutionary conceptions of law as are surely not to be adopted by the revolution of the proletariat." (24)

To quote from Petradjetsky : " How disgusting the guillotines of revolution seem and how disgusting also the destruction of the centres and nests of culture ! Yet all these appear to be unavoidable consequences of the injured people's feelings. They are due to elemental revenge for the trampling down of right "—that is, the trampling down of the people's conception of right.

" The conclusion," Lunarchasky says, " is clear ; the people carries within itself a new intuitive conception of law which demands, first of all, the destruction of the institutions of the old law which it regards as the greatest and most complete injustice. That intuitive conception of law which reflects in itself the class interests of the masses, and corresponds to the newly born economic order, may only be embodied in distinct form by the process of immediate revolutionary law-creation. Such is the law of revolutions, and,

## JUSTICE UNDER THE SOVIET REPUBLICS 277

especially, of the great overthrow which preceded ours. Down with the justice of the mummy, down with the altars to dead law! Down with judges and bankers, who are prepared to drink the blood of the living upon the fresh grave of the unshared dominion of capital! *Vive* the people that creates in its boiling, brewing courts [i.e. places in which fermentation is going on] new ' law,' ' justice for all,' the law of a great fraternity and equality of the workers! "

These long extracts and condensed passages have been taken from Lunarchasky's article, because this article expresses with more authority, candour, and ability than any other the overt Bolshevik position in relation to the question of justice, and because, in the only forms in which the article is at present available, it is not readily accessible.

It cannot be denied that the argument of Lunarchasky is plausible and interesting. It is, however, conceived in a spirit of romantic anarchism rather than in that of Marxian socialism. If, after the elimination of the *bourgeoisie* and the abolition of *bourgeois* " ideology," as well as of all *bourgeois* institutions, the peasants and workmen of Russia had been left to the development (of their own initiative and in correspondence with their own emergent needs) of a wholly new and original system of law, the process would have been worthy of the most attentive study of students of legal philosophy throughout the world. The details of the actual working of the " new justice " which have been given above show, as far as they go, that while to some extent the local tribunals were left to make their own law or rather to form their own decisions upon individual cases, however inconsequent and inconsistent these decisions might be, they were also bound by general edicts issued by the central government. These edicts were not by any means always concocted by unsophisticated peasants or workmen evolving the terms of the laws out of their " revolutionary state of mind " ; but were in general devised by *bourgeoisie* like Lenin, for instance, whose minds found great difficulty in orienting themselves entirely afresh, and who therefore resorted to the forms and methods of the autocracy which they had overthrown. Nor was their intention otherwise. In establishing what they called the dictatorship of the proletariat, the Bolsheviks meant clearly the dictatorship of the communist party ; and the principles of that dictatorship were derived from an " ideology " that was not indigenous, but was ostentatiously and slavishly Marxian.

Lunarchasky's " new justice " to be developed *ab ovo* by the peasant must have experienced difficulty in finding nourishment owing to the deliberate destruction of its yolk ; but these difficulties

## 278 THE RUSSIAN REVOLUTION

became insurmountable when the peasant was deprived of his freedom of action by a central authority which knew no mercy in the exercise of its " autocratic will."

---

### NOTES

(1) The strike was futile, in face of the abolition of legal procedure.

(2) The case of the Luga Soviet, cf. supra, p. 72.

(3) Mayer, N., *Service in the Commissariat of Justice and the People's Court* in *Archives of the Russian Revolution* (Berlin, 1923), vol. viii, p. 59.

(4) Krasekov was a member of the Executive Committee of the Petrograd Soviet, elected in September 1917 (Spiridovich, A. E., *History of Bolshevism in Russia*, Paris, 1922, p. 368).

(5) N. Mayer was procureur in the Ministry of Justice during the war.

(6) Mayer, N., op. cit., p. 59.

(7) That is, by the Government.

(8) Mayer, N., op. cit., p. 59.

(9) This phrase was much in use in 1917–1918 (cf. infra in Lunarchasky's argument, p. 274).

(10) This condition also obtained in China during the revolution of 1911.

(11) N. Mayer (who had been procureur under the old *régime* and was a lawyer by profession) goes farther than this. He says, without mentioning the name of the person, that the head of the criminal department had not been more than a candidate for service in the Ministry of Justice. He had received temporary employment on probation, and he had simply been allowed to remain in the department. In his (Mayer's) " private opinion and from his observation, undoubtedly he was half a madman " (Mayer, N., op. cit., p. 60).

(12) Pleshko, N., *The Last Provincial Intelligent* in *Archives of the Russian Revolution* (Berlin, 1923), vol. ix, p. 202.

(13) Ibid.

(14) Ibid.

(15) The course of legal history in Russia had been characterized by the gradual suppression of varied and inconsistent local customary laws and the formulation of a general code. Bolshevism reversed this process in spite of its general tendency towards centralization.

(16) E.g., the Luga Soviet.

(17) Mayer, N., op. cit., vol. viii, p. 56.

(18) The article by Lunarchasky from which the succeeding part of the text of this chapter is condensed appeared in *Pravda*, No. 193, December 1–14, 1917. It was reprinted in *Materials of the People's Commissariat of Justice : Popular Courts*, Extract II (Moscow, 1918), pp. 15–19.

(19) *Pravda*, loc. cit.

(20) Ibid. Lunarchasky might with more point have referred to other *Utopias* —especially those of Sir Thomas More and Samuel Butler.

(21) Cf. supra, p. 272.

(22) In support of this statement, Lunarchasky cites Borolzheimer, *System der Rechts* ; Anton Menger, *Neue Staatslehre* ; Jellinck, *Verfassungsänderung und Verfassungswandlung* ; and Petradjetsky, *The Theory of Law.*

(23) Petradjetsky, *The Theory of Law.*

(24) Lunarchasky wrote this before the beginning of the Red Terror. When rumours reached Petrograd that the Kremlin had been bombarded and the church of St. Basil damaged by the mob, Lunarchasky resigned ; but on learning that the reports were exaggerated, he withdrew his resignation. However interesting the two buildings may be as memorials of the history of Russia, their importance as works of art hardly justifies so much concern. Lunarchasky does not seem to have been disturbed by the mass executions, or the retention of political prisoners for years in the fortresses.

## CHAPTER IV

# THE PRESIDIUM OF THE ALL-RUSSIAN SOVIET OF PEOPLE'S ECONOMY

THE task before the High Soviet, or Supreme Council of People's Economy, was nothing less than that of rapidly organizing the supply of necessaries for the millions of people in Russia who were not themselves actually engaged in the direct production of food. The majority of the Russian people lived in self-contained communities, and their power of consumption of the goods manufactured in the industrial centres had always been small, compared with that of the agricultural groups of central and western Europe. The people by whom these goods had been chiefly consumed had been as a class annihilated by dispersal, imprisonment, judicial murder, or depression into the lowest ranks, and their consuming power had vanished with them. Yet, although its character had been altered, social parasitism had not been abolished ; there were, in fact, more parasites than before. Working men rejoicing in their " liberty," and belonging to the " armed proletariat," were little inclined for the drudgery of work, thus aggravating, in the early days of the October Revolution of 1917, the disorganization which previously had infected industry. Even if the factory workers had been willing to work, the failure in production of those industries subject to exploitation deprived the factories of the raw materials necessary for manufacture. The collapse of domestic production, extinction of credit, the blockade maintained by the Allies, the absence of skilled direction, and the dilapidation of the railways, all caused a cessation of external trade and conduced to stagnation of production, unemployment, and the disappearance of industrial discipline. Meanwhile there was an enormously increased and increasing personnel of civil servants owing to the nationalization of industries, and these had to be fed ; moreover, supplies had to be provided for the Red Army, as well as for the people engaged in the operation and maintenance of railways and river transport. In all these groups distress was spreading rapidly. Thus, in the aggregate, the demand for food became enormous, and could only be satisfied from the surplus products left over from the requirements of the peasants. Satisfaction of this demand presented grave difficulties, because immense numbers of the producing classes had been withdrawn. The industrial proletariat were not yielding tangible equivalents for their

## THE RUSSIAN REVOLUTION

maintenance, while the civil servants upon whom fell the responsibility of direction were too incompetent to render adequate services in return for the food they consumed.

Under any political and social system, the recovery of Russia from the exhaustion of the war must have been slower than that of the central and western European countries; under the Soviet political plan and communist system it seemed wellnigh impossible.

The mechanism of exchange and transport had been destroyed, confidence in the stability of communism did not exist, yet the movement of food from the peasant farms to the towns was an urgent necessity. The Soviet Government approached its task with singular optimism. (1) It clung to the belief that somehow everything would organize itself. The " higher spheres " occupied themselves in a futile fashion with details of this or that industry, or with visions of a remote future, while their real problems—the formulation of a general economic plan in conformity with their fundamental ideas, and the co-ordination of effort towards the carrying out of that plan—were not even approached. None of the leaders had any sense of proportion; the Bolsheviks were evidently in revolt against the multiplication table, for they proposed to divide among the peasants more agricultural implements than could be imported or produced in Russia; and again, the suggested " steel programme " would have required four times as much iron as could have been provided under the iron-smelting scheme.

The following conversation illustrates the mood of the Bolshevik leaders at this period (1918). It occurred at a meeting of the Presidium (2) for the discussion of the iron programme. After hearing a statement from one of the members in which plans for the future were expounded, N. Pavlovich, one of the few economists among the Bolsheviks, pointed out that iron production was dependent upon the supply of coal, and that a coal supply adequate for the production contemplated was impossible. He was answered ·by a member of the Presidium, G. I. Oppokov, (3) who said :—

" You are discussing too narrowly, comrades. In the period of planning, of organizing economy, all plans and accounts may be spoiled by some unforeseen circumstances; but our plans do not require to have the detail of a drug-shop. They must be in accordance with our future aims, even though we have not the means of accomplishing them now. We may not be able to reach them to-day; but they will not lose their power to-morrow, and they will stand before us as the ideal for leading the industry. Only in this way, and not by limiting our aims, can we control." The Presidium agreed with Oppokov, (4) and the estimated quantity was, of course, not nearly attained.

## PRESIDIUM OF THE ALL-RUSSIAN SOVIET

Such estimates were all made hurriedly "for to-morrow's meeting," a very usual practice in the case of people who have not had systematic training. Preliminary analytical work in technical and statistical details is indispensable for reliable estimates ; but this was wholly neglected, (5) and, in consequence, plans which had been ratified were frequently subjected to successive alterations, and were sometimes cancelled after work in connection with them had begun. In the case of complex products, co-ordination of production was thus impossible. Corruption also crept in. The managers of private enterprises who were desirous of securing orders from the Government bestowed "gratuities" in appropriate quarters, and received advances, and though the statistical returns of production bore a gratifying proportion to these advances, their relation to the quantity actually delivered was remote. (6) Such machinations were not unknown under the imperial *régime* ; and from time to time persons, even in high places, were severely punished for corrupt practices. (7)

The habit of forming pretentious and unreal estimates, and undertaking recklessly enterprises beyond their experience and their powers, is probably associated with a mood which manifested itself among the Bolsheviks about the time when they leaped into notoriety. The explanation of this mood is suggested in a passage by Maxime Kovalevsky.

"That the character of the Russian *mujik* has been modified by the system of the ' great family ' is proved by the fact that wherever a division of the common property has taken place, wherever the peasant has been reduced by his own will to depend entirely upon his personal industry for his success in life, he has become the pushing, unscrupulous man with whom the American novelist has made us familiar." (8)

In recent Russian memoirs, the expressions "headstrong activity," "primitive diplomacy," "sincerity, fearlessness, and vigour of attack" are all associated—and are evidently regarded as synonymous—with what is called in the same memoirs "business Americanism." Very few Bolsheviks had had real experience of American life ; none of them could have had any conception of the hard, continuous, co-ordinated studies, the discipline of mind and body, the sound and rapid judgment, most valuable, most rare, and most difficult to acquire, which go to produce the competent man of affairs in America as in other countries. Evidently, as Kovalevsky suggested, they were indebted for the business man of their fancy to American novelists, many of whose works were indifferently translated into Russian. Kovalevsky's penetrating observation has, moreover, an important bearing upon the Bolshevik psychology.

## THE RUSSIAN REVOLUTION

The rank and file of the Bolsheviks are of peasant origin. Even men like Lenin, for instance, who was the son of a small landed proprietor, belonged to a class in general scarcely distinguishable in its habits from the peasantry. In parts of Russia remote from the capitals, the small proprietors and the peasants formed the only society. In both groups the large undivided household was the rule, but in both " separations " had been going on. In the peasant group these " separations " were greatly accelerated by the land laws of 1906 and by subsequent extension of these, till the peasant communities and the families of the small landowning class gradually came to be disintegrated. Youths having cast off the family restraints which had hitherto kept in subjection the aggressive traits native to their character, exhibited that truculent and cynical disregard of moral scruple (9) so conspicuous in the conduct and utterances of the Bolsheviks. Their communism, fluctuating as it was owing to the circumstances of its establishment, gave them a career in which their native propensities could find ample scope for development.

It is remarkable that the kind of communism adopted by the Bolsheviks should apparently have had its origin in a protest against the variety practised in the " great " Russian household. (10) The encouragement given by the Stolypin land legislation of 1906 (11) to the breaking up of the large family may be regarded as the efficient cause of Bolshevism.

Struvë and other Russian writers have dwelt with justice upon the foreign origin of the doctrines of the Russian Communist party, but it is obvious that these doctrines would never have obtained a hold upon the mass of the Russian people, unless they had expressed more or less plausibly a mood indigenous to the peasant mind.

The naïve belief of the Bolshevik leaders that, if they could only enlist a few *intelligentsia*, order would quickly be brought out of chaos, suggests that the quality of effectiveness to which they aspired was regarded by them as characteristic of the educated classes and as the means by which miracles could be performed. They appear, indeed, to have abandoned one set of superstitions only to fall victims to another.

In the year 1918 and in the early part of 1919 the president of the Presidium of the High Soviet of the People's Economy was A. I. Rykov, and among the members were G. I. Oppokov, L. Karpov, I. Chubar, J. Weinberg, and L. B. Krassin, (12) with one or two others who rarely attended. Larin, whether he was a member of the Presidium or not, often attended the meetings. Rykov (13) was a man of peasant origin, of middle height, " very badly dressed, worse washed, with a rather clever face, and a not unpleasant aspect. He reminded me of one of those provincial *zemstvo* agronomists or

## PRESIDIUM OF THE ALL-RUSSIAN SOVIET 283

statisticians of radical tendencies. I think he was one of these in the past." Rykov had no special education. He had a bad stutter which compelled him in public speaking to avoid abstract discussion, even if he had been competent to engage in it, and to confine himself to concrete matters. His short phrases and his stammer made his speeches seem very forceful. He thus acquired the reputation of being a good man of business and of possessing " a strong and honest character." Because of this favourable opinion Rykov became manager of interior affairs in the first Soviet of People's Economy. (14) But, according to Yurovich, the real man was a wholly different person from the imaginary one. Lacking in those very qualities of practical and businesslike sagacity which had been attributed to him, Rykov could speak in a fashion not too halting, and with a confident air, upon unimportant schemes for important affairs. He could talk in general terms ; but when any concrete question about actual work arose he was quite helpless and even naïve, saying, after the characteristic peasant fashion, " This is a specialist's business," or, " It will come out somehow." Because of this helplessness in practical matters Rykov was at times credulous and at other times sceptical and obstinate. Thus speculators who were cunning enough to impose upon him secured advantages which were refused to more honest applicants. He had no definite plan of economic organization, only the desire that it should correspond with his rather nebulous social doctrines. In these doctrines he was a disciple of Lenin : " For Rykov, Lenin's words were absolute truth." (15) During the early days of the dictatorship, the economic policy, which was wholly determined by Rykov, involved the nationalization of all large undertakings and the control only of small establishments. A few months later he changed this policy and embarked upon a reckless destruction of private enterprise ; both were due to the influence of Lenin.

The next most influential person in the High Soviet of People's Economy in 1918 was G. I. Oppokov, manager of the department of economic policy. In this department the reactions of any project of law relating to economic life ought to have been carefully studied before the corresponding edict was put in force. Yet nothing of this sort was done. Oppokov imagined himself to be a business man of the type of the American of Russian fancy. If a project bearing the stamp of " America " were placed before him, he was sure to adopt it, and his good will was thus exploited by speculators more shrewd than himself. For instance, according to Yurovich, Oppokov handed over the lead industry in Russia to one firm, because the idea of concentrating in this manner appealed to his imagination as characteristically " American." Accordingly, machinery and raw materials were transferred from other lead enterprises to the favoured plant, with ruinous results to the lead industry. (16) Oppokov was certainly one of the earliest, if not the first, to advance the idea of giving concessions to private persons and companies. He was so naïve and so susceptible to flattery that he was peculiarly exposed to unsound grandiose schemes promoted by international adventurers. One of these schemes, the furtherance of which is alleged by Yurovich to have been accompanied by bribery, was approved and advocated by Oppokov, together with Rykov, Bonch-Bruyevich, and other followers in the High Soviet, but the affair excited the suspicions of someone in the *Che-Ka*, and it was therefore terminated.

Another member of the High Soviet whose attitude of mind was somewhat similar to that of Oppokov was J. Weinberg. This man had been a clerk in a provincial pharmacy, and in so far as it related to party politics, his education was meagre. He was an extreme Bolshevik, perfectly honest, strong-willed, and full of self-confidence. He could make long speeches and impress his audiences with his sincerity, and so he was sent by the trade unions to represent them in the High Soviet. Yurovich remarks that " at that time the Bolsheviks were flirting with the labour masses, and therefore representatives of these masses were taken into " the High Soviet. Weinberg was entrusted with the conduct of the department erected for the purpose of directing nationalized establishments. His principle of management was to make " quick decisions " and to take rapid action, after the fashion of American business as it was conceived by the Russians. Weinberg's " quick decisions " were " always childishly fantastic or simply ignorant, and his rapid action was shown only in his shoutings to engineers. . . . His orders were practically always ruinous to the establishments under his control, but they had to be carried out. When comment was made about his management, he became furious, and accused his colleagues of *sabotage*, and his critics of lack of understanding of socialist methods. His colleagues learned to let him alone. It was better, they thought, that nationalized establishments should be ruined, than that colleagues should quarrel with one another." He spoke on every subject brought before the Presidium and very often carried his point, after the characteristic fashion of a peasant debater, by shouting down his opponents and winning because they were the first to be exhausted. His arguments were usually of the vaguest, and his proposals were generally impracticable.

Of a type very different from Rykov, Oppokov, and Weinberg was the manager of the chemical department of the Presidium, L. Karpov, an engineer. Karpov was a sound expert, not young, very calm and level-headed. He saw quite clearly that the

## PRESIDIUM OF THE ALL-RUSSIAN SOVIET

economic policy of the Bolsheviks as carried out by the Presidium of the Soviet of People's Economy was rousing the hatred of the people, and he prophesied its speedy destruction, though he himself was a member and had his share in its activities. But Karpov was an old Bolshevik, and was reluctant to separate himself from his political friends. Yurovich remonstrated with him on his retention of office in a party with which he had ceased to be in sympathy, but he answered, " Imagine yourself in the army, and in the last fight with the enemy. You can see that the army is not disciplined, very badly instructed, very badly equipped, disorganized, full of murderers and swindlers. The leaders are making one blunder after another. In short, you can see clearly that the affair is hopeless. Would you therefore leave the army during the struggle ? I cannot do that. I would rather die with these swindlers." (17) Karpov objected strongly to the *Che-Ka* and its terrorism, and he spoke of Dzerjensky, the head of the *Che-Ka*, as " that *bête humaine*." (18)

I. Chubar, another trade-union representative upon the High Soviet, had been a railway employee, and for that reason he was made manager of the department of transport. He was a Little Russian, with the practical sense of his people, had a calm manner, and was " quite intelligent." His confidence in the soundness of the socialist doctrines was sufficient to neutralize the pessimistic tendency of his mind. In the department managed by him he was clever and careful so long as questions of only minor importance had to be settled ; but when big problems of policy arose, he was incapable of dealing with them, and the result was confusion.

Nobody could stand more in need of a privileged *advocatus diaboli* than the High Soviet of the People's Economy. The person who performed this *rôle* was Michael Solomonson Lurie, who, although he had other names, was best known as Yorie Larin. In a group whose members in general had but scant respect for economic science, Larin was the conspicuous economist, although his economics had little in common with any recognized economic principles. " Half paralysed," he attended the meetings of the Presidium with a nurse and a hospital attendant. Tall, melancholy, and with a look of suffering, he had a gleam of sardonic humour in his eyes that gave him a resemblance to Mephistopheles. Clever and educated, speaking in a clear, concise, logical, and sarcastic fashion, he exposed the weak points in the projects of the members of the Presidium, and his exposition must have acted like a cold douche upon minds unaccustomed to hard thinking, upon peasants like Rykov, trade unionists like Weinberg and Chubar, and banal *bourgeoisie* like Oppokov. After launching his criticisms, Larin seems to have been in the habit of making constructive suggestions,

286 THE RUSSIAN REVOLUTION

as if, having denounced false currency, he felt himself called upon to replace it with something genuine. Yurovich remarks that " it is hard to explain the strange contradiction between the critical and constructive intelligence of this talented man, although this contradiction was his main characteristic." (19) In his writings, one of which is noticed in a later chapter, Larin discloses a certain logical coherence. Probably he alone of all the Bolsheviks realized clearly the inevitable implications of the Bolshevik abolition of private property. It is not clear, however, that his talent for analysis went so far as to make him see that there was a contradiction between the logically coherent economic system devised by him, and certain fundamental characteristics in human society which must prevent it from ever being realized.

It is not surprising that Larin's criticisms disturbed the other Bolsheviks who fancied themselves to be economists, and that his constructive ideas appeared to them to be merely scholastic phantasmagoria impossible to associate with the processes of real life with which, at every moment in their stormy career, they were coming into actual contact. Yet, by the magnetic influence of his personality, Larin convinced his colleagues at the end of 1919 that the next step would have to be the abolition of money.

When the commissariat of finance introduced a scheme for dealing with the rapid devaluation of currency, Larin sharply criticized the project, and made the drastic proposition that the simplest and best plan was to abolish money, and to substitute " natural " exchange or exchange in kind for a currency based even indirectly upon metal. He seems to have had in his mind a system similar to the Labour Notes of Robert Owen, involving the exchange of a definite quantity of goods of the first necessity for another definite quantity of similar objects. Larin proposed that on January 1, 1920, the Soviet Government should begin to pay in that way, and that at the same time it should call in all the money in circulation. He suggested further that each receipt for labour service should be valid for a definite time only, and in this way the accumulation of pecuniary capital would be prevented.

The Soviet ratified his proposal, and orders were apparently given to print these " receipts," otherwise Larin's " natural money." But the printing-presses were choked with the supply of paper roubles which were being demanded in phenomenal quantities, and delay occurred in getting the " natural money " through. Meanwhile other difficulties emerged, and the Presidium began to entertain doubts about the scheme. The result was that the projected " reform " of Larin, to the fury of its author, was not carried into effect, and a less drastic currency reform was subsequently adopted.

## PRESIDIUM OF THE ALL-RUSSIAN SOVIET 287

Meanwhile another personality of a different type was introduced into the High Soviet: this was Leonid Borisovich Krassin. Krassin was a Siberian, born in 1870 at Kurgansk in the *gub* of Tobolsk. He was educated at the St. Petersburg technological institute, and was implicated in the student disorders of 1890 and again in the demonstrations of 1891. He became a member of the Bolshevik faction of the Social-Democratic party soon after its formation, but from 1905–1907, though still belonging to the party, he did not take any active part in the revolutionary movement. After receiving the education of an engineer, he embarked upon a business career, and became the manager of a succession of large industrial enterprises and sat on the direction boards of others. For some years before the war he acted as a director in Russia of the Russian branch company of the electrical firm of Siemens-Schuckert, Berlin, and managed some of its enterprises. This firm had pursued an aggressive commercial policy, by means of which, sometimes at the cost of temporary pecuniary sacrifice, it obtained an important share of electrical business. Krassin was reported to have been in receipt of large salaries and to have accumulated thereby a considerable fortune.

He resumed interest in his party in 1917, but even after the October Revolution he did not for some time take a prominent part in its activities. Only after the dictatorship appeared to be firmly established did he accept any share of responsibility, and even then he would occupy only the position of manager of one of the departments of the Petrograd Soviet. Later he became a member of the All-Russian Soviet of People's Economy, and from that time played an important though varying *rôle* in Russian affairs.(20) In the group of theorizing emigrants, journalists, self-educated workmen and peasants, and quite uneducated people who occupied the Bolshevik stage, Krassin was conspicuous as the one man who had behind him " a really solid commercial and administrative past."(21) He corresponded to the aggressive, successful, " American " type of which the Russian peasant dreams, consequently his fellow-Bolsheviks deferred much to him, and even stood in awe of him as a kind of Russian Rockefeller or Stinnes whom they had been lucky enough to enlist on their side. Krassin had an imposing manner, and never condescended to the intimate familiarity customary among the Bolsheviks. Though standing aloof, he seemed to impress his fellows with a sense of strength and power held in reserve which might be available on occasion. He dressed well, even when times were very hard, and was a careful, rather than a good, speaker. The simple-minded rank and file of the Bolsheviks looked upon him as someone they could lean on, who could take upon his shoulders

288 THE RUSSIAN REVOLUTION

all their practical troubles and enable them to get rid of the harassing and uncomfortable feeling of ignorance and helplessness in face of the urgent problems that were continually confronting them. (22)

Only rarely did he say or do anything which recalled the fact that he was a Bolshevik; in general, his projects and utterances had little in common with the ideas of any of the socialist parties. Yet he never argued against even the most fantastic of socialist doctrines; indeed, he always expressed agreement with the Soviet decrees. Yurovich remarks that the Bolsheviks believed in him; but to Yurovich himself and to others as well he " appeared to be very insincere." This impression was confirmed by two or three incidents. When people went to Rykov demanding concessions to start private enterprises, Krassin was usually called in for consultation. On such occasions he adopted a very sharp socialistic tone, and proposed to Rykov that the matters in question be held over for detailed examination by Krassin himself, to whose office the applicants were then invited. He at once expressed himself as satisfied with the justice of their demands, and gave them more than they anticipated. Yurovich ventures upon a diagnosis and a prophecy : " Some people have come to the conclusion that Krassin is not a Bolshevik at all; and perhaps this is true. I am inclined to agree. He was one when he was a boy; and the only reason why he did not break away from the party was that the *intelligentsia* were glad to help any revolutionary organization, even though the party programme was quite different from their ideas. In 1917, when people were hurrying to attach themselves to one party or another, Krassin attached himself to passivism. . . . It might be that, being far-sighted, he saw, as did many other people, in which direction the labouring masses would go, and thought that if he adhered to the Bolshevik party he might be able to save the industrial enterprises of which he was director; and then, after a time, he looked round and saw before him a career which turned his head. . . . From the Russian Carnot to the Russian Barras, that might be his road. To become actual dictator of Bolshevik Russia under the Bolshevik flag, and then to bring Russia from the Bolshevik phantasy to normal order (naturally saving for himself in the new Russia the wealth that he had accumulated on the road) : that is the engineer L. B. Krassin; that is—as I see it—the secret of this man." (23)

The activities of the High Soviet of People's Economy, attempting as it did to control every transaction and to draw into its net all economic relations, involved the employment of a large number of so-called counter-agents—really police—whose business lay in discovering breaches of the stringent trade laws. In the summer of

## PRESIDIUM OF THE ALL-RUSSIAN SOVIET 289

1918 there was a large number of these agents, and at that date there were still many enterprises unnationalized, but kept in operation as far as possible. The owners, or the technical employees and managers, were supplied with subsidies because the absorption of the banks by the Soviet had extinguished the usual sources of credit. There thus grew up a kind of partnership between the Soviet and private enterprises, but the managers of the businesses concerned found great difficulty in inducing the Soviet to keep to the terms of its contracts (24), though through its counter-agents the Soviet sought to detect any breach of contract on the part of the managers.

Yurovich's detailed account of the working of the Soviet system with its complicated series of Soviets, committees, commissariats, departments, sub-departments, and sections, together with his criticism that the whole lacked a definite plan of construction, and that officials were more numerous than necessary, might be applied to any government in any country ; as also his account of the personnel of the Presidium of the All-Russian Soviet of People's Economy (chief guardians of the economic interests of the people) with its commonplace level of ability and character. Governmental administration everywhere presents more or less the same features—lack of plan and too many officials—but the chief point of difference between the Soviet and other systems lay in the total absence of administrative experience on the part of the persons in power. The object-lesson of Soviet Russia would therefore seem to prove that it takes something over and above a revolution to work a radical change.

The technical newspapers occasionally criticized minutely the methods of the Government, yet it was not very safe to do so. There was a prevailing spirit of confidence in the future and indifference to detail, precisely the attitude of mind that is found in politicians in what are described as new countries, and which, though good up to a point, leads, when pushed to extremes, to economic and other disasters. " Some sort of ridiculous optimism makes them [the Bolshevik leaders] believe that they are doing a very large business. . . ." (25) They were not disturbed when they were reproached for the carelessness with which their plans were drawn up and the divergence between these plans and actualities, and they usually laid the blame of failure upon *bourgeois* opposition.

Lenin knew better. " We have not yet been able," he said, speaking in December 1920, (26) " to learn [the lessons of] our practical experiment. . . . We make mistakes—in that we are masters ; but we are not able to study our own experiment and to correct [our errors in] it."

T

## THE RUSSIAN REVOLUTION

An obvious and convincing proof of the defect noticed by Lenin is the sternness with which the Bolsheviks suppressed all criticism.

A phase of the futile activities of the All-Russian Soviet of People's Economy was the frequent creation of new departments. These were generally set going through some communist, interested in economic questions, who had made a report upon some subject to the High Soviet, only to find himself appointed as the head of a new department formed for the purpose of carrying out his suggestions ; or through some *bourgeois* specialist who contrived, through the High Soviet, to get control of a branch of industry.(27)   The result of this casual formation of departments was that their respective functions were not defined, and that they often competed with and overlapped one another with regard to the carrying out or cancelling of work.   Some of the more timid heads of departments rendered neutral reports upon everything to the Presidium, others, more courageous, acted on their own responsibility ; even "nationalization" and "confiscation" were carried out by them without reference to the Presidium.

The relations between the All-Russian Soviet of People's Economy and the commissariats and departments under the commissars were very ambiguous.   With some of the commissariats the Soviet exhibited a tendency to restrict their power sharply and to use them merely as advisory and executive bodies, requiring them to act only under orders and to refrain altogether from proceeding on their own initiative.   The commissariats or administrative departments with which the All-Russian Soviet of People's Economy was most continuously interfering were those of trade and industry, labour, agriculture, food, and transport—those, in fact, which were most directly concerned with economic life.

There seemed to be a tendency to regard the Soviet system as represented by the All-Russian Soviet of People's Economy as an ideal organization for the establishment of a communist order. Therefore the administrative departments which represented a hierarchical, as opposed to a conciliar system were subordinated to the Soviet, and came to be regarded as technical advisers and servants whose duty lay in obedience to orders rather than in the development of independent initiative.   This meant that the politicians desired to obtain, and did obtain, complete control over the administrative departments, and since the actual functioning of the economic life of the country in every aspect was placed under the control of the administration by violent seizure, supplemented by legislation, all economic power fell into the hands of the Soviet. Yet there was a more or less continuous struggle against this tendency.   The politicians were members of the Soviet ; but the heads

## PRESIDIUM OF THE ALL-RUSSIAN SOVIET

of departments were members also, and their view of their relation to the Soviet was coloured by their own relation to the department. As departmental heads, they disliked the idea of subordination, and this led to frequent disputes. The Soviet cancelled or amended regulations issued by the commissariat of trade on the relation of employers and employed during the period of gradual nationalization, and later when the New Economic Policy came into operation. Sometimes it would take upon itself duties which had previously been departmental, e.g. the distribution of agricultural machinery, although that was the function of the department of agriculture. Sometimes, again, the Soviet would issue food regulations and give orders relating to railway administration, although there were special governmental organs for both these duties. The departments protested, and attempted to retain in their own hands the exercise of functions within their sphere ; but the Soviet always managed to defeat them. Yet the result of any one conflict was not always speedily known, and it was impossible to foresee what the Soviet might do next, or what view it might take upon a particular subject. Thus the administration was speedily reduced to chaos.

The relation of the Soviet to the individual citizen was even more uncertain. Its various proceedings clearly indicate that it recognized no limits to its authority, for even after endowing a commissariat with definite powers, the Soviet still reserved to itself the right to interfere whenever it saw occasion to do so. Moreover, it conceived that not only should it regulate and manage in detail those industries which had been explicitly nationalized by itself or by some other authority, but should also exercise similar functions with regard to any question with which the economy of the people was in any degree concerned. Such matters, for instance, as would otherwise have been settled by the courts of law, or submitted for arbitration by mutual consent, were now brought before the Soviet to be dealt with summarily and without possibility of appeal against its decisions. The Soviet of the People's Commissars—corresponding to the Council of Ministers of the old *régime*—was powerless, excepting in so far as the members of that body were also members of the Soviet of the People's Economy. While the Soviet thus performed the functions of a civil court, it also acted as a criminal court, even on occasion reviewing the decisions of the already existing criminal tribunals. If, for example, a decision was made of which it disapproved, the Soviet might order the arrest of anyone, and the actual orders of arrest were generally given by managers of departments, their assistants, secretaries, or even clerks, although the number of arrests after this manner was not very great. When this happened, however, the prisoners found their position very hard,

## THE RUSSIAN REVOLUTION

for they were often forgotten, since no one knew their place of imprisonment, nor by whose order they had been arrested, and sometimes not even the offence of which they stood accused. When inquiries were made by the relatives of persons imprisoned under such circumstances, the only answers were, "We know nothing about the matter," "We have had nothing to do with this prosecution." Occasionally, by chance, through promise of a bribe, or some other means, a prisoner obtained his freedom.

In exercising the functions of legislator and executive, the Soviet came to disregard all consistency, and therefore all law. It had slender regard for the terms of an agreement into which it had entered. "It thought that it had the right to annul the contract, or to amend it, and did not recognize any claim for compensation on the ground of breach of contract." The Soviet position rested upon two bases, first, by its doctrines it had the right to limit or abrogate private rights, and thus also it could alter, by extension or otherwise, the rights of the Soviet itself; and secondly, in a socialistic *régime* the economic freedom of citizens has no existence.

Yurovich remarks that the effect of this doctrine was to make the public authority the possessor of a private property right, (28) the relationship between the State and individual being that of possessor and possessed. There is nothing new in this; it was the legal conception of the State under the older or Kalita dynasty. The land, and the people upon it, were the heritable property of the sovereign—his *votchina*; but under the Romanovs the State ceased to be the *votchina* of the Tsar. (29)

Thus, by abolishing individual rights, the dictatorship revived an old private right vested in the possessors of power which gave them control over the lives and property of the inhabitants of the State territory. Instead of advancing, they went back more than three centuries to a legal position which had been an important factor in originating the Revolution and the subsequent anarchy of "the period of troubles;" (30) the circumstance that the power was held in one case by a single individual and in the other by a self-perpetuating group is an insignificant detail. Sometimes the people's provincial courts, at a loss for principles to guide them, employed the old methods and forms of procedure. Should the decisions arising from the use of the old methods not suit the Soviet, it took no notice of them, ignored all protests made against its action by the provincial courts, and sought no aid from them in carrying out its own decrees. (31)

The character of the officials who were engaged in conducting the business of the Soviet as described above may be gathered from the following account by A. Yurovich. He says that the general

## PRESIDIUM OF THE ALL-RUSSIAN SOVIET 293

opinion entertained by the people in Moscow who had to deal with the Soviet officials was that the majority of them in 1918 were party communists, or at least Left Social-Democrats or Internationalists near to the communist platform, and that no material difference in the officials from the point of view of political and social opinions could be traced. This, however, by no means accurately represented the Soviet bureaucracy. In the superior ranks of the Soviet service, and also among the crowd of less important workers, there were communists, but most of these persons were not Bolsheviks. The majority was composed of " counter-revolutionists of different categories. The inferior places were taken by numerous girls and young men who had previously been book-keepers, shopmen, clerks, students, and boys from the gymnasium. These young people were working for the Soviet because the pay was relatively high, and because they were so numerous that there was very little work for each of them. All day they were running about in the corridors, flirting, hurrying out to buy cakes, dividing among themselves tickets or beef conserves, swearing profanely at the Bolsheviks, and talking about Myrbach coming to Moscow with German soldiers. If anyone went to the office on business, he would have to wait a long time." When he found someone to attend to him, he was usually told that the person who had charge of the matter in question was absent. " If the girl was amiable, she would take the trouble to go and find the official ; but generally she would send the visitor to another department," where he would have to go through the same procedure all over again.

There were, however, many honest officials of the old *régime* who prepared their reports laboriously and conscientiously in the form prescribed by previous custom, only to find that the matter had long before been decided off-hand without regard to precedent or serious examination. (32) These conscientious officials were tied to their desks bacause they could not live otherwise. There were some romantic people who imagined that working in the enemy's citadel was an adventure, and there were also dishonest officials who robbed everyone with whom they came in contact. The process by which they did this was very simple. They obtained large advances on account of some important expenditure, and by retaining these advances in their own hands for a time, or even altogether, they were able to make large profits, in fact, many previously honest people resorted to this practice. The use of public funds in this way could rarely be detected because no accurate accounts were kept ; the collection of taxes from private enterprises was thus a fruitful source of illicit revenue. There was also " the grandiose field of bribery." Some people were willing to pay to be

## 294 THE RUSSIAN REVOLUTION

kept off the list for nationalization or to be put on the list of those to whom Soviet contracts might be given ; others simply paid out of fear. " The officials would frighten such persons by threatening them with arrest for some offence or alleged offence in contravention of some real or imaginary law, and they opened their pockets, not as in the old cheap time, but sometimes in ' Homeric ' fashion. The dishonest officials were rarely caught ; and if they were, they could resort to bribery in order to escape. Only if the *Che-Ka* interfered " might escape be difficult. (33)

### NOTES

(1) Yurovich calls it " light-headedness."

(2) Of the All-Russian Soviet of People's Economy.

(3) G. I. Oppokov (known also as A. Lomov), son of a rich bank director of Saratov. Educated as a lawyer, but did not practise. Young, inexperienced, except in party affairs. Was Commissar of Justice in Lenin's first list, but was soon replaced. Became manager of the department of economic policy in the High Soviet of People's Economy.

(4) Yurovich, A., op. cit., p. 311. The variety of Bolshevism represented by Oppokov is very familiar ; it is rampant wherever what is known as " public ownership " is advocated by politicians who are ignorant of the subject.

(5) The Bolsheviks are not the only public officials who produce fantastic estimates.

(6) Yurovich, A., op. cit., p. 310.

(7) Under the Bolsheviks, the critics of the Government were sent to jail, not those who took bribes.

(8) Already quoted in Mavor, J., *An Economic History of Russia*, vol. ii, p. 266. The passage is from Kovalevsky, Maxime, *Modern Customs and Ancient Laws of Russia* (London, 1891), p. 61.

(9) Lenin says of the Russian landowners, " they were committing all sorts of brutality and crime " (*Collected Works*, vol. xiv).

(10) For the character of the " great " or undivided household (two or more generations living commensally), see Mavor, J., op. cit., vol. ii, pp. 266 et seq.

(11) Ibid., p. 342.

(12) Properly Krasen.

(13) Yurovich, A., op. cit., p. 319.

(14) On the death of Lenin, Rykov succeeded him as President of the Soviet of People's Commissars.

(15) Yurovich, A., op. cit., p. 320.

(16) Ibid., op. cit., p. 321.

(17) Karpov died of typhus in 1921. He and his wife refused to purchase food illegally, although their ration was extremely slender.

(18) Yurovich, A., op. cit., p. 322.

(19) Ibid., op. cit., p. 324.

(20) In 1924 he became Soviet ambassador at Paris, where, as in his residence in London, he attracted attention by his ostentatious manner of living.

(21) Yurovich, A., op. cit., pp. 324–25.

(22) Ibid., op. cit., p. 325.

(23) Ibid., op. cit., p. 326.

(24) Ibid., op. cit., p. 313.

(25) Ibid., op. cit., p. 311.

## PRESIDIUM OF THE ALL-RUSSIAN SOVIET 295

(26) Lenin, N., *Transition to the New Economic Policy of 1921 : Address to the Communist Party, 8th All-Russian Soviet Congress,* December 30, 1922 (*Collected Works*, Moscow, 1923, vol. xviii, Part i, p. 16).

(27) Yurovich, A., op. cit., p. 311.

(28) Ibid., op. cit., p. 314.

(29) Cf. Mavor, J., op. cit., vol. i, p. 155.

(30) 1598–1613.

(31) Yurovich, A., op. cit., p. 315.

(32) This practice is not unknown outside Soviet Russia.

(33) Yurovich, A., op. cit., p. 318.

# CHAPTER V

## THE CONCRETE ECONOMIC PLAN OF THE BOLSHEVIKS

DURING the first six months of their rule the leaders in the Soviet Government were few in number ; they had many external distractions and they had little leisure for the formulation of an economic programme and practically no trained assistance for carrying such a programme into effect. It is not surprising, therefore, that very slight progress was made in that period towards the building up of a new society. But the processes of social existence do not remain inactive nor do they await the convenience of legislators. Spontaneous readjustments of social changes induced by the two phases of the Revolution pursued directions which were by no means in accordance with the preconceived ideas of any of the socialist parties. When more or less logically coherent schemes were formulated, intended to be uniformly applicable throughout the immense Russian area, the difficulties of their application in presence of these spontaneous readjustments became manifest.

Lenin had been of opinion that definite plans for the morrow of the Revolution, concocted beforehand in the leisure of the study, were futile. He thought that such plans if they were made would simply hamper a revolutionary government, because, at the best, they must be adapted to special circumstances, and at the worst, would be likely to be thrown aside, while a plan hastily produced on the spur of the moment, and under the pressure of events, might better serve the Government's purpose.

M. S. Lurie, (1) writing under the *nom de plume* of " Yo. Larin," on May 1, 1918, published a significant article, (2) in which he says : " It is the misfortune of the proletariat and its leaders that there was a lack of system in the first moments after the overthrow. . . . Only through experience could there be found a sufficient basis for a plan. From now onwards the finding of a programme will be easier and more successful, because the leading circles of the proletariat have shown considerable ability in the understanding of life and the retention of power. In this sense the proletariat ' has passed its examinations.' I want now to do again what I did in November (1917), viz. summarize an economic policy as a programme for the coming period.

" Some months ago I wrote in *Izvestia* various recommendations about economic measures. Many of these have already been

## CONCRETE ECONOMIC PLAN OF BOLSHEVIKS 297

adopted—1st, Nullification of loans. 2nd, Establishment of main committees in different branches of industry. 3rd, Establishment of barter. 4th, Turning every *volost* into a unit for the supply of bread and for receiving manufactured products.

" In the midst of the leading circles I have always had to fight against various tendencies and against the lack of a common, definite economic plan."

The new programme recommended by Larin was as follows : 1st, Nationalization of the banks. 2nd, Refusal of permission to foreign banks to establish themselves in Russia. 3rd, Nationalization of industry, branch after branch. Mixed State and capitalistic trusts not to be allowed. 4th, Settlement of accounts between different industries to be arranged [by cheque] without money. 5th, Private transactions to be replaced by co-operative commerce controlled by the " main " committees. 6th, State purchase of goods. 7th, Organization of imports. 8th, Diminution of the numbers of the army to 300,000, costing 3 millions instead of 30 milliards of roubles. 9th, High property and income taxes. Adoption of a sales tax. 10th, Abolition of compulsory labour service. 11th, Establishment of a leading centre in each locality for the carrying out of State enterprises. 12th, The economy of the State to be spread gradually over agriculture, beginning with the organization of state sowing upon landowners' lands.

In this programme there is a strange mixture of naïveté and shrewdness.

1. The banks have now all been nationalized.
2. No foreign bank was at all likely to embark upon business in Russia under the conditions imposed by the Soviet Government. This item in its extended form contains the naïve suggestion that loans might be contracted in Europe and America on the security of a mortgage on a part of Kamtchatka !
3. Industries were all nationalized ; but under the New Economic Policy, precisely such mixed state and capitalistic trusts are encouraged, although up to now there has been reluctance on the part of investors to embark funds in Russia.
4. Settlement of accounts by cheque as an item in a revolutionary programme is amusing.
5. The control of commerce by political committees is precisely the most doubtful point in the whole economic programme. It has not been shown to be either effective or advantageous in any sense. Delay and additional cost seem inevitable consequences of such control.

# THE RUSSIAN REVOLUTION

6, 7. The state purchase of goods and the organization of imports are dealt with later.

8. The costs of the army have been reduced because of the cessation of civil war, but they are still understood to be very high.

9. The provision in this new programme for an income tax, a property tax, and a sales tax, suggests that six months after the Bolshevik Revolution the process of nationalization was still incomplete, that there remained some taxable private property, some incomes received otherwise than from wages paid by the State for services rendered in state enterprises, and that there still existed private trade upon which a sales tax might be levied. No doubt there did exist such property, such incomes, and such transactions. The disclosure of these for purposes of taxation does not in other countries lead to confiscation, and therefore taxes upon them are collectable. In Russia, disclosure of property in any form was almost certain to result in its expropriation, and the disclosure of an income would have equally undesirable results, whilst the revelation of sales upon which a tax could be levied might lead at once to charges of speculation before the new tribunals.

10. Compulsory labour service seems to have been abolished. The reason given for the suggested abolition is that it places the proletariat at the mercy of the peasantry, in other words, the compulsion can be enforced upon the factory hand, but cannot be enforced upon the field worker. Larin suggests that compulsory service should be retained only for members of the previously dominant classes. Obviously this is merely a vindictive suggestion, and is not determined by any economic motive.

11. This seems a reasonable administrative measure.

12. The spreading of the state economy over agriculture can have only one meaning in this connection : it is designed to make all the peasantry in effect state peasants. Since the peasants had succeeded, through the legislation of Stolypin, in throwing off what they considered as the yoke of the *mir*, and since in the summer and autumn of 1917 they had by their own acts discarded the burdens placed upon them by their landlords, they were not likely to submit themselves to the yoke of the State unless they encountered invincible force.

In May 1918 the First All-Russian Congress of the Soviets of People's Economy met at Moscow. There were present about

## CONCRETE ECONOMIC PLAN OF BOLSHEVIKS 299

250 delegates from central and northern Russia, and also from Siberia, Ural, and Turkestan. They were drawn from such divergent centres as Vladivostock and Vitebsk, Archangel and Astrakhan, and were divided into two categories : 103 had a decisive vote and 149 had no vote at all. The members represented regional Soviets, trade unions, supply organizations, and co-operative societies. This congress was significant, for in it there were gathered all the most important people who were actually engaged throughout the immense Russian region in attempting to work out in practice the semi-communistic, semi-collectivist system introduced by the Bolsheviks.

The central authorities had performed their share in the process of destruction throughout the country, as had the peasants and the workmen by " direct action." The members of the Congress of Soviets of People's Economy were now trying to construct. They were, indeed, undertaking a task of immense difficulty, and they encountered on all sides most formidable obstacles—technical, administrative, and social—and they could look back upon only five and a half months of experience.

The work of this congress was divided into three parts : 1st, Analysis and study of the contemporary economic structure of Russia, including (a) the study of the internal situation as a whole as well as of the different branches of economic life ; and (b) the study of the international situation, especially in connection with the Brest-Litovsk Treaty. 2nd, The planning of an economic programme for the future. 3rd, The organization of economic life, e.g. instruction in the art of administering nationalized enterprises, in the turning over of goods, in building up a supply of agricultural machinery, and the organization of the Supreme Council of People's Economy.

The members of the congress were almost all communists. There were only a few Left Socialist-Revolutionaries, a solitary Syndicalist, and one Independent. The communists were divided into Right and Left groups, the former being in the majority. The resolutions brought forward by the Left communists were none of them passed. The unanimous view of the congress was that the economic situation of Russia was depressed ; but regarding the measure of that depression and the means to be taken to overcome it there was profound disagreement. Those who took an optimistic view were Lenin, Radek, (3) and others of extreme Bolshevist tendency ; those who were pessimistic included Obelensky, Ryazanov, (4) Gastiev, and Pletniov. The latter group refused to admit any possible outcome of the situation other than catastrophe. " An engineer cannot build a railway without first making a survey, and we cannot build a new social structure and lay down a new

# THE RUSSIAN REVOLUTION

way without learning first what we have [by way of resources] and where our way is to be laid down. Without estimating correctly the economic situation we cannot formulate correctly the approximate economic programme." (5) Clearly the congress was unwilling to accept a mere statement of hopelessness, and was glad to adopt the alternative of studying the situation with a view to formulating a constructive policy. In the carrying out of this they might at least hope to avoid disaster. The first point to which the congress addressed itself was an estimate of the change in economic life produced by the separation of the Ukraine and Poland from what had been the Russian Empire. Many reports dealt with that important question. (6) Radek said : " We have lost the Donetz basin with its iron and coal. We have lost 90 per cent. of our sugar industry. (7) We have lost regions from which Russia used to receive its surplus bread-stuffs which served as a means of exchange. Because of the separation of the Ukraine we lost about 516 million *pùdi* of bread-stuffs which the Ukraine had as a surplus, and we lost coal to the extent of 300 to 350 million *pùdi*." (8)

The Russian Soviet Government does not seem to have contemplated at this time (May 1918) the policy of coercion which it afterwards applied to the Ukraine, for Radek goes on to point out that even the economic losses suffered through the secession of that State were by no means irremediable, for what was there lost might be replaced by the development of production in regions like the Ural Mountains and Western Siberia. There was a surplus of bread-stuffs in Central Russia, Siberia, and the Caucasus. Coal was available in Soviet Russia to the extent of 300 to 350 million *pùdi*, and there is iron in the Urals. Finally, the textile industry was in the hands of Soviet Russia. Even if Russia were isolated, the reserves in hand would enable her to live. " Political developments may overthrow any estimate, but that has nothing to do with estimating the economic situation." Besides, Radek adds, " The Brest-Litovsk Treaty has put an end to the isolation in which Russia existed at the time of the October overthrow." The Treaty of Brest-Litovsk compelled Russia to seek economic relations with other countries. Moreover, the mere ending of the war had made an enormous difference, for whereas it consumed from 60 to 75 per cent. of the whole output of the Russian industries, (9) its conclusion meant that the iron, steel, copper, cloth, etc., which were used for military purposes, which entailed a colossal waste of the people's wealth, could now be employed for the productive needs of the country. (10) Sokolnikov read a report upon the financial situation, in which he said :—

" The *bourgeois* press has spread sensational news to the effect

## CONCRETE ECONOMIC PLAN OF BOLSHEVIKS 301

that Russia is face to face with a budget of 160 to 200 milliards of roubles. In reality, the expenses for the first six months of 1918 will be 14 milliards . . . and for the whole year will be between 25 and 30 milliards. Our financial policy aims at balancing the budget at this amount." (11)

The following are the chief points in the main resolution adopted by the congress :—

" The process of destruction and the process of construction are in reality one and indivisible. In our economic practice we destroyed the *bourgeois* ways of regulating and administering the economic life of the country. We have nationalized the banks, the commercial fleet, and more than 300 large enterprises. We have created central organs whose business it is to look after production and distribution in different branches [Centro-Textile, Glava-Kozha (hides), Glava-Liess (timber), Central Chai (tea), etc.]. (12) All these administrative institutions were created in the centre and in the provinces, on the basis of certain principles. With a few exceptions these institutions consisted of representatives of Soviets or of workers' trade unions or co-operative organizations. With regard to exchange and distribution, we endeavoured to carry out, with the participation of the whole population, the most correct distribution possible. We financed industries and did not allow them to die. . . . The basis of all our economic policy is the strengthening of the dictatorship of the proletariat and the accomplishment of socialist measures. The economic situation of the country and the relations of the social forces require the prosecution of that programme. The carrying out of nationalization, its extension over the fundamental branches of industry and over private commercial undertakings, the establishment of equitable exchange of goods between the city and the village, the enforcing of industrial discipline and the increase of the productivity of the workers—these are the main tasks of our economic activity." The resolution was adopted by the congress by an overwhelming majority. All except six members voted for it ; thirteen members abstained from voting. Milyutin remarks that " those who opposed the resolution, the Right Socialist-Revolutionaries and the Mensheviks, had no economic programme of their own, nor could they have while the proletariat remained in power." They certainly had a programme while the *bourgeoisie* was in power, but " that programme was one of negotiation and bargaining."

Milyutin nevertheless admits that although the Bolsheviks had a plan, or rather a thesis for a plan, of a general character, there was no single scheme for nationalization of enterprises, and no uniform system for their subsequent administration. He admits also that

302 THE RUSSIAN REVOLUTION

the proceedings of the congress illustrated the lack of co-ordination between the central and the local administrative organs, as well as the weakness of the local organizations. " All this," he says, " is undoubtedly true. There are many faults and shortcomings in our work ; only by hard work and merciless self-criticism can we get rid of them. It would be indeed strange if such a great affair as the rebuilding of the whole present economic order into a new socialistic system could be done easily, smoothly, without errors or faults. These imperfections are quite remediable ; but it is necessary to understand them clearly and to give concrete and definite suggestions for correcting them. The congress has given concrete indications how to remedy the defect." (13) Lenin, in his speech to the congress, remarked : " If we may withdraw ourselves a little from the immediate unpleasantness of frequent alteration of decrees, and if we look a little deeper and farther into that gigantic, all-world historical affair which is to be carried out by the Russian proletariat through its own inadequate forces, then we shall understand at once that even more frequent alterations and trials of different methods of administration . . . are unavoidable. In such a gigantic undertaking we could never expect, and no reasonable socialist who ever wrote upon the possibilities of the future could conceive, that we could be able, according to some plan given in advance, to build at once and shape at one stroke ready made forms for a new society. . . . We do not close our eyes to the fact that we alone could not carry out the socialist Revolution in a country even if it were much less backward than Russia, and even if we were living under easier circumstances than after four years of an unthinkable, hard, difficult, and destructive war ; but forces are growing with the process of fighting and with the advancement of the Revolution. When the country started along the road of the greatest changes, then to the credit of the country, and of the workers' party that conquered that country, must be placed the fact that we have approached, closely and in practice, tasks which formerly were known only in theory. We are sure that in the near future historical events will bring the proletariat of western Europe to office, and we shall not then be solitary in the world's arena, as we are at present. Thereby the movement towards socialism and its incarnation in the life of all nations will become comparatively easy." (14)

While the Bolshevik leaders were constantly urging their " principles " and were frequently obliged to excuse departures from these, most of their administrative acts were carried through under the spur of necessity, and many of them would have been done by any governmental authority under similar conditions. For example, nationalization of industry and protection of the plants by

## CONCRETE ECONOMIC PLAN OF BOLSHEVIKS 303

troops were the only possible preventive measures against rapine. The workmen were already " taking over " the factories as the peasants were " taking over " the land. The nationalization of the factories was also rendered necessary by the collapse of credit, and by the blockade to which Russia was subjected from 1914 to 1918. After this was finally raised, the state of the currency rendered the control of exports necessary, and this control could be most effectively exercised by means of a monopoly of foreign trade. Whether the adoption of such measures could have been advantageously maintained when normal conditions returned is questionable, but there seems no doubt that in the absence of private credit and private capital, and the desertion of many of the employers who had been obliged to evacuate their factories in consequence of the attitude of their workmen or because they took a hopeless view of the situation, the nationalization of industry, at least as a temporary measure, was absolutely necessary. The Bolshevik error lay not in the nationalization of industry itself, but in the way in which it was done, the ruthless destruction of the whole mechanism of production, commerce, and private finance, without any possibility of replacing the ruined system by any other, except after long and fatal delay.

The requisitioning of grain from the peasants was essential to keep the town inhabitants from want. Nor was this requisitioning a new precaution; it had been adopted in 1916 by the imperial minister of agriculture during a food crisis resulting from the war, and a State monopoly of grain had been introduced by the Provisional Government in March 1917, immediately after it assumed office. What was new was the absence of any adequate inducement to the peasants to produce a surplus in order to supply the demands of the Government, an omission which ultimately wrecked the whole scheme.

The provisions council of the *gub* of Petrograd ordered all local administrative bodies in the *gub* to increase the production of crops. The district communes were required to distribute the assessment of food-stuffs over the rural population, allowing the people to retain only the quantity necessary to meet their own needs. The council also ordered that the crops in all collective enterprises, as well as all others, must be subjected to a strict stocktaking. (15) The provision of rest-houses for workmen who were under medical supervision was the care of the *gubernie* or provincial authorities. In the Petrograd *gub* the provision during the month of September 1920 for each resting person was on the average 3,514 calories per day. The dietary included 164 grammes of albumen and 35.7 grammes of fats. The average norm, according to the Russian

## 304 THE RUSSIAN REVOLUTION

practice, for each healthy person was 75 to 100 grammes of albumen and 50 grammes of fats. (16)

The " campaign " in Petrograd for the collection of the assessment in kind was in 1920 attended by a considerable measure of success. By October 20th of that year, even in the regions most affected by diminished production, more or less satisfactory collections had been made. (17)

---

### NOTES

(1) Michael Solomonovich Lurie, otherwise known as " Yorie Larin," " Lurie-Larin," " Larin," and " Yoriev," was a member of a group composed of Bukharin, Vallach-Litvinov, Lunarchasky, A. Malmovsky, and Sverdlov, who held the views of the old *Narodnaya Volya*. (Cf. Mavor, J., *An Economic History of Russia*, vol. ii, pp. 114–34.) Lurie was arrested in 1903, and again in 1904. In 1906, under the name of Yorie Larin, he wrote some pamphlets on the relation of the peasant question to social democracy. These were published in St. Petersburg. (Cf. Spiridovich, A. E., op. cit., pp. 53–54.)

(2) Larin, Yo., *The Economic Programme* in *Labour Control (Rabochi Kontrol)* (Moscow), No. 4, May 1, 1918.

(3) Karl Sobelson, known also as " Radek."

(4) Goldenbach, known also as " Ryazanov."

(5) The words quoted are from Milyutin, V., in *The Results of the Congress of the Soviets of the People's Economy* in *People's Economy* (Moscow), No. 4, June, 1918. They are said to represent the views of the pessimistic group.

(6) There were reports by Radek, Lomov, and Milyutin.

(7) Chiefly in the Ukraine.

(8) *People's Economy*, loc. cit.

(9) This is probably an exaggeration. A more moderate estimate places the proportion at one-half.

(10) There is here an assumption that the production of the war period would be maintained in time of peace and under the communist *régime*.

(11) *People's Economy*, loc. cit.

(12) The activities of these were made the subject of a report by Rykov.

(13) Milyutin, V., op. cit.

(14) *People's Economy* (Moscow), June 1918.

(15) *Pravda* (Petrograd), No. 228, October 12, 1920.

(16) Ibid., No. 229, October 13, 1920.

(17) For details see *Pravda* (Petrograd), No. 235, October 20, 1920.

# APPENDIX E

## NOTE TO CHAPTER II

THE possibility of utilizing the power of the numerous rivers in European Russia and in Siberia was a subject of discussion before the outbreak of war in 1914. Various estimates were offered of the quantity of power available—ranging from 12 to 20 million horse-power. About 10,000 horse-power was actually produced (cf. *Economic Russia, Her Actuality and Her Possibilities*, New York, 1917). Since most, if not all, of this development was in Finland, it is unlikely that there was any material quantity of hydraulic power actually being utilized in Soviet Russia before 1924. The feasibility of developments depends upon the proximity of the site of the origin of the power to the region in which the industrial enterprises dependent upon it are to be developed, and upon the comparative costs of other forms of power. It also depends upon the credit of the country, by means of which the enormous capital necessary for development can alone be secured. (The hydraulic power utilized in the United States and Canada in 1924 was about 5 million horse-power, and in the whole of western Europe about 5,400 horse-power. The proportion in each case of utilized to utilizable hydraulic power was about $12\frac{1}{2}$ per cent. The presumption is that the balance was not at the time economically exploitable.)

# CHAPTER VI

## THE NATIONALIZATION OF INDUSTRY AND ITS CONSEQUENCES

THE great mining centres of Russia were the Ural Mountains and the basin of the River Don. Although the environs of Moscow had long been of industrial importance, industry on a large scale was carried on chiefly in the St. Petersburg district. Ironworks, cotton, wool, and paper mills, electrical engineering plants and the like had been established there, some of them since the eighteenth century. Russia was a pioneer in this field long before large-scale enterprises were prominent in Great Britain or in western Europe. The area of the country, however, was so enormous, and the population, though great, so reluctant to leave the land, that in spite of the magnitude of her natural resources, Russia was only thinly organized in an industrial sense. Yet in the aggregate the development of Russian industry was very considerable.

The condition before the war was not unfavourable. Earnings of industrial enterprises, compared with those of similar undertakings elsewhere, were high. Many of the companies had adopted the expedient of " stock watering," and had by this means disguised the relation between the annual profits and the amount of capital actually engaged in the enterprises. Precise and reliable statements cannot therefore be made ; but from statistics available it appears that the average net profits (1911–1913) ranged from 8·3 per cent. in sawmills, to 30·3 per cent. in rubber manufacture ; and the dividends paid in the same years varied from 4·1 per cent. in saw-mills to 14·4 per cent. in rubber factories. The total amounts invested in the principal industries in 1913 were as follows :— (1)

|  |  | Millions of Gold Roubles. |
|---|---|---|
| Metallurgical Industries | .. .. | 904·5 |
| Cotton ,, | .. .. | 603·4 |
| Oil ,, | .. .. | 452·7 |
| Wool ,, | .. .. | 129·6 |
| Rubber ,, | .. .. | 89·8 |

The amount of Russian and foreign capital invested in Russian industries was, of course, not large when compared with the amounts invested in the industries of countries with a higher industrial development and greater political and social security. The credit

## THE NATIONALIZATION OF INDUSTRY 307

of Russia suffered a severe blow in the revolutionary years 1905–1907, and was wholly destroyed in October 1917.

The total amount of capital invested in industry in Russia in 1913 has been estimated at about 4 milliards of gold roubles.(2) It is impossible to state with accuracy how much of this amount was contributed by foreign investors. Including government and all other securities, however, the amount of foreign investments in Russia between the years 1904 and 1912 amounted to about 2,300 million gold roubles. There were no doubt extensive investments of French, Belgian, and British capital before 1904, so that probably the total amount of foreign investment in 1914 was at the least about 3 milliards of gold roubles.

During the first two years of the war foreign loans were made to the Russian Government ; but as they were expended abroad in the purchase of munitions, which were used in the campaign, the amounts of those loans do not appear in the deposits of the Russian banks. These deposits, however, increased two and a half times between 1915 and 1917,(3) large sums having been withdrawn from Russian investments abroad.

Although the February Revolution (1917) was political in the strict sense of the word, it was accompanied by a sharp social change. The demands of labour increased, the political power which working men began to exert, or began to feel that they could exert through the Petrograd Soviet, caused them to claim increased wages and shorter hours, while the demand for labour for munitions compelled those in authority to grant the workers' demands, no matter how extravagant they might be. When the war was brought to an end by the armistice which immediately followed the October Revolution, the industrial system, which latterly had been directed chiefly to war service, was suddenly checked. In the other belligerent countries, and in those which had remained neutral, the final armistice of the following year (1918) brought a similar arrest of those industries which had been devoted directly or indirectly to the purposes of the war. In the most stable, highly organized, and efficiently administered of these countries, the sudden cessation of those specialized industries produced very considerable social consequences ; but in Russia in 1917 the results were proportionately graver, because the arrest of industry occurred simultaneously with a social upheaval in which the successful revolutionaries announced their intention to abolish private property and to nationalize industry. It is probable that owing to the collapse of her foreign credit which she suffered on account of her defeat, and owing to the overwhelming demand for money for war purposes, the greatest difficulty would in any case have been experienced by the Russian manufacturers in

## THE RUSSIAN REVOLUTION

securing the capital required for their enterprises. When to these general economic disasters there was added a condition peculiar to Russia, that of extreme instability, political and social, Russian industry in October 1917 was in a highly parlous state. It is improbable that the factory wheels could have been kept running except by the assistance in some form of the Government. There was nothing bizarre in the suggestion, taken by itself, that certain industries should be nationalized. Indeed, in many cases, the actual undertaking by the State of the finance and control of an industry may have been the only alternative to dismissing the workmen and closing the doors.

The Soviet Government's first idea was to nationalize the large industrial establishments, but there was no intention of doing this simultaneously. A preliminary process was to be the concentration of several enterprises in one trust, after which nationalization would ensue ; but this scheme was not followed out. Various organs of the Government began to " nationalize " immediately and directly. The War-Revolutionary committee, several executive committees, and the Soviet of People's Economy all engaged in " nationalization " of industrial and other establishments, while the *Che-Ka* also confiscated and " nationalized " after its own fashion. All was done without a plan and from a variety of motives. Sometimes a factory owner had made himself obnoxious to the Government or had incurred the dislike of the *Che-Ka*. His factory was " nationalized " by the first or " confiscated " by the second. Or perhaps a factory found itself without fuel, whereas there might be a reserve in an opposition factory ; then the owner of the first factory, by means of gifts in the proper quarter, succeeded in closing up the second by having it nationalized, afterwards transferring the fuel to his own premises. Occasionally an engineer who was not satisfied with his position in a nationalized factory proposed to the All-Russian Soviet of People's Economy that they should nationalize another plant and place him in charge.

A struggle gradually arose between the High Soviet and the provincial and municipal Soviets. The local authorities wanted to appropriate factories and the like, and so did the central authority as represented by the High Soviet ; with the result that when some works were compulsorily transferred to that body, they were found to be destroyed. (4)

In May 1918 the Supreme Council of People's Economy became very pessimistic. The following summary of the situation, as it was at that date, is condensed from an article on *The Nationalization of Production*, (5) and illustrates the way in which this pessimism was reflected in the Soviet press.

## THE NATIONALIZATION OF INDUSTRY 309

" Our industrial apparatus is quite ruined and we are enduring a very acute crisis of under-production. The best indicators of the state of industry are the figures relating to fuel and metal—the fundamental elements of production.

" While in 1916 the output of coal was 1,373 million *pùdi*, in 1917 it was 1,182 million ; and now every month [since the close of the year] the output is falling, and besides that the deliveries from the places of output are declining also. In 1918 we shall have to rely upon naphtha and wood fuel as well as on the coal of the Ural basin. With regard to metals, in place of 21 million *pùdi* of iron and steel which were produced in 1916, we have in 1917 only 16 millions. Pig-iron in 1916 was 19·5 million *pùdi*, and in 1917, 15·9 million *pùdi*. How can we fight this crisis of under-production ?

" The Soviet Government is carrying on the broadest nationalization of industry, (6) the fundamental motto of the policy of the Soviets is " workers' control " ; but the growth of workers' control meets with *sabotage* on the part of the managers of industrial enterprises. It becomes clear that the control over production is insufficient. In some cases it does not reach its aim, being only control on paper, whereby the proprietors of the enterprises can shield themselves. In other cases it has led to the seizure of the enterprises by the workers engaged in them. For that reason the Supreme Council of People's Economy conceived the idea of nationalizing all branches of industry and credit. On account of the *sabotage* on the part of the employers, many enterprises had to be nationalized ; nationalization was thus brought from below. The State had to finance the whole of nationalized industry, and that was the result of the absence of any plan. Nationalization of all branches of industry will be carried through, and instead of being punitive, which was sometimes necessary, it will be systematic. The administration by the workers themselves which has been brought about for the first time in the world's history could not at once find its proper forms. Experience makes us reject most decisively syndicalization of enterprises . . . because in such cases the single master was replaced by a group of new masters whose interests not seldom were in contradiction to those of the whole of the working class. Therefore at present the Supreme Council of People's Economy has decisively adopted a concentrated administration of industrial enterprises in the hands of the whole proletariat. The administration is in the hands of the representatives of the Soviets, the committees of plants and factories, trade unions, etc. The workers in some particular branch will be given one-third of the places (in the administrative organ). At present nationalization is being applied by degrees to the metallurgical and coal

## THE RUSSIAN REVOLUTION

industries. Afterwards the textile, rubber, and paper industries are to be included.

" For the transition period there is being established an apparatus for the guidance of these branches, and main committees, such as centro-textile, main rubber committee, main paper committee, etc., are to be formed. But we must not conceal from ourselves that production, besides being affected by general causes of an economic and political character, is being ruined by the decline in the productivity of labour. The Soviet authorities resolved to fight that evil by establishing an iron industrial discipline by means of the fixation of a normal minimum of production, and also by means of compulsory labour service." With this last end in view, a census of the working and non-working population had to be made.

As regards agriculture, the Government intended to organize the state working of land in cases where the people were unable to organize themselves, and demobilization would gradually restore the man-power in the peasants' economy. Agricultural machinery to the value of 160 million dollars would probably be imported in 1918–1919 from America.

" It is self-evident that the *bourgeoisie* will be removed from industry as a class, but not as an organizing power ; and in the latter capacity they will certainly be attracted to creative work in the interests of the whole nation."

The principle of nationalization of industry involves logically the nationalization of banks. So far this measure had not justified the hopes that were entertained of it, because the people had not become accustomed to that new form of credit, and had been in the habit of keeping their money in their own hands instead of depositing it in banks.

A series of new branch banks will have to be opened. The people will learn to employ the new forms of credit and money apparatus will be " restored." The next measure will be the union of the People's Bank (which arose through the absorption of nationalized private banks) with the Bank of Russia.

The exchange of goods must be placed upon a new basis. The concrete plan of the Government to that end was as follows :—

1. Introduction of a series of monopolies.
2. Gradual removal of private commercial apparatus, and, as a transitional measure, the most systematic and severe control over private commerce.
3. Affiliation of everyone to one or other co-operative, the co-operatives covering all regions.

# THE NATIONALIZATION OF INDUSTRY

4. Organization of exchange in real goods—without money notes—between different producing regions. The meaning of this measure is that each branch of industry will have a state credit in the form of a current account, in the name of the main committee and in the books of the state bank. When, for example, a purchase of fuel takes place, the appropriate amount is then to be withdrawn from the current account and transferred to the credit of the current account of the coal enterprise. So the raw materials, fuel, etc., will move from one branch to another without the transference of money. The cheques which are given to the workers in payment of wages will be paid in money, and besides that all proprietors of commercial enterprises will be compelled to surrender monthly their whole revenue into the current account, that is to say those commercial enterprises that remain unnationalized during the gradual process of nationalization.

All the above-mentioned measures do not involve an immediate transition to socialism, but they are socialistic in tendency.

Soviet writers point out quite reasonably that nationalization of enterprises, especially in an " atmosphere of struggle," should not be regarded exclusively from the point of view of pecuniary profit and loss—" It was necessary to safeguard production and to safeguard the workers from unemployment. The interference of the State was necessary in order not to allow enterprises to perish." (7) It might well be suggested in this connection, that in an " atmosphere of struggle," under economic conditions inevitably depressed, and with a widespread disorganization of finance and industry, the expatriation of the greater number of those most qualified to direct and organize is not necessarily the best way to effect reorganization. Indeed, it might be held that the interference of the State was the ruin, rather than the salvation, of the undertakings.

Milyutin says that the Ukrainian capitalists " threw the workers into the streets, and closed their enterprises," and that the same would have happened in Soviet Russia but for nationalization.

The following cases serve to illustrate this process :—

### 1. NATIONALIZATION BECAUSE OF REFUSAL TO CONTINUE PRODUCTION.

" Because of such a refusal by the management of the plant of Sestro Riesk Metallic Company (near Petrograd), the Council of the People's Commissars decreed the confiscation of all the property of

## 312 THE RUSSIAN REVOLUTION

the said company, whatever that property might be, and declared it to belong to the Russian Republic."

" In view of the categorical refusal of the owners of Rostoikin factory, Moscow *gub*, to continue production, notwithstanding the stock of fuel and raw material in hand," the factory was nationalized.

" In view of the announcement by the management of Samolotni-Stroitelni *Zavod* (Aeroplane Construction factory) . . . of unwillingness to comply with the decree of demobilization and their desire to dismiss all workers, nationalization was proclaimed."

" In view of the refusal of the management of the automobile shops of the International Wagon-Lit Company, the Cardboard factory (Kibbel's), and others, to continue the employment of the workers, the workshops and factories were nationalized."

### 2. NATIONALIZATION BECAUSE OF REFUSAL TO SUBMIT TO THE CONTROL OF THE WORKERS.

" In view of the refusal of those who controlled the Joint Stock Company of the Serganiko Ufaleskoy Mining District (*gub* of Ufa) to obey the decrees of the Council of the People's Commissars, or to submit to the workers' control over production, the Council of People's Commissars resolved to confiscate all the property of the said company."

On the same ground they seized upon the property of the Bogoslav Mining Company, the Russo-Belgian Metallurgical Company, the Company of Kushtin Mining District, etc. The decrees concerning workers' control formed the principal basis for nationalization during the first period.

### 3. NATIONALIZATION ON THE GROUND OF ECONOMIC EXPEDIENCY.

During the first period there were very few cases of deliberate nationalization of industrial enterprises on economic grounds. This third motive applied, in the first instance, to the banks, the river and sea mercantile fleets, and similar enterprises. The preparation of schemes for the deliberate transference of industries to the State took time, and not until the second half of the year 1918 were they fully developed. Then the economic council seemed to think that nationalization on purely economic grounds might be greatly extended. (8) The technical consequences of this transference varied greatly. The Mackaev mines increased production by 50 per cent., but this is represented as being by no means typical. The technical reports to the Soviet show that while there was great enthusiasm for

# THE NATIONALIZATION OF INDUSTRY 313

nationalization and for the destruction of capitalistic influence and the dominance of the workers, " the increase of production, the creation of new forms of economic activity, the improvement of technique—are subject to gradual organic growth."(9)

" The nationalization of industry, the systematic working out of a plan for organizing the system of the people's economy, opens the door to a broad creative effort by human genius, and attracts for the first time the working masses to conscientious participation in the process of production, and to the organization of a people's economy in the interests of the whole society. The results of these changes must appear in the immediate future." (10)

Seizures of industrial establishments by the workmen employed in them began at least as early as the outbreak of the October Revolution. The process was very simple. The workmen went to their employers and told them that henceforward they would conduct the factory themselves. They had no objection, as a rule, to the employer remaining, but he must do as directed by a committee elected by the workers.(11) These seizures embarrassed the Soviet Government, for the policy of the Bolsheviks was not revolutionary syndicalism, it was revolutionary Marxism. They desired that the factories should be nationalized, not that they should be handed over to the workmen who happened at the time of the Revolution to be within the walls. But there were other obstacles in the way of gradual nationalization. Technical managers and foremen were not always willing to transfer their services from private employment to the State. Many of them preferred to go abroad, and those who remained were often reluctant to assume responsibility in the absence of industrial discipline, and under conditions of *espionage*, with the probability of being denounced on some fictitious ground always hanging over their heads. Notwithstanding these and other difficulties, a large number of industrial enterprises had been transferred to the State less than six months after the October Revolution. The following table (see p. 314) shows the number which were nationalized within the period November 7, 1917, to June 14, 1918. (12)

The industries included in the table on p. 314, under the heading " Nationalized," were those which were regarded as suitable by one or other of the numerous authorities on the ground that they were large enterprises engaged in the production of staple goods. Under the heading " Sequestrated " were included those in which the proprietors or managers were accused of refusing to obey the law.

The owners, directors, and the financial and technical managers of all enterprises were stigmatized as *bourgeois*, and as such war had been declared against them ; but immediate and universal

## 314 THE RUSSIAN REVOLUTION

| | Groups. | Belonging to the State before the Revolution. | Nationalized. | | | Sequestrated. | | | Total. |
|---|---|---|---|---|---|---|---|---|---|
| | | | By Soviet of People's Commissars and Supreme Council of People's Economy. | By Regional Soviet of People's Economy. | By Local Bodies. | By Soviet of People's Commissars and Supreme Council of People's Economy. | By Regional Soviets of People's Economy. | By Local Bodies. | |
| 1 | Mining, Metallurgical. | 23 | 50 | 39 | 2 | — | 7 | 1 | }218 |
| | Metallic. . . . . | — | 18 | 26 | 5 | 1 | 45 | 1 | |
| 2 | Fuel . . . . . | 4 | 4 | 2 | 11 | — | — | — | 21 |
| 3 | Electro-technical . . | — | 5 | 1 | 2 | — | 10 | — | 18 |
| 4 | Textiles. . . . . | — | 3 | 5 | 7 | — | 7 | 4 | 26 |
| 5 | Chemical . . . . | — | 4 | 21 | 4 | — | 8 | 5 | 42 |
| 6 | Timber and Paper. . | — | 3 | 7 | 24 | — | 22 | 6 | 62 |
| 7 | Minerals . . . . | — | — | 4 | 1 | — | 5 | — | 10 |
| 8 | Food Products. . . | — | 9 | 19 | 16 | — | 10 | 7 | 61 |
| 9 | Animal Products . . | — | — | 1 | 6 | — | 1 | 5 | 13 |
| 10 | Printing and Publishing | — | 1 | 9 | 5 | — | 2 | — | 17 |
| 11 | Transport . . . . | — | 1 | 2 | 4 | — | — | — | 7 |
| 12 | Miscellaneous . . . | — | 1 | 16 | 6 | — | 2 | 1 | 26 |
| | Totals . . . | 27 | 99 | 152 | 93 | 1 | 119 | 30 | 521 |

nationalization was not possible without the risk of complete idleness in a large number of undertakings. The workmen, unprepared by education and training for the responsibilities of management, could not direct the factories, arrange for the regular supply of raw materials, or take measures for the distribution of the finished products. Even if they had been competent to perform all these services, their management might not necessarily have been in accordance with the conception of nationalization. The process had to move more or less deliberately, and the management had to be brought definitely into relation with the new central organs which had been instituted for the purpose of controlling nationalized enterprises. When, however, the owners of enterprises not as yet nationalized refused to be controlled by competent authority, the undertakings had to be sequestrated, even although the necessary preliminary arrangements had not been made.

While this was true of large enterprises in general, there were some of medium dimensions which were nominally nationalized and really permitted to conduct their affairs as before, without disturbance of either personnel or methods.

# THE NATIONALIZATION OF INDUSTRY 315

" The capitalist system in Russia had been broken by depriving the capitalists of their functions " (13) ; but the State had not replaced the organization of capital by any other system. The Bolshevik writers naïvely admit that " it will take not a little time before the capitalist system will be replaced entirely and finally by a new one ; but the process of replacement will go on inevitably." (14) This is very characteristic of the point of view current in Russia in 1918, that everything will come out all right somehow. The same writer goes on to say : " It is to be regretted that the process of creating new economic forms does not proceed with due rapidity and breadth of conception, and that it is late in comparison with the demands of rapidly moving events." (15)

There were three stages in the movement of nationalization. First, from November 1917 till June 1918 ; second, from June 1918 till the end of the year 1919 ; and third, from 1919 till the beginning of the New Economic Policy in 1922.

During the first period it was largely punitive and therefore economically haphazard, and was conducted by many public authorities. From June 1918 there was gradually evolved a system by means of which the administration of nationalized enterprises was centralized and further nationalization accomplished. The productive branches of the Supreme Council of People's Economy gradually took into its hands the task of management, and inspection and accounting were provided for. Thus in the beginning of the second period the direction of future policy in respect to nationalization was laid down by the First All-Russian Congress of Soviets of People's Economy (May 26th till June 4, 1918). The principal resolution was as follows :—

" With regard to the organization of production it is necessary for complete nationalization. From the nationalization of separate enterprises it is necessary to proceed to the successive nationalization of whole industries in all their various branches, especially, at an early date, of metals, mechanical engineering, chemicals, naphtha, and textiles. Nationalization must not be haphazard. It must be carried out exclusively either by the Supreme Council of the People's Economy or by the Council of the People's Commissars on the recommendation of the Supreme Council of the People's Economy." (16)

This resolution was followed by various decrees issued by this Supreme Council, providing for nationalization in detail—for example, the decrees for the nationalization of the whole of the naphtha industry, as well as of a group of engineering plants at Sormova near Nijni-Novgorod and also at Kolomna, and other decrees involving almost all the large inudstrial enterprises in nearly all branches of industry. (17)

# THE RUSSIAN REVOLUTION

By the end of August 1918, according to Milyutin, practically all the large enterprises in Russia were in the hands of the State. He adds jubilantly: " The economic overthrow was completely accomplished. If the *bourgeois* thinkers believed the capitalist system to be the alpha and omega of economic development, then the Revolution in Russia proved the falsity of that idea. It is true that the new system is very far from perfection; but when and where in history was a new social system built up all at once in a perfect form? It is to be considered as an achievement that we in Russia, by means of the nationalization of industry, are arriving, for the first time in the history of the world, at a realization, albeit in a coarse and imperfect form, of a new economic system and the downfall of capitalism." (18)

In a report to the All-Russian Congress of Workers in the Chemical Industries, (19) the following statistics are given; they must, however, be accepted with reservation, as it is not at present possible to verify in every case. Between 1900 and 1914 the chemical industries increased out of all proportion to other undertakings in Russia. While the average growth of all industries was from two to two and a half, they increased nearly four times. The number of persons employed in the chemical industries in 1914 was 200,000, while the value of the undertakings was about 3 milliards. The production was of the annual value of about 600 millions of gold roubles. This means, according to the report, that each worker was producing goods to the value of 3,000 roubles. The average wages were 350 roubles per year, or about 11·6 per cent. of the value of the product. The report, by a miscalculation of its own figures, says that the average wage of the workers in the chemical industry was about 5 per cent. of the product, thus understating them by more than one-half. Without specifying the exact figures, either of the numbers employed or of the production, the report says that now (that is in May 1918) wages in the chemical industries have increased, and on the average are from 5 to 10 per cent. of the value of the produce. (20) If the figure of 11·6 per cent. for the earlier period is correct, the wages of chemical workers have fallen from this figure to 5 to 10 per cent. of the value of the produce.

The report entertains hopes of the development of the manufacture of dye-stuffs in the Altai district and in Kusnetsky, as well as in the Don region. In the two first mentioned there is abundance of water power. Already, the report says, simple dye-stuffs are produced in Semipalatinsk and Middle Asia, and probably also in Altai, to serve the local cotton, wool, and silk industries. It further remarks that the textile industries—this was in 1918—were being

## THE NATIONALIZATION OF INDUSTRY 317

brought under state control ; but the by-products of the manufacture of gas for illuminating purposes cannot be counted upon for dye-stuff manufacture, because they are under municipal control. This remark illustrates that extraordinary and astonishing lack of collaboration which had all along characterized the Soviet-communist system. The Soviet chemists have been recommending the installation of large plants for the " dry transfusion " of wood, the products of which—turpentine, pitch, birch-tar, acetone, acetic acid, etc.—are used in domestic trade and may also be exported. The report goes on to say that the development of this industry is the task of the local *Zemstvo* ; that is true, but the active spirits in the *Zemstvos* been expatriated, and it does not yet appear that the " poorest peasants " are interested in chemical engineering.

The report further notices the absence of development in the manufacture of soap, candles, and glycerine because of the scarcity of fats, and its author hopes that the increase of agriculture will result in greater production of animals, and naïvely suggests that an increase in fishing in the North Sea might be expected to provide more fats. He says that the fat industry is being syndicated under the control of the State. Matches used to be manufactured in sufficient quantity to meet the demands of the home market ; now, taking into account the abolition of the excise duty, the cheapness of wood, and the production of phosphorus, the report anticipates that Russia should soon be again exporting matches abroad. The policy of the Government was to demolish the small and semi-domestic industries for making matches, and to replace them by large plants, well equipped with improved machinery. Production was to be nationalized in the naphtha, kerosene, and benzine plants, and a great export trade was to be the result. Mechanism for the manufacture of explosives was being broken up, and already production had diminished to one-fourth of the 1918 standard. The acid plants used during the war were being converted into plants for the manufacture of superphosphates, and the report considers that, since Russia has all the raw materials necessary for the production of sugar, hides, cellulose, naphtha products, glycerine, rubber goods, and cotton cloth, an export trade in these commodities must develop. It also looks forward to an important export business in fertilizers, as well as an increased domestic demand.

It further notices that Germany, of recent years, has been increasing the yield per acre of her farm crops. Since the comparison is in terms of Russian measurement, this form has been preserved.

## 318 THE RUSSIAN REVOLUTION

### GERMANY

At the beginning of the 19th century, yield in *pùdi* per *dessiatine*, 60 ; about 1900, 90 ; in 1913, 135.

Tilled surface, 26,000,000 *dessiatines*, or about 50 per cent. of total area.

Annual production, 2,000,000,000 *pùdi* grain and 3,000,000,000 *pùdi* potatoes.

### RUSSIA

Tilled surface, 120,000,000 *dessiatines*, or about 6 per cent. of total area.

Annual production, 4,000,000,000 *pùdi* grain, and 2,000,000,000 *pùdi* potatoes.

Thus the productivity of the German tilled surface is about four times that of Russia. This is explained in the report as due to the inferior cultivation in Russia, owing to lack of agricultural inplements, to the " many field " system, and to the lack of fertilizers. Germany spends annually 400 million marks on fertilizers, Russia spends upon a tilled surface five times larger than that of Germany, only 30 million roubles, or about 60 million marks. According to the report, if the fertilization were adequate, Russia should consume annually 600 million *pùdi* of phosphates, 1,200 million *pùdi* of nitrogenous fertilizers, and 600 million *pùdi* of calcium fertilizers. Russia has the phosphates and the nitrogen, but the supply of calcium is inadequate. If, however, the new lime beds in the *gub* of Perm were exploited, this deficiency might be made good. Russia used to import annually from Germany 5 million *pùdi* of calcium salts. The report estimates that if only 1 *pùd* of superphosphates per *dessiatine* were applied (instead of about 5 *pùdi* as in Germany), the demand would be for 120 million *pùdi* annually. To manufacture this quantity would require 60 million *pùdi* of sulphuric acid. In 1918 the manufacture of sulphuric acid was not greater than 20 to 25 million *pùdi*. Therefore the report recommends that all existing sulphuric acid plants and all explosives plants be applied to the manufacture of superphosphates, and also to the development at the earliest date of the deposits of minerals containing phosphorus in Podolsk, Kiev, Kursk, Orel, Viatka, Kama, Kostroma, and Saratov. It also recommends the employment of various known methods for obtaining nitrogen. In this connection it advocates the use of peat by the Monda Carro process. " Russia must start the state use of peat, and the sooner the better." (21)

The report anticipates a great increase in agricultural production, the higher productivity of labour being due to the increased interest of the workers in the profits.

The author also speaks of an " Economical Liberty Loan " of 10 milliards of roubles for productive purposes, and appeals to all

## THE NATIONALIZATION OF INDUSTRY 319

citizens of Russia to subscribe, saying that " the shares in this loan would represent the whole wealth of Russia and would make every citizen a participant in the building up of the homeland, and would give a stable form of money which would not need any gold security at all because it would represent crystallized labour, not of the printing-press, but of life itself, of the toiling people who are building up its economy. It is necessary also to execute this programme with our own money, otherwise our industry will be seized by foreigners. There is only one way to the building up of a new people's economy, and that is by means of free, duty-less commerce and nationalization, by means of state construction, mass production, and a commercial monopoly of ' sale, purchase, and distribution ' over some of the most important products."

This report is very instructive because it states candidly the point of view of the technician who has become a convert to " public ownership." He is evidently not concerned about the political peculiarities of Bolshevism, nor about the distribution of the product upon a commensal basis or otherwise. What he is concerned about is the utilization of the natural resources of the country for the benefit of the Russian people. He sees also quite clearly that, under the present conditions of Russian economic life, private enterprise can do nothing. All must be done by the State. His plea for the issue of a paper currency, with the natural resources of Russia as security, is made in terms curiously similar to those of John Law of Lauriston when he offered for his paper money " the magnificent security of the land of France." The natural resources of Russia were already mortgaged ; paper money had been issued to excess ; while the credit of the country had disappeared and could not be recovered until a government was in power with *bourgeois* views upon financial integrity.

The chief difficulty in carrying out the programme of production which the report develops is not the provision of capital, but the supply of competent and hard-working people. The peasant straight from the plough is apt to waste much material before he learns how to use a machine, whilst the artisan of Petrograd or Moscow had scarcely recovered from his elation at being told that he was now the " master of the situation," or that the time had come for his dictatorship. To step from that elevation to work in a sulphuric acid chamber or to shovel lime into a furnace could not be very congenial to him. The idea that the workman would sit in the office while the manager did the shovelling seems to have been prevalent ; but even if all the managers were set to shovelling, the programme of production could not possibly be maintained.

The nationalization of production and the exploitation of natural

## THE RUSSIAN REVOLUTION

resources on a large scale can be accomplished, but only by means of labour which will submit to discipline. Such labour must receive payment not much higher than the cultivation of land would yield, for otherwise the land would be denuded of labourers, production of food-stuffs would decline, and precisely the same fluctuations of employment and production would ensue as those with which " capitalistic production for profit " has made everyone familiar.

Even if the Soviet Government had in every one of its offices an expert like the reporter of the chemical industries, and even if every item on his programme were carried out, the difficulty of bringing the vast expanse of Russia, with its population, increasing with appalling rapidity, into economic equilibrium on the basis of any system, commensal or otherwise, is staggering beyond all power of expression.

While the distribution of the products of the great staple industries, such as iron, the coarser textiles, and the like, might conceivably be placed on a more or less effective basis, there were many industries which did not belong to this category and which yet employed large numbers of workmen. Among these were many engaged in the manufacture of goods for which there existed at present no market in Russia. The *bourgeoisie* who had been the chief consumers of miscellaneous goods had been killed, expatriated, imprisoned, or impoverished, thus for some of the goods consumed by them there could be no demand until a new *bourgeoisie* made its appearance, and unless an altogether new range of manufactures could be devised, the factories in question must be closed. As the difficulty of devising new manufactures with sufficient rapidity was practically insuperable, insufficient demand with consequent unemployment continued.

The Revolution practically closed the Russian mines and put a stop for a time to the exploitation of minerals. There may have been some local exploitation on a small scale ; but in spite of the fact that the minerals had been nationalized at a stroke, nothing was done for more than six months towards organizing a new department of mines after the former one had been abolished. Early in April 1918 the Mining Council was organized, consisting to begin with of " a single table," at which there was a chairman, destitute of the equipment or the staff appropriate to an office of such responsibility. The following details are condensed from a *Report on the Activities of the Mining Council* submitted to the Supreme Council of People's Economy in August 1918. (22) The initial impetus towards organization seems to have come, not from the Supreme Council of People's Economy, nor from the Council of the People's Commissars, but from the mining regions. The people there very naturally desired

# THE NATIONALIZATION OF INDUSTRY          321

to have some understanding with the central authorities before they resumed mining operations on any scale. Small spontaneous Soviets had been formed in these regions, and deputies had been elected after the loose and indefinite manner of the Soviet procedure. The abolition of the mining department of the old *régime* had thrown such of its functions as had been to any extent preserved, into the hands of new Soviets in which there were no persons with mining knowledge. Thus the local organs, such as they were, could not correspond with or seek advice or assistance from any central organ, for that had been destroyed and no new system had been instituted to take its place. In order to meet the urgent demands from the mining regions, an effort was made to form a new Mining Council as a branch of the Supreme Council of the People's Economy, and experienced and good workers among the former employees of the department of mines were invited to act upon it. It soon became apparent that a new mining law adapted to the changed economic system must be formulated, and in order to draft this law, the Mining Council appointed a special commission of jurists, mining engineers, geologists, etc., who prepared a new code as well as a series of by-laws for the guidance of the Mining Council. The Soviets in the mining regions were all linked up together, and the former Institute of District Engineers was preserved. Then began the " purification " of the personnel, the dismissal of engineers who were regarded as men of routine and their replacement by active persons in order that the work might be more efficiently performed. (23) By this means the Mining Council attempted, ostensibly, to collect about it " the best technical forces of the country who might render substantial help by their experience and business knowledge." (24) To these specialists were allocated certain tasks. One of them, for example, was set to work on a project for forming new sections of the Mining Council, as, for instance, an intelligence section which had as its task a survey of the mineral resources of Russia, and within a short time of its organization it had made a survey of the coal areas along the Orenburg-Orsk Railway as well as of a part of Ilmen Mountain (in the Urals). Another section of the Mining Council had charge of the mineral water and salt industry, and made detailed investigations of the Staraia-Russa (*gub* of Tambov) and Lipetsk (Sergeievsk) health resorts with regard to their suitability for summer season activities. The same section has established local administrations for the health resorts in association with the local Soviets of Workers' and Peasants' Deputies.

The technical section, besides carrying out its special work, co-operated with the geological committee in organizing the output

**322**  THE RUSSIAN REVOLUTION

of the ores of rare metals—tungsten and molybdenum. The main gold committee, besides a large amount of current work, organized a special expedition to Siberia for the purpose of re-establishing the ruined gold mining industry.

The Mining Council had also to undertake the necessary measures for maintaining a food supply at the mines. Besides the branches of which details have been given, it included sections on ores, building materials, precious stones, and fuel.

The report mentions that the Mining Council inherited from the former mining department a library and extensive archives with much valuable scientific material, although, strangely enough, without a catalogue. The Mining Council was not less indebted to the old *régime* for the education of the engineers and scientific persons without whom it would have been helpless.

A cardinal characteristic of State socialism is the fusion of political and economic relations. Every point of contact between one man and another becomes a political affair. No surprise, therefore, need be occasioned by the fact that insistence of political discussions proved disturbing, especially since this political atmosphere was altogether new to Russian life.(25) It permeated not merely the Supreme Council of People's Economy and its numerous branches, but made its appearance also in the local Soviets. Political discussions were especially acute in those places where, under the old *régime*, extensive works employing large numbers of persons had been installed. The workers in the old state establishments looked upon themselves as privileged, and resented interference by the local Soviets. Their contact, by long established tradition, was especially with the central government, and they had never had experience of local control.

Thus, wherever there were old state works (and there were many of these), conflicts arose between the management and the local organizations. So also difficulties arose between the state works and the numerous departments, commissions, and committees of a central as well as of a local character with which they had to deal. The multiplication of organs led to hypertrophy of organizations, with the result that frequently the organs neutralized the functions of one another. The following example is taken from the correspondence columns of *Rabochi Kontrol*.(26)

In the Council of People's Economy for the *gub* of Tula there is a section charged with the supply of agricultural implements to the peasants. But the *Protcom*, or supply committee, which is charged with the supervision of the exchange of commodities, very naturally looks upon agricultural implements as coming under that category, and therefore regards the furnishing of them as being

# THE NATIONALIZATION OF INDUSTRY     323

within its competence. But the committee on schemes and factories and the union of workers and peasants have also an interest in the question of agricultural implements, and in consequence of this multiplication of effort no one of these organizations was able to accumulate the necessary statistical data, " and the peasants remained without any assistance in obtaining tools."

Everywhere there were Soviets, sections, sub-departments, branches, and committees without adequate co-ordination, and when a difficulty arose, a new committee had to be formed to deal with it, with consequences such as those described.

The history of state and private enterprise alike during the earlier years of the *régime* of the Soviets was a history of crises. Raw materials were delivered most irregularly. There were cotton crises when the Moscow stores could not or did not deliver cotton, " notwithstanding repeated demands upon the cotton committee " (27); timber crises when timber deliveries were delayed because rival committees competed for the timber; and naphtha crises occurred when the steamers on the Volga could not get the supplies which ought to have been stored for their first trip of the season. (28)

The Council of People's Commissars (in other words, the Cabinet) issued a decree on April 16, 1920, upon requisitions and confiscations, and supplemented this decree by another on July 16th, headed " Confiscation of money and valuables." The following were regarded as susceptible of confiscation, irrespective of their number or weight : (*a*) Platinum, gold, or silver coins ; (*b*) Platinum and gold in bullion and in raw condition ; (*c*) Interest and dividend-bearing obligations, excepting those which, by special regulations, might circulate as bank-notes ; (*d*) Bank-notes, if the People's Court found that they were destined for purposes of speculation. (29)

The following were to be confiscated : (*a*) Gold and platinum ware, exceeding 18 *zolotniks* (30) per person ; (*b*) Silver ware exceeding 3 lbs. per person ; (*c*) Brilliants and other precious stones in total more than 3 carats, and pearls more than 5 *zolotniks* per person.

The quantities of the above which might be retained by the owner had to be kept exclusively for personal and household use, and surplus above the norms stated was requisitioned. Cases where the chief and essential parts of the articles were not of precious metal (e.g. gold-mounted spectacles, gold watches, and the like) were excluded from the decree of confiscation.

All money in cash, over and above a certain small amount (not very clearly stated in the decree), must be deposited with the State Bank to the proprietor's credit in current account, and it was further

## THE RUSSIAN REVOLUTION

prescribed that a formal act of arrest should be drawn up in which the articles arrested were fully detailed. These were required to be transferred within three days to the nearest office of the People's Commissar of Finance. (31)

In July 1920 the executive committee of the Petrograd Soviet determined to exterminate private commerce by closing up all un-nationalized shops, warehouses, and factories. In order to carry out the orders of the committee a force was mobilized composed of Communist party workers, troops from the Red Army, and sailors. The process of extermination went on from early morning until three o'clock in the afternoon of July 30th. Goods in the shops and warehouses, etc., were checked and sealed up, and the proprietors were arrested and taken to the district Soviets. During the evening of the same day the merchants and others who had been under arrest were brought before a special commission composed of representatives of the Petrograd Soviet, of the Workers' and Peasants' Inspectorate, and of the Extraordinary Commission (the *Che-Ka*), and were detailed to various nationalized works. (32)

At a meeting of the Presidium of the Petrograd Council of the People's Economy held on October 2, 1920, reports were read upon the state of industry in the Petrograd district at that time. Factories manufacturing food-stuffs were reported to be handicapped for lack of fuel, and of raw materials, both main and subsidiary, but scarcity of labour was not so acute here as in others. The report notices an increase in the manufacture of bread in one factory where the output was 1,000 *pùdi* per day.

The Presidium suggested the working out of plans to remedy the shortage of raw materials, especially by establishing agencies and by offering premiums to the peasants in the form of manufactured products in exchange for raw materials delivered. Two suggestions of an original character appear to have been made by the Presidium. One concerned the construction of a floating preserve factory to collect its material at the sources of supply ; the other was a design for a train factory for drying eggs, preserving milk, and making butter, which should collect its raw material and do its work at the same time. (33)

### Nationalization of Houses.

The nationalization of industry must inevitably be a gradual process, but the communization of dwelling-houses might be carried out more speedily. The simple method adopted by the Bolsheviks of dealing with people who were experiencing insufficient or no accommodation was to take them to the nearest large house and force the owners or occupants to receive them. (34) In some cases,

## THE NATIONALIZATION OF INDUSTRY 325

no doubt, rude justice characterized the proceedings ; but in others the method was employed not so much to provide for the poor as to punish the well-to-do. (35)

"There were many cases in which houses and their contents were simply requisitioned and the owners required to quit within twenty-four hours." (36) In other cases the owners were left with the garret or the cellar only, and families were installed in the living rooms. "During three days in Moscow, just before my departure, the population of a whole quarter, near the *Che-Ka*, were turned out of their houses, and not only the *bourgeoisie* but poor people as well." (37)

Smelg-Benario narrates a case with which he had to deal officially, and describes it as " a characteristic example." In a large eighteenth-century house in the Moscow district a lunatic asylum had been established for a long time. The president of the regional Soviet, who was also " regional war commissar," having a personal quarrel with the manager of the asylum, ordered the house to be cleared in four days. The order was not complied with, and on appealing to the commissariat on housing, it was cancelled ; but policemen were sent by the war commissar with orders to throw the lunatics and the asylum furniture into the street. This was prevented at the last moment by a threat to bring the affair before the Revolutionary Court. The dismissal of the regional war commissar was also demanded ; but that functionary was an old communist and could not be discharged " for such a small thing." (38) In this way, as Smelg-Benario says, the dictatorship of the party (i.e. the Communist party) came to be changed through force of circumstances into the unlimited rule of individual persons. (39)

---

### NOTES

(1) Goldstein, Joseph M., *Russia, Her Economic Past and Future* (New York, 1919), Diagram No. 66.

(2) This is the estimate of Dr. Goldstein (op. cit., p. 7). The amount given is equal to £400,000,000, or $2,000,000,000. According to a report by A. E. Makevetsky to the All-Russian Congress of the Workers in the Chemical Industry, the value of all industrial undertakings in Russia before the war amounted to 30 milliards of gold roubles. The difference between 4 billions and 30 billions is not irreconcilable. In one case all the state enterprises may be omitted as well as all the small enterprises, whereas in the other all these may be included, as well as the estimated value of forests, etc., of state, ecclesiastical, and private enterprises. (Cf. A. E. Makevetsky, *The Chemical Industry in Russia* in *People's Economy*, Moscow, No. 3, May 1918.)

(3) Increase in deposits was not confined to the larger banks. This is shown by those in the Moscow People's Bank.

(4) Cf. Yurovich, A., *The Highest Soviet of People's Economy* in *Archives of the Russian Revolution* (Berlin, 1924), vol. vi, p. 311. Yurovich says : " Some day the

# 326 THE RUSSIAN REVOLUTION

archives of the High Soviet of People's Economy will lay open before the historian all the tragedy of unity " (Ibid.).

(5) In *Rabochi Kontrol (Workers' Control)*, Moscow, No. 4, May 1, 1918.

(6) In May 1918 Nationalization had not yet reached its height.

(7) Milyutin, V., *On the Question of Nationalization of Industry* in *People's Economy* (Moscow), No. 5, July 15, 1918.

(8) Ibid.

(9) Ibid.

(10) Ibid.

(11) It seems that an idea was prevalent that clever workmen should not be elected to the committee in case they might deceive the workers. Occasionally the chairman of the committee was the man who swept out the office.

(12) Milyutin, V., op. cit., p. 5. It is difficult to institute a comparison between the numbers of establishments in the above table and in the same industries before the war. The above figures include practically all factories in existence in 1917.

(13) Ibid.

(14) Ibid.

(15) Ibid.

(16) Ibid.

(17) Ibid.

(18) Ibid.

(19) Makevetsky, A. E., *Report* cited.

(20) Ibid.

(21) The experience of the Canadian Government in attempting the exploitation of its resources in peat has been very costly.

(22) This report is printed in *People's Economy* (Moscow), Nos. 6–7, August 15, 1918.

(23) This was no doubt the principle ; but there is reason to believe that one of the qualifications of a mining engineer was ability to pass a really stringent examination in the history and theory of socialism. Adherence to socialist opinions may have been enforced in certain cases, but, in general, knowledge of the subject appears to have been held to be sufficient.

(24) *Report* cited.

(25) While travelling in Russia before the war and the Revolution, the author frequently met with the observation: "We enjoy a great advantage over you western European peoples. We have no politics. Our political affairs are in the hands of the Government. We are not interested in them."

(26) *Rabochi Kontrol (Workers' Control)*, Moscow, No. 4, May 1, 1918.

(27) Ibid.

(28) Ibid.

(29) I.e. destined for the purpose of buying goods and selling them again at a profit.

(30) 1 lb. Troy = 84 *zolotniks.*

(31) *Pravda* (Petrograd), No. 164, July 27, 1920.

(32) Ibid., No. 168, July 31, 1920.

(33) Ibid., No. 221, October 3, 1920.

(34) Russia was not alone in adopting this expedient. Under the emergency laws passed in Germany during the war, owners of large houses were obliged to allow others to share them.

(35) Smelg-Benario says that punishment was the usual motive. Cf. *In the Service of the Soviet* in *Archives of the Russian Revolution* (Berlin, 1921), vol. iii. p. 154.

(36) Ibid.

(37) Ibid.

(38) Ibid., p. 155.

(39) Ibid.

# CHAPTER VII

## OBLIGATORY LABOUR, NORMALIZING PRODUCTION, AND THE SYSTEM OF RATIONING

THE foundation of the system of obligatory labour was laid in a resolution of the Third All-Russian Congress of Soviets. (1) When the outbreak of cholera occurred in Petrograd, Zinoviev, then president of the Executive Committee of the Soviets, asked the regional Soviets to impose obligatory labour upon the *bourgeoisie*, and advised that in the event of any difficulty the recalcitrant members should simply be arrested in the streets and sent to forced labour.

In the middle of October 1918 the commandant of the 6th army, which was on the northern front, demanded from the war commissariat of the Petrograd district " that 800 labourers should be sent for building roads and digging trenches. For this gang the war commissariat decided to utilize the persons who were called up for obligatory labour." (2)

Pozern, the commissar, ordered Smelg-Benario, who was a member of the war commissariat, to undertake the task of finding the 800 men, but Smelg-Benario refused, saying, " You know, comrade, what my political ideas are, and you will understand why I refuse to carry out the so-called mobilization of the *bourgeoisie*." (3) Pozern made no reply. He called for Ryashkin, who was in charge of foreign labour in " the first-town region," and he undertook to furnish the 800 members in eight days. Smelg-Benario meanwhile was required to make the necessary arrangements for transport. The mobilization was carried out by Ryashkin in the following manner :—

" To the Soviet were summoned various citizens, chiefly of the merchant class, to be registered in view of possible future ' forced labour.' When the citizens came to the Soviet for registration, they were arrested and sent to the Semenovsky barracks, where they had to remain until their departure ; but in spite of this clever *ruse*, less than 800 people were collected. Then Ryashkin and other members of the regional Soviet, in obedience to the advice given by Zinoviev, decided upon the following extraordinary plan : Three days before the departure of the group of ' obligatory labourers ' to the northern front, the Nevsky Prospekt, by order of Ryashkin, was surrounded by soldiers, and everybody who was in the street and who could not show his party ticket or some

## THE RUSSIAN REVOLUTION

certificate from a government establishment was arrested and sent to Semenovsky barracks. Among the mobilized were many women, but on the following morning they were liberated, and the men only were left. On the third day this party was sent to Vologda, where by agreement they were taken under the supervision of the sixth army. Not one of the mobilized persons was allowed to arrange his affairs, see his family, or obtain necessary clothing. Neither Pozern nor I had any idea at the time how this mobilization was being carried out." (4)

Very many of those who were arrested in order that obligatory labour might be forced upon them were over fifty years of age. "Once," Smelg-Benario narrates, "an old man almost deaf and dumb came [to the commissariat]. He was so weak that his niece had to accompany him. What was my surprise when I learned that he had been ordered to undertake obligatory labour. He asked me to give him an exemption certificate ; I refused, saying that it was not necessary, as no one would take him. But next day he came again and showed me the order by which he had to go to work. Then I gave him the certificate." (5)

Such incidents were frequent at the outset of the institution of obligatory labour, but later haphazard methods were abandoned and a more or less regular procedure was adopted.

On August 11, 1920, the Council of Labour and Defence issued the following order headed " Mobilization of Workers in the Fish Industry " :—

" Because of the necessity of securing a sufficient number of experts for the fish industry, the Council of Labour and Defence decrees the mobilization of all persons who have worked during the past ten years in public or private fish enterprises, and who are between 18 and 50 years of age.

" Persons serving with the Red Army and in institutions under the care of the war and navy commissars, and in the main fish or branch fish enterprises, are exempt." (6)

There is a singular want of specification in this notice, for it does not state in what capacity the persons to be commandeered will be required to act, whether as fishermen, cleaners of fish, or canners.

Although the system of obligatory labour had been in operation for two years, so many difficulties had arisen that on January 2, 1920, the Council of the People's Commissars decreed the formation of a commission for the purpose of determining the measures which should be taken for the introduction of universal labour service and for the mobilization of labour. (7)

# OBLIGATORY LABOUR

### Normalizing Production.

In order to stimulate production a system of premiums was devised. As a preliminary to the fixation of these, the character of the normal day's work in the various industries had to be determined. For the purpose of establishing norms the normalizing commission was appointed, and it was also entrusted with the determination of wages. It proceeded to establish in the workshops subordinate bureaux whose duty was the working out in detail of the norms of production. Thus in the metal trades, for example, each turner, moulder, pattern-maker, and so forth, must produce a definitely established number of pieces in " each unit of working time." (8) The practice of determining the normal quantity of product per unit of time is well known in many countries, but in Russia it was a novelty—both to the workers and to the new labour administrators. " In our industry this is a new idea, and in literature it has not been made sufficiently clear." (9) The process proceeded very slowly. After four months the commission had succeeded merely in dividing the workers into groups for the purpose of arriving at a means of fixing the norms, (10) but the norms themselves were not yet established. Normalizing could not be accomplished satisfactorily except by experts, and these were few in number. Thus up to October 1918 no fixed methods had been developed, either in the industrial centres or elsewhere. This delay was due largely to hostility on the part of the artisans. The workers knew well enough, in individual cases, what they could accomplish in a given time without too much pressure, but they were reluctant to have exceptional or even usual production regarded as normal. They seemed to be afraid that the political situation might change, and that in consequence the profit of any increase in productivity might go into private hands. (11) This point of view was so widespread that, as the year 1918 wore on, normalization still remained an open question.

The official (Bolshevik) point of view is as follows : " We are sure that the question of normalizing production will be moved from the dead point, only when the broad circles of the workers understand the connection between their own interests and the interests of the State. The officials on the spot must show sufficient energy and they must prepare the masses of the workers psychologically and practically to understand the question as a whole. It would be very difficult to work unless this were done. We must take into consideration the lack of confidence and the enmity prevalent among the workers." (12)

## THE RUSSIAN REVOLUTION

Although the process of normalizing was still in a rudimentary stage, the Soviet of Trade Unions, together with the Soviet of People's Economy, worked out, in 1920, a draft scheme to be applied to the Petrograd district for the payment of premiums in money and kind. Under this scheme premiums were to be allowed only for, and to conform strictly to, increased productivity, and were never to be permitted to appear as " a veiled addition to wages." In each enterprise to which the scheme applied norms of production were to be fixed in the first instance in respect of each article or operation, and norms of the general productivity of the enterprise as a whole were to be determined also. Every increase above the fixed norms entitled the workers to a premium in kind.

The following was the suggested scale of premiums :—

> For 5 per cent. above the norm, 5 per cent. premium.
> For 50 per cent. above the norm, 50 per cent. premium.
> For 75 per cent. above the norm, 75 per cent. premium.
> For 100 per cent. above the norm, 100 per cent. premium.

It is to be presumed, although it is not so stated, that the premiums constituted a percentage of the normal wages. The premiums in kind might be awarded to individuals, to groups, or to all the employees in an enterprise. Where the work was done by a group, distribution of the premium within the group was in terms of the actual time during which each man was at work. In cases where a collective premium was paid to an enterprise, it was distributed in terms of "the intensiveness of the work done by each worker." (13)

In 1923 the process of " normalizing " production and wages had not been completed. In the Twelfth Congress of the Russian Communist party the following resolution was passed :—

" The general policy in regard to wages has in future to be directed towards more or less equalizing the average wages in all branches of industry, [provided that] workers of similar or equal qualifications be paid approximately the same in different branches of industry." (14)

As far as possible, wages were to be unaffected by casual movements of market prices ; the state institutions were to act in accordance with the trade unions, and wages in particular industries were to be considered in relation to the interests of the working class as a whole.

Thus five years after the Bolshevik Revolution the problem of wages was still unsolved. There was no open market for labour or for goods ; there were neither competitive wages nor competitive prices. Arbitrary scales satisfied few, and those adjustments which

# OBLIGATORY LABOUR

were neither competitive nor arbitrary, but merely fair to everyone concerned, were found extremely difficult to devise. The experience of the communists in the field of both wages and production fully justified the prognostications of the economists.

## THE SYSTEM OF RATIONING.

The rationing of the people was determined by three authorities : (1) the Council of the People's Commissars ; (2) the Council of Labour and Defence ; and (3) the Central Commission on Supply for Workers. For rationing purposes the population was divided into certain categories.

The normal worker (15) was entitled to what was called the " armoured ration " or fixed supply to be delivered to his class after the requirements of the army had been satisfied. All workers did not receive the " armoured ration "; only those were eligible who were regarded by the Central Commission as occupying the status of " normal " workers. The following was the normal ration in Petrograd :—

> Bread, 1¼ *funti* (16) per day ;
> Sugar, ½ *funt* per month ;
> Salt, 1 *funt* per month ;
> Fish and Meat, 4 *funti* per month ;
> Fats, ⅓ *funt* per month ;
> Soap, ¼ *funt* per month ;
> Coffee substitute, ¼ *funt* per month ;
> Matches, 2 boxes per month ;
> Vegetables, 20 *funti* per month.

Members of the worker's family received one-half of this norm, provided they belonged to one of the following categories :—

(a) Those who were free from labour service.
(b) Those who lived continuously with the worker.
(c) Those who were under his full care and incapable of working (parents, brothers or sisters, children under sixteen years of age).

Children enrolled as members of the family of a worker were not entitled to cards for individual free rations. The normal ration was delivered only for actual days of work and days of rest, the number of the latter being fixed by a tariff. In case of illness, on production of a medical certificate, the worker was entitled to his normal ration.

The Central Commission on Supply for Workers issued in January 1921 a series of regulations regarding the food supply to certain categories of employees. The " normal " ration (the so-called " armour plated " or irreducible minimum upon which those who were entitled to it might absolutely rely) was fixed for

## 332 THE RUSSIAN REVOLUTION

those workers who, in the judgment of the Central Commission, were entitled to be placed in the category of persons having the first claim upon available food supplies after the needs of the army had been satisfied. This ration is identical with the Petrograd ration just quoted and was to be delivered only for the actual days of work and days of rest as fixed by the tariff. Workers on leave or while sick (a medical certificate being required) were entitled to the normal ration, but if the worker went into a hospital or rest-house, this lapsed, but rations were delivered to his family as usual. In case of wilful absence from work without sufficient reason for a period of more than three days, the absent worker together with the members of his family was deprived of the normal ration for the period of absence. If workers were required owing to the conditions of the industry (as in chemical works, for example) to work overtime, they were entitled to receive, in addition to the normal ration, $\frac{1}{8}$ *funt* of baked bread for each hour so employed.

Workers in certain enterprises were to receive the following supplementary ration :—

> Bread, $\frac{1}{4}$ *funt* per day ;
> Salt, $\frac{1}{2}$ *funt* per month ;
> Meat or Fish, $3\frac{1}{2}$ *funti* per month ;
> Fats, $\frac{1}{4}$ *funt* per month ;
> Coffee substitute, $\frac{1}{4}$ *funt* per month ;
> Vegetables, 20 *funti* per month ;
> Groats, $3\frac{3}{4}$ *funti* per month.

The list of enterprises in which the above supplementary ration obtained was to be drawn up by the Central Committee and sent to the *gubernie* commissions for the control of workers' supplies. (17) This ration is by no means generous. In any case, it is hardly practicable to devise a uniform scale for a country which presents so great a variety of climatic conditions as does Russia.

According to Yurovich, the ration in Moscow in 1921 differed considerably from that in Petrograd, as is shown by the following statement :—

> Bread, $\frac{1}{2}$ *funt* per day ;
> Beetroot, 5 *funti* per month ;
> Potatoes, 8 *funti* per month ;
> Rice, 1 *funt* per month ;
> Herrings, $1\frac{1}{2}$ dozen per month.

The special ration for the workers in the Soviet offices, etc., excepting for those in the war department, did not exist at that time. (18)

The ration as given for Petrograd was certainly the highest, yet it cannot be regarded as adequate. In 1895, investigations (19) into the consumption of bread by peasants showed that the quantity of bread-stuffs which barely sufficed to meet the minimum needs of

# OBLIGATORY LABOUR

labouring people was an average of 19 *pùdi* per head annually, while the quantity required to meet these needs fully was 26·5 *pùdi* per head. The daily quantity of 1¼ *funti* in the Petrograd ration amounts only to 11·3 *pùdi* annually. The fish and meat (4 *funti* per month) are not sufficient to make up the dietary to the equivalent of the minimum mentioned in the 1895 investigations. The deficiency of the ration is shown in the relatively large quantity of vegetables (6 *pùdi* annually), which were presumably chiefly potatoes.

The central committee of the Textile Workers' Union recommended (in January 1920) the introduction of a uniform assured ration for all workers and employees in the various branches of industry and labour. It also recommended that payment to workers in kind of their own products should not be permitted.(20) This interesting recommendation shows that the normalizing process had not been producing satisfactory results. Evidently the sting of inequality remained, or the total produce available for rationing purposes was inadequate, possibly the distribution of the produce was wasteful; all these causes no doubt lay at the root of the recommendations. An assured ration which would be impervious to influences of any kind is an impossibility, but in 1921 the Soviet Government went as far as they could towards providing one for their dependents, or those upon whom they depended, by securing the requisite quantity of produce from the peasants through the pressure of armed force.

The hostility of the Textile Union to payment of wages in kind did not avail to prevent an edict of the Supreme Council of People's Economy from being issued. This edict is dated July 23rd, and is headed "Norms for self-supply workers," that is, for the supply to workers of the products in the manufacture or sale of which they are themselves engaged. The norms are monthly: Main Tea, 1 lb. of coffee; Main Sugar, 1½ lbs. sugar; Main Starch, 3 lbs. molasses or 4 lbs. potato flour; Main Confections, 2 lbs. confectionery products; Main Vegetable Oil, 1 lb. vegetable oil; Main Match, 10 boxes of matches; Central Fat, 4 cakes of toilet soap or 1 lb. of inferior soap; Main Textile, 7½ *arshini* of cotton cloth for a man and 10 *arshini* for a woman per year.(21)

---

## NOTES

(1) Smelg-Benario, *In the Service of the Soviet* in *Archives of the Russian Revolution* (Berlin, 1921), vol. iii, p. 166.

(2) Ibid.

(3) Ibid.

(4) Ibid.

# 334 THE RUSSIAN REVOLUTION

(5) Smelg-Benario, *In the Service of the Soviet* in *Archives of the Russian Revolution* (Berlin, 1921), vol. iii, p. 166.

(6) *Pravda* (Petrograd), August 11, 1920.

(7) Ibid., January 3, 1920.

(8) " I. D.," *Tasks of Normalizing* in *Metallist* (Moscow), October 30, 1918.

(9) Ibid.

(10) Ibid.

(11) Ibid.

(12) Ibid.

(13) *Pravda* (Petrograd), No. 213, September 27, 1920.

(14) *The Communist Calendar* (Moscow, 1924), p. 251.

(15) See infra.

(16) 1 Russian *funt* = $\frac{9}{10}$ lb. *avoirdupois*.

(17) *Pravda* (Petrograd), No. 11, January 18, 1921.

(18) Yurovich, A., *The Highest Soviet of People's Economy* in *Archives of the Russian Revolution* (Berlin, 1924), vol. vi, p. 323.

(19) Mares, *The Production and Consumption of Bread-stuffs in Peasant Economy* in *The Influence of Yield and Bread-stuff Prices on Some Sides of Russian Economic Life*, ed. by Chuprov and Posinkov (St. Petersburg, 1895), p. 35. See also Mavor, J., *An Economic History of Russia*, vol. ii, p. 290.

(20) *Pravda* (Petrograd), No. 14, January 21, 1920.

(21) Ibid., No. 161, July 23, 1920.

## CHAPTER VIII

## THE CO-OPERATIVE MOVEMENT AND THE SOVIET REPUBLIC

FROM about the year 1900 the co-operative movement, especially in the field of consumers' co-operation, had achieved great success in Russia. In certain regions, notably in the Moscow district and in Kharkov *gub*, the co-operative societies were vigorously and intelligently conducted. Their efforts were directed, on the one hand, towards stimulating the interest of the peasants in the use and care of agricultural machinery, and on the other, towards securing for the peasants a readily accessible interior market for their produce.

In the year 1917, the last year in which the co-operative societies worked under the old *régime*, there were in All-Russia 23,000 consumers' co-operative societies, with a membership of between nine and ten million. The turnover of the societies for that year was more than five milliards of roubles. Thus, if four-fifths of the number were rural societies, there was one co-operative society for every 1,000 householders. (1) This really important achievement was accomplished, not by the spontaneous efforts of peasants and workmen, but chiefly by intelligently directed enthusiasm among the middle classes. In addition to the societies founded in this way, there were many smaller ones for consumers and producers which were formed spontaneously by working people and peasants. Six months after the assumption of power by the Bolsheviks, i.e. in the spring of 1918, the whole fabric of co-operation was destroyed.

" A wide-spread wave of destruction of the co-operative societies swept over the provinces. These societies were nationalized, confiscated, or subjected to compulsory contributions. Such measures ruined quite uselessly the whole of a huge economic organization which under proper business-like management could have been of the first importance in carrying out socialist measures in the country." These words were not written by a critic of Bolshevism, but by the Bolshevik writer, V. Milyutin. (2)

The destruction of the co-operative movement, however, was not an illogical proceeding ; it was the inevitable consequence of Soviet legislation. The economic system of Russia had been completely altered ; the co-operative system could not possibly escape change and remain isolated from the new economic life. While the theory of Marxism as adopted by the Bolsheviks implied co-operation, the meaning they attached to this word was not the

# THE RUSSIAN REVOLUTION

same as that understood by the movement, either in Russia or elsewhere. The latter meaning, according to Tugan-Baranovsky, is as follows : A co-operative society is an economical enterprise of voluntarily associated persons, which has as its object, not the acquisition of the utmost profit for the invested capital, but, through common action in production and sale, the increase of the incomes of its members. (3) The Bolshevik definition is as follows : " The co-operative society is first of all a social organization which includes all persons in a certain territory—an organization the object of which is the correct and expedient distribution of products among all persons who live in that territory." (4)

Since the territorial organizations were to cover the entire country, they were intended to include the whole population. The legislation which was to bring this policy into operation was contained in a decree of April 12, 1918, issued by the Soviet of People's Commissars. (5) By this decree membership in a local co-operative society was obligatory upon all persons residing in the locality in which the society was situated. By way of preventing evasion, a 5 per cent. " turnover tax " was imposed on the society, and then a proportionate amount of this tax was returned to members ; the amount yielded by the tax on non-members remained in the public treasury. There was also an entrance fee of half a rouble which all had to pay. As soon as the co-operative stores received supplies of products, wages were to be paid in the form of labour certificates entitling the wage-earners to obtain products for consumption from the stores. This last paragraph is of the utmost importance, because in it is to be found the legislative form of the particular variety of quasi-communism adopted by the Soviet Republic. The Bolshevik writers saw quite clearly that unless there was a continuous and reliable supply of food-stuffs to the co-operative stores, no validity could be attached to the labour certificates. They saw with equal clearness that if a dependable supply could be secured, there would be placed in their hands " a mighty weapon for the effective regulation and administration of economic life," (6) and that the requirements of the people, as indicated in the books of the consumers, would form a guide to production in the state factories, etc.

The decree of April 12th was followed on October 4th, (7) by a resolution of the Presidium of the Soviet of People's Economy. This October resolution prohibited the existence of more than two co-operative stores in each town, one for the " civil " population (i.e. medical men, teachers, etc.), and the other for the working people. It also ordered the compulsory union of all co-operative societies founded upon the old model (i.e. founded in accordance with the principles of co-operation as these were understood in

# THE CO-OPERATIVE MOVEMENT

Russia before the Revolution) with the new co-operative bodies formed under the decree of April 12th. The "civil" co-operative stores were compelled to unite in Moscow, for example, with the society "Co-operation," and the workers' co-operative stores with the Moscow Central Workers' Co-operative. Forced union of these prosperous voluntarily organized societies with new institutions controlled by the Government and composed of compulsory co-operators was resisted, and sharp criticisms of the measure made their appearance in the co-operative journals. These criticisms stated bluntly that the measure was inspired by animus against co-operation as a free social organization for the distribution of the necessaries of life, and that it struck at the root of a workers' institution which had been laboriously created and expanded. "It is impossible to overestimate the deadly significance of this measure to the life of the Moscow Consumers' Co-operation. . . . The Consumers' Co-operative Society, which was established by various groups of Moscow people with great effort, is not going to be destroyed so quickly as it may seem at the first glance." (8) The critic went on to point out that the requirement of the resolution of the Presidium that union should be effected by November 1, 1918, could not be carried out, because much time would be required to liquidate the existing co-operative societies, creditors must be paid, shareholders reimbursed, and so forth. These objections were cogent enough to delay somewhat the actual absorption of the voluntary unions, but eventually this was accomplished, and their voluntary character once destroyed, the organization they represented became a function of the Government.

Voluntary consumers' co-operation had been greatly promoted by the establishment in 1912 of the Moscow People's Bank, with a paid up capital of one million roubles. This Bank succeeded in attracting deposits, and, by means of these, financed co-operative societies all over Russia. The following indicates the growth of the business of the Bank :—

|  | Deposits. | Turnover in Loans. |
|---|---|---|
|  | In Million Roubles. | In Million Roubles. |
| 1912 . . . . | 0·65 | 2·81 |
| 1913 . . . . | 2·26 | 7·37 |
| 1914 . . . . | 3·85 | 11·54 |
| 1915 . . . . | 10·96 | 24·87 |
| 1916 . . . . | 33·07 | 98·42 |
| 1917 . . . . | 153·32 | 506·85 |
| July 1, 1918 . . . . | 495·02 | — |

# 338    THE RUSSIAN REVOLUTION

During 1917 the Bank lent to co-operative societies three and a half times more than in all the preceding years taken together. Between 1915 and 1917 the deposits in all the Russian joint-stock banks increased two and a half times, and in the Moscow People's Bank twelve times. The Bank had branches in all the principal cities in Russia, and even after 1917 it established new branches. In doing so it incurred, as such a policy must incur, the reproach of extreme centralization ; but the management was easily able to show that centralized administration had enabled it to occupy a financial position independent of the State Bank, and at the same time to supply money when and where required by the co-operative groups. At the beginning of 1918 it served 250 unions of co-operators, including 25,000 groups, and in addition 4,000 separate co-operative societies. (9) When almost all other banks carrying on domestic and foreign business in Russia were nationalized, the Moscow People's Bank remained independent ; but after three years (in 1920) it also was absorbed by the Soviet State. (10)

The legislation in respect to co-operation excited much sullen antagonism and some active hostility. Yet the Supreme Economic Council persevered in the task of reducing the co-operators to submission. When, however, the New Economic Policy came into being, the attitude of the Soviet authorities towards the co-operative movement changed. Not only were the co-operative societies, which had been brought under control to a certain extent, released, but the burdens upon these societies were from time to time reduced by the modification of income taxes and licence fees. (11) Yet the movement is not now autonomous ; it is subjected to rigid control by the Government.

The economic statistics of Russia as now published are of varying value. Occasionally they bear evidence of having been prepared with care by competent hands, but very frequently they show want of experience on the part of the statistician. The following figures regarding the numbers of co-operative societies are taken from official sources, but they can with difficulty be correlated for purposes of comparison with the figures given for earlier years :—

|  | Numbers of Active Consumers' Societies. | Stores. |
| --- | --- | --- |
| January 1, 1922 . . | 15,079 | 19,600 |
| October 10, 1923 . . | 18,713 | 27,225 |
| January 1, 1923 . . | 19,110 | 28,744 |

## THE CO-OPERATIVE MOVEMENT

| | Numbers of Inactive Consumers' Societies. | Stores. |
| --- | --- | --- |
| January 1, 1922 . . | 25,220 | 51,985 |
| October 10, 1923 . . | 23,223 | 35,032 |
| January 1, 1923 . . | 22,494 | 31,419 |

These figures indicate that during one year the number of societies previously moribund, but resurrected into life by the New Economic Policy, was over 2,000 ; that the number of stores similarly awakened was nearly 20,000, and that there were additions of 4,000 new societies and 9,000 stores. (11) While there was evidently a movement towards an increase in the membership of societies, there was also a tendency, less readily observable, towards the absorption of smaller by larger groups, and therefore towards a relatively smaller number of co-operative societies in proportion to the number of members. Simultaneously there was a noticeable falling off in the number of employees. In 1920-1921 the consumers' co-operatives employed 420,100 persons (of these, 70,000 were in the two capitals, Moscow and Petrograd). On January 1, 1923, the number had fallen to 200,000. During the same period those employed by Centro-Soyus diminished from 5,500 to 2,800. The administrative expenses of the state co-operative societies were in 1922 as follows :—

> Centro-Soyus, 4·8 per cent. of turnover.
> Provincial Unions, 11 per cent. of turnover.

These relatively high costs are said by the critics (within the ranks of the Bolsheviks) to handicap the co-operative societies in their competition (under the New Economic Policy) with private enterprise. The administration of the co-operatives expects that the increase of the turnover will bring the administrative costs to a much lower percentage.

The following shows the turnover in 1922 :—

| | | |
| --- | --- | --- |
| Centro-Soyus . . . | 65 million gold roubles | |
| Provincial Unions . . | 88 ,, | ,, |
| District Branches. . . | 77 ,, | ,, |
| City and Workers' Societies | 127 ,, | ,, |
| Ural Mountains Societies . | 88 ,, | ,, |
| | 445 ,, | ,, |

Rather more than half of this amount was contributed by the cities and towns, and rather less than one-half by the villages.

## THE RUSSIAN REVOLUTION

According to the estimates of interior trade made by the Soviet authorities, the villages altogether experienced in 1922 a " turnover " of 500 to 600 million roubles. The co-operative societies passed through their hands 110 millions, that is, 20 to 25 per cent. of the total turnover. The aggregate turnover of the cities and towns is similarly estimated at 800 milions, the co-operative societies passing 15 per cent. through their hands.

TURNOVER IN INTERIOR TRADE.

| | Co-operative Societies. | State Organizations. | Private Enterprises. | Total. |
|---|---|---|---|---|
| | Per Cent. | Per Cent. | Per Cent. | Per Cent. |
| Cities and Towns. . | 15 | 42·5 | 42·5 | 100 |
| Villages . . . . | 20–25 | — | 75–80 | 100 |
| *In Millions of Gold Roubles.* | | | | |
| Cities and Towns. . | 126½ | 340 | 340 | 806·50 |
| Villages . . . . | 110 | — | 490 | 600 |

The following relates exclusively to important commodities and their transference from the producer to the consumer during the year 1922 :— (12)

| | Millions of Gold Roubles. | Percentage. |
|---|---|---|
| Co-operation . . . . . | 80 | 20 |
| State Institutions . . . . | 120 | 30 |
| Private commercial enterprises . | 200 | 30 |
| | 400 | 80 |

Thus, after having absorbed practically all industrial and distributing enterprises, the Soviet State was obliged, immediately after the adoption of the New Economic Policy, to relinquish its direct control over 20 per cent. of these to the co-operative societies, and of 50 per cent. to private enterprises.

The Centro-Soyus is now attempting to increase the proportion (30 per cent. in 1922) of its share in the turnover of important commodities by means of the formation of, or agreement with, syndicates and trusts. (13)

The intention of the Soviet Government as disclosed in the resolutions of the Twelfth Congress of the Russian Communist

# THE CO-OPERATIVE MOVEMENT

party (1923) was to develop the so-called co-operative system as organized under the decree of April 12, 1918, modified by that of October 4, 1918, and by the New Economic Policy, in such a way that the co-operative system would become a " mediator " between the peasant and the townsman—between agriculture and industry—for the purpose of effecting exchange of agricultural and industrial products.

---

## NOTES

(1) Milyutin, V., *A New Way of the Co-operative Movement* in *People's Economy* (Moscow), No. 3, May 1918.

(2) Ibid., loc. cit.

(3) Tugan-Baranovsky, M., *The Socio-Economic Nature of Co-operation* in *Courses on Co-operation*, vol. i, p. 8. The substance only of the definition is given.

(4) Milyutin, V., loc. cit.

(5) For text of this decree, see *People's Economy* (Moscow), No. 2, April 1918.

(6) Milyutin, V., loc. cit.

(7) Text in *Izvestia*, October 5, 1918.

(8) Muraviev, N., *The Decree on the Compulsory Union of Moscow Co-operatives* in *The Voice of the Workers' Co-operation* (Moscow), Nos. 20–21, October 1918.

(9) The details are taken from Schurmann, M., *The Moscow People's Bank and Consumers' Co-operation* in *The Voice of the Workers' Co-operation* (Moscow), Nos. 20–21, October, 1918.

(10) The Moscow People's Bank greatly increased its business between 1917 and 1920 no doubt because of the general conviction that the Soviet Government would not expropriate the Bank ; but expropriation came in 1920.

(11) *The Communist Calendar* (Moscow, 1924), p. 570.

(12) Ibid., p. 572.

(13) Ibid.

CHAPTER IX

# THE CIVIL WARS, CHIEFLY IN RELATION TO THEIR ECONOMIC CONSEQUENCES

### A. The South Russian Campaign.

THE manifesto to the army, promulgated by the Bolsheviks immediately after their assumption of power, explicitly invited the troops to hand over their officers, and the soldiers apparently regarded the manifesto in the light of a permission to murder. Many officers indeed were murdered, but some of the higher military leaders who survived, refused to take refuge abroad, and declined to submit without a struggle to the Bolshevik dictatorship. Generals Alekseiev, Denikin, and Kornilov had all been arrested ; Alekseiev and Kornilov were liberated, Denikin escaped, and these three met at Ekaterinodar in South Russia, where they established a government and began the organization of an army to fight the Bolsheviks. The forces collected by them formed the Volunteer Army, and by means of it the Red Army was kept at bay for three years. The adventure came to an end with the defeat of General Wrangel in November 1920.

The series of campaigns in which the Volunteer Army was engaged may be divided into four periods :—

1. The period of Kornilov and Alekseiev, from November 1917 to April 1918.
2. The period of Denikin and Alekseiev, from April to September 1918.
3. The period of Denikin, from September 1918 to March 1920.
4. The period of Wrangel, from March to September 1920.

The organization of an armed force formed for the express purpose of overthrowing the Bolsheviks was begun in November 1917 by General Alekseiev at Novo-Tcherkask, (1) and known afterwards as the Volunteer Army, and it was largely, although not exclusively, composed of Cossacks. General Alekseiev remained with it, looked after its finances, and held communication with the political groups who were opposed to the Bolsheviks and were for that reason interested in putting an end to their rule. On the formation of the Volunteer Army, the actual command was placed in the hands of Kornilov, who, general headquarters having been

# THE CIVIL WARS

recently established at Ekaterinodar, issued the following political programme :—

1. Re-establishment of the rights of citizens. All citizens of Russia to be equal before the law without distinction of sex or nationality. Abolition of class privileges. Inviolability of person and home. Freedom of travelling, living, etc.
2. Re-establishment of free speech and the press.
3. Re-establishment of freedom of production and trade. Abolition of nationalization of private financial enterprises.
4. Re-establishment of private rights.
5. Re-establishment of Russian army on the basis of military discipline. The army should be formed on a volunteer basis, on the principle of the British army, without committees, commissions, or elected persons.
6. Re-establishment of international treaties signed by Russia. The war should be brought to an end with the united efforts of " ourselves and our allies." The peace should be signed by all and should be honourable and on democratic principles, i.e. with the right of independence for the conquered nations.
7. Re-establishment of compulsory education, with a broad regional autonomy of the schools.
8. The Constituent Assembly dissolved by the Bolsheviks should be re-convened. Elections to the Assembly should be free without pressure upon the will of the people and should be held all over the country. The personality of the elected members should be sacred and inviolable.
9. The Government established by the programme of General Kornilov is responsible for its actions only to the Constituent Assembly, to which it will surrender all its powers. The Constituent Assembly, as the only proprietor of All-Russian soil, should determine the basis of the Russian law and constitution and eventually erect a permanent government.
10. The Church shall receive complete autonomy in religious affairs. . . . Religious freedom will be complete.
11. The complicated agrarian question will be decided by the Constituent Assembly. Before this question is decided . . . and the new agrarian law is passed, no seizures of any kind will be permitted.
12. All citizens will be equal before the law. Capital punishment is left in force, but it will be exercised only in extreme cases of treason against the State.

## 344                 THE RUSSIAN REVOLUTION

13. Workmen will retain all the politico-economic victories of the Revolution, in the sense of limitation of working hours, freedom of labour unions, meetings, and strikes. Forcible socialization of enterprises and labour control which have contributed to the ruin of national commerce will not be permitted.

14. General Denikin is recognized by the different nationalities in Russia as the representative of broad regional autonomy. (2)

General Kornilov commanded the Volunteer Army for three months, and then lost his life in an engagement at Ekaterinodar on March 3, 1918. He was succeeded in the command by General Denikin, who, like Kornilov, was a Cossack, the son of a Cossack peasant. Denikin, by his own energy and ability, had risen high in the imperial service. Meanwhile General Alekseiev continued to exercise the functions above mentioned, and on August 31, 1918, he took the title of Chief Director of the Volunteer Army.

This army had acquired control of a large part of South Russia, and its responsible heads had performed many of the functions of government. It had been joined in the course of the summer of 1918 by two former members of the Duma—B. Shulgin and V. N. Lvov, and Shulgin now suggested to Denikin the expediency of forming a kind of Cabinet or ministerial council or committee in order to relieve General Alekseiev of his increasing civil as well as military responsibilities.

Denikin adopted this advice, and a body called " Special Committee of the Commander-in-Chief of the Volunteer Army " was organized. This name (3) was chosen because the Council was intended to perform, among other functions, those of the Imperial Council of Defence, of which both Shulgin and Lvov had been members.

Shulgin drew up, with the assistance of General Dragomirov, a project of organization as follows, the terms being abbreviated :—

1. The functions of the Special Committee are—

(a) To discuss all questions relating to central and local government in all places over which the influence of the Volunteer Army extends.

(b) To prepare temporary laws to be operative within the same regions. These laws to be conceived in the interests of All-Russia.

## THE CIVIL WARS

(c) To organize diplomatic relations with all the provinces of the late Russian Empire so as to discover the real position of affairs within these provinces, and to open negotiations with a view to forming a united front for the re-establishment of Great Russia.

(d) To organize relations with the Allies and to discuss plans for united action against the Central Powers.

(e) To get into communication with the dispersed Russian statesmen and leading representatives of different branches of the former central government as well as of the *Zemstvos*, and to obtain assistance from these in the task of reorganizing the administration.

2. The Special Committee consists of the following departments: (a) State organization: imperial affairs. (b) Diplomatic relations. (c) Finance. (d) Trade. (e) Production and Supply. (f) Agriculture. (g) Ways of Communication. (h) Justice. (i) Education. (j) Control (audit, etc.)

3. At the head of each of the above departments is a manager and two assistants.

4. There is to be appointed a director, who will prepare the business for the Special Committee. He will have at his service an information bureau.

5. The chairman of the Special Committee will be the Chief Director of the Volunteer Army, General Alekseiev. His subordinates in order of rank are: (a) Commander of the Army, Lieut.-General Denikin. (b) Vice Chief Director, General Dragomirov. (c) Vice Commander, Lieut.-General Ukhomsky.

6. The permanent members of the Special Committee are Generals Denikin, Dragomirov, Ukhomsky and the Chief-of-Staff, General Romanovsky, and all the managers of the above-mentioned departments.

7. In addition to the permanent members, other persons may be co-opted by special permission of the chairman.

8. Appointments to the departments are made by the Chief Director of the Volunteer Army.

9-17. These sections relate to appointments and meetings.

18. The meetings, small as well as large, have exclusively a character of debate. Their resolutions are not necessary for the Chief Director or for the Commander-in-Chief, who may act on their own initiative and may give the force of law to what they do.

# THE RUSSIAN REVOLUTION

The document from which these extracts are taken is endorsed : "Approved. General of Infantry, Alekseiev. Ekaterinodar, August 31, 1918." (4) The first meeting of the Special Committee took place on September 28th, the acting chairman being General Dragomirov.

On December 27, 1918, General Denikin issued an order concerning the aims and functions of the Special Committee, from which the following is condensed :—(5)

1. *Aims.* (a) One great undivided Russia, the defence of religious belief, the establishment of order, the establishment of a productive force of people's economy, and increased production. (b) Resistance to the Bolsheviks to the end.

2. *Methods.* A military dictatorship. Pressure from political parties to be prevented. The question of the form of government an affair of the future. . . . Union with the people, and the quickest possible union with the Cossacks, with a view to establishing a South Russian Government are essential steps. The support of the Caucasus to be obtained.

3. *External Policy.* National Russian. In spite of the fickleness of the Allies on the Russian question, it is necessary to work with them, because any other combination is- not morally permissible, and is also practically impossible. Slavonic unity ! Not an inch of Russian soil to be alienated to those who may assist us.

4. All possible guarantees must be given to the families of fighters. The administrative organs of supply must utilize all the wealth of the country and not merely rely upon external help . . . the rich population must provide the means of supplying munitions to the army, and the army must be given a sufficient amount of money irrespective of other claims upon the treasury. At the same time unpaid requisition and robbery of military stores must be punished without mercy.

5. *Internal Policy.* The Special Committee will act as guardians of all sections of the population. They will carry out the projects for agriculture, the agrarian division of the land, and the labour-laws in the sense of the previous declaration, and the *zemstvo* law. They will aim at an organization of society to increase the people's economy, and they will further efforts on the part of the people for the improvement of their economic position by means of co-operatives, trade

# THE CIVIL WARS 347

unions, and the like. The anti-state activity of some movements must be stopped. The press which is on our side must be helped. Those newspapers which do not agree with us will be tolerated, but those which are attempting to destroy us must be destroyed. There will be no class privilege, no discrimination in administrative, financial, or moral assistance. Revolt, anarchical movements, speculation, robbery, bribery, desertion, etc., will be suppressed by means of the Department of Justice. The death penalty will be maintained. The course of rehabilitation will be hastened and simplified. Those who show symptoms of Bolshevism or Petlurism will be forgiven, provided that is their only fault and they are otherwise good for business. Only persons of business capacity will be appointed to the public service, and everyone who is incompetent will be summarily dismissed.

6. Officials of the local governments, although they may not be under the control of the central authority, must be dismissed and punished if they do not work. Officers must be appointed and given wide powers to make the front and also the interior sanitary. These officers will be assisted by field courts, which should take strong measures to clear out counter-*espionage* and criminal detectives, and to introduce more of the juridical elements.

7. The value of the rouble must be increased. Transport and production are to be conducted chiefly for the defence of the State. Taxes are to be imposed mainly upon wealthy people who do not render military service. Trade is to be carried on only for the supply of ammunition and of the most necessary objects of consumption.

8. Temporary militarization of water transport.

9. The condition of the families of the men at the front will be improved by giving them more food.

10. Propaganda directed against Bolshevism should be conducted by the Government with a view to rousing the consciousness of the people and the will to struggle against anarchy.

This document was signed by General Denikin as Commander-in-Chief of the " Military Forces in South Russia " at Taganrog, December 27, 1918. Three days later, on December 30th, Denikin dissolved the Special Committee by a General Order, and, while retaining in substance the various administrative departments, altered the distribution of them and reserved to himself the right to bring projects of law before the Government—measures which

## 348 THE RUSSIAN REVOLUTION

practically placed the Government wholly in the hands of the Commander-in-Chief. This state of affairs lasted until February 20, 1920, when an agreement was made between General Denikin and " high Cossack circles " to the effect that the group of ministers should form a Soviet or council, and that this body should be responsible through the law courts to the representatives of the people. No legislative act was, however, published by this body, and in less than a month it was dissolved by order of General Denikin. This order empowered M. V. Pernatsky to simplify the administration in correspondence with the reduced area occupied by Denikin's army and to admit the population of that region to co-operate in the government. This order was issued on March 17, 1920, at Theodosia in the Crimea, to which place Denikin had retreated from Ekaterinodar under the pressure of the Red Army. (6)

In spite of the obstinacy with which they clung to the foothold they had obtained in South Russia, Denikin and Wrangel failed. The reasons for their failure seem to have been chiefly these : (1) The absence of support by and the unfriendly attitude of the population in whose interests they regarded themselves as struggling, which was itself due to three causes : (a) They identified the Volunteer Army with Kornilov, who, although popular among the Cossacks, was looked upon by the people in general as being desirous of restoring the monarchy. (b) They feared the re-establishment of private rights, especially in land, for the land had been distributed ; and they feared also the reimposition of a centralized authority from which, during the troublous times since 1917, they had been free. (c) They were not given any share in the administration, nor were they necessarily consulted in any way regarding the government of the region they inhabited. [The documents cited and largely quoted above do not mention the people as an element worthy of consideration until the issue of Denikin's Order of December 27, 1918, (7) after the campaign had been going on for two years and when the end was approaching.] (2) The absence of the necessary capacity to lead on the part of Denikin as well as of Wrangel. General Denikin was a good staff officer, conscientious in obeying orders, but without the grasp indispensable for the conduct of a campaign, especially a campaign in a civil war. General Wrangel was a man of exceptional courage, but he also lacked the grasp of affairs and the commanding personality which were necessary to attract from all parts of Russia the best elements in the population, from which alone an effective military force might be built up. (3) The conduct of the troops of the Volunteer Army towards the population. Officers and men alike seemed in general to regard everyone who was not in their force as a Bolshevik,

# THE CIVIL WARS 349

and therefore as someone who might be killed or robbed with impunity. When the Army was in retreat, the country was laid waste. Hence, from the point of view of the people, the conduct of the Volunteer Army was no better than that of the Red Army; there was little to choose between them; both were equally ruining the country. (4) Insistence upon unity in the manifestos of Denikin created a prejudice in the minds of the people of the separated nations. They feared to be drawn once more under the yoke of an arbitrary or even of a democratic central authority. (5) The lack of activity shown by Denikin and his staff and the Special Committee (during the short period of its existence) in organizing the region as it came under their control within the lines of the Volunteer Army. If, during the two years in which Denikin and Wrangel were occupying the greater part of South Russia, they had succeeded in bestowing upon it a model government, they might have convinced the peasants that they were better rulers than the Bolsheviks. Probably through lack of persons suitable for such a task they failed in this essential particular, with the result that when they retired, as they had to retire before the advancing Bolsheviks, the Volunteer Army was regarded by the peasants with the keenest hostility. The absence of simultaneous action and co-ordinated effort against the Bolsheviks in parts of Russia other than the south was due to the circumstances that those regions which had gained their freedom by separation from Soviet Russia were themselves still in a precarious position, that communication between the armies was slow and difficult, and that the programme of Denikin, in which he proposed the reunion of the elements which formerly constituted the Russian Empire, did not harmonize with the views of Finland, Poland, or the new Baltic States. The people of these regions desired to crush the Bolsheviks, but they hesitated about joining in a doubtful adventure which, if it succeeded, would result in the loss of their independence. Whether Denikin really meant to absorb Poland and Finland is doubtful; but his rough method of dealing with such questions seemed to suggest that he placed a higher value upon " Slavonic unity " than he did upon the national independence of distinctively non-Slavonic peoples.

The assistance received by Denikin and Wrangel from Great Britain and France was given by these Powers, in the spring of 1918, for the purpose of keeping on the eastern front a Russian force sufficient to prevent the withdrawal of the German and the Austrian armies. In November 1917 the formation of the Volunteer Army by General Alekseiev undoubtedly prevented the German High Command from withdrawing many divisions which it would otherwise have been able to transfer to its western front. When

## THE RUSSIAN REVOLUTION

Austria and Germany sued for peace, the interests of Great Britain and France would have been served by immediate recall of their military missions from Russia ; but the obligations of both Powers to the Russian oppositional generals on different fronts of the Civil War rendered abrupt withdrawal impossible, for it would have meant leaving them to the merciless hands of the Bolsheviks. Yet after the Armistice, and still more after the conclusion of Peace, the assistance rendered by Great Britain and France was both too much and too little. It was great enough to identify these Powers with the Volunteer Army and everything it did and failed to do, and it was too small to enable that army to succeed in its enterprise. Denikin blames the Allied Powers for the uncertainty of their support ; but vacillation upon their part was natural, in view of the unfavourable reports constantly coming through from the military missions. There was a conspicuous lack of discipline and *esprit de corps* in the Volunteer force, due largely to the previous demoralization of its constituent elements while they were yet in the Russian army. (8)  Among the events which had a bearing upon the course of the Civil War between November 1917 and the close of the southern campaign in September 1920 were the following :—

On December 8, 1917, the Bolsheviks issued a manifesto denouncing Kaledin and Kornilov as enemies of the people and as organizers of counter-revolution. The *gubernie* of Orenburg, Ufa, and Perm proclaimed their independence, and on December 15th Kaledin, *Ataman* of the Cossacks, entered Rostov-on-Don after six days' fighting. (9)  On the same day the Russian troops evacuated Finland. (10)  On December 21st the Ukraine stopped its supplies of wheat and sugar to Petrograd, (11) and Kerensky and General Verkhovsky offered their services to the Ukraine Government. (12) Trotsky issued (December 23rd) an official note demanding that the foreign military missions in Russia should cease to meddle in the Civil Wars, and threatening that if Germany did not agree to a democratic peace Soviet Russia would be obliged to wage a revolutionary war. (13)  The Government of the Ukraine sent a delegation to Brest-Litovsk, (14) and General Alekseiev (December 24th) declared that the Ukraine would not submit to the consequences of the peace which the Bolsheviks were preparing to conclude. He also complained that the regiments which were being sent against the Ukraine by the Bolsheviks were commanded by German officers. (15)  Meanwhile, on December 19, 1917, the Crimean Tartars declared their independence, (16) whilst on January 1, 1918, the Congress of Cossacks gave full powers to Kaledin, and at the same time their forces were joined by the Kalmuck Tartars. (17)

# THE CIVIL WARS

Events moved quickly in January 1918. Both France and the Executive Committee of the Soviet recognized the independence of Finland, the Bolsheviks took Vladivostock, but were themselves defeated on the 8th of the month by the Cossacks, who captured four large cannon and 300 machine guns. On January 4th Novorossisk fell to the Soviet troops, the Ukrainians seized Imerinka, but their 3rd regiment was disarmed on the 13th when the Bolsheviks took Kharkov. In Petrograd, on January 11th, there were strikes of tramway employees and postal and telegraph services ; the Soviet Government convened a meeting to discuss the formation of a socialist army, instituted a revolutionary tribunal, and recognized the autonomy of Armenia. (18) Sir Auckland Geddes announced in the House of Commons (January 14th) that the defection of Russia would result in the augmentation of the effective German forces on the western front by 1,600,000 men, (19) and on the same day Count Diamandi, the Roumanian Minister, was arrested and sent to the fortress of St. Peter and St. Paul, but was set at liberty after a protest by the diplomatic corps. (20) Purishkevich was accused of being engaged in a monarchist plot and sentenced to four years' " forced social labour." (21) An attempt was made upon the life of Lenin, and on January 16th he summoned to Petrograd a division of Lettish troops and a number of war vessels. The Russian army, which during the negotiations at Brest-Litovsk was holding the western front, was threatened with famine. (22) The Bolshevik troops reached Odessa, where the French military mission had organized a White Russian force ; but on the departure of the French troops, this force was easily overwhelmed. The Volunteer Army retreated to the Crimea, and there it was dissolved, thousands of refugees finding their way on British vessels to Constantinople.

### B. The North Russian Campaign.

Although there was an active Bolshevik group at Archangel during the spring of 1918, that city became the resort of officers who had belonged to the imperial army and navy. These officers, assisted, according to a Russian writer, (23) by the British intelligence department and by private persons, had succeeded in introducing themselves into the Soviet army organizations and in keeping in touch with the British and French intelligence services.

The regional commissars appointed by the Soviet Government were no doubt aware of the presence at Archangel of a more or less important " White " element, but they were afraid to provoke an open rupture because this might bring about an attack by British ships from Murmansk, where the Allies had established themselves. (24)

# THE RUSSIAN REVOLUTION

The Soviet Government was, moreover, " negotiating for retention of supplies at Archangel " (munitions of war sent there by Great Britain), and meanwhile " removing such supplies at the rate of a hundred cars daily." (25)

The commander of the Red forces, Colonel Potapov, and the commander of the Red fleet, Admiral V., were both in communication with the Allied military authorities at Murmansk, and in spite of the efforts of the local commissar, Kedrov, were able to make such a disposition of the Red troops as to facilitate at the proper time the landing of the Allied forces at Archangel. Major N., also in the " White " interests, organized a cavalry regiment—the Byelomovsky Horse—in which were officers from Petrograd. Potapov sent the majority of the Red Army to the south of Archangel across the northern Dvina, and Admiral V. disobeyed the orders of the Soviet war office by refraining from laying submarine mines for the defence of the entrance to the port. As a matter of fact he sent two ice-breakers ostensibly for this purpose, but these vessels were sunk. When the Allied fleet arrived off the port, it was received by the fire of only one battery, the Mudiojsky, and that was soon silenced. (26)

As rumours that the fleet was in sight spread in the town of Archangel, commissars and officers of the Red Army fled by rail or otherwise, and the rank and file were quickly disarmed by Major N.'s cavalry. Thereupon there was formed " The Provisional Government of Northern Russia," of which the leading figure was Nicholas Tchaikovsky, (27) a national socialist. The other members of his Government were Lekhach, Maslov, Ivanov, and Gukovsky, all being Left Socialist-Revolutionaries. (28) Apart from the White military element, there were practically no other anti-Bolsheviks in Archangel from whom a governing body might have been selected. The *bourgeoisie* had been dispersed or carried off to be imprisoned at Moscow.

The embassies of the Allies and the United States had left Petrograd on February 27, 1918, and had established themselves at Vologda, where they remained until July 25th, when they went to Archangel. (29) The Tchaikovsky Government assumed power in the morning of August 2nd, and four hours afterwards the British force arrived off the port. An advance guard landed at the pier and telephoned to the town, " What Government is in control here ? " The answer was, " The Provisional Government of Northern Russia."—" Will you permit us to land ? "—" Yes, come quick." (30)

The landing was effected by General Poole with about 2,000 men ; the Bolsheviks fled in panic, and in a very short time the whole of the *gub* of Archangel was cleared by the Allied force,

# THE CIVIL WARS

supplemented by the Whites, other Russians in the towns, anti-Bolshevik peasants, and Polish volunteers.(31) Meanwhile there had taken place one of those disagreeable episodes which too frequently occur in Russia to mar otherwise fine achievements. When Major N.'s Horse occupied the quarters of the staff of the Red Army, they found a chest containing military funds amounting to four million roubles. This sum Major N. seemed to regard as legitimate loot, and he accordingly divided it among his officers and men, the officers receiving from 150,000 to 400,000 roubles, and the men 10 to 20 roubles each. This transaction very naturally made a disagreeable impression, and diminished greatly the moral authority of the Whites. An inquiry was instituted, and the culprits were brought before a military court and sentenced to various terms of imprisonment.(32) Major N. had declared himself Commander-in-Chief of the Russian forces at Archangel, but Tchaikovsky, on the ground of this episode, compelled him to retire, and the command was given to Subcaptain Chaplin of the Russian navy, who had been on General Poole's staff.

The Provisional Government of Northern Russia had not an auspicious beginning, and subsequent proceedings gave little promise of its being able to vindicate its existence. The only sign of activity given by the Government was the promise to re-establish the *zemstvo* and municipal organizations which had been shattered by the Bolsheviks. Otherwise it seemed to be simply turning over in its mind the Utopian ideas (33) of the Tchaikovsky circle of fifty years earlier. It could not have retained its power without the assistance of the Allied troops and the foreign diplomatic representatives. Even these were unable to prevent the dissatisfaction of the White elements, who had made important contributions towards the driving out of the Bolsheviks and the installation of the Government. This dissatisfaction brought about an adventure which involved a few White officers, led by Subcaptain Chaplin.

On September 4th a contingent of about 4,500 U.S. troops, commanded by Colonel Stewart, landed at Archangel. One or two days afterwards, (34) Subcaptain Chaplin and a group of officers arrested the members of the Government and despatched them in a steamer to the monastery of Solovietsk, which is situated upon an island in the White Sea. According to Dobrovolsky, the reason for this action was that the White officers, who had really put Tchaikovsky in power ; distrusted him and feared that he was preparing, on the quiet, for union with the Bolshevik Government of Soviet Russia ; (35) for the moment, therefore, Northern Russia was without a government, the White officers not having found substitutes for those whom they had arrested. (36) Two of the ministers, however,

z

354        THE RUSSIAN REVOLUTION

Lekhach and Ivanov, who had escaped arrest, issued a manifesto denouncing the violence of Chaplin, the Commander-in-Chief, declaring that he intended to restore the Tsardom, and had for this purpose concealed the Grand Duke Michael in Archangel. This manifesto was circulated among the surrounding peasants, many of whom armed themselves, and, under the leadership of a Socialist-Revolutionary agronomist, Kapoustin, marched to Archangel. (37) Mr. Francis, the United States ambassador, received a deputation from these peasants and others who protested against the action of Chaplin and the White officers in arresting Tchaikovsky's ministry, whilst the British military mission erected barricades in Archangel and patrolled the town. A meeting of the diplomatic and military representatives of the Powers, under the chairmanship of General Poole, decided to have the members of the Government brought back from Solovietsk and to arrest the officers who had kidnapped them. They further decided to request Tchaikovsky to form a new government of a character somewhat different from the former, and accordingly the ministers returned on September 8th at nine o'clock in the evening.

Tchaikovsky and his colleagues met the diplomatic representatives on the following day, and they all agreed that it was expedient to re-establish his Government on a firm basis. However, two days afterwards, on the afternoon of September 11th, the ministry of Tchaikovsky intimated its intention to resign after appointing a Governor-General, who would be responsible to the Government which had been formed at Samara. (38) The explanation given for this change of front was that the Government was disappointed at the result of a mobilization order which had been issued, only three officers having responded out of the three hundred who should have come forward. According to Mr. Francis, they also spoke of friction between the British and the Russian military officials. (39) Mr. Francis adds : " General Poole appointed a French Military Governor, Colonel Donop, for the city of Archangel, and he has had friction not only with the ministry, but with the ministry's military appointees ; he is sustained by the French ambassador, who has suggested a *modus vivendi*, which leaves the sovereign Government a government in name only." (40)

On September 18th Colonel Durov was appointed Governor-General and also Commander-in-Chief in place of Subcaptain Chaplin, who, besides having compromised himself by the kidnapping exploit, was reported to have reduced his staff to chaos through his inexperience in military matters. Soon another scandal occurred in connection with the staff. A Subcolonel N. was accused of embezzling 50,000 roubles, and being found guilty by a military

# THE CIVIL WARS

court, was sentenced to eighteen months' imprisonment in a penitentiary. This sentence was afterwards modified, and he was sent to the front as a private soldier.

A week after Colonel Durov's appointment Tchaikovsky changed his mind again and selected a new ministry. This ministry was composed of himself as President; P. Iv. Zubov, member of the Union for the Re-establishment of Russia (Minister of Agriculture); Prince Kurakin (Finance); Dr. Mefodiev, formerly member of the State Duma and Constitutional Democrat (Trade and Commerce); S. N. Gorodetsky (Justice); and M. M. Fedorov, Populist-Socialist (Education). A commission was appointed to inquire into the kidnapping of the ministers and to examine the armed peasants, but by order of the Government, on October 1st, all the persons concerned were amnestied. (41)

The Russian troops which were available through local mobilization were evidently looked upon by the allied military authorities on the spot as having experienced too deeply the demoralization of the Russian army to justify any confidence being placed in them. The front of the Northern Government was held almost wholly by Allied troops, very few Russian soldiers being employed, and in the city of Archangel there were only one infantry regiment, one battery of artillery, and one automobile division of Russian troops. These were regarded as of so little consequence that no care was taken either as to their rationing or their discipline : they were simply left to their own devices. No doubt it would have required much hard and conscientious work to drill them into efficient soldiers, but it does not seem to have been even attempted. All the orders of Colonel Durov bore a resemblance to what had come to be called in the army " kerenskchina," (42) which was characterized by demagogic talk and lack " of firmness, force, and discipline " among the officers. " Under such circumstances no army could exist." (43) The Bolsheviks had successfully adopted quite different methods ; they employed the committees and commissars, by whose means they had disorganized the Russian army, to build up in the Red Army a new military discipline as severe as that which had existed before the collapse. The Red Army soldiers were compelled to abandon all ideas of self-government. In the army of the north measures of that kind seem to have been fruitless or to have been condemned as counter-revolutionary. Fear that their orders might be denounced in this manner led Colonel Durov, and those who were about him, to devote their efforts, not towards infusing military discipline into the soldiers, but towards placating them—forgiving men who insulted their officers, conducting meetings with them, and explaining everything to them. Colonel

## THE RUSSIAN REVOLUTION

Durov himself had been abroad from the time of the February Revolution during the whole period of the demoralization of the army, and he was therefore unfamiliar with the signs and consequences of wholesale military disintegration.

It is not surprising that under these circumstances riots occurred among the troops left in Archangel, nor is it to be wondered at that the British military authorities should have been infuriated (44) by the conduct of the Russians—officers and men alike. Those who were unwilling to endure the kind of life then being led in the Russian military units volunteered for the organized Slav-British and French legions, and many officers joined these units, although they had to enlist in the ranks. The British military authorities also opened in Archangel an artillery school for Russian officers. This school was only partially successful, because the Russians did not readily submit to the methods of instruction and the lurid vocabulary so characteristic of the British drill sergeant. (45) The continued reliance upon the Allies, and the failure to mobilize and train Russian troops for the defence of the north, led to universal dissatisfaction. The Provisional Government, therefore, with the consent of the representatives of the Allies, decided to call to its assistance two officers who had distinguished themselves elsewhere. These officers were Generals Miller and M——sky, the latter having seen service in France, where he had commanded a brigade. At the same time General Poole was succeeded as British commander by General Ironside. General M——sky was the first to arrive. He immediately reorganized the staff, appointing as his chief-of-staff the young Colonel J. The first steps of the new military administration were energetic, and though they were followed by an attempt at riot by an infantry regiment, this was sternly suppressed. These active measures resulted in renewed confidence on the part of the Government and the population, and the return to the Russian service of many officers who had joined the foreign legions in the British and French armies.

General Miller, who was recommended to Tchaikovsky by Tereshtchenko, (46) was apparently invited to Archangel to serve as a " buffer " between the British military commander and the Provisional Government. When he arrived at Archangel, the Governor-General was General Mikhailovsky, assisted by V. E. Ignatiev, whose office was the commissariat of the province. Ignatiev, who had in his hands the control of the civil administration of the Northern Province, was a Populist-Socialist (*Narodnik*). On the second day after his arrival General Miller was appointed Governor-General, and at the same time was given charge of the department of the Interior. Ignatiev was not satisfied, and warm

# THE CIVIL WARS

disputes took place in the Provisional Government. An ambiguous compromise was effected by which Ignatiev was to be under the control of General Miller as Governor-General, but not under him as head of the department of the Interior. Dobrovolsky (47) says that the apparent reason for this was that Ignatiev was supposed to be more familiar with administration than General Miller, who was a soldier, while General Miller's presence as Governor-General was a guarantee to the commander of the British military mission. According to Dobrovolsky, Tchaikovsky, who was the head of the Government, was anxious to prevent General Miller from exercising any influence in interior affairs. Dobrovolsky finds this attitude very natural in one who all his life had been opposed to militarism, and who was therefore suspicious of anyone who wore a soldier's uniform. This reason might have sufficed to explain opposition to the presence of any military man in a position of authority at Archangel, but it could hardly justify measures to neutralize the usefulness of a man whose co-operation Tchaikovsky had himself expressly invited. In this confused state of the administration of the Northern Province, Tchaikovsky, leaving Zubov in his place as president of the ministry, left Archangel on January 24, 1919, and went to Paris as a member of the All-Russian Diplomatic Delegation. The other members of this body were Sazonov, (48) Maklakov, (49) Prince Lvov, and Savenkov. (50). In April 1919 Prince Kurakin went to Siberia in order to establish connections with Admiral Koltchak, leaving the department of Finance, of which he had been the head, to Zubov. Under these circumstances the chief influence in the Government was that of General Miller, who, at the end of January 1919, drew up the reply to the note of the Allies in connection with the projected conference at Prinkipo, and who also drafted, at the end of March 1919, the letter which recognized Admiral Koltchak as dictator.

In September 1919 news reached Archangel that Yudenich had been thrown back from Petrograd, and that his army had fallen to pieces, that Denikin was retreating southwards in disorder, and that the army of Admiral Koltchak was " in agony." The northern army was not defeated ; but when the other anti-Bolshevik armies were eliminated from the various fronts, its turn would inevitably come. The population of Archangel became very nervous, and manifestos and appeals failed to reassure them. Dissatisfaction now began to manifest itself among the officers ; the front was very extended (about six hundred miles) ; periods of rest were infrequent, reserves were inadequate, and the situation both at the front and in the rear became more and more unfavourable. In the night of September 26–27 the Allies evacuated Archangel, slipping

## 358     THE RUSSIAN REVOLUTION

away in the darkness, and when the Russian front fell to pieces, as it soon did, and the troops began to fall back upon the town, the Government fled, and the Northern Province was no more.

### C. SIBERIA AND THE REVOLUTION.

The administrative reforms in the government of Siberia which had been initiated by the Tsar Alexander II (51) about the time of the emancipation of the serfs were swept aside in the reaction which followed the Polish uprising of 1863. The expectations to which these projected reforms had given rise remained however, and the idea of an autonomous Siberia within the Russian Empire gradually developed. The idea of autonomy had at its root a desire to benefit the country, by securing adequate administration of the education of the people, improvement of the condition of the native Siberian tribes who were being exploited by unscrupulous traders and others, development of the natural resources of the region, and freedom from the centralized and incompetent bureaucracy.

In 1865 proceedings were instituted by the Government against a small group of persons who had had the audacity to publish, in a pamphlet, their views on the future of Siberia. Among these were a retired sublieutenant, G. N. Potanen, Colonel Usov, and eight or ten others—all young men. Their pamphlet was intended to prove the possibility and the necessity of forming Siberia into an economically independent country within the Empire. " We Siberians offer like brothers our hands to the Russian patriots for a united struggle against our common foe. (52) When this struggle is finished, Siberia should call together its popular assembly to settle its future relations with Russia." The pamphlet concluded with these words : " Long live Siberia from the Ural Mountains to the shores of the Pacific." (53) This small group had formed branches of " the Society of Independent Siberia " in several of the Siberian towns, and they were accused of organizing a movement for the separation of Siberia from Russia, but there is no proof that they proposed independence in that sense. Although the originators of the society were not revolutionists, they were joined by Ph. V. Volkhovsky and other *Narodnovoltsi.* (54)

The idea at this time was cherished only by a small number of persons ; it found no echo in the masses of the Siberian population ; indeed, it was practically impossible to spread ideas, even supposing them to be in the interests of all, amongst peoples separated from each other by so many racial and geographical barriers, as, for example, Bashkirs, Khirgiz, Yakuts, Buriats, besides Polish, Ukrainian, Great Russian, and German colonists.

# THE CIVIL WARS

The question of Siberian autonomy slumbered until 1908, when it was revived by the publication of an article by G. N. Potanen, (55) one of the writers of the 1865 pamphlet. In spite of the revolutionary movement of 1905–1907, little interest was excited among the Siberian public, because increased speed of communication by means of the Trans-Siberian railway had somewhat mitigated the inconvenience of highly centralized control. In 1917, however, after the February Revolution, the people began at last to take a lively interest in the subject, and the idea of a united and autonomous Siberia under a Siberian Government was widely discussed. The moderate socialists advocated a federation of Siberian provinces, each to have a measure of local autonomy, (56) a system which should comprise the whole of Russia. They saw in such a federation a means of resisting the Bolshevik influence. In August 1917 the representatives of the Revolutionary Democratic organizations in Siberia met at Tomsk for the purpose of discussing the formation of a popular government. This meeting resulted in an All-Siberian Congress which met in October, and passed a resolution convening a Siberian Extraordinary Regional Assembly in December. When this assembly met it decided to call a Siberian Regional Duma, fixed the regulations for provisional appointments to certain offices, and elected a Provisional Siberian Government Council. It also decided that the Council should initiate legislation, which was then to be presented to the Duma for approval.

The representatives who met as described were inevitably drawn largely from the organizations which had sprung up spontaneously in Siberia, as they had over the whole of European Russia. These local institutions were of very varying character. They were loosely formed and equally loosely dismissed, and in some places a Soviet had no sooner begun to exercise its functions than public clamour insisted upon its being superseded; similarly in the case of its successor. In spite of such fluctuations, the Soviets were the only organized bodies, and they were necessarily used for the purpose of attempting to build up a stable governmental system. Those who were endeavouring to shape the future government of Siberia were obliged to adapt themselves to circumstances; thus the early personnel of the Siberian Regional Duma could hardly be conspicuous for its wisdom. Almost half of the members were elected by the Soviet organizations, the Soviet of peasants, of Cossacks, and the deputies of the Khirghiz. To these were added the representatives of the Siberian soldiers at the front (the Russian-German front) and of the " semi-intellectual and semi-political unions," (57) as, for example, the post-telegraph, railway employees, teachers', and students' unions. Many

## THE RUSSIAN REVOLUTION

representatives were drawn from the co-operatives, the trade unions, and from the members of the national (properly tribal) organizations. The *bourgeoisie* were not given any representation ; sovereign power was confided to the Duma, which thus kept the ministers under its control. (58)

Opposition to the Siberian Duma soon began to develop. Exclusion of many of the *intelligentsia* from representation aroused the opposition of the members of the Cadet party. The idea of Siberian autonomy began to look like separatism. The Bolsheviks, who were not numerically strong, were hostile because they feared that they would be continually outvoted. Some of the more influential Siberian newspapers were opposed to it because they thought it likely to develop a socialistic bias, (59) and others because they were so much in favour of decentralization that they regarded as fantastic the idea of a centralized authority embracing the European steppe and the whole of Siberia. (60) The Krasnoyarsk Soviet denounced the scheme of Siberian autonomy with a popular assembly as counter-revolutionary, and the Soviet of Achensk took the same view. They asked the Tomsk deputies to take " all measures," including dispersal of the assembly and arrest of its members, to prevent the scheme from being carried into effect. The Soviets of Petrograd and Moscow were equally antagonistic. The obvious reason for all this hostility to Siberian autonomy was the conviction that the influence of the local Soviets was threatened. The members who had been elected to the Siberian Duma became nervous about their position, and only slowly and reluctantly made their appearance at Tomsk.

In December 1917 and January 1918 there arrived G. N. Potanen, Derber, Patushensky, Shatelov, Novoselov, and Zakharov, who had been elected members of the Provisional Council. This Council was endowed legally with very limited powers ; its sole duty was to convene the Duma, but force of circumstances led it to exceed this duty, and to exercise some of the functions of government. The Council was obliged to enter into negotiations with the newly formed Regional Council, which had been acting as the governing authority in Trans-Baikalia. It had to deal also with the so-called " Napoleon of Siberia," Colonel Semenov, (61) who had sent his greetings, declaring that he also was fighting for a Constituent Assembly and against the Bolsheviks. It also had to be in communication with various representatives of foreign countries who had made their appearance at Tomsk, and with the Chinese Government, through Kudashev, the former imperial ambassador to Peking, with regard to the closing to traffic of the railway station at Manchuria. But beyond writing and negotiating, the Council

# THE CIVIL WARS

could do nothing, as it had no administrative staff and no pecuniary resources, and only a personnel of five employees. The Provisional Council, however, added to itself a financial and military section entrusted with the duty of working out the project of law for the coming regional Duma.

The G. N. Potanen mentioned above as one of the members of the Provisional Council was, as has been already pointed out, the same G. N. Potanēn who in 1865 was subjected to prosecution for taking part in the publication of a pamphlet advocating Siberian autonomy. In 1918 he was eighty-three years of age, and by far the most popular and widely respected man in Siberia. He had devoted his life to the service of his country, and through his researches had extended the knowledge of its resources, as well as adding to a knowledge of the neighbouring countries, especially Mongolia. Potanen was no fanatic, but a very clear-headed man, whose judgment was so sound that " everybody wanted his support." (62) He was thus the centre of a struggling group. Great age and physical weakness rendered his influence less commanding than it would have been had he been even ten years younger, but he kept his head clear in the political storm, though he could not subdue the over-excited emotions of the people about him, who were intoxicated by their sudden and unaccustomed freedom and power. Potanen was president of the Provisional Council, but when it began to compromise itself with the Soviets he felt himself obliged to resign, and the task of guiding the destinies of Siberia fell to younger men, less experienced and less personally disinterested.

After Potanen's resignation, the most energetic and influential member of the Council was P. J. Derber, who had for a long time been a salaried member of the Socialist-Revolutionary party. Derber was a dwarf whose small, childish face afforded no indication of his extraordinary ability, especially in grasping at once the salient points in a political situation ; but his honesty was not above the suspicion even of the members of his own party who were closely associated with him. (63)

By January 20, 1918, in spite of the boycott (64) by the working men's associations, and in spite also of the numerous objections which have been mentioned, and the enormous distances which many of the members had to traverse, a hundred members had arrived in Tomsk, and the Duma was duly opened on February 1, 1918. The members could be divided into two large and several small groups. The large groups were the Socialist-Revolutionaries, and a more moderate one was composed of non-Russian Siberians— members of colonies or indigenous tribes—Buriats, Khirgiz, etc., together with Polish, Ukrainian, and German colonists. The most

## THE RUSSIAN REVOLUTION

important subject of discussion was the electoral law which should govern the elections to the Constituent Assembly to be opened in March 1918, and especially the franchise. The chief point at issue was the admission or exclusion of wealthy landowners, peasants, and merchants, of whom there were large numbers in Siberia, and the Duma finally decided to elect a Provisional Government which should be responsible for the conduct of the elections.

Meanwhile the Bolsheviks in Siberia began to aim at acquiring political power in the same manner as had been done in Petrograd and Moscow in October 1917. In the middle of December Omsk fell into their hands ; but the Socialist-Revolutionaries were not disturbed by this occurrence because they thought that they would be overwhelmingly in the majority in the Constituent Assembly which was to meet in Petrograd in January 1918 (which indeed turned out to be true), and that they would be able to overthrow the Bolsheviks. If the Bolsheviks used force to crush the Assembly (which is what occurred), then they expected that the whole of Russia would rise and overthrow them (which, as a matter of fact, did not happen). In January 1918 the Bolsheviks began to acquire influence in Tomsk, but they did not dare at once to act openly against the Regional Council and the Duma.

There was, however, no unanimity, even among the other parties, about the expediency of holding an election. The Socialist-Revolutionaries, with the solitary exception of Derber, opposed an election because they thought the times too abnormal, and that the only result would be the re-election of the Council and the formation of a regional Duma on a larger scale. The group, composed of various tribal representatives and of colonists, including Poles and Ukrainians, as well as some foreign elements, was opposed to the election of a government with full powers. Derber alone persisted in advocating it, suggesting that, when elected, it should leave Tomsk and go farther east. Eventually his proposal was carried, and the Socialist-Revolutionaries gave their adhesion on condition that enough representatives of their party should be included to ensure them a majority. Since the Socialist-Revolutionaries did not have in their immediate circle a sufficient number of persons suitable for ministerial positions, judged even by the inferior standards of the time, they proposed to elect as members of the Government two men from the district Soviet, Shatelov and Zakharov, as well as a local Socialist-Revolutionary, Kudryartsev, although these three were no better qualified than many others. The tribal and foreign group on its part demanded to have two representatives in the ministry, one of them to be Minister of Education. Then, at a secret meeting held in a private house, about

# THE CIVIL WARS

twenty members of the Regional Duma, out of one hundred and fifty, elected a Provisional Government, which consisted of sixteen ministers with portfolio and four without, six of the members of the Duma present being among those elected. Some of the new ministers were previously almost unknown, like Mikhailov, for instance, who became Minister of Finance, apparently only because his name had been mentioned by someone, whilst many ministers were elected without their knowledge or consent. Among these were Vologodsky (who afterwards played a conspicuous *rôle* in Siberian politics), Ustrugov, Serebrenikov, and Krutovsky. The elections were according to the old Russian custom, not by ballot, but by acclamation. Seven only agreed to act, and many others did not even learn of their election until long after the proceedings.

The whole affair had been conducted in secret out of fear of communist interference, and the consequence was that Derber took the reins into his own hands and succeeded in having himself elected as head of the Government, with Vologodsky, Krutovsky, and Mikhailov as his allies ; whilst the others quickly disappeared from the scene. (65)   The affairs of Siberia were thus for the time in the hands of a small *junta* irregularly and secretly elected by a fraction of the Duma. When the Bolsheviks became aware of what had happened, they determined to disperse the Duma, and, if possible, arrest the members of the Government. On the night of January 26, 1918, they made a raid upon both and succeeded in capturing a few, but Derber and some others evaded arrest, and decided to hold the meeting of the Duma as arranged and to proceed to the election of the Government. On February 27, 1918, Derber issued a manifesto to the following effect :—

The hope of all regions and of all Russian nationalities was the Constituent Assembly, but this body was violently dispersed by the Bolsheviks and the Socialist-Revolutionaries of the Left wing. The Constituent Assembly had been the dream of successive generations of revolutionaries in their struggle with the Tsar. To convene the Assembly and to support it offered the only way of saving the Revolution. Yet this Assembly, the only means of securing self-government by the people, was " destroyed and sold " by the Bolsheviks. The Soviet of the People's Commissars which dispersed the Assembly was the enemy of the nation. The Bolsheviks who brought against the Constituent Assembly the Soviets of Workmen's, Peasants', and Soldiers' Deputies were traitors. The Assembly was not opposed to the Soviets, on the contrary it regarded them as the representatives of the democratic forces of the country.

The All-Russian Constituent Assembly had already recognized the federative character of the All-Russian Democratic Republic,

## THE RUSSIAN REVOLUTION

which involved the autonomy of Siberia and of all other constituent elements. The Siberian Duma would take all necessary steps towards the convocation of a Siberian Constituent Assembly which would support the All-Russian Constituent Assembly. The Duma protested against a separate peace with Germany, and, should the Bolsheviks conclude such a peace, the Duma would not assume any moral or material responsibility for an action so " dishonest." If peace were concluded, the Duma would insist upon the return to Siberia of all soldiers belonging to that region and upon the demobilization of ￣ troops in Siberia. The way would then be clear for the formation of a Siberian Volunteer Army, whose duty would lie in defending the All-Russian Constituent Assembly as well as the autonomy of Siberia. Peoples who lived in territories annexed to Russia at different periods of history would be allowed to decide by way of congress and referendum whether or no they would remain as members of the Russian Federated Republic. The agrarian policy of Victor Chernov was declared to be the policy of the Siberian Duma. This policy involved the nationalization of all land, waters, forests, and minerals previously in the possession of the State, the Church, landowners, and others, without compensation, " so that everyone who works (66) can have full right to the earth." The new agrarian law would take into account all the ethnographical and historical conditions. As regards industry, the mines would be nationalized and organized under social control.

There was no suggestion of nationalizing the factories or of instituting government monopolies of manufacture or trade ; nor was there any proposal to interfere with the co-operative societies which were widespread in Siberia. Either Derber, who may be presumed to be the principal author of the manifesto, was unaware of the conditions owing to his being a total stranger to the country, or the scheme of nationalization of the land was a mere verbal bid in competition with the Bolsheviks. The fact was that the land, the waters, the forests, and the minerals were already national property. The clause relating to nationalization, however, created much opposition, because under it grants and leases of public land made to tribes and individuals might be held to be subject to resumption. The Khirgiz, Buriats, and other tribes, as well as the Cossacks and the colonists, began to fear that they might be deprived of lands which had been granted on certain terms by the Imperial Government, and were now looked upon by them as their own.

In February 1918 the members of the Duma and of the Government decided to move eastwards separately in order to avoid possible hostile demonstrations by the Bolsheviks. Derber remained for a time in Tomsk organizing military anti-Bolshevik groups

# THE CIVIL WARS

which were put in touch with the various secret societies of officers of the former imperial forces.

Meanwhile affairs in the Far East were undergoing rapid changes. The Bolsheviks who made their appearance in Trans-Baikalia were dispersed by the first Siberian Cossack regiment on its return from the front. When, however, some members of the Duma arrived at Chita, the Soviet controlled by the Bolsheviks was again in power, and the Duma members were therefore obliged to continue their journey. They went to Harbin, and later to Vladivostok, but only five of them reached the last-mentioned place, the remainder being scattered in different places in Siberia. Several members of the Government, being unaware of their election, had not left their homes, and so great was the confusion that two of the elected members actually took part in hostilities against their own Government : one joined the Bolsheviks and the other General Khorvat.

At that moment (March 1918) Harbin was the principal centre of the anti-Bolshevik forces in Siberia, as well as of those which had been obliged to leave European Russia. When the Siberian Provisional Government, whose history has just been narrated, arrived at Harbin, they found there the Far East Committee for Active Defence of the Fatherland and the Constituent Assembly. In addition to this committee, and holding himself apart from it, but nevertheless exercising an important influence, was General Khorvat, who had been the director of the Chinese Eastern Railway Company. (67) Appointed as he was by the Chinese Government, and being in close communication with it and with all the financial groups engaged in the exploitation of Manchuria and Eastern Mongolia, General Khorvat was inevitably very influential. He enjoyed, moreover, wide personal popularity. There were also two other military figures each of whom played an important part in later events. One was Captain Semenov, and the other was Admiral Koltchak. Captain Semenov was a Cossack officer who had been elected *Ataman* of the Siberian Cossacks. He was under thirty years of age, and his father was a member of a well-known Trans-Baikalian Cossack family, whilst his mother was a Buriat. He spoke both the Mongolian and the Buriat languages, and his energy, reputation, and association with the more adventurous elements in the Amur Region enabled him during the Kerensky *régime* to form a cavalry regiment composed of Buriats and Mongols. This regiment came to be known as the Special Manchurian detachment, and its headquarters at the time of the October Revolution was at Manchuria station, which was on the frontier between the Russian and Chinese territories. Semenov at once declared his intention of supporting the All-Russian Constituent Assembly, and of devoting

# THE RUSSIAN REVOLUTION

himself to a merciless struggle against the Bolsheviks. In accordance with his antecedents, Semenov was anti-Chinese and was a partisan of Mongolian independence. (68) His attitude towards the Chinese led to his being supported by the Japanese, who, according to the Bolsheviks, supplied him with munitions. (69) His association with the Cossacks and the Buriats led him to sympathize with them against the " old-established peasants " of Siberia in their long-standing territorial disputes, and by these means Semenov secured the support of the large Cossack and Buriat population.

Bolshevism made its appearance in Trans-Baikalia only after the return from the front of some Bolshevized Siberian troops, who told the " old-established peasants " that the Bolsheviks had declared that the land belonged to the people. The peasants, who considered that they alone were the people, interpreted this to mean that the land belonged to them—Buriats and Cossacks did not belong to that category. Since the " old-established peasants " were in the minority, Semenov was able to appeal to the majority of the population, and, according to the Bolsheviks, Semenov's troops, who were probably not really inspired by any lofty motives, shot down and robbed the Bolshevized soldiers who returned through Manchuria station. (70)

The new Government at Omsk succeeded in establishing itself without difficulty. The Bolshevik Commissars disappeared, carrying off large amounts of money from the Omsk branch of the State Bank and many cargoes from a flotilla of steamers on the Irtish. These depredations might possibly have been prevented, but no one interfered—indeed the Government seemed glad to get rid of the Bolsheviks on any terms. Power was now in the hands of the Provisional Siberian Government, consisting of Paul Mikhailov, who had been a member of the All-Russian Constituent Assembly, Boris Markov, Michael Lindberg, and Basil Sederov, the last mentioned having been the head of the local government of the Tomsk district. Its powers were strictly limited to executive affairs, legislation being wholly in the hands of the Siberian Regional Duma. The chief tasks to which the Duma and the Government set themselves were the rebuilding of a system for the exchange of goods (which had been completely upset by the Bolsheviks), the organization of food supply, and the prevention of interference from the east. They were also to arrange for an early meeting of the Siberian Constituent Assembly, elected by a direct, equal, and secret ballot on a basis of proportional representation. The more general aim was a complete union of the forces of revolutionary democracy for the purpose of uniting all the separated regions into the All-Russian Federated Democratic Republic.

The difficulty lay in carrying into effect the policy which had

# THE CIVIL WARS

been so evolved. There was no administrative machinery, and even if it had existed there were few competent people to work it. Unknown volunteers turned up in all the towns. When Mikhailov arrived at Omsk, and set to work vigorously day and night to bring order out of chaos, he called a conference of social workers, explained to them the financial and transport problems with which they had to deal, and began to organize the different departments of the Government and to find suitable persons to put in charge. In spite of protestations of equality, the *bourgeois* elements were completely excluded. Before the arrival of Mikhailov, the former munitions committee had succeeded in putting its own members into important places in the Council of People's Economy, and some of these people were experienced persons. The most important member of the munitions committee had been Dvenarenko, a Siberian peasant who had begun life as a sailor, and become a millionaire; now, along with his assistants, he was employed in active administrative work. Departments were organized for the administration of hygiene, municipal self-government, posts and telegraphs, defence, justice, food supply, trade and industry, labour, agriculture and colonization, traffic, and native population. There was besides a Manager of Affairs, G. K. Guins, who had been a civil servant under the old *régime*, and was the only person in Omsk at this time who had had legal and administrative work in the Central Government at Petrograd, although several had had local experience. The Administrative Department was given into the hands of Sezekov, who was a Socialist-Revolutionary, and had been active in the disintegrating propaganda conducted in the army at the front after the February Revolution. He was put into this administrative position, although he was not in the least suitable, because the Socialist-Revolutionaries wanted one of their own members to occupy it. For the commissariat of the military department, Formen, a young man of twenty-eight years, and a member of the All-Russian Constituent Assembly, was proposed. He was not a military man, but Guins advocated the separation of the military commissariat from the office of commander-in-chief in order that the finances of the Department might be regulated by a civilian. Formen, however, was not appointed, the separation was not made, and military influence became predominant.

On the whole, it was extremely difficult to secure suitable persons for the commissariat offices. Few of those who were fitted for them would undertake them, fearing to make themselves conspicuous whilst the issue of the confused state of affairs could with difficulty be foreseen. Although the co-operators were numerous and strong in Siberia, and many of them had experience in the management

**368**     THE RUSSIAN REVOLUTION

of their societies, yet none of them would take places in the commissariat, refusing to interfere in politics on the ground that their talents lay exclusively in economic organization. (71)

The West Siberian Commissariat being thus formed, it began at once to experience certain difficulties. It considered itself as the representative of supreme rule in Siberia, which had but a shadowy form in the Far East. Yet important questions of general policy had to be decided by the departmental heads without the possibility of reference to any other authority. They had been appointed on the explicit understanding that policy was no concern of theirs, and that as executive officers they were to do as they were told. But if they were to act at all, they must act upon some plan; thus from the beginning they were compelled to formulate policies. The Department of Agriculture, for instance, decided to abolish the land committees which had been established by Victor Chernov while he was a member of the Provisional Government at Petrograd, and to restore private landownership. There had never been large estates in private possession in Siberia, and so there had been little reason for the existence of the land committees. The Department of Commerce decided to denationalize the industrial enterprises which had been nationalized under Soviet rule. The Department of Justice found itself in conflict with the Soviet of Workmen's Deputies, which still existed and still had control over the popular courts which had been erected. In all these matters, however, the commissariat hesitated about making sudden practical changes; although its very existence was a protest against Soviet control, it nevertheless allowed the Soviets to remain and to influence the administration, and decided to denationalize only those industries which were not of the nature of public utilities. But as in Siberia practically all the industries might be regarded as belonging to this category, they remained nationalized, the nominal change in policy notwithstanding. The Department of Agriculture was not permitted to abolish the land committees because these had been erected by Victor Chernov, who was a Socialist-Revolutionary. It was hard for them to abandon collectivism, for they had always advocated universal nationalization of land and industry, yet in spite of the tragic experiences of the immediate past, the Socialist-Revolutionaries who formed the commissariat clung to the long-cherished ideals of their party. Their party programme had been appropriated by the Bolsheviks, and in their hands its application had obviously ruined the country; but the programme remained, and the Socialist-Revolutionaries were not convinced of its impracticability. The methods only of the Bolsheviks were objectionable, not the principle of collectivism. Of the truth of this many of the Socialist-Revo-

# THE CIVIL WARS

lutionaries were obstinately convinced. Markov, for example, was accustomed to say that when he adhered to Socialist-Revolutionary formulæ he never made mistakes. (72) Two members of the commissariat, however, had a genuine understanding of the situation. These were Sederov, who had had experience as a *zemstvo* official, and Mikhailov, who possessed real administrative ability, and might have exercised a greater influence on the general policy, if he had seen his way to forgo journeys which he deemed necessary and to stay more continuously in Omsk.

During the Russian advance on the Carpathians, a large number of Czechs belonging to the Austrian army had been made prisoners of war, and there were besides numerous instances of desertion by whole regiments. The latter circumstance caused the Russian military and civil authorities to treat the Czechs in Russia, on the whole, in a very different manner from that in which the German prisoners were treated. Other causes also contributed to the same result. The Czechs were Slavs, and the possibility of a new Bohemian State being formed independent of Austria, together with the influence of Professor Masaryk, who was an ardent advocate of Czech independence, and the known hostility of the Czechs to German Austrians and to Germans, were all important factors. The consequences were that the Czech troops were permitted to retain their organization and their arms, and some were prepared for transference to France, or to the Russo-German front. When the Revolution of October 1917 took place, there were about 300,000 Czech troops in Russia, most of them being in Siberia. The disorganization following upon the Civil War in European Russia prevented them from returning to their native country by the western route, and their leaders therefore determined to assemble and prepare them for fighting their way if necessary through Siberia. This advance began at the end of May 1918, simultaneously with the beginning of the Siberian Civil War. This war endured for two years, during which the Czechs played an important part in Siberian politics.

When they eventually left Siberia, they realized that their conduct had been so ambiguous as to demand an explanation. They therefore issued a manifesto in which they declared their policy in these words : " We supported the democracy and assisted in the struggle against reaction." In carrying out this policy, they declared that they had supported the Siberian Regional Duma in its struggle against the Siberian Government, and had upheld the committee of members of the All-Russian Constituent Assembly ; they further alleged that the creation of the Directorate at Ufa was their doing. The Czechs had been guarding the Trans-Siberian Railway, partly

# THE RUSSIAN REVOLUTION

to secure their own transport, and partly because, having taken this office upon themselves, the Siberian Government left them to it. They stated in their manifesto that they had ceased to guard the railway when they saw " the cruelty that was practised by the punitive detachments of the government forces who tried to put down the uprising of the peasants." " We declare to the whole world," they said, " that it is not possible for us to remain in a country governed by such a government of blood and violence as the Siberian Government. We took the transport in our hands when the Russians could not manage it ; we took the gold into our care, and we gave it to the popular rulers in Irkutsk. We guarded Admiral Koltchak and then handed him over to the popular court, not only as a reactionary, but as an enemy of the Czechs. He ordered Semenov to blow up the tunnels [through the mountains south of Lake Baikal] in order to prevent the retreat of the Czechs to the east."

This manifesto is very candid. The facts of the case seem to be quite simple. The Czechs first betrayed the Austrians and then the Russians who had reposed confidence in them. At the end of May 1918 the Czech forces were spread over the Russian and Siberian railways from Penza to Vladivostok. The Soviet Government at Moscow, at the instance of the Germans, (73) had insisted upon their surrendering their arms. There was much reason in this demand. The Czechs had been armed and equipped by the Russian Government, the munitions in their hands were the property of that Government, and its representatives conceived that they had a right to require that a foreign force armed by them should not engage in military operations outside their control and should not carry the equipment out of the country. The Czechs, however, refused, and kept their arms, for they had to provide for their own safety until they left Russian territory, and they intended to go to France in the interests of the Allies. Their leaders declared that they felt certain that Germany would be beaten in the campaign, and that, in making a separate peace, the Russians were merely ruining themselves. " We will secure the independence of our country by keeping faith with the Allies."

The failure of the attacks upon the Bolshevik rule from many sides was due to the following causes : the want of co-operation of the various commanders, the absence of support of these by the general population within the areas occupied by them, the lack of a political programme sufficiently attractive to the people in the rear of the armies within the region over which the Bolsheviks ruled, or to the volunteers in the White forces, and lastly to the absence of discipline in these armies. General Denikin, and perhaps

# THE CIVIL WARS

anti-Bolshevik Russians in general, were inclined to blame the want of support from the Allies ; but it is doubtful whether any Government could have risked the disapproval of its own people by continuing a series of campaigns in the heart of Russia long after peace had been declared in Europe. It is true that Bolshevism appeared to be a menace to Europe, and that a struggle against it might one day have to be undertaken ; but a defensive struggle is one thing and an aggressive campaign, which might result in the re-establishment of the autocracy from which Russia had already suffered too long, is quite another. Even had the Allies, by means of an expeditionary force operating on their own account, effected the capture of Petrograd and even Moscow, that would have been the beginning, rather than the end, of the trouble. The Allies could not undertake to govern Russia, yet the Russians seemed incapable of governing themselves ; there would thus have emerged an insoluble dilemma. There was really nothing to be done but to leave the Russians to work out their own salvation in their own way, however grievous that way might be.

During the Civil Wars and the blockade which accompanied them, the population of the cities suffered almost incredible hardships, and the peasantry were not much better off because of the forced levies in kind to which they were subjected. Perhaps only a country like Russia, where the mass of the population is inured to a low standard of life, could have survived. For three years Soviet Russia was cut off by the Civil Wars from the bread and beef regions—the Ukraine and Siberia—as well as from the coal-fields of the Don and the oil-fields of the Caucasus. She was also cut off from other countries by the blockade and by the impossibility of producing, in the absence of raw materials, sufficient goods to exchange for adequate food supplies, and by the further difficulty, in the absence of credit, of obtaining these supplies on promise of future payment. The centre and north of Russia do not customarily produce sufficient food for the people who inhabit them : these people have been accustomed to rely upon the rich agricultural regions of the south and east, and have increased and prospered thereby.

The population of the two capitals and of the industrial towns was still large, though it had been depleted, immediately after the conclusion of the war in November 1917, by the decline of industry, the dispersal to the villages of the industrial population, and the voluntary exile of the upper classes in consequence of the proletarian revolution. Thus the Soviet Government was in a cleft stick. The army, now numbering about 700,000, had to be fed, so had the people of the capitals. The mechanism of supply, exchange,

# THE RUSSIAN REVOLUTION

and credit, damaged during the European war, was subjected to sudden and enormous strain immediately upon its cessation, partly from inevitable economic causes, but chiefly because the Bolsheviks, from political motives, heedless of economic consequences, had destroyed it wilfully and completely. Even if the mechanism of credit and exchange had been preserved, and even if the elements in the population accustomed to perform the functions associated with this mechanism had not been driven out of the country and thereby into hostile relations with the Government, the difficulties would have been enormous. Under pre-war conditions, the exports of grain took place principally from the large estates and to a relatively small extent from the peasants' holdings. In the best years the peasants had very little surplus over their own needs. Under the pressure of necessity, the Soviet Government took from them, not only that surplus, but even what was necessary for their subsistence, the food for their animals and the seed for succeeding crops. Lenin fully admits that this was done, (74) but excuses the action on the ground that the Civil War had to be waged by all elements, that a common stand had to be made against Denikin and Wrangel, and that, hardship being inevitable, the peasant must bear his share. Thus the peasantry, impoverished during and immediately after the Civil War, were called upon to face the inevitably deficient harvest of 1920, followed by the famine of the succeeding year.

---

## NOTES

(1) Novo-Tcherkask is the capital of the Cossacks of the Don. It was here that the Tsarevich was formally invested as their *Ataman*.

(2) *Archives of the Russian Revolution* (Berlin), vol. ix, p. 284.

(3) The word employed is *sovieshchanie* = council, committee, or simply meeting.

(4) General Alekseiev died on September 25, 1918.

(5) Text in *Archives of the Russian Revolution* (Berlin, 1922), vol. iv, pp. 241–51,

(6) Ibid. These details are derived from copies of the documents in question.

(7) *Prekaz*, No. 175, December 14, 1919 (O.S.), quoted above.

(8) Private reports made to the writer dwell upon the indolence of Denikin's and Wrangel's officers.

(9) *Chron. de la Guerre*, 7ᵉ vol., p. 245.

(10) Ibid.

(11) Ibid., p. 250.

(12) Ibid., p. 252.

(13) Ibid., p. 253.

(14) Cf. supra, p. 208.

# THE CIVIL WARS

(15) *Chron. de la Guerre*, 7<sup>e</sup> vol., p. 253. These German officers were taken from the camps of the prisoners of war in Russia.

(16) Ibid., p. 248.

(17) Ibid., 8<sup>e</sup> vol., p. 6.

(18) Ibid., p. 22.

(19) For the reasons explained above, although the German High Command withdrew some troops, it was not possible to transfer the whole army which had been holding the German eastern front.

(20) Dennis, A. L. P., *The Foreign Policies of Soviet Russia* (New York, 1924), p. 25 ; and Francis, David R., *Russia from the American Embassy, April 1916–November 1916* (New York, 1922), pp. 216–22.

(21) *Chron. de la Guerre*, 8<sup>e</sup> vol., p. 23.

(22) The shortage of food for the army is not to be associated with the cessation of supplies from the Ukraine.

(23) Dobrovolsky, S., *The Fight for the Re-establishment of Russia in the Northern Provinces* in *Archives of the Russian Revolution* (Berlin, 1921), vol. iii, p. 19.

(24) According to David R. Francis, United States ambassador to Russia, the landing at Murmansk was permitted by Trotsky at a moment when he thought that the Brest-Litovsk negotiations were going to break down (op. cit., pp. 264–65.)

(25) Francis, D. R., op. cit., p. 20.

(26) Dobrovolsky, S., op. cit., p. 20.

(27) Nicholas Tchaikovsky (b. *circa* 1840) was leader of the Tchaikovsky circle of 1872–1874 (cf. Mavor, J., *An Economic History of Russia*, London, vol. ii, pp. 75, 75 n., 76).

(28) Dobrovolsky, S., op. cit., p. 21.

(29) The ambassadors were M. T. Noulens (France), Signor de la Toretta (Italy), and Mr. D. R. Francis (U.S.). The British commissioner was Mr. F. O. Lindley. For the experiences of the embassies at Vologda, see Francis, D. R., op. cit., pp. 234 et seq.

(30) Ibid., p. 264.

(31) Dobrovolsky, S., op. cit., p. 20.

(32) Ibid.

(33) Ibid., p. 21.

(34) Dobrovolsky gives the date as September 6th. Mr. Francis gives September 5th. The arrests took place between 2 and 3 a.m.

(35) Dobrovolsky, S., op. cit., p. 21.

(36) The following characteristic dialogue is reported by Mr. Francis (op. cit., p. 270).

> September 5, 1918. Time, 10.15 a.m.
> *General Poole :* " There was a revolution here last night."
> *Mr. Francis :* " The hell you say ! Who pulled it off ? "
> *General Poole :* " Chaplin."
> *Mr. Francis :* " There is Chaplin over there now."
> *General Poole :* " Chaplin is going to issue a proclamation at eleven o'clock."
> *Mr. Francis :* " Chaplin, who pulled off this revolution here last night ? "
> *Captain Chaplin :* " I did. I drove the Bolsheviks out of here ; I established this government. The ministers were in General Poole's way, and were hampering Colonel Donop (the French Provost Marshal). I see no use for any government here, anyway."
> *Mr. Francis :* " I think this is the most flagrant usurpation of power I ever knew, and don't you circulate that proclamation that General Poole tells me you have written until I can see it and show it to my colleagues."

" Chaplin's manner indicated that he was proud of the deed, and expected commendation." (Report by Mr. Francis to U.S. Secretary of State, September 10, 1918.)

(37) Mr. Francis says : " We [the ambassadors] told Dyedushenko [Lekhach must be meant] not to circulate the proclamation, and he went to the telephone in my apartment and gave an order to that effect." (*Russia from the American Embassy, April 1916–November 1916* (New York, 1922), p. 274. The statement in the text is from Dobrovolsky, S., op. cit., p. 21.)

# 374 THE RUSSIAN REVOLUTION

(38) The Government at Samara consisted of Alekseiev, Avksentiev, and Stepanov.

(39) Francis, D. R., op. cit., p. 276.

(40) Ibid.

(41) Dobrovolsky, S., op. cit., p. 22.

(42) " After the manner of Kerensky."

(43) Dobrovolsky, S., op. cit., p. 23.

(44) Dobrovolsky, who was in Archangel from the beginning of September 1918, and who was in a position to examine all the documents, says the attitude of the Russian soldiers " made the English mad " (op. cit., p. 23).

(45) Dobrovolsky makes some naïve comments upon what he calls " the rudeness of the English sergeants," and cites one case in which a sergeant struck a Russian officer (op. cit., p. 23).

(46) A member of the Provisional Government at Petrograd.

(47) Dobrovolsky, S., op. cit., p. 25.

(48) Foreign Minister under the imperial *régime*.

(49) Maklakov was a Moscow barrister, member of the Constitutional-Democratic party in the Second, Third, and Fourth Dumas. After the February 1917 Revolution he was appointed commissar of the Ministry of Justice, and in the summer of the same year Russian ambassador to France.

(50) Socialist-Revolutionary.

(51) Cf. Kropotkin, P., *Memoirs of a Revolutionist* (Boston, 1899), p. 170.

(52) The common foe being the centralized bureaucracy.

(53) Guins, G. K., *Siberia, The Allies, and Koltchak* (Peking, China, 1921), vol. i, p. 69.

(54) Cf. Mavor, J., op. cit., vol. ii, p. 109, etc.

(55) In the magazine *The Needs of Siberia* (St. Petersburg, 1908).

(56) This idea was said by Prince Kropotkin to have been embodied in the constitution drawn up by the Grand Duke Constantine before the assassination of the Tsar Alexander II in 1881.

(57) That is, the politico-intellectual unions.

(58) Cf. Guins, G. K., op. cit., p. 71.

(59) E.g. the *Siberian Ryech*.

(60) E.g. *Golos Preamurya*.

(61) Cf. infra, note (68).

(62) Guins, G. K., op. cit., p. 73.

(63) Ibid., p. 74.

(64) The word " boycott " long since found its way into the Russian language.

(65) The details are derived from Guins, G. K., op. cit., vol. i, pp. 75–78.

(66) The word used, *trudyashchagosya*, implies work of any kind, manual or mental.

(67) For the text of the Agreement, dated August 29, 1896, between China and Russia relating to this railway, see Kent, P. H., *Railway Enterprise in China : An Account of its Origin and Development* (London, 1908), App. A., No. 3, p. 211.

(68) According to the Bolsheviks, Semenov was a mere bandit ; according to those who shared his political views, he was a " very honest man." Subsequent to the Bolshevik triumph in the Far East he spent a short time in the United States, where, at the instance of the Bolsheviks, he was arrested on an accusation of stealing furs. He took refuge later in Japan.

(69) *Izvestia* (Petrograd), No. 102, 1918.

(70) Headquarters of the Special Manchurian detachment in October, 1917.

(71) Cf. Guins, G. K., op. cit., p. 89.

(72) Ibid., p. 94.

(73) According to Guins, G. K., op. cit., vol. ii, p. 517.

(74) Lenin, N., *Collected Works* (Moscow, 1923), vol. xviii, p. 190.

## CHAPTER X

## THE RED TERROR

THE helpless passivity and pacifism of the Russian *intelligentsia* became more and more marked after the violent closure of the Constituent Assembly, and it was largely this forced acquiescence on their part which enabled the Bolsheviks not only to rise to power, but, in the process, both to disarm and ride rough-shod over them. Pacifism has in past times, both in the individual and in the group, alternated with periods of febrile energy, and has sometimes tended to remorseless cruelty. There is thus nothing inexplicable about Russian pacifism. The Bolsheviks bore ostentatiously on their banners, " A democratic peace without annexations and without indemnities " (1)—although they signed a peace involving both. The Socialist-Revolutionaries had turned from faith in conspiracies to faith in meekness of spirit—in other words, to a fatalistic scepticism as to the benefits of activity. Nothing mattered, when all effort was useless.

If pacifism was characteristic of the Socialist-Revolutionary party, which commanded by far the largest number of votes of any of the numerous political parties, it was still more characteristic of the other groups and of the large number of non-party people. Even westernized liberals like Miliukov became pacifist, for the apparent uselessness of struggling against inevitable fate paralysed all energy.

What really happened was that the *intelligentsia* of Russia, numbering probably about ten millions, became exhausted with the strain of the war. After finding themselves subjected to a momentary stimulus under the influence of which they got rid of the old *régime*, they fell back into their customary attitude of indifference to politics. " Politics are someone else's business, not ours. They are not an agreeable mode of spending time ; and when they are profitable, then they are discreditable. It is very fortunate that some people seem to have a talent and a liking for the affairs of government. Such a taste seems foolish and inexplicable ; but those who choose a trade of that kind are welcome to it, and to the profits of it too, if there are any. I have my profession, my business, or my estate, and they take up all my time. I do not like people to exercise authority over me, to exact taxes from me, and to conscript my sons for the army ; but to all these I must submit.

## 376 THE RUSSIAN REVOLUTION

In any case, I do not understand politics and do not want to do so. It is a great mistake to dabble in them. I would rather pay someone to take the trouble off my shoulders." This was the pre-war standpoint ; and, strange to say, many have returned to it in spite of the tragedy to which this apathetic attitude has so largely contributed.

Shrewdly realizing that they had crushed internal opposition, and that they had won the Civil War, the Bolsheviks in 1921 moderated the reign of terror that they had established after the dispersal of the Constituent Assembly. Up to that time the terror was very real, and it is impossible to estimate accurately the number of people who suffered death (some by torture), long terms of imprisonment, loss of property, or exile. Up till the middle of August 1918 the loss of life in the Bolshevik Revolution had not been very great. Such casualties as occurred were in the field, in street riots in the capitals, or in one or other of the phases of the Civil Wars.

On August 17, 1918, Moses Solomonson Uritsky, a Jew, president of the *Che-Ka* or Extraordinary Commission, was shot and killed in the Warsaw Square, Petrograd, near the Winter Palace. Smelg-Benario describes this event and its immediate consequences as follows :—

" On a *triste*, foggy morning in August, I was sitting in my office (the War Commissariat). My windows looked on to the Warsaw Square ; on the right was the Winter Palace, and on the left the huge building of the former General Staff. . . . I heard shots in the square. We went to the windows and saw that someone was being followed by men on bicycles. I went down quickly. 'What has happened ? ' I asked some of the military people who were standing in the square. ' Uritsky, the president of the *Che-Ka*, has just been killed,' a soldier answered excitedly. In a few minutes a car from the sanitary department came and took away the body of the murdered man—who had been a few minutes before the harsh president of the *Che-Ka*. His death, from a shot in the head, was instantaneous. . . . The murderer of Uritsky was a student of the Polytechnic Institute, Kannegiesser. I knew him well at the Institute, where we worked in the same department. The murderer himself, as well as the murder, had a great effect upon me. My heart was very heavy when, an hour later, there came to the commissariat, in an excited state, the Commissar of War Control, a young communist, Dukhvinsky, with whom I was on very friendly terms. He began to tell me with joy how, under his direction, Kannegiesser had been arrested.

" After the murder of Uritsky, as is well known, an awful terror began. Everyone who was in Petrograd during these dreadful days knows what wild licentiousness, what anarchy reigned in

# THE RED TERROR

the capital. No one who was not a communist and an important service man felt himself safe. Armed Red Army men and sailors were entering houses and arresting people on their own initiative. The captives were sent without any inquiry to prison, and were held as hostages, although their only fault was that they were *bourgeoisie* and *intelligentsia*. The wave of Red Terror flowed all over Russia. Petrovsky, the Commissar of Interior Affairs, issued an order requiring all Soviets to seize a definite number of citizens (2) and to hold them as ' pledges.' In the event of any counter-revolutionist *bourgeois* or *kulak* (3) daring to revolt, the Soviet had the right to shoot those who were held as hostages. All Russia was under the Bolshevist terror. No one knew what the next hour would bring forth for him.

"Life in Petrograd became more and more unbearable. The hand of terror was pressing heavily. Every day there were arrests and executions. The Government not only refrained from putting a stop to the slaughter, but on the contrary tried to inflame the savage instincts of the masses of the soldiers. Zinoviev, the president of the Petrograd Executive Committee, was not afraid to throw watchwords of this kind to the masses :—

"'You *bourgeoisie* kill separate individuals; but we kill whole classes.'

" These words were not empty phrases ; the state press seized upon them and did everything possible to inflame the masses with a thirst for blood. Zinoviev and his companions had won a victory.

" Kannegiesser was killed without trial. A few days later when I arrived at the commissariat I did not see Pozern, who was usually at his desk early in the morning. . . . I found that he had been called to Kronstadt. The sailors had entered the prison there and had shot the imprisoned *bourgeois* hostages without trial. It is said that they shot nearly five hundred people."

Smelg-Benario goes on to describe several incidents in which relatives of his were arrested, their only offence being that they were regarded as belonging to the *bourgeoisie*. The following extracts from one of these descriptions are typical :—

" At two o'clock in the morning I was aroused. . . . Some armed men entered. ' Are you Citizen T—— ? We want to search your house. . . .' Nothing was found. Then the commissar asked me, ' To what party do you belong ? ' ' To none.' . . . . He arrested me, saying that I belonged to the *bourgeoisie* and that was sufficient. . . . I found that the armed men had demanded from the porter the list of those who received bread in the 4th category, and that their arrests were based on this list. He [the commissar] was making arrests on his own initiative. . . ."

## 378 THE RUSSIAN REVOLUTION

The prisoner was carried off and thrown into the Troutbetskoy bastion of the fortress of St. Peter and St. Paul, where he endured damp, starvation, darkness, and constant fear that he would be shot. Always after midnight, about three o'clock, " we heard shots in the fortress. We had no doubt as to the meaning of these shots. . . . ' Why should I be tortured ? Is it because I was the owner of a shop ? That is my only fault. . . .' Such was the freedom at which our people were aiming ! " This man emerged from the fortress, through the influence of his brother-in-law, but during the few days that he spent there his hair turned grey and his body became bent as if with age.

Another extract narrates how four engineers disappeared. Inquiries were made about them, and their relatives were told by the *Che-Ka* that they " had been shot through a misunderstanding." Smelg-Benario says that up to this time he had been sceptical regarding alleged Bolshevik cruelties because the Moscow newspapers were sometimes given to exaggeration. After repeated cases with which he came in close contact, he was convinced that these incidents represented the real Bolshevism. " As a democrat and socialist," he says, " I never agreed with Bolshevist methods, but the shock of the terror alienated me from the Bolsheviks. I began to get more and more critical of the movement, and at every step I saw more clearly that our Revolution, under the patronage of the Bolsheviks, was nothing but riot and anarchy." (4)

" I was detailed as a member of a committee to go to Yamburg, our business being to settle a dispute between the regional Soviet and the military control. . . . During the journey I had some talk with Barshovsky (a member of the Presidium of the Central *Che-Ka*). I asked him about the fate of Kannegiesser. 'Is it true that Kannegiesser is still alive ? ' ' Yes, it is true,' answered Barshovsky. ' How do you explain that ? I thought that he had been shot a long time ago.' ' You see,' said Barshovsky, ' we have a reason for not shooting him. Why the devil should we shoot him now ? Let him suffer for a while. We shall always have time to shoot him.' . . . I was talking (at another time) with Koslovsky, a member of the collegium of the People's Commissariat of Justice, about the orders which were in force in the All-Russian Extraordinary Commission (the *Che-Ka*) for the struggle with the counterrevolution. I asked him why the Commissar of Justice did not take measures against the crude and criminal elements which had crept into the *Che-Ka*.

" ' Don't you think it is very necessary to cleanse the *Che-Ka* ? These elements are simply compromising our Revolution.'

" ' Yes, comrade, that is very easy to say,' said Koslovsky ;

# THE RED TERROR

' but do you think that such people as you and I are any good for the *Che-Ka*? Certainly not. We are now engaged in a merciless struggle—a fight not for life but for death, with the counter-revolution, and for such a fight we *intelligentsia* are not fit. For such a struggle only thick-skinned people are suitable. It is true that among the crude elements in the *Che-Ka* there are many with a very dark past. We cannot do anything against them, so we must conciliate them.'

" I thought to myself that we might make a stand against this terrorism; but they simply do not want to do anything. Only later it became clear to me that the whole system of Bolshevist government is based on the crude and criminal elements which have now the opportunity to develop their ' activities.' " (5)

Smelg-Benario narrates a conversation between Borshchevsky, a member of the *Che-Ka*, and an old Jew of the Jewish town of Yamburg. The Jew was an acquaintance of long standing, and he put many questions to the Bolshevik without regard to the formidable power with which he was invested. Borshchevsky answered, using frequently such words as " mercilessly, death, shooting," etc. Then he spoke in general about " the necessity of crude measures in a struggle with enemies." He spoke of many cases in his own experience. The old Jew listened very attentively, and finally said :

" ' I am already old . . . and that may be why I cannot understand very well the aims of the younger generation. I know that in the past there were many injustices and evils ; but I tell you, you will not be able to destroy evil by your methods. First of all, you must value human life. Our old holy religion, our prophets and learned men, always told us that human life is the highest gift. Humanity should be the aim and not the means. Young man,' he said, addressing Borshchevsky, ' you smile ; but I assure you that your actions and those of your party comrades cannot come to any good. It is possible that there may come a time when you will remember my words. The Tsar and his servants acted (for a time) without incurring punishment, just as you are doing now. During the autocracy a man's life had no value—and you know now to what straits the autocracy came. Let me tell all of you that your opinions and your actions bring only bloodshed and savagery, and cannot produce any good fruit.' " (6)

Much of the hardness and cruelty of the Soviet Government's methods was due, undoubtedly, to the presence in its ranks of inferior elements brought over from the old *régime*. The following instance illustrates this fact :—

" I knocked at a door. No answer. I knocked again ; a drowsy voice answered ' Come in ! ' I opened the door. Just before me,

## 380  THE RUSSIAN REVOLUTION

by the window, there was a table upon which lay a sword and two revolvers. On the left, in the corner, were standing many rifles. On the right was a bed on which was stretched a man in military uniform. He remained as he was when I entered. ' Are you the commandant ? ' ' Yes,' he answered. I told him who I was. He immediately rose and with a deep bow and amiable smile asked me to sit down. ' Please excuse my lying down just now,' he said, ' but you know that I work so much at night that I must rest during the day. You see [and here he lowered his voice] every night I make a search in our region and arrest officers and other counter-revolutionists. You know how afraid of me they are. Immediately night falls I go hunting.' He seemed to like this word very much, because he smiled vindictively. ' You know, comrade, I am not like others who take money from the Government and do nothing. I really try to do my work, not out of fear, but conscientiously. If I get tired, I have still the gratification of knowing that I am serving the Soviet Government faithfully and well.' I looked the commandant attentively in the face. He was a typical regional inspector or sergeant of the old *régime*. By his crude, hard expression one could at once see that his profession was to torture men who fell into his hands. In his servile manner one could trace the ' brave ' soldier that he was in the old time, arresting revolutionary youth, just as here and now, with the same indifference, he was arresting counter-revolutionists. This was a common type of those days [October 1918], and I am sure it was very often met with in the Soviet organizations. Former policemen and sergeants—old Tsarist bureaucrats—very quickly transferred their services to the new *régime*, changing their colour to Red." (7)

The terror was applied not merely to those who had enjoyed the possession of property under the old *régime*, many working people suffered also. Workmen were arrested, imprisoned, and shot as *bourgeoisie* without delay, inquiry, or trial. (8)

That there was no cohesion or co-operation between the different elements of the Soviet system is illustrated by the following incident :—

A group of five hundred alleged *bourgeoisie* was sent to Vologda to be put to " forced labour," but they were thrown into prison instead. The prison was cold and damp. " On the first night many became insane and many committed suicide." They were then divided into parties of ten and sent to the front. There they were compelled to dig trenches and carry machine guns under the fire of the British troops. The Red Army looked upon them as serfs. The decree under which these people were sent to Vologda provided for their being employed on obligatory labour for not more than three

# THE RED TERROR

months; but the authorities at Vologda said they had nothing to do with the laws passed at Petrograd. "We have our own laws." "All power to the Regions!" These poor people died because they were insufficiently clad and nourished, for they were not allowed to have clothes from their homes, and it was useless to send parcels surreptitiously because they would be seized *en route* by the soldiers, who said, "We are communists, everything is ours." (9)

The Red Terror was the result of fear. Fear had caused the fall of the Tsar; fear had brought the Duma over to the side of the Revolution; fear had compelled the Provisional Government from the outset of its career to submit to the Petrograd Soviet; fear had brought Kerensky into power and had caused his fall; and now fear of counter-revolution impelled the Bolsheviks to meet it with savage and indiscriminate terror, for, from their point of view, to impress the population of Petrograd with a sense of fear was essential to their own retention of power. (10)

---

### NOTES

(1) The people of the victorious countries could not have viewed such a peace with favour, and did not when the time came. Thus peace without annexations and indemnities would not have been a democratic peace.

(2) The word employed in the order is vulgar and unquotable.

(3) Well-to-do peasant.

(4) Smelg-Benario, *In the Service of the Soviet* in *Archives of the Russian Revolution* (Berlin, 1921), vol. iii, pp. 149–54.

(5) Ibid., pp. 156–57.

(6) Ibid., p. 157.

(7) Ibid., p. 159.

(8) For instances, see Smelg-Benario, op. cit., pp. 152, 162, 163.

(9) Ibid., p. 164.

(10) For Trotsky's apology for the terror, see his *Defence of Terrorism* (London, 1921).

*BOOK V*

# ECONOMIC CRISIS, COLLAPSE OF COMMUNISM, AND THE NEW ECONOMIC POLICY

## CHAPTER I

# THE ECONOMIC CRISIS OF THE WINTER OF 1920-1921 AND THE FAMINE OF 1921

THE pressure of Germany upon Russia after the Peace of Brest-Litovsk, the occupation of a large part of the country by Germany, the revictualling of Germany and Austria from the Ukraine, and the outbreak of the Civil War, led inevitably to the extension of the blockade against the Central Empires in order to include Russia. This blockade was intended to assist the anti-Bolshevik forces, and also to prevent Germany or Austria from procuring, through Russia, materials urgently wanted by them for the prosecution of the war.

On the conclusion of the European war, however, the blockade of the Central Empires was raised, but the blockade of Russia remained until the conclusion of the Civil War. Under ordinary circumstances, a blockade of Russia, whether by land or sea, or both, would not affect the livelihood of the inhabitants. Up till the period of the war she had exported food, and her imports of food-stuffs were insignificant. But in the autumn and winter of 1917–1918 Petrograd was being inadequately supplied by the villages, and was cut off by the blockade from importing anything.

When eventually the Civil War ended, so also did the blockade. The land was all nationalized, and the peasants, the communes, and the working men's unions were granted the use of the land on certain terms. The Government proclaimed a firm monopoly of foreign trade and restricted interior trade within certain limits. Private commerce of almost any kind was prohibited. The reason for this rigid prohibition was that the Soviet Government was attempting to plant its power firmly by means of the food ration. So long as it held the keys of every larder, life was impossible without submission to the Communist party which controlled the Government.

The state-collectivist system instituted by the Bolsheviks in 1917 reached its height during the autumn of 1920. Nationalization had been carried to its fullest extent. No doubt there were cases of illegal hoarding, trade, and speculation ; but the bulk of the economic resources was in the hands of the Government, and the people in general were obedient.

## THE RUSSIAN REVOLUTION

The high-water mark of " public ownership " had been reached. Enthusiasts had anticipated that when such a moment came everyone would at least have the material means of being happy. One condition, however, was lacking. The Government owned everything, but by itself it could neither use nor produce anything. The people were reluctant to work, neither peasants nor workmen were inclined to produce for the Government as much as would easily have been forthcoming if they were working for themselves. The political communists, led by Kalinin, president of the Soviet Republic, carried on an active propaganda. They tried to persuade the peasants that in working for and handing over their grain to the Government they were working for the whole nation and incidentally for themselves. They tried to convince the working men that in toiling for subsistence rations they also were working for their country. But when the peasants found that the purchasing power of their grain diminished, and that the Government left them scarcely sufficient for food for themselves and their animals, and to serve for seed for the next crop, they determined to save their labour, to sow less, and thus have less to give. In a competitive market such a policy would have led to an increase in the price of grain as expressed in goods, and a corresponding decline in the price of goods as expressed in grain, but by means of arbitrary fixation of prices the Soviet authorities endeavoured to prevent the advance of grain prices. The forces of human nature were, however, too strong. Beneath the surface there was going on, collectivism notwithstanding, a perpetual struggle between the agrarian and the industrial interests, between country and town.

The Bolshevik police were well organized, pervasive, even ubiquitous, yet illegal trade increased. Notwithstanding the enormous risk, the peasants sold their produce to the people at high prices rather than sell to the Government for what the Government might choose to give ; and the people in the towns bought at these high prices rather than permit their dependents to starve upon the inadequate government ration. Mothers, formerly rich, whose children needed bread, went into the country and besought the peasants to exchange flour or potatoes for clothing or jewels which they had been fortunate enough to conceal. Working women were in the same plight. There is an air of actuality about the following narrative by an officer in the War Commissariat of the Petrograd region. He had been into the country upon an official mission with a member of the *Che-Ka* and another functionary. The three officers went to the food department of the town they were visiting and asked for some potatoes, and by grace of the department they were each given about half a hundredweight. When

# THE ECONOMIC CRISIS OF 1920–1921

they arrived at the Baltic station in Petrograd the officers had to undergo the scrutiny of the station guards who were examining the belongings of every passenger, but their cards of identification enabled them, with their sacks of potatoes on their backs, to proceed without impediment. As they passed the guard " a soldier stopped a woman and took from her some flour which she was carrying. The woman as usual began to shout terrifically, but neither tears nor begging availed anything. We came to the automobile which was waiting and threw our three sacks into it, but I was not altogether pleased. It was very clear to me how unjust is this government control by which three of us, by virtue of our service position, have the opportunity of bringing in the produce necessary for life whilst ordinary men are deprived of it. But at home, when my valuable bundle was disclosed, I was met with such sincere happiness that the depressed feeling passed away immediately." (1)

Rationing notwithstanding, the people in the capitals and in the other centres of population were on the verge of starvation. (2) The ruined nation was involved in a vicious circle. The peasants would not sow more than they needed for their own support, because they feared any surplus would simply be taken from them, the workman could not produce the manufactures wherewith to purchase his food, unless he had food to sustain him while he was working. Neither would or could trust the other. The customary connecting-link had been broken. That link was credit, which had provided the means to pay the peasant ; and the peasant's produce provided the artisan with the means of supporting himself while he made the goods, which were then bought on credit and held until the peasant needed them.

In smashing capital, the Government had destroyed credit. The connecting apparatus of exchange had gone, and no other had been supplied. The complicated system of Soviets, commissariats, committees, and departments, with their army of officials, were so many encumbrances on the back of peasants and workmen. The " firm communists " who were sent to see what was out of gear were only talkers, who brought nothing in their hands and whose hungry eyes merely distressed the peasants without weakening their obstinate determination.

Peasant tradition, with its accustomed tenacity, had vaguely preserved the memory of payment of taxes in kind in old Russia. (3) Taxes of every sort were objectionable to the peasant, but those in kind were more displeasing than any other, because the payment of them could not be postponed, so long as he had any produce which might be seized. The payment of taxes in money might be delayed or handed over in minute instalments. The peasant

# THE RUSSIAN REVOLUTION

might on occasion earn enough in ready cash to pay the tax without the amount of it being a burden upon the household exchequer. An absent member of the family might even be able to remit a portion or the whole. For these and other reasons taxation in kind had been abandoned. Under the imperial *régime* the taxes were relatively small in amount. Stringent means of collection were seldom resorted to, and sometimes the taxes were suffered to fall into arrears over long periods. (4)

The plan of the Bolsheviks as indicated above was to induce or compel the peasants to yield up the whole of their surplus produce and to receive for this produce the manufactured goods they consumed. By this plan there would be no necessity to make direct impositions upon the peasant, because a profit might be obtained through the turnover of agricultural produce, and this profit would go to the treasury. The plan included delivery of the peasants' surplus to the Soviet " co-operatives," and the handing over through them to the peasant of the equivalent in goods, the terms being in effect fixed by the local co-operative management acting under the regulations and instructions of the Supreme Economic Council in the capital.

This plan clearly implied a coincidence as regards time and equivalence in value, of agricultural and industrial products, and it also implied exchange of these products whether the peasant desired or not. The plan did not work. The goods which the peasant wanted could not always be had from the co-operatives, and when they were obtainable the terms of the exchange were looked upon by the peasant as being unfavourable to him. These terms became more and more unfavourable with every increase in the cost of production, an increase which was due to the enhanced demands of the artisans, to greater scarcity of raw materials, or to uneconomical management. When the peasants could not get the exchange they wanted, the Government endeavoured to induce them to take payment in paper money ; but this measure suited them even less than " natural " exchange, for the eventual return exhibited a constant tendency to decline through depreciation.

Thus in 1921 the peasants refused to give up their surplus produce unless they obtained a satisfactory equivalent, and thus, in order to avoid starvation in the capitals, the Soviet was compelled to secure a certain amount of bread-stuffs by armed forces. (5) As this situation afforded too precarious a means of supply, the Government was driven to devise a method of placating the peasants. The plan of " natural exchange " was abandoned, and another, permitting the pecuniary payment of taxes, was substituted.

A single direct agricultural tax was imposed, which provided

## THE ECONOMIC CRISIS OF 1920–1921

in the villages for the unification, in one impost, of all direct taxes levied by the central authority—sales tax, labour tax, etc.—as well as levies for local purposes. The intention of the new levy was to put an end to plurality of taxation, of which the peasants had always complained. Theoretically, the single tax was to be based upon the capacity of the peasant to pay, all his circumstances being taken into account—the area of arable land occupied by his household, the number of cattle, the average crop, and the number of consumers in the family. It was expected that by this plan he would not be unduly assessed, and that the poor and middle peasants would be protected against excessive taxation. A resolution of the Twelfth Congress of the Russian Communist party (held in 1923) urged the Communist party to explain to the peasants the advantages of direct taxation, and impressed upon the officials in charge of the collection the necessity of avoiding any breach of the law and even any contemptuous or inconsiderate treatment. In the event of offences being committed by the collectors they might expect the " resolute condemnation " of the Communist party and severe punishment by the Soviet authorities. (6)

With all its disadvantages and its difficulties in satisfying the physical appetite, the Bolshevik collectivist system was at least able to satisfy the appetite for statistics.(7) This could be done very readily, since, for a time, all the economic life of the country flowed, as it were, through one pipe. The new great roll contained such figures as these : " There are wanted for the supply of Petrograd in terms of the norms for September the following goods :—

| | *Pùdi.* | | | *Pùdi.* |
|---|---|---|---|---|
| Flour . . . . | 452,600 | Meat and Fish . . | 112,458 |
| Sugar . . . . | 22,687 | Onions. . . . | 5,564 |
| Salt . . . . | 64,506 | Dried fruit . . . | 3,198 |
| Vegetables . . . | 412,979 | Potato Flour . . | 2,312 |
| Eggs . . . . | 1,992,090 | Coffee and Chicory . | 4,787 |
| Grits . . . . | 67,000 | Fats . . . . | 10,304 " (8) |
| Sweets . . . . | 5,338 | | |

What proportion of these supplies was actually procured dues not appear.

The Petersburg (9) committee of the Russian Communist party at its regular meeting in the middle of November 1920 occupied itself with the new problems which had arisen in consequence of the cessation of the Civil War and the demobilization of the Red Army. The most acute question was " the strengthening of economic life and the necessity of pouring fresh forces into factories and plants." The committee resolved to send groups of qualified workers who had been engaged in Soviet institutions. The first

## THE RUSSIAN REVOLUTION

group sent was to be headed by a number of " responsible political workers, members of the Petersburg committee and the executive committee." (10) That is to say, the economic system was placed more and more in the hands of politicians in order that the grasp of the Soviet administration over the resources of the country and the produce of its labour should be more and more secure.

Meanwhile there were other signs of economic decay. The housing question was not, in one sense, acute in Petrograd. The palaces of the nobility and the town houses and apartments of the *bourgeoisie*, large and small, had been seized ; the owners were sometimes permitted to occupy a small part of the house, often the cellar, while the members of the Communist party or others occupied the rest. Although houses were subject to very rapid deterioration, both externally and internally, they were inhabited by larger numbers of people than ever before, while the total population of the city was declining. When the seat of government was moved from Petrograd, the commissariats and their staffs, now very numerous, were also transferred to Moscow. The subsequent additions to the civil service, together with the deterioration of property which had been going on because of the want of private interest together with public neglect, led to great congestion of population in Moscow and to an acute housing crisis. The most injurious deterioration consisted in damage done by frost to the sanitary appliances. According to reports made to the executive committee of the Moscow Soviet, on November 11, 1920, there were in Moscow about 15,000 dwelling-houses unfit for habitation. During the winter of 1919–1920 5,000 houses had been broken up for fuel. Notwithstanding these adverse circumstances, about 30,000 workers moved into comfortable dwellings, and the housing department provided accommodation for about 6,000 medical students. By transferring institutions to different quarters and by putting up several in one building or group of buildings, detached houses and apartments were set free for the general public. The conditions of 1920 did not, of course, favour the erection of new buildings, owing to obvious adverse circumstances, such as the scarcity of labour and, consequently, of timber and brick for building purposes ; but the reporters took occasion to remark that the apartments system had been shown to be unsuitable for the housing of working people. (11)

The economic depression, producing as it did great physical suffering, reacted upon the mood of intelligent Russians and brought to many of them a sense of reality which they had not experienced for a long time. This was manifest in the ranks of former revolutionists of various types, but especially among the Socialist-Revo-

## THE ECONOMIC CRISIS OF 1920-1921

lutionaries. They subsided into a state of extreme passivity, which was, indeed, characteristic of the Russian psychology. So long as they had any hope of the fall of Bolshevism, they fought against it, and especially during the years 1917 and 1918, and more particularly in December of the former year and January of the latter—the critical period—they were energetic and as yet hopeful. Even then they came in contact, among the general mass of the people, with " a dead wall of passivity," a lethargic mood, the *leitmotif* of which was the Russian " perhaps " and " everything will be organized." Even the leaders of the political parties were preaching against action and deriding any activity as " adventurism " and " flightiness." (12) Some of the Socialist-Revolutionaries who engaged in " adventures " were sent to prison, and when they emerged they also succumbed to the prevailing apathy. They became fatalists : " Everything will somehow be arranged. To fight ? To live a life of active politics ? To concoct plots ? All these are useless, unnecessary, harmful." (13) This passivity was consistent with hatred of Bolshevism and contempt for Bolsheviks, but it was ineffective. It was the sign of a fresh outbreak of the neurasthenia which followed the revolutionary movement of 1905–1907. (14) Therefore, in spite of the obvious failure of the Bolshevik plans, the security of the Soviet Government was not imperilled.

The coincidence of numerous unfavourable conditions in the year 1921 brought on a famine, not only on the Volga, where famine has frequently been acute, but in those parts of Russia which had always been looked upon as exceptionally productive. The most important of these conditions was the bad season which was experienced. In times past Russia has known acute famine in certain districts, but never in the country as a whole. There was a widespread deficiency in the harvest in 1891, and again in 1899, chiefly in the region of Kazan. When the season was not exceptionally good, there was deficiency in many *gubernie* without actual famine. In all the famines of recent years, the Imperial Government was able to transfer produce from those parts of Russia where there was plenty, to those parts where there was a need, and either by the action of the State or by private benevolence the famine-stricken areas were always relieved, for there was never any difficulty in obtaining grain from peasants who had it for sale.

As the railway system was extended, and especially as branch lines were constructed, the movement of grain was facilitated. Improved cultivation on the great estates of the Government and of private owners, together with these improved means of transport, had neutralized the effect of any unfavourable season to such an

## 392 THE RUSSIAN REVOLUTION

extent that since 1899 there had been no famine, and since 1891 no acute or widespread scarcity.

In 1921 the shortage was general; even the Black Soil region, celebrated for its fertility, was seriously affected. The season was bad; but the disorganization of the system of transport, and of the system of exchange coinciding with this poor harvest, rendered the movement of grain exceedingly difficult, and caused the famine in some localities to be the most acute of any recorded in Russian economic history. Appeals were made to the benevolence of foreign countries, and immense systems of relief were organized by forty distinct foreign agencies. (15) The Soviet Government appeared to be very willing to transfer its obligations to other shoulders, for when a foreign relief agency undertook to send supplies into a famine-stricken area, the Government ceased to supply the normal ration in that district even to its own officials.

The serious decline in agriculture was fully disclosed by the Bolshevik writers, as for example in the following survey :—

" Before the war [i.e. in 1913] the acreage sown [in bread-stuffs, i.e. wheat, rye, barley, and oats] was 86·4 million *dessiatines*. In 1920 it diminished to 60·5 million *dessiatines*, i.e. by 28·8 per cent. . . . The average harvest of all bread-stuffs in 1909–1913 was 3,788 million *pùdi*." In 1913 the harvest was 4,500 million *pùdi*. " In 1921 the harvest was only 1,600 million *pùdi*. Thus, although the area sown had diminished by only 28·8 per cent., the harvest fell off by 58 per cent." (16)

The peasant had always rightly or wrongly blamed the Government for famines, and he had been encouraged in this attitude by socialists of all groups because they found in it " rich material for agitation." Now that the peasants were experiencing the worst famine in history, they were not more inclined to exonerate the Government.

The All-Russian Central Executive Committee (popularly known as the *Tsik*) organized measures in the autumn of 1921 and throughout 1922 with the object of preventing a repetition of the conditions of the preceding disastrous year. In two years this committee distributed among the peasants 15,000,000 *dessiatines* of forests. It flattered itself that by this means " the peasant fortune was founded." (17) But the peasant is not a good forester; he has been so much accustomed to having his labour directed for him, that when he is called upon to manage his own he is helpless. In most cases where peasants have acquired forest lands, they have simply cut down the trees and used or sold them, leaving the stumps in the ground, and taking no trouble to replant or clear the land for cultivation.

# THE ECONOMIC CRISIS OF 1920–1921     393

The Soviet Government in 1922 gave " seed loans " amounting to 50 million *pùdi*, and in 1923 to 30 million *pùdi*, and also established seed stations. (18)

The result of these various measures, together with improved weather conditions and the adoption of the New Economic Policy (to be noticed shortly), was an increase in the yield of the harvest, which came to about one-half of the pre-war yield.

Among the troubles of the Soviet Republic in the year 1921 was an epidemic of theft from nationalized enterprises. The Government issued instructions to the boards of management of the plants, requiring exact accounting and control over raw materials as well as finished goods. The instructions also suggested withdrawal of the premiums in kind either for the whole institution or for the department in which pillage was being practised. (19) The prevalence of thefts in Russian factories has always been a problem. Up till a short time before the downfall of the old *régime*, every workman was examined before he was allowed to leave work, in order to detect theft of tools or of manufactured goods. This inspection had fallen into desuetude, until the relaxation of industrial discipline rendered it again necessary.

Pilfering from factories was a small affair compared with the wholesale robberies of goods in transport. " During the first period of supply work 50 per cent. of the cargoes were lost on the road. Statistics for the recent period give another picture, and show a good percentage of deliveries of cargoes of provisions despatched from the provinces to the Petrograd *gub* . . . During November [1920] . . . the Kharkov *gub* shows the least percentage [of deliveries]—66·7 per cent." Other places delivered up to 93·1 per cent. (20)

---

### NOTES

(1) Smelg-Benario, *In the Service of the Soviet* in *Archives of the Russian Revolution* (Berlin, 1921), p. 158.

(2) A friend living in Petrograd during the winter of 1920–1921 told the writer that, without parcels sent by his friends abroad, he could not possibly have survived.

(3) There is a vivid picture of the process, by the modern Russian artist S. V. Ivanov. He shows the Boyars sitting in an inner room, and in an outer chamber the clerks receiving payment from the peasants, who bring live ducks, vegetables, etc., and receive a quittance. A peasant is evidently effecting a private arrangement with one of the officials.

(4) The writer has before him the tax-books of peasants before 1914, showing payment in small instalments.

(5) The writer was informed in 1921, on excellent authority, that artillery was sent to the villages to intimidate the peasants into yielding up their grain.

(6) *Resolutions of the Twelfth Congress of the Russian Communist Party* in *The Communist Calendar* (Moscow, 1924), pp. 254–55.

## 394 THE RUSSIAN REVOLUTION

(7) Perhaps this appetite should properly be regarded as carnal ; it is certainly not spiritual.

(8) *Pravda* (Petrograd), No. 197, September 5, 1920.

(9) This is the word used.

(10) *Pravda* (Petrograd), No. 258, November 17, 1920.

(11) Ibid., No. 255, November 13, 1920. The report as printed does not go into detail, but as it observes that the housing department had been urging the people to "self-service," it seems likely that the reason for this was that the apartment system involved an amount and kind of household service for which no servants could be found under the new conditions, and that, unless the people contrived to serve themselves, the apartment system must be condemned. The housing department also appealed to the people to take an interest in the working of the department.

(12) Sokolov, Boris, *Defence of the All-Russian Constituent Assembly* in *Archives of the Russian Revolution* (Berlin, 1924), vol. xiii, p. 6.

(13) Ibid.

(14) Cf. Mavor, J., *An Economic History of Russia*, vol. ii, p. 599.

(15) Some of these reported frequent cases of cannibalism on the Volga.

(16) *The Communist Calendar* (Moscow, 1924), p. 550.

(17) Ibid.

(18) Ibid.

(19) *The Fight against Stealing in State Enterprises* in *Pravda* (Petrograd), No. 144, July 12, 1921.

(20) *Pravda* (Petrograd), February 6, 1921

## CHAPTER II

## THE COLLAPSE OF COMMUNISM

LENIN frequently gave it as his opinion that the Communist party was the advance guard of the Russian proletariat, and that the dictatorship of the Communist party must precede the dictatorship of the proletariat as a whole. These ideas were advanced as the reason and the apology for the seizure of power by the leaders. What then were the numbers of that party upon which the leaders of the October Revolution relied? The Bolshevik statisticians may be accused of exaggeration, but they must at least be acquitted of minimizing their extent and influence. Their own account is as follows :—

" The statistics of the party are very complicated. The territory of the S.S.R. [the Socialist Soviet Republic] is very large, and to collect complete figures from all the regions is a task which simply cannot be accomplished. If we add to this the extreme fluctuation of the membership of the party, frequent initiation into and exile [or dismissal] from it, the difficulty of compiling statistics would seem to be still greater." The following figures are given :—

| | | | | | | |
|---|---|---|---|---|---|---|
| 1914 | . | . | . | 40,000 | | |
| 1917 | . | . | . | 200,000 at the time of the 6th Congress | | |
| 1919 | . | . | . | 300,000 | ,, | ,, | 8th | ,, |
| 1920 | . | . | . | 612,000 | ,, | ,, | 9th | ,, |
| 1921 | . | . | . | 705,000 | ,, | ,, | 10th | ,, |
| 1922 | . | . | . | 532,000 | ,, | ,, | 11th | ,, |
| 1923 | . | . | . | 380,000 | ,, | ,, | 12th | ,, |

" The decrease in the membership of the party during the two past [last-mentioned] years is explained, firstly, by the general cleaning up of the party in 1921, during which many unnecessary elements were thrown out ; and secondly, by the continuation of this process through the work of the Committee of Control, together with voluntary resignations of members . . . who are opposed to party discipline and party etiquette. The significance of this cleaning up is very great. The proletarian membership of the party is continually increasing." In 1922 the following were the constituent elements :—(1)

| | | | | | | Per Cent. |
|---|---|---|---|---|---|---|
| Labourers | . | . | . | . | 235,700 | 44·3 |
| Peasantry | . | . | . | . | 142,600 | 26·8 |
| Civil Servants | . | . | . | 118,100 | 22·2 |
| Others | . | . | . | . | 35,600 | 6·7 |
| Total | . | . | . | . | 532,000 | 100·0 |

## 396 THE RUSSIAN REVOLUTION

In Petrograd the percentage of labourers was 58·1 per cent., and of peasantry 6·3 per cent. In Moscow the percentage of civil servants was 32·1 per cent. No statistics are given which might afford a comparison with years earlier than 1914. *The Communist Calendar*, from which the above figures are taken, says :—

" A consideration of the total statistics will show that the proletarian composition of the party is much higher than at the beginning. The cleaning-up, and especially the last measures of the Committee of Control for purging the party of antagonistic elements, have liberated it from 200,000 parasitic (moon-baying) *intelligentsia*, and have made of the communists a very strong force which can withstand any influence from outside—a real iron advance guard of the labouring classes." (2)

These *ex-parte* statements are quite candid and honest, but underlying them is undoubtedly the fact that the mood of passivity, disillusionment, and weariness which so deeply affected the *intelligentsia* and the wide circles of working men and peasants, had also begun to affect the communists. Enthroned as they were in power, their rank and file had little influence with the oligarchy, in whose strong and remorseless hands they and the country alike felt themselves powerless.

In place of " dictatorship of the proletariat," there was dictatorship of a small group of merciless leaders, while the proletariat, never numerous as a class in Russia, had disappeared from the industrial towns and been absorbed into the village life from which its members originally came. The destruction of industries further decimated the towns and in effect destroyed the proletariat as a class. The following statistics of production illustrate the fluctuations of industry :— (3)

### OIL

|      |   |   |   |   |   | Million *Pùdi*. |
|------|---|---|---|---|---|------|
| 1913 | . | . | . | . | . | . 554 |
| 1920 | . | . | . | . | . | . 243 |
| 1921 | . | . | . | . | . | . 246 |
| 1922 | . | . | . | . | . | . 277 |

The exploitation of oil was thus about one-half of the pre-war quantity. (4)

### COAL

|      |   |   |   |   |   | Million *Pùdi*. |
|------|---|---|---|---|---|------|
| 1913 | . | . | . | . | . | . 1,738 |
| 1918 | . | . | . | . | . | . 731 |
| 1919 | . | . | . | . | . | . 511 |
| 1920 | . | . | . | . | . | . 467 |
| 1921 | . | . | . | . | . | . 520 |
| 1922 | . | . | . | . | . | . 594 |

# THE COLLAPSE OF COMMUNISM

The exploitation of coal was about 35 per cent. of the pre-war quantity.

### METALLIFEROUS MINES

| | Million *Pùdi.* |
|---|---|
| 1913 | 638 |
| 1920 | 10 |
| 1921 | 8 |
| 1922 | 12·5 |

The mining of metals almost ceased.

### PIG IRON

| | Million *Pùdi.* |
|---|---|
| 1913 | 256·8 |
| 1919 | 6·9 |
| 1920 | 7·7 |
| 1921 | 7·0 |
| 1922 | 14·2 |

The programme of production for 1922–1923 was 16·5 million *pùdi.* Of this quantity only 51·3 per cent. was actually produced.

### SIEMENS-MARTIN STEEL

| | Million *Pùdi.* |
|---|---|
| 1913 | 259·3 |
| 1919 | 12·2 |
| 1920 | 10·0 |
| 1921 | 11·0 |

The programme for 1922–1923 was 30·7 million *pùdi.* The production fell short by 6 million *pùdi.*

### MANUFACTURE OF METALS

| | | Million *Pùdi.* |
|---|---|---|
| | 1913 | 214·2 |
| | 1918 | 21·8 |
| | 1919 | 10·0 |
| | 1920 | 12·2 |
| | 1921 | 8·5 |
| ¼ year | 1921–1922 | 8·9 |
| ½ year | 1922–1923 | 11·8 |

The programme for 1922–1923 was 25 million *pùdi.* The production fell short by 5 million *pùdi.*

The production of gold and platinum declined to about 8 per cent. ; of raw cotton to about 40 per cent. ; of thread to about 25 per cent. ; of woollen yarn to about 33 per cent. ; of paper and pulp to about 30 per cent. ; of sugar to about 15 per cent. (5)

Lenin shows in many of his writings that his aim was to bring his conception of communism into relation with what he conceived to

## 398 THE RUSSIAN REVOLUTION

be modern progress, by declaring that the two objects of the dictatorship of the proletariat were (1) a struggle against the production of goods upon a small scale, and (2) a struggle against the preservation and revival of capitalism. (6)

Within two years of the seizure of power by the Bolsheviks he was able to say :—

" Labour is communistically united in Russia. Private property in the means of production has been abolished, and the proletarian government has organized, upon an all-national scale, great production in the lands and enterprises of the State. The proletarian government divides labour among the different branches of economy and distributes among the toiling people mass quantities of consumable products. . . ." But there remains a portentous problem. " The economy of the peasants continues as a small-scale production. In this state of things we have an extremely large [in the aggregate] and strongly rooted basis of capitalism, on which capitalism is preserved and revived ; the consequence is a severe struggle against communism. The forms of that struggle are bag commerce (7) and speculation directed against the state supply of bread and other products, and in general against state distribution of products." (8) Lenin gives the following statistics, applying to the year 1919, quoting from a report by the central statistical board. (9) The statistics do not apply to the whole of Soviet Russia, but only to twenty-six, or about one-third, of the total number of *gubernie*.

PROPORTIONS OF STATE AND PRIVATE (ILLEGAL) TRADE.

| 26 *gubernie* Soviet Russia. | Population in Millions. | Production. Bread without Seeds and Cattle Fodder in Million *Pùdi*. | Bread supplied. | | Total of Bread. | Consumption per Head. |
|---|---|---|---|---|---|---|
| | | | By Commissar of Supply. | By " Bag Commerce." | | |
| Productive *gubernie* { Cities, 4·4 | | — | 20·9 | 20·6 | 41·5 | 9·5 |
| Villages, 28·6 | | 625·4 | — | — | 481·8 | 16·9 |
| Consuming *gubernie* { Cities, 5·9 | | — | 20·0 | 20·0 | 40·0 | 6·8 |
| Villages, 13·8 | | 114·0 | 12·1 | 27·8 | 151·4 | 11·0 |
| Total | 52·7 | 739·4 | 53·0 | 68·4 | 714·7 | 44·2 |

These figures seem to prove that of the 121·4 *pùdi* of bread-stuffs which were exchanged by the peasants for manufactured goods, 56·35 per cent. were exchanged illegally in " bag commerce." They also appear to show that the peasants' bread-stuff ration was largely in excess of that for the urban population, especially in the consuming

# THE COLLAPSE OF COMMUNISM 399

*gubernie.* Since all the cases of " bag commerce " are unlikely to have been discovered, illegal trade probably amounted to even more than is disclosed by the figures.

By the year 1919 it thus became evident that the communist experiment was being wrecked by both working men and peasants, especially by the latter. Lenin found it convenient to attribute the phenomenon to capitalism, but that he himself was misled is hard to believe. A principle in human nature older than capitalism, and surviving the destruction of capitalism in Russia, explains the phenomenon very simply. Notwithstanding the discouraging failure to convert the peasantry to communism, Lenin still hoped that force of circumstances would bring it about. In a speech delivered at a conference of factory committees and trades unions held on July 29, 1919, he indicates clearly the course of action he intended to take. " We know," he said, " that when bread is sold in a country, that is a main source of capitalism. At this moment the last and decisive fight against capitalism is going on. . . ." By this he means the struggle by the peasants to prevent the direct sale of bread. He continues : " The peasant must change his relation to his product ; otherwise when he sells bread at any price to the worker he certainly becomes a *bourgeois* and proprietor. We say that the bread must be sold at the price fixed by the State—that will help us to get rid of capitalism. When we tear the peasantry away from property, when we turn them to our state work, then we shall [be able to] say that the difficult part of our road is passed." (10)

This means clearly that when the peasant has had what he looks upon as his property torn from him, and when he has been made a serf of the State, those who control the State will be able to determine the rate of exchange between the products of the soil and those of the factory. Lenin delivered his speech to workmen in the towns, but he ran a grave risk of betraying the terms to the peasants. Inert as they are, any overt attempt to deprive them of the land, which they have suffered a revolution to acquire must meet with universal resistance. An armed rebellion by the peasantry might be suppressed by the Red Army, but universal sullen and prolonged under-production would present a very different problem.

All the belligerent countries, and even those which remained neutral, have suffered from the reactions of the war ; but all of them, even France and the Central Powers, which suffered in different ways, have to a great extent recovered their powers of production. Yet not one of these countries is ever approximately self-supporting, all have to import necessary food-stuffs. Russia, on the other hand, is practically self-contained in so far as her resources are concerned. The country has been at peace, both externally and internally, since

# THE RUSSIAN REVOLUTION

1919, yet her industries are still dormant, and agriculture is, compared with the past, seriously unproductive.

If there had been no change in government, the blame for this condition would everywhere have been laid, and justly laid, upon the autocracy. Yet even the autocracy undertook no such responsibilities as the Soviet has taken on its shoulders. The autocracy allowed a large freedom of economic action ; the Soviet Government left no freedom either in domestic or foreign trade. It assumed the function of universal organizer and provider, and it expected the people to work for it; but the statistics of production show conclusively that, at the dates indicated above, the people were not working at nearly their full capacity. This was very clearly recognized by the Bolshevik leaders, who were fully aware of the danger to themselves of industrial and agricultural lassitude, and no " *bourgeois* capitalism " could have engaged more strenuously in propaganda for increase of work and for the extension of working hours. The " firm communists " were called upon to set the example.

The central committee of the Russian Communist party issued an appeal for " Work in a revolutionary manner," in which they adjured the communists to throw into industry the energy they had concentrated upon the Revolution. The gist of this appeal is contained in an article contributed to *Pravda* of May 17, 1919, by A. J. (11) " The appeal [of the Central Committee] gave a strong impetus to communists and communist organizations. The general animation [excited by the appeal] sent many communist railwaymen to the [labour] front, though most of them [communist railwaymen] could not leave their responsible places for new forms of revolutionary work. Local complaints about the slowness of mobilization [of labour] and about office delays compelled the Moscow-Kazan railway to turn its attention to the mechanism of railway economy. It [the administration of the railway] proved that because of lack of labour and because of the want of intensive labour, urgent orders, including pressing repairs to locomotives, were neglected." On May 7 (1919), at a general meeting of communists of the Moscow-Kazan railway sub-region, the following resolution was passed : " Because of the grave internal and external situation [the Koltchak campaign in Siberia was still in progress] . . . the communists and sympathizers . . . resolve to give one hour of their rest to work (i.e. to increase their working day by an hour) . . . and on Saturday by six hours . . . in order to produce results of real value. Since the communists do not spare their lives and health in the cause of revolution, this work shall be done free of charge. The communist Saturday will be introduced throughout the sub-region until

# THE COLLAPSE OF COMMUNISM    401

a victory over Koltchak is obtained." After deliberation, the resolution was passed unanimously.

On May 17th at Alexandrovsk, on the first communist Saturday, ninety-eight communists and sympathizers, according to the resolution of the meeting, worked gratuitously for five hours beyond the normal working day. They received only the right to have dinner and ½ *funt* of bread each. Although this work was not properly arranged and organized, its productivity was two or three times greater than the normal.

On June 5th at Saratov the communist railwaymen "answered the call of the Moscow comrades," and at a general party meeting, decided to work five hours gratuitously beyond the usual time on Saturdays for the sake of the People's Economy.

The system of premiums, noticed in a previous chapter, the difficulty of discovering the normal productivity of labour, the conviction reached by experience that the economic relations of the peasant to the artisan could not be arbitrarily determined, the decline in the membership of the Communist party, the diminution alike in agricultural and in industrial production, the sheer impossibility of obtaining an adequate ration for the urban populations, the difficulty of suppressing illegal trade—all these circumstances indicated that the idea of controlling the people through the rationing system had not worked. This system implied the acquiescence of the peasants, and the receipt of constant supplies from them on terms fixed by the Government. But they would not agree, and the system came to grief. Since rationing lay at the root of communism, it became clear that the adoption of that system was either premature or wholly unsound. Lenin was reluctant to admit that an organization upon the success of which he had built such high hopes, was unstable, therefore he fell back upon the declaration that it was premature, and proposed to modify it sharply, promising to return to the more rigid application of the system at a more opportune time. This attitude gave rise to the New Economic Policy.

---

### NOTES

(1) *The Communist Calendar* (Moscow, 1924), p. 257.
(2) Ibid.
(3) These figures are taken from *The Communist Calendar*, p. 532.
(4) The production of oil probably declined in 1924 owing to the revolt in the Caucasus and the interruption of the pipe-line between Baku and Batum.
(5) *The Communist Calendar*, p. 532.
(6) Lenin, N., *Collected Works* (Moscow, 1923), vol. xvi, p. 348.

# THE RUSSIAN REVOLUTION

(7) By " bag commerce " Lenin means trade carried on with the peasants by people in the towns who carry bags into the country and fill them with produce illegally purchased from the peasants.

(8) Lenin, N., op. cit., 1923, vol. xvi, p. 349.

(9) Ibid., p. 350.

(10) Ibid., pp. 288–93.

(11) This article was considered by Lenin as so important that he printed it *in extenso* in an article of his own (see Lenin, N., op. cit., vol. xvi, p. 242).

## CHAPTER III

## THE NEW ECONOMIC POLICY

THE famine resulting from diminished cultivation and deficient harvests brought the Bolshevik leaders to an *impasse*. The agrarian revolution had gone beyond their control. The peasants refused to allow themselves to be coerced into cultivating the soil which they themselves had seized, when the produce of their cultivation was wholly or almost wholly taken from them; and although the industrial centres had lost heavily in population through migration of working men to their native villages, the small number of townsfolk left could not be supported without supplies from the surplus produce of the peasants.

Up till the moment of the adoption of the New Economic Policy at the instance of Lenin, the Soviet press, even technical journals, constantly referred to the necessity of " the extirpation of the remnants of the capitalist system, the carrying out of socialist measures, and the creation for that purpose of appropriate organs." (1) But the creation of appropriate organs was not speedy enough to keep pace with the destruction of those already existing, whose fitness had stood the test of centuries. When the new organs were established, their lack of technical efficiency, as well as their complicated character, prevented them from performing the services which had previously been rendered by the spontaneous co-operation of private groups, and the consequence was absence of co-ordination between industrial and agrarian production. The reasons for the adoption of the New Economic Policy, which, after the Russian fashion of applying nicknames, came to be known as Nep, and the actual outcome of that policy during the first two years of its operation, may be gathered from a description in *The Communist Calendar*, (2) of which the following is an abstract :—

In 1920 the Soviet Government found itself embarrassed by the administration of a large number of small industrial undertakings. In that year the Government had under its control 37,017 establishments, employing 615,064 workmen. Of these, 13·9 per cent. were *kustarni* (i.e. domestic) in character, and the number of employees per establishment was very small. In addition to the *kustarni* workshops, there were other small enterprises employing not more than 15 workers. Altogether the small establishments numbered 67·6 per cent. of the whole, and employed 5·9 per cent. of the workers, while the large establishments (with more than 15 workers) numbered 32·4 per cent., and employed 94·1 per cent. of the workers. The New Economic Policy liberated the small establishments and retained the larger—thus releasing 5·9 per cent. of the employed workers from under the control of the Government and exercising control over 94·1 per cent. These small enterprises were thus handed back to their former owners. In March 1921 a decree provided for the renting from the Government of industrial establishments where less than 20 workers were employed. By January 1, 1923, this provision had been utilized to the extent of 4,384 such undertakings. Of the tenants only one-half were former owners, the rest were co-operators, syndicates (of workmen), etc. The number of labourers employed in rented industry was 63,263 in 1923.

There remained in the hands of the Government 7,500 establishments, and of these, 5,000 only were in operation, the remaining 2,500 being idle. (3) These 5,000 were organized into 507 trusts, employing 833,000 workers. When this figure is compared with that representing the employees of private capital (viz. 63,000), the infinitesimal *rôle* which the New Economic Policy allowed to private capital can readily be seen.

It is obvious that the fundamental reason for the adoption of the New Economic Policy was the impossibility of preventing illegal trade between the town inhabitants and the villages, without which the town inhabitants would have been unable to subsist. Therefore the supreme economic council decided to permit private persons to engage in retail trade, and to allow the individual operation of the smaller enterprises, which were very numerous in Russia, but it meant to retain its hold upon large industrial establishments.

At the same time every effort was to be made to develop the large enterprises in such a way as to crush the smaller out of existence. This expectation has not been so far realized. Under Russian capitalism there had been, during the previous twenty-five years, a tendency towards " mergers " of large factories, towards the increase in numbers of intermediate factories, and towards the maintenance of numerous small workshops in certain industries. Thus, even under capitalism, intermediate and small industry had not been ousted wholly from the field. When the Revolution occurred, the workmen deserted the towns for the villages, and in consequence of the difficulty of exchange with the towns, there was a great increase of village industry. The villages could not depend upon the towns, and the reinforcement of village labour by skilled artisans enabled them to satisfy their own demands within the limits of their ability to procure raw material.

# THE NEW ECONOMIC POLICY

Meanwhile an improvement in the food supply of the towns resulted from the New Economic Policy, and the reopening of the retail shops, which speedily came to be filled with the wardrobes and possessions which the people had contrived to conceal from the newly appointed agents of the Soviet, brought about a certain briskness in legalized retail trade. For a short time there was a boom, which was held to indicate revival of economic prosperity; but as soon as the stocks were disposed of, the shelves of the shops were again empty, because production had not yet been reinvigorated.

Then the New Economic Policy began to affect production for retail trade, and the intermediate and large factories in the hands of the Government began to cater for public patronage. The newspapers of Petrograd and Moscow printed columns of advertisements inserted by state establishments, commending their wares after the manner of competitive trade. (4)

In this and other ways the Soviet industry and commerce exhibited a tendency to adopt the methods of capitalist enterprise, and the conclusion was very naturally drawn that the Bolsheviks possessed a " capitalist psychology " and that they could not rise above it. Repeated declarations by Lenin and others show that the Soviet economic authorities aimed at playing in Russia the part which they naïvely suppose is played by " Rockefeller and Morgan " in the United States. It is not at all clear that any of the Bolshevik bureaucrats or politicians had any conception of the function of capital. If they had, they would have realized that it is not the existence of capital, but the use which is made of it in the organization of credit, that is the important point; and that in order to organize and maintain this credit the prime qualifications are skilful management and, above all, scrupulous honesty in the making and fulfilling of engagements. To attempt the *rôle* of great financiers and industrial organizers without these prime qualifications is absurd. When the Bolsheviks denounced capitalists as robbers they probably believed that they really were robbers, and that robbery of the same kind might be as easily committed by themselves.

In a series of decrees and resolutions beginning in 1921, the Soviet Government and the other central authorities in economic affairs endeavoured to stimulate agricultural " co-operation." The conception involved in these measures has been explained in a preceding chapter. The provincial agricultural co-operatives, as also the consumers' co-operatives, were allowed access to foreign markets for sale and purchase, through the All-Russian Central Rural Union. (5) The trade tax upon them was reduced and a system of agricultural credit was organized. A special department of the State Bank, with an assigned capital of twenty million gold roubles,

**406** THE RUSSIAN REVOLUTION

was established for the purpose of managing agricultural credit, and the State Bank and the People's Commissar of Agriculture founded twenty-two district agricultural societies. Provincial banks were also set up, and their capital was allotted in part to local organs of public economy, including co-operatives, and also peasants, who were given " specially cheap shares."

Sufficient time has not elapsed for a judgment to be pronounced regarding the success of these measures. They appear, however, to have stimulated somewhat the increase in the production of flax, cotton, tobacco, wine, and butter.

By the beginning of 1923 there had been organized 25,000 primary agricultural co-operatives and 300 district and provincial societies. These united in economic affairs three million peasant households, or approximately ten millions of people. The agricultural co-operatives were united in the All-Russian Union of Agricultural Co-operatives. The above-mentioned societies were of a general character, and, in addition, groups were organized to include those interested in some special branch of agriculture, as, for example, the flax union and potato unions, which united the *artels* and companies of flax and potato growers respectively. The insurance union and the Useco Bank were also organized for the purpose of concentrating co-operative finance in a single bank. The aggregate capital of the agricultural co-operatives was about eighty million gold roubles, and of this amount thirty-two millions were subscribed by provincial and district unions, forty millions by primary co-operatives, and eight millions by the central union.

The Central Agricultural Union (*Selsko-soyus*) began with a capital of 10,000 gold roubles, and in 1923 it had risen to eight millions, whilst the capitals of all the unions were increased by a subscription of 20 per cent. from the state treasury. The central union was also given about five million gold roubles which had formerly belonged to the shareholders of various agricultural co-operatives. In the first eighteen months of its existence agricultural co-operation as a whole appeared to come up to the expectations which had been formed. Through the hands of the organs of the movement passed seven million *pùdi* of bread-stuffs, 235,400 *pùdi* of flax seed, 100,000 *pùdi* of vegetables and food seeds, 1,600 mowing machines, 675 cutting machines, 16,000 ploughs, and 600,000 scythes. The agricultural co-operatives transferred to the Soviet foreign trade authorities for export 2·5 million roubles' worth of furs, about 84,000 gallons of peasant wine, and 110,000 *pùdi* of fruits grown on peasants' farms.

The creamery *artels* (small co-operative societies) had been abolished by the Bolsheviks, but in 1923 these were restored, and by

# THE NEW ECONOMIC POLICY

the end of that year numbered 25,000, with 500,000 cows contributing to them. In 1923 these *artels* produced one million *pùdi* of butter.

The potato *artels* had eighty-eight potato-grating factories which utilized four million *pùdi* of potatoes, a quantity amounting to three-quarters of the total potato crop within the region of potato co-operation. In this region there are eighteen electrical plants, the capital for which was subscribed by one hundred villages.

On June 10, 1923, the Shungen agricultural electrical plant of 500,000 h.p. was inaugurated, to supply electric light for forty-two villages as well as power for ploughing.

In so far as the New Economic Policy means release of private enterprise from the strangulation which it was suffering, and from constant or spasmodic interference by politicians, Soviets, or committees, there is some prospect that it will contribute, within the limits of its operation to the economic recovery of Russia. These limits, however, are not extensive, since, as regards industry, it liberated only 5·9 per cent. of the workers from Soviet control. Moreover, under the state monopoly of banking, the small industries must seek financial assistance from the State Bank, and to that extent are still under political control. While the effects of the New Economic Policy upon retail trade are considerable, and upon industry perhaps less, its influence upon the granting of concessions within Russia and upon foreign trade has been very slender.

The notion seems to have been entertained by the Supreme Economic Council that they had only to announce their willingness to grant mineral, timber, and petroleum concessions to foreigners, in order to obtain large sums of money from *concessionnaires*. They do not seem to have realized that, except in the case of a concession that had not previously been sold, it was not in their power to give a satisfactory title. They could not guarantee their stability as a government, and therefore any purchaser of a concession which had been formerly granted to and paid for by another individual, must run the risk of dispossession should a new administration decline to be pledged to the validity of his purchase. The Soviet Government was therefore unable to do any business in disposing of confiscated concessions, but succeeded in selling some new ones in mines, timber-lands, and other national resources. No important concession of this kind was taken, however, because of the risk attaching to the operation. There was in every case a danger of " direct action " on the part of the workmen, which the Soviet Government might be powerless, even if it desired, to prevent or arrest ; it approached some of the foreign *concessionnaires* whose property had been confiscated, with the idea of inducing them to

**408** THE RUSSIAN REVOLUTION

return in order to operate their plants, but in such cases serious risks had to be taken into account by the *concessionnaires*. As a preliminary, they required compensation for the losses they had already experienced, and, according to the Soviet Government, placed these losses at prohibitive figures. (6)   In any case, nothing came of these attempts.

The conditions of all concessions provide for confiscation at will by the Soviet Government—a condition under which none but mere adventurers would undertake any enterprise.   Only quick and huge profits could justify acceptance on such terms.

Foreign trade under the New Economic Policy has been slowly increasing, although the excessive profits exacted by the state monopoly have constituted a serious impediment.   The addition to the export prices of some goods in the form of duties and taxes, apart altogether from transport charges, amounted in some cases to 100, 200. or even 350 per cent.   These cases occurred in small shipments ; probably in larger consignments the charges and profits were not so heavy.

The course of events has altered the course of Russian foreign trade.   Before the disruption of the Empire and the separation of the Baltic States from Great Russia, the ports of Libau and Windawa in Kurland, of Riga in Latvia, and Reval in Esthonia, were the channels for the greater part of the sea-going trade of the north of Russia.   A comparatively small part of the shipping entered the port of St. Petersburg.   Now, although part of the foreign trade of northern Russia passes through Riga, there is a strong inducement for the Soviet Government to develop the port of the northern capital. (7)

Although the foreign trade of Russia up till the year 1924 had recovered only a small fraction of its former dimensions, the Soviet foreign trade commissariat was so unused to the technique of foreign commerces, that it was compelled to call to its assistance some of those who had before the October Revolution been engaged in the business of import and export.   These persons were quickly able to establish themselves as middlemen between the foreign trade commissariat and the foreign merchants.   Their profits or commissions were probably not less than those they had been formerly accustomed to charge, so that the Russian buyers or sellers were obliged to pay a profit to the State in addition to the customary charges of shipment.

In addition to the legal trade from and to Russia through the Baltic ports, there was an extensive illicit commerce through Reval in Esthonia, which has direct railway communication with Petrograd, and through Riga in Latvia, which has easy access to Moscow.

## THE NEW ECONOMIC POLICY

A trading agreement between the British Government and the Soviet Republic was signed on March 16, 1921, (8) but difficulties in the way of the actual conduct of trade immediately arose. Two months after the agreement was concluded, Krassin had to admit that no exports from Russia had yet been made to Great Britain, because, before the signing of the agreement, a small quantity of timber had been seized at the port of entry in England by " a pretended owner who alleged that it had been taken from his estate." Krassin denied this charge, saying that the timber had actually been cut upon estates of the imperial appanage ; (9) but goods could not be sent to England until there was no longer any risk of seizure on the ground of their being stolen property. The export of gold was in a similar position. The Russian Soviet Republic was not recognized by Great Britain, therefore exported gold might be seized by those who held claims against the former Imperial Government on the ground that the gold in the State Bank under the care of the ministry of finance had formed the initial security for the repayment of loans advanced to the public treasury. There were also other impediments. Instances occurred in connection with textiles and also with timber, in which the Soviet Republic was accused of lack of the most elementary commercial morality. (10)

Throughout the year 1921 the principal industrial nations were perturbed by the changes in demand and in prices due to the passing of the conditions which prevailed during the war. The Bolsheviks were not alone in regarding this agitation as a crisis through which capitalism was passing, nor were they alone in supposing that it presaged the fall of capitalism. Such surmises proved to be without foundation. The practice of providing reserves during periods of inflation to form a support in the inevitable subsequent periods of depression had long been prevalent in Great Britain, and had become widespread among large enterprises in the United States. On the whole, these reserves were adequate, and the critical years 1921, 1922, and 1923 passed without disaster.

During the year 1920 an opinion was prevalent in Great Britain, especially in the Independent Labour Party, that all that was necessary to relieve the unemployment situation in Great Britain was a trade agreement with Russia. That this opinion was without foundation is proved by the circumstance that four years after the trade agreement was signed Russian trade had not attained any importance. The reason was very clear, viz. that trade depended, not upon an agreement, but upon the internal condition of Russia. Export of grain was impossible because the peasants would not grow it. Import trade was impossible, partly because there were no exports to pay for it, and partly because the classes consuming

## THE RUSSIAN REVOLUTION

British goods in Russia had been exterminated. Therefore, until a complete social change took place through the extension of the New Economic Policy by the Soviet Government, or through the substitution of another government with a more effective economic system, there could not be an external trade of any moment.

During the summer of 1921 the Bolshevik leaders were negotiating with German bankers in order to discover what were the prospects of financial assistance for the Soviet Government in the event of their abandoning the policy hostile to capital, upon which its economic system had been founded.(11) High hopes were entertained in Germany that the Soviet Government would make a drastic change in its economic policy, and in the following year at Rapallo a treaty between Germany and Russia was concluded in which Germany made large concessions for the purpose of securing Russian trade. The mode in which this treaty was negotiated aroused a storm in Europe, but the tangible benefits to Germany have yet to appear.

Up till the spring of 1925 the New Economic Policy had accomplished very little, except that it had made life in Russia more tolerable. It came to be possible to buy and sell without running the risk of imprisonment and obligatory labour. The shopkeepers were recalled from the manual work to which they had been sent, and ordered to reopen their shops. The peasants were able to get a return for their produce, and were therefore induced to cultivate more of their land, and the risk of famine was proportionately diminished.

Yet the Soviet Government was evidently afraid to go too far or too fast in the work of freeing private enterprise. A member of the Soviet Government is reported to have said in the summer of 1924: " We must not go too fast because so many people have benefited by the system we have established, that we should incur some risk if we attempted to change it too quickly." In other words, vested interests have already arisen, and these interests will fight hard against any system which might involve a change in the existing individual advantages. Timorousness of this kind, however, must have disillusioned the enthusiastic members of the Supreme Economic Council, who looked forward with Lenin to the industrialization of the peasant, to the development of mechanical power, and to huge exports of Russian manufactured goods. These results could only follow the adoption of new financial and administrative methods with which a purely communist policy is wholly inconsistent.

# THE NEW ECONOMIC POLICY

## NOTES

(1) The example is taken from an article by V. Milyutin, *A New Way of the Co-operative Movement* in *People's Economy* (Moscow), No. 3, May 1918.

(2) *The Communist Calendar* (Moscow, 1924), pp. 523–24.

(3) The Government offered these to *concessionnaires* or for sale (*The Communist Calendar*, p. 524).

(4) The argument has often been put forward in defence of socialism, that under it no one would resort to the " wasteful expedient " of advertising. The Soviet factories had a monopoly of production, except for the village industries and yet, because the government factory managers competed with one another, they found advertising necessary.

(5) Resolution of the Council of Labour and Defence of May 9, 1923.

(6) This was conveyed to the writer in a private communication.

(7) For some reason as yet obscure, the heavy shipments of flour which were made to Russia in the spring of 1925 were ordered to be sent to Vladivostok.

(8) Canada entered into a similar agreement on July 3, 1922. Recognition by Great Britain followed in 1924.

(9) Interview with Krassin in Petrograd (*Pravda*, May 7, 1921).

(10) Two such cases were brought in detail to the attention of the author. The presumption of right seemed in each case to be on the side of the British firms. These cases appear both to have been influential in impeding commercial relations, the trade agreement notwithstanding.

(11) The author was personally informed in 1921 in Hamburg of these negotiations. Paul Scheffer, special correspondent in Moscow of the *Berliner Tageblatt*, writing in February 1922 (see that newspaper of February 19, 1922), referred to a conversation with Trotsky " some time before," in which Trotsky remarked upon the " reserve " shown by European capitalists in their dealings with Russia. " Trotsky said that the western peoples showed very little courage, and feared or expected in Soviet Russia all sorts of difficulties arising out of the proletarian-communist ideas upon which that State was based. Trotsky pledged his word that the property, profits, and personal security of foreigners would remain unmolested. There was, it is true, one situation in which communization would occur, namely, if the communistic revolution should be also successful outside Russia and if the proletariat in the rest of Europe entered upon the inheritance of the capitalists."

## CHAPTER IV

## SOVIET FINANCE

NATIONALIZATION of banks and confiscation of their assets in every form threw currency and credit entirely into the hands of the Government. Lenin had declared his intention of instituting a method of " natural exchange " or barter in kind and to eliminate monetary currency from economic life. His purpose in doing so was to prevent the accumulation of readily realizable capital, and so to facilitate the destruction of the power of the *bourgeoisie* by striking at them through finance. By these means he hoped to render impossible their re-emergence as a class.

Reversion to forsaken habits, even by a peasantry among whom many primitive customs have survived, is not easy. Since a system of purely urban barter is impossible, and since the peasants refused to accommodate themselves to the terms of exchange which the Soviet Government attempted to force upon them, the institution of " natural exchange " was slow in coming into effect.

For purposes of exchange there was available only the currency which had been confiscated. This was reissued, but the Government soon realized that the extravagant demands of the working men could not be satisfied by wages determined on a scale in correspondence with the financial position of the Soviet, notwithstanding confiscation of private property.(1) It thus found itself confronted by a dilemma. There were no more private fortunes to confiscate ; no internal loan could be procured ; therefore either a foreign loan must be raised, or a paper currency must be issued with a view to effecting a forced internal loan. As a foreign loan was not procurable, the issue of paper currency was the only expedient until the produce of the national enterprises and of taxation of such private enterprises as had been permitted to remain, should yield a surplus sufficient for the services of the Government. These services consisted in (a) provision for the Red Army and (b) provision for the civil service, which had been enormously increased in personnel and cost, owing to the increased duties imposed upon it. Many items of expenditure under the old *régime* had been wholly eliminated, e.g. the service of the external and internal debt, the cost of the imperial household in so far as that fell upon the State, (2) the cost of the diplomatic service (only gradually did

## SOVIET FINANCE 413

some of the Powers receive Soviet representatives), and the cost of the State Duma.

The currency had become depreciated in the last days of the Tsardom, and still more so during the reign of the Provisional Government; but in October 1917 it still retained a purchasing power not seriously below that of gold. During the Civil War the issues of paper currency were grotesque. The Soviet Government issued enormous quantities, as also did the numerous authorities, military and civil, which had set themselves up in the various parts of what had been the Russian Empire. Such authorities comprised: Archangel; the army of General Vaudam (at Pskov); Riga (communist issue); Avalova-Bermondt army; General Yudenich's army; army of General Rodzianko; municipality of Odessa; government of Ukrainia; municipality of Elizavetgrad; the Crimea; the region of the Don; municipality of Astrakhan; municipality of Ekaterinograd, Northern Caucasus; the Volunteer Army (under Denikin and Wrangel); city of Tiflis; Gruziya; Batum; Sochë; Baku; Armenia; Trans-Caspian government; Turkestan; Semeryechye; Orenburg; Siberian temporary government; Chēta; Blagovieshtchensk; Khabarovsk; Kharbin; Vladivostok; Nikolaevsk (Amur); Japanese army of occupation; German and Hungarian prisoners of war; and the Chinese Eastern Bank. (3) The amounts issued by these numerous authorities cannot and need not be stated. The total, if it were known, would have to be expressed in figures hitherto employed exclusively in calculations of celestial distances. Instead of abolishing money, Lenin had set in motion forces which produced an unprecedented flood of currency. Certainly all this money became discredited; but when this happened, the people took refuge, not in barter, but in a return to currency based upon metallic reserves.

Before this return could be made, however, several operations were necessary: the budget had to be balanced, the process of printing paper money had to be severely controlled, and the sharpest economy observed in every department of state expenditure. Since the Soviet State had extended its functions more widely than any other modern State, it incurred a greater risk of waste. Until the Civil War was over, it could do little to stop the tide of currency, or to economize and thus balance its budget; but when the Civil War was concluded, the Government set itself to work to bring its finance out of the chaos into which it had fallen.

Had production been restored, and the peasant farms and the agricultural enterprises of the State (of old-standing or confiscated from proprietors of large estates) been cultivated to the pre-war level, the financial position of Russia could have been righted with

## THE RUSSIAN REVOLUTION

the greatest ease ; and no foreign loans need have been raised, or concessions granted to foreigners or to Russians. The fatal error of the Bolsheviks was that, at a moment when every kind of stimulus was necessary to bring Russia out of the pit into which she had sunk, the stimulus which comes from security of possession was denied to the labourer. The peasants might have refused to exert them-selves even under that stimulus, but its absence at any rate rendered certain a deficiency of production.

The doctrines of the Bolsheviks proved too heavy a handicap to carry, and when they adopted at Lenin's suggestion the New Economic Policy, they threw some of these doctrines overboard. At the same time they devoted themselves to economies in adminis-tration. They rigorously cut down the number of officials, and transferred communists from one department to another in their endeavour to find them the work for which they were best adapted. The result of these reforms was " the first more or less tolerable budget "—that of 1922–1923.

It is practically impossible to compare the Bolshevik budgets with those of the old *régime*. The latter included the revenues from State lands, mines, and from the customs duties upon imports, excise duties, direct taxes, etc. The former include the same individual features, but their yield is much depleted ; the state lands, mines, etc., no longer yield what they did under former conditions ; imports are diminished because of the dispersal or destruction of the classes consuming foreign goods ; government monopolies have absorbed excise duties ; and the elimination of private property, in so far as that has been carried out, has rendered direct taxation unproductive. Thus, in spite of confiscation of every movable and immovable property, the Soviet State has less at its disposal than had the Imperial Government. The confusion of industrial finance with administrative finance—the inevitable consequence of the unification of economic and political activities—renders impossible comparison with any other budget in which this confusion does not occur.

The " total " revenue of 1922–1923 was 800 million roubles, and the expenditure about 1,300 million. There was thus a deficit of 500 million roubles, and there was no way of meeting this deficit except by a forced loan disguised by a fresh issue of paper money. The consequence of this issue was a further fall in the Soviet rouble.

The All-Russian Central Executive Committee then ordered the limitation of the issue of paper currency to the equivalent of 30 million gold roubles per month. (4)

The Bolshevik writers attribute the deficiency in the budget of 1922–1923 to the following causes : demands of the railways and

## SOVIET FINANCE

of the heavy industries, difficulties in the collection of taxes, and in controlling expenditure in the provinces. (5)

The estimates for 1923–1924 were: Revenue 1,400 million roubles, and expenditure 1,600 million roubles. The increase in revenue was only apparent because a change in the system of accounting brought into the estimated revenue some items which had not previously been included. On the side of expenditure, the demands of the railways and of heavy industry were less than those of the previous year. The demands of the latter were reported to have diminished owing to reduction in the rates of freight, and to increase of income.

Efforts on the part of the Soviet Government to concentrate authority led to centralized control of revenue collection and expenditure. Too much concentration led inevitably to inconvenience and loss. The 1923–1924 budget was dealt with under two categories —state finance and local finance. (6) In the latter budget were charged the expenses of the local Soviets, schools, hospitals, roads, prisons, militia, etc., and the collection of local revenues was provided for. (7) Not only did the administrative organs acquire in this manner a certain amount of financial freedom, but the quasi-independent republics, of which the Union of Soviet Socialist Republics was composed, also gained a degree of financial independence. There came about, as an inevitable corollary, the separation of the budget of the Union as a Union from the budgets of the individual States of which the Union was composed.

The system of centralization thus broke down owing to the difficulties of centralizing the finance of the Union without paralysing the activities of its constituent States. If a difficulty arose in any locality, an official of the Government was sent there to inquire into, and decide upon, the question at issue; but so inexperienced were the Bolshevik politicians in matters of any magnitude that their interference in local affairs only served to aggravate disputes which they were expected to examine and adjust.

---

### NOTES

(1) Lenin speaks with an air of disappointment of the results of confiscation.

(2) The imperial household was maintained chiefly from the income of the Udelny or imperial estate. This was confiscated by the Bolshevik Government, and, if it had been managed as formerly, would have yielded a large revenue.

(3) Facsimiles (with dimensions in millimetres) of the originals of all the currencies issued by the above mentioned authorities are given in *Archives of the Russian Revolution* (Berlin, 1923), vol. viii.

(4) *The Communist Calendar* (Moscow, 1924), p. 555.

(5) Ibid.

(6) Arriving independently at the same solution reached by the British system many years ago.

(7) This led to multiplication of taxes and to subsequent unification and division.

CHAPTER V

# THE ECONOMIC SITUATION IN RUSSIA IN THE YEARS
## 1923–1925

DURING the two years from 1923 to 1925 the New Economic Policy was developed, and a great improvement in the conditions of life was observable.

The industrial conditions at the beginning of the period are indicated in the following resolution passed at the Twelfth Congress of the Russian Communist party held in Moscow in 1923 :—

" A system of unified authority must be brought about from top to bottom in the organization of industry. Selection of workers, control of their removal and dismissal are necessary conditions of the real leadership of industry. . . . Recommendations . . . by trade organizations (such as trade unions) must meet with full consideration, but in no case can the responsibility of the competent authority be evaded. The work of managers, etc., in decreasing the costs of production and in realizing a profit meets with enormous obstacles, which cause frequent conflicts, removals, and dismissals. The manager who practises economy encounters two dangers : either he incurs the displeasure of the workers who have increased their demands, together with that of their representative organizations, local party, and Soviet institutions ; or he is apt to proceed along the line of least resistance and thereby to forgo the profitableness of the enterprise and to compromise its future. The directors of a Soviet plant must pay the greatest attention to the material and spiritual interests of workers and to their feelings and impressions ; but he must never forget that his supreme duty towards the working class as a whole is increase of the productivity of labour and in the quantity of material goods for the workers' State, and decrease of the cost of production. To these ends the party and the workmen must render the Soviet manager every assistance. Attention, persistence, and economy are the necessary qualifications of a Soviet manager. The best test is the balance of the enterprise. The working man must be helped to understand management, which, tending towards profit, thereby serves the interests of the working class, as much as those of the trade union advocate, who endeavours to raise the standard of life of the worker and to preserve his health." (1)

A report on the economic situation in 1924 was submitted to the Combined Council on Public Projects by V. G. Groman in September

# THE ECONOMIC SITUATION IN RUSSIA 417

of that year, (2) immediately after the close of the agricultural year, which, for statistical purposes, takes place on August 31st. V. G. Groman is a well-known and very reliable writer on economic statistics. His report shows that the acreage sown in 1924 was greater by 6 per cent. than that sown in the previous year ; but the crop as a whole was less by 15·6 per cent. than that of 1923, because of the poor harvests in some localities. In 1923 the total crop, exclusive of that in the Far East, Turkestan, and Trans-Caucasia, was rather more than 3 milliards of *pùdi*. In 1924 it was estimated at 2,675 milliards of *pùdi*, a figure which shows a diminution of about 11 per cent. Stock-breeding had been increasing at the following rates : horses 4·6 per cent., cattle 11·3 per cent., sheep 2 per cent., goats 8 per cent., hogs 64 per cent. In August prices of grain fell in comparison with prices current in July, but they were much higher than those of August 1923. Wheat was 1 rouble 64 *kopeks* per *pùd*, as against 92 *kopeks* ; and rye was 99·7 *kopeks* as against 42 *kopeks*. Yet in comparison with pre-war prices, those in August 1924 were not high.

The relatively low prices of 1924 are probably attributable to the immobility in the crops due to the decline of the railways, and to the absence of the old organized export system, which carried grain to foreign countries, thereby diminishing the quantity available for sale in the local markets. It is important to remember that there was a diminished demand on the part of the people due to the decline of industry, and the consequent migration of the industrial population from the towns to the villages, where their consumption of grain is a first charge upon the local crop, and is to be found as a more or less vague estimate in the agricultural statistics. The following is the estimated balance sheet of food grains for 1924 :—

| | In Million *Pùdi.* | |
|---|---|---|
| Reserves brought over from 1923 :— | | |
| Ascertained quantities | 74 | |
| Estimated additional quantities | 150 | |
| Total reserves | 224 | |
| Crop of 1924 | 2,675 | |
| | | 2,899 |
| Required for seed | 630 | |
| „ for consumption of rural population | 1,400 | |
| „ for consumption of town population | 243 | |
| „ for feeding cattle | 365 | |
| „ for Turkestan | 12 | |
| Total requirements | 2,650 | |
| Estimated surplus | 249 | |
| | | 2,899 |

2 D

418 THE RUSSIAN REVOLUTION

The reporter (V. G. Groman) regarded this estimate of the surplus as too high. He placed the ascertained surplus at 50 million *pùdi* with a hypothetical additional surplus at 100 million *pùdi*. If, then, the surplus was only 150 million *pùdi*, the consumption during the year 1924 must have absorbed the production, and about 74 million *pùdi* must have been drawn from the reserves brought forward from 1923 —about one-third of their quantity. Under these circumstances exportation of wheat or rye was out of the question. The balance sheet for the year 1924 as given above may be compared with the following :—

Average production of grain food-stuffs in 1901–1910 : (3) In Million *Pùdi*.

| | |
|---|---|
| (a) 50 *gubernie* of European Russia . . . . | 4,425·8 |
| (b) Caucasus . . . . . . . . | 287·1 |
| (c) Siberia . . . . . . . . | 199·3 |
| (d) Steppes . . . . . . . . | 55·4 |
| (e) Ural Cossacks . . . . . . . . | 11·2 |
| | 4,978·8 |

Poland and Finland have been omitted, and the Far East, Turkestan, and Trans-Caucasia have also been left out in accordance with the balance-sheet for 1924. The figures of production are therefore strictly comparable, and show that the production of food grains in 1924 was 56·3 per cent. of the average production of 1901–1910. In other words, the production of food grains had not yet reached much more than one-half of the pre-war scale.

According to the official report for August 1924, the production of manufactured goods for that month exceeded that of July by 6 per cent. The value of all goods produced in August 1924 was 124·4 millions, being 31 per cent. more than in August 1923. The number of workers in the workshops was greater in August 1924 than in July of the same year, by 4 per cent.

In the Moscow exchanges the turnover for August was 116 million roubles. (4) This was 20 per cent. less than the July turnover. In forty provincial exchanges the turnover was 127 million roubles, 20 per cent. more than in July.

The amount of paper money issued amounted on September 1st to 630·23 gold roubles—an increase of 10 per cent. for the month. Owing to the requirements of harvest time, the banks were obliged to restrict the credit of their customers.

The average wages per month in industrial employments were 16·5 roubles, an increase over the preceding month of 4 per cent., and over the year 1923 of 36 per cent.

The exports for August 1924 were 20·7 million roubles ; the imports 20·9 million roubles. Timber exports amounted to 6·3

## THE ECONOMIC SITUATION IN RUSSIA 419

million roubles. The chief import was cotton—12·8 million roubles. (5) The author of the report from which the above particulars are cited adds :—

" Notwithstanding the inferior harvest, the process of rebuilding production did not stop. Great difficulties are being experienced in the regulation of crop prices. The storing of the crop is going on better than was expected. The rate of the development of industry is not less than that of the previous year. While (in textile and metallic industries) there is a decrease in the disposal of the produce, that is due to difficulty of transport. Increase in the quantity of money was not followed by a rise in prices." (6)

The letter (7) of which the following is a translation, was written in the *gub* of Saratov on May 27, 1924, by a mechanic in the employ of the railway department :—

" So long as the Bolsheviks do not take the land from the peasants, the peasants will help to keep the Bolsheviks in power. We expect the harvest to be good, (8) although the cultivated acreage is much smaller than it was before the war. The decline in acreage is due to the lack of implements. The peasants use wooden ploughs. (9) Animals are scarce ; there are few horses. Fertilizers are not used. Thus the harvest must be small, notwithstanding that the yield per acre may be relatively high. Even on good estates cultivation has declined. The following are the prices at the present time : (10) Rye, 65 *kopeks* (100 *kopeks* = 1 gold rouble) per *pùd* (36·11 lb. *avoirdupois*). Wheat, 1 *rouble* 10 *kopeks* per *pùd*. Meat (best), 18 *kopeks* per *funt* ($\frac{9}{10}$ lb. *avoirdupois*). Pork, 50 to 60 *kopeks* per *funt*. Milk, 25 *kopeks* per *krujka* (2·88 imperial quarts, English measure). Eggs, 10 for 44 *kopeks*. Printed calico (medium quality), 50 *kopeks* per *arshin* (2·33 feet English measure)."

### THE RUSSIAN RAILWAYS.

In the beginning of January 1920 an Extraordinary Commission on the state of the railways, which had been appointed in December, made its first report to the Council of People's Economy. The conclusions of this report were to the effect that the chief causes of the delay in repairing the railways were : (*a*) shortage of qualified workers ; (*b*) lack of special parts (of locomotives, wagons, and carriages, and of the machinery for building and repairing these) ; (*c*) the fuel crisis ; and (*d*) decline in the discipline of labour. Hence the numbers of locomotives, wagons, and carriages which were withdrawn from use were increasing rapidly. For instance, on the Nicolai railway there were under repair 7,134 cars (including wagons and carriages) and 457 locomotives ; and on the Moscow-Windawa-

420 THE RUSSIAN REVOLUTION

Rybinsk line 1,372 cars and 22 locomotives. On some railways the number of locomotives out of repair surpassed the number in commission.

The Commission recommended the adoption of several measures designed to check the tendency towards deterioration of the railway system. The first of these was to increase the productivity of labour through the introduction of a system of premiums—which were to be paid in kind in the form of bread. For that purpose the Commission asked for a special supplementary appropriation of 6,000 rations, and also recommended the return from the army of all experts in the mechanics of transport. (11) These measures, while harmless in themselves, seem to have been hardly sufficient. Probably the most effective means of hastening repair of the railway system would have been to employ a competent German manager, who might have been obtained from one or other of the Baltic Provinces. He would in all likelihood have been able to select efficient heads of departments and to have enough pressure brought to bear upon the heads of the ancillary industries—coal-mining, iron-smelting, steel-manufacture, locomotive-engineering, and the like—to bring their production up to the required limits. Then, with the rigorous expulsion of " supervising communist politicians," the railways might quickly have been brought into working order. (12)

In 1920 the Central Committee of the Communist party resolved to mobilize 5,000 of their members for railway transport. (13) These communists were to be occupied in raising the spirits of the railway workers, in instilling into the minds of the railwaymen's children sound communist doctrine, in diffusing a communist atmosphere, and above all in seeing that the railwaymen did not shirk their work or exhibit any anti-Bolshevik or counter-revolutionary tendencies.

During the succeeding three or four years these and similar measures effected an important improvement in the railway system. The discipline of the employees was improved, locomotives and other rolling stock were repaired and placed in commission, the time-tables were better observed, and passenger traffic on the great through lines, including the Trans-Siberian, was resumed. The movement of goods, however, remained in an unsatisfactory condition. In the centre of Russia and around Petrograd the goods service was improving, but it still remained poor in the south. In the Caucasus, for example, trains were kept until a sufficient quantity of goods was offered. The train only left the station, as a tramp steamer leaves the docks, when it was loaded. Those who wished to despatch goods had no means of learning even approximately when the train would start, except by employing someone to wait

## THE ECONOMIC SITUATION IN RUSSIA 421

in the station and to warn them when the train was likely to begin its journey.

The granaries and " elevators " on the large estates and at the great shipping ports were, before the war, of the most modern construction, equipped with the best machinery for cleaning the grain and preparing it for the market. As a consequence, Russian grain cargoes from the Baltic or the Black Sea supplied the most attractive samples on the counters of the Liverpool grain brokers. A visitor to Russia in the summer of 1924, who was especially skilled in such matters, found that not a single elevator was in working order, that the grain offered for sale was heavily adulterated by foreign seeds, and that it was far dirtier than that of any other country. (14)

The difficulties in the management of nationalized enterprises which have been detailed in previous chapters had not been overcome fully in 1924, but certain improvements were observable. The former owners and managers had in some cases been induced to return. Demand even for articles of luxury was slowly though fitfully returning, and some factories, previously idle, were beginning to function now that workmen had returned to the towns from their villages, doubtless having found village life, especially under the new conditions, dull after the relative liveliness of the centres of industry and population. Yet this fact brought about a condition which in former times had been extremely rare in Russia—the existence of a great mass of unemployed men and women. Formerly, when employment could not be obtained in the town factories, the workmen simply returned at once to their villages and remained there until demand for labour revived. Now they remained in the towns demanding rations from the Government whether they were employed or no. The burden of unemployment, therefore, in spite of nationalization of industry and compulsory labour, was, and is, very heavy.

The Government, in Moscow especially, took pains to provide the proletariat with amusement. Two opera houses were heavily subsidized, and conductors, orchestras, and actors were employed on terms which bore no relation to wages or normal rations. Russian, (15) German, French, and Italian music was rendered by great artists, and the productions were on an extraordinarily magnificent scale. (16)

Meanwhile the question of education had become extremely perplexing. The assumption that the peasantry was eager for teaching was not found to be in a general sense justified, but there were ambitious young peasants who desired higher education, and who expected it to be administered to them in strong, frequent, and

**422        THE RUSSIAN REVOLUTION**

effective doses. The qualification for admission to the universities had been greatly diminished, and the halls of the institutions of higher learning were crowded by inadequately prepared students, and measures had to be taken, first to deal with those who had already presented themselves, and, secondly, to check the stream, which threatened soon to become overwhelming. In former days, the number of Jews admitted to the universities had been restricted, and many were thus denied, irrespective of their qualifications. Some of these were driven abroad, especially to the universities of Switzerland, Germany, and Belgium, where they formed compact groups, nourishing hostile feelings against Russia. Under the Soviet *régime* the proscribed class was that of the *bourgeoisie*. Thousands of students who were the sons of *bourgeois* parents were expelled from the universities, and the courses in the institutions were readjusted to the needs of the new type of student. The consequence has been a marked decline in educational standards.

In former days the primary schools were of two orders. One was promoted and managed by the *zemstvo* authorities, the other by the Government, which was often subject to ecclesiastical influence. The *zemstvo* schools were excellent. There were few primary school systems anywhere to compare with them as effective educational instruments, but during the period of the quarrel between the Imperial Government and the *zemstvo* authorities the *zemstvo* schools were frowned upon. (17) The Church schools attached predominant importance to religious instruction, and although secular education could not be said to be neglected, it was overshadowed by the religious element. Under the Bolshevik system many new schools have been opened, but in these schools communism as a definite subject of instruction has taken the place of religion and has dominated all other subjects.

When the New Economic Policy had ameliorated life in the cities, many officials of the old *régime* were induced to return to their posts, (18) and technical experts, chemists, engineers, and the like resumed service, either in the old state enterprises or in nationalized plants. High hopes were entertained that under the New Economic Policy a large revenue would be derived from concessions for the exploitation of natural resources. These hopes had not been realized, for only to a small extent had concessions been granted.

In the spring of 1925 the Soviet Government bought large quantities of flour, the equivalent of between three and four million bushels of wheat, from Great Britain, Canada, and the United States. The purchase of flour instead of wheat was due to the fact that there were few large flour mills in Russia, most of the milling being done in small village or domestic mills, whilst those

# THE ECONOMIC SITUATION IN RUSSIA 423

in Eastern and Western European Russia were not sufficiently numerous or adequately enough equipped for the task of grinding wheat in the required quantities. It was not certain that there would be any serious deficiency of bread-stuffs in the summer of 1925 before the harvest, but provision was made to some extent against a shortage and against a consequent advance in prices. In spite of the Government's fixation of prices to be paid to the peasants for grain, the competition of the private market, which had now been legalized by the New Economic Policy, made it possible for the price to be advanced beyond the government standard. The Soviet State has simply adopted the means which were employed as an emergency measure by Great Britain during the war.

-------

## NOTES

(1) Resolution of the Twelfth Congress of the Russian Communist party in *The Communist Calendar* (Moscow, 1924), pp. 253-54.

(2) *Izvestia*, September 10, 1924.

(3) *Collection of Statistics and Economics of the Agriculture of Russia and of Foreign Countries* (5th year, St. Petersburg, 1912), pp. 33 et seq.

(4) Gold roubles.

(5) Groman, V. G., Report cited.

(6) Ibid. The word used is "drop in prices"; but it is evident that the author meant rise in prices. It is quite usual for an interval to elapse between the issue of an additional amount of paper money and an advance in prices; but if the amount issued is in excess of the market's power to absorb the new issue, prices expressed in paper must rise within a short time.

(7) From private correspondence.

(8) The harvest of 1924 was fairly good.

(9) There is much to be said for the wooden plough. It is light, and can easily be transported on the back of a horse—a matter of great importance where the peasant's fields are at a distance from his house yard. It is not easily damaged when working in stony ground, and can be soon repaired by the peasant himself. It does not plough more than 4 or 5 inches, but the peasant defends shallow ploughing.

(10) These prices, except the price of calico, are probably determined by the commune or by the local Soviet.

(11) *Pravda* (Petrograd), No. 8, January 13, 1920.

(12) Cf. supra, where the railway servants demanded the separation of the railways from the State. In so far as the railways have been rehabilitated, this has been effected through the application of more economy and discipline and less politics and agitation.

(13) *Pravda* (Petrograd), No. 56, March 11, 1920; *Party Mobilization for Transport.*

(14) From private information.

(15) Some of the Russian operas have been edited by Bolshevik censors.

(16) The writer has been so informed by an eminent musician.

(17) This circumstance affords the sole ground for the accusation frequently made against the Imperial Government that it denied schools to a peasantry who were clamouring for them. Neither of these statements is true. The peasantry did not clamour and the Government did not withhold.

(18) The staff of the Russian Foreign Office in 1925 was wholly composed of former imperial officials.

## CHAPTER VI

## THE THIRD INTERNATIONAL

THE story of the formation of the International Working Men's Association at a meeting held in London in September 1864, as well as its subsequent history until its death in 1876 in New York, has been told elsewhere. (1) It is interesting to note, however, that a Russian section was formed at Geneva in March 1870, (2) but between 1876 and 1899 there was no International Working Men's Association, till at a Labour Congress held in Paris in 1889 the Second International was formed. During the European war international socialists came to be divided into three groups, which Lenin distinguishes as follows :—

" 1. Social patriots, that is, socialists in words and *chauvinists* in fact, who agree to defend their fatherland in an imperialistic war, and particularly in this imperialistic war. . . . They count among their numbers the majority of socialists in every nation—Plekhanov and others in Russia ; Schiedemann in Germany ; Renaudel, Guesde, and Sembat in France ; Bissolati and others in Italy ; Hyndman, the Fabians, and the Labourites in England ; Branting and others in Sweden ; Troelstra and his party in Holland ; Stauning and his party in Denmark ; Victor Berger and other defenders of the fatherland in America, etc.

" 2. The second group, which might be called the centre, is hesitating between social-patriotism and actual internationalism. . . . The centre is for union and against any sort of schism. . . . The fact is that the centre is not convinced of the necessity of a revolution against the government of its own country ; it does not preach that kind of revolution. . . . Historically and economically, the centre does not represent any special stratum of society ; it only represents the transition from the old-fashioned labour movement as it was from 1871 to 1914 (which rendered inestimable services to the proletariat through its slow, continuous, systematic work of organization in a large, very large field) to the new movement which was objectively necessary at the time of the first world-wide war of imperialism, and which has inaugurated the social-revolutionary era. The main leader and representative of the centre is Karl Kautsky, who dominated the Second International (from 1889 to 1914), who has been responsible for the complete downfall of Marxism, who has shown the most unheard of lack of principle

# THE THIRD INTERNATIONAL 425

and the most pitiful hesitancy, and who has betrayed the cause since August 1914. Among these centrists are also Haase, Lebedour, and the so-called Labour group in the Reichstag; in France, Longuet, Pressman, and the so-called minority; in England, Philip Snowden, Ramsay MacDonald, and other leaders of the Independent Labour Party, and a part of the British Socialist Party; Morris Hilquit and many others in the United States; Turati, Treves, and Modigliani and others in Italy; Robert Grimm and others in Switzerland; Victor Adler and others in Austria; the Mensheviks, Akselrod, Martov, Chkheidze, Tseretelli, and others in Russia.

"3. The third, the true internationalist group, is most accurately represented by the so-called 'Zimmerwald Left.' It is characterized by its complete schism from the social-patriots and the centrists. It has been waging a relentless war against its own imperialistic government and its own imperialistic *bourgeoisie*. Its motto is, 'Our worst enemy is at home.' It has fought ruthlessly the phraseology of nice and respectable social pacifists, for those people who are social pacifists in words are *bourgeois* pacifists in deeds. . . . They have been employing every form of sophistry to demonstrate the impossibility, the inopportuneness of keeping up the proletarian struggle or of starting a proletarian social revolution in connection with the present war. The members of this group in Germany are known as the Spartacus (3) or International group, to which Karl Liebknecht belongs. . . . Rosa Luxembourg is also a member and leader of the Spartacus group. . . . In France those who stand closest to real internationalism are Loriot . . . and Henri Guilbeaux. . . . In England, the supporters of the review *The Trade Unionist* and some of the members of the British Socialist Party and of the Independent Labour Party. . . . In the United States, the Socialist Labour Party and certain elements of the opportunist Socialist Party (4), which began in 1917 to publish the paper *The Internationalist*. In Holland, the party of the 'Tribunists' . . . In Sweden, the section of the younger men and of the Left. . . . In Denmark, Trier and his friends who have left the purely *bourgeois* Social Democratic party headed by Minister Stauning. In Bulgaria, the '*Simon-Pure*.' In Italy, Constantine Lazzari, Secretary of the Socialist Party, and Serrati, editor of the organ *Avanti*. In Poland, Karl Radek, Ganetsky, and other leaders of the social democracy forming the Kraev group; Rosa Luxembourg, Tyshka, and others forming the main group of social democracy. In Switzerland, the 'Left,' which put through the referendum of January 1917, in order to fight the social-patriots and the centre, and which, at the session of the Socialist party in

426 THE RUSSIAN REVOLUTION

the canton of Zürich on February 11, 1917, carried a revolutionary resolution against the war. In Austria, the youthful friends of Friedrich Adler, whose activity . . . was ended by the reactionary Austrian Government, which imprisoned Adler for his heroic but ill-considered attempt upon the life of Count Stuergkh." (5)

These extracts sufficiently indicate the position of the Third International in relation to the other socialist groups, and its birth has been noticed in a previous chapter. Its headquarters was at Moscow in 1919. The president of the executive committee was Zinoviev, who had been president of the Petrograd Soviet. Although nominally not a department of the Soviet State, the relations of that Government with the dominating members of the Third International were from the beginning too close for their respective activities to be otherwise than formally differentiated. There can be no doubt that the funds for the activities of the committee of the International were supplied by the Government. The materials for an impartial account of them are not yet available ; they exist for the most part in the intelligence departments of the Governments of the various countries in which they have been conducted.

The destructive aims of the Third International do not admit of dispute. These are to destroy nationalism by breaking down national boundaries, to foment class war everywhere, and to exterminate the *bourgeoisie* of every country. The constructive aims are not so obvious. From one point of view, they seem to imply a high degree of centralized power, the centre being the headquarters of the executive committee of the International. At present this is at Moscow, but it might be moved to another centre. The world revolution at which the International aims is apparently to be directed by its committee, which, according to the quotations which have been given, has widespread connections with groups in many countries. Attempts at revolution by internationalists were made in Buda-Pesth and in Germany ; the uprising in Hungary was put down by the Roumanian army, that in Berlin by German republican forces, and both were suppressed with much loss of life.

The pretence that the committee of the Third International is an international committee, and is therefore altogether separate from the Russian Soviet Government, cannot be taken seriously ; it is clearly financed by the Russian Government, and its foreign policy, in so far as it may be so described, is the foreign policy of that Government, whilst the leading figures are also its members. The apprehension prevalent in all countries that the Third International may, through subversive propaganda, become a formidable power is similar to the sensation caused by the First International in the decade from 1865 to 1875. Then, partly by means of measures taken against it,

# THE THIRD INTERNATIONAL

chiefly in France, and partly through the internal disputes which have so often broken up such organizations, these apprehensions passed away with the passing of the International. Yet the mere fact that history has shown the menace of the International to be less formidable than was anticipated does not warrant the assumption that all contemporary apprehensions are without foundation.

The French journalist Claude Anet (6) lucidly expresses the megalomaniac dream which inspired the leaders of the Third International :—

" We Russian socialists are going to show the whole world how a revolution is made. In reality, all the revolutions in the west have failed ; but we shall make a revolution such as has never been seen before, extraordinary, unheard of, complete and final, in a word, *à la russe*. And we shall make the principles of Social-Democracy reign throughout the whole world." (7)

---

## NOTES

(1) In Mavor, J., *An Economic History of Russia*, vol. ii, pp. 87–89. See also Meyer, R., *Der Emancipationskampf des vierten Standes* (Berlin, 1892), vol. i, p. 114 et seq. ; Mehring, F., *Geschichte der deutschen Socialdemocratie* (4th edition, Stuttgart, 1909), vol. iii ; Malon, B., *l'Internationale, son Histoire et ses Principes* (Lyons, 1872) ; Tcherkesoff, W., *Précurseurs de l'Internationale* (Brussels, 1899) ; and Testut, Oscar, *L'Internationale* (7me edn., Paris, 1871).

(2) Testut, O., op. cit., p. 209.

(3) Called after the pseudonym Spartacus (derived from the Thracian brigand and gladiator Spartacus, who with two Celts led a revolt of slaves who had been kept in Capua for the gladiatorial games ; cf. Mommsen, Th., *History of Rome*, translation, New York, 1895, vol. iv, p. 357), adopted by Dr. Adam Weishaupt, professor in the University of Ingolstadt, Bavaria, who was an advocate of world revolution (cf. Blanc, Louis, *Histoire de la Révolution*, vol. ii, p. 84).

(4) The Socialist Party (U.S.A.) refused without reservation to join the Third International. Neither it nor the Socialist Labour Party (U.S.A.) was affiliated to the Third International.

(5) Lenin, N., *The General Programme of the Bolsheviki* in *The Proletarian Revolution in Russia*, by N. Lenin and Leon Trotsky, edited by L. C. Traina (New York, 1918), pp. 145–49.

(6) Correspondent of *Petit Parisien* in Russia on the outbreak of the February Revolution.

(7) Anet, Claude, *Through the Russian Revolution* (London, 1918), p. 134.

# CHAPTER VII

## CONCLUSIONS

An attempt has been made in the foregoing pages to trace the various immediate causes of the Russian Revolution, and to examine its effects in so far as these have developed in Russian life. The problem now is, can we go behind these immediate causes and discover the living but less obvious forces which inspired a series of movements upon a scale so vast and so bewildering ?

No one who has had experience of Russian life can fail to have met with the belief, traditionally held and expressed by men of widely different characters and temperaments, that Russia is the bearer of a gospel to the world. Not merely do we notice among the Slavophils and even among Russian intellectuals in general the conception of a national or racial gospel to mankind, but we find also in certain individuals an idea, sometimes ecstatically expressed, of a personal religious mission. Tolstoy, for example, voices this conviction vividly and directly in his Diary, under the date of March 5, 1855, while he was in the fourth bastion at the siege of Sevastopol.

" A discussion on God and faith brought me to a great, a stupendous conception, to the realization of which I felt able to devote my life. The idea is to create a new religion corresponding to the development of mankind, a religion of Christ purified from dogma and mysticism, a practical religion, not promising bliss in the future, but giving happiness on earth. I understand that this idea can be realized only by generations consciously working to that end. One generation will bequeath it to the next, and some day by fanaticism or by reason it will be realized. To work consciously for this union of mankind through religion—that is the fundamental idea which I hope will be my inspiration."

In another entry in his Diary (written three years earlier, in 1852) Tolstoy had already said, " Something within me makes me think that I am not born to be as others." (1) There can be no doubt that he regarded himself, although perhaps vaguely, as a Messiah, and that he definitely looked upon Russia as the chosen people among the nations.

Professor Peter Struvë, in an illuminating and suggestive article, has pointed out that, " On the one hand men with minds of a profoundly religious temper have believed in such a mission. For

## CONCLUSIONS 429

them it signified that Russia, by its spiritual essence and creative genius, would in some way recall and reassert the highest truth of Christianity. Such is the profound idea, at once historical, philosophical, and religious, of the Slavophils and Dostoevsky. This conception, this attitude, is not only religious in an abstract sense : it is definitely mystical. It is an experience akin to the eschatological aspirations of the early Christians. Side by side with this there is an idea, in form identical with that just described, but set in a different context. This is the conception of a militant realization of socialism, an atheistic faith, a belief not in the kingdom of God on earth, but in a godless supersession of all that is historic, including religion, of all that has happened irrationally and exists on the earth. Thus, side by side with an apocalyptic Christian Messianism, there emerges a Messianism, if we may so call it, of atheism, which has swollen and exacerbated the general anti-religious tradition, combining it with Maximalism in all other spheres—in economic, in social, and in political thought." (2)

With regard to the conception of a religious call to Russia, Professor Struvë observes that "two ideas, two principles have been strained to their utmost limits. The first is the idea that a nation is a collective individuality, that each human personality is an organic part of it and is sustained and fed by its willing obedience to it ; the second is the conception of a blessing conferred, of an individual and collective call from God. . . ." But there is the second idea, the content and the psychology of which are anti-religious. " Reduced to a modest expression, this content and psychology may appear as a respectable sort of 'free thought' of the type which in the historical development of thought attains its classical expression, for instance, in English philosophical radicalism. Neither Marx nor Lenin, neither Owen nor Bentham, can be brought into any association with Dostoevsky and the Slavophils. Here are two principles which, even if they repudiate their forms and expressions, cannot be blended. . . .

" Now the Russian Revolution is precisely the historical conflict of two such spiritual principles, and the struggle in it of political ideals and social aspirations is, in a certain cultural and philosophical sense, only a superficial expression and reflection of this profound conflict, which is by no means ended ; on the contrary, it has passed through one phase only so far, and is now approaching another. The fundamental character of this conflict is only vaguely understood by those who have taken or are taking part in it, and by outside observers." (3)

Here it seems worth while to go back to the perspicacious

## 430 THE RUSSIAN REVOLUTION

prophecy regarding the course of Russian history made nearly seventy years ago by Joseph de Maistre :—(4)

> Or cette puissance conservatrice et préservatrice n'existe pas en Russie. La religion y peut quelque chose sur l'esprit humain, mais rien du tout sur le cœur où naissent cependant tous les désirs et tous les crimes. Un paysan pourra peut-être s'exposer à la mort plutôt que de manger gras un jour prohibé ; mais s'il s'agit d'arrêter l'explosion d'une passion, il ne faudra pas s'y fier. . . . On peut soutenir, en thèse générale, qu'*aucune souveraineté n'est assez forte pour gouverner plusieurs millions d'hommes, à moins qu'elle ne soit aidée par la religion, ou par l'esclavage, ou par l'une et l'autre.* Ce qui est vrai surtout lorsque la population, quoique très-grande, considérée d'une manière absolue, cesse néanmoins d'être telle relativement à l'immensité du territoire.
>
> C'est à quoi il faut bien réfléchir avant de rien entreprendre relativement à l'affranchissement des serfs ; car dès qu'une fois l'impulsion légale sera donnée, il se formera une certaine opinion, un certain esprit général qui entraînera tout ; ce sera une mode, puis une passion, puis une fureur. La loi commencera et la rébellion achèvera. Et le danger sera porté à un point qu'il est impossible d'exprimer, par le caractère particulier de la nation la plus mobile, la plus impétueuse, la plus entreprenante de l'univers. . . .
>
> On ne saurait trop insister sur une maxime aussi certaine qu'une proposition de mathématiques : *Jamais un grand peuple ne peut être gouverné par le gouvernement.* J'entends par le gouvernement *seul.* . . .
>
> Ces serfs, à mesure qu'ils recevront la liberté, se trouveront placés entre des instituteurs plus une suspects et des prêtres sans force et sans considération. Ainsi exposés, sans préparation, ils passeront infailliblement et brusquement de la superstition à l'athéisme, et d'une obéissance passive à une activité effrénée. La liberté fera sur tous ces tempéraments l'effet d'un vin ardent sur un homme qui n'y est point habitué. Le spectacle seul de cette liberté enivera ceux qui n'y participent point encore. Que, dans cette disposition générale des esprits, il se présente quelque Pugatscheff d'université (comme il peut s'en former aisément, puisque les manufactures sont ouvertes), qu'on ajoute l'indifférence, l'incapacité, ou l'ambition de quelques nobles, la scélératesse étrangère, les manœuvres d'une secte détestable qui ne dort jamais, etc., etc. . . . l'État, suivant toutes les règles de la probabilité, se *romprait*, au pied de la lettre, comme une poutre trop longue qui ne porterait que par les extrémités : *ailleurs, il n'y a qu'un danger à craindre ; ici, il y en a deux.*
>
> Si l'affranchissement doit avoir lieu en Russie, il s'opérera par ce qu'on appelle *la nature.* Des circonstances tout à fait imprévues le feront désirer de part et d'autre. Tout s'exécutera sans bruit et sans malheurs (toutes les grandes choses se font ainsi). Que le souverain favorise alors ce mouvement naturel, ce sera son droit et son devoir ; mais Dieu nous garde qu'il l'excite lui-même ! (5)

The Savoyard gentleman, catholic and conservative, predicted very confidently what must come to pass where neither religion nor serfdom exist to aid the government in controlling the people. When Joseph de Maistre wrote, serfdom was about to be abolished. Professor Struvë agrees with his conclusion regarding the absence

# CONCLUSIONS 431

of religion as a conservative and preservative force : " In Russia there was a religion and a religious sense, but religion did not penetrate into everyday life as a principle of discipline." (6) Thus from Joseph de Maistre's point of view, when serfdom was abolished, autocracy, and indeed government of any kind, became impossible.

Professor Struvë attaches importance to this prediction, not because it is psychologically profound, but because it gives the coming Revolution a religious interpretation.

The question remains : does such an interpretation solve the problem ? The answer depends upon the conception which is formed of the Revolution—that is to say, in what it consisted. If it was expressed in the bread riots in Petrograd in February 1917, and in the subsequent manœuvres and seizure of power by the Bolsheviks in October of the same year, then the spiritual struggle between two groups, represented by the modern Slavophils on the one hand, and the anti-religious and materialistic Lenin on the other, would seem to have no clear connection with the Revolution. If, on the other hand, this struggle was the essence of the Revolution, it was not merely a matter of bread riots in February or the manœuvres of the Bolsheviks in October.

But let us take a more comprehensive view. If the Russian Revolution did not begin in 1917, when then did it begin ? The thesis might be maintained that it originated with the Cossack and peasant rebellion associated with the name of Pugachev at the end of the third quarter of the eighteenth century. There is no question of a religious motive in that revolt. It was undoubtedly a spontaneous movement, having its origin in minor Cossack grievances, and deriving its force from the dissatisfaction of peasants. Or it might be argued that the Revolution began in 1824 with the revolt of the Decabrists. That revolt did not arise directly out of Russia's internal struggles, but rather out of the impact of the liberal movement of the immediately preceding years in France and Germany upon the minds of the younger members of the Russian nobility. The new ideas thus imbibed led them to realize the inevitability of a similar movement in Russia towards political equality and decentralization of government. While spiritual motives may have influenced some of the Decabrists, there is no evidence that their revolt was caused by, or accompanied by, any religious struggle, (7) or to be in any sense susceptible of a religious interpretation.

During the period between the suppression of the Decabrists in 1825 and the Emancipation of the Peasants in 1861 a great fermentation was in progress in Russia. Russian literature began in this period, and the sudden splendour of it cannot be exaggerated. Pushkin, (8) Lermontov, (9) Byelinksy, (10) Herzen, (11) Gogol, (12)

## 432 THE RUSSIAN REVOLUTION

Turgeniev, (13) Nekrassov, (14) Dostoevsky, (15) and, at the end of the period, Tolstoy, (16) all these are universally recognized as among the great men of letters of the nineteenth century. (17) The Russian literary movement was inseparably connected with Slavophilism, which involved, not merely enthusiasm for the Slav race, (18) but the idea of a Slavic mission. It is open to doubt whether any two of the Slavophils would have agreed upon the precise or even the general terms in which that mission would be expressed. Some of them shared the romanticism of Pushkin and Lermontov (19) ; some were artists, as Turgeniev and Dostoevsky ; some were critics, as Byelinsky ; but each expressed the Slavic spirit in his appropriate form, and in that way all fulfilled the Slavic mission. With the exception of Chaadaiev, who denounced Russia as irreligious, and regarded the Orthodox Church as schismatic, none of the Slavophil group represented religious points of view. The religious motive became dominant in Tolstoy only at a later period, after he had written all his great works of fiction, and in his case it was an individual religion and practically independent of the current thought of the time. No other contemporary Russian author of even approximate fame exhibited in his writings a definitely religious tone.

Of the Slavophils, probably Chaadaiev alone assumed a distinctively religious standpoint. President Masaryk describes him as having " moved away from the rationalist outlook of Voltaire to romantic mysticism." (20) To Chaadaiev, " human history is the history of Christianity and the Church, the history of the realization of God's kingdom upon earth, the history of religious education. To him the Christian religion is no mere system of morality. Above all it is the eternal, divine energy, not acting upon the individual alone, but infused into society at large. The dogma of the one true Church implies such a social influence. Christianity has organized society ; Christianity has actually realized God's kingdom upon earth. . . . Despite the individuality of separate nations, he considers that in the spiritual sphere the medieval Church realized cultural unity. . . . The Russians were Christians only in name. . . . The masses are blind ; none but heaven-sent great men can be accepted as representatives of the people, and there are no such men in Russia. Moreover, Russian life is not inspired with a genuinely Christian spirit." Chaadaiev points to the English as exemplars of a truly religious people. " The ideals of duty, justice, law and order, are at home only in the west, not in Russia." (21)

Although the revolutionary movements in western, central, and eastern Europe during the years 1848-1849 did not leave Russia unaffected, their influence was more noticeable in the seventies than

# CONCLUSIONS

**433**

when they occurred. The Russian revolutionary movement of the seventies may perhaps more properly be described as humanitarian, although during that period, as well as during the pre-Emancipation days, the impetus may well be regarded as having had a spiritual origin. In the *Narodnaya Volya* movement, those who took part in it did so in general from ethical motives. They counted it disgraceful that they should concern themselves with letters and science when the peasants were suffering, as they were at that time, from famine as well as from ignorance. To this extent only may the *Narodnaya Volya* be regarded as a religious movement.

The revolution of 1905–1906 may be definitely regarded as the first stage of the Russian Revolution, although the preliminary phases which have been mentioned cannot be ignored. This revolution, which occurred at the close of the Russo-Japanese war, had among its causes not only the war itself, but its conduct and consequences. The first definite signs of revolt came from the soldiers when they returned from Manchuria, and the ostensible leaders were social democrats of the type of Lenin, who was indeed one of them, and many Socialist-Revolutionaries. The aims of these parties at that time were similar, although as individuals they did not work very well together. Their principles were those of the materialistic group of Professor Struvë's analysis, and with whatever fervour they advocated these principles, they were, in the ordinary acceptation of the word, deeply anti-religious. After the revolt was suppressed by the Government, there was an outbreak of mysticism among some groups of the *intelligentsia*, which found expression in a book of essays, one of which was written by Professor Struvë. This book, called *Vyekhë* (from the tall posts erected along the Russian roads to mark them when snow covers the steppe in winter), attracted much attention, and a mass of similar literature grew up in connection with it. (22) But the mystical enthusiasm of which this literature was the expression seemed to evaporate, and when the Revolution of 1917 came, the *intelligentsia* were evidently unprepared for the problems in government with which they were then confronted. Although the educated classes cannot be said to have made the Revolution, they at first placed themselves at its head ; but after a few months of unstable power, they were compelled to surrender their places to the Bolsheviks, who were strategically and tactically superior. For that reason, and not because they held one or other religious view, the *intelligentsia* went down in the struggle, and, so far as Russia was concerned, were annihilated as a group ; albeit individuals survived, and accepted the Bolshevik terms with what grace they might.

It is to a large extent although not wholly true that the Russian

## THE RUSSIAN REVOLUTION

spiritual movement has now passed from Russia with the Russian refugees. Except for those " tougher souls " who have remained to do their duty by their country as best they can, there is little evidence of any movement in Russia which might fairly be described as religious. Suffering may evoke such a movement ; and suffering the Russians have certainly had in full measure. Thus, even if we look upon the Russian Revolution as a tragic drama played against a background symbolizing, in an obscure and mystical sense, a struggle between opposing religious ideals, the interpretation does not seem to go very far towards a clear understanding of the great upheaval.

The other principle to which Professor Struvë refers is the idea that " a nation is a collective individuality, and that each human personality is an organic part of it and is sustained and fed by willing obedience to it." Against this idea the whole force of the Bolshevik propaganda is directed. From the Bolshevik point of view, a nation is a fortuitous collection of individuals, without organic relation with one another ; there are no racial divisions, and frontiers are artificial, and merely provocative of disputes and wars. The idea of nationality must be opposed and overcome because the real issue is not between nations but between classes. In this conflict the working class must be victorious, and therefore in every nation it must be induced to engage in a class war against the *bourgeoisie* by whom the political structure of the modern State, now to be smashed, has been devised and maintained. Bolshevism is thus the antithesis of nationalism, and yet the particular form which the Bolshevist State has assumed in Russia is that of a highly centralized bureaucracy. The Bolsheviks have, however, strenuously maintained that this is a transitory phase, and that when class divisions are wholly eliminated society will be found to consist of communist groups, between which only simple economic relations involving exchange of products will form the connecting links.

The history of Bolshevism so far does not appear to support this view of the future. Not merely have the peasants refused to accept the method of exchange by barter which is inconvenient for their economy, but the tendency of Bolshevik industry seems to involve the elimination of small industrial groups and the concentration of State industrial enterprise in large units. In this sense the Bolshevik State is more capitalistic than any other, for it possesses a monopoly of credit and of the organization of industrial enterprise. The New Economic Policy has not affected this situation. It has been directed chiefly towards relieving the State of the burden of managing the details of small enterprises, and especially of retail trade. The large enterprises remain fully under the care of the State even in those cases in which the former owners or managers have been

# CONCLUSIONS

induced to return. It is obvious that the organization of mines, factories, etc., upon a State-collectivist basis is not compatible with communism. This has been discerned by the Bolsheviks, and the originally projected communist system has been qualified by premiums and other payments, which have been found necessary in order that production may be maintained upon a scale sufficient to sustain the weight of the mechanism of government. Owing to various causes, chief among these being the absence of administrative skill, many enterprises are idle because the products of their manufacture cannot be disposed of, and the result is widespread unemployment. As already noticed, unemployment in Russia was formerly rare, because when workmen were out of employment they returned to their native villages. If these workmen were now allowed to go back to their old homes, they would only reinforce the peasantry, which is already sufficiently hostile to the Bolshevik rule. They must therefore be maintained in the towns, whether they are actually working or not.

Although the attitude of the peasantry is hostile to the Soviet authority, a rising of the peasants against the Government is not likely, because they fear that if the Soviet Government were replaced by another, they might lose some of the advantages which they owe to the Revolution. Under these circumstances, the continuance of at least a nominal Bolshevik *régime* seems for the present to be secured. It is certain, however, that many changes are in progress. Economic difficulties have forced the Government to make many concessions and frequently to alter its plans. The growth of rivalries among its members, especially since the restraining hand of Lenin has gone, has already resulted in the beginning of disintegration. Yet so many persons have been able in the stormy period to entrench themselves in positions politically advantageous to themselves, that the strength of the Bolsheviks has increased rather than diminished in recent years. The Imperial Government survived for more than two centuries, and during that period it was guided sometimes by persons of great ability, and sometimes by feeble and irresolute rulers. It fell because at a critical moment it was controlled wholly by a group whose weakness and vacillation were notorious. Incompetent as the Bolsheviks have shown themselves to be, they have been neither feeble nor irresolute, and therefore they have maintained a position to which their lack of administrative talent gives them no title.

While it is not suggested that the Russian Revolution is susceptible of adequate interpretation on economic and political grounds alone, these grounds may be held to account for a large number of the phenomena of which it consisted. The gradual growth of an

## THE RUSSIAN REVOLUTION

urban proletariat, especially in the two capitals, furnished the rank and file of a revolutionary army. The calling up of more than fifteen millions of conscripts and the arming of these under conditions of imperfect discipline and defective leadership, provided favourable soil for an uprising. The disastrous issue of the war broke down the confidence which, almost to the end, the people retained in the Government, and the war weariness that beset peasant and workman alike led them to desire peace at any price. The Government paid heavily for its aloofness from the people and for the distrust with which it regarded them ; and the Tsar paid with his life for his own faults and for his lack of discrimination in the appointment of ministers.

While these economic and political causes may be held to account in part for the Revolution, the completeness of the *bouleversement*, the incompetence and cruelty of the Bolshevik rule, suggest deep-seated faults in the character of the Russian people. The tragedy of it is that the Revolution is not yet completed. The process of demoralization has not yet ended, physical and economic deterioration are rapidly sapping the strength of the people, whilst the organic process, by means of which alone the Russians can regain spiritual and economic vigour, has yet to begin.

The uprising by which the Tsar was dethroned appears as the culminating act of a century and a half of struggle against autocracy, under which the majority of the people were oppressed by a minority numerically insignificant. In this way it marks the end of an epoch. What may be the character of the life of the new age has yet to be determined, for the experiments of the communists cannot be said to suggest the direction which the new life is likely to take. For some reason the Russian people have brought the Revolution to dust by again permitting themselves to be enslaved by another small minority. That explanation cannot, however, be dissociated from fundamental defects in the life and character of the people, defects which may include, as both Joseph de Maistre and Professor Struvë suggest, the absence of the disciplinary influence of religion, as well as faults which even religion may be powerless to overcome. One fact has been illustrated with startling vividness during the Revolution, that is, the relatively small number of persons capable of taking an effective share in any capacity in the political life of the country. Thus the real Revolution has not yet taken place, and cannot take place until, by organic means, the Russian people acquire the capacity for government and the disposition to change the personnel of their ministry without resorting to violence. To this end the Bolshevik rule seems so far to be making little or no progress.

It is difficult to see how the message of modern Russia to the

# CONCLUSIONS 437

world can be of a positive character. It may be that the mysticism which strongly colours the Russian outlook is merely a belated survival of medievalism, and that Russia cannot fulfil any new or important mission ; but it may be also that the conspicuous lesson which modern Russia teaches is economic rather than spiritual, and amounts to this : that communism and State-collectivism bear only a negative relation to progress, and that the sooner public illusions about them are dispelled the better.

The immediate function of a people is to live ; yet under the influence of a compromise between the two systems manipulated by the group which seized power in 1917, the Russian people began to die physically and spiritually. Many of the important and numerous tribes out of which the Russian peoples were compounded—for example, the Avars—have dwindled to insignificance and then wholly disappeared from history. Many races more civilized than the Slavs have died out except as individuals, many political societies more highly developed than the Soviet society of the present time have succumbed to internal decay or to foreign conquest. It would not be surprising or unprecedented if the valuable intellectual elements of Russia were to be permanently, as they have been temporarily, absorbed by other nations, and if the remainder of the population were to continue for an indefinite period in the stage of primitive culture to which they have reverted. (23)   It is difficult to see how Soviet Russia can have any other mission to mankind than to serve as an awful warning and example.

The general conclusions, therefore, may be ventured that, in the Russian people, and therefore in the national army which comprised more than one-half of the adult male population, the historical past had produced a soil peculiarly favourable for the growth of ideas adverse to social order. Absence of a secure sense of property owing to remote causes, impatience of discipline, and ignorance of the world outside the narrow circle of village interests, made the peasant obstinate in his opposition to gradual reforms. The way in which the middle and superior classes were deprived of administrative influence during the imperial *régime* rendered them so unused to political action, that when the dynasty fell there was no effectively organized group of persons able and willing to take the control of the country into its hands. The Duma tried to do so, but the Government appointed by it failed to maintain its position. Thus the way was clear for the extreme elements, which had been for the most part excluded from the country, to return under new conditions —free speech, free press, etc. Revenge for lives damaged by imprisonment and exile was a powerful incentive ; the dynasty was gone, but the structure of Russian society which supported it re-

## THE RUSSIAN REVOLUTION

mained, therefore that structure must share the same fate. Both the peasantry and the working men had for many years been in a revolutionary state of mind, but they had hitherto lacked definite objectives. These could now be supplied. A counter-revolution might be organized which would not only secure the defeat of the revolutionary Provisional Government, but at the same time wipe out the superior classes. Thus the Revolution begun in February 1917 by all grades of the people was ingeniously and rapidly defeated in October of the same year by the seizure of power by one class only, the working men. The peasantry had sent the Constituent Assembly to Petrograd, but it was dispersed and many of its members thrown into prison. Again and again the peasants had intimated their disapproval, inarticulately but effectively, by refusing to surrender their surplus grain or by taking care that there should be no surplus grain to surrender, but machine guns and artillery were ready to stifle any overt action. The manufacturers, merchants, and shopkeepers were killed, imprisoned, sent to obligatory labour, or forced to expatriate themselves, and their property was confiscated. The landowners, large and small, even the peasants who were. considered to possess more land than their families could cultivate, were deprived, wherever possible, of the excess. By means of the rationing system, the Soviet had hoped to control the whole of the economic life of Russia, but the system broke down because the peasants would not keep it going.

Not merely the system of rationing, but the whole Bolshevik scheme of things collapsed—not because it was a communist system, but because, in the strict sense of this word, it was not a system of any kind. In any system the essential feature is that the parts should be co-ordinated with one another and be either organically or mechanically interactive. What the Bolsheviks did was to tear up social life by the roots. Even from the mechanical point of view, they scrapped the existing social mechanism before they had thought of that which should succeed it, and when they had got rid of the old, they found that they had dispersed the mechanics who might have furnished the new. They shattered the social structures and destroyed the material of which they were made, before they had even opened the quarries from which, by necessarily long and laborious processes, the materials for the new structure could alone be obtained. Instead of guiding the backward people of Russia, as they pretended to do, along a new path of social progress, they have plunged them into a primitive condition from which it must take them many long years to emerge, and they have wasted the products of centuries of human progress by threatening to induce in the societies of western Europe, an epidemic of indiscriminate

# CONCLUSIONS 439

destructiveness. Thus the experiment would seem to prove beyond question that under Bolshevik policy and methods no social advancement is possible, for Bolshevism is in its essence the very antithesis of progress.

---

## NOTES

(1) Biriukov, Paul, *The Life of Tolstoy* (London, 1911), p. 83. See also account of last conversation with Tolstoy in Mavor, J., *My Windows on the Street of the World* (London, 1923), pp. 84–85 and 90.

(2) Struvë, P., *Russia* in *The Slavonic Review* (London, 1922), vol. i, p. 25.

(3) Ibid., p. 26.

(4) Professor Struvë uses a paragraph from Joseph de Maistre as a motto for his article.

(5) De Maistre, Comte Joseph, *Quatre Chapitres inédits sur la Russie* (Paris, 1859), pp. 19–28.

(6) Struvë, P., op. cit., p. 36. In spite of the combined authority of Joseph de Maistre and Professor Struvë, it is well to hesitate before accepting their conclusions. Spirituality is imponderable, and for that reason hard to measure.

(7) Chaadaiev " described the philosophy of the Decabrists as mere frigid deism, culminating in doubt " (Masaryk, T. G., *The Spirit of Russia*, London, 1919, vol. i, p. 226).

(8) 1799–1837.

(9) 1814–1842.

(10) 1810–1848.

(11) 1812–1870.

(12) 1809–1852.

(13) 1819–1883.

(14) 1821–1877.

(15) 1821–1881.

(16) 1828–1910.

(17) Prince Kropotkin remarks on the interest taken in Russian writers as shown by English reviews between 1832 and 1845 and by French translations and criticisms about the same time (see Kropotkin, P., *Russian Literature*, London, 1905, p. 39).

(18) In the case of Bakunin, Masaryk speaks of Sarmatiophilism as though Slavism did not embrace a sufficiently wide category. Note also the enthusiasm among the Bolsheviks for Scythianism.

(19) To be associated with the earlier and contemporary romantic movement in Scotland (Scott) and England (Byron).

(20) Masaryk, T. G., *The Spirit of Russia*, vol. i, p. 226. President Masaryk adds : " From available evidence it is impossible to determine whether and to what extent he returned to Voltairism."

(21) Ibid., vol. i, pp. 222–23.

(22) *Vyekhë, As Sign of the Times* (Moscow, 1910) ; *Intelligentsia of Russia* (St. Petersburg, 1910); etc. (See also Mavor, J., *An Economic History of Russia*, London, 1914–1925 ; vol. ii, pp. 585–96.)

(23) Large groups of the Russian population have never been otherwise than primitive in their culture ; e.g., the Bashkirs, the Ziranes, and many others. (See the ethnographical sketch in Mavor, J., op. cit., vol. i.)

# BIBLIOGRAPHY OF BOOKS, PERIODICALS, ETC., USED BY THE AUTHOR

## AUTHORS OF BOOKS, ARTICLES IN NEWSPAPERS, ETC.

A. J.   Article in *Pravda* (Petrograd, May 17, 1919).

AKHMANOV.   *Red Sketches.*

ANET, CLAUDE.   *Through the Russian Revolution : Notes of an Eyewitness from March 12–May 30, 1917* (Hutchinson, 1918).

ANON.   Article " *The Tsar* " in *The Quarterly Review* (London, July, 1904).

ANTONELLI, ÉTIENNE.   *Bolshevist Russia : A Philosophical Survey,* trans. from the French by Charles A. Carroll (S. Paul, 1920).

BALLIN, ALBERT.   *Memorandums* of July 1916 and September 1917, quoted by B. Huldermann in *Albert Ballin* (London, 1922).

BEAZLEY, C. R., RAYMOND, C. (and others).   *Russia from the Varangians to the Bolsheviks* (Clarendon Press, 1918).

BIRIUKOV, PAUL.   *L. Tolstoy, his Life and Work* (Heinemann, 1906, etc.).

BLANC, LOUIS.   *Histoire de la Révolution.*

BLOK, ALEXANDER.   *The Last Days of the Old Régime* in *Archives of the Russian Revolution* (Berlin, 1922).

BOROLZHEIMER.   *System der Rechts.*

BUCHANAN, SIR GEORGE.   *My Mission to Russia* (London, 1923).

BURTSEV, VLADIMIR.   *The Enemy who is forcing his Way into our Homes.*

CHERNOV, VICTOR.   *Disintegration of Classes in Russia* in *Foreign Affairs* (New York, 1923).

CZERNIN, COUNT OTTOKAR.   *In the World War* (Cassell & Co., 1919).

DENIKIN, GENERAL A. I.   *Notes on the Russian Turmoil : Memoirs Military, Social, and Political* (New York, 1923).

DENNIS, A. L. P.   *The Foreign Policies of Soviet Russia* (Dent, 1924).

DOBROVOLSKY, S.   *The Fight for the Re-establishment of Russia in the Northern Provinces* in *Archives of the Russian Revolution* (Berlin, 1921).

DOSTOEVSKY, F.   *The Brothers Karamazov,* trans. from the Russian by Constance Garnett (Heinemann, 1917).

FLETCHER, G.   *The History of Russia, or The Government of the Emperour of Muscovia, with the Manners and Fashions of the People of that Country* (1643, orig. pub. 1591).

FRANCIS, DAVID R.   *Russia from the American Embassy : April 1916– November 1916* (New York, 1922).

GOLDSTEIN, JOSEPH M.   *Russia, Her Economic Past and Future* (New York, 1919).

GOURKO, GENERAL BASIL.   *Memories and Impressions of War and Revolution in Russia 1914–1917* (Murray, 1918).

GROMAN, V. G.   *Report on the Economic Situation in 1924* to the Combined Council on Public Projects, in *Izvestia* (Petrograd, September 10, 1924).

GUINS, G. K.   *Siberia, The Allies and Koltchak* (Peking, China, 1921).

HINDENBURG, MARSHAL VON.   *Out of My Life,* trans. from the German by F. A. Holt (Cassell, 1920).

HULDERMANN, BERNHARD.   *Albert Ballin* (London, 1922).
Also *Reconstruction in Europe* in *The Manchester Guardian* (May 18, 1922).

# 442 THE RUSSIAN REVOLUTION

I. D. *Tasks of Normalising* in *Metallist* (Moscow, October 30, 1918).

ISVOLSKY, ALEXANDER. *Memoirs*, ed. and trans. by C. L. Seeger (Hutchinson, 1920).

JELLINCK. *Verfassungsänderung und Verfassungswandlung*.

KENT, P. H. *Railway Enterprise in China : An Account of its Origin and Development*, App. A. (P. Arnold, 1907).

KERENSKY, A. F. *The Prelude to Bolshevism : The Kornilov Rebellion* (Allen & Unwin, 1919).

KOVALEVSKY, M. *Modern Customs and Ancient Laws of Russia* (Nutt, 1891).

KOVARSKY, B. *N. K. Mikhailovsky and the Social Movements of the Seventies* (St. Petersburg, 1909).

KRASSNOV, V. *Memories about 1917–1920* in *Archives of the Russian Revolution* (Berlin, 1924).

Also *The Internal Front* in *Archives of the Russian Revolution* (Berlin, 1921).

KROPOTKIN, PRINCE PETER. *Memoirs of a Revolutionist* (Smith and E., 1899).

Also *Russian Literature* (Duckworth, 1905).

KRYLOV. *Young Lion's Education*, trans. by Sir Bernard Pares in *The Slavonic Review* (London, 1922).

KUPRIN. *Instantaneous Photographs* (Paris, February 21, 1921).

LANDAU-ALDANOV, M. A. *Lénine* (Paris, 1919).

LARIN, YO (M. S. LURIE). *The Economic Programme* in *Labour Control* (Moscow, May 1, 1918).

LENIN, N. *Collected Works* (Moscow, 1923), including *The First Stage of the First Revolution : Letters from Far Away ; Dual Government ; The Reflection of Marxism in Bourgeois Literature ; Upon Punishment ; The Economic Basis of the Narodnochestvo ; The Revolutionary Year 1905 ; Louis Blancovism ; Transition to the New Economic Policy of 1921 : an address to the Communist Party 8th All-Russian Soviet Congress, December 30, 1922*.

With Trotsky: *The Proletarian Revolution in Russia*, ed. by L. C. Traina (New York, 1918).

LUNARCHASKY, A. V. *Three Plays of A. V. L., Faust and the City : Vasilisa the Wise : The Magi*, trans. by A. L. Magnus and K. Walter (Broadway Translations) (Routledge, 1923).

Also Article in *Pravda* (Petrograd) reprinted in *Materials of the People's Commissariat of Justice : Popular Courts*, Extract II (Moscow, 1918).

LYADOV. *History of the Russian Social Democratic Working Men's Party* (St. Petersburg, 1906).

MAISTRE, JOSEPH DE. *Quatres Chapitres inédits sur la Russie* (Paris, 1859).

MAKAROV, NICOLAS P. *The Russian Agrarian Movement* in *World Agriculture* (Amherst, Mass., 1922).

MAKEVETSKY, A. E. *The Chemical Industry in Russia* in *People's Economy* (Moscow, May 1918).

MALON, B. *L'Internationale, son Histoire et ses Principes* (Lyons, 1872).

MARES. *The Production and Consumption of Bread-stuffs in Peasant Economy* in *The Influence of Yield and Bread-stuff Prices on Some Sides of Russian Economic Life*, ed. by Chuprov and Posinkov (St. Petersburg, 1895).

MARX, KARL. *Revolution and Counter-Revolution* (Chicago, 1907).

MASARYK, T. G. *The Spirit of Russia* (Allen & Unwin, 1919).

MAVOR, J. *An Economic History of Russia* (Dent, 1914–1925).

Also *My Windows on the Street of the World* (Dent, 1923).

# BIBLIOGRAPHY 443

MAYER, N. *Service in the Commissariat of Justice and the People's Court* in *Archives of the Russian Revolution* (Berlin, 1923).

MEHRING, F. *Geschichte der Deutschen-Social-Democratie* (4th ed., Stuttgart, 1909).

MENGER, ANTON. *Neue Staatslehre.*

MEYER, R. *Der Emancipationskampf des vierten Standes* (Berlin, 1892).

MILIUKOV, PAUL. *Bolshevism : an International Danger : Its Doctrines and its Practices through War and Revolution* (Allen & Unwin, 1920).

MILYUTIN, V. *A New Way of the Co-operative Movement* in *People's Economy* (Moscow, May 1918).

Also *The Results of the Congress of the Soviets of the People's Economy* in *People's Economy* (Moscow, June 1918).

Also *The Nationalisation of Industry* in *Pravda* (Petrograd).

MOMMSEN, THEODORE. *History of Rome* (New York, 1895).

MURAVIEV, N. Article in *The Voice of the Workers' Co-operation* (Moscow, October 1918).

NAUDEAU, L. Article in *Le Temps* (Paris, April 14, 1918).

NEKLUDOV, A. *Diplomatic Reminiscences : Before and During the World War 1911–1917*, trans. from the French by Alexandra Paget (Murray, 1920).

PALÉOLOGUE, MAURICE. *La Russie des Tsars pendant la Grande Guerre* in *La Revue des Deux Mondes* (Paris, January-May, 1921). English translation by F. A. Holt under title *An Ambassador's Memoirs* (Hutchinson, 1924).

PARES, SIR BERNARD. Translation of Krylov's fable *Young Lion's Education* in *The Slavonic Review* (London, 1922).

PETRADJETSKY. *The Theory of Law.*

PLEKHANOV, G. V. Article in *Rabochaya Gazeta* (*Workmen's Gazette*).

PLESHKO, N. *The Last Provincial Intelligent* in *Archives of the Russian Revolution* (Berlin, 1923).

POSVOLSKY, L. Article in *The Russian Review* (1919).

PRICE, MORGAN PHILIPS. *War and Revolution in Asiatic Russia* (Allen & Unwin, 1918).

Private correspondents. Letters.

RODZIANKO, M. V. *The State Duma in the February 1917 Revolution* in *Archives of the Russian Revolution* (Berlin, 1924), in Russian.

SCHEFFER, PAUL. Article in *Berliner Tageblatt* (February 19, 1922).

SCHELKING, E. DE. *The Game of Diplomacy, By a European Diplomat* (London, n.d.).

SCHURMANN, M. Article in *The Voice of the Workers' Co-operation* (Moscow, October 1918).

SHULGIN, BASIL. *The Months before the Revolution* in *The Slavonic Review* (London, 1922).

SIMEONIEV. *German Money and Lenin* in *The Last Information*, No. 299 (April 10, 1921).

SMELG-BENARIO. *In the Service of the Soviet* in *Archives of the Russian Revolution* (Berlin, 1921).

SOKOLOV, BORIS. *Defence of the All-Russian Constituent Assembly* in *Archives of the Russian Revolution* (Berlin, 1924).

SPIRIDOVICH, A. E. *History of Bolshevism in Russia* (Paris, 1922), in Russian.

STANKEVICH, V. B. *Memoirs 1914–1919.*

STRUVĚ, PETER B., *Russia* in *The Slavonic Review* (London, 1922).

Also essay in *Vyekhě, As Sign of the Times* (Moscow, 1910).

**444** THE RUSSIAN REVOLUTION

TCHERKESOV, W. *Précurseurs de l'Internationale* (Brussels, 1899).
TESTUT, OSCAR. Article in *L'Internationale* (7ᵐᵉ ed., Paris, 1871).
TOLSTOY, COUNT LEO. *Diary.*
TROTSKY, L. D. (Pseudonym Nicholas Trotsky). *Defence of Terrorism* (Labour Publishing Co., Allen & Unwin, 1921); *Literature and the Revolution*, trans. from the Russian by Rose Strunsky (Allen & Unwin, 1925); *The October Revolution* in *Archives of the Russian Revolution* (Berlin, 1918); *Rôles and Problems of Trade Unions.* With Lenin, *The Proletarian Revolution in Russia*, ed. by L. C. Traina (New York, 1918).
TUGAN-BARANOVSKY, M. Article in *Courses on Co-operation*, vol. i.
TYRKOVA-WILLIAMS, MRS. ARIADNA. *From Liberty to Brest-Litovsk : The First Year of the Russian Revolution* (Macmillan, 1919). ·
VANDERVELDE, ÉMILE. *Three Aspects of the Russian Revolution*, trans. by Jean E. H. Findlay (Allen & Unwin, 1918).
VORONOVICH, N. *Memoirs of a President of a Soviet of Soldiers' Deputies* in *Archives of the Russian Revolution* (Berlin, 1923), in Russian.
WILCOX, E. H. *Russia's Ruin* (Chapman & Hall, 1919).
WINDISCHGRAETZ, PRINCE LUDWIG. *My Memoirs*, trans. by Constance Vesey (Allen & Unwin, 1921).
WITTE, COUNT. *Mémoires du Comte Witte 1849–1915* (Paris, 1921 ; Eng. trans. by A. Yarmolinsky, Heinemann, 1921).
Also *The Autocracy of the Zemstvo.*
WITTE, COUNTESS. Preface to *Mémoires du Comte Witte* (Eng. trans.).
YUROVICH, A. *The Highest Soviet of People's Economy* in *Archives of the Russian Revolution* (Berlin, 1924).
ZAVADSKY, C. V. *On the Great Cleavage : The Report of a Citizen upon Life in 1916–1917* in *Archives of the Russian Revolution* (Berlin, 1923).


## PERIODICALS, NEWSPAPERS, REPORTS, ETC.

*Archives of the Russian Revolution* (Berlin).
*Berliner Tageblatt* (February 19, 1922).
*Brockhaus and Ephron's Encyclopedia* (St. Petersburg, 1900).
*Cause Commune, La* (Paris). Russian ed. *Obshoyé Dielo.*
*Chroniques de la Guerre.* 7ᵉ et 8ᵉ vols.
*Collection of Statistics and Economics of the Agriculture of Russia and Foreign Countries*, 5th year (St. Petersburg, 1912).
*Communist Calendar* (Moscow, 1924).
*Complot Germano-Bolshevist, Le* (Document No. 5).
*Courses on Co-operation*, vol. i.
*Daily Review of the Foreign Press* (London).
*Débats* (Paris).
*Écho de Paris* (Paris, January 25, 1919).
*Economic Russia, Her Actuality and Her Possibilities* (New York, 1917).
*Foreign Affairs* (New York, 1923).
*Influence of Yield and Bread-stuff Prices on Some Sides of Russian Economic Life*, ed. by Chuprov and Posinkov (St. Petersburg, 1895).
*Intelligentsia of Russia* (St. Petersburg, 1910).
*Izvestia* (Helsingfors).
*Izvestia* (Petrograd).
*Journal de Genève* (January 13, 1918).

# BIBLIOGRAPHY

*Labour Control (Rabochi Kontrol)*, (Moscow).
*Labour Leader, The* (London, August 12, 1915).
*Last Information, The*, No. 299 (April 10, 1921).
*Letters* from private correspondents.
*Literature of the Social Revolutionary Party (Narodnaya Volya)*, Paris, 1905.
*Manchester Guardian, The* (May 18, 1922).
*Manifestos* of Bolsheviks and various persons and political parties.
*Materials of the People's Commissariat of Justice : Popular Courts*, Extract II
    (Moscow, 1918).
*Metallist* (Moscow, October 30, 1918).
*Narodnaya Volya (Literature of the Social Revolutionary Party)*, Paris, 1905,
    in Russian.
*Needs of Siberia, The* (St. Petersburg, 1908).
*Obshoyé Dielo* (Petrograd). Paris ed., *La Cause Commune.*
*Order No. 1.* March 1, 1917 (O.S.), March 12, 1917 (N.S.).
*Peace Negotiations between Russia and the Central Powers* (Washington, 1918).
*People's Economy* (Moscow, May–June 1918).
*Pravda* (Petrograd).
*Prekaz*, No. 175, December 14, 1919 (O.S.).
*Proceedings of the Brest-Litovsk Peace Conference* (Washington, 1918).
*Proclamations* reprinted in official organs.
*Proletarian, The* (Detroit, Mich.), vol. iii, No. 4, January 1921.
*Quarterly Review, The* (London, July 1904).
*Rabochaya Gazeta (Workmen's Gazette).*
*Rabochi-Kontrol (Labour Control)*, Moscow.
*Radiograms* reprinted in official organs.
*Recueil des Données Statistiques et Économiques* (St. Petersburg, 1912).
*Reports on the Activities of the Mining Council ; on the Economic Situation in
    1924 ; to the All-Russian Congress of Workers in Chemical Industries,*
    etc., etc., reprinted in official organs.
*Resolutions* of congresses, conferences, etc., reprinted in official organs.
*Revue des Deux Mondes* (Paris, January–May 1921).
*Russian Review, The* (1919).
*Slavonic Review, The* (London, 1922).
*Statesman's Year Book, The* (London, 1920).
*Telegrams* from M. V. Rodzianko to the Tsar Nicholas II.
*Temps, Le* (Paris, April 14, 1918).
*Texts of the Russian Peace* (Washington, 1918).
*Times, The* (London, September 24, 1917).
*Voice of the Workers' Co-operation, The* (Moscow, October 1918).
*Volnost*, Cossack organ ed. by Amfitreatov.
*Vyekhĕ, As Sign of the Times*, Essays (Moscow, 1910).
*Workmen's Gazette (Rabochaya Gazeta).*
*World Agriculture* (Amherst, Mass., 1922), vol. ii.

# INDEX

Abrahamov, Comrade, 264
Adler, F., 426
Adler, Victor, 425
Aeroplane Construction Factory, 312
Agricultural Tax, 388
Agriculture. See under *Peasants ; Land tenure*, etc.
Akselrod, M., 244, 246, 425
Alekseiev, General, Chief of Staff to Kerensky, 122, 123
                    Defence of counter-revolution by, 135
                    Volunteer Army command, 342 *et seq.*
Algasov, M., 269
All-Russian Central Executive Committee. See *Tsik.*
All-Russian Central Rural Union, 405
All-Russian Conference, August 25, 1917, 111
All-Russian Congress of Peasants, 74
All-Russian Congress of Soviets, 161
All-Russian Congress of Soviets of People's Economy, 298, 315
All-Russian Congress of Workers in Chemical Industries, Report to the, 316
    *et seq.*
All-Russian Congress of Workmen's and Soldiers' Soviets, 89, 170
All-Russian Constituent Assembly. See *Constituent Assembly*
All-Russian Diplomatic Delegation, 357
All-Russian Soviet of People's Economy, 279 *et seq.*
All-Russian Soviet of Workmen's and Soldiers' Deputies. See *Petrograd Soviet*
All-Russian Union of Service, 184
All-the-World Workers' Movement, 160
Altai Mountains, 316
America. See *United States of America*
American Federation of Labour, 138
Amsterdam, 243
Anet, Claude, 427
Antonov, M., 146, 159, 161, 162
Archangel, 351 *et seq.*
Ardahan, 214
Armenia, 210, 351
Armistice 1918, 307, 385
Armistice, The Separate, 170 *et seq.*, 307
Army, Civil Wars, 342 *et seq.*
        Constituent Assembly, 185
        Costs of, 298
        Demoralization of, 99 *et seq.*, 113
        Equipment of, 48, 52, 75, 124, 126
        Food of, 81
        Forty-year-old reservists, 90
        Kerensky-Kornilov affair, 119 *et seq.*
        Petrograd garrison, 88

**448** THE RUSSIAN REVOLUTION

Army, Petrograd military district in " Red October," 146, 152
  Separate Armistice, 170 *et seq.*
  Soldiers' Soviets, 133. See also *Labour Army ; Red Army ; Volunteer Army*
*Aurora*, cruiser, 155, 158
Austria-Hungary, 22, 106, 203, 205, 208
Autocracy, 27 *et seq.*, 51, 181, 436
  A Jew on, 379
  Economic situation under, 400. See also *Nicholas II, Tsar*
*Autocracy and the Zemstvo, The* (Count Witte), 30
*Avanti*, 425


" Bag commerce," 398
Bagratin, General, 159
Balabanova, Angelica, 246
Ballin, Albert, 105
Baltic Fleet, Central Committee of, 107
Baltic Provinces. See under names as *Lithuania ; Esthonia*
Baltic Sea, 39, 113
Banks and Banking, Bank-notes confiscated, 323
  Bank of Russia, 156
  Deposits, 307
  Moscow People's Bank, 337
  Nationalization of Banks, 297, 310
  Peasants' Bank, 35
  Provincial Banks, 406
  Seizure by Soviet, 255, 289
  Under New Economic Policy, 407
Baravtin, Lieutenant, 76
Basilevich, Captain, 127
Batum, 214
Bauermeister, Major, 163
Belgium, 208, 242
Belke, Major von, 163
Benedict XV, Pope, 205
Bentham, J., 429
Berger, Victor, 424
Berne, 246
Berzine, M., 244
Bessarabia, 172, 175, 207
Bissolati, M., 424
Bistritz, 110
Bitsenko, Madame, 203
Black Hundred Bands, 112, 156
Black Sea, 39
Black Soil Region, 44
Blockade, 279, 371, 385
Blok, Alexander, 46, 50
Bobrov, M., 246
Bogoslav Mining Company, 312
Bolsheviks and Bolshevism, Anti-Bolshevism of classes, 139, 347

# INDEX                                                        449

Bolsheviks and Bolshevism, Antithesis of nationalism, 434
    Characters and Ideology of, 235, *et seq.*
    Count Czernin's view of, 209
    Definition of co-operation by, 336
    Economic Plan of, 296 *et seq.*
    Education under, 421
    In " Red October," 142–168
    Problems of Power, 254 *et seq.*
    Programme of, 239
    Propaganda by, 91, 100, 104, 113, 127, 144, 180, 247
    Provision of amusements by, 224, 421
    Psychology of, 281
    Trotsky joins, 78
Bonch-Bruyevich, Vladimir, 170
Bourderon, A., 246
*Bourgeoisie*, As consumers, 320
    As organizers, 310
    Revolutionary meaning of, 224, 255
Branting, Hjalmar, 138, 247, 424
Bread riots, 51–53, 57, 106
Breschkovskaya, Madame, 139
Brest-Litovsk Peace Treaty, 202 *et seq.*
Brody, 106
Brussels, German occupation of, 242
Brussilov, General, 108, 145
Buchanan, Sir George, In " Red October," 151, 157, 159
    Note to Foreign Office, 173
    On Bread riots, 53
    On July 1917 rising, 117
    Refuses reply to Trotsky, 172
Budget.  See *Finance*
Bukharin, M., 235
Bunge, M., 33
Burtsev, V., 137, 147
Byelinsky, M., 431
Byelomovsky Horse, 352


Cadet Party, Capital of, 56
    Discusses legality of Soviet, 110
    In Fourth Duma, 29
    Joins Kerensky, 109
    Moscow Conference delegates, 112
    Resignation of Cadet Ministers, 90, 92
Canada, Hydraulic power in, 305
    Land-holding in, 37
Cannibalism, 394
Capital, Amount invested in Russia, 307
    Destruction of, 387
    Under New Economic Policy, 404 *et seq.*
Capital punishment, 112, 343, 347

2 F

## 450 THE RUSSIAN REVOLUTION

Catherine II, Empress of Russia, 221
Central Agricultural Union.  See *Selsko-Soyus*
Central Land Committee, 75
Central Powers.  See *Germany* ; see also *Austria-Hungary*
*Centro-Soyus*, 339, 340
Chaadaiev, M., 432
Chanetsky, M., 246
Chaplin, Captain, 353 *et seq.*
*Che-Ka* (Extraordinary Commission), 285, 386
        Murder of Uritsky by, 376 *et seq.*
        Nationalization of industry by, 308
Chemical Industries, Report to the All-Russian Congress of Workers in, 316 *et seq.*
Cheremesov, General, 165
Chernov, Victor, Agrarian policy of, 80, 109, 364
        Becomes Bolshevik, 123
        On flight of capital, 76
        President of Constituent Assembly, 195–198
Chicherin, M., 172, 175, 213
Chikhachov, M., 30
China, 77, 365
Chkheidze, M., Address to crowd in 1917, 107
        Answer to Nekrassov, 110
        Member of Second International, 425
        Opposes Coalition Government, 79
        President of Pre-Parliament, 135
        Proclamation against Bolshevik demonstration, 89, 90
        Resignation of, 123
Cholera epidemic, 327
Chubar, I., 282, 285
Chudnovsky, M., 146, 158
Civil Wars of 1917–1920, 342 *et seq.*
Coal, Exploitation of, 397.  See also *Mines*
Coalition Government, 78 *et seq.*
        Elections for, 135
        Personnel, 80, 86
Committee for the Saving of the Homeland and the Revolution, 164
Communism, Collapse of, 395 *et seq.*
*Communist Calendar*, 396, 403
Communist Party, Russian, Foreign origin of doctrines of, 282
        Twelfth Congress of, 264, 330, 389
Communist Saturday, 400
Concessions to foreigners, 407
Constituent Assembly, Account of, 177 *et seq.*
        Elections for, 145
        General confidence in, 91
Constitutional Democrats, 48, 132, 142, 235
Co-operative Movement, 335 *et seq.*
Copenhagen Conference, 243
Cossacks, In " Red October," 158
        In Volunteer Army, 342, 348
        Kaledin as *Ataman*, 120, 123, 168, 350

# INDEX

451

Cossacks, Kerensky-Kornilov affair, 143
   Repudiate anarchy, 111
   Soviets of, 162
   Support Provisional Government, 108, 110
Courland, 206, 210, 212
Crimea, 215, 350
Currency. See *Money;* see also *Paper Money*
Czechs in Siberia, 369
Czernin, Count, 203 *et seq.*
Czernovitz, 109, 112

Dago Island, 136
Dashkov, Count Vorontsev, 30
Death penalty, 112, 123, 343, 347
Dekabrists, 235, 431
Denikin, General A. I., 76, 86, 342 *et seq.*
Derber, P. J., 360, 361
Diamandi, Count, 351
Dibenko, M., 162
" Direct Action " by peasants and artisans, 70, 78 *et seq.*, 104, 124, 131, 407
Dobrovolsky, S., 353, 357
Dolgurukov, Prince, 31
Donetz mines, 76, 217, 300
Donop, Colonel, 354
Dostoevsky, F., 225, 429
Dragomirov, General, 123, 344–346
*Dual Government* (Lenin), 57
Dukhonin, General, 167, 170 *et seq.*
Dukhvinsky, M., 376
Duma, Aims of First and Second Dumas, 28
   Aims of Third and Fourth Dumas, 29–32, 48
   A sailor's description of, 110
   Joins Revolution, 55, 63
   " Toil Group " in, 65, 140
Durnovo, I. N., 33
Durov, General, 354
Dvenarenko, M., 367
Dye industry, 316
Dzerjensky, M., 146

East Prussian Campaign, 46, 125
Economic plan of Bolsheviks, 296 *et seq.*
Economic situation, In 1908–1914, 86
   In 1914, 100 *et seq.*
   In European War, 47
   In 1920–1921, 385 *et seq.*
   In 1923–1925, 416 *et seq.*
   Under New Economic Policy, 403 *et seq.*
Economical Liberty Loan, 318
Education, Kornilov's programme, 343

**452** THE RUSSIAN REVOLUTION

Education, Soviet schools in 1923–1925, 421
Ekaterinodar, 344–348
Electrical power, 265, 305
Emancipation of Labour. See *Osvobojdenie Truda*
Emancipation of serfs in 1861, 35, 358, 431
England. See *Great Britain*
*Entente*, Anglo-French, And Kerensky, 105
      Efforts to keep Russia in war, 170
      Separate peace, 172
      War-weariness of, 114
*Entente*, Franco-Russian, 100
Entin, M., 273
Eremiev, M., 146
Esthonia, 206, 210, 212
European War, Economic effects on Russia, 45 *et seq.*
      Failure of Germans in West in 1914, 242
      International socialist groups during, 424
      Responsibility for, 21–24, 100, 170 *et seq.*
      The Separate Armistice, 170 *et seq.*
      War-weariness, 91, 99 *et seq.*, 115. See also *Army*
Exchange of goods. See *Natural Exchange*
Extraordinary Commission. See *Che-Ka*


Fabians, 424
Famine, In Kazan, 39
   In Lithuania, 109
   Of 1921, 391
Fats, scarcity of, 317
Federov, M. M., 355
Finance, Budget of 1922–1923, 414
   In 1914, 83, 101 *et seq.*
   Soviet Finance, 412 *et seq*
Finland, Autonomy of, 108
   Economic crisis in, 116
   General strike, 111
   Government formed, 168
   Timber trade, 39
Finland, Gulf of, 113, 123
Fish industry, 317, 328
Flotow, Baron, 118
Foch, Marshal, 111
Food supply, At the mines, 322
     Difficulty of organization, 254, 279
     Economic crisis, 1920–1921, 387
     Fixation of prices, 81
     Grain from Ukraine, 175, 179
     Hunger in Army, 172
     In Civil Wars, 371
     Petrograd Provisions Council, 303
     Riots, 51–53, 57, 106, 122, 124
     Riots in Tashkent, 135, 136

# INDEX

**453**

Food supply, Riots in Vienna, 203
    Under New Economic Policy, 405. See also *Rationing*
Foreign Trade under New Economic Policy, 408
Forestry, 392
Formen, M., 367
France, Albert Thomas's attitude to Russia, 92
    Anglo-French capital for war, 56
    Efforts to keep Russia in war, 170
    French Governor for Archangel, 354
    Help for Volunteer Army, 349
    Refuses recognition of Soviet, 115
    Responsibility for war, 100
    Stockholm Conference representatives, 100, 138
    Training of Russian troops, 110. See also *Entente, Anglo-French*
Francis, David R., 354
Franco-Russian factory, 180, 189, 198


Ganetsky, M., 425
Gantchev, Lieutenant-Colonel, 202
Gastiev, M., 299
Gatchina, 166
Geddes, Sir Auckland, 351
Gerard, M., Governor of Finland, 30
Germany, Bolsheviks fight in interests of, 143
    Brest-Litovsk Peace, 202 *et seq.*
    Declaration of War by, 45
    *Espionage* by, 110
    Farm crops in, 317
    German bankers and Soviet, 410
    German money for Bolsheviks, 109
    German officers for Bolshevik forces, 154
    Hampered by Volunteer Army, 349
    Military strength of, 99
    Plan to seize Paris and Calais, 204
    Pre-war mercantile interests of, 102
    Propaganda by, 43, 75, 113, 246
    Responsibility for European War, 21–24, 100 *et seq.*
    Russian branch of German General Staff, 163
    Stockholm Conference, 138
Glyebov. See *Idelov, N. P.*
Godnov, L., 64
Gogol, N., 431
Gold, Confiscation of, 255, 323
    Decline of production of, 397
    Export of, 409
    Mines in Siberia, 322
    Reserve of, 84
Golitzin, Prince, 54
Gompers, Samuel, 138
Goremikin, M., 21, 30
Gorodetsky, S. N., 355

**454** THE RUSSIAN REVOLUTION

Gourko, General, 110, 120
Grain, Appliances for shipping, 39, 421
 Fixation of prices, 81
 Payments of, to Germany, by Ukraine, 175
Great Britain, Anglo-French capital for war, 56
 Arthur Henderson and Russia, 92
 Efforts to keep Russia in war, 170
 Help for Volunteer Army, 349
 Lenin on responsibility for war, 100
 Liberation of British subjects, 175
 Refusal to recognize Soviet, 172
 Stockholm Conference, 138
 Supplies for Archangel, 352
 Training of Russian troops by, 110
 Trotsky on English law, 212
 Unemployment in, 409
 Unprepared for war, 46.  See also *Entente, Anglo-French*
" Great Households," 35, 282
*Grey Cloak, The* (*Sieraya Shinel*), 186, 198
Grimm, Robert, 246, 425
Groman, V. G., 417
Grozden, M., 159
Guchkov, A. S., 64, 122
Guesde, M., 424
Guilbeaux, Henri, 425
Guins, G. K., 367
Gushelin, Lieutenant-Colonel, 66


Haase, M., 425
Harbin, 365
Hartvin, Lieutenant, 163
Hegland, M., 246
Helsingfors, 76
 Resolution, 107
 Soviet, 137
Henderson, Arthur, 92, 138
Herzen, M., 431
Hilquit, Morris, 425
Hindenburg, Marshal von, On *Entente* and Russia, 170
 On Kerensky, 105
 On Russian peace, 164
Hoffmann, General, 202, 211, 214
Housing, 262, 390
 Nationalization of houses, 324.  See also " *Great Households* "
Huldermann, Bernhard, 116
Hydraulic Power, 265, 305
Hyndman, H. M., 138, 424


Idelov, N. P., 163
Ignatiev, V. E., 356

# INDEX

455

Income Tax, 261, 298

Independent Labour Party, British, 409, 425

Industry, Russian, Specific industries, 311, 314. See also *Economic situation ; Nationalization of Industry ; Co-operative Movement*

*Intelligentsia*, Changes of opinion amongst, 260

Effect on *émigrés* of, 224

Employment of, 257, 282

Inertia of, 237, 375, 391

Mysticism of, 433

Renunciation of institution of property by, 37

International Groups, 247

The Third International, 424 *et seq*

*Internationalist, The*, 425

International Wagon-Lit Company, 312

International Working Men's Association, 424

Ioffé, A. A., At Brest-Litovsk, 202, 208

On War Revolutionary Committee, 146

Ironside, General, 356

*Iskra (The Spark)*, 86

Ismaelovsky regiment, 185, 190, 198

Isvolsky, Alexander, 32

Italy, 242, 246

Ivanov, M., 352, 354


Japan, 366. See also *Russo-Japanese War*

Jews, A Jew of Yamburg, 379

*Bund* represented at Zimmerwald Conference, 244

In Universities, 422

Posts held by, 224

Jugashbeli, J. B., See *Stalin*

Justice under Soviets, 269 *et seq.*


Kaledin, *Ataman* of Cossacks, 120, 123, 168, 350

Kalinin, M., 386

Kamenev, M., At Brest-Litovsk, 203

In " Red October," 146

On seizure of power, 123

Kannegesser, murderer of Uritsky, 376–378

Kapoustin, S. R., 354

Karakhan, M., 146, 203

Karpov, L., 282, 284

Kars, 214

Kartachov, M., 155

Kautsky, Karl, 424

Kazan, 39, 112, 391

Kerensky, A. F., In Provisional Government, 65

In " Red October," 142 *et seq.*

Kerensky-Kornilov affair, 108, 119 *et seq.*

Manifesto to Navy, 137

Plan of offensive in 1917, 105 *et seq.*

## 456 THE RUSSIAN REVOLUTION

Kerensky, A. F., Speech to Petrograd Soviet in March 1917, 68
Khabalov, General, 53
Kharkov, 335
Khorvat, General, 365
Kibbel's cardboard factory, 312
Kieff, 112
Kienthal, 246
Kiev, 105
Klembovsky, General, 120
Koldrov, Basil, 246
Kollontay on " Red October," 147
Koltchak, Admiral, 357, 365
Konovalov, A. L., 65, 136, 151, 157
Kornilov, L. G., Commander-in-Chief, 108, 110
     Denounced by Bolsheviks, 350
     Kerensky-Kornilov affair, 119 *et seq.*
     Telegram to Foch, 111
     Unpopularity of, 348
     Volunteer Army command, 342 *et seq.*
Kovalevsky, Maxime, 281
Kraev group, 425
Krasekov, M., 270
Krassin, L. B., 282, 287, 409
Krassnov, General, 165
Krilenko, N. V., 147, 162, 174, 190
Krivoshein, land laws of, 38
Kronstadt, Sailors from, 89, 108, 119, 123, 155, 158, 194 *et seq.*
     Soviet, 136
Kropotkin, Prince Peter, 153, 439
Krutovsky, M., 363
Krymov, General, 120
Kudashev, M., 360
Kühlmann, Baron von, 203, 210–212
Kuprin's *Instantaneous Photographs*, 85
Kurakin, Prince, 355, 357
Kushtin Mining District, 312
Kuskov, Comrade, 261
Kusnetsky dye industry, 316
Kuzmin, M., 185
Kvostov, M., 110


Labour Army, 217–221
Labour certificates, 336
*Labour Leader, The*, 243
Lamezan, Baron, 209
Land tenure, Central Land Committee, 75
     Chernov's agrarian policy, 80, 109, 364
     Distribution of, in villages, 113
     Pre-war, 35 *et seq.*
     State ownership of peasants' land, 298
     Stolypin Reforms, 31, 36, 226, 228. See also under *Peasants*

## INDEX

457

Lapinsky, M., 244, 246
Larin, Yorie (M. S. Lurie), 263, 282, 285, 296
Lashchevich, M., 146, 149
Latvia, 208
Lavrov, Peter, and Lavrism, 235, 240
Law Courts.  See *Justice under Soviets*
Law of Lauriston, John, 319
Lazari, Constantino, 246, 425
Lebedour, M., 425
Lekhach, M., 352, 354
Lenin, Nicholas, Arrival at Petrograd, 78
  Attempted assassination of, 351
  Career, 84
  Disappearance of, 110
  Hiding in Petrograd, 145
  In " Red October," 150
  No economist, 235
  On aims of Communism, 397–399
  On causes of February 1917 Revolution, 55–57
  On electrical development, 265
  On International Socialism, 424
  On Social Democracy, 241
  On Trotsky's pamphlet on Trade Unions, 248–250
  On world revolution, 302
  Popularity of, 192
  Programme of Bolsheviks in " Red October," 160
  Separate Armistice, 170 *et seq.*
  Signs Brest-Litovsk Peace, 213
  Speech in 1920, 289
  Speeches of, 100 *et seq.*
  World-wide invitation to revolutionaries, 247
Leobertz, Major, 163
Leopold of Bavaria, Prince, 202
Lermontov, M. Y., 431
Letts, 351
Libau, 39
Liberation, Union of, 30
Liebknecht, Karl, 78, 425
Lindberg, Michael, 366
Lindley, F. O., 373
Lipetsk health resort, 321
Literature, Russian.  See *Russian Literature*
*Literature and the Revolution* (Trotsky), 236
Lithuania, 109, 206, 210
Livonia, 206, 213
Livovsky regiment, 155
Lomov, A. A.  See *Oppokov, G.*
London, Conference in, 208
  Socialist Congress in, 242
  Treaty of, 172
Longuet, M., 248, 425
Loriot, M., 425

# 458 THE RUSSIAN REVOLUTION

Lugano, Peace proposal at, 242
Luga Soviet, 72–74, 88, 92
Lunarchasky, A. V., A Commissar, 163
    Arrest ordered, 110
    Dramas of, 235
    On Soviet Law, 273 *et seq.*
Luxembourg, Rosa, 425
Luzhof garrison, 191
Lvov, Prince G. E., Member of Provisional Government, 60, 64, 266
    Resignation of, 108
Lvov, Vladimir N., 64, 120, 344


MacDonald, J. Ramsay, 425
Mackaev mines, 312
Maistre, Comte Joseph de, 430
Maklakov, M., 357
Manchuria, 365
Mankov, a sailor, 150
Manuilov, A. A., 65
Marie Palace, 54, 139, 158
Markov, Boris, 366, 369
Marne, Battle of the, 242
Marrheim, A., 246
Martini, M., 244
Martov, L., 78, 242, 244, 425
Marx, Karl, 84, 177, 219, 235, 240, 277
Masaryk, T. G., On Chaadaiev, 432
    On Russian Revolution, 125
Matches, manufacture of, 317, 333
Maximalists, 211
Maximov, Vice-Admiral, 75
Mayer, N., 259, 270
Mefodiev, Doctor, 355
Mekhanoshchin, M., 146
Menshevik Party, And Constituent Assembly, 180, 183
    Groups in, 142
    Opposes Petrograd Soviet in " Red October," 161
    Sokolov on error of, 140
    Under Kerensky, 108, 126
Menshikov Palace, 89
Michael, Grand Duke, As possible Tsar, 63, 179
    Message from Rodzianko to, 53
    Murder of, 75
Michael Artillery College, 157
Mikhailov, Paul, 363, 366
Mikhailovsky, General, 235, 356
Mikhailovsky stables, 165
Military Missions, British and French, 350 *et seq.*
Miliukov, Paul, Blames A. Thomas and A. Henderson, 92
    Member of Provisional Government, 64
    On Berne Resolution, 248

# INDEX

459

Miliukov, Paul, On Zimmerwald Conference, 243
        Speech in Fourth Duma, 48
Miller, General, 356
Milyantovich, S. D., 137, 157, 159
Milyutin, V., On Bolshevik economics, 301
        On Co-operative Movement, 335
        On Nationalization of Industry, 311, 316
Mines, 76, 217, 306, 320–322, 397. See also under specific names as *Donetz mines*
Mining Council, 320–322
Minsk, 211, 241
Mirsky, Prince Svyatopolk, 30
Modeliani, G. E., 246, 425
Moeseënko, Boris, 127
Mohilev, Anti-Bolshevik headquarters at, 168, 174
Moldavian Republic, 207
Money, Cash deposits, 323
        Depreciation of, 413
        Natural exchange, 286, 311
        Not deposited in Banks, 310. See also *Paper Money*
Moscow, All-Russian Conference in, 111
        Congestion of population in, 390
        Congress of March 1919, 247
        Co-operatives in, 335
        Municipal elections, 144
        Ration in 1921, 332
        Seat of Government, 136, 139
        Street fighting in, 168
Moscow-Kazan Railway, 400
Moscow People's Bank, 337


Nakhaikess, M., 147
*Narodnaya Volya* movement, 84, 358, 433
*Nashé Slovo* (newspaper), 78
Nationalization of Houses: See under *Housing*
Nationalization of Industry, 306 *et seq.*, 385
        In Siberia, 364
*Nationalization of Production*, 308
Natural Exchange, 286, 311, 388
Navy, Baltic fleet, 107
        Kerensky's Manifesto to, 137
        Kronstadt sailors, 89, 108, 119, 123, 155, 158, 194 *et seq.* See also *Koltchak, Admiral*
Nekludov, A., 128
Nekrassov, N. V., Alleged intrigues of, 75
        In Provisional Government, 65
        Vice-President of Council, 109
Nenn, Charles, 246
N.E.P. See *New Economic Policy*
Nessimy Bey, 203
New Economic Policy, 264, 297, 338, 401 *et seq.*, 434

# 460 THE RUSSIAN REVOLUTION

Nicholas II., Tsar of Russia, Abdication of, 51 *et seq.*
      Alleged suggestion of separate peace, 56
      Blame for war reverses, 99
      Choice of ministers by, 27
      Declining prestige of, 21
      Facial characteristics of, 258
      Refuses dictatorship of Grand Duke Michael,
        53
      Reply to *Zemstvos*, 33
Nicholas, Grand Duke, 46
Nikitin, M., 159
Nogën, V., 163, 267
Normalizing Production, 329–331
North Russian Campaign in Civil Wars, 351–358
Noulens, M. T., 373
Novorossisk, 39, 351
Novoselov, M., 360
Novo-Tcherkask, 342


Obligatory Labour, 272, 298, 327. See also *Labour Army*
Obolensky, V., 263, 299
October 1917 Revolution. See *Revolution of October 1917*
Octobrists, In Fourth Duma, 29, 48
      In Provisional Government, 65, 142
      *Intelligentsia* amongst, 235
      Lenin's allegation concerning, 56
Odessa, 39
Oesel Island, 136
Oppokov, G., 163, 280, 282
*Order No. 1* of the Petrograd Council of Workmen's and Soldiers' Deputies,
    66, 109
      Text of, 94
      Withdrawal of, 152
*Order No. 1* to Petrograd Labour Army, 218
*Osvobojdenie Truda* (Emancipation of Labour), 240
" *Our Affair* " (newspaper), 86
Ovceënko, V. E. See *Antonov, M.*
Owen, Robert, 286, 429


Paderewski, I. J., 141
Paléologue, Maurice, 49
Paper Money, Bolshevik issue of, 255, 412
      Groman's Report on, 418
      In 1892, 33, 83
      Peasants' dislike of, 388
      Provisional Government's issue of, 128
      Security for, 319
      Workers in Government factory, 189
Pares, Sir Bernard, 268
Patushensky, M., 360

# INDEX

Paul I., Emperor of Russia, 33
Pavlovich, N., 280
Pavlovsk regiment, 53
Peace terms at Brest-Litovsk, 202 *et seq.*
Peasants, Bank of, 35
    Character of, 225
    Conference of, 172
    Congresses of, 74, 178
    Disturbances. See *Direct Action by Peasants and Artisans*
    Landownership by, 35 *et seq.*, 228–230
People's Economy. See *All-Russian Soviet of People's Economy*
People's House, Petrograd, 147
Perekrestov, M., 167
Pernatsky, M. V., 348
Peter the Great, Emperor of Russia, 221, 250
Petradjetsky, M., 276
Petrograd, Attitude of citizens to Bolsheviks, 192–194
    Industrial establishments in, 134
    In " Red October," 145
    In the Red Terror, 376
    Municipal elections, 173
    Ration in, 332
    Riots in, 106
Petrograd Labour Army, 218
Petrograd Provisions Council, 303
Petrograd Soviet, And Kerensky, 107 *et seq.*
    Announcement of November 5, 1917, 148
    Declining influence over Army, 88
    Favours Coalition, 79
    Helsingfors Resolution, 107
    Issue of *Order No. 1*, 66
    Resignation of Chkheidze, 123
    Revival of, in February 1917, 64
    Trotsky as president of, 136
Petrov, B., 172, 175, 186
Petrovsky, M., 213, 377
Plehve, M. von, 30
Plekhanov, G. V., On Soviet programme, 145
    Socialist views of, 240
    Social Patriot, 424
Pletniov, M., 299
Podolia, 112
Podvoësky, M., 146
Poincaré, M., 43
Pokorny, Lieutenant-Colonel Hermann, 202
Pokrovsky, M. N., 203
Poland, Autonomy of, 111, 206
    Economic crisis in, 116
Polkovenekov, Colonel, 148
Poll, Herr von, 163
Polovtsev, General, 117
Poole, General, 352, 354

# 462 THE RUSSIAN REVOLUTION

Pope Benedict XV, 205
Popoff, M., 203
Population of Russia, Depletion of, 371
    Growth of, 22, 44
    Racial composition of, 40, 437
Potanen, G. N., 358–361
Potapov, Colonel, 352
Pozern, M., 258, 327, 377
Preobrashensky regiment, 53, 185
Pre-Parliament, Institution of, 135
    Presidency of Madame Breschkovskaya, 139
    Termination of, 158
Presidium of the All-Russian Soviet of People's Economy, 279 *et seq.*, 324
Press, The, Burtsev's warnings, 147
   Printing of secret treaties, 171
   Printing-presses in " Red October," 155
   Soviet Press, 403
   *The Grey Cloak*, 186. See also names of newspapers as *Rabochaya Gazeta; Labour Leader*, etc.
Pressman, M., 425
Prohibition, 83
Prokhorov factory, 112
Propaganda. See under *Bolsheviks ; Germany*, etc.
Protopopov, M., 42, 52
Provisional Government, Bolsheviks try to overthrow, 88 *et seq.*
    Compared with Soviet, 266
    Finance of, 83
    Formation of, 51 *et seq.*
    Lenin's view of, 57, 79
    Loyalty of Cossacks to, 108
    Personnel of, 64
    Powerlessness of, 130, 136
    Proclamation by, 59
    Provisional Council in " Red October," 151
    Revival of Soviets and, 63 *et seq.*
    V. Burtsev on, 137
Provisional Government of Northern Russia, 352
Provisional Siberian Government, 359, 366
Provisional Workers' and Peasants' Government. See *Soviets*; *Soviet of the People's Commissars*
Pskov, 123
Pugachev's revolutionary movement, 221, 431
Pulkov, 166
Purishkevich, M., 351
Pushkin, A. S., 431
Putilov ironworks, 218
Pyategorsky, M., 262

Quadruple Alliance, 205, 209

*Rabochaya Gazette* (*Workmen's Gazeta*), 240, 242
*Rabochi-Kontrol* (*Workers' Control*), 322

# INDEX

**463**

Radek, Kar Sobelson, 299, 425
Radoslavov, M., 207
Railways, Russian, 39, 111, 419. See also under specific names, as *Moscow-Kazan ; Trans-continental*, etc.
Railway Workers' Union, 191
Rapallo, Treaty of, 410
Raskolnikov, M., 163
Rasputin, M., 46
Rationing, 219, 331–334, 385
Rausch, O., 163
Red Army, After Civil War, 217
      Discipline of, 355
      Food for, 279
      Havoc made by, in Poland and Ukraine, 215
      In Red Terror, 377
      Not heroic, 185
      Pozern's control of, 258
      Volunteer Army and, 342 *et seq.*, 352
      Volunteers from the front join, 199
Red Cross, 188, 199
Red Fleet, 352
Red Guard, 107, 125, 150, 158, 194. See also *Red Army*
" Red October," Preparation, 142 *et seq.*
      Explosion, 155 *et seq.*
Red Terror, 237, 375 *et seq.*
Refugees, Russian, 224, 351
Reichstag, Labour group in, 425
Reisner, Professor, 270
Religion, In Russian Literature, 432 *et seq.*
      Religious freedom, 111, 131, 343
Renaudel, M., 424
Rest-houses for workmen, 303
Reval, 138, 408
Revolution of February-March 1917, 51 *et seq.*, 223
Revolution of October 1917, Russian People and, 223 *et seq.* See also *Red October*
Riazonov, M., 147, 244, 299
Riga, 113, 207, 408
Rochal, M., 166
Rodzianko, M. V., Food supply measures of, 53
      On Dumas, 29–32
      On outbreak of war, 45
      President of Duma, 110
      Telegrams to Tsar, 59
*Rôles and Problems of Trade Unions* (Trotsky), 248
Roman Catholic Church, Abolition of restrictions on R.C.s, 111
      Analogy of the Soviet system, 131
Romanov dynasty. See *Nicholas II, Tsar*
Romanovsky, General, 345
Rostoikin factory, 312
Roumania, 101, 105–112, 243
Rudnev, M., Mayor of Moscow, 167

**464** THE RUSSIAN REVOLUTION

Rudnyeb, V. V., 184
Russian Empire, Dissolution of, 99 *et seq.*
        Specific causes, 115
Russian Literature, 225, 431
Russian Railways. See *Railways, Russian*
Russian Social Democratic Working Men's Party, 241, 253
Russky, General, 123, 145
Russo-Belgian Metallurgical Company, 312
Russo-Japanese War, Defeat of Slavs in, 23
        Effect on Duma, 28, 433
        Military re-organization after, 46
Ryashkin, M., 327
Rykov, A. J., 162, 236, 282, 288


Safronov, a sailor, 191
Sailors. See under *Kronstadt*
St. George, Chevaliers of, 186
St. Peter and St. Paul, Fortress of, 149, 155, 158
St. Petersburg, Congress, 30
        Industries in, 221, 306
Samarin, Colonel, 128
*Samolotni-Stroitelni Zavod*, 312
Saturday, Communist, 400
" Savage Division," Caucasian, 119
Savenkov, M., 119, 357
Sazonov, S., 22, 357
Scheffer, Paul, 411
Schenemann, Herr von, 163
Schiedemann, Herr, 424
Schlaknikov, A. R., 162
Schools. See *Education*
Schröder, M., 269
Sederov, Basil, 366, 369
Seed loans and Seed stations, 393
*Selsko-Soyus* (Central Agricultural Union), 406
Sembat, M., 424
Semenov, Colonel, 360, 365
Semenovsky regiment, 149, 185, 190, 193
Semipalatinsk, 316
Serbia, ultimatum to, 21
Serebrenikov, M., 363
Serganiko Ufaleskoy Mining District, 312
Serrati, M., 425
*Sestro Riesk* Metallic Company, 311
Sezekov, M., 367
Shatelov, M., 360, 362
Sheremetev, Count, 31
Shingarev, A. S., 65
Shreider, M., Mayor of Petrograd, 164
Shulgin, Basil, 344

# INDEX

Shungen electrical plant, 407
Siberia, Confederation, 207
     Demands autonomy, 112
     Gold mining in, 39, 322
     Railways of, 39
     Revolution and, 358–372
     Trotsky in, 86
Siberian Regional Duma, 359, 364
Siemens-Martin steel, 397
Siemens-Schuckert electrical firm, 287
*Sieraya Shinel.* See *Grey Cloak, The*
*Simon-Pure* group, 425
Sipiaghin and *Zemstvos*, 30
Skobelov, M., 79, 86
Slavs and Slavophils, Balkan Slavs, 101
     In Russian Literature, 428, 432
     Nature of, 225, 235
     Slavic peril, 22
     Treatment of Cossacks by, 369
Smelg-Benario, On the Red Terror, 376 *et seq.*
     Opposes obligatory labour by *bourgeoisie*, 327
     Service with the Soviet, 258
Smirnov, A. P., 189
Smithovich, V. G., 267
Smolny Institute, 146, 149 *et seq.*, 166, 191
Snowden, Philip, 425
*Sobranie.* See *Constituent Assembly*
Social Democratic Congress, October 1st, 1917, 135
Social Democratic Party, Countenances violence, 182
     Divisions of, 133, 142
     Helsingfors Committee of, 107
     Lenin's leadership of, 100
     Manifesto of, 253
     Plekhanov's description of, 240
     Trotsky's membership of, 79, 86
Social Democratic Working Men's Party, Russian. See *Russian Social Democratic Working Men's Party*
Socialists. See names of Socialist parties, as *Bolsheviks ; Social Democratic Party*, etc.
Social patriots. See *International groups*
Social Revolutionary Party, Calibre of members of, 235
     Chernov's appeals to peasants, 80
     Defence of Constituent Assembly by, 179 *et seq.*
     Groups in, 142
     Helsingfors Committee, 107
     In " Red October," 161
     War Committee of, 192
Sokolnikov, G. J., 213, 300
Sokolov, Boris, 125, 140, 178 *et seq.*
Sokolovsky, Aleksandra (Madame Trotsky), 86
Soldau, 46
Solovietsk, Monastery of, 353

# 466 THE RUSSIAN REVOLUTION

South Russian Campaign in Civil Wars, 342–351
Soviets, " All power to the Soviets," 90, 100, 130 *et seq.*
    All-Russian Congress of Soviets, 89, 161
      Finance of, 412 *et seq.*
      Justice under, 269 *et seq.*
      Luga Soviet, 72–74, 88
      Mining Soviets, 321
      Presidium of All-Russian Soviet of People's Economy, 279 *et seq.*
      Provisional Government and, 63 *et seq.*, 88 *et seq.*
      Provision of amusements by, 224
      Soviet of Labour and Defence, 220, 328
      Soviet of the People's Commissars, Address to Army, 171
                  Establishment of, 162
                  On Co-operation, 336
                  Organization of Labour Army, 217
                  Personnel of, 162
      Soviet Press, 403
      Village Committee of, 73
Spain, 172
Spartacus group, 425
Special Army, 124 *et seq.*
Special Committee of Commander-in-Chief of Volunteer Army, 344
Special Manchurian Detachment, 365
Spiridovich, A. E., 86
Spiridovna, Marie, 195
Squartsov, I. I., 163
Stalin, M., 146, 163, 171
Stanislau, 106
Stankevich, V. B., 166
Staraia-Russa health resort, 321
Stauning, a socialist, 424
Steinberg, M., 269
Stewart, Colonel, 353
Stockholm, 208
Stockholm Conference, 138
" Stock-watering," 306
Stolypin's Reforms, 31, 36, 226, 228
Strikes, In 1905–1907, 35
        In 1917, 52
        In Petrograd, 351
        Lawyers' strike, 269
        Railways' strike, 111
        Threat of general strike, 184
Struvë, Peter, 242, 282, 428, 431, 433
Stuergkh, Count, 426
Stürmer, Prime Minister, 32, 42
Submarine Campaign, 113, 123, 204
                Albert Ballin on, 106
Sukhomlinov, Minister of War, 49, 111, 124
Switzerland, 242
Syndicalism, 313

# INDEX

Taganrog, 347
Tarnopol, 106, 108
Tartars, 350
Tashkent, food riots in, 135
Taurida Palace, 64, 69, 107
  Constituent Assembly in, 183, 185, 194 *et seq.*
Taxes in kind, 387
Tchaikovsky, Nicholas, 352 *et seq.*
Tereshtchenko, M. S., 64, 136, 151
Terror, The.  See *Red Terror*
Textile industries, 316
Textile Workers' Union, 333
Theodorovich, I. F., 163
Thomas, Albert, 92, 141
" Toil Group."  See under *Duma*
Tolstoy, Countess Sasha, 135
Tolstoy, Count Leo, 428
Toretta, Signor de la, 373
*Trade Unionist, The*, 425
Trade Unions, Lenin on, 248
  Soviet of, 330
Trans-Baikalia, 360, 365
Trans-continental Railway, 39
Trans-Siberian Railway, 359, 370, 420
Tretiakov, M., 151
Treves, M., 425
Tribunists party, 425
Trier, M., 425
Troelstra, a socialist, 424
Trotsky, L. D. (Nicholas Trotsky), Arrival, 78
  Brest-Litovsk, 203, 208 *et seq.*
  Career, 85
  Chairmanship of Petrograd Soviet, 124, 136
  Character of, 236
  Czernin's view of, 209
  In " Red October," 142 *et seq.*
  Popularity of, 192
  Separate Armistice, 170 *et seq.*
  Supports Soviet claims in 1917, 107
Trotsky, Madame, 86
Tsarskoë Selo, 166, 170
Tsekki Pasha, 202
Tseretelli, M., 80, 86, 109, 425
*Tsik*, 392
Tugan-Baranovsky, M., 336
Tumanov, Prince, 159
Turati, M., 425
Ture-Nermann, a socialist, 246
Turgeniev, Ivan, 432

# 468    THE RUSSIAN REVOLUTION

Turkestan, 207
Tver, Report of a landlord of, 71, 228
Tyshka, M., 425


Udelny estate, 415
Ukhomsky, Lieutenant-General, 345
Ukraine, And Brest-Litovsk Peace, 205, 209, 213
  Dispute with Petrograd, 179
  Economic crisis in, 116
  Government formed, 174
  Grain from, 175
  Landownership in, 229
  Local Government, 267
  *Rada* set up, 111
  Republic federated to Russia, 171
Ulianov, Alexander, 84
Ulianov, Vladimir Ilich.  See *Lenin, Nicholas*
Unemployment, In Great Britain, 409
  In Russia, 421, 435
Uniats, 111
Union of Liberation, 30
United Internationalists, 161
United States of America, American Federation of Labour, 138
  Armies of, 170
  Bolshevik view of American business men, 281, 283, 287, 405
  Embassy at Vologda, 352
  Hydraulic power in, 305
  Labour party, 425
  Reserves of currency, 409
  Stock Exchange in 1914, 102
  Troops at Archangel, 353
  Trotsky on American Independence, 212
Ural Mountains, Coal in, 306, 309, 321
  Societies, 339
Uritsky, Moses Solomonson, 146, 376
Useco Bank, 406
Usov, Colonel, 358
Ustrogov, M., 363


Vandervelde, Émile, 138
Varsky, M., 246
Verkhovsky, General, 123
Vienna, food riots in, 203
Village Committee of Soviet, 73
Virubova, M., 46
Vishnyak, Mark, 183
Vitebsk, 108
Vladimir College, 165
Vladimir Soviet, 268

# INDEX

469

Volhynia, 112
Volhynsky regiment, 53
Volkhovsky, P. V., 358
Vologda, 352, 380
Vologodsky, M., 363
Volunteer Army, 342 *et seq.*
*Vyekhë, as Sign of the Times* (Essays), 433


War Revolutionary Committee, 144 *et seq.*, 174, 217
Weinberg, J., 282, 284
Weishaupt, Dr. Adam, 427
*Western Observer, The,* 86
Whitehouse, M., 157
White Russians, Congress of, 211
      In Archangel, 351–353
White Sea, 353
William II, Emperor of Germany, Enters Riga, 113
       Telegram from Tsar to, 22
Windawa, 39
Winter Palace, 155, 157, 159
Witte, Count, Manifesto of 1905, 27
    On *Zemstvos,* 30
Wolff, N., 163
Women, Careers open to, 138
    Sempstresses commandeered, 221
    Women's Battalion, 151, 159
*Workers' Control.*  See *Rabochi-Kontrol*
*Workmen's Gazette.*  See *Rabochaya Gazeta*
Wrangel, General, 342 *et seq.*


Yasnaya Polyana estate, 135
Yudenich, M., 357
Yurovich, A., 260–263, 283 *et seq.*


Zakharov, M., 360, 362
Zavadsky, C. V., 41
Zbrucz, 109
*Zemstvos,* Arbitrariness of, 226
    Promise to re-establish, 353
    Schools of, 422
    To control chemical industries, 317
    Tsar's hostility to, 30, 81
    Union of, 64
Zenzinov, M., 122
Zimmerwaldism, 92, 142
     First Zimmerwald Conference, 242 *et seq.*
     Second Zimmerwald Conference, 246
Zinoviev, O. G. A., Arrival at Petrograd, 78
     At Luga, 88

# 470 THE RUSSIAN REVOLUTION

Zinoviev, O. G. A., Disappears, 110
        Obligatory labour imposed by, 327
        On Constituent Assembly, 189
        President of Third International, 426
        Supports Soviet claims in 1917, 107
Zubov, P. I., 355, 357